SOCIOLOGY

J. ROSS ESHLEMAN

Wayne State University

BARBARA G. CASHION

Georgetown University

SOCIOLOGY

An Introduction

Second Edition

LITTLE, BROWN AND COMPANY
BOSTON   TORONTO

Library of Congress Cataloging in Publication Data

Eshleman, J. Ross.
   Sociology, an introduction.

   Bibliography: p. 647
   Includes indexes.
   1. Sociology.   I. Cashion, Barbara G.   II. Title.
HM51.E84 1985   301   84-21299
ISBN 0-316-24961-0

Library of Congress card number 84-21299

ISBN 0-316-24961-0

9 8 7 6 5 4 3 2 1

RRD

Published simultaneously in Canada by Little, Brown & Company (Canada) Limited

Printed in the United States of America

Text Credits

Chapter 11, p. 288: From Cary S. Kart, *The Realities of Aging*, Boston: Allyn and Bacon, 1981. Reprinted by permission.

Chapter 16, pp. 463–464: From Harold Freeman, *Toward Socialism in America*. Copyright © 1979 by Schenkman Publishing Company, Inc. Reprinted by permission.

Chapter 18, pp. 528–529: From Ralph H. Turner "Collective Behavior and Conflict: New Theoretical Frameworks," *TSQ* 5:2 (Spring 1964). Reprinted by permission of the *Sociological Quarterly*.

Chapter 20, p. 593: Adapted by permission of Macmillan Publishing Company from *Defensible Space* by Oscar Newman. Copyright © 1972, 1973 by Oscar Newman.

(Continued on page 658)

To Janet, Jill, and Sid
and
to Janet and Libby

Preface

As in the first edition, our purpose in writing this text is to convey both the excitement of sociology and its relevance to students' lives. We feel that the excitement of sociology comes from its subject matter: social life and social organization. Sociology encompasses all aspects of society, including those that involve us in a direct and personal way: family life, community change, religion, and gender inequality, to name just a few. It involves a unique way of looking at the world in which we live, forcing us to question the obvious and understand how society and behavior are patterned and organized. More and more people are discovering that sociology provides them with unique skills and abilities: in research methods, in applying social theory in the working world, and in using their knowledge and understanding of social processes, organization, and change.

Changes in This Edition

Before we began this revision, we contacted people who had been using the text — both instructors and students — and asked them for feedback on what worked and what didn't work for them. Using this information, we have both made some significant revisions and retained those aspects of the text which made the first edition so popular. We are pleased with this revision and hope that you will be as well.

Major Changes. We have made several major changes in organization and coverage.

1. We have moved the chapter on Social Groups and Social Organizations to follow the material on Culture and Society.

2. We have combined the material on Socialization and on Social Interaction to provide a more unified discussion of how we learn to interact.

3. Gender Differentiation and Age Differentiation are now covered in two separate chapters so that each topic can be discussed in more detail.

4. A new chapter on Health Care Groups and Systems has been included in Part IV: Social Institutions.

5. The chapter on Population now includes ecology.

Additional Changes. We have made other revisions that are no less important in terms of coverage, clarity, and timeliness.

1. Additional material has been included on topics such as cultural lag, dual labor market, political parties, and computers and technology, to name just a few areas.

2. We have enhanced our coverage of the various sociological perspectives throughout the text.

3. All census and research material has been updated to reflect the most recent information available.

4. The Appendix, Exploring a Career in Sociology, has been expanded to include information on cover letters and résumés as well as on job networking.

5. Five of the eight Part Readings are new to this edition.

6. Last, but certainly not least, are our popular "Sociologists at Work." One-third of these profiles are new for this edition. In response to your suggestions, we have included more profiles of people with bachelor's degrees to show the undergraduate major what is open to him or her.

Features

The following features, which significantly enhance our text's effectiveness for both instructor and student, have been retained from the last edition:

□ *Sociologists at Work.* Twenty-one profiles show what career options are available to sociologists. Thus, each chapter contains the profile of an individual whose training has been in sociology at the BA, MA, or PhD level. Some teach, but others are working as sociologists in areas outside of academia. Instructors and students alike have found these profiles fascinating and are amazed by the range of careers these people have chosen.

□ *Summaries.* Each chapter is followed by a summary that highlights the key ideas and concepts discussed in the chapter. These can be helpful to students who want a quick review of the chapter.

□ *Key Terms.* Following each chapter summary is a list of the terms and concepts discussed in the chapter. Like the summaries, these lists can serve as useful review tools for the student. Each of these terms is defined in the Glossary at the end of the text.

□ *Suggested Readings.* Following the key terms, each chapter provides a list of sources to supplement the material in the chapter. Each of the suggestions is annotated with a brief description of the suggested material.

□ *Boxed Inserts.* Each chapter contains supplemental materials in the form of boxed inserts. Most are short excerpts from books or newspapers and illustrate a point under discussion.

□ *Tables and Figures.* Each chapter includes tables and figures to supplement the written content. Whether the material is from the

United States Census, the United Nations, or survey data, we have used the most up-to-date figures available to us at the time of writing.

□ *Full-Color Art Program.* Careful thought went into selecting photographs, fine art, and movie stills that will be of interest to students and reinforce concepts discussed in each chapter. We are also pleased to have commissioned a well-known Boston artist, Karen Watson, to create original art for the cover and part-opening pieces.

□ *Part Readings.* Each of the five parts concludes with one or two brief readings. Because readings are included in the text, there is no need for a separate readings text.

□ *Appendix: Exploring a Career in Sociology.* Sociology majors frequently ask for practical advice on careers, the level of degree needed for jobs in sociology, finding a job, locating professional organizations, and sources available to assist in educational training and career advancement. Our Appendix answers these questions in great detail. This Appendix, in conjunction with our "Sociologists at Work" feature, provides students with a real sense of the timeliness and relevance of sociology.

□ *Glossary.* The extensive glossary serves as a quick and easy reference. It is especially useful for checking on the meanings of terms listed at the end of each chapter and for reviewing.

Supplements

1. *Study Guide.* A thorough and practical student study guide includes learning objectives, chapter outlines, and a special feature called "Workshops" that applies sociological concepts to everyday life by using newspaper articles and raising questions based on them.

2. *Instructor's Manual.* A comprehensive manual provides a wealth of teaching sugges-

tions, objectives and resources, outside activities stressing the importance of sociology to personal lives, suggested readings from short stories and novels, a guide to films, and much more.

3. *Test Bank.* An extensive test bank of approximately 2100 items is available to instructors, in both booklet and computerized format. The questions are primarily multiple choice with many true-false and a number of short essays as well. The test bank is in two parts so that differently worded but similar questions can be given to different classes. Each question is referenced to the appropriate text page to make verification quick and easy.

Acknowledgments

As in the first edition of this text, we wish to acknowledge the contributions of many people. How does one express an intellectual debt to the scholars, researchers, teachers, and students who provided the ideas, data, and findings expressed here? Obviously that is impossible. One can, however, acknowledge those people who have helped in the preparation of specific aspects of this book.

We thank, of course, our own personal groups — our families and friends who have supported our efforts as we have studied and worked in our chosen field. We especially thank our children who have taught us as much as we have taught them. We also thank our teachers, those people who have sparked our interest in sociology and helped us develop our ability to think through the issues of the discipline. Certain professors have been especially influential: Professors Muriel Cantor, Edward Dager, John Pease, Barbara Hetrick, Larry Hunt, Jennie McIntyre, A. R. Mangus, Leonard Kercher, and numerous colleagues at Wilson College, Western Michigan University, Georgetown University, and Wayne State University.

Special thanks are due to two people who were instrumental in organizing and writing a first draft of two chapters in the first edition. Dr. Melinda Bacol-Montilla wrote the original draft for the chapter on racial and ethnic differentiation, and Dr. James E. Gruber wrote the original draft for the chapter on the changing community. A note of appreciation is due to Lillian Motis who assisted with some of the typing.

We wish to thank the many instructors who used the first edition of our text and provided us with valuable feedback. We are especially grateful for the comments and suggestions offered by the reviewers of both the first and second editions. In particular we wish to thank: David Alcorn (Angelo State University); Henry Barlow (Cleveland State University); Howard Standish Bergman (Manchester Community College); David Brinkerhoff (University of Nebraska-Lincoln); Jack Dison (Arkansas State University); Stephen Green (North Adams State College); Arthur Greil (Alfred University); David Karp (Boston College); Mark Kassop (Bergen Community College); Abraham Lavender (University of Miami); Kathryn Mueller (Baylor University); Suzanne T. Ortega (University of Nebraska-Lincoln); Anthony Orum (University of Texas-Austin); Brian Pendleton (University of Akron); Evan T. Peterson (Brigham Young University); Beth Rubin (Indiana University-Bloomington); Richard Shaffer (California Polytechnic State University-San Luis Obispo); Robert Smith (Framingham State College); Charles Tolbert (Baylor University); Thomas Van Valey (Western Michigan University); Charles Vedder (Stetson University); Joan Weston (Brookhaven Community College); and Ronald Wohlstein (Eastern Illinois University).

A special word of thanks goes to the people behind the scenes who made significant contributions to the text and played a major part in the final product. None of them perceived themselves as sociologists several years ago, but several of them may feel they now qualify. Our deepest thanks and appreciation to Lesley Ripley, Development Editor, whose expertise and assistance was invaluable in seeing both editions through to a successful completion. A number of people on the production staff should be commended for their superb performance, particularly Virginia Shine, Billie Ingram, and Victor Curran. Bradford Gray, the Sociology editor, and Garret White, the Editor-in-Chief provided the approval, support, and encouragement to produce the text. Many other individuals made specific contributions and need to be recognized, including Barbara Anderson and Anne Bingham. Daniel Otis took our submitted drafts and did the reorganizing, rewriting, and polishing essential for publication. The remarkable skills, support, and enthusiasm of these individuals made the project proceed smoothly and resulted in a final product that we believe is superior to any of the competing texts.

J.R.E.
B.G.C.

Contents

SOCIOLOGISTS AT WORK
Helping Children Live
Within the System   46

Chapter 3
Methods of Studying Society   51

SOCIOLOGISTS AT WORK
Analyzing Data on
Pharmaceuticals   68

Part I Reading
The Promise   73

Part II
Individuals
Within Society   79

Chapter 4
Culture and Society   81

SOCIOLOGISTS AT WORK
Redirecting Juvenile Offenders   188

Part II Readings

Part III
Social Inequality   203

Chapter 8
Social Differentiation
and Stratification   205

SOCIOLOGISTS AT WORK
Co-hosting on
National Public Radio   226

Part III Readings

Part IV
Social Institutions   327

Chapter 12
Family Groups
and Systems   329

Chapter 13
Religious Groups
and Systems   363

SOCIOLOGISTS AT WORK
Helping Religious Refugees
Adjust   386

Chapter 14
Educational Groups
and Systems   391

SOCIOLOGISTS AT WORK
Selling College Textbooks   412

Chapter 15
Political Groups
and Systems   417

SOCIOLOGY

PART I

Sociology: Perspectives and Methods

Sociology is about people, but we learn about people in history, psychology, business, anthropology, political science, biology, and many other disciplines. So why study sociology? Because the perspective is different. Sociologists study people as they interact with other people, at work, at play, at home or in school, in small groups, in large groups, or in large organizations. We learn not only about people but also about social groups and social systems, a major goal in sociology.

The first chapter in this textbook describes what sociology is, what sociologists do, and how sociology differs from other disciplines. Chapter 2 introduces you to the history of sociology and the development of a variety of theories sociologists use to describe social groups and social systems and how people interact in them. The third chapter explains how sociologists gather and use evidence to test their theories.

We hope that as you begin to learn how sociologists view people and their activities, you too will use their perspective in your own observations of people. We believe that with a sociological perspective you will better understand yourself and others and realize how social groups and social systems shape your life and the lives of those around you.

CHAPTER 1

The Nature and Uses of Sociology

People who like to avoid shocking discoveries, who prefer to believe that society is just what they were taught in Sunday School, who like the safety of the rules . . . should stay away from sociology.

— Peter Berger

Our lives are governed by the society we live in. Social rules and conventions influence every aspect of our daily lives. We begin to learn them before we can talk, and they are reinforced, altered, or contradicted every time we enter a social situation, whether new or familiar. By the time we reach college age, we have internalized them so completely that we obey them without thinking, which does not diminish their importance or pervasiveness, however.

The answers to many of the questions we wonder about have at least some social components. Why, for example, do roommate situations with three people almost always have problems? Do sororities or fraternities serve any real purpose? Why do they choose to admit some people but not others? Have you had an argument with anyone lately? If you have, the chances are that it arose at least in part from having different perceptions about how people should behave — perceptions influenced by social surroundings. The housing offices of most schools recognize this important factor and try to place people from similar backgrounds as roommates. Why do most of us feel uncomfortable with a group of people we don't know? Part of the reason is that we don't know how to behave — our social behavior is determined by a constant exchange of social cues, and these cues may vary from group to group. Indeed, why are you attending college, taking this course, and reading this book right now? (Rates of college attendance vary dramatically from one social group to another.)

The list could be extended indefinitely, but our point should be clear: whether or not we like it or are even aware of it, the social fabric that surrounds us dictates many aspects of how we live. One of the pleasures of studying sociology is that it has both "scientific" applications and very personal ones. It attempts to explain not only the factors that draw group members together but also why we feel uncomfortable talking to most athletes and yet feel very comfortable talking to most members of the drama club (or vice versa). Although we may not recognize them, there are reasons for our social behavior, and a knowledge of them is useful both in our daily lives and in understanding trends in the world around us. At its best, an understanding of sociology can bring to light an entire new dimension of social forces that influence us constantly.

What Is Sociology?

What is *sociology?* There are several ways to try to answer this question. The dictionary will tell you that it is the study of social relationships, social institutions, and society. The term itself, often credited to Auguste Comte (1798–1857), the founder of sociology, is derived from two root words: *socius,* which means "companion" or "associate," and *logos,* which means "word." At its most basic, then, it means "words about human associations or society."

Another way to find out what sociology is would be to check the table of contents of an introductory sociology text. There you would find that it is concerned with such topics as social interaction, culture, stratification, bureaucracy, population, age and sex roles, collective behavior, ecology, power and politics, norms and values, urban development, and crime and deviance.

A third method would be simply to ask people. You might get such responses as "Sociology is much like social work" and "Sociology is similar to socialism, I think."

Another procedure would be to find some sociologists and observe them at work. Some

might spend most of their time poring over volumes from the census bureau or travel to northern Alaska every year to talk to Eskimos about their hunting practices. Some might investigate sexual behavior in a clinic or study kinship systems among natives of the South Pacific. Others might look into how college students perceive their professors or how television has influenced family life in the United States.

If you pursued all these approaches, you would probably find yourself with a bewildering variety of responses. What do they have in common? They all suggest that sociology is concerned with every aspect of the self in relationships with others and every aspect of the social world that affects a person's thoughts or actions. As stated by the American Sociological Association in a booklet called *Careers in Sociology* (1977), sociology is *the study of social life and the social causes and consequences of human behavior.* The term "social life" encompasses all interpersonal relationships, all groups or collections of persons, and all types of social organizations. The "causes and consequences of human behavior" encompass how these relationships, groups, and organizations are interrelated; how they influence personal and interpersonal behavior; how they affect and are affected by the larger society; how they change or why they remain static; and what the consequences of these factors are. This definition reflects the belief that people can be understood only in the context of their contacts, associations, and communications with other people.

Thus, sociologists may consider questions such as the following (general topics are followed by specific studies that a sociologist might undertake):

□ How do groups influence individual human behavior? (How is student participation in class influenced by the size and composition of the class?)

Sociologists attempt to understand social life and social organization in a variety of contexts. Here are two locations where people purchase basic food, clothes, or household products. But note the contrast in physical structure, social organization, and interaction patterns: one has a permanent structure where products remain from one day to the next while in the other unsold products are removed by the owner at day's end; one has fixed market prices but the other, very likely, involves bargaining or haggling; one has products raised or produced by one's family while the other is an intermediary between producer and consumer. Understanding such contrasting patterns of everyday life are the concerns of the sociologist.

□ What are the causes and consequences of a particular system of social order? (Why are women the principal landowners in some societies while men are in others?)

□ What social factors contributed to a particular social change? (Why has a larger percentage of women been working outside the home during the last thirty years?)

□ What purpose is served by a particular social organization? (Why do people join the Rotary Club?)

□ What are the causes and consequences of a particular social system? (How do the patterns of social interaction in a small village differ from those in a large city?)

Other areas investigated by sociologists include racial and ethnic relationships, prejudice and discrimination, power and politics, jobs and income, families and family life, school systems and the educational process, social control, organizations, bureaucracies, groups and group dynamics, leisure, health, military systems, women's movements, and labor movements. The stratification of people by wealth, education, power, and differences due to sex or age may also be examined. As you can see, sociology is an extremely broad field. In its most comprehensive sense, it can be regarded as including every aspect of social life — its causes, its forms and structures, its effects, and its changes and transformations.

The Sociological Perspective

Up to this point, we have been discussing the content of sociology. Sociology is also a perspective, a way of looking at society and social behavior. Like the blind men who described the elephant differently depending on whether they felt its trunk, tail, body, or leg, everyone regards the world from his or her own point of view. A school building may be seen as a place of work by a teacher, as a place of study by a student, as a tax liability by a homeowner, as a fire hazard by a firefighter, and as a particular structural design by a builder. In the same way, sociologists consider the social world from their own unique perspective.

What is *the sociological perspective?* It is a conscious effort to question the obvious, to remove ourselves from familiar experiences and examine them critically and objectively. This sort of empirical (based on observation or experiment) investigation enables us to determine whether our generalizations about society are accurate. These investigations could involve asking questions about poverty in a wealthy nation, about the social forces leading to unionization, or about the effects of divorce on family life and children.

This perspective also entails efforts to see beyond individual experiences. The sociologist tries to interpret patterns, the regular, recurrent aspects of social life. An awareness of interaction patterns and group processes can help us understand the relationship between our personal experiences and the society we live in.

Human behavior is to a large extent shaped by the groups people belong to, by the social interactions that occur, and by the social and cultural context in which the behavior takes place. Apart from the social and cultural context, for example, it may be extremely difficult to understand the spontaneous, simultaneous, and collective shout that occurs when a person with a wooden stick hits a round object over the head of a person wearing a glove on one hand but not the other. It may be difficult to understand the anger of people in a neighborhood when children are bused to a school in a different neighborhood. Behaviors such as these reflect the group, the institution, and the society in which they occur. Since individual behavior can be understood only in its social and cultural context, the sociological perspective considers the individual as part of the larger society. It notes how the society is reflected in individuals and attempts to discover patterned behaviors and regularity in events.

The sociological perspective operates at two levels, which sociologists term *macro* and *micro*. The difference is related to the size of the unit of analysis. *Macrosociology* deals with large-scale structures and processes: broad social categories, institutions, and social systems such as war, unemployment, and divorce; solutions to these problems are sought at the structural or organizational level.

Microsociology, on the other hand, is concerned with how individuals behave in social situations. The social problems of a veteran, unemployed worker, or divorcé would be subjects for microsociological research; solutions would be sought at the personal or interpersonal level. The sociological perspective involves investigations of problems on both scales.

Perhaps the macrosociological/microsociological distinction can be clarified by elaborating on the issue of divorce. At a microlevel we can observe husbands and wives in interaction and

Macrosociology deals with large-scale structures and processes. At this level the sociological perspective might involve examining how systems such as the military influence or are influenced by types of governments or cooperation between nations, or how events such as war affect marriage and divorce rates or the gross national product. Macrosociology focuses on patterns of behavior and forms of organization that characterize entire societies.

Microsociology deals with people's everyday interactions. It focuses on individuals in the workplace, in marriage, or in any group interaction. It is concerned with how acts, motives, and meanings of individuals shape their social interactions, which in turn maintain or change social structures.

note that divorce is more likely to occur if the persons involved can't agree on important issues, if one person takes a rigid or inflexible stance, or if the personalities of the persons involved are incompatible. At a macrolevel we can observe how divorce rates vary cross-culturally by degree of societal modernization or how divorce rates are related to various systems of mate selection, lineage, or place of residence. At microlevels the unit of analysis is the person or persons in interaction; thus "solutions" to divorce may be re-lated to personal counseling, marital education programs, or small group workshops. At macro-levels the unit of analysis is the organization, in-stitution, or system, and solutions to divorce may be related to decreasing "free choice" of mates in favor of "parental choice," or moving to a single (patrilineal or matrilineal) lineage system rather than a multilineal one, or living with the kin group rather than in a separate residence or lo-cale. At a microlevel we may try to change the person, the behavior, or the interaction pattern.

How to Read a Table

Sociologists make frequent use of tables to present the findings of their own research, to provide numerical evidence to support or reject statements they make, or to show comparisons between groups, categories, events, or different points in time. Numerous tables are presented throughout this text, not so much to present our own research findings but to lend numerical support to substantive content and to show comparisons between groups or periods of time. You will be able to understand the contents of a table more easily if you follow a systematic procedure. The first table in this text will be used as a model (Table 1-1) in leading you

through steps to follow in reading a table.

1. *Examine the title.* A good table will have a title at the top of it that tells precisely what the table contains. The title in Table 1-1 informs us that this table includes information on marriages, divorces, and rates for both in the United States for the years 1960 to 1982.

2. *Check the source.* The source of the information presented will usually appear at the bottom of the table. Unless it is original data, it will most likely list the research journal or publication that contains that original

us where the data comes from and where we can go to locate it, it helps us judge how reliable the information is. In Table 1-1, the data comes from U.S. Census material as published in the *Monthly Vital Statistics Report* and *The Statistical Abstract of the United States.*

3. *Look for any headnotes or footnotes.* Headnotes generally appear below the title while footnotes are likely to appear below the table but above the source. Headnotes or footnotes may tell how the data was collected, how a question was asked, what numbers or headings mean, why certain information is lacking, the statistical measure used, or why the data was presented as it was. Table 1-1 has no headnote but has a footnote "a" indicating that rates are figured annually per 1,000 popu-

At the macrolevel we may attempt to change the structure, the organization, or the social system. Sociologists study and analyze society and social life at both levels.

Sociology and Popular Wisdom

It is widely assumed, sometimes accurately so, that research findings tend to support what we already know. We all have some idea why people act the way they do and understand how society works. As social beings, most of us were raised in families and communities. Everyone has learned to obey traffic signals and danger signs. We have all heard the debate and rhetoric of presidential and local political campaigns. We have all read newspapers and heard television reports that remind us continually of crime, ra-

cial conflicts, poverty, inflation, pollution, and teenage pregnancies. We all understand social life — our own experiences make us experts in human behavior and in the nature of society. Let us examine a few examples to prove our point. Is it not obvious that

1. with divorce at an all-time high, the institution of marriage is breaking down and the number of families is decreasing drastically?

2. since the Catholic church opposes the use of artificial means of contraception, far fewer Catholics than Protestants in the United States use contraceptive devices?

3. since capital punishment leads people to give serious thought to the consequences before committing crimes, crime rates are much lower

lation. It is important to know what the figures indicate. Are they actual numbers, rates, percentages, or something else?

4. *Read the column and row headings.* Tables contain two important types of headings. The column headings appear at the top and tell what appears below them. The row headings appear on the left and tell what exists to the right of them across the table. In Table 1-1, you can note a double column heading. The top one indicates that one set of figures below the heading refers to marriage and the other set refers to divorce. The second column headings indicate year, number of marriages, rate of marriages, number of divorces, and rate of divorces. The first column heading (year) tells us what is in the row headings. Keep both column and

row headings in mind as you look at the table.

5. *Make comparisons.* Now that we know what the figures mean (numbers and rates), what the column headings refer to (marriages and divorces), and what the row indicates (year), we are ready to read the table and make comparisons. We can tell that in 1975 there were 2,152,000 marriages at a rate of 10 marriages per 1,000 population. By looking at the vertical column we see that the general pattern was an increase in the number of marriages between 1960 and 1982 with a drop in number in 1974 and 1975. Looking at the horizontal row, we can compare the number and rates of marriage with the number and rates of divorce, and so forth. Comparing columns and rows we can note similarities, differences,

or trends. By doing this, we are ready for the final and highly important step: drawing conclusions.

6. *Draw conclusions.* What can we conclude from the material presented? Has the marriage rate increased, decreased, or done both at different times? What about the number and rate of divorce? How might we explain the drop in the number of divorces in 1982, the only decrease in number from one year to the next in the entire table? Does this data support the popular wisdom mentioned in the text that the institution of marriage is breaking down drastically?

Tables will vary considerably in format and complexity, but following these six steps should assist you in understanding and grasping the information presented in any table you encounter.

---

in states that have capital punishment than in those that do not?

4. since women in most societies are confined to the home, receive relatively low pay, and are dependent and oppressed compared with men, more women than men commit suicide?

5. since blacks in the United States are the "last to be hired and first to be fired," have lower average levels of education, are disproportionately represented below the poverty level, and are discriminated against in most areas of social life, more blacks than whites experience low self-esteem?

6. when natural disasters such as tornadoes, floods, and fires wipe out homes and communities, panic sets in, social organization breaks down, and looting becomes rampant?

Many other examples could be given, but these common sense ideas should illustrate our point. Although you may agree with all of them, research findings indicate that all these statements are false. It is true that divorce rates are close to an all-time high, but it is not true that marriage is breaking down, nor that the number of families is greatly decreasing. Most people who divorce remarry. People are tending to marry at a later age, and an increasing number of young people are choosing to remain single longer, but most people eventually marry. Combined with the increasing number of persons in society, neither the number of marriages nor the rate of marriages per thousand people is decreasing (see Table 1-1).

The second statement suggests that because

Table 1-1

Marriages, divorces, and rates: United States, 1960–1982

	MARRIAGE		DIVORCE	
YEAR	NUMBER	RATE	NUMBER	RATE[a]
1982	2,495,000	10.8	1,180,000	5.1
1981	2,438,000	10.6	1,219,000	5.3
1980	2,390,000	10.6	1,189,000	5.2
1979	2,331,000	10.4	1,181,000	5.3
1978	2,282,000	10.3	1,130,000	5.1
1977	2,178,000	9.9	1,091,000	5.0
1976	2,154,000	9.9	1,083,000	5.0
1975	2,152,000	10.0	1,036,000	4.8
1974	2,229,000	10.5	977,000	4.6
1973	2,284,000	10.9	915,000	4.4
1972	2,282,000	11.0	845,000	4.1
1971	2,190,000	10.6	773,000	3.7
1970	2,158,000	10.6	708,000	3.5
1969	2,145,000	10.6	639,000	3.2
1968	2,069,000	10.4	584,000	2.9
1967	1,927,000	9.7	523,000	2.6
1966	1,857,000	9.5	499,000	2.5
1965	1,800,000	9.3	479,000	2.5
1964	1,725,000	9.0	450,000	2.4
1963	1,654,000	8.8	428,000	2.3
1962	1,577,000	8.5	413,000	2.2
1961	1,548,000	8.5	414,000	2.3
1960	1,523,000	8.5	393,000	2.2

[a] Rates are based on an annual basis per 1,000 population.

SOURCES: Monthly Vital Statistics Report, *Annual Summary for the United States, Births, Deaths, Marriages and Divorces*, DCHS Publication, vol. 30, no. 13, December 20, 1982, p. 1, and vol. 31, no. 12, March 14, 1983; U.S. Bureau of the Census, *Statistical Abstract of the United States: 1984*, 104th ed., U.S. Government Printing Office, Washington, D.C., 1983, no. 83, p. 63.

the Catholic church opposes contraception, the proportion of Catholic users would be far lower than that of Protestants. This "obviously true" statement was accurate until fairly recently. Today, however, national survey data of married women under age forty-five show that except for sterilization, Catholic and non-Catholic contraceptive practices are quite similar (Westoff and Jones, 1977). In 1975, between 75 and 80 percent of each group were using contraception. Only slight differences exist in the use of the pill (34 percent for both non-Catholic and Catholic), IUD (9 percent versus 7.6 percent), diaphragm (4.1 percent versus 3.5 percent), condom (9.6 percent versus 14.9 percent), or foam (3.9 percent versus 2.6 percent). Thus, in this regard, the position of the church is not followed by most persons who define themselves as Catholics, at least in the United States.

The third statement suggests that crime rates are lower in states that have capital punishment than in states that do not. The evidence, however, suggests that there is very little relationship between the rate of murder and other crimes and the use of capital punishment. The murder rates in states that have the death penalty are not consistently lower than in states that do not have it. In general, the death penalty is not a deterrent to murder or other crimes. Even imprisonment does not seem to be a major deterrent, as is evident from the recidivism (repeat) rate of people who have been in prison. Rather than changing people's attitudes, punishment may make them more cautious and promote extra efforts to avoid apprehension.

The fourth statement, that women are more likely than men to commit suicide, is also without support. For a variety of reasons, the suicide rate is much higher among men than among women (see Table 1-2). This is true regardless of race for both the number and rate of suicides. In 1980, for example, of 26,869 suicides, 20,505 were by males (76 percent). The rate of suicide per 100,000 population is more than three times as high for men as for women.

The fifth statement suggests that since blacks are socially and economically oppressed, have lower levels of training and skills, and are frequent victims of racism, they have low levels of self-esteem. Studies (Hunt and Hunt, 1977; Turner and Turner, 1982) consistently call into question the prevailing view that blacks have negative self-evaluations, however. Guterman (1972, p. 87) reviewed studies comparing blacks

Table 1-2

Number of suicides by race and sex, 1950–1980

YEAR	TOTAL	WHITE		BLACK AND OTHER	
		MALE	FEMALE	MALE	FEMALE
1950	17,145	12,755	3,713	542	135
1960	19,041	13,825	4,296	714	206
1970	23,480	15,591	6,468	1,038	383
1975	27,963	18,206	6,967	1,416	474
1980	26,869	18,901	5,928	1,604	436
	RATE PER 100,000 POPULATION				
1950	11.3	19.0	5.5	6.8	1.6
1960	10.6	17.6	5.3	7.1	1.9
1970	11.5	17.9	7.1	8.6	2.9
1975	12.7	20.1	7.4	10.6	3.3
1980	11.9	19.9	5.9	10.6	2.6

SOURCES: U.S. Bureau of the Census, *Statistical Abstract of the United States: 1980*, 101st ed., U.S. Government Printing Office, Washington, D.C., 1980, no. 310, p. 186; NCHS, *Monthly Vital Statistics Report*, "Annual Report of Final Mortality Statistics, 1980," vol. 32, no. 4, supplement, August 11, 1983.

and whites on measures of self-esteem and concluded that the level of self-esteem among blacks is either the same as or higher than that of whites.

The sixth statement suggests that natural disasters lead to panic, looting, and the breakdown of social organization. Interestingly, disasters are more often followed by more centralized decision making, the creation of emergency operations groups, and a highly organized mode of operation. An immediate reaction of many people is to rejoin their families and friends. The looting or pillaging of homes and businesses is infrequent, and crime rates tend to decrease. Martial law (in which military forces are called upon to maintain order) has never been declared in the United States following a natural disaster.

These examples illustrate that although some popular observations may be true, many others are not supported by empirical data. Without social research (see Chapter 3), it is extremely difficult to distinguish what is actually true from what our common sense tells us should be true. Even if this is the only sociology course you ever take, we hope that, after completing it, you will have a far greater understanding of yourself, of your society, and of human behavior, as well as an increased ability to question many of the popular observations widely accepted as truth by the press and by our citizens.

Sociology and the Other Social Sciences

All branches of science attempt to discover general truths, propositions, or laws through methods based on observation and experimentation (see Chapter 3). Science is often divided into two categories: the social sciences and what are often referred to as the natural sciences. The natural sciences include (1) the biological sciences — biology, eugenics, botany, bacteriology, and so forth, which deal with living organisms, both human and nonhuman; and (2) the

physical sciences — physics, chemistry, astronomy, geology, and so on, which deal with the nonliving physical world. The word "natural" must be applied to these sciences with caution, however. The *social sciences* are just as natural as those that comprise the natural sciences. The organization of cities, the collective action of a football team, and the patterns of interaction in a family system are just as natural as electricity, magnetism, and the behavior of insects.

Sociology is a social science, but it is important to realize that a complete understanding of a society or of social relationships would be impossible without an understanding of the physical world in which societies exist and an understanding of the biological factors that affect humans. Like the other social sciences — psychology, anthropology, economics, and political science — sociology deals with human relationships, social systems, and societies. Although the boundaries among the various social sciences are sometimes hazy, each tends to focus on a particular aspect of the world and tries to understand it. Scientists who devote their lives to the study of rocks, birds, plants, childrearing, or poverty do not deny the importance of other aspects of the world. They find, rather, that the area they have chosen to study requires their full concentration.

Each social science focuses on selected aspects of social relationships or social systems. Scientists in each field generally devote their attention to "what is" rather than "what should be." The social sciences are also likely to have as a goal the acquisition of knowledge rather than the direct utilization of that knowledge. Each is likely to seek general laws or principles instead of isolated descriptions of particular cases or events. Thus they differ little in their focus on social phenomena, in their methods, and in their goals, but they do vary in their particular focus of attention. Also, it's not unusual for the social sciences to overlap somewhat. People living in poverty, for example, may be of equal interest to the sociologist, the demographer, and the historian. Each of them, however, would concentrate on a different aspect of the situation. As a result, an introductory course in sociology is very different from an introductory course in economics, political science, anthropology or psychology, and a brief description of the other social sciences may help us understand the nature of social science in general as well as the nature of sociology in particular.

Economics is the study of how goods, services, and wealth are produced, consumed, and distributed within societies. Figures about the gross national product, balance of payment deficits, or per capita income may seem to belong more to the realm of statistics or mathematics than to a social science, but these statistics reflect individual behavior, the relationships among groups, and the functioning of society. The effect of supply and demand on prices and the distribution and consumption of material goods serve as indicators of social exchange. Although sociologists also study factors such as these, they devote their attention to different aspects of them. Few economists, unlike sociologists, pay much attention to actual behavior or attitudes, to business enterprises as social organizations, or to the impact of religion or education on levels of productivity or consumption. Economists may provide us with import and export figures, ratios of savings to investment, and information about the rate at which money changes hands, but they would be unlikely to interpret these factors as the results of people buying new cars to gain prestige or starting new businesses because they are frustrated with their jobs or their bosses.

Political science studies power, governments, and political processes. Political scientists study different kinds of governments as well as interpersonal processes and means through which power is exercised, focusing on both abstract theory and the actual operation of government. During elections, it is political scientists who provide us with information about voting patterns, changes from previous elections, and the characteristics of voters. Traditionally, political scientists have been interested primarily in political theory and government administration. Recently, however, they have begun to devote more attention to matters of interest to the sociologist, such as the acquisition of political beliefs, the social backgrounds of the political activists, and the role of women and minorities in political outcomes.

Anthropology, like sociology, is a broad and varied discipline. It includes physical anthropology, archaeology, cultural history, social linguistics, and social and cultural anthropology, Physical anthropologists attempt to understand both primitive and modern cultures by studying physical traits such as the shape and size of skulls, artifacts such as pottery and weapons, and genetic mutations of both human and nonhuman forms of life. The work of cultural or social anthropologists, on the other hand, is very similar to that of sociologists. Like sociologists, they are concerned with social institutions, patterns of organization, and other aspects of society. There are differences in the two fields, however. Anthropologists generally study a society as a whole, whereas sociologists are likely to concentrate on one aspect of a society. Also anthropologists often live in the culture or community they are studying so that they can observe behavior directly. Sociologists are more likely to rely on statistics, questionnaires, or secondary data, and are frequently interested in comparing information about the social processes and structures of different cultures, whereas anthropologists often study cultures or communities individually.

Psychology is concerned primarily with human mental processes and individual human behavior. Frequent areas of study include learning, human development, behavior disorders, perception, emotion, motivation, creativity, personality, and a wide range of other psychic and behavioral processes. In addition to being studied by psychologists, some of these areas are also studied by sociologists and by members of a field known as *social psychology*. These three branches of social science have different emphases, however. Psychology is concerned with individuals. Social psychology is the study of how an individual influences his or her social interactions with other individuals or with groups, and of how social behavior influences the individual. Sociology deals primarily with groups and social systems. Much of the material covered in sociology textbooks is technically social psychology.

History is considered either a social science or one of the humanities and provides a chronological record of important past events. Sociology is an analytical discipline that tries to derive general truths about society. History, on the other hand, is basically descriptive; historians traditionally consider every event to be unique, assuming that attempts at classification or generalization may impair their ability to understand exactly what happened. A sociologist studying the Bolshevik revolution, therefore, might try to determine whether revolutions evolve through a standard series of stages or whether certain social situations are common to most prerevolutionary societies. A historian studying the same revolution would be more interested in discovering the exact sequence of the events that actually occurred.

Increasingly, however, many historians are becoming more sociological in their orientation. Instead of concentrating exclusively on events — names, dates, successions of kings, details of battles — they are analyzing broad social movements and general social patterns. Many are turning to sociological methods of analysis to determine what social forces influenced specific historical events.

Geography is concerned with the physical environment and the distribution of plants and animals, including humans. Geographers may study such things as why a particular trade route evolved or how the formation of nations is influenced by the physical landscape. The physical geographer investigates climate, agriculture, the distribution of plant species, and oceanography. Social and cultural geographers, like sociologists, may be interested in how the distribution of people in a particular area influences social relationships. Sometimes urban geographers and urban sociologists work together on such problems as how various types of housing affect family life and how a given transportation system affects employment and productivity. Although often not considered a social science, social geography clearly shares many areas of interest with the other social sciences.

Is *social work* a social science? Technically, it is not. Social work is the field in which the principles of the social sciences, especially sociology, are applied to actual social problems in the same way the principles of physiology are applied in medicine and principles of economics are applied in business. The *applied sciences* — those that directly use these principles — are often considered distinct from the *pure sciences* — those that seek knowledge for its own sake — but they can actually be considered to occupy different points on the same continuum. At one end of the continuum would be the disciplines that use knowledge to solve actual problems. A social worker might, for example, use information obtained from family research to try to place children in foster homes or to establish centers of spouse abuse. At the other end of the continuum would be the disciplines involved in research, not to solve a specific problem, but simply to increase our understanding of the world. A researcher of this sort might study childrearing or spouse abuse as a function of income or education levels. But few social scientists do only pure research and few social workers do only applied science. For example, social workers devise their own research and techniques to help people

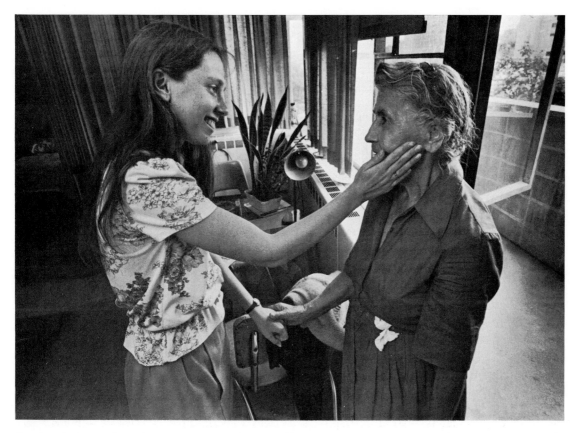

Social work is to sociology what engineering is to physics and business is to economics. Social workers try to influence and help people directly through personal or group contact with those who need assistance: the poor, dependent aged, abused children, disrupted families, and the like. Social workers draw heavily upon the principles of sociology, psychology, and the other social sciences in directing their activities.

solve personal and group problems, and the resulting applications contribute to our existing body of knowledge. For their part, sociologists have recently begun to become more involved in applied research. Sociologists and social workers do share some common tasks, then, but it is a mistake (albeit a common one) to regard sociology as equivalent to social work or social welfare.

Sociological Careers and the Uses of Sociology

Beginning students of sociology often ask a number of related questions. Some of the more common ones are (1) "Why should I take sociology? If I'm not interested in a sociological career,

The Sociologist's Image

It is, of course, true that some Boy Scout types have become sociologists. It is also true that a benevolent interest in people could be the biographical starting point for sociological studies. But it is important to point out that a malevolent and misanthropic outlook could serve just as well. Sociological insights are valuable to anyone concerned with action in society. But this action need not be particularly humanitarian. Some American sociologists today are employed by governmental agencies seeking to plan more livable communities for the nation. Other American sociologists are employed by governmental agencies concerned with wiping communities of hostile nations off the map, if and when the necessity should arise. Whatever the moral implications of these respective activities may be, there is no reason why interesting sociological studies could not be carried on in both. Similarly, criminology, as a special field within sociology, has uncovered valuable information about processes of crime in modern society. This information is equally valuable for those seeking to fight crime as it would be for those interested in promoting it. The fact that more criminologists have been employed by the police than by gangsters can be ascribed to the ethical bias of the criminologists themselves, the public relations of the police and perhaps the lack of scientific sophistication of the gangsters. It has nothing to do with the character of the information itself. In sum, "working with people" can mean getting them out of slums or getting them into jail, selling them propaganda or robbing them of their money (be it legally or illegally), making them produce better automobiles or making them better bomber pilots. As an image of the sociologist, then, the phrase leaves something to be desired, even though it may serve to describe at least the initial impulse as a result of which some people turn to the study of sociology.

SOURCE: Peter Berger, *Invitation to Sociology: A Humanistic Perspective.* Garden City, New York: Doubleday, Copyright © 1963 by Peter L. Berger, pp. 2–3. Reprinted by permission of Doubleday & Company, Inc.

what use will it be to me?" (2) "What is the value of sociology to society? Why should this field be supported?" (3) "What do sociologists do? If I decided to become one, what career options would be open to me?" Let us explore some answers to these questions.

What Sociologists Do

First, we should separate the discipline from the person. Sociology is the discipline. Sociologists are the people who have been trained in the discipline and practice it. They use their skills in a wide variety of jobs, many of which seem far removed from sociology, as you will see in the "Sociologists at Work" sections at the end of each chapter.

One type of training sociologists receive concerns statistical techniques and analysis. Skills in this area are useful in a surprising variety of tasks. Most social programs, for example, try to produce changes of some kind, and the effectiveness of these programs is often assessed by choosing a representative sample of the people served and determining how much they benefited. Millions of dollars of government funding can depend on the results of such statistical surveys. Technical skills of this sort have been used to assess the effects of sex education on parents and adolescents; to study innovations in the federal court system; to find out how large a factor personal wealth is in determining who attends prestigious colleges; and to help department stores decide whether it would be profitable for them to move from a central-city location to a suburban shopping mall. Statistical surveys are used by city planners, bankers, large corporations, personnel departments, government at all levels, and people in countless other professions.

A knowledge of the results of sociological inquiry is also useful for many other areas in the workplace. Suppose you are an elementary school teacher who wishes to increase the involvement of your Hispanic students' parents in your school. The knowledge that childrearing is traditionally the primary responsibility of mothers in Hispanic cultures might help you plan and schedule your program. In a white middle-class community, on the other hand, both parents are more likely to be involved in childrearing, and you might plan your program differently. Doctors, nurses, and other health professionals would find it useful to know that members of different ethnic groups tend to have different attitudes toward modern medicine and hospitals. Factory and union management alike would be interested in knowing what aspects of the work environment workers consider most important. In Philadelphia, city planners made use of sociological information to produce seven scenarios of what the city might be like in twenty-five years as an aid in planning for development. The list goes on and on — it's difficult to think of a job in which a knowledge of sociology would not be valuable.

Most people who have advanced degrees in sociology and think of themselves as professional sociologists use both their statistical and substantive knowledge in their work. The majority of these people work as teachers, researchers, administrators, and policy consultants.

Sociologists as Teachers. More sociologists are employed as teachers than in any other capacity. There are more than fifteen thousand sociologists in the United States today, and at least two-thirds of them consider teaching their primary responsibility. Most teaching sociologists also serve other functions — researcher, administrator, or social critic, perhaps. Most teaching positions are found in liberal arts colleges or colleges of arts and sciences, in departments devoted to sociology exclusively or to some combination of sociology, anthropology, and social work. Increasingly, sociologists are being hired in professional schools of such fields as medicine, nursing, law, social work, business administration, theology, and education.

Sociologists as Researchers. In addition to teaching, most sociologists do research. The research function is often regarded as contributing to the society at large by providing new knowledge about society. Most researchers engage in *basic or pure research,* the acquisition of knowledge for its own sake with little thought about how the results will be used. Increasingly, funding and social agencies are asking for *applied research* that will help solve specific problems. Both types of researchers, for example, may be interested in crime. The basic researcher may seek information about the causes of crime, its prevalence, and its distribution by age, sex, or geography. The applied researcher may study existing social policies, police or court practices, or ways to decrease or eliminate a particular type of criminal activity. Both types of research make important contributions to our society.

Sociologists as Administrators. Sociologists serving as administrators work as coordinators, decision makers, or managers of a social organization. Increasingly, they are applying their knowledge of interpersonal relationships, bureaucracies, and organizations to improve employment practices in hospitals, schools, businesses, and government agencies. The trained sociologist should have a solid understanding of organizational structure, role conflicts, status

Sociologist Rosabeth Moss Kanter is both a teacher and a management consult-ant. Kanter's book Men and Women of the Corporation *explores the pres-sures and problems of work in a large corporation.*

differentiation, primary group relationships, both material and symbolic rewards, and the re-lationship of a particular institution or organiza-tion to the larger community and society. Although not all sociologists make good admin-istrators, sociological training should provide many of the intellectual resources and concep-tual tools necessary to serve effectively in this capacity.

Sociologists as Policy Consultants. As an outgrowth of their role as academicians and re-searchers, sociologists are often sought out by

governments, businesses, and communities to offer suggestions or advice. Their services have been requested in court decisions on busing, in neighborhood programs for crime prevention, in the development of personnel policies for insur-ance companies, in discrimination cases involv-ing automotive companies, and in the creation of community mental health centers. Sociologists seldom work as full-time consultants, however. They are used in specific situations, such as of-fering methodological advice to groups doing evaluation studies, assisting in data analysis, or explaining the probable consequences of a set of alternative courses of action. Many people consider this capability of social scientists to be an underutilized national resource. Sociologists, economists, political scientists, anthropologists, and psychologists, all of whom are experts in a particular aspect of society, could often make a much greater contribution to society if they were given an opportunity to do so.

Uses of Sociology

As can be seen from the previous discussion, sociologists serve in a variety of capacities. Although teaching, research, administration, and consulting are not reserved exclusively for sociologists, they have a unique contribution to make in these roles. Since most of you are not studying sociology to make it a career, you might well ask: What else does it have to offer us?

First, because it is concerned with every aspect of social life, sociology should interest every social being. Just as we should have an understanding of sickness without being doctors and an understanding of money without being economists, an understanding of sociological principles can be useful in our daily lives because they are concerned with an enormous range of events. Sociologists may study topics as diverse as the intimacy of husband and wife and the dynamics of mob violence. Violent crime may be the subject of one study, the communion of persons in a religious institution the subject of another. One investigator may be concerned with the inequities of race, age, and sex, while another may investigate the shared beliefs of common culture. Sociology is interested in both the typical or normal and the unusual or bizarre.

Second, even if you are not interested in a career in sociology, it offers valuable preparation for other types of careers. If your interest lies in business, law, education, medicine, architecture, ministry, social work, public administration, politics, or any profession dealing with people, social life, or the social order, sociology can be a

Sociologists are often called upon to provide advice in their areas of expertise. A criminologist with a Ph.D. in sociology worked with the Detroit Police Department to set up this neighborhood crime watch program.

useful major since it provides a wealth of knowledge that can be applied to any of these fields.

Third, sociology can teach us to consider perspectives other than our own and to look beyond the individual in our efforts to understand individual behavior. It encourages us to look not merely at how people and events are unique and different, but at how people share perceptions and how events occur in patterns. It familiarizes us with a range of theoretical explanations of how people think and act, how societies' structures change, and how society operates.

Fourth, since research is basic to sociology, even a brief introduction to the field will acquaint you with a range of research techniques and methods that can be applied to any social area: family, education, poverty, delinquency, war, ecology, and so on. Whether we use simple observation, formal structured interviews, content analysis, experimental designs, or elaborate statistical computations, a knowledge of the variety of research techniques available should be useful in many settings.

Fifth, and perhaps most important, sociology can help us understand ourselves. Humans are social animals, and people can understand themselves only in the context of the society in which they live. A knowledge of the social constraints that bind us can be frustrating — we may feel trapped, angry about our inability to control our lives, and disappointed at the social inequities that surround us. It is only through understanding our society, however, that we can appreciate what is good about it and try to improve conditions we believe to be bad.

Joel Charon (1980) provided a good summary of the uses of sociology when he listed some of the insights he has gained from his studies in this field:

1. To be different is not to be wrong. Others may think us funny, immoral, or dumb, but these judgments are merely aspects of their social definition, not absolute truths.

2. We are prisoners of social organization. Much of what we do is determined by the structures of the cultures we live in. This knowledge can be liberating, however — through understanding society we can achieve the freedom to live as we choose.

3. Things are not what they seem to be. We adopt the views transmitted to us by our culture, but these views are often limited and superficial and do not constitute understanding.

The study of sociology also made Charon more realistic about what is possible in society. Certain ideals are worth working for and can be achieved. By devoting our efforts to conditions

SOCIOLOGISTS AT WORK
Clinical Sociology and Personal Change

Roger A. Straus is a clinical sociologist. He made that career choice while a graduate student at the University of California at Davis. "I became increasingly committed to the principle that all our theories, concepts, and knowledge, if they are truly worth anything, can be applied to resolving problems in the real world. I came to feel that the test of valid theory and knowledge was in its ability to be brought back into the real world usefully. At the time, however, I had no interest in working for the state or federal government or for a consulting firm. My commitment was to the development and practice of sociologically grounded interventions to serve people and their groups. There was no such institutionalized role. Even now there is none."

What Straus did, therefore, was to create his own role. He set up a private practice as a clinical sociologist. "My goals in turning to clinical practice," he explains, "involved an extension of my conventionally sociological interests. I wanted to discover realistic theory through clinical data and

that can be changed, we can influence the direction of the social evolution that is always occurring, both in our own lives and in society.

Summary

Sociology is the study of society, social life, and the causes and consequences of human social behavior. The terms society and social life are as-

feedback from theoretically guided interventions, and I wanted to do something useful with sociological perspective and methods." As an undergraduate and later as a graduate student he had done research on the nature of religious conversion and the function of new religious movements. He concluded that such groups were successful not because they brainwash or process recruits "like pigs being converted into so much bacon," but because they hold out to potential recruits what he calls "proprietary technologies for personal transformation" — that is, methods, practices, or answers that only they claim to offer. Outsiders who are seeking to change or improve their lives may then choose (or be persuaded) to become involved with one of these groups in order to realize those promises for themselves.

"Following up this line led me to the phenomenon of hypnosis," Straus says. "I found myself getting involved in working with hypnosis at the same time that I was conducting research into the nature of hypnosis and personal change processes generally. I operated within the context of a hypnosis practitioner — although this was quickly transformed into a much wider role." One application was weight loss counseling. Straus would focus on the social origins of weight problems in America. "I'd typically begin by discussing how we are trained as children to use food to reward ourselves, to compensate for difficulties or illness, and to manage stress and make ourselves feel better, generally." The client would then be guided to replace such definitions with new ones facilitating the desired self-control.

After three years of private practice, Straus closed his office and shifted gears. "I had found out what I wanted to learn," he says. "Since 1980 I have directed my efforts at writing for the general public and working with community groups. In both cases, my aim has been to do clinical sociology on a wider scale than would be possible in a conventional practice." He has had one book published (*Strategic Self-Hypnosis*, 1981) and is at work on a second, a self-help book on weight control. He has organized the Center for Clinical Sociology, which serves as a resource center for the clinical sociology movement. And he has expanded his clinical activities to the areas of community mental health and politics. "My role is a logical extension of traditional sociology to interventions designed to empower individuals and their groups to deal with the social systems, problems, and dynamics affecting their lives," he says. "Conventional sociology has almost invariably stopped at seeking to define the ways social context influences, shapes, and constrains human beings. That's only half the story. Clinical sociology is an extension of the educational function, but we must extend our concept of education to embrace pragmatic training — showing people how to translate theory and concept and perspective into action."

sumed to include interpersonal relations within and among groups and social systems. Sociology is concerned with all aspects of the social world. Concerns range from such subjects as the family, sibling rivalry, and small-group dynamics to international conflict, organizational processes, and bureaucracies like the federal government.

In their efforts to understand social life, sociologists question the obvious, seek patterns and regularities, and look beyond individuals to social interactions and group processes. They try to assess individual behavior in the context of the larger society. This perspective is applied both to microsociology, which considers problems at the level of interpersonal and small-group processes, and to macrosociology, which considers large-scale problems, structures, social organizations, and social systems.

Although many people believe that the structure and workings of society are a matter of common knowledge, countless sociological findings disprove popular conceptions and provide surprising insights.

Sociology is one of the social sciences, disciplines that try to systematically and objectively understand social life and predict how various influences will affect it. Each social science attempts to accumulate a body of knowledge about a particular aspect of society and the social world. Economics deals with the production, consumption, and distribution of goods and services. Political science deals with power, governments, and political processes. Anthropology deals with social and physical aspects of both primitive and contemporary cultures. Psychology is concerned with the bases of individual human behavior and with mental and psychic processes. History explores past events, and geography investigates the relationship between people and their physical environment. Strictly speaking, social work is not a social science — it is not concerned chiefly with accumulating a body of basic knowledge. Rather, it is considered an applied discipline that uses the knowledge of the social scientist to improve social life.

At the end of the chapter, we raised and answered three questions about sociology: (1) What do sociologists do and what career options are available to them? (2) Why should students who are not interested in sociology as a career take it as a course? (3) What is the value of sociology to society? In answering these questions, we noted that most sociologists are employed as teachers, researchers, administrators, consultants, or some combination of these roles. Sociology is of value even to people uninterested in making it their career because it (1) provides a basic understanding of social life, (2) is a useful preparation for other careers, (3) broadens the range of perspectives from which we try to understand the social world, (4) provides an orientation to the use of

research techniques applicable in a wide variety of contexts, and (5) helps us understand ourselves and our positions in society.

In the next chapter, we consider sociology from a historical perspective, noting its development in Europe and America and examining the theoretical orientations predominant in the field today.

Key Terms

anthropology
economics
geography
history
macrosociology
microsociology
political science
psychology and social psychology
pure and applied science
social science
social work
sociological perspective
sociology

Suggested Readings

Berger, Peter. **Invitation to Sociology: A Humanistic Perspective.** *Garden City, N.Y.: Doubleday Anchor, 1963.* A brief introduction to sociology, written in a nontechnical, easily understood style.

Careers in Sociology. *A publication of the American Sociological Association, Washington, D.C., 1977.* A booklet providing a series of vignettes that illustrate careers in sociology at various levels of education.

Charon, Joel M. **The Meaning of Sociology.** *Sherman Oaks, Calif.: Alfred Publishing 1980.* A concise, easy-to-read overview of the field of sociology.

Freeman, Howard E., Russell R. Dynes, Peter H. Rossi, and William Foote Whyte. **Applied Sociology.** *San Francisco: Jossey-Bass Publishers, 1983.* An examination of the roles and activities of sociologists in diverse settings.

Harris, C. C. **The Sociological Enterprise.** *New*

York: St. Martin's Press, 1980. This book critically examines sociological inquiry and some of its fundamental concepts. It may be difficult reading for undergraduates.

Inkeles, Alex. **What Is Sociology?** *Englewood Cliffs, N.J.: Prentice-Hall, 1964.* A brief overview of the history, approaches, and schools of sociological thought.

Lazarsfeld, Paul F. and Jeffrey G. Reitz. **An Introduction to Applied Sociology.** *New York: Elsevier, 1975.* A book about applying the principles of sociology to real problems.

Mills, C. Wright. **The Sociological Imagination.** *New York: Grove Press, 1959.* This brief book, a classic in sociology, provides a readable overview of the sociological perspective.

Scott, Robert A. and Arnold R. Shore. **Why Sociology Does Not Apply: A Study of the Use of Sociology in Public Policy.** *New York: Elsevier, 1979.* A serious critique of the purpose of sociology in society. The authors are particularly concerned with the relationship between pure and applied research and their actual relevance to social policy (as distinct from their relevance to intradisciplinary concerns).

CHAPTER 2

The Development of Sociology

The human eye with all its warps and astigmatisms, can yet be trained to see more clearly than it does at present.

— Kai T. Erikson

The Development of Sociology in Europe

The study of sociology is a recent development in social history. Philosophers such as Aristotle and Plato had much to say about society and human relationships, but until the late nineteenth century, no writer we know of could appropriately be considered a sociologist. In fact, the label "sociologist" was not applied to the early practitioners of the field in their own time — they have been identified as such only in retrospect. Most early writers were interdisciplinary in orientation, drawing their ideas from philosophy and the physical and biological sciences. As a result of developments in the natural sciences, much early writing in sociology was based on the assumption that laws of human behavior could be discovered in the same way that laws of nature had been discovered by astronomers, physicists, and other natural scientists. These early writers also had great faith in the power of reason, assuming that it could be used to formulate laws that could be applied to improve social life and eliminate or diminish social problems.

These assumptions were rapidly put to a test as the industrial revolution presented new challenges and social problems. People began to migrate to towns and cities for factory jobs. With many of these jobs came low wages, long working hours, child labor practices, housing and sanitation problems, social alienation, social conflict, crime, and a range of other social problems that provided an abundance of conditions for concern, study, and solution. The industrial revolution that began in England, social revolutions in France under Napoleon, and political upheavals throughout Europe provide the backdrop for the emergence of the discipline known today as sociology.

We can begin to understand this discipline, now less than two hundred years old, by briefly examining a few of the early writers who were influential in its development. An understanding of the origins of sociology may improve our grasp of what the discipline is today. We will discuss the ideas of five theorists: Comte, Marx, Spencer, Durkheim, and Weber. These men all lived in the nineteenth century, and their ideas stemmed from their personal circumstances and social settings.

Auguste Comte

Auguste Comte (1798–1857) was born in southern France, the son of a minor government official. Educated in Paris, his studies were concentrated in mathematics and the natural sciences. Before completing his schooling, he was expelled for participating in a student insurrection against the school's administration. He then became secretary to Henri Comte de Saint-Simon, an influential political leader and advocate of a pre-Marxist version of socialism — a system in which the means of production (e.g., industry) is owned by the people. Comte was greatly influenced by Saint-Simon, but their relationship ended when Comte was accused of plagiarism, a charge he denied. He held another job in Paris for approximately twelve years, but was again dismissed. He had made too many enemies and too few friends.

Comte is usually credited with being the "father of sociology" since he coined the term sociology. he first called this new social science "social physics" because he believed that society must be studied in the same scientific manner as the world of the natural sciences. Like the natural sciences, Comte said, sociology would use empirical methods to discover basic laws of society, which would benefit mankind by playing a major part in the improvement of the human condition.

Comte is best known for his *law of human progress*, which states that each of our leading conceptions, each branch of our knowledge, all human intellectual development, passes successively through three different theoretical conditions: the *theological*, or fictitious; the *metaphysical*, or abstract; and the *scientific*, or positive. In addition, each mental age of mankind is accompanied by a specific type of social organization and political dominance. In the first stage, the theological, everything is explained and understood through the supernatural. The family is the prototypical social unit (the model or standard to which others conform) and the political dominance is held by priests and military men. In the second stage, the metaphysical, abstract forces are assumed to be the source of explanation and understanding. The state replaces the family as the prototypical social unit and, as in the Middle Ages and the Renaissance, the political dominance is held by churchmen and lawyers. In the third and highest stage, the scientific, the laws of the universe are studied through observation, experimentation, and comparison. The whole human race replaces the state as the operative social unit, and the political dominance is held by industrial administrators and scientific moral guides. It was Comte's assertion that the scientific stage of human knowledge and intellectual development was just beginning in his day. According to Comte, sociology, like the natural sciences, could henceforth draw on the methods of science to explain and understand the laws of progress and the social order.

A related concept originated by Comte was the view that society was a type of "organism." Like plants and animals, society had a structure consisting of many interrelated parts, and it evolved from simpler to more complex forms. Using this organic model as a base, he reasoned that sociology should focus on *social statics*, the structure of the organism, and on *social dynamics*, the organism's processes and forms of change. Comte believed that sociology was the means by which a more just and rational social order could be achieved.

Karl Marx

Karl Marx (1818–1883) was born in Germany. His father, a lawyer, and his mother were both descended from long lines of rabbis. Marx attended college, planning to practice law, but after becoming involved with a radical antireligious group he decided to devote his life to philosphy. Unable to get a university position, he became a writer for a radical publication and wrote a series of articles on certain inhumane social conditions. His articles attracted the attention of government officials who opposed his views, and he lost his job. Shortly thereafter he moved to Paris and met the leading intellectuals of the radical movements of Europe, completing his conversion to socialism. He began his lifelong friendship with Engels, with whom he wrote the now famous *Communist Manifesto* (1847). Having joined the Communist League in Brussels, he returned to Germany. He was again exiled for his activities. He moved to London where, with his friend Engels, he continued to promote his views until his death in 1883.

The theme common to all the writings of Marx and Engels was a profound sense of moral outrage at the misery produced in the lower classes by the new industrial order. Marx concluded that political revolution was a vital necessity in the evolutionary process of society and that it was the only means by which the improvement of social conditions could be achieved.

Marx was a major social theorist and contributor to economic and philosophical thought. He believed that *social conflict* — struggles and strife — were at the core of society, the source of all social change. He asserted that all history was marked by *economic determinism*, the idea that all change, social conditions, and even society itself are based on economic factors and that economic inequality results in class struggles between the

Karl Marx (1818–1883) addressed his writings to the inequalities between the producers of wealth (labor) and the owners of its production (management). He believed that as a social scientist he should not only observe, but work to change the inequalities that existed between the different classes.

bourgeoisie, or owners and rulers, and the *proletariat*, the industrial workers. These conflicts between the rich and the poor, the managers and the workers, lead to feelings of alienation among the workers. The recognition among workers that they share the same plight leads to a sense of "class consciousness" and ultimately, according to Marx, to revolution.

These ideas were in sharp contrast to those of Comte and many other key figures of the nineteenth century. Comte proposed that the social order be modified by science and research findings, but Marx believed that conflict, revolution, and the overthrow of capitalism were inevitable.

Today, regardless of whether they agree or disagree with Marx's ideas, few sociologists deny the importance of the contributions he made. Sociologists are still trying to understand the influence of economic determinism, social conflict, social structure, social class, and social change on society.

Herbert Spencer

Herbert Spencer (1820–1903) was born in England, the son of a school teacher. Like Comte, he received considerable training in mathematics and the natural sciences but little in history and none in English. Feeling unfit for a university career, he worked as a railway engineer, a draftsman, and finally as a journalist and writer.

One of Spencer's major concerns was with the evolutionary nature of changes in social structure and social institutions. He believed that human societies pass through an evolutionary process similar to the process Darwin explained in his theory of natural selection. It was Spencer who coined the phrase "survival of the fittest," and he was the first to believe that human societies evolved according to the principles of natural laws. Just as natural selection favors certain organisms and permits them to survive and multiply, societies that have adapted to their surroundings and can compete will survive. Those that have not adapted and cannot compete will encounter difficulties and eventually die.

Spencer's ideas on evolution, that is, his *evolutionary theory*, paralleled Darwin's theory of biological evolution in other ways. He believed that societies evolved from relative homogeneity and simplicity to heterogeneity and complexity. As simple societies progress, they become in-

creasingly complex and differentiated. Spencer viewed societies not simply as collections of individuals, but as organisms with a life and vitality of their own.

In sharp contrast to Comte, the idea of survival of the fittest led Spencer to argue for a policy of noninterference in human affairs and society. He opposed legislation designed to solve social problems, believing it would interfere with the natural selection process. He also opposed free public education, assuming that those who really wanted to learn would find the means. Just as societies that could not adapt would die out, Spencer contended, individuals who could not fit in did not deserve to flourish.

As you can imagine, Spencer's ideas had the support of people of wealth and power. His theories strengthened the position of those who wanted to keep the majority of the population impoverished and minimally educated. His ideas also tended to support a discriminatory policy — was it not a natural evolutionary law that kept people unequal? Like Marx, Spencer thought conflict and change were necessary parts of the evolutionary process. Unlike Marx, however, he believed that planned change would disrupt the orderly evolution of society, which he thought would eventually improve the social order. His goals are a radical departure from those of Marx in other respects, too, of course.

Spencer was one of the earlier writers to be concerned with the special problem of objectivity in the social sciences. Comte never seemed concerned with potential conflicts among his personal views, his religious mission, and his analysis of society. Marx denied that objective social science was possible, believing that theory was inseparable from socialist practice. Spencer, however, devoted attention specifically to the problem of bias and other difficulties that sociologists face in their work.

Those familiar with contemporary politics in the United States will recognize a recent resurgence of ideas similar to those espoused by Spencer, but today few sociologists accept his ultraconservative theory of noninterference in social change. There is, however, widespread acceptance of the idea that societies grow progressively more complex as they evolve.

Emile Durkheim

Emile Durkheim (1858–1917) can be considered the first French academic sociologist. Before Durkheim, sociology was not a part of the French education system, although such related fields as education, social philosophy, and psychology were studied. In 1892, the University of Paris granted him its first doctor's degree in sociology. Six years later he became the first French scholar to hold a chair in sociology. In addition to teaching, Durkheim wrote critical reviews and published important papers and books. His best known books include *The Division of Labor in Society, The Rules of Sociological Method, Suicide,* and *The Elementary Forms of Religious Life.*

Durkheim is responsible for several important ideas. He refused to explain social events by assuming that they operated according to the same rules as biology or psychology. To Durkheim, social phenomena are *social facts* that have distinctive social characteristics and determinants. He defined social facts as "every way of acting, fixed or not, capable of exercising on the individual an external constraint" (1933, p. 13). Being external to the individual, they outlive individuals and endure over time. They include such things as customs, laws, and the general rules of behavior that people accept without question. Stopping at traffic lights, wearing shirts, and combing one's hair are behaviors most people perform without dissent. In short, individuals are more the products of society than the creators of it.

Although an individual can come to know and be a part of society, society itself is external to the individual. For this reason, Durkheim

concentrated on examining characteristics of groups and structures rather than individual attributes. Instead of looking at the personal traits of religious believers, for example, he focused on the cohesion or lack of cohesion of specific religious groups.

Durkheim's work *Suicide* deserves special attention for several reasons. It established a

Emile Durkheim (1858–1917) advanced social theory as well as social methodology in central ways. He was especially concerned with the problem of social order: how individuals can live together in a harmonious society. He advanced sociological research with a classic statistical study that showed how the incidence of suicide will vary from one population group to another and that it is influenced by social forces.

unique model for social research, and it clearly demonstrated that human behavior, although it may seem very individual, can be understood only by investigating the social context in which the behavior takes place. After looking at numerous statistics on different countries and different groups of people, Durkheim concluded that suicide was a *social* phenomenon, related somehow to the individual's involvement in group life and the extent to which he or she was part of some cohesive social unit. Durkheim's central thesis was that the more a person is integrated into intimate social groups, the less likely he or she is to commit suicide. Thus, people who have a low level of social integration and group involvement, such as the unmarried and those without strong religious convictions, would be expected to have higher suicide rates. Durkheim found that this was true.

He believed that social integration was achieved through people's mutual dependence and acceptance of a system of common beliefs. An important element in the system of beliefs was religion, whose ceremonies become common experiences, symbols shared by the association of a group of people.

Durkheim played a key role in the founding of sociology. Although Comte, Marx, and Spencer introduced new ideas about society and helped convince the public that sociology and the other social sciences deserved a hearing, it was Durkheim who made sociology a legitimate academic enterprise.

Max Weber

Max Weber (1864–1920) was born in Germany, the son of a wealthy German politician. He was trained in law and economics, receiving his doctorate from the University of Heidelberg at the age of twenty-five. For the next several years he taught economics, but he soon succumbed to the severe mental illness that kept him an invalid and recluse for much of his life.

Max Weber (1864–1920) developed a sociological perspective that balanced two views. On the one hand he believed that social scientists should study the subjective values and meanings that individuals attach to their own behavior and that of others. At the same time he believed that social scientists should study these values and meanings objectively, remaining morally neutral or value-free. His own investigations covered very diverse fields, including law, politics, economics, religion, and authority.

Despite this condition, Weber was a prolific writer. His best known works in sociology include *The Protestant Ethic and the Spirit of Capitalism, The Sociology of Hinduism and Buddhism, Theory of Social and Economic Organization,* and *Methodology of the Social Sciences.*

Weber's mixed feelings toward authority, familial or political, are reflected in his writings on the topic of power and authority. Weber discussed why men claim authority and expect their wishes to be obeyed. (Typically for his period, women were not considered.) His approach to sociology, however, has probably been as influential as his ideas. His predecessors considered societies in terms of their large social structures, social divisions, and social movements. Spencer based his studies on the belief that societies evolved like organisms, Marx considered society in terms of class conflicts, and Durkheim was concerned with the institutional arrangements that maintain the cohesion of social structures. These theorists assumed that society, although composed of individuals, existed apart from them. In Weber's work, the *subjective* meanings that humans attach to their interactions with other humans played a much greater role. Weber believed that sociologists must study not just social facts and social structures, but *social actions,* the external objective behaviors as well as the internalized values, motives, and subjective meanings that individuals attach to their own behavior and to the behavior of others. He also contended that social actions should be studied through qualitative, subjective methods as well as objective and quantitative techniques. The goal, Weber believed, was to achieve a "sympathetic understanding" of the minds of others. He called this approach *verstehen:* understanding human action by examining the subjective meanings that people attach to their own behavior and to the behavior of others. Once values, motives, and intentions were identified, Weber contended, sociologists could treat them objectively and scientifically.

This approach is evident in Weber's interpretation of social class. Whereas Marx saw class as rooted in economic determinism, particularly as related to property ownership, Weber argued that social class involves subjective perceptions of power, wealth, ownership, and social prestige, as well as the objective aspects of these factors.

Besides the scholars we have discussed, many other European thinkers have made important contributions to sociology, including Georg Simmel, Henri de Saint-Simon, Vilfredo Pareto, Ferdinand Tönnies, and Karl Mannheim. With rare exceptions, they viewed society as a social unit that transcended the individual or was greater than the sum of individuals. It was for this reason, in part, that they did not investigate the means by which individual humans come to accept and reflect the fundamental conditions and structures of their societies — a question that was an important concern of some early American sociologists.

The Development of Sociology in America

The earliest sociologists were Europeans, but much of the development of sociology took place in the United States. The first department of sociology was established in 1893 at the University of Chicago, and many important early figures of the discipline were associated with that institution. Sociology is such a young discipline that your instructors may have met or studied with many of the leading early sociologists.

Most of the earlier American sociologists shared with their European forerunners an interest in social problems and social reform, in part because of the rapid social change that had been taking place in this country. These scholars focused on urbanization and urban problems — ghettos, prostitution, drug addiction, juvenile delinquency, immigration, and race relations.

The Chicago School
Until the 1940s, the University of Chicago was the leading sociological training and research center in America. Seven of the first twenty-seven presidents of the American Sociological Association taught or were educated at that institution. The city of Chicago served as a living laboratory for the study of many early social problems.

One leading figure in this group was Robert E. Park (1864–1944), who studied in Germany with a sociologist named Georg Simmel. Park worked as a secretary to Booker T. Washington, and also as a journalist, before beginning his work at the University in 1914, and he was the author of several important books. With another writer he wrote an early textbook in sociology (1921) and a book called *The City* (1925), which showed how urban communities are areas of both cooperation and competition much like ecological habitats that occur in nature. The multidisciplinary approach he established became known as *social ecology* (described in Chapter 20).

After World War I, a group of scholars at the University of Chicago developed an approach to social psychology known today simply as the "Chicago School." Previously, human behavior had been explained primarily in terms of instincts, drives, unconscious processes, and other innate characteristics. The Chicago School, whose members included Charles Horton Cooley, George Herbert Mead, and W. I. Thomas, emphasized instead the importance of social interactions in the development of human thought and action. Mead was the chief advocate of the view that humans respond to symbolic and abstract meanings as well as concrete experiences, and that self and society are one and the same in that individuals internalize social role expectations, social values, and norms. Humans are both actors and reactors, they are self-stimulating and can produce their own actions, responses, and definitions. To most members of society, for example, the act of burning a flag is more than a need for heat. People have learned to attach a special significance and meaning to a flag and respond with agreement or anger over a particular symbolic act, in this case, burning the flag. They might turn to others to ask why this is happening or to tell others what to do. This ability to internalize norms, share meanings, and anticipate responses

Robert E. Park (1864–1944) was one of the most influential members of the "Chicago School" of sociology. He brought his interest in the city and in urban processes into the university and into the lives of his students more than any other scholar.

is what makes social order and social systems possible. These ideas are basic to what was later called the *symbolic interactionist perspective*, which is explained in more detail in this chapter and those that follow.

The decade of the 1930s was a period of rapid change in American sociology. It was during this time that the field developed its "service" relationship to national public policy, its theoretical focus on macro systems, and its methods of large-scale quantification. In the words of Lengermann (1979, p. 196), "The societal crisis of the thirties raised new empirical and theoretical questions for sociologists, brought new demands from public and state to bear on the professional community, opened up new sources of employment and research support, created career anxiety for many sociologists and helped produce the regional associations." Lengermann claims, however, that the depression of the 1930s was not the cause of changes in sociology during this decade, since the methodological, theoretical, and professional transformation was in process prior to 1929. Rather the changes were brought about by factors such as the growth and differentiation of the profession, by emerging elitist coalitions, and by the loss of momentum of the Chicago scholars.

The Shift of Influence to the East

In the 1940s the center of sociological research shifted from Chicago to schools like Harvard and Columbia. Talcott Parsons (1902–1979), who founded the sociology department at Harvard, rapidly became the leading social theorist in America, if not the world. Drawing heavily on the work of European thinkers such as Weber and Durkheim, he developed a very broad "general theory of action" (Parsons and Shils, 1951), in which he attempted to analyze the influence of a great variety of social factors. He applied his conclusions in many areas, including the family, health, education, the economy, religion, and race relations. Although generations of graduate students have joked about the difficulty of understanding his complex abstract writing style, he had an undeniable influence on American sociology.

Robert K. Merton (1910–   ), a student of Parsons, began his teaching career at Harvard. From 1941 until his official retirement in the 1970s, however, Merton was affiliated with Columbia University. Although his general orientation was similar to Parson's, Merton was much less abstract and more concerned with linking general theory to empirical testing. This approach came to be known as the *middle range theory*. His contributions to our understanding of such concepts as social structures, self-fulfilling

Robert K. Merton (1910–   ) is an American sociologist whose teaching and writing career has been based at Columbia University. Some of his contributions are noted throughout this text in discussing topics such as middle-range theories, deviance, bureaucracy, and discrimination. Here Merton is shown in his study in front of his "wall of friends" portraits that includes Talcott Parsons (third photo down on left), Charles Cooley, W. I. Thomas, Paul Lazarsfeld, Pitirim Sorokin, and Sigmund Freud.

Why Not Dispense with Theories and Simply Get Down to Earth?

Why not dispense with theories and simply get down to earth? Why not select some concrete problem, such as urban slum life . . . and design studies to shed light on this problem? In short, why not deal primarily with our important social problems as they arise? This is certainly an important kind of criticism of current social science research, and it must be answered. One answer can be given in terms of knowledge for its own sake. The scientist is not concerned with how his theories and findings are to be applied. He is basically an intellectual whose curiosity has been aroused, and our aesthetic appreciation of his work ought to be sufficient justification in and of itself.

While I think there is much to be said for this position, I do not believe that it would appeal to most students or laymen nor even to many scientists themselves. We have seen too many examples of scientists producing weapons of destruction, and of, in effect,

selling themselves to the highest bidder, to give credence to the naïve assumption that, in the long run, scientific advances will necessarily work toward the benefit of mankind. Social scientists, in particular, are sensitive to this kind of problem. They see billions being spent on rocket research while people are starving and discrimination is producing serious social problems. Yet most social scientists seem to believe that basic or nonapplied research is absolutely essential, even where the ultimate objective is to shed light on practical problems of the day. Why should this be the case?

The difficulty with purely applied research and attention to current practical problems is that the problems change much more rapidly than our ability to study them. By the time we had conducted a thorough study of one phenomenon, it might have given way to another. In fact, activists argue that "research" is often used as an excuse for doing noth-

ing. What they seem to mean is that it will take so long to conduct the research that the problem will have either disappeared or been obscured or forgotten. This is sometimes true and must be freely admitted. Even if the phenomenon has not changed completely, many of the specifics may change with sufficient rapidity that by the time the research report has been made available the findings will no longer accurately describe the true state of affairs. For example, the study may report that 53 percent of whites favor school integration, but a series of riots that have intervened between the time of the interviews and the time of the report may have shifted the true percentage downward to 20 percent. An action policy based on this dated finding might fail because of its inaccuracy. . . .

The most useful scientific laws, then, are those that do not refer directly to concrete events (e.g., the position of Venus at 8:05 P.M. July 1, 1970) but are instead phrased more generally in the form of "if-then" statements. *If* a body is moving with a particular velocity and momentum in a specified gravitational field, *then* its position can be expected to

---

prophecies, deviance, and bureaucracies place him among the leading American social theorists.

C. Wright Mills, Lewis Coser, George Homans, Erving Goffman, and Herbert Blumer will also be mentioned throughout the book as major contributors to the development of sociology. These are just a few of the many influential

scholars we do not have room to discuss. It is perhaps sufficient to say that sociology is stronger in the United States than in any other country although the field is also well established in many other parts of the world. The American Sociological Association currently has about fourteen thousand members, a number far greater than in any other country.

change according to some specified law. If one then wants to refer to a particular historical event, such as the position of Venus on a given day, this general law can be applied to the concrete case. In addition to the law itself, however, it will be necessary to supply some concrete facts about the mass and present velocity of Venus and its present position in relation to the sun and other planets. It will also be necessary to make certain simplifying assumptions about the lack of disturbances from outside factors (e.g., nearby stars). . . .

One of the most serious and difficult problems confronting the social scientist is that of developing reasonably general laws of social behavior that are not so restricted as to time and place that they can be applied only under very limited circumstances. The more restrictive the law, the less likely that it will remain appropriate for use in practical situations, which means that its implications cannot be continually tested. Even if a general theory of "hippie" behavior could be constructed and tested, and even if it predicted hippie behavior extremely well, its usefulness would disappear with the last hippie

colony. Perhaps a variation of the hippie theme might later appear, in which case the theory might again be applied with minor modifications, but clearly a theory restricted to this single kind of deviant behavior will be useful only to the extent that the phenomenon continues to persist. The theory would be much more useful if it could be generalized to include, let us say, all forms of "escapist" deviance. But such a more general formulation would undoubtedly be less specific regarding details, and its predictions would be much less precise.

Thus we have a peculiar kind of dilemma in many of the social sciences owing to the fact that the phenomena we study are often not as persistent and regular — relative to the time it takes to study them — as in some of the physical sciences. Yet many social phenomena appear to be all too persistent: wars, prejudice and discrimination, crime, and many kinds of interpersonal conflict. Many less "problematic" phenomena are also persistent: the formation of friendship cliques, authority relationships within bureaucratic organizations, socialization patterns within the family, and the like. It

would seem possible to develop reasonably specific theories of these phenomena, even in the absence of highly general laws that are relatively timeless. . . .

Let me illustrate in terms of dominance-subordinance relationships. It would certainly be useful if we could explain many different forms of dominance relationships in terms of a single theory of power. For example, what is there in common in the parent-child, white-black, citizen-criminal, and large nation-small nation relationships? Can we spell out the conditions under which increasing punishment by the dominant party will lead to increased resistance by the subordinate party, as contrasted with the conditions under which the subordinate party will yield? If a really adequate theory existed, then it would be possible to apply it to some new power relationship not yet systematically studied (e.g., power relationships between college administrations and student rebels).

SOURCE: Hubert M. Blalock, Jr., *An Introduction to Social Research,* © 1970, pp. 81–85. Reprinted by permission of Prentice-Hall, Inc., Englewood Cliffs, New Jersey.

Contemporary sociology, like most academic disciplines, is concerned with many subject areas. It uses a wide variety of methodological tools and procedures and offers a range of theories to explain the phenomena with which it is concerned. These social theories and major theoretical orientations are discussed in the next section.

The Major Theoretical Perspectives in Sociology

Theories are explanations offered to account for a set of phenomena. Social theories are explanations of social phenomena — why people choose to marry as they do or why people behave differently in different social situations.

We all develop theories (to use the term in its broadest sense) to help us explain a wide variety of events. Even when the explanations are wrong, they may help us develop guidelines for behavior and hypotheses that can be tested.

Suppose, for example, that several sociologists are trying to determine why the rate of armed robbery has risen in Metropolis in the last ten years. One sociologist might suggest the proposition that it was due to the increase in unemployment, which forced people to rob to get money for food. Another might hypothesize that the crime rate is largely the result of the increased availability of heroin — addicts are robbing to get money for a fix. A third might suggest that armed robbery is related to the incidence of divorce — children from broken homes are spending too much time on the street and getting into trouble.

After they develop their theories, the sociologists would begin to test them. They could examine statistics, interview parents, check police records, and use other means to acquire information. In this greatly oversimplified example, let us assume that the sociologist with the "broken home" idea discovers that most of the robbers who have been caught are in their twenties and thirties. This conclusion argues against his theory — the robbers would probably have been living away from their families. Is it possible, though, that the robbers are alienated and incapable of holding jobs because of experiences they had as children? (This is an example of a theory leading to new avenues of exploration even though it appears to be wrong.) The sociologist, upon further investigation, determines that the divorce rate in Metropolis underwent a sharp decline in the 1940s and 1950s, contrary to the national trend. This assumption means that his secondary theory — that the robbers are the victims of homes disrupted by divorce when they were children — is also wrong.

Let us assume, however, that the other propositions are supported by the information discovered. The robbery rate began to climb shortly after the local air conditioner factory closed, and it jumped dramatically at about the time the police say heroin began to be sold on the street.

Does the fact that both of these theories received support from research mean that one of them is wrong? Not necessarily. Sociology offers multiple explanations of most phenomena. Explanations can be different without being incompatible, and even those that seem unlikely or illogical should be evaluated in the context of the events they were designed to explain.

In the example given above, the term theory is used rather broadly. To be more precise: a theory is a set of interrelated statements or propositions intended to explain a given phenomenon. It is based on a set of assumptions and self-evident truths, includes definitions, and describes the conditions in which the phenomenon exists.

Although sociological theories exist to explain everything from childrearing to automobile sales, a small number of basic theories predominate in the field. These are explained below and will be described in more detail and applied to specific topics later in the book.

Evolutionary Theory

The evolutionary approach is associated with biological concepts and concerned with long-term change. *Evolutionary theory* suggests that societies, like biological organisms, progress through stages of increasing complexity. As with ecologists, evolutionists suggest that societies, again like organisms, are interdependent with their environments.

Most of the early sociologists and some recent ones adhere to an evolutionary view. Early sociologists often equated evolution with progress and improvement, believing that natural selection would eliminate weak societies and those that could not adapt. The strong societies, they believed, deserved to survive because they were better. It was for this reason that early theorists such as Spencer opposed any sort of interference that would protect the weak and interfere with natural evolutionary processes.

Contemporary evolutionists, on the other hand, rarely oppose all types of intervention. They tend to view evolution as a process that results in change, but they do not assume that the changes are necessarily for the better. Almost all would agree that society is becoming more complex, for example, but they might argue that the complexity brings about bad things as well as good. The telephone is a good illustration of a technological improvement that makes our lives more complex. Surely it is an improvement — it permits us to be in contact with the whole world without stirring from our homes — but a contemporary evolutionist might point out that a phone can also be an annoyance, as students trying to study and harried office workers can attest. Early evolutionists, on the other hand, would have been more likely to regard the telephone as a sign of progress and hence an unmixed blessing.

Evolutionary theory provides us with a structural perspective from which to judge a wide range of social influences. If its basic premises of directional change and increasing complexity are valid, it should provide better comprehension of current trends, and even help us predict the future.

Structural Functional Theory

Structural functionalism also has its roots in the work of the early sociologists, especially Durkheim and Weber. Among contemporary scholars, it is most closely associated with the work of Parsons and Merton. Many would argue that structural functionalism is the dominant

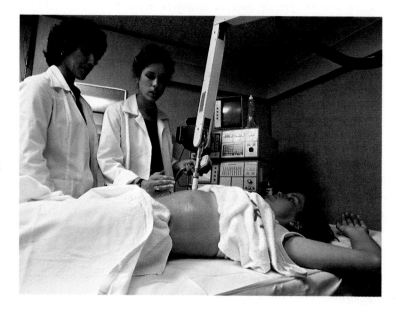

All social systems are made up of interrelated statuses with certain behaviors attached to them. The structural functionalist, in analyzing our health care system, notes that people of varying statuses — physicians, nurses, technicians, patients — have differing role expectations and perform differing functions. Here a technician or medical assistant works with a physician in running tests on a patient. The expectations associated with these statuses make it inappropriate for the patient to operate the equipment or to direct what tests should be given.

theoretical view in sociology today. It is sometimes referred to as *social systems theory, equilibrium theory,* or simply *functionalism.*

The terms *structure* and *function* refer to two separate but closely related concepts. Structures can be compared with the organs or parts of the body of an animal, and functions can be compared with the purposes of these structures. The stomach is the structure; digestion is its function. In the same way, health care organizations and the military are social structures (or social systems), and caring for the sick and defending the country are their functions. Like a biological structure, a social system is composed of many interrelated and interdependent parts or structures.

Social structures include any component or part of society: clubs, families, nations, groups, and so forth. Central to an understanding of social structures are the concepts of *status* and *role.* Simply defined, a status is a socially defined position: female, student, lawyer, or Catholic. Some of these are *ascribed statuses,* that is, given to us at birth (age, sex, race) whereas others are *achieved statuses* (college graduate, father, teacher). Sets of interrelated statuses or positions are *social systems.* For example, the interrelated statuses of mother, father, and children constitute a family system. The interrelated statuses of teachers, students, and school administrators constitute an educational system.

You can easily list many personal statuses, such as age, sex, marital status, education, occupation, or religion. Each of these statuses has a dynamic aspect, a set of expectations and behaviors associated with it in a given group or society. These are termed *roles.* As a result, different roles (expectations for behavior) are associated with different statuses (positions) such as infant or adult, male or female, student or teacher, married or single. To occupy certain statuses is to have a general idea of appropriate behavior. The

roles or expectations of a baseball team manager, for instance, differ from that of the batter, pitcher, or fielder. What is expected of a pitcher or batter, however, and what that pitcher or batter actually does may differ. In other words, role performance does not always match role expectations. The learning of these role expectations and behaviors is accomplished through the socialization process, described in Chapter 6.

As we mentioned earlier, interrelated statuses constitute social systems. Each social system performs certain functions that make it possible for society and the people who comprise that society to exist. Each serves a function that leads to the maintenance or stability of the larger society. The educational system is intended to provide literary and technical skills, the religious system is intended to provide emotional support and answer questions about the unknown, families are intended to socialize infants, and so on. The functionalist perspective assumes that these social systems have an underlying tendency to be in equilibrium or balance; any system that fails to fulfill its functions will result in an imbalance or disequilibrium. In extreme cases, the entire system can break down when a change or failure in any one part of the system affects its interrelated parts.

A social system can be regarded as having two types of functions: (1) what the system does and (2) the consequences that result from a particular type of structure or organization. In a biological system, the function of the eyes is to obtain information about the environment. This function provides one with the ability to seek food and shelter and the ability to avoid danger. In a social system, one function of government might be to maintain order. An advantage of this function is that people can carry on their affairs — running businesses, raising families — without having their lives disrupted.

According to Merton, a social system can

have both *manifest functions* and *latent functions.* Manifest functions are intended and recognized; latent functions are neither intended nor recognized. One manifest function of education systems is to teach literary and technical skills. They also perform the latent functions of "sitting" for children while parents work and providing contacts for dating and marriage. Correctional institutions have the manifest functions of punishment and removing criminals from social interaction with the larger society. They may also perform the latent functions of providing advanced training in breaking and entering.

Merton recognized that not all consequences of systems are functional — that is, they do not all lead to the maintenance of the system. Some lead to instability or the breakdown of a system. These consequences he termed *dysfunctions.* Families have a manifest function of rearing children. The intensity of family interactions, however, can lead to the dysfunction, or negative consequence, of violence and child abuse. This dysfunction may lead to the disruption of relationships within the family system or even to the total breakdown of the system.

Sociologists who adhere to the functionalist perspective examine the parts of a given system and try to determine how they are related to one another and to the whole. They observe the results of a given cluster or arrangement of parts, attempting to discover both the intended (manifest) and the unintended (latent) functions of these parts. In addition, they analyze which of these consequences contribute to the maintenance of a given system and which lead to the breakdown of the system. It should be noted that what may be functional in one system may be dysfunctional in another. A function that is good for corporate profits may not be good for family solidarity, while one that is good for religious unity may not be good for ethnic integration.

Competition for limited resources and inequalities between persons or groups may lead to disharmony, even violence, but they may also be a source of constructive change. Shown here is one situation of status and power inequality.

According to the functionalist perspective, social systems exist because they fulfill some function for the society. Functionalists focus on order and stability, which has led some critics to argue that it supports the status quo. With the emphasis on equilibrium and the maintenance of the system, the process of change, critics say, receives little attention. In this respect, functionalism differs greatly from conflict theory, which is described below.

Conflict Theory

Conflict theory also had its origins in early sociology, especially in the work of Marx. Among its more recent proponents are such people as Mills, Coser, and Dahrendorf. They share the view that society is best understood and analyzed in terms of conflict and power.

Karl Marx began with a very simple assumption: the structure of society is determined by economic organization, particularly the ownership of property. Religious dogmas, cultural values, personal beliefs, institutional arrangements, class structures — all are basically reflections of the economic organization of a society. Inherent in any economic system that supports inequality are forces that generate revolutionary class conflict, according to Marx. The exploited classes eventually recognize their submissive and inferior status and revolt against the dominant class of property owners and employers. The story of history, then, is the story of class struggle between the owners and workers, the dominators and the dominated, the powerful and the powerless.

Contemporary conflict theorists assume that conflict is a permanent feature of social life and that as a result societies are in a state of constant change. Unlike Marx, however, these theorists rarely assume that conflict is always based on class or that it always reflects economic organization and ownership. Conflicts are assumed to involve a broad range of groups or interests: young against old, male against female, or one racial group against another, as well as workers against employers. These conflicts result because things like power, wealth, and prestige are not available to everyone — they are limited commodities, and the demand exceeds the supply. Conflict theory also assumes that those who have or control desirable goods and services will defend and protect their own interests at the expense of others.

In this view, conflict does not mean the sort of event that makes headlines, such as war, violence, or open hostility. It is instead regarded as the struggle that occurs day after day as people try to maintain and improve their positions in life. Neither should conflict be regarded as a destructive process that leads to disorder and the breakdown of society. Theorists like Dahrendorf and Coser have focused on the integrative nature of conflict, its value as a force that contributes to order and stability. How can conflict be a constructive force? The answer is basically that people with common interests join together to seek gains that will benefit them all. By the same token, conflict among groups focuses attention on inequalities and social problems that might never be resolved without conflict. Racial conflicts, for example, may serve to bind people with common interests together and also lead to constructive social change.

There is an obvious contrast between the views of the functionalists, who regard society as balanced and in a state of equilibrium, and the views of conflict theorists, who assume that society is an arena of constant competition and change. Functionalists believe the social process is a continual effort to maintain harmony; conflict theorists believe it is a continual struggle to "get ahead." Functionalists view society as basically consensual, integrated, and static; conflict theorists believe it is characterized by constraint, conflict, and change. Whereas functionalists have been criticized for focusing on stability and the status quo, conflict theorists have been criticized for overlooking the less controversial and more orderly aspects of society.

Symbolic Interaction Theory

Symbolic interaction theory, although influenced somewhat by early European sociologists, was developed largely through the efforts of Mead, Thomas, and Cooley, who all belonged to the Chicago School. The key difference between this perspective and those discussed earlier revolves around the size of the units used in investigation and analysis. Macrosociological orientations — the evolutionary, structural-functional, and conflict theories — interpret society in terms of its large structures: organizations, institutions, social classes, communities, and nations. Microsociological orientations such as symbolic interaction theory, on the other hand, study individuals in society and their definitions of situations, meanings, roles, interaction patterns, and the like. Although these levels of analysis overlap considerably, they operate from different assumptions and premises.

The question of how individuals influence society and how society influences individuals is central to sociology. As you recall, early sociologists (Spencer, Durkheim, and Marx, for example) regarded society as an entity existing apart from the individual. Symbolic interactionists, however, assume that society exists within every socialized individual and that its external forms and structures arise through the social interactions taking place among individuals at the symbolic level.

What is meant by "the symbolic level"? It can be explained this way: suppose you are driving down the road in your car and you come upon a brick wall running across the road. You stop, of course, because you have learned you cannot pass through a physical object. If, however, you perceive the brick wall to be a mental picture, a mirage, you won't "of course" stop. Let us suppose next that you are riding down the same road and you come to a stoplight. Once again you stop — but why? There is nothing physical to keep you from progressing. Your reason for stopping is that you have learned that the red light is a *symbol* that means stop. The world around us can be said to consist of these two ele-

Symbolic interaction theory alerts us to the importance of shared meanings and definitions attached to objects and behaviors. Here we have the seal of the President of the United States. To nonsocialized humans or to animals, for example, this symbol carries no importance or significance. To others, however, it represents the highest office in the United States and a position of great power and prestige.

ments: physical objects and abstract symbols. Thus language is a system of symbols. It represents physical objects or concepts that can be used to communicate.

According to George Herbert Mead, who played an important role in the development of symbolic interactionism, it is the ability of humans to use symbols that sets us apart from animals and allows us to create social institutions, societies, and cultures. People in a society share an understanding of certain symbols (the stoplight, for example). Social learning takes place at both symbolic and nonsymbolic levels. In interaction with others, we learn (internalize) social expectations, a specific language, and social values. In interaction with others, we learn to share meanings and to communicate symbolically through words and gestures. As humans, we can interact at both a physical (a slap) as well as a symbolic level (showing a fist or making a verbal threat). Because we can relate symbolically, we can carry on conversations with ourselves. We can also imagine the effects of different courses of action. We can imagine what will happen if we throw a rotten tomato in the face of a police officer. By thinking through alternate courses of actions, we can choose those believed to be most appropriate for a given situation. The fact that others share similar expectations makes life patterned and relatively predictable. Those who fail to recognize that red traffic lights mean stop will have trouble getting any place safely in their cars.

The interactionist perspective examines patterns and processes of everyday life that are generally ignored by many other perspectives. It raises questions about the self, the self in relationships with others, and the self and others in the wider social context. Why do some of us have negative feelings about ourselves? Why can we relate more easily with some persons than others? Why do we feel more comfortable around friends than strangers? How is it possible to interact with complete strangers or to know what to do in new situations? How are decisions made in families? Symbolic interactionists try to answer such questions by examining the individual in a social context. The starting point of this examination is the social setting in which an individual is born and the interactions he or she has with parents, siblings, teachers, neighbors or others. From these interactions, we learn what is

proper or improper, whether we are "good" or "bad," who is important, and so forth. A more complete explanation of this perspective is given in Chapter 6 and in other sections throughout the book.

Although symbolic interaction theory is the most widely used and recognized interaction perspective, exchange theory also falls within this general orientation.

Exchange Theory

Exchange theory has a diverse intellectual heritage, drawing from sources in economics, anthropology, and psychology as well as sociology. This perspective is based on the belief that life is a series of exchanges involving rewards and costs. In economic exchanges, people exchange money, goods, and services, hoping to profit or at least break even in the exchange. In anthropological, psychological, and sociological exchanges, the items of exchange include social and psychic factors as well. In return for your companionship, I'll invite you to my house. In return for your positive teacher evaluation, I'll work extra hard to be a good instructor. Work, gifts, money, affection, ideas — all are offered in the hope of getting something in return.

Social exchange theory seeks to explain why behavioral outcomes like marriage, employment, and religious involvement occur, given a set of structural conditions (age, race, gender, class) and interactional possibilities. Women, for example, marry men of a higher social status more frequently than men marry women of a higher social status. Exchange theorists would attempt to explain this finding by examining the desirable qualities men and women have to exchange. In the United States, for men to have money or a good job is viewed as desirable. For women to be physically attractive is viewed as desirable. Thus, we might expect that very attractive lower-status women could exchange their beauty for men of a higher economic and occupational status, which seems to be what happens.

Exchange theory assumes that people seek rewarding statuses, relationships, and experiences and try to avoid costs, pain, and punishments. Given a set of alternatives, individuals choose those from which they expect the most profit, rewards, or satisfaction and avoid those that are not profitable, rewarding, or satisfying. When the costs exceed the rewards, people are likely to feel angry and dissatisfied. When the rewards exceed the costs, they are likely to feel that they got a good deal (unless they got it through exploitation or dishonesty, in which case they may feel guilty and choose to avoid further interactions). For both parties to be satisfied with the interaction there must be some type of equity in the exchange, a feeling on the part of both that the rewards were worth the costs.

Although people may work selflessly for others with no thought of reward, it is quite unusual. The social exchange perspective assumes that voluntary social interactions are contingent on rewarding reactions from others. When rewarding reactions cease, either the actions end or dissatisfaction results.

There are two different schools of thought in the exchange theory perspective. George Homans, the theorist responsible for originating exchange theory, represents a perspective consistent with that of behavioral psychologists, who believe that behavior can be explained in terms of rewards and punishments. Behaviorists focus their attention on actual behavior, not on processes that can be inferred from behavior but cannot be observed. In exchange theory, the rewards and punishments are the behavior of other people, and those involved in exchanges assume that their rewards will be proportional to their costs.

Peter Blau is the advocate of a different school of exchange theory, one that is consistent with symbolic interactionism. Blau does not attempt to explain all exchanges in terms of observable behavior. He argues that the exchange is more subjective and interpretative and that the exchanges occur on the symbolic level. As a result, money may be a just reward only if it is defined by the receiver as such, and psychic rewards of satisfaction with doing a good job or of pleasing someone may be as important as money, gifts, or outward responses of praise.

Both Homans and Blau agree that what is important is that each party receives in the exchange something perceived as equivalent to that which is given (to Homans, *distributive justice*; to Blau, *fair exchange*). All exchange involves a mutually held expectation that reciprocation will occur. If resources or exchange criteria are unequal, one person is at a distinct disadvantage and the other has power over and controls the relationship. As a result, in marriage, unequal exchanges between husband and wife are likely to result in dominance of one over the other or may even end the relationship. In employment, if employee and employer do not recognize a fair exchange of rewards and costs, dissatisfaction may result, the employee may quit, or the employer may dismiss the employee.

In exchange theory, then, social life is viewed as a process of bargaining or negotiation, and social relationships are based on trust and mutual interests.

Summary

Compared with the other sciences, sociology is of recent origin. Not until the 1800s was a scientific methodology applied to social phenomena. The industrial revolution and political upheavals in Europe encouraged various scholars to try to explain social change and the social order. Five theorists who had an especially im-

SOCIOLOGISTS AT WORK
Helping Children Live Within the System

Henry Lewis is a group leader and counselor at New Horizons Ranch and Center, outside Goldthwaite, Texas. New Horizons is a residential treatment center for children who have problems living within "the system" — be it their family, their school, or the community at large. The center's goal is simple. As Lewis puts it, "We help them get their act together." The people who run the center think Henry Lewis has a solid credential that can help them achieve that goal: a B.A. in sociology, which he earned at Angelo State University in nearby San Angelo.

If New Horizon's goal is simple, the ways of reaching it are not. "Every child comes here with a different problem, and every child is dealt with differently," says Lewis. "They're referred to us by their school systems, by the Texas Department of Human Resources, and by the Texas Youth Council. We're a private, nonprofit organization. We're not an institution per se. We're located out in the country, and there are no locks, no fences, nothing like that. We run a school, and we get the kids involved in work around the ranch or for businesses in town. We go fishing, we go skating, we go to movies — we try to set up a family environment. And we do a lot of individual counseling."

There are about fifty children at New Horizons at any given time. "They come to us because they've had school problems or home problems," Lewis says. "Or they might have been taken out of their homes because they've been neglected or physically or sexually abused. Or they might have been abandoned. None of our kids have criminal records. They've come to the Texas Youth Council because there's no other place for them to go at the time. Students who are referred to us have to come up here for pre-placement — we accept about one in ten. They have to assure us that they *want* to work on their problems, that they *want* to be in our program. Then we draw up an individual treatment plan." The average stay at the center is about eleven months, although some children stay only a month or two and some have stayed as long as three years. Then they move back to their homes, or on to foster homes

portant influence on the development of sociology are: Comte, Marx, Spencer, Durkheim, and Weber.

Auguste Comte is credited with being the father of sociology. He first called it social physics because he believed society must be studied in the same scientific manner as the natural sciences. He believed that human progress evolved through three stages: the theological, the metaphysical, and the scientific. Karl Marx, one of the most radical thinkers of his time, made major contributions to our understanding of social conflict. He believed that all history was based on economic determinism, which resulted in class struggles between the rich and powerful bourgeoisie and the working class proletariat. Herbert Spencer, like Comte, focused his attention on evolutionary schemes, emphasizing in particular the social survival of the fittest. Unlike Comte, however, he argued for a policy of

or to other treatment centers. One girl left recently to enroll in Henry Lewis's alma mater, Angelo State University. At present there are about forty-five boys and nine girls at the center. They are divided into groups according to age, background, educational level, and size — four groups of boys and one of girls. Lewis is the group leader for the youngest group, eight boys aged ten to fourteen.

The staff of thirty includes people with degrees in psychology and sociology and other counseling backgrounds, and others with no degrees who have been with the center from the beginning (in 1971) and understand and are committed to its ideal of treatment in a family atmosphere. When they were looking for someone with training in sociology, a friend in the Texas Department of Corrections referred them to Lewis. "My study of sociology really helped me prepare for this work," he says. "I was interested in juvenile delinquency, family violence, and that whole spectrum of social problems. The most important thing is to understand the reality — that the sort of stuff we deal with really does happen. To a lot of people it's hidden. Studying sociology, studying families and children in families and in groups, gave me an awareness of the problem and the need."

The problems Lewis encounters are a varied lot. He cites the case of a young black boy who grew up in a completely segregated setting and had little experience of white people. "He grew up in an environment where whites were foreign, the bad guys. We had to work with him just to get him to the point where he could feel comfortable around a white person." Another boy was adopted at a young age. After three or four years it became clear that his adoptive family didn't want him. He was neglected and abused. He reacted to this several ways: soiling his underwear, fighting in school, attacking his teachers. "We had here a child who could not really fit in with any social group. Wherever he went — to school, to the store — you could be sure he would cause some disturbance." The center set a goal for him: to increase his patience and his attention span. After about a year the results were noticeable. "Now you can send him into a store and know he's not going to pull anything. We had to offer him an alternative to his behavior. We had to show him that he *could* go out with a group, that he *could* live in a world of families and groups." That is something New Horizons Ranch and Center excels at. "For some of these children, this is the only real home, the only family, they've ever had."

government noninterference in the course of human history and change.

Emile Durkheim made major contributions to our understanding of social facts. He rejected explanations of social events that assumed that society operated in a fashion parallel to biology. In a classic study, he demonstrated that suicide was related to the degree of involvement in a cohesive group or social unit. Max Weber focused his writing on a new methodology for studying social life. He emphasized the need to focus on subjective meanings (*verstehen*) in studying human interaction and social systems.

The development of sociology in America drew heavily from European writers, especially at the macrosociological level, but America was also very influential in the development of microsociology. Important contributions were made by men like Cooley, Mead, and Thomas who stressed the importance of social interaction and the influence of society on human thought and action. Not until the 1930s did sociology shift from the University of Chicago to other major educational institutions. In the East, Parsons, Merton, Mills, Coser, Homans, and Blau were influential in the development of social theory.

A social theory is a systematically interrelated proposition that seeks to explain a process or phenomena. Five major theories, three at the macro level and two at the micro level, have had an important influence on contemporary sociology. These are the evolutionary-ecological theory, structural functional theory, conflict theory, symbolic interactional theory, and exchange theory.

An evolutionary theory suggests that societies, like biological organisms, go through transitions or stages and are interdependent with the environment or world about them. A structural functional theory focuses on the parts of a system, the relationships among these parts, and the functions or consequences of social structures. These functions can be either intended and recognized (manifest) or unintended and unrecognized (latent). Some consequences are dysfunctional in that they lead to the instability and breakdown of the system. Structural functional theories assume that systems have a tendency toward equilibrium and balance.

Conflict theory assumes that conflict is a permanent feature of social life and a key source of change. The Marxist orientation toward conflict assumes that it is rooted in a class struggle between the employers and the workers or between the powerful and the powerless. Many conflict theorists assume that conflict serves an integrative function and acts as a source of constructive change. Symbolic interactionism, a micro theory, emphasizes relationships between individuals and between individuals and society. According to this theory, society has as its basis shared meanings, language, social interaction, and symbolic processes. It is the mind that differentiates humans from nonhumans and permits people to develop a social self, to assume the role of others, and to imaginatively consider alternative courses of action.

The basic assumption of an exchange theory is that social life involves a series of reciprocal exchanges involving rewards and costs. Exchange theories endeavor to explain why certain behavioral outcomes result from a given set of structural conditions and interactional possibilities.

The next chapter looks at methods of studying society. Upon completion of this first part of the book, you will have a clearer understanding of sociology and the close relationship between theory and research.

Key Terms

ascribed and achieved status
bourgeoisie and proletariat
Chicago School
Comte's law of human progress
conflict theory
dysfunctions
economic determinism
evolutionary theory
exchange theory
manifest and latent functions
Marx and social conflict
middle range theory
roles
social facts
social statics and social dynamics
social system
Spencer's evolutionary scheme
structural functionalism
symbolic interaction theory
theories
verstehen

Suggested Readings

Coser, Lewis A. **Masters of Sociological Thought: Ideas in Historical and Social Context, 2d ed.,** *New York: Harcourt Brace Jovanovich, 1977.* A look at the lives and ideas of major figures in the development of sociological theory.

Hinkle, Roscoe C. **Founding Theory of American Sociology 1881–1915.** *Boston: Routledge and Kegan Paul, 1980.* An advanced work that compares, contrasts, and classifies the theories of early American sociologists.

Merton, Robert K. **Social Theory and Social Structure.** *Glencoe, Ill.: The Free Press, revised and enlarged ed., 1957.* The original statement of structural functionalism. Merton also discusses the development of his theory of the middle range, the consequences of anomie, and the self-fulfilling prophecy.

Poloma, Margaret M. **Contemporary Sociological Theory.** *New York: Macmillan, 1979.* A text designed and written for undergraduate students of sociology covering the major sociological theories.

Rossides, Daniel W. **The History and Nature of Sociological Theory.** *Boston: Houghton Mifflin, 1978.* An introduction to social theory with an emphasis on a critical investigation of problems of social science.

Turner, Jonathan H. **The Structure of Sociological Theory.** *Homewood, Ill.: The Dorsey Press, revised ed., 1978.* An analysis of the historical roots and contemporary forms of four dominant paradigms of social theory: functionalism, conflict, interactionism, and exchange.

Warshay, Leon H. **The Current State of Sociological Theory: A Critical Interpretation.** *New York: David McKay, 1975.* A comprehensive and integrated overview of the present state of contemporary sociological theory, with a discussion of current trends.

CHAPTER 3

Methods of Studying Society

It is a capital mistake to theorize before one has data.

— Sir Arthur Conan Doyle

People arrive at their opinions and beliefs through a number of different routes, and notions about reality vary greatly. Some people believe that politicians are crooked, others that they are dedicated public servants. Some believe that hard work will lead to success, others that it is a waste of time and that for them, failure is inevitable.

We get ideas such as these from a number of different sources. We derive some from everyday experiences and common sense: our past experiences and personal observations convince us that certain things are true. We see blondes having a good time and are convinced that blondes have more fun. We talk to women who want children and assume that a desire for children is instinctive in women. Experience and common sense may lead others to different conclusions, however.

We get other ideas from "authorities," people assumed to be knowledgeable because of their experience or position. We may consider the Pope, the President of the United States, our personal physician, our professor, or our parents to be authority figures. We seldom bother to investigate the source of their expertise or the information they used to reach their conclusions because we feel that their information is not subject to question. Like ideas derived from common sense, however, the opinions of authorities may differ. The conclusions of one doctor are not always identical to those of another doctor. Parents sometimes do not agree with each other, much less with other parents.

A third source of ideas or knowledge is revelation. Revelation may be thought to result from divine experiences, prayer, or magic. Knowledge acquired through revelation is often considered sacred and absolute, so it is not subject to question. Some people, for example, believe that wives should submit to their husbands' authority because the Bible says they should do so.

A fourth source of ideas is tradition. The wisdom of previous generations is passed on and accepted as accurate. We may plant corn by the phase of the moon and take a sip of brandy to cure a chest cold. Why? Because that's the way it's always been done.

A fifth source of knowledge is research that uses empirical methods. Some sociologists do not reject personal experience, common sense, authority, revelation, and tradition as sources of knowledge, but most rely heavily on methods considered empirical or scientific. Empirical methods focus on observable phenomena, which means that others should be able to observe the same phenomena and check our observations for accuracy. Unlike the common sense observations made as part of our daily experience, however, researchers using empirical methods strive to be objective. In this chapter, we will consider the use of scientific methods in sociology. We will also examine standards of scientific inquiry, types of sociological research, research methods, and the process of research.

Is Sociology a Science?

As you saw in Chapter 2, Comte, Spencer, and other early sociologists regarded their new discipline as a science. The natural sciences had successfully formulated laws, principles, and theories about the physical world through the use of the *scientific method*, a procedure that involved systematically formulating problems, collecting data through observation and experiment, and devising and testing hypotheses. Early social theorists believed that the same method could be used to develop laws, principles, and theories about the social world. There was also a practical reason for adopting science as the model of inquiry. The Western world, particu-

larly the United States, has regarded science as almost sacred. Sociologists seeking legitimacy for their new discipline wished to convey to a skeptical world that they too could be objective, systematic, precise, and predictive in their field of study. They also hoped to develop a social technology that could be used to direct change and resolve social problems.

Not everyone regards sociology as a science, however. Some contend that, defined strictly, science does not include the descriptions, hunches, opinions, and statistical tendencies of sociology. It has also been argued that human behavior is too complex and unpredictable to be studied scientifically and that sociology is too young a discipline to have developed a body of laws and principles like those found in the natural sciences. An additional criticism is that sociologists are part of the societies they observe, which makes it extremely difficult for them to prevent bias from affecting their perceptions.

Defenders of sociology as a science assert that any subject may seem complex to an untrained observer and that people have been "doing" sociology on an informal basis for thousands of years. In response to the criticism that sociologists must be biased because of their closeness to their subject matter, it can be argued that they can be objective by separating themselves from the subject, by repeating studies using multiple observers, and by making crosscultural and historical comparisons. Thus, although one can argue correctly that many sociologists are biased, naive, simplistic, limited in cultural perspective, and bound by the present, this type of argument tells us little about whether sociology can be considered a science.

How then does one proceed? To determine whether sociology is or is not a science, we have to rephrase the question, asking what distinguishes the scientific mode of inquiry from nonscientific modes of inquiry. Can sociology and the other social sciences follow the scientific mode? To answer this question, we will consider

The invention and widespread dissemination of computers for reading and processing data have greatly expanded the research capabilities of social scientists. Today, sociologists can work with thousands of cases and engage in sophisticated statistical analysis in a relatively brief time due to the hardware and programming technology readily available to them.

the nature of scientific theories and standards of scientific inquiry.

The Components of Scientific Theory

A theory is an attempt to find patterns and consistencies in seemingly idiosyncratic and inconsistent events. Good theories are a key source of

ideas for researchers to test; the information they discover through testing may be used in turn to modify and refine the theory. The building blocks of theories are concepts and variables, conceptual frameworks, and propositions and hypotheses.

Concepts and Variables

A *concept* is an abstract system of meaning that enables us to perceive a phenomenon in a certain way, which may sound complex and difficult, but it really isn't. Concepts are simply tools that permit us to share meanings. Most of the terms in the Glossary are sociological concepts: norm, status, stratification, group, mob, folkway, and so on. The concept of "stratification," for example, represents a certain type of inequality that exists in society; developing the concept made it possible for people to think and communicate about the social differentiation of people by wealth, sex, age, social position, and other characteristics.

When concepts can have two or more degrees or values, they are referred to as *variables.* "Husband" is a concept; "years married" is a variable. "Dollar" is a concept; "level of income" is a variable. "Years of marriage" and "level of income" can both vary, but the meanings of the words "husband" and "dollar" remain constant.

Conceptual Frameworks

When a set of concepts is interrelated to describe and classify phenomena, the concepts are generally referred to as a *conceptual framework,* which might be defined as a cluster of interrelated concepts for viewing a phenomenon and for describing and classifying its parts. In the strictest sense of the term, a conceptual framework is not a theory. Theories explain, conceptual frameworks do not. For purposes of research, using a particular concept or variable within a framework of related concepts or variables proves to be useful in understanding the meaning of or the manner in which the concept is used. The concept "role," for example, when used within a structural-functional framework, is generally defined as an expectation for behavior associated with a given status such as male, married, or student. Role to an interactionist, however, may mean expectations for behavior developed in interaction between persons and mutually shared by them.

Propositions and Hypotheses

A *proposition* is a statement about the nature of some phenomenon. It generally consists of a statement about the relationship between two or more concepts. The statement "Social activity is related to student grades" would be a proposition. If this proposition is formulated so that it can be tested, it is considered a *hypothesis*. A testable hypothesis would be "Students who attend more than one social activity a week have higher grade point averages than those who do not." Hypotheses and propositions are identical, except that hypotheses indicate how the stated relations can be tested.

Frequently, as in the example above, a hypothesis states that if one variable changes in some regular fashion, a predictable change will occur. Thus, as social activity goes up, grade point averages go up. This is known as a *direct relationship. Inverse relationships* are also possible — as social activity goes up, grade point averages go down. Hypotheses that involve direct or inverse relationships are called directional hypotheses. Null hypotheses, which state that there is no relationship between the variables of interest, can also be formulated: there is no relationship between social activity and grade point averages.

Theory

A *theory* is a set of logically interrelated propositions that explains some process or set of phenomena in a testable fashion. A good theory should be stated in abstract terms and allow predictions to be made. Theories also serve as important sources of new hypotheses.

There are many theories to explain crime, for example. Early explanations were based on biological theories and propositions were established that attempted to relate crime to the shape of the head, the size of the body, or chromosome abnormalities. Some psychological theories of crime lead to propositions linking criminal activity to emotional immaturity, a certain personality type, or a mental defect or illness. Sociologists have developed theories of crime based on social and cultural factors. These theories have led to propositions and testable hypotheses linking crime with social inequality, socialization or learning experiences, disorganization in the social order, and lack of effective controls. All these theories are sets of interrelated propositions that attempt to explain crime or some criminal activity. A theory provides direction in what we research and enables us to develop hypotheses that we can test.

The formulation of theories is just one aspect of the scientific method. Measured against this standard alone, sociology would certainly be considered a science. Most sociologists are keenly aware of the importance of organizing concepts, testing hypotheses, and developing theories. In addition to using this framework for their investigations, however, scientists adhere to a number of widely accepted standards of inquiry.

The Standards of Scientific Inquiry

Objectivity

The scientific standard of objectivity asserts that in the study of any phenomenon, social or nonsocial, the personal biases and values of the people doing the research must never influence the data reported or the interpretation of results. The political, religious, racial, or other beliefs of the investigators should in no way determine the findings of a study. Two independent researchers who study the same phenomena should produce identical results regardless of their differences in status, belief, or personal behavior.

Whether totally objective social research is possible has been seriously questioned. The literature from social psychology itself shows that people's interests and perceptions are influenced by their social background, social class, level of education, and numerous other factors. It also indicates that they are selective in what they perceive, remember, and report. Male and fe-male researchers studying marriage often report different perceptions of the same married couple. Sociologists studying race relations have found that a journalistic account of an event by a black writer differs from an account of the same event by a white writer. It is argued that human beings cannot be totally objective.

If absolute objectivity is to be regarded as a requirement, then sociology can be dismissed from the realm of scientific inquiry. There are, however, many procedures for minimizing the level of subjectivity. One procedure is to recognize the influence of existing biases and assumptions and strive to eliminate the influence of those we can control. Another procedure is to

All aspects of social life are areas for sociological research. Shown here are Lebanese mothers and children searching through rubble following bombing destruction in Beirut. Specific events may be difficult to replicate since they may happen only once. Similar but different events, however, may reveal patterns and consistencies that make generalization and prediction possible.

base research on a particular theory and test it by seeking evidence that could either support or reject it. Other methods of minimizing the level of bias and subjectivity will be discussed in the following sections on the other standards of science and the scientific method.

Replication

The scientific standard of replication asserts that research should be conducted and reported in such a way that someone else can duplicate it. The use of similar subjects and measuring procedures under similar conditions should produce results virtually identical to those of the original study. Thus, another way to reduce investigator bias is to have identical or similar studies undertaken by people who have differing biases and personal values.

In the physical sciences, replication of studies under identical conditions is often easier than it is in the social sciences, but even in the physical sciences it is sometimes impossible to re-create identical conditions. A California earthquake or a space shuttle explosion cannot be duplicated. In the social sciences, the problems of replication are compounded by human factors. Some studies may be impossible to duplicate because of the nature of the problems studied. It would not be possible, for example, to duplicate studies of the wives of the Marines killed when their barracks were bombed at Lebanon's Beirut airport in 1983, or to duplicate studies of the residents of a particular town destroyed by flood or fire. It is possible, however, to perform studies on the residents of other communities or on other wives of husbands killed in military activities and to note patterns of psychological adjustment, points of greatest stress, changes in kin and child relationships, or other conditions. The principle of replication of studies is based on the conviction that similar conditions and circumstances should produce highly similar results.

Precision of Measurement

The scientific standard of precision of measurement asserts that the phenomenon being studied should be measured in precise, reliable, and valid ways. The more accurate our measurements, the better we are able to test our ideas about the social world. An ability to test or study anything, whether it be height, a religious practice, or a theory, is in large part dependent on the ability to measure it accurately. Theories could be debated endlessly without progress if no one determined how to observe and measure the ideas or concepts central to them. No one has developed a precise, reliable, or valid measurement of the influence of angels, for example, so there is no way to prove or disprove their existence.

Some concepts or variables are much easier to measure than others. We all agree on how to measure the number of males and females in a room, because we know how to measure quantities of people and how to determine gender, but how would we proceed with a study of the relationship between gender and happiness? "Happiness" is an abstract term that means different things to different people, and opinions would vary on how to measure it. In general, the more abstract a variable is and the further it is removed from direct observation, the more difficult it is to reach a consensus on how it should be measured. This is not to say that the variable happiness cannot be measured — it can.

The process of arriving at a means of measuring a concept or variable is referred to as operationalization. In this procedure, the sociologist selects quantitative indicators of an abstract concept, determining what will be observed and how it will be measured. In the example given above, this would involve determining some criteria for assessing happiness. We might decide that happiness is whatever the individuals themselves think it is and simply ask them whether they are happy or not, or ask them to rate their own happiness on a five-point scale. On the other hand, we might decide that factors such as absence of depression, high levels of self-esteem, or the ability to function successfully are indicators of happiness and attempt to measure those. Although opinions may differ on whether the criteria selected actually reflect happiness, the operationalization of the definition ensures that we understand the term happiness and thus know what it is that we are measuring. An *operational definition*, then, is a definition of a concept or variable such that it can be measured during research. Operationalization makes an abstract variable measurable and observable and permits another researcher to objectively replicate our study. This process also improves the precision of our measurements.

Now that we have discussed some of the methods and attributes of scientific inquiry, we can return to our original question. Should sociology be considered a science? Like most questions, this one cannot be answered with a simple yes or no. The issue is not so much whether sociology is a science, but to what extent it is pursued with scientific modes of inquiry. According to the criteria we have discussed, some sociological studies would certainly be regarded as scientific. A sociologist studying the correlation between age at marriage and divorce rates would develop operational definitions and precise measurements to objectively examine a phenomenon in a replicable study. Studying a problem such as the relationship between gender and happiness might have to use methods that, strictly speaking, would not be considered scientific. In short, the techniques used by sociologists range from those that meet the strictest standards of scientific inquiry to those that, although still useful, fall short of that standard.

Now that we have discussed the basic procedures of science and sociology, we can turn our attention more specifically to research methods and the logic of proof.

Types of Sociological Research

The distinction between scientific and unscientific sociology can be clarified by examining the methods used to prove a hypothesis. One criterion that social scientists use to evaluate theories and propositions is the extent to which they can be empirically researched. This research is of two basic types, descriptive and explanatory.

Descriptive Research

Descriptive research describes social reality or provides facts about the social world. A descriptive study would be undertaken to determine whether people who have served time in prison have more trouble finding jobs than people who have not been in prison, or to determine what percentage of college students smoke marijuana more than once a week.

All descriptive studies share the goal of providing data on social facts, which are reliable and valid items of information about society. A fact could be a behavior (John scored three touchdowns), an attitude (women want equal pay for equal work), a law (the speed limit is fifty-five), or even a statistic (the median family income in 1982 was $23,430). The information must be reliable and valid. *Reliability* is the extent to which repeated observations of the same phenomena yield similar results. *Validity* is the extent to which observations actually yield measures of what they are supposed to measure. If a bathroom scale registers different weights each time you step on it, it is not reliable. If it gives the same weight each time but it isn't an accurate measure, the bathroom scale may be reliable (same results each time) but not valid (inaccurate weight). For a measure of your weight to be considered a fact, the scales must be reliable (consistent) and valid (accurate). A key goal of

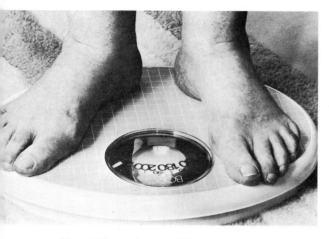

Oh my! This scale may well be reliable if it registers the same weight for the same person every time. But it may not be valid, unless it registers an accurate weight every time.

descriptive research is to provide an accurate view of social reality by providing social facts that are both valid and reliable.

Explanatory Research

Explanatory research attempts to explain why things happen or don't happen. Why do people with prison records have trouble finding jobs? What factors are related to students smoking marijuana? Questions like these are concerned with the problem of causation. What factors make a designated phenomenon happen or change? What is the cause of a given effect?

In all scientific studies, the variable that causes an effect is known as the *independent variable*. The variable that is affected by the independent variable is the *dependent variable*. In a study of child abuse, the abuse itself would be the dependent variable, the effect; the causes of child abuse — perhaps such factors as stress and the abuse of parents when they were children themselves — would be the independent vari-

ables. In another study, lung cancer (effect) could be the dependent variable and smoking (cause) the independent variable.

The same variable may be independent in one context and dependent in another. In a study of the causes of divorce, for example, divorce would be considered the dependent variable (effect), and the causes of divorce, the independent variable. In a study of factors that influence job performance, however, divorce might be found to be an independent variable (a cause), and job performance (the effect) the dependent variable.

Sometimes independent variables are known and the investigator focuses on dependent variables. A study of this sort was undertaken to determine whether soldiers exposed to atomic fallout during nuclear tests suffered any ill effects. The cause, or independent variable (nuclear radiation), was known and the effect, or dependent variable, was being investigated: Did these soldiers develop health problems?

In other cases, dependent variables are known, and investigators focus on independent variables. Studies of this sort were recently undertaken at various sites in Michigan, New York, and other states. The investigators knew that farm animals were dying, that meat was contaminated, and that people in certain areas were suffering from a number of health problems; that is, they knew the effect, the dependent variable. They had to search for the independent variable, the cause of the health problems. They found that the farms and homes in these areas were located near waste disposal dumps in which toxic substances had been disposed of and that the residue was causing serious health problems.

When a clear relationship in time exists between an independent and dependent variable, they are easy to distinguish. The independent variable (cause) must precede the dependent variable (effect). Lung cancer does not cause smoking. In the social sciences, however, cause and effect are sometimes hard to distinguish clearly. For example, do sexual problems cause marital problems, or do marital problems cause sexual problems?

To establish a cause-effect relationship, researchers must establish an *association* between two variables. Variables that are not associated cannot be causally related. The age of one's grandparents is not related to one's driving ability — obviously, neither causes the other. Even when two variables can be associated, however, it is not safe to assume that one causes the other. Hours of daylight begin to increase at the same time the rate of drowning begins to increase, but it would be absurd to argue that one causes the other. Thus, we can see that there must also be a logical rationale for relating two variables before they can be considered to comprise a cause-effect relationship.

How do sociologists go about their research, whether it be descriptive or explanatory? How do they determine facts, associations, or cause-effect relationships? What procedures do they use to observe and generalize in a scientific manner? Some of the methods used in sociological research are reviewed in the following section.

Sociological Research Methods

Sociological research involves methods of two types, qualitative and quantitative. Qualitative methods are used to study conditions or processes that are hard to measure with numbers, such as self-image, manners, how police make a decision to arrest someone, or the pain parents feel as they spank a child. This type of research often involves case studies and participant observation, in which the observer takes part in the activity being observed. Quantitative methods are designed to study variables that can be measured in numbers: age, income, years married, or crime rates, for example. This type of research usually involves surveys or experiments.

Citizens of the Love Canal community in New York determined that their disproportionate number of health problems (dependent variable) were caused by (independent variable) chemicals dumped close to their homes. The homeowners joined together in order to get legal assistance, increase public awareness of the seriousness of the problem, and to find a solution to their dilemma.

Throughout the research process, careful consideration must be given to the range of alternative methods or procedures that might meet one's objectives, and a variety of suitable procedures and methods do exist. Expense, facilities, access to people with computer and statistical skills, time, and other factors will influence the choices made. By carefully choosing a research design and methods, a great deal of time and money can be saved, and the research can be done more efficiently. Observation studies, survey research, and experimental designs are the research options considered most often.

Observation Studies

One qualitative method of obtaining information about social processes is through *observational research*. The researcher or research team watches what is happening and makes no attempt to control, modify, or influence the ongoing activity. The researcher systematically observes what is happening, and the focus is specifically on the variables or dimensions defined by the hypotheses, propositions, or theory.

Systematic observations may take several forms. One type is the laboratory observation, in which the sociologist controls the environment in which a particular activity takes place. Sometimes one-way windows are used to reduce the chances that the activity will be influenced by the researcher. This technique might be employed to study how aggression in children's play is influenced by their watching violence on television or to explore interactions between men and women in a small group.

A second type of observation takes place in a natural setting rather than in a laboratory. Often termed field observation, this type is done by the researcher "on location." One might observe student behavior in a classroom or the interactions between salespersons and customers at a store, for example.

A third observation technique is participant observation, in which the researcher is an active participant in the event being studied. Anthropologists frequently use this method to study a particular community or subculture. Sociologists have been participant observers in studies of nudist camps, bars, prisons, the drug trade, and entire communities. Unlike laboratory or field observers, the researchers become directly involved in the group or community activities. As participants, they may learn about some of the subtleties involved in personal interactions. The researcher may therefore acquire a deeper understanding of the emotions and beliefs that bind the group together than would be possible if observations were made by a person not participating in the group.

Most participant observation research takes the form of a case study, in which an individual person, group, community, or activity is observed. Although case studies and participant observation generate new insights and hypotheses, they also present serious difficulties. It may be impossible to generalize on the basis of observations of a single group because an examination of a single case or example may not prove or illustrate anything. Furthermore, a researcher who is also a participant can have difficulty remaining objective and making unbiased observations. It may be impossible to separate personal emotions and feelings from actual events: we tend to see what we want to see. Another problem is that in some instances the researcher is more an intruder than a longtime member of a group. Does the presence of a newcomer affect what takes place? In spite of difficulties such as these, however, participant observation can familiarize us with certain social realities that would be impossible to understand with other data-gathering procedures.

Survey Research

The procedure used most frequently to obtain information about the social world is *survey research*. This quantitative technique involves systematically asking people about their attitudes, feelings, ideas, opinions, behaviors, or anything else. Usually, the researcher uses a questionnaire to guide the questioning. You may have participated in a survey at some point, either an informal survey in a magazine — "How masculine or feminine are you?" — or a formal survey of your attitudes toward birth control or some other issue.

Surveys have a number of advantages over many other data-gathering procedures. They are usually easy to administer and often permit researchers to gather data on identical variables from many people simultaneously. Unlike most participant observation studies, which may take months or years, surveys provide a lot of information in periods ranging from a few minutes to several hours. When highly structured, survey responses are uniformly categorized, which makes tabulation easier. Finally, the precise categorical data provided by surveys is highly amenable to statistical quantitative analysis.

There are problems with surveys too, of course. First, if questions concern personal information about age, income, sex life, or criminal activities, for example, the respondents may not answer honestly. Second, if the questions or responses are highly structured, the results of the survey may not reflect the actual beliefs of the people being questioned but rather the researcher's conceptions of how the questions should be asked and what people's answers are likely to be. To give an exaggerated example, a survey question about attitudes toward abortion that listed as the only possible answers "I think abortion should not be allowed under any circumstances" and "I think abortion is permissible in situations involving rape or danger to mothers' health" would not yield valid information. Third, do surveys assess only the most superficial aspects of social life or cover only a limited part of the respondents' thoughts on a subject? Surveys may fail to assess areas that are difficult to examine, and people's beliefs may be far more complex than a survey indicates.

A survey is a study, generally in the form of an interview or questionnaire, used in gathering information about people's attitudes and behavior. "Person-on-the-street" surveys are not necessarily an accurate reflection of the entire population or community. A major concern about such surveys is how the questions are worded and who is selected for interview.

Despite problems such as these, survey research has gained increasing methodological sophistication and is widely used by social scientists. Public opinion pollsters use surveys to gather information about the popularity of politicians. Market researchers employ them to discover why people use a particular product. Census takers use them to learn the characteristics and size of the population. They are helpful to sociologists in getting information on a great variety of factors and in testing hypotheses.

One major problem in research is identifying a group of people to be studied. The group might be doctors, students, taxpayers, voters in a

A Research Note on College Students and Drinking Behavior

Introduction
Educators, parents, and the public in general have noted a dramatic increase in the consumption of alcoholic beverages among the nation's youth, particularly college students. How much of a problem is drinking and do different patterns of drinking occur among students?

Problem
Susan M. Vaughn conducted a study to describe patterns of drinking behavior among college students and to test the relationship between normative structures and drinking behavior. She wanted to find out why students drink, how often, how much, when, and what type of beverage they consume. She also wanted to find out if rules of conduct

(norms) and beliefs influence drinking behavior.

Literature Review
In reviewing the literature, Vaughn discovered that over the past twenty-five years, the prevalence of drinking has increased appreciably among college women but only slightly among men. She also found that differences in the drinking patterns of freshmen and seniors had not changed and that drinking-related problems such as property damage and trouble with the law had not increased. Of particular interest was the finding that persons who received few guidelines concerning acceptable drinking behavior were more likely to become heavy drinkers than those who were given specific normative guidelines.

Hypotheses Developed
Based on the literature review, three types of normative structures were examined. Those who received guidelines prohibiting drinking and believed that drinking alcoholic beverages was not acceptable were classified as having *proscriptive* normative structures. Those who received positive guidelines and believed drinking was acceptable but only in certain situations were classified as having *prescriptive* normative structures. The third group, who did not receive definite guidelines or know how they felt about drinking were classified as *nonscriptive*. The hypotheses were that: 1) Proscriptive students would abstain or drink very little. 2) Prescriptive students would drink on a regular basis but have few alcohol-related problems. 3) Nonscriptive students were most likely to drink the most and misuse alcohol.

Design, Sample, and Data
To conduct the survey, students at five colleges (three Catholic

given election, or any selected group that can provide the information needed to prove or disprove the hypotheses. This group is usually called the population. Since we can rarely study all doctors, students, or taxpayers due to such factors as cost and time, we must pick an appropriate sample. A *sample* is a group of people chosen from the population who are thought to represent the population. The sample is questioned, and their answers should reflect the beliefs of the population as a whole.

Samples are chosen by a variety of methods. A *random sample* is chosen by chance, so that every member of a group has an equal chance of being selected. Since it is usually impossible to place all names in a hat, as is often done at prize drawings, sociologists often assign a number to each name and use a table of random numbers to select which persons should be included. They may also use a method known as *systematic sampling,* in which a specific pattern of selection is followed, such as selecting every twentieth name.

and two state-related) in north-western Pennsylvania were given a questionnaire. An effort was made to get a representative proportion of freshmen, sophomores, juniors, seniors, and graduate students. 548 respondents completed the three-page questionnaire, which asked about their alcohol consumption, drinking behavior, and beliefs.

Findings

Less than 10 percent of the entire sample were abstainers or barely drank, about 75 percent were drinkers but had no alcohol-related problems, and 16 percent were classified as alcohol misusers. Thirty-three percent of the students drank every weekend; 12.6 percent drank several times a week. Most drank because they liked the taste (71 percent), but some (13 percent) drank because they felt nervous, tense, or full of worries. Most drank with friends their own age, had mixed drinks and enjoyed the effect of getting high. Although three-fourths of

the respondents were under age twenty-one, the legal drinking age in Pennsylvania, most got their liquor from friends (60 percent), 25 percent used false identification, and 10 percent got it through parents and relatives.

Of the total sample, 86 percent had prescriptive normative structures (drinking acceptable); 5 percent had nonscriptive normative structures (lacked norms); 2.4 percent had proscriptive normative structures (drinking was not acceptable); and the rest were classified as "other." The nonscriptive respondents were most likely to drink every weekend or every day, were most likely to drink to relieve tension and for the taste, and were most likely to misuse alcohol by drinking until high or drunk. The prescriptive respondents started drinking at the earliest age and were likely to drink regularly, but had no alcohol-related problems. The proscriptive respondents were most likely to never drink and only had one drink if they did.

Conclusions and Discussion

The data wholly support the hypotheses. Students with different types of normative structures had different patterns of drinking behavior. The nonscriptive students were most likely to drink most often and misuse alcohol; the prescriptive students were likely to drink regularly but have few alcohol-related problems; and the proscriptive were most likely to be abstainers or barely drink.

One implication of this study is that alcohol abuse is related to sociocultural phenomena. Responsible use of alcohol can be taught. Children who are given specific guidelines for drinking alcohol will internalize these norms and rules and carry them to college and into adulthood.

SOURCE: Susan M. Vaughn, "The Normative Structures of College Students and Patterns of Drinking Behavior," *Sociological Focus* 16 (August 1983):181–193.

A third method is *stratified sampling,* in which the population is divided into groups and then chosen at random from within those groups. If our population were students, we might stratify them by class rank, sex, or race and then randomly select from each of these groups.

Regardless of how the sample is chosen, if every person has an equal chance of being chosen, it should be representative — it should reflect the attitudes of the total population. A small representative sample is likely to provide

far more accurate data about a population than a large nonrepresentative one. There are obvious benefits in being able to study a few hundred people and make accurate generalizations about an entire population on the basis of one's findings. These procedures are used daily in the ratings of television programs, by market researchers of consumer purchasing patterns, and by sociologists testing hypotheses.

The survey is not completed with the selection of a sample, of course. It is necessary to administer our tests or ask our questions of the sample. The questions themselves must be formulated according to the principles of scientific inquiry, which were discussed earlier. Our questions must be carefully worded, precise, operationally defined, free from investigator bias, valid, reliable, and so forth. Imagine how the responses might be influenced if we were to ask a question such as this: "Do you agree with my view and that of all patriotic Americans that an increase in the military budget is vital to our national defense?" As you can see, it is important to ask questions that aren't slanted toward a particular type of response or are unclear. Care should be taken to ensure a complete set of possible response choices. The use of improper questions, regardless of the representativeness of the sample, will yield data that cannot be used to prove or disprove a hypothesis and adequately complete the research process.

Experimental Designs

A third procedure for obtaining information about the social world is through the *experimental design,* a classic scientific procedure used to determine cause-effect relationships in carefully controlled situations. In an ideal experiment, it is possible to control all relevant factors and manipulate, statistically or in the society itself, one variable to determine its effect.

To carry out an experiment, two matched groups of subjects are selected. In the *experimental group,* an independent variable is introduced, and it is the effect of this variable that is tested. The *control group* is identical to the experimental group in every respect, except that the variable is not introduced into this group. If we were studying the effects of dim lighting on social interaction, for example, we might randomly choose two groups of students. The experimental group would be placed in a dimly lit room, whereas the control group would be in a normally lit room.

The researcher would note differences in the behavior of the two groups: frequency of interaction, level of noise, number of subgroups formed, and other behaviors considered germane. Differences in the social behavior of the two groups would presumably be due to the influence of the independent variable, dim lighting.

Experiments are most frequently done in a laboratory setting where it is easier to control conditions than it is in a natural or field (nonlaboratory) setting. It has been argued, however, that laboratory settings are artificial and yield distorted results.

Among the social sciences, the experimental design is used most often in psychology, and extensive experimental work has been done in the study of learning, perceptions, attachments, frustration, and similar behaviors. Students often ask how it is possible to conduct experiments with humans in either a laboratory or non-laboratory setting. Can we lock people in rooms, withhold food, punish them, or remove them from friends and family? We can't, of course, because such research would be highly unethical. But scientists can study circumstances that already exist in the social world: populations of starving people, families who abuse their children, jobs that provide little variation in activity, neighborhoods destroyed by floods or fire, hospitals that isolate people from their loved ones, and prisons that put people in solitary confinement. The social world also contains populations of well-fed people, families that do not abuse their children, and so forth. It is often possible to find existing experimental and control groups that have all characteristics in common except the independent variable chosen for observation.

Suppose we wish to find out whether playing music to workers in a factory influences their productivity. We could design an experiment in which music was played to one group (the experimental group) and withheld from another group. An alternative method would be to find existing settings in which music was provided or not provided and compare their productivity. A third method would be to statistically compare two groups in which the selected variables could be controlled. Sociologists have used each of these procedures, and, as you can see, a variety of alternatives are available with an experimental type of design.

One of the best-known experiments in sociology resulted in what is widely referred to as the "Hawthorne Effect." Before World War II at the Hawthorne plant of Western Electric, Elton Mayo separated a group of women (the experimental group) from the other workers and systematically varied their lighting, coffee breaks, lunch hours, and other environmental factors (Roethlisberger and Dickson, 1939). In the control group, work conditions went on as usual. Much to the amazement of the researchers, the

productivity of the experimental group (the dependent variable) increased regardless of the variables that were introduced, including returning the workers to their original conditions. Obviously, the desired result, increased productivity, was not being caused by a specific independent variable. On the one hand, the experiment seemed to be a success — the experimental group differed from the control group when independent variables such as lighting and coffee breaks were introduced. The experiment appeared to be a failure, however, in that one independent variable seemed to have as much influence as another. The researchers concluded that the women were trying to please the researchers and enjoyed the attention they were getting. The very presence of the researchers "contaminated" the experiment to the point that they became a significant independent variable and caused a change in the dependent variable — work productivity. The Hawthorne Effect can

These employees at the Hawthorne plant run by the Western Electric Company in Chicago were part of an experimental study conducted by social scientists more than fifty years ago. The researchers discovered the importance of human factors in job performance and productivity. Any steps taken by the researcher — even negative ones such as reducing the lighting — seemed to increase output. The increased attention, the informal cliques of workers, and other factors related to the workers themselves were found to be highly related to productivity.

be a potential problem whenever an experiment is conducted.

The Research Process

Most research proceeds in accordance with a sequence of rules and procedures basic to the scientific method. The first step in this process is to *formulate the problem*. But sociologists using scientific methods can choose only those problems that are amenable to observation and testing, and the problem must be articulated such that the researchers know exactly what they are trying to determine. Let us suppose that the problem we want to investigate concerns the effects of age at marriage on the number of children a couple has.

Having decided what to research, the next step is to *review the literature*. Examining texts and articles in periodicals will tell us what is already known, where there are gaps in our knowledge, and more specifically what we should investigate. For our example, we will suppose that our review indicates that little work has been done in this area.

The third step is to *develop hypotheses for testing*. Hypotheses, you will remember, are statements of relationships between two or more variables that can be empirically proved or disproved. We might state our hypothesis as follows: "Age at marriage is negatively related to

family size." Unlike the concept of happiness discussed earlier, these variables are easy to operationally define.

The fourth step is to *choose a research design*, which is the process of establishing procedures to gather the evidence that will be used to support or reject the hypothesis. These procedures include the methods to be used to gather the data (observation, survey, experiment), the sample to be selected, the type of questions to be asked, and the general plan to make it possible to collect and analyze the data. Many factors must be considered, including the time and money available, the reliability and validity of various designs, and so on. It is important to keep in mind that aspects of the design may have to be changed once the process is begun. For our example, we might choose to mail a questionnaire to a representative sample of one thousand married couples, to search public documents and link marriage and birth records, or to seek the information from U.S. Census Bureau material.

The next step in the research process is to *collect the data* as described in the research design. In this case we could note each person's date of birth, marital status, date of marriage, and number of children. To check the validity of data, we should gather it from several different sources.

When the data are collected, they must be

Not all observation experiments or research require laboratories or one-way mirrors. In fact, many observation studies conducted by sociologists use nonlaboratory settings. Studies of driving patterns, dress codes, or smoking behavior, for example, are often done in informal natural settings by a nonparticipating observer.

Figure 3-1

Variability of age at marriage: three examples

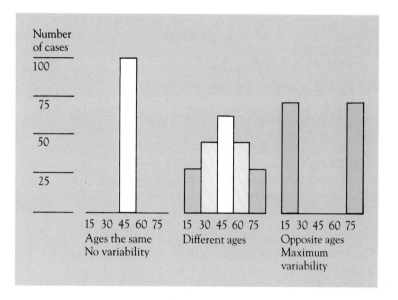

assembled, organized, and classified so that the hypotheses can be tested. This is the stage in which we *analyze the results*. In most cases, it is necessary to arrange the data in a manageable form. With our example, it might be desirable to organize age information into different categories such as five-year intervals. It would then be a simple matter to make a graph or table of results that could easily be interpreted.

In addition, we might want to include some descriptive data about each of the variables. The *mode* is the most frequent response. We might discover that the mode of male age at marriage was twenty; that is, more males married at twenty than at any other age. The *median* is the point at which one-half of the respondents are above and one-half are below. We might discover that half the women were married before age eighteen and half after age eighteen. The *mean* is the average, the sum of the age at marriage divided by the number of people involved. Suppose, for example, that the first seven people in our study were married at ages 30, 22, 20, 18, 16, 16, and 16. The

most frequent age at marriage (mode) is 16. The age at which half are below and half are above (median) is 18. The average age (mean) is 19.7 — the sum of the ages divided by seven. These figures are measures of central tendency.

We may also wish to discover the *range* of a variable, the distance between the largest and smallest amount. Suppose that the youngest person in our study was age fifteen and the oldest was seventy-five, giving us an age range of sixty years. For the variable age at marriage, we might discover that the fifteen year old married at that age, and the seventy-five year old also just married. The range for age at marriage, therefore, would be sixty years.

Variance is a related concept. In descriptive research, the variance tells us how the data are spread over the range. Three groups could all have an age range from fifteen to seventy-five, for example, but the distribution of the age of those married in the three groups could differ.

In Figure 3-1, all three bar graphs have an age range of sixty years, yet the example on the

SOCIOLOGISTS AT WORK
Analyzing Data on Pharmaceuticals

Lisa Eig works for Drug Distribution Data (DDD) in Wayne, New Jersey. Her job involves the statistical analysis of what she describes as "an enormous data base" concerning the sales of pharmaceutical products by major drug manufacturers. She finds her training in sociology useful in several aspects of her job. She learned her statistical skills in a sociology program, and she also finds her sociological knowledge helpful in interacting with her co-workers. Her education includes a year of graduate study in sociology at New York University and an undergraduate degree in sociology and psychology from Kean College in Union, New Jersey.

DDD is the only company of its kind. It was founded by a group of pharmaceutical manufacturers to meet a need for more information on where and when their prescription and over-the-counter drugs were being sold. The problem, Eig explains, was that pharmaceutical manufacturers sell to wholesale warehouses, not directly to hospitals, drugstores, or doctors. As a result, detailed information on how a specific product was selling in a specific region was lacking. The manufacturers wanted to know what happened to their products after they were sold by the wholesaler to the retailer. They also wanted a system for "auditing" information from other sources to con-

firm that it was accurate. Drug Distribution Data was created to meet these needs.

Eig's title is "data quality assurance analyst." She is responsible for the forty warehouses in the state of California. "We work on a monthly cycle," she says. "We buy detailed information from the wholesaler's warehouses in the form of a computer tape on which all the sales for the month are recorded. After we've transformed the information from tape to print-out, we do a statistical analysis of the results and sell our information back to the original manufacturers. We have about 150 client companies, including major pharmaceutical companies such as Abbott and Lillie.

"The sales of most pharmaceutical products are fairly consistent," she adds. "A given product will sell about the same amount from one month to the next. One of the things we watch for is a sudden variation in the sales pattern — a tremendous increase or decrease in sales, for example. Once we've made sure that the product is coded correctly in our computer, we try to determine why the sales have changed so dramatically. In some cases, we expect fairly substantial variations in the sale of a product from month to month. Sales of cough and cold remedies shoot up in the winter, while suntan lotion sells more in the sum-

left shows no variance in the age at marriage — everyone who married did so at age forty-five. The middle example shows a normal variation with the most people marrying at age forty-five and fewer at older and younger ages. The example on the right illustrates maximum variance,

with half the group marrying at age fifteen and half at age seventy-five.

After the analysis of the data, the final activities of the research process are begun. We *interpret our findings, draw our conclusions, and confirm, reject, or reformulate our original hypothesis, proposi-*

mer. Certain prescription drugs also have seasonal sales variations. Other variations, however, may indicate that a mistake has been made. This is where I find my statistical training useful. Statistics is really just a way of using mathematics to find out why something is occurring or not occurring."

Problems do arise. In one instance, a warehouse changed the way it was marketing "injectables" such as insulin. Originally, they were sold in packages of ten, but the warehouse began selling them individually without changing the code used to identify the product in the computer. The warehouse should have informed DDD about this change, but they didn't — they kept reporting their sales in terms of packages of ten. Thus, DDD thought they were selling ten times as many items as they actually were and was reporting this exaggerated figure back to the manufacturer. The manufacturer realized that the figure was too high, and notified Eig. Eig's job was to return to the figures for the period when the error had been made — a period of almost six months — and bring them into conformity with the actual sales.

What do the manufacturers do with the information DDD provides to them? According to Eig, the report has two functions. First, it is used to determine how much salespeople will be paid. Second, it has a variety of uses in market research.

The report's use in compensation is necessary because, unlike salespeople in most fields, those who sell pharmaceutical products do not take orders directly from the people they are trying to sell to — doctors. A drug company with a new product to sell may send a salesperson to describe the product to a group of doctors, but the doctors will order it through their hospital or pharmacy. How, then, can a manager determine how much various salespeople should be paid? The usual commission system will not work. The reports from DDD, however, are detailed enough that a manager can determine which members of the sales force have been most successful.

The report's potential uses in market research are almost unlimited. In fact, Eig considers what she does to be basically a form of market research. The report can be used to assess trends from month to month, determine if a new product is doing well in a test market, judge the effectiveness of an advertising campaign, and generally determine how best to approach the sales of a particular product. Have the sales dropped? The report may show that the drop coincided with a price increase or the entry into the marketplace of a new product from the competition. Eig's technical training helps her be sure that her company is using the most accurate data possible to make their decisions.

Eig also draws on her knowledge of sociology in an entirely different realm of her working life. "I think it helps me deal with people," she says. "People who have training in sociology seem to express themselves more clearly and understand other people's points of view. They may not accept what another person is saying, but they are more likely to understand why the other person feels that way. This sort of basic understanding makes working together much easier."

tion, and theory. Then the results are disseminated. These final activities can be very difficult, however. Suppose we found that people who married at a young age did have larger families but that they were only slightly larger than the families of those who married when they were older. If people who married before age twenty had an average of 1.9 children and those who married after age twenty had an average of 1.8 children, should we accept our hypothesis? Would this finding be significant, or could the difference be the result of chance or a bias in the sample we investigated? Interpretations must take into account any factor in the research process that could have influenced our results.

By reporting our findings and conclusions, we make them subject to public review, criticism, and application. Sociologists frequently publish their results in professional journals, where they are reviewed by other sociologists. Sometimes the results are published in books, monographs, or popular magazines. When the results have been disseminated, the research process is complete.

Summary

Although we learn about society from everyday experiences, common sense, authority, revelation, and tradition, sociology is heavily dependent on empirical research that uses the scientific method.

Is sociology a science? Some argue that it is, some that it isn't. It may be more constructive to note what distinguishes scientific modes of inquiry from nonscientific modes of inquiry and then consider whether sociology can follow a scientific mode.

There are certain standards of inquiry basic to science. Objectivity involves excluding personal values, beliefs, and biases from the research process, findings, and interpretations. The standard of replication requires that research be undertaken and reported such that someone else can duplicate it. The precision in measurement standard requires that whatever is studied be measurable and that measurements be precise, reliable, and valid.

Sociological research is of two basic types: descriptive and explanatory. Descriptive research provides reliable, valid data on social facts. Explanatory research goes beyond description to determine why a certain social situation occurs and to discover cause-effect relationships. Dependent variables in explanatory research are

those the investigator wants to explain; they are dependent on or determined by other variables. Independent variables are those that cause the variations in the dependent variable.

Sociological methods are often categorized into two types: qualitative and quantitative. Qualitative methods are used to study variables that cannot be measured in numbers without great difficulty. These methods include case studies, laboratory observations, field observations, and participatory observations. Quantitative methods are used to study variables that can be measured in numbers. Experimental research and surveys are quantitative methods. Surveys, the most frequently used method of sociological research, involve systematically asking people about their attitudes or behaviors, which is usually accomplished with the use of questionnaires. Choosing an appropriate sample and wording questions carefully are crucial parts of the survey method. The experimental method involves the use of two or more similar groups. An independent variable is introduced into the experimental group but withheld from the control group.

Research generally involves a sequence of tasks, including the following: formulating the problem, reviewing the literature, developing hypotheses for testing, choosing a research design, collecting data, analyzing the findings, drawing conclusions, and disseminating the results. There are often many different ways to categorize the data, formulate tables, and use statistical measures such as the mode, median, mean, range, and variance. When the data analysis is finished, conclusions are drawn and the results are made available to the public.

Key Terms

concept
conceptual framework
control group

dependent variable
direct relationship
experimental design
experimental group
hypothesis
independent variable
inverse relationship
mean
median
mode
observational research
operational definition
proposition
random sample
range
reliability
sample
scientific method
social facts
stratified sampling
survey research
systematic sampling
theory
validity
variables
variance

Suggested Readings

Bailey, Kenneth D. **Methods of Social Research.** *New York: Macmillan, 1978.* A survey of sociological methodology, emphasizing quantitative methods.

Cole, Stephen. **The Sociological Method, 3d ed.** *Chicago: Rand McNally, 1980.* A short book de-

signed to give the beginning student a conceptual understanding of empirical social research. Paperback.

Denzin, Norman K. **The Research Art.** *New York: McGraw-Hill, 1978.* A look at sociological research methods from an interactionist point of view, with an emphasis on qualitative methods.

Hoover, Kenneth R. **The Elements of Social Scientific Thinking, 3rd ed.** *New York: St. Martin's Press, 1984.* A short explanation of social science for those who used the results of social science research and those who are beginning their own research. Paperback.

Labovitz, Sanford and Robert Hagedorn. **Introduction to Social Research, 3rd ed.** *New York: McGraw-Hill, 1981.* A brief, understandable introduction to social research. Paperback.

Rossi, Peter W., James D. Wright, and Andy B. Anderson (eds). **Handbook of Survey Research.** *New York: Academic Press, 1983.* Comprehensive state-of-the-art essays by acknowledged authorities, who discuss techniques and practical applications of survey research.

Walizer, Michael H. and Paul L. Wienir. **Research Methods and Analysis: Searching for Relationships.** *New York: Harper & Row, 1978.* A textbook that integrates methodological considerations with statistical processes.

Weiss, Carol H. **Evaluation Research: Methods of Assessing Program Effectiveness.** *Englewood Cliffs, N.J.: Prentice-Hall, 1972.* A brief paperback that discusses the application of research methods to the evaluation of social programs.

Williamson, John B., David A. Karp, and John R. Dalphin. **The Research Craft: An Introduction to Social Science Methods.** *Boston: Little, Brown, 1977.* A comprehensive textbook designed for use in a first course on social research methods.

The Promise

by C. Wright Mills

In this classic of sociological literature C. Wright Mills discusses "the promise and the task" of the sociological imagination: to guide us to an understanding of the life of the individual, the history of society, and the relations between the two.

Nowadays men often feel that their private lives are a series of traps. They sense that within their everyday worlds, they cannot overcome their troubles, and in this feeling, they are often quite correct: What ordinary men are directly aware of and what they try to do are bounded by the private orbits in which they live; their visions and their powers are limited to the close-up scenes of job, family, neighborhood; in other milieux, they move vicariously and remain spectators. And the more aware they become, however vaguely, of ambitions and of threats which transcend their immediate locales, the more trapped they seem to feel.

Underlying this sense of being trapped are seemingly impersonal changes in the very structure of continent-wide societies. The facts of contemporary history are also facts about the success and the failure of individual men and women. When a society is industrialized, a peasant becomes a worker; a feudal lord is liquidated or becomes a businessman. When classes rise or fall, a man is employed or unemployed; when the rate of investment goes up or down, a man takes new heart or goes broke. When wars happen, an insurance salesman becomes a rocket launcher; a store clerk, a radar man; a wife lives alone; a child grows up without a father. Neither the life of an individual nor the history of a society can be understood without understanding both.

Yet men do not usually define the troubles they endure in terms of historical change and institutional contradiction. The well-being they enjoy, they do not usually impute to the big ups and downs of the societies in which they live. Seldom aware of the intricate connection between the patterns of their own lives and the course of world history, ordinary men do not usually know what this connection means for the kinds of men they are becoming and for the kinds of history-making in which they might take part. They do not possess the quality of mind essential to grasp the interplay of man and society, of biography and history, of self and world. They cannot cope with their personal troubles in such ways as to control the structural transformations that usually lie behind them.

Surely it is no wonder. In what period have so many men been so totally exposed at so fast a pace to such earthquakes of change? That Americans have not known such catastrophic changes as have the men and women of other societies is due to historical facts that are now quickly becoming "merely history." The history that now affects every man is world history. Within this scene and this period, in the course of a single generation, one sixth of mankind is transformed from all that is feudal and backward into all that is modern, advanced, and fearful. Political colonies are freed; new and less visible forms of imperialism installed. Revolutions occur; men feel the intimate grip of new kinds of authority. Totalitarian societies rise, and are smashed to bits — or succeed fabulously. After two centuries of ascendancy, capitalism is shown up as only one way to make society into an industrial apparatus. After two centuries of hope, even formal democracy is restricted to a quite small portion of mankind. Everywhere in the underdeveloped world, ancient ways of life are broken up and vague expectations become urgent demands. Everywhere in the overdeveloped world, the means of authority and of violence become total in scope and bureaucratic in form. Humanity itself now lies before us, the super-nation at either pole concentrating its most co-ordinated and massive efforts upon the preparation of World War Three.

The very shaping of history now outpaces the ability of men to orient themselves in accordance with cherished values. And which values? Even when they do not panic, men often sense that older ways of feeling and thinking have collapsed and that newer beginnings are ambiguous to the point of moral stasis. Is it any wonder that ordinary men feel they cannot cope with the larger worlds with which they are so suddenly confronted? That they cannot understand the meaning of their epoch for their own lives? That — in defense of selfhood — they become morally insensible, trying to remain altogether private men? Is it any wonder that they come to be possessed by a sense of the trap?

It is not only information that they need — in this Age of Fact, information often dominates their attention and overwhelms their capacities to assimilate it. It is not only the skills of reason that they need — although their struggles to acquire these often exhaust their limited moral energy.

What they need, and what they feel they need, is a quality of mind that will help them to use information and to develop reason in order to achieve lucid summations of what is going on in the world and of what may be happening within themselves. It is this quality, I am going to contend, that journalists and scholars, artists and publics, scientists and editors are coming to expect of what may be called the sociological imagination.

1

The sociological imagination enables its possessor to understand the larger historical scene in terms of its meaning for the inner life and the external career of a variety of individuals. It enables him to take into account how individuals, in the welter of their daily experience, often become falsely conscious of their social positions. Within that welter, the framework of modern society is sought, and within that framework the psychologies of a variety of men and women are formulated. By such means the personal uneasiness of individuals is focused upon explicit troubles and the indifference of publics is transformed into involvement with public issues.

The first fruit of this imagination — and the first lesson of the social science that embodies it — is the idea that the individual can understand his own experience and gauge his own fate only by locating himself within his period, that he can know his own chances in life only by becoming aware of those of all individuals in his circumstances. In many ways it is a terrible lesson; in many ways a magnificent one. We do not know the limits of man's capacities for supreme effort or willing degradation, for agony or glee, for pleasurable brutality or the sweetness of reason. But in our time we have come to know that the limits of "human nature" are frighteningly broad. We have come to know that every individual lives, from one generation to the next, in some society; that he lives out a biography, and that he lives it out within some historical sequence. By the fact of his living he contributes, however minutely, to the shaping of this society and to the course of its history, even as he is made by society and by its historical push and shove.

The sociological imagination enables us to grasp history and biography and the relations between the two within society. That is its task and its promise. To recognize this task and this promise is the mark of the classic social analyst. It is characteristic of Herbert Spencer — turgid, polysyllabic, comprehensive; of E. A. Ross — graceful, muckraking, upright; of Auguste Comte and Emile Durkheim; of the intricate and subtle Karl Mannheim. It is the quality of all that is intellectually excellent in Karl Marx; it is the clue to Thorstein Veblen's brilliant and ironic insight, to Joseph Schumpeter's many-sided constructions of reality; it is the basis of the psychological sweep of W. E. H. Lecky no less than of the profundity and clarity of Max Weber. And it is the signal of what is best in contemporary studies of man and society.

No social study that does not come back to the problems of biography, of history and of their intersections within a society has completed its intellectual journey. Whatever the specific problems of the classic social analysts, however limited or however broad the features of social reality they have examined, those who have been imaginatively aware of the promise of their work have consistently asked three sorts of questions:

1. What is the structure of this particular society as a whole? What are its essential components, and how are they related to one another? How does it differ from other varieties of social order? Within it, what is the meaning of any particular feature for its continuance and for its change?

2. Where does this society stand in human history? What are the mechanics by which it is changing? What is its place within and its meaning for the development of humanity as a whole? How does any particular feature we are examining affect, and how is it affected by, the historical period in which it moves? And this period — what are its essential features? How does it differ from other periods? What are its characteristic ways of history-making?

3. What varieties of men and women now prevail in this society and in this period? And what varieties are coming to prevail? In what ways are they selected and formed, liberated and repressed, made sensitive and blunted? What kinds of "human nature" are revealed in the conduct and character we observe in this society in this period? And what is the meaning for "human nature" of each and every feature of the society we are examining?

Whether the point of interest is a great power state or a minor literary mood, a family, a prison, a creed — these are the kinds of questions the best social analysts have asked. They are the intellectual pivots of classic studies of man in society — and they are the questions inevitably raised by any mind possessing the sociological imagination. For that imagination is the capacity to shift from one perspective to another — from the political to the psychological; from examination of a single family to comparative assessment of the national budgets of the world; from the theological school to the military establishment; from considerations of an oil industry to studies of contemporary poetry. It is the capacity to range from the most impersonal and remote transformations to the most intimate features of the human self — and to see the relations between the two. Back of its use there is always the urge to know the social and historical meaning of the individual in the society and in the period in which he has his quality and his being.

That, in brief, is why it is by means of the sociological imagination that men now hope to grasp what is going on in the world, and to understand what is happening in themselves as minute points of the intersections of biography and history within society. In large part, contemporary man's self-conscious view of himself as at least an outsider, if not a permanent stranger, rests upon an absorbed realization of social relativity and of the transformative power of history. The sociological imagination is the most fruitful form of this self-consciousness. By its use men whose mentalities have swept only a series of limited orbits often come to feel as if suddenly awakened in a house with which they had only supposed themselves to be familiar. Correctly or incorrectly, they often come to feel that they can now provide themselves with adequate summations, cohesive assessments, comprehensive orientations. Older decisions that once appeared sound now seem to them products of a mind unaccountably dense. Their capacity for astonishment is made lively again. They acquire a new way of thinking, they experience a transvaluation of values: in a word, by their reflection and by their sensibility, they realize the cultural meaning of the social sciences.

2

Perhaps the most fruitful distinction with which the sociological imagination works is between "the personal troubles of milieu" and "the public issues of social structure." This distinction is an essential tool of the sociological imagination and a feature of all classic work in social science.

Troubles occur within the character of the individual and within the range of his immediate relations with others; they have to do with his self and with those limited areas of social life of which he is directly and personally aware. Accordingly, the statement and the resolution of troubles properly lie within the individual as a biographical entity and within the scope of his immediate milieu — the social setting that is directly open to his personal experience and to some extent his willful activity. A trouble is a private matter: values cherished by an individual are felt by him to be threatened.

Issues have to do with matters that transcend these local environments of the individual and the range of his inner life. They have to do with the organization of many such milieux into the institutions of an historical society as a whole, with the ways in which various milieux overlap and interpenetrate to form the larger structure of social and historical life. An issue is a public matter: some value cherished by publics is felt to be threatened. Often there is a debate about what that value really is and about what it is that really threatens it. This debate is often without focus if only because it is the very nature of an issue, unlike even widespread trouble, that it cannot very well be defined in terms of the immediate and everyday environments of ordinary men. An issue, in fact, often involves a crisis in institutional arrangements, and often too it involves what Marxists call "contradictions" or "antagonisms."

In these terms, consider unemployment. When, in a city of 100,000, only one man is unemployed, that is his personal trouble, and for its relief we properly look to the character of the man, his skills, and his immediate opportunities. But when in a nation of 50 million employees, 15 million men are unemployed, that is an issue, and we may not hope to find its solution within the range of opportunities open to any one individual. The very structure of opportunities has collapsed. Both the correct statement of the problem and the range of possible solutions require us to consider the economic and political institutions of the society, and not merely the personal situation and character of a scatter of individuals.

Consider war. The personal problem of war, when it occurs, may be how to survive it or how to die in it with honor; how to make money out of it; how to climb into the higher safety of the military apparatus; or how to contribute to the war's termination. In short, according to one's values, to find a set of milieux and within it to survive the war or make one's death in it meaningful. But the structural issues of war have to do with its causes; with what types of men it throws up into command; with its effects upon economic and political, family and religious institutions; with the unorganized irresponsibility of a world of nation-states.

Consider marriage. Inside a marriage a man and a woman may experience personal troubles, but when the divorce rate during the first four years of marriage is 250 out of every 1,000 attempts, this is an indication of a structural issue having to do with the institutions of marriage and the family and other institutions that bear upon them.

Or consider the metropolis — the horrible, beautiful, ugly, magnificent sprawl of the great city. For many upper-class people, the personal solution to "the problem of the city" is to have an apartment with private garage under it in the heart of the city, and forty miles out, a house by Henry Hill, garden by Garrett Eckbo, on a hundred acres of private land. In these two controlled environments — with a small staff at each end and a private helicopter connection — most people could solve many of the problems of personal milieux caused by the facts of the city. But all this, however splendid, does not solve the public issues that the structural fact of the city poses. What should be done with this wonderful monstrosity? Break it all up into scattered units, combining residence and work? Refurbish it as it stands? Or, after evacuation, dynamite it and build new cities according to new plans in new places? What should those plans be? And who is to decide and to accomplish whatever choice is made? These are structural issues; to confront them and to solve them requires us to consider political and economic issues that affect innumerable milieux.

In so far as an economy is so arranged that slumps occur, the problem of unemployment becomes incapable of personal solution. In so far as war is inherent in the nation-state system and in the uneven industrialization of the world, the ordinary individual in his restricted milieu will be powerless — with or without psychiatric aid — to solve the troubles this system or lack of system imposes upon him. In so far as the family as an institution turns women into darling little slaves and men into their chief providers and unweaned dependents, the problem of a satisfactory marriage remains incapable of purely private solution. In so far as the overdeveloped megalopolis and the overdeveloped automobile are built-in features of the overdeveloped society, the issues of urban living will not be solved by personal ingenuity and private wealth.

What we experience in various and specific milieux, I have noted, is often caused by structural changes. Accordingly, to understand the changes of many personal milieux we are required to look beyond them. And the number and variety of such structural changes increase as the institutions within which we live become more embracing and more intricately connected with one another. To be aware of the idea of social structure and to use it with sensibility is to be capable of tracing such linkages among a great variety of milieux. To be able to do that is to possess the sociological imagination.

SOURCE: From C. Wright Mills, ed., *The Sociological Imagination*. New York: Oxford University Press, 1959, pp. 3–11. Copyright © 1959 by Oxford University Press, Inc. Reprinted by permission.

PART II
Individuals Within Society

There would be no society if there were no people talking, acting and interacting, cooperating, and competing with one another. But how do people know how to behave in their own society? How does society teach them what is right and what is wrong, what is appropriate behavior and what is not? Each society has its own special set of rules, its own customs and traditions, its own set of values and beliefs, and each must teach its members how to fit into the society. Chapter 4 looks at the components of culture. Chapter 5 introduces us to social groups, one of the key elements of sociology. In Chapter 6 we discuss how society teaches its members appropriate behavior and how social interaction affects the way we look at ourselves. In addition, this chapter describes how sociologists study interaction, what they look for in the interaction, and whether interaction is consistent with the rules, customs, traditions, and beliefs of the society. But what about those people who do not conform? Most of us at some time or other do not behave as expected, and some of us never seem to behave according to any of society's rules. When and why people deviate from what is considered normal behavior is taken up in the final chapter of this section.

CHAPTER 4

Culture and Society

Customs may not be as wise as laws, but they are always more popular.

— Benjamin Disraeli

The term "culture" means different things to different people. In the minds of many people, it is associated with such activities as attending the opera, listening to classical music, and going to art museums. According to this definition, relatively few of us have culture. If one wanted to acquire it, one might begin by studying Mozart, Rembrandt, and Chaucer.

As used by sociologists and cultural anthropologists, however, culture has a different meaning. To a sociologist, a *culture* is a system of ideas, values, beliefs, knowledge, norms, customs, and technology shared by almost everyone in a particular society. A *society* is a group of interacting people who live in a specific geographical area, who are organized in a cooperative manner, and who share a common culture. A culture is a society's system of common heritage. Each of us has a culture, because we were all raised in a society. We express our culture continuously in our dress, food, work, language, and other activities. We learn our culture from our forebears and contemporaries and then we pass it on to future generations.

In general terms, a culture can be said to include all the human phenomena in a society that are not the products of biological inheritance. Culture includes all learned behavior, not just the behavior of the wealthy or the highly educated. It consists of both the nonmaterial aspects of a society such as language, ideas, and values, and the material aspects, such as houses, clothes, and tools. Both the skills needed to make a product and the product itself are parts of culture. Sociologists do not judge culture on the basis of the taste or refinement of the society it is a part of. Bowling and fox hunting, rock groups and symphony orchestras, wood carvings and museum paintings — all are human products and all reflect culture.

Elements of Culture

In most discussions of culture it is assumed that the various groups of people within a society share certain expectations about how it works and how its members should behave. In America, people live in houses or apartments. We buy food in a supermarket or grow it ourselves, we have jobs, and we generally expect our spouses to be sexually faithful to us. In traditional Eskimo culture, by contrast, people lived for part of the year in houses made of snow. They hunted for food because no one had jobs in our sense of the word. In some circumstances, sexual infidelity was not merely tolerated, it was encouraged. Since behaviors of these types vary from one group or society to another, they are viewed as products of culture rather than as basic aspects of human nature. In other words, these behaviors are not programmed genetically, as in most animal life — they are determined by the culture. Humans are not born knowing which beliefs and behaviors are appropriate. They must be learned.

Symbols

The existence of culture is dependent on people's ability to create and understand symbols. A *symbol* is something that is used to represent something else. Words, numbers, flags, crosses, and kisses are symbols. During World War II, raising the middle and index fingers of one hand was the symbol "V" for victory. During the 1960s, the same gesture came to symbolize "peace." Raising the middle finger, putting thumbs up or thumbs down, and spreading one's thumb and little finger ("hang loose" in Hawaii) all convey a particular meaning. In the same way, a stop sign is a symbol meaning "halt" and a cross

is a symbol of Christianity. The ability to use symbols is uniquely human. Unlike animals, human beings can use symbols to understand reality, to transmit messages, to store complex information, and to deal with an abstract symbolic world.

Symbols are arbitrary designations. There is no necessary connection between a symbol and what it represents. There is nothing inherent in the act of holding one's thumb up that indicates we approve of something. Similarly, the word "tree" is just a label we give to an object. If a group of children designate a tree a "goal," it becomes a goal. Symbols are often completely unrelated to the objects they represent.

As stated in Chapter 2 in our discussion of the symbolic interaction perspective, only humans can assign symbols to represent the objects around them, which is what makes humans different from animals and enables us to create cultures. The difference is not one of degree. It is not that humans have better reasoning ability than animals. Rather, it is a fundamental difference in kind. Most sociologists agree that animals do not reason, communicate symbolically, or deal with abstractions.

Language

The most important set of symbols is *language*. Language, among humans, refers to the systematized usage of speech and hearing to convey or express feelings and ideas. It is through language that our ideas, values, beliefs, and knowledge are transmitted, expressed, and shared. Other media such as music, art, and dance are also important means of communication, but language is uniquely flexible and precise. It permits us to share our experiences in the past and present, to convey our hopes for the future, and to describe dreams and fantasies that may bear little resemblance to reality. Some scientists have questioned whether thought is even possible without language. Although language can be

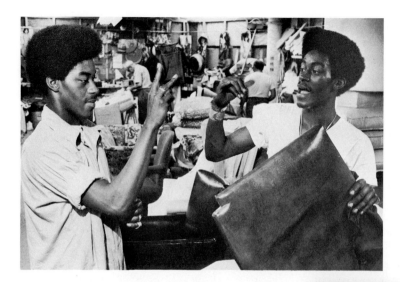

Two of the key elements of culture are symbols and language. Both are abstractions used to represent some aspect of the culture. Fingers, for example, are used symbolically to point, indicate numbers, convey approval or disapproval. A handshake, pat on the back, or smile symbolically represent friendship, warmth, and acceptance. Such symbols generally are used in conjunction with verbal symbols, or language.

used imprecisely and seem hard to understand, it is the chief factor in our ability to transmit culture.

All human societies have languages. Although there are thousands of different languages in the world, linguistic behavior as such is universal. Some societies cannot read or write their language, but they all have a spoken language. Like symbols, language is uniquely human, which is one of the most basic distinctions between human beings and other forms of life.

The importance of language to humans and to our cultural heritage is illustrated by the reports of two experiments in which young chimpanzees were reared for a time in the homes of psychologists (Hayes, 1951; Kellogg and Kellogg, 1933). The first study, conducted in the 1930s, involved a husband and wife, both psychologists, who raised their own child with an infant chimpanzee. The infants were the same age, and careful attention was given to treating them similarly. In many respects, their development was almost identical. In motor skills, the chimpanzee

Several experiments have been done comparing the development and social organization of animals, often chimpanzees, with children and adults. The ability for humans to use language, signs, and symbols is believed to be a crucial factor in their development and in the existence of culture. Shown here is a chimpanzee being taught to use sign language.

even outpaced the child, but as soon as the child began to speak, the child's cognitive development greatly outpaced that of the chimpanzee. Efforts were made to teach the chimp to speak, but the psychologists reported that they were completely unable to train their animal to utter any words or to imitate human speech.

A similar experiment was conducted in the 1940s, again with a human infant and a chimpanzee and a husband-and-wife team of psychologists. The results were about the same, but this research team reported that their chimpanzee acquired a vocabulary of three words: mama, papa, and cup. Observers reported, however, that the imitation of words was so crude that the sounds could hardly be identified and could be called words only by a stretch of the imagination. It was also clear that these words were used mechanically and without understanding.

These studies demonstrated a major gap between the human infant and the chimpanzee, a difference in kind, not merely in degree. The chimpanzee, one of the most intelligent animals,

lacked the neural equipment to either generate or comprehend language. Although chimps emit sounds and respond to commands, their sounds do not constitute a system of symbols and their responses do not involve a system of shared definitions and meanings. Chimpanzees also lack the type of pharynx found in humans, whose size, shape, and mobility are crucial to the production of speech.

More recently, studies have been done on teaching chimpanzees to use sign language. The most famous of these chimpanzees was Washoe. Washoe was taught to use American Sign Language, a system of hand signs used by the deaf. During the four years that Beatrice and Allen Gardner worked with her, Washoe amassed a vocabulary of 160 signs (Gardner and Gardner, 1969). She not only used the appropriate sign for an object but also put signs together in meaningful ways and occasionally invented her own names for objects. Since Washoe, other chimps have been taught to use different types of symbols to communicate. Some of the most exciting research has involved teaching two chimpanzees to use sign language with each other. However, the verdict is still out on whether the use of sign language by chimpanzees really constitutes "language." We may eventually find ourselves changing our description of language as uniquely human.

Language is so basic to culture and essential for human interaction and social organization that it is often taken for granted, but we can only speculate as to its origins. Did it begin with the imitation of sounds of nature such as running water or wind in the trees? Did it start with the utterance of grunts, sighs, coughs, and groans? Did it originate in calls and sounds that came to be shared by group members and later expanded to include new experiences and objects? We don't know, but there do seem to be attributes shared by many of the world's languages.

By studying the structures and other characteristics of the world's languages, linguists have been able to classify them into about nine families on the basis of their similarity. Languages in these families are spoken by almost 90 percent of the world's population. English belongs to the Indo-European family, which also includes Hindi, Sanskrit, Greek, Russian, French, German, and a number of other languages. The inclusion of certain languages in a common language family was determined by noting regular phonemic changes that took place from one language to another over time and place. For example, the Sanskrit word *brata* (brother) became *phrater* in Greek, *frater* in Latin, *broder* in Old English, and *bratu* in Slavonic. Regularities such as these suggest that these languages are related and descended from a single original Indo-European tongue. In addition, related words for milk, yoke, and wheel, which are widespread, suggest the availability of cattle and wagons in most cultural communities. These regularities of words over time and place, and the widespread use of certain words, indicate that language is an integral and universal part of culture. Linguistic

traits are learned and shared just like other cultural traits.

Language influences people's thought and experience to a greater degree than is generally recognized. In 1929, Edward Sapir argued that people see and interpret the world through the grammatical forms, labels, and categories provided by their language. He contended that societies with different languages actually perceive the world differently; that is, they don't just use a different set of labels to describe the same things. This idea is known as the *Sapir-Whorf Hypothesis*. Benjamin Whorf, a student of Sapir, noted while working for an insurance company that workmen handling barrels of gasoline were very careful about matches and cigarettes when the barrels were full but that they became careless and caused many accidents once the label "empty" had been applied to a barrel. In other words, the application of the word "empty" to a barrel influenced the workers' perception and consequent behavior (Whorf, 1941). Intrigued by this finding, he began to study different cultures to see whether people's behavior was influenced by the language they used. He found that language does influence the way we perceive things and how we behave. The Eskimos, for example, have no general word for snow, but they have more than twenty words for different kinds of snow, depending on whether it is falling, drifting, fresh, crumbling, and so on. To most Americans, a banana is just a banana, but Filipinos have different words for bananas of different sizes, colors, and uses. Interpreters of languages such as Hebrew, Russian, or German often find that no parallel word exists in English for the word they are trying to translate. Thus they can only try to convey in English the "reality" of the word they are translating. The Sapir-Whorf Hypothesis appears to be valid: our perceptions of reality are greatly influenced by our language. Languages are learned, shared, and transmitted from one generation to another and they are a central element of culture.

Values

Values are ideas shared by the people in a society about what is important and worthwhile. Our values are the basis of our judgments about what is desirable, beautiful, correct, and good as well as what is undesirable, ugly, incorrect, and bad. Most values have both positive and negative counterparts, which are reciprocally related. If you place a high positive value on fighting for one's country, for example, you probably place a high negative value on those who refuse to fight. If you value marital sexual exclusiveness, you probably disapprove of those who engage in extramarital sexual relationships. Values are often emotionally charged because they stand for things we believe to be worth defending.

Most of our basic values are learned early in life from family, friends, the mass media, and other sources within society. These values become part of our personalities. Because we learn them from society, few people possess unique sets of values. They are generally shared and reinforced by those with whom we interact. Placing a high value on God, money, honesty, cleanliness, freedom, children, education, or work serves as a general guide for our behavior and the formation of specific attitudes. Since values indicate what is proper or improper, they tend to justify certain types of behavior and forbid others.

When basic values are in conflict, we usually place them in a hierarchy of importance and behave in ways consistent with the most important. During a war, for example, the value of patriotism may overcome the value that human life is precious. When it is impossible to place our values in a hierarchy to resolve a conflict, we may feel guilty or suffer mental stress.

To give another example of value conflict, consider the case of a husband who enjoys spending time with his family. If job demands take him away from his family for extended periods, he is likely to feel stress. To avoid stress, he could quit his job, take the family along on job trips, justify the job demands as in the best interests of the family, compromise on both family and job demands, or leave the family. Some of these choices may be impossible, however. Quitting the job or taking the family along may not be realistic alternatives, and divorce may conflict with social and religious values. Mental stress is likely to result when choices are impossible. The alternative courses of action, as well as the choice selected, will generally be consistent with the values of the society and those most important to us.

Sometimes our stated values and our behavior are inconsistent. We may place a high value on freedom of the press but want to censor communist writings. We may place a high value on individualism but want to punish people whose behavior is inconsistent with our definition of appropriate behavior. Our true values are often reflected more by what we do than by what we say. If we say we value education but have no interest in attending classes, or if we say we value simplicity but spend money conspicuously to display our wealth, it is our actions that expose our real values.

Since values are learned cultural products, they differ from one society to another. One society may value political independence, another may place a higher value on political conformity and obedience. One society may value individual achievement, another may emphasize family unity and kin support. In the United States, despite the tremendous diversity of our population, certain value patterns tend to be shared by almost everyone. Robin M. Williams, Jr., in a sociological interpretation of American society (1970), described fifteen major value orientations in our culture. These included a belief in achievement and success, stressing personal achievement, especially secular occupational achievement; external conformity, emphasizing

Values are ideas shared by people in a society about what is important or worthwhile. Sometimes certain books and other literature are believed to violate values of sexual morality, patriotism, racial purity, or religious doctrines. In such instances it is not uncommon to ban, even destroy, such literature. A scene from the movie Fahrenheit 451 *vividly portrays this situation.*

the adherence to similarity and uniformity in speech, manners, housing, dress, recreation, politically expressed ideas, and group patterns; and democracy, advocating majority rule, representative institutions, and the rejection of monarchical and aristocratic principles. Other American values are described in Table 4-1.

It must be kept in mind that these are general themes in American values, which change constantly. They are often in conflict, and they are not all exhibited in a single person's behavior. As you may have noted, some of them appear to be inconsistent. How can we value both independence and conformity, or equality and racism? Some of the explanations for these inconsistencies lie in whether the value is applied generally or specifically. For example, a person might say, "Our society believes strongly in freedom of the press, but I don't want my town library to carry novels with explicit sex in them." Other explanations may reflect the beliefs of different regions of the country. Williams states that most conflicts between value systems in the United States occur between those centering around individual personalities and those organized around categorical themes or conceptions. Group discrimination and racism, as categorical themes, are contrary to other central values of the society. Each of these values has a historical base and a complexity far greater than is evident in this brief discussion. Evidence does suggest, however, a decline in racist beliefs over several decades: legislation has forced movements away from enforced segregation and public discrimination, and Congress has passed a civil rights act and a series of laws that forbid discrimination because of race, sex, religion, nationality, place of birth, or place of residence. Thus, while a central value may continue to exist that grants privilege based on group or racial affiliation, some evidence suggests that this particular theme may be fading.

Table 4-1

General themes in American values

Achievement and Success — An emphasis on personal achievement, especially secular occupational achievement.

External Conformity — An emphasis on the adherence to similarity and uniformity in speech, manners, housing, dress, recreation, politically expressed ideas, and group patterns.

Democracy — Advocacy of majority rule, representative institutions, and the rejection of monarchical and aristocratic principles.

Activity and Work — An emphasis on haste and bustle, strenuous competition, ceaseless activity, busyness.

Moral Orientation — Thinking in terms of ethics: right or wrong, good or bad.

Humanitarian Mores — An emphasis on any type of disinterested concern and helpfulness such as personal kindliness and comfort, spontaneous aid in mass disasters, philanthropy, etc.

Efficiency and Practicality — An emphasis on getting things done, standardization, mass production, technological innovation, adaptability, expediency.

Progress — An emphasis on the future rather than the past or present; a belief that forward is better than backward, that new is better than old, and that changes proceed in a definite direction and make life better.

Material Comfort — A focus on adequate nutrition, medical care, shelter, transportation, and an increasing emphasis on obtaining maximum pleasure with minimum effort.

Equality — An emphasis on equality of opportunity rather than equality of condition, and a rejection of rigid class distinctions — particularly on the level of overt interpersonal relationships.

Freedom — A belief that people should run their own lives and be independent, that government should not deny freedom of the press, freedom of worship, or freedom of private enterprise.

Science and Secular Rationality — An interest in controlling nature, and a belief in an ordered universe in which human beings can improve their situation and themselves by approaching problems rationally and scientifically.

Nationalism-Patriotism — Preferential treatment for one's own culture, demanding loyalty and allegiance to national symbols and slogans and pride in one's country.

Individual Personality — Placing a high value on the individual development of responsibility, independence, and self-respect.

Racism and Related Group-Superiority Themes — The ascription of value and privilege to individuals on the basis of race or membership in a particular group.

SOURCE: Robin M. Williams, Jr. "Values in American Society" in *American Society: A Sociological Interpretation*, 3d ed. Copyright © 1951, 1960, 1970 by Alfred Knopf, Inc. Reprinted by permission.

Norms

Social *norms* are another element of culture. Norms are rules of conduct or social expectations for behavior. These rules and social expectations specify how people should and should not behave in various social situations. They are both prescriptive (they tell people what they should do) and proscriptive (they tell people what they should not do). Examples of important changes in the norms guiding American life can be seen in Figure 4-1.

Whereas values are abstract conceptions of what is important and worthwhile, social norms are standards, rules, guides, and expectations for actual behavior. Norms and values are likely to be con-

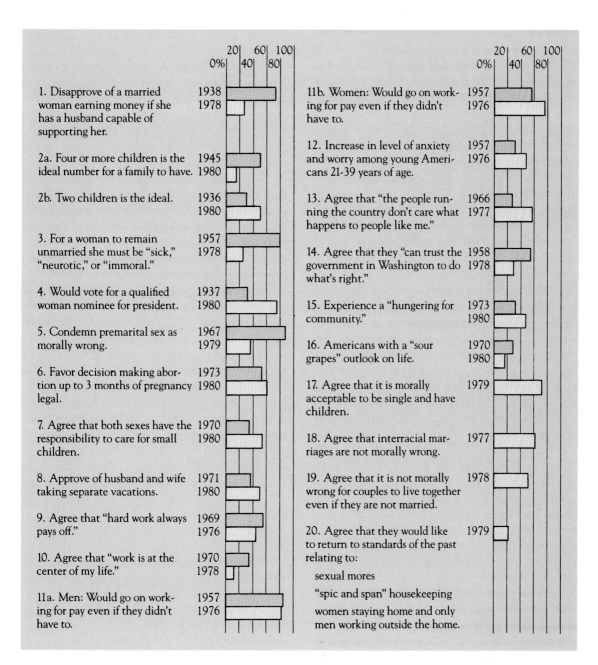

Figure 4-1

Twenty major changes in the norms guiding American life

ceptually consistent, but values are less situation-bound and more general and abstract. Norms link values with actual events. "Honesty" is a general value; the expectation that students will not cheat on tests is a norm. Most norms permit a range of behaviors; that is, certain kinds and degrees of overconformity and underconformity are expected and tolerated. We would not criticize a starving man for lying to get food, for example.

An early American sociologist, William G. Sumner (1840–1910), identified two types of norms, which he labeled "folkways" and "mores." They are distinguished not by their content but by the degree to which group members are compelled to conform to them, by their degree of importance, by the severity of punishment if they are violated, or by the intensity of feeling associated with adherence to them. *Folkways* are customs or conventions. They are norms in that they provide rules for conduct, but violations of folkways bring only mild censure. In the United States, most adults are expected to eat vegetables with a fork rather than a spoon or knife, and most students attend classes in pants or skirts rather than gowns or bathing suits. If you eat vegetables with a spoon or attend class in a gown or bathing suit, the chances are you will not be arrested or beaten, but you may receive some smiles, glances, or occasional comments from others. Why? It may be easier to use a spoon for eating vegetables, and on hot days a bathing suit may be more comfortable attire. The reason people would express mild disapproval is that these behaviors violate middle-class folkways.

Like other norms, folkways are learned in interaction with others and are passed down from generation to generation. Folkways change as culture changes or when we enter different situations. Our tendency is to accept the folkways as appropriate without question. Why do suburbanites fertilize lawns and keep them trimmed?

Why do people avoid facing one another in elevators? Why are people expected to chew food quietly and with their mouths closed? No written rules are being violated in these situations, and no one is being physically harmed. These are simply the folkways of our culture, the set of norms that specify the way things are usually done, and people who violate these norms are punished only mildly if at all.

Mores are considered more important than folkways, and reactions to their violation are more serious. They are more likely than folkways to involve clear-cut distinctions between right and wrong, and they are more closely associated with the values a society considers important. Violations of mores inspire intense reactions, and some type of punishment inevitably follows. The punishment may involve expulsion from the group, harsh ridicule, imprisonment, or in some cases even death. Why don't people masturbate in public? Why don't physicians end the life of elderly people who have a terminal illness? Why don't people betray their country for money? Actions such as these violate cultural mores. Mores that prohibit something, that state "thou shalt not," are called *taboos*. To love and care for one's children is a mos (singular of mores); to commit incest with them or neglect them is a taboo. In the United States, people who murder, commit treason, or engage in incest are widely regarded as sinful and wicked. They violate the mores of society by engaging in taboo behaviors.

Since folkways and mores differ only in degree, it is sometimes difficult to tell them apart. Furthermore, since folkways and mores are elements of culture, they vary from one society or subculture to another. The physical punishment of children may be a folkway in some cultures and a taboo in others. Killing may be rewarded in war but condemned in one's local community. Marriage between blacks and whites may be a norm in Hawaii and a strong taboo in some other states. To function effectively in a culture, one must learn the appropriate folkways and mores.

Certain norms that a society feels strongly about may become *laws*, which are formal, standardized expressions of norms enacted by legislative bodies to regulate certain types of behaviors. Laws do not merely state what behaviors are not permitted; they also state the punishment for violating the law. Ideally, the punishment should reflect the seriousness of the crime or civil offense and be carried out by a judicial system. This system legitimizes physical coercion and is above the control of any individual member of a society. Within the boundaries of their duties, members of a judicial system can use physical force, kill, or imprison without retaliation. Laws, therefore, are formalized legislated norms that are enforced by a group designated for that purpose. In contrast, folkways and mores (unless they are made into laws) are enforced by the members of society themselves, not by a group designated to do the enforcement.

When a law does not reflect folkways and mores, its enforcement is likely to be ignored or given low priority. Although certain actions may be formally defined as illegal in certain communities (shopping on Sundays, smoking marijuana, having sex outside of marriage), enforcement is ignored because of changing folkways or mores that grant a degree of social approval to the behavior. This suggests that conformity to the norms of society does not come from formal law enforcement officials but from the informal interaction of members of society. Most norms are followed by members of society, but adherence is not rigid. Adaptations to changing conditions are possible, and a certain degree of deviation from existing norms is both possible and beneficial for the effective functioning of society. The process of violating norms beyond the range of group acceptability is termed "deviance," and

the process of applying sanctions to obtain social conformity is known as "social control." These topics are explored in Chapter 7.

Technology and Material Culture

In addition to the nonmaterial aspects of culture — symbols, language, values, norms, and laws — there are certain material techniques and products used by societies to maintain their standards of living and lifestyles. The practical production and application of these techniques and products is a culture's *technology*. Technol-

The video craze that began in the late 1970s with the arrival of Pacman is a vivid indication of the impact of new technology on children and families. The adoption of hundreds of other video games quickly spread from the community arcades to the homes of millions of families.

ogy applies the knowledge gained by science in ways that influence all aspects of culture. It includes social customs and practical techniques for converting raw materials to finished products. The production and use of food, shelter, clothing, as well as commodities and physical structures, are also aspects of a society's technology. These physical products are called *artifacts*. A society's artifacts can be very diverse: beer cans, religious objects, pottery, art, pictures, typewriters, computer terminals, buildings and building materials, clothes, books, and even contraceptive devices. Material artifacts reflect the nonmaterial culture — symbols, beliefs, values, norms, and behaviors — shared by the members of a society.

Artifacts provide clues to a society's level of technological development. Americans, especially those of European descent, take great pride in their level of technology. The ability to perform heart transplants, split atoms, and produce sophisticated nuclear weapons, supersonic jets, computers, and environmentally controlled living and working conditions leads us to perceive our type of culture as superior, advanced, and progressive. This perception is often accompanied by a belief that cultures with a low level of technological development are inferior and nonprogressive. These are subjective perceptions, however, not scientific criteria for evaluating cultures. A more objective evaluation of "less developed" cultures indicates that they possess an amazing degree of skill and ingenuity in dealing with the environment. Many apparently crude techniques are based on fundamental principles of engineering. Today, people marvel at the rice terraces built several thousand years ago on mountainsides in Asia, which included water distribution systems that seem difficult to improve upon today. These rice fields produced food for generations of families and communities without the aid of diesel tractors, complex machinery, or hybrid rice plants, and many are still

in use. Anthropologists know of countless instances of the survival of people under conditions that few members of "highly developed" cultures could endure. The adobe huts of American Indians, the igloos of the Eskimos, or the bamboo houses of rural southeast Asia, none of which have indoor plumbing, heating, or air conditioning, would be inadequate homes for most members of more techologically advanced cultures. Yet these people's technology is suited to and perfectly adequate for their particular lifestyles. It could be argued that in more developed nations the technology is developed by a handful of specialists, so the general population is less technologically proficient than members of "primitive" groups.

The goals and consequences of technology and the production of material goods are being seriously questioned today. Does a high level of technology increase happiness and improve family life? Do complex technologies bring us clean air and pure water and help us conserve natural resources? All cultures possess a technology so that they can apply knowledge to master the environment and control nature. It is a mistake to dismiss a culture's technological system because it is less developed or complex than our own.

Cultural Lag

Technology and material culture are cumulative; that is, when a more efficient method or tool is found, the old one is replaced. Within the past decade, for example, word processors have begun to replace typewriters and microcomputers have begun to replace calculators. The new method or tool must be consistent with the values and beliefs of the culture it is used in, however. When changes in technology and material culture come more rapidly than changes in nonmaterial culture, we have a phenomenon known as *cultural lag* (Ogburn, 1950). In a rapidly changing society, cultural lag is inevitable. Although many effective means of controlling

This African village has no large buildings, or streets. It may be perceived by some as a culture with an inferior and nonprogressive level of technological development. Yet ethnographic investigations disclose a highly sophisticated culture with architecture that expresses communal organization and human figures sculpted from tree trunks that rank among the best of African art.

population have been developed, they have not been adopted in some cultures because they are inconsistent with societal beliefs and values. In the United States, for instance, contraceptive devices such as condoms, IUDs, diaphragms, foams, jellies, and birth control pills are widely used and available to the general population. Yet many adults view their use among adolescents as inappropriate and immoral and believe they are a cause of high rates of illegitimacy among teenagers. In Latin America, these same contraceptive devices are not suitable to many cultures because of their inconsistency with religious values, even though these devices are available and have proven to be highly effective when properly used. Many other examples could be given. The development of nuclear weapons may

surpass our techniques of world diplomacy and statesmanship. Medical advances that prolong life may surpass our ability to provide meaningful tasks for the elderly. The production of handguns may surpass our willingness and our ability to control their sale, distribution, and use. Cultural lag indicates that various elements of culture change at different rates and shows how the technological and material aspects of culture affect and are affected by the nonmaterial aspects of culture.

Our attention is often focused on material aspects of culture because of their concrete nature. When archeologists dig up the remains of an ancient civilization, they may find pots, shells, stones, jewelry, building foundations, and bones. When people visit other countries, they notice the goods in the markets, the means of transportation, and the types of housing, whereas the values, beliefs, and meanings associated with symbols and the language system are less obvious. The material and nonmaterial are both significant elements of culture, however, and they have a strong influence on each other.

Interpreting Culture: Our Own and Others

There is an enormous variety of cultural symbols, languages, values, norms, and technologies available to us. How do members of a society decide which to accept or use? When a society chooses one cultural system, how do its members perceive the systems of other cultures? Answers to such questions can be found by examining such concepts as ethnocentrism, xenocentrism, temporocentrism, and cultural relativism.

Ethnocentrism

Do you know of any culture that is better than your own? Do you think other types of families, religions, races, school systems, athletes, or artists are superior to those found in your society? Most people assume that their own culture, group, and behaviors are superior to those of others. The attitude that one's own culture is superior to others, that one's own beliefs, values, and behaviors are more correct than others, and that other people and cultures can be evaluated in terms of one's own culture is known as *ethnocentrism*. Ethnocentrism was defined by Sumner (1906) as "that view of things in which one's own group is the center of everything and all others are scaled and rated with reference to it" (p. 13).

Most groups in any society tend to be ethnocentric. Religious groups believe they have the "truth" and are more moral than others. Some even send out missionaries to convert the "heathen" and change the pagan lifestyles of the "backward" and "lost" people of the world. Sci-

entists are equally likely to believe that their methods are the best way to approach problems. Countries spend vast sums to defend their economic and political system, believing that their way of life is worth dying for. Most Americans believe that monogamy is more "proper" than polygamy and that capitalism is far superior to communism. Most of us consider the practice of

The dynamic contrast between traditional culture and modern transportation technology is evident in this scene in Bombay, India. To the Hindus, the dominant religious group in India, cows are viewed as sacred objects. They cannot be killed and are permitted to roam freely in large cities.

Flag-waving Americans believe that the values and behavior of their culture are the best and should be honored and respected. This ethnocentrism is also illustrated by bumper stickers reading: "Buy American," and "God Loves America."

eating worms disgusting and consider people who scar their bodies to be masochists. We are likely to believe that people who refuse to drink milk are ignorant and that people who walk around half-naked are shameless. Each of these views illustrates ethnocentrism: we judge other cultures according to the perspectives and standards of our own. We think it quite natural that American women paint their lips and hang jewelry from their ears, that men tie a strip of cloth around their necks, and that people eat corn, which is considered chicken food in many cultures.

Most people spend their entire lives in the culture in which they were born, and ethnocentrism is particularly strong among people who have had little contact with other cultures. Yet ethnocentric attitudes are maintained even among people who have considerable formal education, access to the mass media, and extensive experience traveling in other countries. Functionalists might argue that this is so because ethnocentrism is functional for a society's and a group's existence since it promotes group loyalty, cohesiveness, and unity. It also improves morale, encourages conformity, and reinforces nationalism and patriotism. Ethnocentric cultures have confidence in their own traditions; they discourage outsiders and thus protect themselves against change. Cultures that consider themselves superior tend to maintain the status quo — if our culture is already best, why change it?

On the other hand, some aspects of ethnocentrism are dysfunctional and have negative consequences. Ethnocentrism can increase resistance to change and encourage the exclusion of outsiders who may have something good to contribute. It can encourage racism, discourage integration efforts, increase hostility and conflicts among groups, and prevent changes that could be beneficial to all. Carried to an extreme ethnocentrism is destructive, as evidenced by the Nazis in Germany who believed in the absolute superiority of the "white Aryan" race and culture. The result was the death of millions of people who didn't fit this category.

Body Ritual Among the Nacirema

In the hierarchy of magical practitioners, and below the medicine men in prestige, are specialists whose designation is best translated as "holy-mouth-men." The Nacirema have an almost pathological horror of and fascination with the mouth, the condition of which is believed to have a supernatural influence on all social relationships. Were it not for the rituals of the mouth, they believe that their teeth would fall out, their gums bleed, their jaws shrink, their friends desert them, and their lovers reject them. They also believe that a strong relationship exists between oral and moral characteristics. For example, there is a ritual ablution of the mouth for children which is supposed to improve their moral fiber.

The daily body ritual performed by everyone includes a mouth-rite. Despite the fact that these people are so punctilious about care of the mouth, this rite involves a practice which strikes the uninitiated stranger as revolting. It was reported to me that the ritual consists of inserting a small bundle of hog hairs into the mouth, along with certain magical powders, and then moving the bundle in a highly formalized series of gestures.

In addition to the private mouth-rite, the people seek out a holy-mouth-man once or twice a year. These practitioners have an impressive set of paraphernalia, consisting of a variety of augers, awls, probes, and prods. The use of these objects in the exorcism of the evils of the mouth involves almost unbelievable ritual torture of the client. The holy-mouth-man opens the client's mouth and, using the above mentioned tools, enlarges any holes which decay may have created in the teeth. Magical materials are put into these holes. If there are no naturally occurring holes in the teeth, large sections of one or more teeth are gouged out so that the supernatural substance can be applied. In the client's view, the purpose of these ministrations is to arrest decay and to draw friends. The extremely sacred and traditional character of the rite is evident in the fact that the natives return to the holy-mouth-men year after year, despite the fact that their teeth continue to decay.

It is to be hoped that, when a thorough study of the Nacirema is made, there will be careful inquiry into the personality structure of these people. One has but to watch the gleam in the eye of a holy-mouth-man, as he jabs an awl into an exposed nerve, to suspect that a certain amount of sadism is involved. If this can be established, a very interesting pattern emerges, for most of the population shows definite masochistic tendencies.

Note: If you didn't recognize who the Nacirema are, try spelling their name backwards.

SOURCE: Horace Miner, "Body Ritual Among the Nacirema," *American Anthropologist* 58 (3) (June 1956): 503–507. Reprinted by permission.

Xenocentrism

The opposite of ethnocentrism is *xenocentrism*. Xenocentrism is the belief that what is foreign is best, that one's own lifestyle, products, or ideas are inferior to those of others. The strange, distant, and exotic are regarded as having special value: cars made in Japan, watches made in Switzerland, beer brewed in Germany, fashions created in France, silks imported from India and Thailand, and gymnasts from eastern European countries are believed to be superior to our own. In some instances, feelings of xenocentrism are so strong that people reject their own group. Thus we find anti-American Americans, anti-Semitic Jews, priests who revolt against the church, blacks who reject a black identity, and family members who scorn the kin network. Xenocentrism may focus on a product, an idea, or a lifestyle. Regardless of the focus, it is assumed that native techniques and concepts are inferior.

Temporocentrism

Temporocentrism is the temporal equivalent of ethnocentrism. It is the belief that one's own time is more important than the past or future. Accordingly, historical events are judged not in their own context but on the basis of contemporary standards. As Bierstedt (1970) stated, "We are all inclined to assume that the present is more important than the past and that the whole of historical time is significant only for what it means to us" (p. 177). Our tendency toward temporocentrism leads us to assume that current crises are more crucial than those of other periods, that problems need to be solved now before it is too late. An associated belief is that actions taken now will have an enormous impact on life in the future. This belief could conceivably be warranted — as in the case of nuclear warfare, which could end world civilization — but in most cases what we do in our time will later be viewed as only a minor ripple on the stream of history.

Just as ethnocentrism is strongest among people with little education or exposure to other nations, temporocentrism is most prevalent among people who lack historical perspective. Even people with extensive educational training and a strong grasp of history tend to focus on the present, however. Politicians and social scientists view today as the critical period. Sermons, newspapers, and teachers stress that we are living in perilous times, that this is the age of transition.

Cultural Relativism

Social scientists who study other cultures tend to be highly temporocentric, but most make special efforts to avoid ethnocentrism and xenocentrism. They attempt to view all behaviors, lifestyles, and ideas in their own context. The belief that cultures must be judged on their own terms rather than by the standards of another culture is called *cultural relativism.*

According to the cultural relativistic perspective, an act, idea, form of dress, or other cultural manifestation is not inherently right or wrong, correct or incorrect. They should be judged only in the context in which they occur; what is appropriate in one culture or context may be inappropriate in another. Nudity in the shower is appropriate, but nudity in the classroom is inappropriate. In some hunting societies, being fat may have survival value and serve as a source of admiration. In America, however, fatness is regarded as unhealthful and rarely serves as a source of admiration. The practice of abandoning unwanted infants would be viewed as intolerable by most contemporary cultures, but many cultures used to follow this practice and some still do. The point is that any aspect of a culture must be considered within its larger cultural context. The aspect may be regarded as good if it is acceptable to the members and helps attain desired goals and bad if it is unacceptable or fails to achieve these goals.

Cultural relativity does *not* mean that a behavior appropriate in one place is appropriate everywhere. It is not a license to do as one wishes. Even though having three wives is acceptable for Moslem men, killing female infants is acceptable in a Brazilian tribe, and wearing loin cloths is acceptable to African bushmen, these behaviors are not acceptable to most Americans in New York or Los Angeles. They are appropriate in some societies because they are part of a larger belief and value system and are consistent with other norms appropriate to that cultural setting. Judging other societies on the basis of cultural relativism makes us less likely to ridicule or scorn the beliefs and habits of people from other cultures.

The Organization of Culture

A culture is not simply an accumulation of isolated symbols, languages, values, norms, behaviors, and technology. It is an organized system of many interdependent factors, and its organization is influenced by physical circumstances — climate, geography, population, and plant and animal life. Eskimos traditionally eat meat almost exclusively, live in igloos or huts made of skins, and dress in furs. Many societies in tropical rain forests have diets composed primarily of fruits and vegetables, live in shelters made of leaves and branches, and wear few clothes. Physical circumstances, however, may have less influence on a culture's organization than such social factors as contact with other cultures, the stage of technological development, or the prevailing ideologies — the assertions and theories characteristic of the group.

Although cultures vary in their symbols, language, behavior, and the way these factors are organized, all cultures share some basic concerns, which are known as *cultural universals*. People in all cultures must have food, shelter, and protection. All people face illness and death, and every society has a kinship system. Like American suburbanites, African bushmen and Mongolian nomads socialize and train their members in the ways of the culture, provide for work and leisure activities, and establish leaders and rulers. Many of these basic social needs are met through social institutions.

Social Institutions

A *social institution* is a system of norms, values, statuses, and roles that develops around a basic social goal. Like the concepts "norm" and "value," the concept "institutions" is abstract. All societies have certain institutions to meet broad goals; indeed, institutions form the foundation of society and supply the basic prerequisites of group life. The family reproduces and socializes children. Religion affirms values and provides an approach to nonempirical questions. Education transmits cultural heritage, knowledge, and skills from one generation to the next. Economic institutions produce and distribute goods and services. Political institutions provide social leadership and protect individuals from one another and from forces ouside the society. Other important institutions include marriage, medicine, transportation, and entertainment.

Social institutions are often confused with social groups and social organizations, which are described in the next chapter. They are not the same, however. Like institutions, groups and organizations exist to meet some goals, but groups and organizations are deliberately constructed bodies of individuals, whereas institutions are systems of norms. Thus education is an institution; the University of Vermont is an organization. Religion is an institution; the Baptist church is an organization.

The confusion between institutions and organizations stems in part from the fact that the names of institutions can often be used to describe concrete entities as well. In its abstract sense, for example, the word "family" is used to refer to an institution. Using the word in this way, we might say, "During the 1960s, the family in the United States began to undergo important changes." We can also use the word "family" to refer to an actual group of people, however. Using the word in this concrete sense, we might say, "I am going to spend my vacation with my family." The speaker is referring to an existing group of individuals — mother, father, sisters, and brothers. The two meanings of the word are closely related but nevertheless distinct. The word "institution" is an abstraction; the word "organization" refers to an existing group. The distinction should become clearer as we discuss social groups and social organizations in the next chapter and specific institutions in Chapters 12 through 17.

Cultural Traits and Complexes

Cultural traits are the smallest meaningful unit of culture. Traits of the material culture would include such items as a handshake or a kiss. Traits such as a salute, handshake, or kiss can be of many different types and have many different meanings. A *cultural complex* is a combination of related traits. Baseballs, bats, and gloves are parts of a sports complex. Kissing, holding hands, and sharing verbal intimacies are parts of a love complex. Textbooks, papers, lectures, and classrooms form part of the complex related to students and education.

One way to analyze a culture's organization is to examine the traits and complexes that comprise it. These factors are not arranged randomly; the technologies, skills, values, behaviors, and other characteristics of a culture tend to complement one another, and all are integrated into a larger unit. The extent of the complementarity of units is often referred to as the degree of cultural integration.

As you might expect, the extent of cultural integration varies widely. Preindustrial, traditional societies are more likely to be highly integrated than less traditional industrial societies, which are generally larger and more complex and contain a greater variety of groups and lifestyles. They are more heterogeneous and possess a wide range of values, work patterns, mate selection procedures, religious rituals, and other conditions. The variety of forces at work in an industrial culture make integration more difficult. Although entire cultures may share many cultural complexes, variations in a culture's values, languages, families, and other elements can be discovered through examination of subcultures, countercultures, and idiocultures.

Subcultures

It is rare to find a society that has a single culture shared equally by all its members. This

The United States is comprised of many subcultures. A well-known religious subculture is that of the Amish who live in agricultural communities in Pennsylvania, Ohio, Indiana, Michigan and a few other states. The distinctive dress, the use of horse and buggies for transportation, and the unwillingness of the Amish to use electricity are unique characteristics.

could happen only in small, isolated, nonindustrial societies. Most societies include groups who share some of the cultural complexes of the larger society yet also have their own distinctive set of cultural complexes. These units of culture are called *subcultures*. Although subcultures exist within the confines of a larger culture, they also have their own norms, values, and lifestyles. They often reflect racial or ethnic differences such as those found among black, Polish, or Chinese Americans. Other subcultures develop around occupations: athletics, the military, medicine, or factory work. The Mormons, Amish, Hutterites, and other groups form religious subcultures; some are based on geography, such as those found in the South and New England; others are based on wealth and age. There are also drinking, drug, disco, and homosexual subcultures. Every society that has diverse languages, religions, ethnic or racial groups, or varying economic levels has subcultures.

All subcultures participate in the larger, dominant culture but possess their own set of cultural elements: symbols, languages, values, norms, and technologies. In heterogeneous societies, a person may be a member of several subcultures at any one time or at different times in his or her life. In the United States, a black adolescent male living in poverty may speak a black dialect, wear a certain style of clothing, enjoy soul food, and obtain money by means considered appropriate to his culture but unacceptable to the dominant culture. An Amish adolescent male living on a Pennsylvania farm might speak a form of German, wear a black suit and hat, part his hair in the middle cut to shoulder length, enjoy sauerkraut and potatoes, be forbidden to dance or go to movies, and turn all earnings over to his father. Both the black and the Amish adolescent are required to abide by the laws of the dominant society, however.

At times, the dominant culture and the subculture may conflict to such a degree that tremendous stresses occur and a crisis results. Members of the subculture may be required by the dominant culture to register for the military even though they value pacifism. The subculture may value the use of certain drugs but be forbidden by the dominant culture to obtain them, or speak a language not used in the public schools. It is important to realize that, in addition to the differences among cultures, there are great variations within cultures as well.

Countercultures

A *counterculture* is a subculture that adheres to "a set of norms and values that sharply contradict the dominant norms and values of the so-

ciety of which that group is a part" (Yinger, 1977, p. 833). Ideologically, countercultures adhere to a set of beliefs and values that radically reject the society's dominant culture and prescribe an alternative one. Because they accept such beliefs and values, members of a counterculture behave in such radically nonconformist ways that they tend to drop out of society (Westhues, 1972). Dropping out may mean either physically leaving or ideologically and behaviorally "leaving" by rejecting the dominant values and working to change them.

Delinquent gangs, the Hare Krishna religious sect, and the youth movement of the 1960s can be classified as countercultures. The norms and values of each of these groups contrast sharply with those held by conventional middle-class groups. Often, these values are not merely different from those of the dominant culture, but in opposition to them. Delinquent gangs may grant prestige and social approval for lawbreaking, violence, theft, or the use of drugs to achieve their goals of dominance and material success. The stated goal of the Hare Krishna religious sect is the salvation of the world through its conversion to Krishna Consciousness. The Krishna counterculture entails considerable ritualism, ceremony, shaved heads, chant-ins, proselytizing in airports, and other activities often viewed as countercultural. The youth movement of the 1960s, which included political activists, dropouts, and hippies, actively challenged the dominant cultural norms of hard work, financial success, dress conformity, sexual restrictiveness, military superiority, and white supremacy. Flacks (1971) indicated that the youth movement of the 1960s stressed cooperation over competition, expression over success, communalism over individualism, being over doing, making art over making money, and autonomy over obedience. Now, however, the hippies have all but vanished and their flourishing communities such as Haight-Ashbury in San Francisco and the East Village in New York have disappeared.

10TH ANNIVERSARY WOODSTOCK REUNION

Studies of the values expressed in counterculture and dominant culture magazines indicate that the counterculture did not appreciably influence the values of the dominant culture (Spates, 1976). It appears that today the pendulum has swung away from countercultural trends among youth.

Idiocultures

Gary Fine (1979) argues that every group forms its own culture to a certain extent. He called these created cultures *idiocultures*. An idioculture is a system of knowledge, beliefs, behaviors, and customs created through group interactions. Members of a group share certain experiences and recognize that references to a shared experience will be understood by other members. Members of one group, for example, might roar with laughter whenever the word "cashew" is mentioned. All small groups have a culture unique to themselves but which is nevertheless part of a larger cultural pattern. A group's idioculture is formed by the group itself, so idiocultures do not exist when a group is first formed. They are created from the opening moments of group interaction when people begin to learn names and other information about one another. With time, rules are established, opinions expressed, information exchanged, and members experience events together.

Suppose, for example, that a newspaper has just been established and that the editors, reporters, typesetters, and other employees have come together for the first time. Initially, they will have shared no experiences, but as they work together they will develop certain unique ways of interacting. At first, the reporters may go out for coffee individually, but eventually they might decide to delegate one person to get coffee for everyone. "Gathering background information" might become a euphemism for wasting time. When the Johnson Warehouse is destroyed in the biggest fire that ever happened in the town, they might come to refer to any big story as a "Johnson." Similarly, stories dealing with improper behavior by politicians might come to be called "Watergates," and the task of writing the relatively uninteresting daily reports about weddings, funerals, and meetings might come to be called the "trivia." After a few unpleasant arguments, the reporters might agree never to comment on one another's stories. After working together for an extended period, the group would develop its own jargon and set of customs that would not be intelligible to an outsider.

Ideal and Real Culture

In most cultures, differences exist between what people are supposed to do and what they actually do. The *ideal culture* consists of the

SOCIOLOGISTS AT WORK
Evaluating Sex Education Programs

Sandra Baxter is a senior researcher at Advanced Technology, Inc., in McLean, Virginia, where she conducts program evaluations for federal government agencies. Previously, she worked at MATHTECH, Inc., in Bethesda, Maryland, as a sociologist researching the effectiveness of sex education programs for adolescents and their parents. Before that, she taught sociology at the university level for five years. She has an undergraduate degree from the University of Chicago and graduate degrees from American University and the University of Michigan — all in sociology.

How did this sociologist get into the business of consulting for the federal government? "I left teaching because my heart was always in research," Sandra Baxter says, "and teaching leaves little time for thoughtful research. I learned about the position at MATHTECH from a friend there. I asked him what the position entailed, and when he told me I remarked that I couldn't have written a better job description for myself. So, like the majority of job changes, this one came through informal knowledge of a vacancy and the encouragement of a friend already located in the new job setting. I was interested in the subject matter because of my training in social psychology and political sociology, but my background in research methodology and statistics is what actually qualified me for the job.

"Initially, my job was to design the evaluation of parent sex education courses my colleagues were constructing and to implement the evaluation at ten sites around the country. One major problem was to identify good teachers who already were offering or were interested in offering a course for parents. Once we identified them we tried to help them gain access to a group of parents, or create a group. How do you create demand for a new course? The answer depends on the characteristics of the communities you've chosen to work in. We offered a course to Hispanic parents in New York City. With knowledge of the importance of the church in Hispanic communities, we knew that the best strategy was to obtain the sponsorship of a local church, or at

norms and values people profess to follow. The *real culture* is the culture they actually do follow. If you were asked to tell a foreign visitor about the norms and values of Americans, for example, you would probably describe the ideal culture, mentioning such topics as freedom, democracy, equal rights, monogamy, marital fidelity, and educational opportunity for all. The actual culture differs considerably from the ideal, however. The very poor are less likely to get a good education, marital infidelity is common, and many people have several spouses during their lives.

This distinction between real and ideal culture is expressed by some anthropologists in terms of "explicit" culture and "implicit" culture. These terms may be more accurate than "real" and "ideal" — both types of culture are real in the sense that they actually exist. The point is that stated cultural traits and complexes are not always practiced. Students should be sensitive to distinctions of this sort. The speed limit may be 55, but many people drive at 65. Honesty in the classroom may be the norm, but cribbing may be widespread. Clashes between

least get permission to hold the course in their building. Who was likely to attend, and how should the course materials be focused? Again, sociological insight suggests that mothers have the primary responsibility for rearing children in Hispanic cultures, so we could expect only mothers at the New York course. The norm in white middle-class communities is for both parents to play some role in overseeing children's development, so we planned to have both mothers and fathers in attendance at those sites. We were correct in both assumptions, and so were able to tailor the courses correctly to their different audiences.

"I also provided methodological and statistical background for an evaluation of exemplary sex education courses taught to adolescents nationwide. I eventually headed my own project, working with local school districts in Maryland to assess their sex education curricula, conduct training for their teachers, and evaluate how their programs improved with our assistance. All of these jobs required some travel, a quick course in the teaching of sex education, sensitivity to the political volatility of our research, and a firm basis in research techniques.

"Research on any educational program is tricky," Baxter warns. "You have to disentangle learning effects from development effects. In sex education, the desired end result of the course — 'responsible sexual behavior' — may not appear for years in adolescents who are not sexually active. How do you measure whether the course has accomplished its goal? There are intermediate indicators, of course, but the challenge lies in identifying them and measuring them. My knowledge of social psychology, particularly peer group dynamics and family sociology, was invaluable. My background in political sociology gave me a broad perspective on sex education as a social movement, the resistance to it that could be expected, and the strategies sex education professionals could follow to ensure their acceptance in communities. My training in sociology gave me an awareness of the social context in which adolescents, their parents, educators, and researchers functioned. It also gave me the tools to identify, measure, and evaluate the complex dynamics of attitudes and behaviors of all these sets of actors.

"But insights alone wouldn't have answered the questions we were contracted to answer: What effects do sex education courses have on adolescents and on parents? These questions could only be satisfactorily answered through solid, scientifically defensible research designs and procedures. The training I received as a quantitative researcher was crucial to doing the job well."

ideal and actual practices may be avoided through rationalizations or flexibility in social control. A student might defend cheating on a test by arguing that "everyone does it." Police rarely arrest all who exceed the speed limit, concentrating instead on extreme violations.

Summary

A culture is a society's social heritage, the system of ideas, values, beliefs, knowledge, norms, customs, and technology that everyone in a society shares. A society is a group of people who share a common culture. Some of the most significant elements of a culture are symbols, language, values, norms, and technology.

Symbols are arbitrary designations that represent something. The use of symbols is a uniquely human capability that allows us to make sense of reality, transmit messages, store complex information, and deal with an abstract world. Our most important set of symbols is language, which enables us to transmit and store our social heritage. The importance of language to humans is illustrated in studies comparing the development of children and chimpanzees. The humans outpaced the chimps as soon as they began to speak. It has been demonstrated that language influences how we perceive and experience the world. The Sapir-Whorf Hypothesis suggests that the use of different languages by different societies causes them to perceive the world very differently. Rather than simply seeing the same world with different labels, they actually perceive different realities.

Values are conceptions about what is important and of worth. They are learned and shared cultural products that justify certain types of behavior. People in the United States tend to value achievement, success, work, a moral orientation, and humanitarian concerns, among others. Americans also tend to believe that some groups are superior to others. Values indicate what is important, whereas norms are rules of conduct, the standards and expectations of behavior. Norms are of two types: folkways, which are customs or conventions that provoke only mild censure if violated, and mores, which are far more important and provoke severe punishment if violated. Laws are the formalized and standardized expressions of norms.

In addition to the nonmaterial aspects of culture such as these, there are material and technological aspects as well. Cultural lag occurs when changes in technology come more rapidly than changes in the nonmaterial aspects.

Members of a society tend to view their own culture in certain ways. Ethnocentrism is the belief that one's own culture is superior to others and that one's own cultural standards can be applied in judging other cultures. Xenocentrism is the belief that what is foreign is best, that one's own lifestyle, products, or ideas are inferior to those of others. Temporocentrism is the belief that the past should be judged in terms of the present, that one's own time is exceptionally important. The idea of cultural relativism suggests that cultures must be judged on their own terms, not by the standards of another culture. Acts, ideas, and products are not inherently good or bad; they must be judged in the cultural context in which they happen.

A culture is not simply a collection of isolated ideas and values. It is an organized system in which all components are interrelated and interdependent. Some aspects of culture are common to all societies. Many social needs common to all cultures are met through social institutions, which are systems of norms, values, statuses, and roles that develop around basic social goals. The smallest units of a culture are called traits; a combination of related traits is known as a cultural complex. The extent to which these complexes are complementary is an index of a society's degree of cultural integration.

Subcultures are groups within a society that share the common culture but have their own distinctive set of cultural complexes. A counterculture is a type of subculture adhering to a set of norms and values that sharply contradict the dominant norms and values of the society of which the group is a part. To a certain extent, all groups possess localized cultures of their own, which are known as idiocultures. The culture a society professes to follow (its ideal culture) differs from the culture it actually does follow (its real culture).

Key Terms

artifacts
counterculture
cultural complex
cultural lag
cultural relativism
cultural traits
cultural universals
culture
ethnocentrism
folkways

ideal culture
idiocultures
institution
language
laws
mores
norms
real culture
Sapir-Whorf Hypothesis
society
subcultures
symbol
taboos
technology
temporocentrism
values
xenocentrism

Suggested Readings

Gordon, Milton M. (ed.). Special Issue, "America As a Multicultural Society," **The Annals of the American Academy of Political and Social Science** *454 (March 1981):1–205.* A special issue devoted to subcultures in America: blacks, Jews, Catholics, Hispanics, Mexicans, Asians, native Americans, Muslims, and others.

Hammond, Peter B. **An Introduction to Cultural and Social Anthropology, 2d ed.** *New York: Macmillan, 1978.* An anthropology textbook emphasizing both cultural evolutionary and cultural ecologi-

cal interpretations of how cultures develop, how societies "act," and how people behave.

McCready, William C. and Andrew M. Greeley. **The Ultimate Values of the American Population.** *Beverly Hills, Calif.: Sage Publications, 1976.* A national survey research study of the values held by people in the United States.

Mead, Margaret. **Sex and Temperament in Three Primitive Societies.** *New York: Morrow, 1935.* A pioneering work by the most famous anthropologist of this century.

Miller, Elmer S. and Charles A. Weitz. **Introduction to Anthropology.** *Englewood Cliffs, N.J.: Prentice-Hall, 1979.* An anthropology textbook covering human biological evolution and cultural variation in today's world.

Spradley, James P. and Michael A. Rynkiewich. **The Nacirema: Readings on American Culture.** *Boston: Little, Brown, 1975.* A look at the complexity of American culture from an anthropological perspective.

Westhues, Kenneth. **Society's Shadow: Studies in the Sociology of Countercultures.** *Toronto: McGraw-Hill Ryerson, 1972.* A book about countercultural movements that discusses definitions, conditions that give rise to them, and what happens once they get started, followed by an examination of the hippie movement.

Williams, Robin M., Jr. **American Society: A Sociological Interpretation, 3d ed.** *New York: Alfred Knopf, 1970.* An excellent sociological analysis of the people and society of the United States, including a discussion of geography, social institutions, value systems, and cultural change.

CHAPTER 5

Social Groups and Social Organizations

We do not mind our not arriving any-where nearly so much as our not having company on the way.

— Frank Moore

Humans are social animals. Even those who think of themselves as loners participate in many groups, and, for most of us, groups are a major source of satisfaction. You may eat with a certain group of friends every day, belong to a drama club, or play tennis every week with your gym class. You probably depend on social groups, social organizations, and social systems for most of your psychological and physical needs. Research indicates that we are influenced not only by the groups we currently belong to and those we identify with but also by those we associated with in the past. In fact, life without groups seems impossible. Without group involvements, infants die, adolescents get depressed, middle-aged people suffer psychologically, and the elderly get lonely and lose their will to live. We learn, eat, work, and worship in groups and depravation of group involvement is damaging.

Because groups play such a large role in our lives, we tend not to recognize the extent of their influence, yet they affect the structure of society as well as our personal interactions. The groups that comprise society are of many different sizes, and they have a wide range of goals. A group of two may join together to raise a child. The group that elects a president consists of many millions. Groups may be based on friendship or family. Others have a different basis. Corporations are economic groups, the Republicans and Democrats are political groups, and stamp collectors share a common interest. Although we may take their existence for granted, it is important to understand how they influence individuals and society. The first step in developing such an understanding is learning what sociologists mean when they use the word "group."

What Is a Group?

The answer to this question may seem obvious: a group is a number of people who have something in common. Like most topics in sociology, however, the problem is not that simple. Although the concept of group is one of the key elements of sociology, no single definition of it is universally accepted. The problem is not that sociologists are unable to decide what a group is; rather, there are many types of groups, and sociologists attach different meanings to their forms, their functions, and their consequences.

In our discussion, we will focus chiefly on social groups — those in which people physically or socially interact. Several other types are also recognized by most sociologists, however, and deserve to be mentioned.

Statistical groups are formed not by the group members but by sociologists and statisticians. In 1982, for example, there were 61,019,000 families in the United States with an average size of 3.25 people per family (U.S. Bureau of the Census, 1983, p. 10). The group of women between 5 feet 1 inch and 5 feet 5 inches tall would be another statistical group. Some sociologists do not consider groups of this sort to be groups at all, because the members are unaware of their membership and there is no social interaction or social organization (see Table 5-1). Many purely statistical groups have more than a statistical sig-

nificance, however, and some can indicate important characteristics of societies. A society in which 5 percent of the population is illiterate is very different from one in which 90 percent of the population is illiterate, and information of this sort can be very useful in making policy decisions.

Another type of group is the *categorical group*, or *societal unit*, in which a number of people share a common characteristic. Drivers of Corvettes, millionaires, redheads, students, women, senior citizens, and virgins are all categorical groups. Members of groups of this type are likely to be aware that they share a particular characteristic and a common identity. Corvette drivers may wave to each other as they pass on the highway.

The importance of categorical groupings is evident in the extent to which people tend to live and associate with others who share certain characteristics. Teenagers, the aged, interracial couples, unwed mothers, widows, the handicapped, the wealthy — all are aware of their similarity to other members of their own social category.

A third type of group is the *aggregate*. An aggregate is any collection of people who are together in one place. You may join a group of this sort buying an ice cream cone, watching a football game, riding a bus, or waiting to cross a street. Aggregates are basically unstructured, and

Table 5-1

A classification of group types

TYPE OF GROUP	AWARENESS OF KIND	SOCIAL INTERACTION	SOCIAL ORGANIZATION	EXAMPLE
Statistical	No	No	No	Average family size
Categorical	Yes	No	No	Redheads
Aggregate	Yes	Yes	No	Football crowd
Associational	Yes	Yes	Yes	Rotary club

the participants interact briefly and sporadically. Most members act as if they were alone, except perhaps to comment about the weather, ask the time, or complain about the service. The members of an aggregate need not converse but may do so; they need not know one another but may see familiar faces. Members are generally not concerned with the feelings and attitudes of the others. Most aggregates meet only once.

A fourth type is the *associational* or *organizational group*, which is especially important in complex industrialized societies. Associational groups consist of people who join together in some organized way to pursue a common interest, and they have a formal structure. Most of us belong to a number of them; they can be formed for almost any conceivable purpose. A university, a volleyball team, a Rotary club, the Democratic party, General Motors Corporation, Protestant churches — all are associational groups. They share the major characteristics of other types of groups, but in addition they also have a formal structure.

As you can see, a number of different kinds of groups are recognized, and their boundaries are not easy to state clearly. Like other classification schemes, the one we have suggested makes use of certain criteria but ignores others that may in some circumstance be equally important. Groups might also be classified on the basis of social boundaries between members and non-members, adherence to a special set of norms, awareness not only of kind, as in Table 5-1, but of membership, or a variety of other factors.

Given this range of definitions and possible classification criteria, what types of collectives can we call social groups? Although sociologists do not accept a single definition, there would be widespread agreement that membership in a *social group* involves (1) some type of interaction; (2) a sense of belonging or membership; (3) shared interests or agreement on values, norms, and goals; and (4) a structure, that is, a definable,

recognizable arrangement of parts. According to this definition, the statistical, categorical, and aggregate classifications would not be considered social groups, but many associational groups would be. Thus, a given family might be considered a social group, but the 61 million families in the United States would comprise a statistical group. The League of Women Voters would be a social group, but the group of all those who consider themselves female would be categorical. A college class riding a bus on a field trip would be a social group, but a crowd of people waiting at a bus stop would be an aggregate. The sociological use of "group" involves a consciousness of membership, interaction, shared interests, and structure.

Social groups are important because they provide us with a social identity, serve as a key to understanding social behavior, link the self with the larger society, and help us understand social structure and societal organization. By studying the individual in a group context, the dynamic interactions within groups, and the organizational network of the larger society, we can improve our understanding of the self, of human interaction, and of the larger social order.

Types of Social Groups

Social groups vary widely in their size, purpose, and structure (see Figure 5-1). Membership in one type does not preclude membership in other types; in fact, it is not unusual for a single group to fall into several different categories. We will cover the types most often discussed in sociology, including primary and secondary groups, in-groups and out-groups, peer groups, reference groups, and small and large groups.

Primary and Secondary Groups

Perhaps the most fundamental distinction is that made between primary and secondary groups. The term *primary group,* coined by

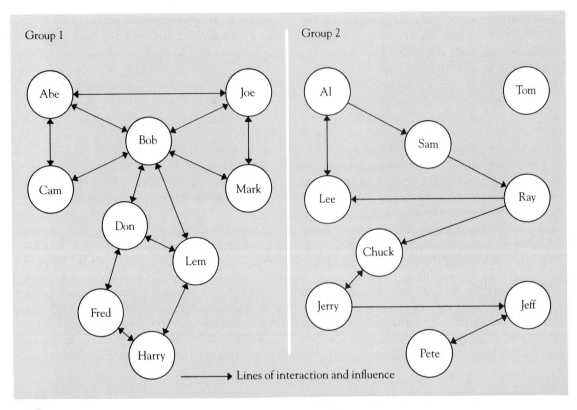

Figure 5-1

Applying sociology to group relationships: A sociogram. Sociologists often use sociograms to chart communication patterns, friendship linkages, and general interaction patterns among the members of small groups. Compare the sociograms of these two groups of nine boys. From the data provided, which group does the most interacting? What conclusions can you draw about these two groups? How might sociograms be useful in actual situations?

Charles H. Cooley (1909), is used to refer to small, informal groups of people who interact in a personal, direct, and intimate way. This category includes such groups as the family and play groups, which Cooley believed were the most important in shaping the human personality. Primary groups involve intimate face-to-face association and interaction, and their members have a sense of "we-ness" involving mutual iden-

tification and shared feelings. Their members tend to be emotionally attached to one another and involved with other group members as whole people, not just with those aspects of a person that pertain to work, school, or some other isolated part of one's life. Your family, close friends, and certain neighbors and work associates are likely to be members of your primary group.

A *secondary group* is a group whose members interact in an impersonal manner, have few emotional ties, and come together for a specific practical purpose. Like primary groups, they are usually small and involve face-to-face contacts. Although the interactions may be cordial or friendly, they are more formal than primary group interactions. Sociologically, however, they are just as important. Most of our time is spent in secondary groups — committees, professional groups, sales-related groups, classroom groups, or neighborhood groups. The key difference between primary and secondary groups is in the quality of the relationships and the extent of personal intimacy and involvement. Primary groups are person-oriented, whereas secondary groups tend to be goal-oriented. A primary group conversation usually focuses on personal experiences, feelings, and casual, open sharing, whereas a secondary group conversation is more apt to be impersonal, purposeful, and limited to socially relevant topics.

Primary and secondary groups are important both to individuals and to society. Primary groups are particularly important in shaping the personality, in formulating self-concepts, in developing a sense of personal worth, and in becoming an accepted member of society. They are also an important source of social control and social cohesion. Such scholars as Erich Fromm (1965) and Lewis Mumford (1962) contend that the strength and vitality of primary groups are the basis of the health of a society. In an increasingly impersonal world, they are sources of openness, trust, and intimacy. People who are not accepted members of some primary group — a marriage, friendship, or work relationship — may have difficulty coping with life or experience greater health problems (see Table 5-2).

Although primary groups are vital to the health of both individuals and society, secondary groups are also important because they tend to meet specific goals. They help societies function effectively and permit people who don't

Table 5-2

Psychological well-being of men and women by marital status

	MEN				
	MARITAL STATUS				
HAPPINESS	MARRIED	SINGLE	SEPARATED	DIVORCED	WIDOWED
Very happy	35	18	7	12	7
Pretty happy	56	63	55	53	56
Not too happy	9	19	38	35	37

	WOMEN				
	MARITAL STATUS				
HAPPINESS	MARRIED	SINGLE	SEPARATED	DIVORCED	WIDOWED
Very happy	38	18	12	11	14
Pretty happy	55	68	45	66	54
Not too happy	7	14	44	23	32

SOURCE: Norman M. Bradburn, *The Structure of Psychological Well-Being*. Copyright © 1966 by National Opinion Research Center. Reprinted by permission.

know one another intimately to perform their jobs more effectively. Most formal organizations such as schools, corporations, hospitals, and unions are comprised of many secondary groups and relationships. The impersonality and formality of the secondary group allows members to focus on skills and specialized interests rather than on personalities. Although pressures may exist to hire a relative or best friend from your primary group, he or she may not be the best trained or most knowledgeable person available for the job. Likewise, people usually avoid romantic involvement with their coworkers because it can disrupt or complicate progress toward a goal. Most jobs, whether they involve driving a bus or performing heart surgery, have clearly defined goals and role expectations, so the personal characteristics of the people fulfilling the roles and the public's need for emotional involvement with them are not of great importance.

It should be recognized that the difference between primary and secondary groups is one of degree. Many formal secondary group situations involve instances of informality and personal openness. In fact, many primary groups develop from secondary groups and organizations. Two students who meet in a formal lecture hall (secondary group) may later marry (primary group); coworkers in a large organization may develop an intimate friendship. Conversely, two friends who join a corporation may grow apart and ultimately have only a secondary relationship. The composition of an individual's primary and secondary groups shifts frequently.

In-Groups and Out-Groups

As mentioned earlier, one of the key characteristics of a group is the members' sense of belonging. Those who belong think of one another as forming a social unit. This unit has boundaries that separate "us" from "them," that differentiate those who are "in" from those who are "out." An *in-group* is a social category to which persons feel they belong and in which the members have a consciousness or awareness of kind (as in Table 5-1). They feel that they share a common fate, adhere to a common ideology, come from a common background, or otherwise resemble the other members. In-groups may be primary groups, but are not necessarily. We can feel "in" with people we have never met or shared personal intimacies with — members of our alumni group, religious group, or veterans group, for example. University of California graduates, Buddhists, or Vietnam veterans may experience feelings of comradeship or a sense of togetherness.

Conversely, an *out-group* is one to which people feel they do not belong. If you are a member of the in-group, the out-group is everyone else. It is made up of those who do not share an awareness of kind. We do not identify or affiliate ourselves with members of out-groups, and we feel little allegiance to them. We treat most members of out-groups with indifference, but at times we may feel hostile toward them because of our tendency toward ethnocentrism (see Chapter 4), the predisposition to perceive our own in-group as superior to others. The out-group, being inferior, does not deserve the same respect as the in-group. Thus the members of an in-group — friends, classmates, doctors, industrialists — may defend other in-group members even when it does an injustice to those who are "out."

The difference between in- and out-groups is sociologically important for several reasons. First, the in-group tends to stereotype members of the out-group. Although we may notice individual differences among members of the in-group, most of us notice only similarities in the out-group, and we label them accordingly. Americans may recognize a wide range of variations in appearance, beliefs, and behavior among our fellow citizens but fail to recognize that all

Sociologists distinguish primary groups from secondary ones. Friends or co-workers engaged in informal conversation and involved in intimate face-to-face association are an example of a primary group. A committee or business meeting is more likely to represent a secondary group. While secondary groups may involve friendly, face-to-face interaction, the relationships are likely to be formal and impersonal.

Chinese do not look alike, that not all Germans love sauerkraut, that not all Iranians are revolutionaries, or that not all Russians are anticapitalistic. Within the United States, whites (in-group) may label blacks (out-group) as lazy, and blacks (in-group) may label whites (out-group) as racists. Republicans may label Democrats as spendthrifts, Democrats may label Republicans as rich and greedy. Students sometimes assume that all professors are absentminded, but exceptions have been known to exist.

A second reason that the two groups are important is that any threat or attack, whether imaginary or real, from the out-group tends to increase the cohesion and solidarity of the in-group. Strange as it may seem, a war with a foreign enemy can have a positive effect on a divided nation. Similarly, economic hardships may bring the members of a family closer together.

Unlike primary groups, which are always small, in-groups and out-groups can vary in size. They may be as large as a nation or continent or as small as a two-person marriage.

We all have many in-group identities and loyalties, some of which overlap and some of which cause conflict. We may, for example, strongly identify with both the women's movement and the Catholic church but find that our belief that a woman should be able to choose whether to have an abortion is in direct conflict with the position of the Catholic church. Whom should you be loyal to when your employer discriminates against your ethnic group? Whom should you root for when your daughter, who plays on the Michigan tennis team, plays against your alma mater? Our affiliation with a particular in-group may provide us with an identity and a sense of belonging, but it also induces conflict and restricts our relationships and interactions with others.

Peer Groups

One type of group from which in- and out-groups draw their members is the *peer group*. A peer group is an informal primary group of people who share a similar status and usually are of similar age. The unique factor in peer groups is equality. In most groups, even small ones such as marriages or committees, one person or more has a higher status or a position of dominance, but in peer groups the members are roughly equal in importance.

Although peer groups are most often discussed in connection with young people, they are found in all age groups. Most friendships, regardless of the friends' ages, share the characteristics of a peer group: they are informal, primary relationships, and the participants are of equal rank and often of the same sex. The emphasis on teenagers in discussions of peer groups might have resulted from the post–World War II baby boom, which produced a large population that came to be associated with a unique subculture. This subculture, with its own dress, language, music, values, and goals was emphasized by the media, which focused on their large rock concerts, the student anti-war movement, and the hippies and flower children of the mid- and late 1960s. This network of age peer group provided support for its members as well as guidance in both attitude and behavior.

Reference Groups

Reference groups are the groups we identify with psychologically. They serve as sources of self-evaluation and influence how we think and act, and what we believe. People need not belong to a group for it to be a reference group for them, and groups we aspire to belong to may also be reference groups. Negative reference groups, those we do not want to be identified with, also serve as sources of self-evaluation. A person might, for example, try to avoid resembling members of a group composed of intellectuals or football players.

Most attention is focused on positive reference groups. These are the ones we want to be accepted by. Thus if you want to be an executive, you might carefully observe and imitate the behavior of executives. If you note that they play golf, wear conservative clothes, and read *The Wall Street Journal*, you might do the same.

Reference groups are an important source of information about our performance in a given area. Just as cultures tend to assess themselves on the basis of their own standards (see the discussion on cultural relativity in Chapter 4), individuals assess themselves in accordance with the standards of their reference group. A B grade may be a source of pride to students if their peer reference group did worse, but it may be a source of disappointment to a family reference group if they expected an A. A professor's income may be good relative to an assistant professor's income, but it may be poor relative to the income of someone employed in industry. In brief, we tend to judge our worth, accomplishments, and even our morality in comparison with groups of reference.

Reference groups serve not only as sources of current evaluation but also as sources of aspiration and goal attainment. A person who chooses to become a professional baseball player, a lawyer, or a teacher begins to identify with that group and is socialized to have certain goals and expectations.

A knowledge of people's reference groups can sometimes help us understand why they behave as they do. It may explain why a teenager who never smokes or drinks at home will do so with a school group, or why politicians may vary their stances on an issue, depending on the audience they are addressing. Our aim is to please and conform to the expectations and behaviors of the groups that are important to us.

Small Groups and Large Groups

Categorizing groups according to size is an imprecise way to differentiate them, but size has a dramatic effect on member interactions. The smallest group, called a "dyad," consists of two people. When just two people are involved, each of them has a special responsibility to interact — if one person withdraws, the group no longer exists. With the addition of a third person, the dyad becomes a "triad" and the interactions change drastically. If one person drops out, the group can still survive. In a group of three, one person can serve as a mediator in a disagreement, or alternatively side with one person and then the other. A third person, however, can also be a

We identify with persons and groups who are significant to us, and we look to these reference groups for direction in how to think and behave. To be recognized as a member of a particular reference group, we may dress or act in certain ways, as is illustrated by the tongue-in-cheek handbook on how to be a Young Urban Professional, or "Yuppie."

source of conflict or tension. The phrase "two's company, three's a crowd" emphasizes the dramatic shift that takes place when dyads become triads. When a triad adds a fourth or fifth member, two subgroups can emerge. As size increases, it may be more difficult to choose a leader, arrive at an agreement or consensus, or decide who will perform certain tasks.

At what point does a small group become large? Is it small if it has two, ten, or twenty members? Is it large if it has 25 or 250 or 25,000 members? Determinations of whether a group is large or small may be influenced by the type of group as well as its goals. In a marriage in most cultures, three would be large. In politics, 30,000 may be small. As you can see, choosing a cutoff

Groups come in all sizes, from as small as two to as large as thousands. As group size increases, so does the division of labor, the formality of interaction, and the type of leadership. This can be seen clearly in these two contrasting photos. In one a dyad engages in a leisure activity — the interaction is highly personal and informal. In the other a board meeting takes place, a meeting that is highly formal and impersonal with a clear-cut division of labor and a defined chair or leader.

point between large and small groups requires that we consider a number of different factors. Even so, such a designation may be largely arbitrary.

Regardless of the distinction between large and small groups, the complexity of group relations increases much more rapidly than the number of members. Two people have only one reciprocal relationship, three people have 6 reciprocal relationships, four people have 24 relationships, five people have 120 relationships, six people have 720 relationships, and seven people have 5,040 relationships. Beyond that, the number of relationships quickly becomes astronomical. Size *does* make a difference.

In addition to the number of relationships, several other characteristics change with increasing size. First, as size increases, so does the division of labor. If the group is small, all the members may engage in the same activities. As size increases, however, activities tend to become specialized. The father of one of the authors, for example, once taught eight grades in a one-room school. He covered the three R's and any other subjects, supervised the playground, did some personal counseling, and occasionally had some transportation responsibilities. As schools got larger, teachers were assigned not only to specific grade levels but also to specific subject areas. They were employed to teach music, art, and other specialized subjects, and a complex system was developed to provide transportation, counseling, lunches, sports, and a wide variety of clubs and other school-related activities. Similar changes in the division of labor occur as churches, families, manufacturing concerns, and other groups grow. Generally, as group size increases, so does the division of labor.

Second, as the size of a group increases, its structure becomes more rigid and formal. Whereas small groups are likely to operate informally according to unwritten rules, large groups usually conduct meetings in accordance with Robert's Rules of Order or some other standard formula. Also, small groups are more apt to emphasize personal and primary characteristics. A small grocery store run by a family, for example, may reflect the tastes of the family members. Jobs may be delegated to various people on the basis of their preferences, and work schedules may be drawn up to accommodate one person's going to college or another person's social life. Large groups, on the other hand, emphasize status and secondary characteristics. In a large supermarket chain, decisions are made by committees. Chair-persons, division heads, or managers are selected, and the problems of bureaucratic red tape begin. In contrast to small groups, employees are expected to conform to the demands of their jobs rather than changing their job to meet their personal preferences.

Third, as the size of a group increases, so does the need for a more formal type of leadership. With increasing size come complex problems relating to the coordination of activities and decisions, and this leads to the emergence of group leaders, persons who have the authority, the power, or the potential ability to direct and/or influence the behavior of others.

In all groups, somebody or some collectivity must make the decisions. In small groups, these decisions may be made informally in a spirit of mutual sharing and agreement with no assigned leader as such. In large groups, which as indicated have more specialized activities and a more rigid and formal structure, the leadership becomes more formal as well and the decision making is more constraining. When the population of these groups bestows the right to leadership, authority exists. Authority is legitimized power (this subject is covered more extensively in Chapter 15 where political groups are discussed). Effective leaders must be able to make decisions, settle disputes, coordinate activities, direct communication, influence behaviors, and bring persons and diverse units together. Seldom do these abilities reside in the same individual. A leader effective in doing one thing may be ineffective in another.

In analyzing leadership in small groups, Bales (1953) found that leaders are of two types, instrumental and expressive. Instrumental leaders organize the group around its goals by suggesting ways to achieve them and persuading the members to act appropriately. Thus the instrumental leader directs activities and helps make group decisions. Expressive leaders, on the other hand, resolve conflict and create group harmony and social cohesion. They make sure that the members can get along with one another and are relatively satisfied and happy. For groups to function effectively, Bales concluded, both types of leaders are needed.

How are leaders selected? In some instances, the persons who are most efficient and resourceful in directing and moving the group in desired directions will be recognized and awarded the leadership positions. They will be looked to for direction, their suggestions will be honored, and they will have considerable influence in the group's behavior.

Groups reflect the characteristics of the societies they are a part of. Suppose, for example, a neighborhood meeting is called to complain about the garbage collection. Ten men and four women show up. What would you guess are the odds that a male will be asked to take the notes or a female will be asked to chair the session or take the formal complaint to the official source? It is unlikely the group will wait to see who can write most effectively (which might be a male) or who can best serve as leader (which might be a female). Similarly, groups may assign the leadership position to the eldest, the most popular, the one with the most formal training, or the one who called the meeting.

Are there particular traits that distinguish leaders from nonleaders? For several decades psychologists and social psychologists have tried to compile lists of leadership characteristics, but most results have been disappointing. Why? One explanation is that the attempt has been to find characteristics or traits that reside within individuals rather than seeking characteristics or traits relative to a task environment or a specific interpersonal and social context. Leaders and leadership qualities do not exist in a vacuum. Assigned cultural and social statuses, skills for specific tasks, and prior experience and training will influence the choice of leaders, which suggests that there is no such thing as a "born leader." Inborn characteristics, in combination with training, experience, skills, and social circumstances, determine the likelihood that a given person will occupy leadership positions. This may partially explain why women and blacks seldom become presidents of corporations or top government officials. They may have the leadership characteristics but not the social status characteristics appropriate to these positions in our culture.

Fourth, as the size of a group increases, communication patterns change. In large groups the leaders tend to dominate the discussions. They talk the most and are addressed the most since the discussion and comments of other members are directed at them. Although similar patterns of communication may exist in small groups, members who never join the discussion in a large group may do so in a small one. Some teachers prefer a large or small class for this very reason. In a large class the communication is both dominated by them and directed toward them. In a small class the chances increase that most members will participate and that a communication exchange may take place among the group members. Social psychologists have been especially fascinated with "small-group dynamics." What happens when two, five, or eight people get together? Who sits where, who talks to whom, and how are decisions made? With committees, families, classes, and other small groups,

Leadership exists in a wide variety of social contexts and is expressed both instrumentally and expressively. How leaders are chosen varies as well with some assuming leadership based on selected personal and status characteristics, others appointed by an authority, and still others selected by a popular vote.

controlled experiments have been conducted to determine how changes in size and composition affect the members' communication, interaction, performance of tasks, and other outcomes. The *Handbook of Small Group Research* (Hare, 1976) is a comprehensive source for the student interested in learning more about these studies.

Fifth, as size increases, cohesion decreases. A group is considered cohesive when members interact frequently, when they talk of "we," when they defend the group from external criticism, when they work together to achieve common goals, and when they are willing to yield personal preferences for those of the group. Membership stability is important for cohesion because a high turnover rate has a negative effect. Conformity is also important — failure to abide by group norms and decisions lessens cohesiveness. Groups induce conformity by formal means such as fines, not allowing participation, or assigning specific tasks as well as by informal means such as verbal chides or jokes. Although these informal means become less effective as group size increases, small groups and informal networks exist within the large group or complex organization. The importance of this small group cohesiveness operating in a large group context was evident in World War II; both American and German soldiers admitted to fighting for their buddies, not for the glory and fame of their country.

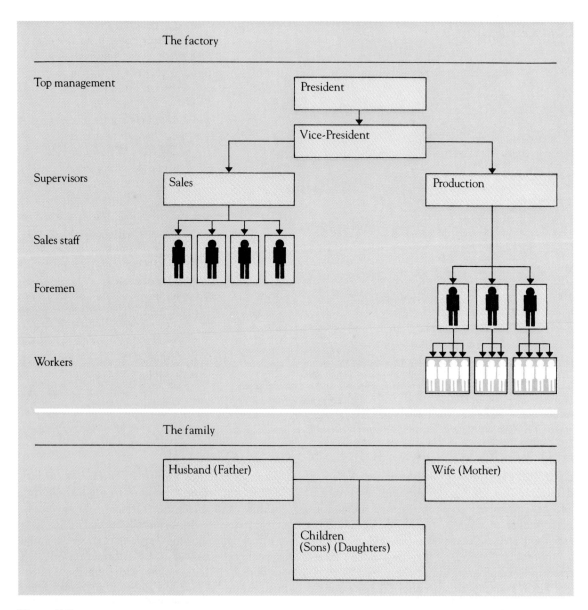

Figure 5-2
The structure of two social organizations

Formal Organizations

Many sociologists view the study of social organizations as the key to understanding society, groups, and personal behavior. The organization, they suggest, is different from the sum of the individuals who belong to it. If all the parts of an automobile are put in one pile, we have all the ingredients necessary for a car, but we certainly do not have an operable means of transportation. Only when those parts are properly assembled and interrelated do we get a car that works. Organizations are much the same. The whole is greater than the sum of its parts. In analyzing organizations, we focus not on the individual but on the group as a whole, which has structures, norms, and roles of its own. (Note the example of the structure of two organizations in Figure 5-2.)

Used generally, "social organization" refers to the way society is organized: its norms, mores, roles, values, communication patterns, social institutions, and the like. Formal organizations are one aspect of social organization. A *formal organization* is a large social group deliberately constructed and organized to achieve certain specific and clearly stated goals. The *Encyclopedia of Associations* (vol. 1, 18th ed., 1983) provides details of more than 17,700 such professional societies, labor unions, trade associations, fraternal and patriotic organizations, and other types of structured groups in the United States consisting solely of voluntary members.

Organizations tend to be stable, often keeping the same structure and continuing to exist for many years. Those who belong to an organization generally feel a sense of membership. Industrial corporations, professional sports, country clubs, trade unions, schools, churches, prisons, hospitals, and government agencies are formal organizations created to meet specific goals. All groups have goals of some sort, but they are often latent, unstated, and general. Group members may even have conflicting goals, but in an organization, the goals are specific, clearly stated, and usually understood precisely by the members.

Consider the case of a family and a school. Both have as goals the education of children. The parents in a family may read to the youngest children and provide the older ones with books, magazines, and newspapers. They may also encourage children to play learning games or take them to museums and concerts. In a formal organization such as a school, however, the education program is much more highly structured. The teachers, administrators, and other staff members have been trained to teach a particular subject to a single age group or meet some other specific goal. The overall goals of the school, although perhaps subject to disagreement, are stated and understood more clearly than those of the family. The same holds true with factories (see Figure 5-2) and all other formal organizations, including voluntary associations, which are described at the end of this chapter.

The Importance of Formal Organizations

The importance of formal organizations in modern complex societies can hardly be overestimated. Every day, we deal with some sort of formal organization in connection with work, food, travel, health care, police protection, or some other necessity of life. Organizations enable people who are often total strangers to work together toward common goals. They create levels of authority and channels of command that clarify who gives orders, who obeys them, and who does which tasks. They are also a source of continuity and permanence in a society's efforts to meet specific goals. Individual members may come and go, but the organization continues to

Professional basketball represents one type of formal organization. What the fans witness is what we see here: a number of players in the action of a game. The organization includes, however, trainers, coaches, general managers, owners, and others, in addition to the players.

function. Thus formal organizations make it possible for highly complex industrialized societies to meet their most fundamental needs and pursue their collective aspirations.

Formalization is the process by which the norms, roles, or procedures of a group or organization become established, precise, and valid, and by which increasing attention is given to structure, detail, and form. The formalization of organizations is the characteristic that distinguishes complex societies from small tribal societies. Herman Turk (1970) goes so far as to state that modern societies are "an aggregate of organizations, which appear, disappear, change, merge, and form networks of relations with one another" (p. 1). The United States, for example, contains many highly professional and often powerful organizations, which are involved in mutually beneficial efforts to serve their own interests and meet their own goals. The American Medical Association and the AFL-CIO are just two of the many such organizations that could be mentioned.

The Goals of Formal Organizations

As you can well imagine, the goals of different organizations vary widely. Businesses are interested chiefly in making a profit. Service organizations assist people with problems like unemployment or illness. Some organizations, such as unions or stamp collectors, exist to promote the interests of their own group; other organizations, such as governments, the military, and prisons, are established to provide services to the general public.

Given this diversity of goals, it is not surprising that certain formal organizations are in conflict with each other. The United Auto Workers, in its attempt to improve the salaries, working conditions, and fringe benefits of its members, is in conflict with the profit goals of the automobile companies. Environmental groups often oppose the goals of government and industrial groups over the use of our natural resources. Organizations such as the Moral Majority have goals that are in conflict with those of the American Civil Liberties Union.

Conflicts appear not only between organizations but within them as well. Universities must determine whether the primary goal of their faculty is teaching or research. Medical organizations must decide whether their chief function is to aid and protect the physician or to improve the health care given to the public. Sometimes an organization's apparent primary goal (e.g., service) is used to conceal its actual primary goal (e.g., profit). A private mental institution, for example, may emphasize the quality of the care it gives in its literature, but decisions about whether or not to provide a certain service to its clients may always be made on the basis of its profitability.

There are often conflicts between the goals of an organization's administration and its employees or the clients or public it serves. In a university, for example, the main priority for the administration may be to balance the budget. The aim of the faculty may be to do research and publish papers. The students may be most concerned with receiving a good education through exceptional teaching and the use of outstanding library and laboratory facilities, which may conflict with cost-saving measures and cut into professors' research time. Finally, certain influential alumni may consider all these goals less important than having an outstanding football team, which brings the school national recognition.

Formal organizations have a certain type of administrative machinery designed to help them meet their goals. This administrative structure is known as bureaucratic organization, or, more simply, as bureaucracy.

Bureaucracy

A *bureaucracy* is a formal organizational structure that directs and coordinates the efforts of the people involved in various organizational tasks. It is simply a hierarchical arrangement of an organization's parts based on the division of labor and authority. A hierarchical structure is like a pyramid — the people at each level have authority over the larger number of people at the level below them. The authority resides in the office, position, or status, not in a particular person. In other words, the responsibilities and authority associated with a particular job in the hierarchy remain essentially the same, regardless of the person occupying the position. Merton (1968) defines bureaucracy as "a formal, rationally organized social structure involving clearly defined patterns of activity in which, ideally, every series of actions is functionally related to the purposes of the organization" (p. 195).

Bureaucracy as an Ideal Type

The classical work on bureaucracy was written by Max Weber (1864–1920), one of the pioneers of sociology. Weber dealt with bureaucracy as an *ideal type,* which is a model of a hypothetical pure form of an existing entity. In other words, he did not concern himself with describing a specific bureaucracy; he examined, rather, a great many bureaucracies in an attempt to discover the general principles that govern how they operate. An ideal type, then, is not to be thought of as a perfect entity in the usual sense of the word "ideal." As we will see later in this chapter, bureaucracies are often far from perfect. Weber (1946) found that bureaucracies typically have the following characteristics.

Division of Labor. The staff and activities of an organization are divided into units called offices or bureaus. Each bureau has certain carefully described responsibilities, and each job is designed to meet a specific need. Thus experts can be hired to meet various organizational requirements, and they can be held accountable for an effective performance in their area of responsibility.

Hierarchy of Authority. Organizations are run by a chain of command, a hierarchy of bosses and workers who are, in turn, the bosses of other workers. As indicated earlier, the hierarchy is in the form of a pyramid: all officials are accountable to those at a higher level for their own responsibilities and those of subordinates. The top of the chain of command is often a board of directors or company officers. Below this level are the middle-level managers, administrators, foremen, and department heads. The largest number of workers is at the bottom of the hierarchy (refer back to Figure 5-2).

Public Office. The office and the organization's written files are in a separate location from the employees' homes and families and are not subject to their influence. The organization's money and equipment belong to the organization, not to individuals, and its activity is separate from the activity of private life.

Merit Selection. Organizations select personnel on the basis of merit, using standardized criteria such as civil service examinations or educational training rather than friendship, political, or family connections. Those who are hired are expected to have the specialized knowledge or skills necessary to perform their assigned task.

Career Pattern. Employees are expected to devote themselves completely to the business of

the organization and recognize that people work their way to the top. As one moves up in the hierarchy, job security and salaries improve. Seniority is recognized, valued, and rewarded. Whether the organization is the U.S. Army, General Motors, or the Catholic church, increasing time with the organization and adequate job performance are supposed to bring promotions, higher pay and status, and stronger tenure.

Objective Rules. The operation of the organization is governed by a consistent set of rules that define the responsibilities of various positions, assure the coordination of tasks, and encourage the uniform treatment of clients. These rules are quite stable and comprehensive, and they can be readily learned and followed.

Although in any given formal organization some members are employed for personal reasons rather than merit, the rules are occasionally ignored, and some customers are not treated impartially, most bureaucracies share the characteristics we have described. A hierarchical organization, division of labor, and the other attributes of the bureaucratic ideal type are essential to efficient functioning. As we all know, however, bureaucracies have their shortcomings, especially government bureaucracies. Most of us associate them with red tape, mountains of forms to complete, and endless lines. How and why do bureaucracies get so bogged down?

Dysfunctions of Bureaucracies

Weber concerned himself almost exclusively with the positive accomplishments of bureaucracies: precision, coordination, reliability, efficiency, stability, and continuity. Merton (1957) was the most important writer on the dysfunctions of bureaucracy. He observed that people in bureaucracies tend to develop what Veblen called *trained incapacity,* a condition similar to ritualism, which is discussed in Chapter 7.

Trained incapacity occurs when the demands of discipline, rigidity, conformity, and adherence to rules render people unable to perceive the end for which the rules were developed. In Merton's words, "Adherence to the rules, originally conceived as a means, becomes transformed into an end-in-itself" (p. 199).

We have all had experiences in which an obsessive adherence to procedures and rules kept us from meeting goals. In corporations, for example, employees are often required to routinely send copies of memos and letters to people who don't look at them and who wouldn't know what they meant if they did. It would be much more efficient simply to stop sending them. Often, our training, habits, or traditional ways of behaving blind us to alternatives that might be far more effective than the ones we are accustomed to.

Another dysfunction of bureaucracies has come to be called the *Peter Principle*. Peter and Hull (1969) have expressed it succinctly: "In a hierarchy, every employee tends to rise to his level of incompetence" (p. 25). In other words, those who do their jobs well are promoted into new jobs. If they can't manage their new jobs well, that's where they stay. Thus many people are moved from jobs they do well to jobs they do poorly, and the whole organization suffers. The authors argue that work is accomplished by the employees who have not yet reached their level of incompetence.

A related dysfunction comes about when

hiring and promotions are based on a rigid set of formal qualifications — five years' experience or a college degree, for example — rather than skill or performance. In one instance, a woman with ten years' experience in her company and an excellent work reputation was passed over for promotion to supervisor because her company's policy dictated that supervisors must have a college degree. There are also instances in which excellent college teachers are denied tenure because they do not have a sufficient number of publishing credits. In bureaucratic organizations, formal qualifications may supersede performance in hiring and promotion.

Another dysfunction of bureaucracy that we are all familiar with is the "runaround." Who among us has not called an organization and had our call transferred to two or three other departments, only to be returned to the first person we spoke to with the problem still unresolved? You will recall that bureaucracies have rules defining the duties and responsibilities of various offices. The legal department handles legal matters, the personnel office handles recruitment, rank, and salary matters, and the payroll department issues checks, withholds money for benefits, and pays taxes. Other departments handle other matters. Now which one would you get in touch with about a lawsuit concerning the payment of salary? The difficulty is that actual problems do not always fit neatly into the compartments designed to handle them. If a problem does not clearly fall within a department's area of responsibility, or if it involves several departments, the runaround is likely to begin.

The Dehumanization and Impersonality of the Bureaucracy

The very impersonality that makes an organization efficient can create problems on the human level. Merton (1957) wrote that bureaucracies stress depersonalization of relationships,

categorization, and indifference to individuals. C. Wright Mills (1951) wrote that middle-class, white-collar employees of bureaucratic organizations were enmeshed in a vast impersonal structure of rationalized activity in which their own rationality is lost. The most logical and efficient way for an organization to operate, for example, is to have one department that does all of the billing. This system may mean, however, that some people will do nothing but put computerized bills in envelopes all day. Even though they know that they are doing necessary work, they are likely to feel as though their work is meaningless, as though they're doing nothing of any consequence. Interestingly, Webster's College Dictionary defines a bureaucrat as a member of a bureaucracy, especially a government official, following a narrow rigid formal routine. To the author, the prevalence of rigidity and formality suggests that bureaucracies will almost inevitably be dehumanized and impersonal.

Kohn (1971) questions some of these notions about the impersonality and rigidity of bureaucracies. In interviews with more than three thousand men employed in civilian occupations, he found a small but consistent tendency for men who work in bureaucratic organizations to be more intellectually flexible, more open to new experience, and more self-directed in their values than men who worked in nonbureaucratic organizations. Kohn attributed these findings in part to the fact that bureaucracies draw on a more educated work force. He suggested, however, that the tendencies he found resulted largely from conditions associated with bureaucratization — most notably, job security, somewhat higher income, and more complex work.

Often, people find ways to get around bureaucratic dysfunctions. In the impersonal structure of bureaucracies, people develop personal relationships. Official rules frequently leave room for interpretations and exceptions that

Networking: A Way To Manage Our Changing World?

Increasingly, bureaucracies exhibit their incapacity to manage the complexities of our global village. At the same time, the alternative structures most likely to succeed these bureaucracies are rapidly emerging. The most common term for these newer structures is "networks."

Networks differ from bureaucracies in several important ways:

Authority tends to be decentralized, residing in individuals with pertinent information rather than in those who occupy assigned positions.

Policies and boundaries tend to be fluid rather than fixed.

Personnel tend to relate, among themselves and with others, as equals rather than subordinates or superiors.

Procedures tend to be people-oriented as much as they are task- or institution-oriented.

Style tends to be sociable rather than officious.

Structure tends to be polycentric rather than monocentric.

Networks Vs. Bureaucracy

The difference between networks and traditional bureaucracies can be illustrated by contrasting a spider web with the bureaucratic "web" characteristic of an organization chart redrawn with the top as its center. The spider web is distinguished by its interconnectivity, which maximizes flexibility and minimizes vulnerability. With its "power" distributed polycentrically rather than concentrated monocentrically, the spider web can survive total destruction of one of its nodes — even the central one — much more readily than a bureaucratic web.

Interconnectivity is a primary characteristic of all networks. This becomes apparent in the following exercise:

On a blank sheet of paper, draw a small circle in the center to represent yourself. Around that circle, draw a dozen other circles, each representing a specific person with whom you regularly interact. Draw lines from their circles to yours, then draw lines to represent all interactions that occur among them. Now make more circles for people with whom you know that the dozen interact. (Even if you do not have direct relationships with these other people, they probably affect your relationships with the dozen.) Draw the connections between the new circles and the dozen — and between one another or with your center circle as appropriate.

You have just portrayed the most immediate influential network in your life. The strength of that influence will tend to be proportionate to the extent of interconnectivity among its members.

Networks, per se, are not new. They are, as anthropologist Virginia Hine noted, "perhaps our oldest social invention." What is new about today's networks is the scale of interconnectivity. What networks and networking once did for the family, neighborhood, workplace, and community, they are now beginning to do on the scale of society, civilization, and world.

SOURCE: Excerpted by permission from Noel McInnis, "Networking: A Way to Manage Our Changing World?" *The Futurist*, June 1984

---

permit adaptations to unique and unanticipated circumstances. The fact that an organization has been deliberately organized to achieve specific goals does not mean that all activities and interactions will conform strictly to the official blueprint. As Blau and Scott (1963) suggest, regardless of the time and effort devoted by management to the design of a rational organization chart and elaborate procedure manuals, the official plan can never completely determine the conduct and social relations of the organization members.

SOCIOLOGISTS AT WORK
Group Therapy

Anthony Reczek is a mental health therapist with a community-based agency in western Massachusetts. "I provide psychotherapeutic services to individuals who have serious mental disturbances," says Reczek. "These people have difficulties in many areas of their lives, including interpersonal relationships, occupations, and sexuality. Often, they are repeatedly hospitalized in a state mental institution to keep them from harming themselves or others. I also work with people who have less severe problems — individuals, couples, and families trying to deal with such problems as alcoholism, drug abuse, obsessive-compulsive personalities, and depression."

In working with his clients, Reczek draws on his academic training, which includes a masters in social work from the University of Connecticut. As an undergraduate at the University of Vermont in the late 1960s and early 1970s, he majored in sociology. Of his undergraduate years, he says, "Revolution was in the air, and it was a good time for sociology. Everything happening in the nation seemed related to one sociological theory

or another — man was examining his institutions and their effect on him, how institutions and culture had shaped generations of human beings, and the continual efforts of individuals to transcend their limits. It was the interplay of man with his social and cultural environment that fascinated me and continues to fascinate me. To understand that interplay, it was necessary to familiarize myself with a wide range of concepts, and that also drew me to sociology — the scope of subjects in its domain, including aspects of psychology, religion, philosophy, economics, and the biological sciences. As I look back on it now, sociology was probably the most natural way to satisfy curiosities in a hundred different areas."

How does Reczek use his sociological training in his work today? "It taught me to appreciate the complex and often less than clear-cut relationship between events in the outer world and their consequences in the minds and personalities of individuals. The person, family, or group who sits in front of me in my therapeutic sessions is, I believe, a composite of forces and reactions to

Voluntary Associations

Voluntary associations are organizations people join because they share their goals and values and voluntarily choose to support them. People join many formal organizations because they are forced to or because they need the income, protection, or training that they offer. Examples include schools, the armed services, insurance companies, and places of work. Voluntary associations, however, are joined out of personal interest, to participate in some social program or as a channel for political action.

Voluntary associations are instances of associational or organizational groups, which were discussed earlier in this chapter. They typically involve awareness of kind, social interaction, and formal organization. Awareness of kind is central to our voluntary involvement because we share the interests and goals of the membership, whether it be the League of Women Voters, the Boy Scouts of America, the Moral Majority, the National Rifle Association, the National Association for the Advancement of Colored People, or the American Sociological Association. We enjoy socially interacting with other members

forces. People must be viewed in their overall context, through their institutions, the values of their ethnic group, and the visions of their parents. Sociology taught me a method of inquiry, an attitude, if you will, that continues to be invaluable in helping me make sense of human complexity."

Of the seventeen or so clients that Reczek is working with at any given time, about two-thirds have chronic problems. "Some chronic patients have been in and out of institutions for thirty or forty years and have few social connections," he says. "We have to be fairly aggressive to stay in contact with them. Often, they've lost touch with their families and have few friends or life goals. Living in institutions, they've developed a fairly limited repertoire of problem-solving skills, and it's easy for them to fall into isolation. Of course, any one of us might feel like holing up for a few weeks, but eventually something will draw us out — we'll have to go to work or make contact with our family or friends. The chronic population faces no such demands, however, and our community outreach program may be the only contact they have."

Reczek believes his agency meets its responsibilities successfully, but he questions some of the practices of other mental health facilities. "For nine years I worked in a private hospital that re-lied heavily on medications," he says. "The use of medications suggests that the problem is biological. Of course, it's very important to look for biological problems, but sociology has given me some idea of the other reasons people are as they are. It's helped me neutralize the biological emphasis and stay open to other possibilties — looking for clues in the family environment, for example."

Many of the problems experienced by Reczek's clients have a social dimension. Now that cocaine is in vogue, for example, it is causing serious difficulties. "One of my clients had used alcohol for a long time, with little financial difficulty. But once he developed a cocaine habit, he began spending something like $400 a week on it — virtually all the money he had. He had to go on welfare for a while, and he was risking his marriage and his future. Fortunately, we were able to help him get over his dependency."

By the same token, social experiences can sometimes help people overcome problems. "This is the basic principle of group therapy," Reczek says. "The other members of the group are at least as helpful in solving a person's problems as the group leader is. If a person is committed to it, group therapy can help provide corrective experiences. People are as they are as a result of their relationships, more often than not."

because of our common focus of attention and shared interests. Since these associations are formally organized, they have officers and bylaws or a constitution. Some associations are small and highly informal; others are large, formal, bureaucratically organized, and demand dues and conformity to established procedures. Because membership is voluntary rather than by ascription, members can leave if they become dissatisfied.

In studies covering several decades, sociologists have learned a good deal about voluntary associations. We know they are highly class-lim-ited — members in any given association usually come from similar class levels. Bowling club members are unlikely to join golf clubs; members of a wealthy businessmen's club are unlikely to join the Ku Klux Klan. Churches are voluntary associations that cover the class and wealth spectrum, but those living at a poverty level seldom attend the same church as the affluent. While people of all ages and socioeconomic levels join voluntary associations, middle-aged people of high social status and education are the most frequent participants. Men are more likely to join than women, but American women are more likely to join associations than women in most other countries. National Opinion Research Center (1982) data show that about two-thirds of all Americans belong to at least one voluntary association and about one person in four belongs to three or more. The rate of turnover is high as well, however. This may be due to the limited objectives of most of these organizations; when personal interests, friends, or objectives shift, the fact that membership is voluntary means that quitting is easy.

Summary

Social groups are so fundamental a part of our existence that it is difficult to imagine life without them. Most social groups involve interaction, a sense of belonging or membership, shared interests and values, and some type of structure. The group concept has been used in many different ways, however. Statistical groups are formed by the social scientist and involve no awareness of kind, no social interaction, and no social organization. Categories, or societal groups, differ from statistical groups only in that the members are conscious that they share a particular characteristic; in other words, their members have an awareness of kind. Aggregates are collections of people who are in physical proximity to one another. They are loosely structured groups that are short-lived and involve little interaction. Members of associational and organizational groups interact, are aware of their similarity, and, in addition, are organized to pursue a common goal.

Although the various types of groups have distinguishing characteristics, it is not unusual for them to overlap or to change from one type to another. Primary groups are small and informal and emphasize interpersonal cohesion and personal involvement. Secondary groups are less personal and intimate, and they are more goal-oriented and purposeful. In-groups are those

that people feel they belong to; everyone else belongs to the out-group. The in-group shares a common allegiance and identity, tends to be ethnocentric, and stereotypes members of the out-group. In-group cohesion is intensified by out-group threats.

Peer groups generally include people of roughly the same age, status, and importance. The members influence one another's socialization and act as sources of support and guidance. Reference groups provide self-evaluation and direct aspirations. They are the groups we use to assess our own performance, even if we do not actually belong to them.

Groups are also differentiated by size. The smallest group possible is a dyad, which has two members. A third person makes it a triad. The addition of even a few people changes group interactions considerably, and, as size increases, there are generally changes in the division of labor, formality, leadership, communication, and cohesion.

Formal organizations are deliberately organized to achieve specific goals. They are particularly important in industrialized societies, in which many relationships are impersonal. Formal organizations are sources of authority and of continuity in our efforts to meet basic societal and personal goals, but conflict within and between organizations is common.

Bureaucracy is a type of administrative structure found in formal organizations. It is a hierarchical arrangement of the parts of an organization based on a division of labor and authority. Positions in the hierarchy are based on position or office, not on individual characteristics. Bureaucracies operate in a location separate from the homes and families of their employees. They also operate according to objective rules, hire and promote people on the basis of merit, and encourage them to rise in the hierarchy through hard work. They can have a positive influence on efficiency, precision, coordination, stability, and continuity, but they can also have negative effects. Trained incapacity, the Peter Principle, the bureaucratic runaround, dehumanization, and impersonality are dysfunctional characteristics of bureaucracies.

Voluntary associations are organizations that people join because they share their goals and values and choose to support them. Since membership is voluntary, members can resign if their interest wanes.

Key Terms

aggregate group
associational or organizational group
bureaucracy
categorical group or societal unit
formal organization
ideal type
in-group
out-group
peer group
Peter Principle
primary group
reference group
secondary group
social group
statistical group
trained incapacity
voluntary associations

Suggested Readings

Corwin, Ronald H. and Ray A. Eddfelt. **Perspectives on Organizations: Viewpoints for Teachers.** *Washington, D.C.: American Association for Colleges of Teacher Education, 1976.* A series of training publications designed to develop an awareness among teachers of what organizations are, how organizations affect them, and how they can deal with organizations.

Etzioni, Amitai. **A Sociological Reader on Complex Organizations, 3d ed.** *New York: Rinehart & Winston, 1980.* An excellent collection of readings on complex organizations, this book covers theories, models for comparing organizations, the structure of organizations, interorganizational relations, change, problems of organizations, and methods of study.

Hall, Richard H. **Organizations: Structure and Process, 2d ed.** *Englewood Cliffs, N.J.: Prentice-Hall, 1977.* A textbook that covers most of the major theories and research relating to bureaucracies.

Hare, A. Paul. **Handbook of Small Group Research.** *New York: The Free Press, 1976.* A review of the literature on small group research covering group process and structure, six variables that affect the interaction process (personality, social characteristics, group size, task, communication networks, and leadership), and performance characteristics.

Kanter, Rosabeth Moss. **Men and Women of the Corporation.** *New York: Basic Books, 1977.* A major study of sex stratification in the corporation, showing clearly the male dominance and sex symbolism that occur at all levels.

Katz, Daniel, Robert L. Kahn, and J. Stacy Adams (eds.). **The Study of Organizations: Findings from Field and Laboratory.** *San Francisco: Jossey-Bass, 1980.* A collection of thirty-eight articles on organization covering environment, motivation, communication, leadership, work and health, conflict, and change.

Ridgeway, Cecilia L. **The Dynamics of Small Groups.** *New York: St. Martin's Press, 1983.* A text that presents an eclectic analysis of small groups as vital units within the larger social structure.

Weber, Max. **From Max Weber: Essays in Sociology,** trans. and ed. H. H. Gerth and C. Wright Mills. *New York: Oxford University Press, 1946.* A classic work on power and the bureaucracy.

Wilson, Stephen. **Informal Groups: An Introduction.** *Englewood Cliffs, N.J.: Prentice-Hall, 1978.* A text covering various aspects of informal groups, this book discusses solidarity, theorists, leadership, and problem solving.

CHAPTER 6

Socialization and Social Interaction

Thus no personal sentiment is the exclusive product of any one influence, but all is of various origin and has a social history.

— Charles Horton Cooley

What Is Socialization?

Socialization is the process of creating a social self, learning one's culture, and learning the rules and expectations of that culture. In the United States, most people learn to speak the English language and to eat with a fork. They learn that cereal, bacon, and eggs are breakfast foods and that sandwiches are appropriate for lunch. They find out that worthwhile people do worthwhile work and that those who don't do anything are of less value. They discover that certain countries and people are friendly and others are dangerous. Women learn to smile when they are tense and to cry at good news as a release of tension. Men learn that they should not cry at all, although some do so at times.

Sociologists are interested in socialization because by studying how people interact we hope to understand people better. By examining our society, ourselves, and our place in society, we can better understand why we think and act the way we do. The study of socialization is also useful in our everyday lives. If we understand why we act as we do, we can change our values, our beliefs, our expectations, and our behavior in ways that might otherwise never occur to us. The study of socialization is a very liberating part of a liberal education.

Is Human Interaction Necessary?

Normal human infants are born with the muscles, bones, vital organs, and all the other biological parts needed to live. They are utterly helpless, however, and cannot survive without human interaction. Babies not only need food

133

and warmth to survive physically, they also need physical stimulation to grow. When they are handled physically by an adult, they are stimulated by touch, tones of voice and facial expressions, which make them aware of their environment and stimulate them to respond to it. Observations of infants who were comparatively isolated from human contact have shown that a lack of social interaction can have very serious consequences.

Children in Institutions

Rene Spitz (1946) observed children who had apparently been healthy when they were born and who had been living in a foundling home for two years. Nutrition, clothing, bedding, and room temperatures in the home were suitable, and every child was seen by a physician at least once a day. A small nursing staff took care of the physical needs of the children, but other interaction was very limited.

Despite their excellent physical care, thirty-four percent of the ninety-one children in the home died within two years of the study, and twenty-one others showed slow physical and social development. They were small, and some could not walk or even sit up. Those who could talk could say only a few words, and some could not talk at all.

Spitz compared these children with infants brought up in another institution, where their mothers were being held for delinquency. Physical care was basically the same as in the foundling home, but their mothers, who had little else to occupy them, enjoyed playing with their children for hours. The infants received a great deal of social stimulation, and their development was normal. Spitz concluded that the difference between the foundling home and the nursing home was the amount of attention the children received, which illustrates the crucial importance of social interactions in child development.

Isolated and Feral Children

Children who have been isolated from others in their own homes also show a lack of development. Kingsley Davis (1940, 1947) described two girls found in the 1930s who had been hidden in the attics of their family homes because they were illegitimate and unwanted.

One child, Isabelle, had been kept in seclusion until age six and a half. Her mother was deaf and mute, and because Isabelle had been confined in a dark room with her mother, she had no chance to develop speech. She communicated with her mother by gestures and could make only a strange croaking sound.

Although it was established that Isabelle could hear, specialists working with her believed she was retarded because she had not developed any social skills. They thought she could not be educated and that any attempt to teach her to speak would fail after so long a period of silence. Nevertheless, the people in charge of Isabelle launched a systematic and skillful program of training that involved pantomime and dramatization. After one week of intensive effort, she made her first attempt to speak, and in two months she was putting sentences together.

Eighteen months after her discovery, she spoke well, walked, ran, and sang with gusto. Once she learned speech, she developed rapidly, and at age fourteen she completed the sixth grade in public school.

The importance of social interaction is also evident in studies of feral children, those who have grown up in the wild. Several feral children were reportedly found in Europe during the past few centuries. Probably the most famous was the wild boy of Aveyron, found in the wilderness in France in 1800 (Shattuck, 1980). It is not known when the boy was separated from other humans or how he survived in the wilderness until he reached puberty, but he did not know any lan-

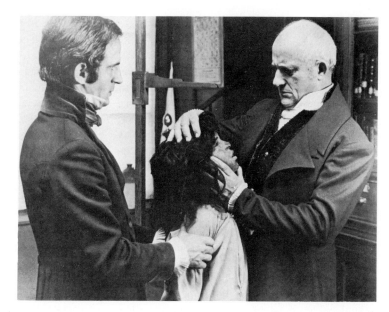

A doctor is shown examining the wild boy of Aveyron in the movie The Wild Child. *The child was apparently healthy yet did not behave at all like a normal boy. Because human behavior develops as a result of social interaction, this boy and others brought up without it do not learn behavior patterns considered to be natural and normal. Our behavior results from our socialization, not from instincts that are present at birth.*

guage, so he might have been separated from humans while very young.

The boy's behavior seemed very strange to those who found him. When given a choice of food to eat, he rejected most of it. He liked potatoes, which he threw into a fire and then picked out with his bare hands, eating them while they were very hot. He could tolerate cold as well as heat, and he was happy to be outdoors in the winter without clothes. He could swing from tree to tree easily, and he was excited by the wind and the moon.

A young doctor took an interest in the boy and taught him to eat a wider variety of foods, to sleep at regular hours, and to wear clothes. It was determined that he could hear noises and make sounds, so an effort was made to teach him to talk. He learned to say a word for milk, but only after he had been given milk — he never learned to use the word to ask for it. After five years of training he had not learned to talk. He did, how-

ever, learn to cry occasionally and to hug his teacher. He survived for twenty-two years after the training stopped, living a quiet life in a cottage with a housekeeper, but he never advanced his learning. Those who studied him were interested to note that he never showed any interest in sexual behavior.

Why do children develop so little when they are isolated from others? Many people assume that the feral boy and the isolated girl had medical problems, that they did not develop normally because they were retarded. Sociologists believe, however, that even physically healthy children could not develop normal social behavior without social interaction. The controversy over whether behavior results from predetermined biological characteristics or from socialization is known as the *nature-nurture debate*. This debate has continued for centuries, but it has drawn more interest recently as a result of the new science of sociobiology.

Sociobiology and the Nature-Nurture Debate

Sociobiology is the study of the biological and genetic determinants of social behavior (Wilson, 1975). Sociobiologists are biologists by training, although some sociologists and other social scientists support their views. Sociobiologists believe that social behavior is determined by inborn genetic traits, which influence human behavior in much the same way that animals are influenced by their genetic inheritance. An example in sociology would be that sexual preference is determined genetically and that humans have a genetic tendency to have only one or a very few mates (Van den Berghe, 1979). Sociobiologists also think that homosexuality is genetically determined, although temporary homosexual behavior (occurring, for example, when opposite-sex partners are not available) may be environmental. They also believe that altruistic behavior (behavior performed to benefit others without regard for oneself) and warlike behavior are biologically based.

Most sociologists criticize the sociobiological viewpoint on the grounds that behavior varies greatly from culture to culture, and sexual behavior, whether with the same sex or the opposite sex, varies enormously. Altruistic behavior also varies widely and is entirely lacking in humans and monkeys who have been raised in isolation. As for warlike behavior, it is completely absent in many societies.

In addition, many physiologists believe that there is no genetic basis for human behavior. Biological drives or instincts that dictate behavior are supposedly very powerful, but so far no powerful, fixed drives or instincts have been discovered in human beings. Insects and birds perform many complex behaviors even when they have been reared in isolation. Honeybees do complicated dances to show other bees where food is located, and birds build intricate nests in the same manner as others of their species. Humans who have been raised in isolation, however, do almost nothing, as the study we discussed indicated.

Money (1980), a physiologist and a psychologist, believes that the nature-nurture controversy is based on an illusion, because environmental factors become part of our biology when we perceive them. When a piece of information enters our minds, it is translated into a biochemical form. Although we don't fully understand the workings of the brain, we do know that the brain stores information permanently and that information in the brain can cause physiological changes in other parts of our bodies. Money contends that the information in our brain shapes our behavior and that distinctions between nature and nurture are irrelevant.

Although a few sociologists emphasize the sociobiological perspective, most believe only that human behavior can be limited by our physiology. We can tolerate just so much heat, cold, or hunger. But how we respond to our physical limits, or how we behave under any other circumstance, is learned from interacting with other people symbolically.

Symbolic Interaction

All animals interact, but we humans are unique in our ability to create societies, cultures, and social institutions. We are also unique in our capacity to use language. It was George Herbert Mead who first described why language makes humans different from all other animals. In *Mind, Self and Society from the Standpoint of a Social Behaviorist* (1934), a compilation of Mead's lectures published by his students after his death, Mead demonstrated that the unique feature of the human mind is its capacity to use *symbols,* both verbal and nonverbal. As discussed in Chapter 4, language is a symbol system. The words in a language have meaning, and when we know the meanings of words and the grammatical syntax in which they function, we can communicate with others who share the same language.

We use language symbols when we think or talk to ourselves and when we talk to other people. When we see another person in the street, we do not simply react to the person instinctively. We interpret the situation by giving meaning to the other person's behavior. We think, "Is this someone I know, or a stranger? Do I want to know this person, ignore her, say hello to her?" If we say "hello" to the other person, we are using a symbol that means, "I wish to greet you in a friendly manner." The other person knows the meaning of the symbol. This is an example of *symbolic interaction*, the social process that occurs within and between individuals as a result of the internalization of meanings and the use of language. By interacting with others, we learn about ourselves, and about other people.

Two theorists who were among the first to explore how this process works were Charles Horton Cooley and George Herbert Mead.

Charles Horton Cooley: The Looking-Glass Self

Charles Horton Cooley (1864–1929) pointed out that when we refer to the self, when we use the word "I," we are usually not referring to our physical body. We use the word "I" to refer to opinions, desires, ideas, or feelings — I think, I feel, I want — or we associate the idea of the self with roles, with what the self is doing. We feel satisfaction as we work well on a project, frustration when things are not going well. We also have a sense of self in relation to other people. We compare and contrast ourselves with others; our uniqueness is based on that comparison. Cooley argues that it is difficult to think about the self at all except to view the self as acting in society, thinking about ideas learned in society, and otherwise being a part of it. Even the word "I" that we use to refer to ourselves must be learned from other people.

From these conclusions, Cooley theorized that the idea of the self develops in a process that requires reference to other people, a process he called the *looking-glass self*. According to Cooley, the looking-glass self has three components: (1) how we think our behavior appears to others, (2) how we think others judge our behavior, and (3) how we feel about their judgments. We know that we exist, that we are beautiful or ugly, serious or funny, lively or dull, intelligent or stupid, through the way other people treat us. We never know exactly what other people think of us, of course, but we can imagine how we appear to them and how they evaluate our appearance. We often respond to these imagined evaluations with pride, mortification, embarrassment, or some other feeling. The looking-glass self concept suggests that we see ourselves and we respond to ourselves, not as we are, and not as others think we are, but as we *imagine* others think we are.

George Herbert Mead: Role Taking

George Herbert Mead (1863–1931), like Cooley, recognized how important it is for people to interact with others in the development of the self. When infants are first born, they cannot differentiate among all the objects they see from their crib. The world appears as a kaleidoscope of color and movement. Very soon, however, they learn to distinguish important objects, such as the bottle and the mother who brings it. Infants can observe the mother and from her actions begin to understand when she is bringing a bottle. In other words, they begin to have expectations about the mother's behavior.

A set of expectations about how a person in a certain situation will behave is known as a "role." Mead used the term *role taking* to describe the process of figuring out how others will act. The ability to role-take is extremely important to children. In fact, *play* is a way of practicing role taking. Children often play "house" or "school,"

Children may not learn to read or write when they play school, but they do learn about the roles of teacher and student. These children have even recruited their dolls and stuffed animals to play the role of student, lining them up in an orderly fashion to face the teacher. By learning to take different roles, the children will know what to expect from other people in these roles.

taking the role of *significant others* — mother, father, or any other person important to them. By taking the roles of these significant others, they can better understand their own roles as children, students, sons, or daughters. By practicing the roles of others in play, they learn to understand what others expect of them and how to behave to meet those expectations.

A child who responded differently to each person in his or her life would never develop an integrated sense of identity and would never know how to behave with strangers. Thus the child learns to see others not as individuals with separate expectations but as a generalized other, a variety of people, all of whom have the same expectations. This hypothetical group is known as *the generalized other*. The influence of the generalized other is evident in the actions of a child playing a game. A child playing baseball does not respond to each team member differently, even though they are different people playing different roles. Instead, he or she treats them all as a team with the same set of expecta-

tions. Because they have just one set of expectations, the child has just one consistent role. As seen through the eyes of this generalized other, the self becomes consistent and unified.

Psychological Theories of Socialization

In addition to the views of Cooley and Mead, two schools of psychological thought have influenced the study of socialization. Unlike sociologists, psychologists focus primarily on individual behavior rather than on interaction among individuals. The psychological perspectives we will consider are behaviorism and developmental theory.

Behaviorism

Behaviorism is the study of observable actions in humans and animals. Behaviorists make no assumptions about the thoughts or interpretations presumed to underlie observable behavior. They distrust efforts to find out what is in someone's mind. Sociologists who are not behaviorists have also benefited from the behavioral stance that caution is necessary in efforts to understand what people are thinking.

Behaviorists believe that children acquire all behaviors through learning. They study how behaviors are learned and what stimulates learning. *Classical conditioning,* first described by the Russian psychologist Ivan Pavlov, involves pairing a once-neutral stimulus with a meaningful stimulus. Pavlov realized that dogs salivate in response to food. When he gave his dogs food, he also rang a bell. The dogs learned to associate the bell with the food; eventually they salivated at the sound of the bell even when no food was present. Similarly, an infant may wiggle and coo when she sees her mother's face, because she has learned to associate her face with being fed just as Pavlov's dogs associated the bell with food.

Operant conditioning, as described by B. F. Skinner, is conditioning in which a behavior is repeated because it has been reinforced in the past. If you study carefully and receive an A in all your courses, you will probably continue to study because your studying has been reinforced. If you receive a D in all your courses, you might soon stop studying. Children's behavior is most likely to be reinforced when they behave in ways that gain their parents' attention, and they repeat behaviors if they are praised. Sometimes an undesirable behavior is reinforced when a parent attends to it, because the child seeks parental attention in any form — even punishment.

Behavior modification is a technique based on the premise that a behavior can be changed by changing the response to it. Psychologists, for example, can teach parents behavior modification to help them reinforce children's good behaviors without reinforcing their undesirable ones.

Sociologists agree that classical and operant conditioning come into play in the socialization process, but we must have some knowledge of a person's thoughts if we are to understand that person's responses to a stimulus. Conditioning may work with very young children because they don't have language and cannot analyze situations. Older children, however, have learned a great deal and attach their own meanings to events. These interpretations of events also influence behavior and should be taken into account.

Developmental Theory

Developmental theories are theories that explain stages of development in terms of the chronological stages of a person's life. Developmental theorists generally agree that, although social learning is influential, the stages of development are determined largely by biological factors. They assume that development proceeds from stage to stage and that the developmental tasks of each stage must be successfully resolved before a person can advance to the next stage. There are a number of important developmental theorists, but we will review only three: Sigmund Freud, Jean Piaget, and Erik Erikson.

Sigmund Freud (1856–1939) was a physician whose contribution to our understanding of personality development has been very influential. *Freudian theory* contends that people possess a number of drives or urges connected with satisfying basic needs, such as the need for food or sexual release. These urges, known collectively as the *id,* seek immediate satisfaction. In society, however, instant gratification is rarely possible, and the id must be controlled. This control is accomplished by what Freud called the *superego,* the part of the mind that incorporates society's rules. The id and the superego are in continual conflict. When you are hungry, for example, your id urges you to satisfy your hunger in the quickest way possible, perhaps by grabbing food from someone else's plate. Your superego, however, tells you that this is an unacceptable way to satisfy your hunger. Freud stated that normally

A child who is frustrated will often throw a temper tantrum. Freud believed this happenes because the child has not yet learned to control the natural desires of the id. Eventually the child will develop a superego by learning that society does not find temper tantrums acceptable. Then the child will develop an ego, or the ability to deal with frustration in a more socially acceptable manner.

developing children develop an *ego*, which reconciles the demands of the id and superego as much as possible.

According to Freud, children develop through a series of five stages: the oral, anal, phallic, latency, and genital. He said that a child developing normally progresses through the five stages, but that under- or overgratification of the child at any stage can cause him or her to remain, or become fixated, at that stage. These fixations can result from improper weaning or toilet training, from demanding too much or too little dependency, from having poor adult models, or from other factors. It is these factors that influence the development of children and shape their personalities.

Jean Piaget (1896–1980), a Swiss psychologist, also contended that development comes in stages as the child develops biologically. Piaget was concerned chiefly with the development of the mind, or cognitive development.

According to *Piagetian theory*, there are qualitative differences in the ways children think at different ages. As they mature, they build upon the learning that took place during previous stages. The first stage, known as the "sensorimotor period," lasts from birth until about age two. During this period, infants are incapable of the process adults call "thinking." They learn about their physical environment, their movements, and the effects of their movements on the environment. They often engage in the same behavior repeatedly if they find that it produces an interesting effect. A baby girl may shake her crib again and again to see the attached mobile rotate. Piaget's studies show that infants and older children seem to enjoy challenges for their own sake, not just because they yield a reward. They also prefer situations that are moderately novel — those that are too familiar may seem boring, and those that are too unfamiliar may be frightening.

The second stage, the "preoperational period," lasts from about age two to age six or seven. Although children become capable of thought during this period, their thinking is illogical and dependent on observable phenomena. They may play with rattles when they see them, but if a rattle is out of sight they don't know how or where to look for it. Their developing ability to use language reflects their growing understanding of symbols, but they do not have a complete understanding of cause-effect relationships or of many other basic concepts, and they tend to be highly egocentric — they cannot distinguish between their own thoughts and perceptions and those of others.

It is during the third stage of cognitive development, the "concrete operational period," that children learn to process information logically and systematically. They can do this, however, only when the information is presented in concrete form because problems presented in abstract form are beyond their capabilities. This period lasts from about age seven to age twelve.

The fourth and final stage, according to Piaget, is the "formal operational period," which begins at about age twelve and which is the level of thinking characteristic of adults. People who have reached this stage can solve complex problems stated in abstract terms. They are capable of thinking logically, so they can test hypotheses, draw inferences, and construct generalizations.

The psychoanalyst, Erik Erikson (1963) believed that people developed in eight stages and that each stage must be successfully completed before the next stage. The first stage is to learn trust instead of mistrust, and the second stage is to learn autonomy rather than shame and doubt about self. In the third stage initiative rather than guilt is learned for performing independently. These three stages should be successfully completed before the child goes to school. The fourth stage, learning industry rather than inferi-

ority, and the fifth stage, learning a sense of identity rather than role confusion, occur in the early school years. During adolescence the child must learn intimacy instead of isolation, especially with the opposite sex.

In adult years a person must learn generativity instead of self-absorption, and integrity instead of disgust and despair. These later stages of development require self-examination and a re-evaluation of moral stance. Some people, according to Erikson, avoid this self-examination and simply conform to the expectations of society. They are likely to remain self-absorbed and suffer from despair.

Psychologists do not agree on the description of stages or which one provides the best theoretical framework for understanding human development. Sociologists tend to argue that all of the stages depend on the culture in which the person is socialized. Monks, scholars, and pioneers, for example, learn isolation rather than intimacy, a trait which is worthwhile both to self and to society. Women are socialized to be doubting rather than autonomous, to have feelings of inferiority rather than industry, and to be self-absorbed about their appearance. They develop as they do because they have been socialized, rather than because they have not developed properly. While sociologists have found the study of child development extremely useful for understanding development in our own society, they do not conclude that these stages occur in all societies.

Agencies of Socialization

Socialization is found in all interaction, but the most influential interaction occurs in particular groups, which are referred to as "agencies of socialization." Among the most important are the family, the schools, peer groups, and the mass media.

The Family

The family is considered the primary agency of socialization. It is within the family that the first socializing influence is encountered by most children and these influencing factors affect them for the rest of their lives. Families give children their geographical location, as easterners or westerners, for example, and their urban or rural background. The family also determines the child's social class, race, religious background, and ethnic group. Each of these factors can have a profound influence on children. They may learn to speak a particular dialect, to prefer certain foods, and to pursue certain types of leisure activities.

Families also teach children values they will hold throughout life. Children frequently adopt their parents' attitudes about the importance of education, work, patriotism, and religion. Even a child's sense of worth is determined, at least in part, by the child's parents.

One of the values instilled in the children of most American families concerns the worth of the unique individual. We are taught that we possess a set of talents, personality characteristics, strengths, and weaknesses peculiar to ourselves and that we are responsible for developing these traits. This view of the value of the individual is not found in all cultures, however. Many people who emigrated from southern Europe, for example, believe that one's primary responsibility is to the family, not to oneself. The son of a European farm family, for example, is expected to be loyal and obedient to the family, to work for its benefit, and eventually, to take over the management of the farm when the parents are old. In our culture, however, staying with the family is often regarded as a sign of weakness or lack of ambition. These beliefs are just two of the many values that people learn primarily through the family.

The Schools

In some societies, socialization takes place almost entirely within the family, but in highly technical societies children are also socialized by the educational system. Schools in the United States teach more than reading, writing, arithmetic, and other basic skills. They also teach students to develop themselves, to test their achievements through competition, to discipline themselves, to cooperate with others, and to obey rules, all of which are necessary if a youngster is to achieve success in a society dominated by large organizations.

Schools teach sets of expectations about the work children will do when they mature. The children begin by learning about the work roles of community helpers such as firefighters and doctors, and later they learn about occupations more formally. They take aptitude tests to discover their unique talents, and with the help of teachers and guidance counselors they set occupational goals.

Schools also teach citizenship in countless ways: they encourage children to take pride in their communities; to feel patriotic about their nation; to learn about the country's geography, history, and national holidays; to study government, explain the role of good citizens, urge their parents to vote and to pledge allegiance to the flag; to become informed about community and school leaders; and to respect school property.

It has been suggested that learning at home occurs on a personal, emotional level, whereas learning at school is basically intellectual. Evidence suggests, however, that learning at school also involves personal factors such as a student's self-image and the teacher's perceptions of the student. In other words, students form a looking-glass self and perform in response to teacher expectations. In one experimental study in the classroom (Rosenthal and Jacobson, 1968), students were randomly divided into two groups. The teacher was told that those in the first group were bright and that those in the second group were not. The students believed to be highly intelligent by the teacher performed significantly better than those believed to be less intelligent. The teacher's expectations of the students influenced their performance.

Most school administrators and teachers reinforce our cultural emphasis on the uniqueness of individuals. Thus, they try to identify the unique talents of students through comparison and competition with other students and then attempt to develop these talents so that they will become useful to the larger society.

Peer Groups

Young people spend considerable time in school, and their *peer group* of people their own age is an important influence on their socialization. Peer group socialization has been increasing in this century because young people have been attending school for a longer period. They no longer drop out at fourteen — most finish high school and about half go on to college.

Young people today also spend more time with one another outside of school. Unlike young people of earlier decades, few are isolated on farms. Most live in cities or suburbs, and increasingly, they have access to automobiles so they can spend time together away from their families. Teenagers' most intimate relationships are often those they have with their peers, and they influence one another greatly. In fact, some young people create their own unique subcultures. Coleman (1974), who refers to these simply as cultures, lists as examples the cultures of athletic groups in high schools, the college campus culture, the drug culture, motorcycle cults, the culture of surfers, and religious cultures. In part because teenagers are often unsure of themselves, the sense of belonging that they get from their subculture may be extremely important to them, although the pressures to conform to group expectations can be quite severe.

The Mass Media

The American *mass media* — television, popular magazines, and other forms of communication intended for a large audience — are paid for by advertising. When dress, music, and other aspects of the youth subculture became big business, advertisers began directing their programs to young people. Radio stations brought new kinds of music not only to youth but also to a wider audience, thus socializing other age groups to the music of the youth subculture. The media also advertised youthful styles of dress. Young people who rejected fashion in favor of blue jeans, however, were later socialized to buy high fashion blue jeans and other garments with designer names. This type of interaction occurs constantly in the socialization process. As young people develop their unique talents, they influence society. Society in turn socializes them to use their unique talents in ways consistent with the values and norms of the society.

Young people are socialized to pursue activities apart from the family. As a result, the movie industry can rely on them to attend movies in theaters and also at school. Because youngsters have learned to be active and competitive, they prefer movies that show action and competition, and movies in turn reinforce this aspect of socialization. Violent horror films have been particularly popular over the last few years. Movies with themes of violent revenge also draw a lot of young people to the theaters, and actors like Clint Eastwood and Charles Bronson have made their reputations by acting in this type of movie.

Television also uses violent programming to appeal to teenagers, but teenagers do not stay home as much as younger children, so they

Studies have shown that children are affected by the violence they see on television. Although it is unclear that they learn to be violent from television, it is clear that they can learn techniques for violence.

watch less television. Younger children, who watch an average of almost four hours of television a day, urge their parents to buy the cereals, snack foods, and toys they see advertised. The shows children watch reinforce the norms of the larger society.

Programs about the family teach children what an American family should be like. Children may develop their conception of the family from what they see on television rather than from the home they live in. They learn, for ex-

ample, that families include both a mother and a father, even though one-fifth of all children have only one parent, and that families live in houses, even though many children live in apartments. Most mothers on television reruns stay home and wear aprons, while real mothers work and wear jeans rather than aprons. We do not know precisely how much children learn about the ideal family from television, but these family shows are undoubtedly influential.

The effects of television violence cannot be

measured accurately because children also learn competition and violence from other sources, and television both socializes and reinforces the socialization they receive elsewhere. Studies do indicate, however, that children can learn new techniques for being violent from watching a movie in an experimental situation, as shown in the classic experiment done by Bandura (1965). A group of children who watched a movie in which a doll was treated aggressively in unusual ways later imitated these unusual aggressive behaviors. Although the mass media are not the only teachers of violence in America, viewers can certainly learn about violence from the media just as they learn it from other experiences.

Socialization of Gender Roles

Socialization plays an especially important part in determining what children believe to be acceptable behaviors for members of their sex. Even though the situation has begun to change, our environment bombards both men and women with subtle and not-so-subtle suggestions that certain types of behavior are acceptable for women and certain types of behavior are acceptable for men. People who diverge significantly from traditional roles often meet with resistance from individuals and the social system as a whole throughout their lives. The same sources of socialization that influence people in other areas of their lives — work, the mass media, education, interactions with others — also affect the socialization of gender roles.

Infant and Childhood Experiences

Gender-role socialization in our society begins at birth. When a baby is born, he or she is wrapped in a blue or pink blanket, and from that moment on parents respond to the infant on the basis of its sex (Bem and Bem, 1976). Parents can

better predict what infant girls will be doing in twenty-five years — being a wife and mother — than they can tell what boys will be doing, since boys have many more options and opportunities. Boys will be expected to be more aggressive, better in mathematics, better problem solvers, and more athletic than girls. When they grow up they will be expected to concentrate primarily on their career, to be task-oriented, and to be interested in performing tasks that lead to the goals they have set for themselves. Sociologists refer to characteristics of this type as aspects of the male's *instrumental role*. Girls will be expected to be more verbal, more expressive, more emotional, and when they grow up, more interested in interpersonal relationships, characteristics that have been labeled the *expressive role* by sociologists (Zelditch, 1955). Infant boys are often described as big, athletic, strong, or alert, but girls are usually described as tiny, dainty, sweet, pretty, delicate, inattentive, or weak. Parents tend to notice the dainty fingernails of the baby girl, even though those of the baby boy look identical. Boy and girl infants are also treated differently. Boys are handled roughly and tossed around playfully, but girls are held more, cuddled, talked to, and treated as if they were very fragile. Even the tone of voice used is different. Boys are talked to in loud voices, while girls are spoken to gently.

Infants respond differently to these very early variations in treatment (Rubin, Provenzano, and Luria, 1974). Children who are touched and talked to cling to their mothers and talk to them more, regardless of their sex, and since girls are held and talked to more than boys, they tend to reciprocate with this kind of behavior (Goldberg and Lewis, 1969; Moss, 1967).

Children also learn gender-role behavior in nursery schools (Serbin and O'Leary, 1975). Classroom observations of fifteen nursery schools showed that the teachers (all women)

Life Without Father

Studies of women raised by mothers alone conclude that "a father's absence makes the girl grow stronger."

How many parents do you need anyway? Although we grew up with the belief that a mother and a father are essential to emotional adjustment and self-esteem, new studies reveal that girls brought up by their mothers alone are stronger and more independent than girls brought up in the traditional two-parent household.

Barbara G. Cashion, assistant professor of sociology at Georgetown University in Washington, D.C., has studied all the social psychological research on female-headed families published between 1970 and 1980. Cashion found that contrary to Freudian and cognitive theories of child development, role modeling plays a minor part in the way children learn from their parents. Instead, *role taking* — figuring out what the parent expects — determines whether the children become independent or dependent. "Children *do* try to please their parents," Cashion says. "So if the mother wants her daughter to be

strong, independent, and helpful, she will be. We don't simply act the way our parents act. We act the way they expect us to act. The research shows also that children choose the most powerful parent as a source of influence."

"If the father is an extraordinary father who treats his daughter in a nonsexist manner," adds Joyce Brothers, psychologist and author of *What Every Woman Should Know About Men*, "she will become independent. But often when there are two parents in the family, the father doesn't expect his daughter to balance a checkbook or fix the plumbing. He expects her to be more dependent than the daughter whose widowed or divorced mother expects a great deal of her. In addition, we see that a rejecting father at home may be worse for a young woman than a father who is gone."

Part of the reason that women from traditional households are less independent than their peers who were raised by a mother alone is that the two-parent family is hierarchical: Mother and father both play powerful roles while the children are subordinate. "In the family with the mother as

head," says Cashion, "there is no such division. Women and children share more in the relationship." A 1977 study of 462 female students by Janet and Larry Hunt at the University of Maryland corroborates that view, pointing out the destructiveness of sex stereotyping and the conflicting relationships often found in nuclear families. The study's conclusion — "a father's absence makes the girl grow stronger" — is a statement with which Cashion concurs. She adds that the close, positive relationships among mother, daughter, and other children in families without fathers contribute to a woman's autonomy in later life.

"A woman alone can raise children brilliantly," agrees Burton White, director of the Center for Parent Education in Newton, Massachusetts, and author of *The First Three Years of Life*. White believes that commitment to a child during the first two years of life from *any* key person — mother, father, or any of the four grandparents — is essential to self-esteem, which in turn is the genesis of high achievement.

SOURCE: Sue Nirenberg, "Life Without Father," *Savvy*, March 1983. © 1983 SAVVY Magazine SAVVY Co., New York, N.Y. Reprinted with permission.

---

treated boys and girls differently. Teachers responded three times more often to disruptive behavior by boys than by girls. The boys usually got a loud public reprimand, whereas the girls

were given a quiet rebuke that others could not hear. Disruptive behavior is often an attempt to gain attention, and because the boys received the attention they were seeking, they continued to behave disruptively. When the teacher paid less attention to the boys, this behavior diminished.

Teachers were also more willing to help the boys find something to do. The girls who were not doing anything were ignored and received attention only when they were literally clinging to the teacher's skirts.

The teachers spent more time teaching boys. In one instance, the teacher showed boys how to use a stapler, but when a girl did not know how to use it, the teacher took the materials, stapled them herself, and handed them back to the girl. Problem solving and analytical ability are related to active participation, but girls were not given the opportunity to try things as often as boys.

The story books read to preschool children also teach gender-role behavior. Weitzman (1972), in a review of picture books, found that little girls were admired for their attractiveness, while little boys were admired for their achievements. Men were admired for their accomplishments, while women were admired for being the wives or daughters of kings, judges, adventurers, or explorers. Women were typically shown as wives and mothers, never as pursuing goals outside of the home. Studies of award-winning children's books have shown that the girls in the stories are usually indoors doing domestic chores or passively watching someone else's activities, while boys do interesting and exciting things like rescuing animals or building space ships.

Textbooks likewise subtly teach gender-role behavior. In a review of mathematics texts published between 1970 and 1975, females were generally portrayed as emotional and domestic. In most textbooks, little boys were shown as significantly taller than little girls of the same age, even though in reality children before puberty are about the same height.

Schools teach gender roles in other ways as well. Most teachers are women, but principals and superintendents are men. Women teachers are more likely to teach young children, but as subject matter becomes more difficult and specialized, more men are found teaching. Children receive subtle messages about the capability of men and women as they observe the jobs they hold. School counselors also encourage children to follow expected gender roles. Girls who want to enter masculine occupations or boys who want to enter traditionally feminine occupations will be defined by career counselors as in need of more extensive guidance. Efforts are sometimes made to steer them into more "appropriate" occupations.

Mass Media and Socialization for Gender Roles

From childhood on, Americans spend thousands of hours watching television, which has a strong tendency to portray gender-role stereotypes. In children's television programming, studies showed that male characters are usually portrayed as aggressive, constructive, and helpful, whereas the female characters are passive and defer to males (Sternglanz and Serbin, 1974). Adult programs, especially the situation comedies, are watched by many children and adults. "I Love Lucy," which was originally produced in the fifties and is still seen in reruns, featured Lucille Ball as a consistently inept housewife who had to be rescued by her harassed but tolerant husband. Every episode revolved around Lucy's getting into some sort of trouble. Current situation comedies are a little more subtle.

Daytime soap operas have tried to show men and women as equals. Nevertheless, the career women on the soaps never let their work interfere with the time spent with their husbands. These same women, however, are expected to understand if their husbands' jobs interfere with their home life. The most successful businesswomen on daytime television, such as Erica Kane

The television series "Magnum, P.I." is popular with viewers as much for the good looks of its star, Tom Selleck, as for the quality of the show itself.

("All My Children"), are considered much too assertive to be able to have a successful marriage.

In general, nighttime television has more male than female characters. The emphasis is on male achievement, which often involves violence. It used to be true that male characters' physical attractiveness was relatively unimportant, but in the last few years there has been a trend toward "beefcake" — the male equivalent of "cheesecake." The popularity of shows such as "Magnum, P.I." and "Matt Houston" is based on the physical attractiveness of the shows' stars. Women characters have always had to be physically attractive regardless of any other attributes they may have. Even when they are portrayed as competent individuals, they either get themselves into situations where they must be rescued by men or else they work for men. The part of Joyce Davenport, the assistant district attorney on "Hill Street Blues," is one of the few roles on television where a woman is competent and independent.

Advertising on television and in the press also tends to stereotype both men and women or to portray roles that are impossible to live up to. Career women are portrayed as "superwomen" who combine a successful career, motherhood, and a terrific marriage while cooking a gourmet meal for a small dinner party of ten. At the other extreme, women are portrayed as beautiful, bewildered homemakers, even when they work outside the home. These ads show the woman arriving home from work to cook the family meal or do the family wash, but apparently overwhelmed by indecision about what to serve or how to get shirt collars really clean. A male voice heard in the background tells the woman how to solve her problem. Men in ads are stereotyped as forceful, athletic, involved in business of some kind, or at least actively watching a ball game, but always knowing exactly what they want or which beer has more gusto.

Many popular songs also reflect male and female gender-role stereotypes. Men sing songs of achievement about how they will be number one and won't be pushed around, while women sing more fatalistic songs about accepting life because there's not much they can do about it. Music videos show men strutting about, rough, tough, even violent. "Their" women follow, or even crawl after the men, waiting, even suffering for a bit of attention. Songs that point up women's strength and self-sufficiency are rare.

Socialization in Adulthood

The knowledge we acquire as children shapes the meanings we give to ourselves and the world, and it can continue to influence us for the rest of our lives. We never stop learning new things, however — every day we have new experiences, learn new information, and add the meanings of these new facts to what we already know. Although new knowledge may be different from knowledge acquired as children, the same agencies of socialization are at work.

Types of Adult Socialization

Like children, adults are socialized by their families. Single people must be socialized when they marry in order to live intimately with their spouses and to share living arrangements. If they have children, they learn the role of parents and will probably rely on the knowledge of child care they acquired from their own parents. Since the two parents were themselves brought up by different sets of parents, they will have learned different childrearing techniques and therefore will have to socialize each other to reach agreement about child-care practices. As the children grow up, the parents must be socialized to allow their children to become independent after years of

Public defender Joyce Davenport, played by Veronica Hamel, interviews a prisoner on the television program "Hill Street Blues." Joyce Davenport is one of the few competent, professional women portrayed on television during prime time. Both men and women are socialized to expect less competent behavior for women, and television usually confirms these expectations. It could, however, teach us that women can be competent by portraying more women like Joyce Davenport.

dependency. All of this learning is a part of adult socialization.

Children themselves are often very active socializers of their parents. As infants, they let their parents know when they need attention. Beginning at about age two, they become aware of themselves, learn to say no, and begin to let their parents know when they need some independence. This process of demanding both attention and independence continues as long as the children are at home. It can result in serious conflicts in some youths, particularly those who rebel, fight, take drugs, or run away from home. The socialization of parents can be quite dramatic.

Adult socialization also occurs in schools. Colleges teach adults of all ages, and the move from home to college can be a period of intense socialization. College freshmen must adapt to their new independence from the family and make their own decisions about health, food, sleep, class attendance, study habits, exercise, and social relationships. They must learn to live in crowded situations and compete with peers. Some avoid these decisions by going along with the crowd. Others drop the values they learned in the family and adopt a new set of values, whereas some continue to maintain family values in the new setting. Each choice entails a certain amount of socialization.

Another type of adult socialization is occupational training, which teaches the attitudes and values associated with an occupation, as well as skills. Medical schools, for example, teach students the technical knowledge required to practice medicine, but they also convey the values of the profession. As students proceed through medical school, the number who want to be general practitioners decreases and the number who want to enter a specialty increases, partly because specialists need to keep up with only a small part of the overwhelming volume of new medical information. In addition, medicine is taught by specialists, who tend to encourage students to enter a specialty.

Rules and values must also be learned in fields that require less training than medicine. A new employee in an office has to learn how to conform to the expectations of the other workers and to the written and unwritten rules. Are men and women expected to wear suits or is less formal clothing acceptable? Do employees address one another by their first names? Is rigid adherence to established procedures expected? Are some department heads more accommodating than others? During socialization, the employee will discover the answers to questions such as these.

Adults, like children, get a great deal of factual information from the mass media — radio, television, books, and newspapers. The news media not only report what is happening, they tell people what to consider important. News items based on press releases may convey only what the agency issuing the release wants to make public, and news broadcasts may not present competing unofficial views. Thus, whether we realize it or not, we may learn to define as important whatever officials are telling us is important.

Soap operas are directed toward working-class women, high school students, and college students who are home during the day. These programs display an upper-middle-class lifestyle to working-class people. The styles of dress and decor and people's conduct in social situations are characteristic of the well-to-do. In subtle ways, soap operas show viewers the evils of drugs and alcohol, proper childrearing techniques, and how to behave during a divorce or other tragedy, to name just a few of the topics they cover. People tend to be either good or evil; generally the good are loved by family and friends whereas the evil suffer as a result of their bad behavior.

Resocialization is usually very dramatic, with a complete stripping away of all personal characteristics. These women marine recruits must learn that originality of dress and fragile presentation no longer matter. For a marine, physical fitness, discipline, and conformity are most important.

Resocialization

Major adaptations to new situations in adulthood may sometimes require *resocialization*. The changes people undergo during this period are much more pervasive than the gradual adaptations characteristic of regular socialization. Resocialization usually follows a major break in a person's customary life, one which requires that the person adopt an entirely new set of meanings to understand his or her new life. *Mortification of self* (Goffman, 1961), the most dramatic type of resocialization, occurs in such institutions as the armed forces, prisons, and mental hospitals. Peo-

ple entering these institutions are totally stripped of their old selves. Physically, they are required to strip, shower, and don institutional clothing. All personal possessions are taken away, and they must leave behind family, friends, and work roles. They must live in a new environment under a new set of rules and adopt a new role as a military person, prisoner, or mental patient. Their previous learning must be completely reorganized.

The "midlife crisis" is another example of a dramatic resocialization. Men may have been socialized by families, schools, peers, the media, and other life experiences to believe that they are unique individuals with special talents that must be developed if they are to be superior to others and attain important positions in society. Men who have learned this — those who have been well socialized — attempt to develop their talents and hold important positions. At some point in middle age, however, a few men learn a revolutionary new set of meanings. They may decide they are unique and valuable people even without their special abilities, important jobs, and high salaries. Once they change the basic set of meanings they have been acting on, everything else changes. Some quit their jobs and take off for the north woods to farm or otherwise work with their hands. Most change in less dramatic ways, but they have still changed the basic set of meanings they learned as children and have begun to act on a new set of meanings.

Retirement from work is sometimes an easy process of socialization to a new situation, but it often requires a great deal of resocialization. Retired people often lose at least part of their income, so they may have to adapt to a new standard of living. With the loss of work, new sources of self-esteem may have to be developed, but society may help in this process by providing education on financial management, health, and housing. Counseling services and support groups for retired persons may also be provided, often by employers, especially when they want employees to retire.

Besides loss of income and self-esteem, retirement creates another resocialization problem. Most roles involve social expectations and provide rewards for meeting those expectations. Retirement, however, is a *"roleless"* role (Riley et al., 1969). There are no social expectations associated with retirement other than the loss of a previous role; as a result, the satisfactory performance of the retirement role goes unrecognized. To compound the problem, the retired person's spouse often dies during this period, so

he or she must relinquish the family role as well as the work role. But if the retired person has enough money to buy nice clothes, enjoy hobbies, and afford travel for social events or volunteer work, then he or she can create a new role that is rewarding.

The Process of Social Interaction

Socialization influences the way we act and interact with each other. In an attempt to analyze how interaction takes place, Goffman (1959) compared interaction to a drama on stage — a comparison known as the *dramaturgical approach.* Whenever we interact we prepare ourselves backstage and then present ourselves as if on stage, according to what we have learned in the socialization process. Most Americans prepare to present themselves by showering, washing their hair, and using deodorant — in our society, cleanliness and a lack of odor are important. Complexions must be smooth, so men shave, women put on makeup, and adolescents use cosmetics to cover up acne. Suitable clothing is selected so that we can present ourselves formally in formal situations and casually in casual situations. A formal setting such as a church, a more informal setting such as a classroom, and a casual setting such as a basketball arena require very different presentations. In some settings one can race for a front-row seat, talk loudly, wave to friends, and eat and drink. In other settings, these behaviors would be quite inappropriate.

The way we present ourselves — the *presentation of self* — gives other people cues about the type of interaction we expect. In formal situations, we usually greet friends with a handshake or a remark, whereas in informal situations we may greet friends with a hug or a kiss. If we are with friends, we talk and laugh, but on a bus or in an elevator we do not speak to strangers and

*In formal situations, such as receiving
a Nobel prize, there are strict rules
for appropriate behavior, which
participants are expected to follow.*

keep a social distance even when space is
crowded and we cannot keep physically distant.
Psychologists refer to our manner of presentation as "body language." We give cues about
ourselves in the way we present and use our
bodies in interaction.

In illustrating the dramaturgical approach,
Goffman described a character called Preedy as
he presented himself on a beach on the Riviera.
Preedy very consciously tried to make an impression on the people around him. It was his
first day on vacation and he knew no one. He
wanted to meet some people, but he didn't want
to appear too lonely or too eager, so he presented
himself as perfectly content in his solitary state.

The following excerpt from Goffman (1959)
describes Preedy's behavior:

If by chance a ball was thrown his way, he looked
surprised; then let a smile of amusement lighten

his face (Kindly Preedy), looked round dazed to
see that there *were* people on the beach, tossed it
back with a smile to himself and not a smile *at* the
people, and then resumed carelessly his noncha-
lant survey of space.

But it was time to institute a little parade,
the parade of the Ideal Preedy. By devious han-
dlings he gave any who wanted to look a chance
to see the title of his book — a Spanish transla-
tion of Homer, classic thus, but not daring, cosmopolitan too — and then gathered together his
beach-wrap and bag into a neat sand-resistant pile
(Methodical and Sensible Preedy), rose slowly to
stretch at ease his huge frame (Big-Cat Preedy),
and tossed aside his sandals (Carefree Preedy,
after all).

The marriage of Preedy and the sea! There
were alternative rituals. The first involved the
stroll that turns into a run and a dive straight into
the water, thereafter smoothing into a strong
splashless crawl towards the horizon. But of

course not really to the horizon. Quite suddenly he would turn on to his back and thrash great white splashes with his legs, somehow thus showing that he could have swum further had he wanted to, and then would stand up a quarter out of water for all to see who it was.

The alternative course was simpler, it avoided the cold-water shock and it avoided the risk of appearing too high-spirited. The point was to appear to be so used to the sea, the Mediterranean, and this particular beach, that one might as well be in the sea as out of it. It involved a slow stroll down and into the edge of the water — not even noticing his toes were wet, land and water all the same to *him!* — with his eyes up at the sky gravely surveying portents, invisible to others, of the weather (Local Fisherman Preedy). (p. 5)

Notice how much Preedy could tell about himself without saying a word. Whether anyone enters the water in as calculated a manner as Preedy is questionable, but whoever watches someone like Preedy will form an opinion of him from his presentation. Likewise we would form an opinion of some other man after watching him walk on the beach. His age, weight, posture, muscle size, suntan, and facial expression will lead us to suppose that he is a newcomer, a beachcomber, athletic, friendly, lonely, happy, or sad. If we interact with him, we would enter the interaction with a preconceived set of expectations about his behavior. Manner and appearance shape interaction in very important ways.

Maintaining the Self

Once we have presented ourselves in a particular role and have begun to interact, we must maintain our presentation. In class, students cannot begin to shake hands with fellow students, wander around the room, or write on the blackboard. It would not only disrupt the class, it would spoil the presentation of the student, who would be considered disruptive, strange, or

worse. If students or others want to maintain the definitions others have of them, they must maintain a performance in accord with the definition.

Sometimes we inadvertently do not maintain our performance, so we try to account for our behavior (Scott and Lyman, 1968). If we are late and want to avoid giving the impression that we are always late, we make excuses: "I am usually very prompt, but my car ran out of gas," or "I thought the meeting was at eight o'clock, not seven o'clock." We may be more fatalistic and say, "I tried to arrive on time, but everyone in my family is late. It's our nature." Or we may blame someone else and say, "The bus was late." On the other hand, we may try to justify our lateness by saying, "These meetings never start on time" or "It doesn't matter. No harm done." We expect others to see us not as irresponsible and inconsiderate but as prompt and considerate, in spite of our lateness. Others often support our claims about ourselves and ignore the contradictory presentation.

We also try to maintain our presentations by *disclaimers,* that is, disclaiming a role even while we are acting in that role. "I usually don't drink, but this punch is so good" disclaims the role of drinker. "I'm not prejudiced, but . . ." followed by a racist remark or "I'm no expert, but . . ." followed by a remark only an expert could make are phrases that tell the audience that the self is not what it appears to be.

Often the audience accepts a person's accounts or disclaimers and the interaction proceeds smoothly, but sometimes the drama does not work out so well. We may present ourselves in the role of someone who knows how to act in social situations but not live up to those claims. We may fall down a flight of stairs as we make our grand entrance. We may stand up at a meeting to give a report, claiming to be an expert, but our trembling hands and factual errors will not support these claims. The speaker and those in the audience may attempt to ignore the errors, but at some point the speaker may get too flustered to continue the pretense of living up to the role or become embarrassed and laugh, cry, faint, or blush. When a group can no longer support the claims made by an individual the whole group may become embarrassed or angry (Goffman, 1967).

Implicit in interactions is the assumption that presentations will be maintained. Each person agrees to maintain the self and to support the presentations of others. If people's presentations are not supported by the people themselves or by others, it may be followed by an emotional response. In some situations, we may become embarrassed, and if our presentation is ridiculed we may get angry. If someone seems to fill a person's image of the ideal romantic love, we may fall in love with that individual. If the person is cruel or unfaithful or behaves in some other way that tarnishes our image of him or her, we may grow angry and eventually fall out of love.

Our feelings about ourselves and others are learned (Hochschild, 1975). Just as we learn self-esteem by understanding how others evaluate us, we learn when to be embarrassed, when to be angry, when to fall in love and with what type of person. If we are angry at someone who deserves our respect, we feel guilty about our own behavior. If we love someone who others define as entirely inappropriate, we become confused. Again, we have expectations about maintaining performances, both our own and others, and we respond emotionally when these expectations are not met.

Humans have very complex minds, of course. People learn a varied set of meanings during their lives, and they interpret each situation on the basis of their own biography and their own definition of the situation. How a person presents self and maintains interaction de-

These two women appear to support each other's definitions of the situation. Both agree to present themselves as glad to see the other and to greet each other in an informal spontaneous way.

pends on his or her unique interpretation of self, others, and the situation. It is this ability to interpret that makes interaction such a varied, interesting, and challenging area of study.

SOCIOLOGISTS AT WORK
Youth Guidance

Barbara Monsor is coordinator of research and statistics at Youth Guidance, a school-based social service program for adolescents in Chicago. A private nonprofit organization founded in 1924, Youth Guidance has offices in middle schools and high schools in five Chicago school districts. Monsor joined them in 1978, after earning a master's degree in sociology at the University of Illinois at Chicago Circle.

Does Monsor find uses for her sociological background in her work at Youth Guidance? "Constantly," she says, "It's an integral part of what I do. My interest — both theoretical and pragmatic — in the field of human development, and particularly child development, is engaged daily." Youth Guidance provides a vast array of services to the children who are referred to it by teachers and school administrators, hospitals, and other professionals. Monsor enumerates some of these services: "We do counseling, we run creative arts programs, we do group counseling and family therapy, we provide referrals to outside therapists and hospitals for problems that are bigger than we can handle, we provide counseling and other services to teachers and counselors who are already in the schools and help them with their counseling overload, and we run a training program for social workers and graduate students in social work."

Being located in the schools is a great help to Youth Guidance in delivering these services. "It's almost axiomatic," Monsor says, "that adolescents don't get these services unless you grab them where they are. We used to have all our offices downtown. Our first move into a school — long before I came here — was something we negotiated with the school district. After that we were asked to move into several other schools. Our office space is an in-kind contribution from the schools, in return for the services we provide."

Children in the schools are referred to Youth Guidance for a wide range of reasons. "They may just have unexplained bad grades," Monsor says. "They may be acting aggressively in the classroom. They may not be showing up for class and be on the verge of dropping out. They may be EMH children — educably mentally handicapped, with many adjustment problems. They may have threatened suicide or have threatened their peers with violence. They may have just been released from the hospital and have problems related to that. They may be pregnant — we have one whole group of pregnant girls. They may have language and cultural problems, especially if they're recent immigrants."

Monsor's role in all this is a busy one. "I am responsible for statistics, in-house evaluation and research, and data to be used in contracts with government and private funders and in meeting their monitoring requirements. I do mainly qualitative research — an annual evaluation of our counseling program based on interviews with clients and school staff people, for example."

Monsor is happy in her job, which she first learned of from the director of Youth Guidance, who is married to one of her professors at Chicago Circle. "I accepted the job," she says, "because I felt I would be able to make use of my academic background, training, and interests, and to work in a setting where I could subscribe to organizational goals. When we deal with children in trouble, we have a systemic approach to *trouble*. We find that problems occur for family, cultural, and economic reasons. We're not one of those mental health agencies that defines our children as 'sick' and wants to lock them up somewhere."

Summary

Socialization is the process of learning how to interact in society. Infants must interact in order to survive, and as they interact they learn about society. Children who have been isolated or who received little attention when very young do not learn to walk, talk, or otherwise respond to people because social interactions are crucial to development.

Sociobiologists believe that inborn genetic traits direct human behavior just as they direct the behavior of animals. They contend that sexual, altruistic, and warlike behaviors occur in humans because we are predisposed to them in our genetic makeup. Most biologists and social scientists, however, sidestep the nature-nurture debate by believing that people's behavior is determined by their biological capacity to learn socially. Human beings are unique because they learn a symbol system — language. Through interaction we develop an idea of who we are.

Charles Horton Cooley used the term "looking-glass self" to describe how people learn about themselves; he argued that our identities are heavily influenced by our perceptions of how others view us. We see ourselves not as we are, and not as others see us, but as we *think* others see us.

Mead used the term "role taking" to describe the process of figuring out how others think and perceive us. According to Mead, children take the role of only one other person at a time at first. Children practice role taking in play and learn to generalize in team games.

Although psychologists are interested in the behavior of individuals rather than social interactions, several psychological orientations are of interest to sociologists. Behaviorists focus on people's observable actions, making no assumptions about underlying processes. They study how behaviors are learned and what stimulates learning. Developmental psychologists deal with the stages of development from infancy on through the life cycle. They study both physical development and cognitive development, the development of thought processes. Many developmental theorists believe that development is predominantly biological rather than social. Freud said that development passes through a series of stages characterized by different sources of drive gratification. Piaget found that the nature of cognitive processes changes as children mature. Erickson described eight stages, but also believed that introspection was necessary for full development.

As youngsters grow, assume the roles of others, and learn about themselves, they are being socialized — learning cultural values and norms. Some of the important agencies of socialization are the family, schools, peer groups, and the mass media.

People's perceptions of behavior appropriate for members of their sex are the result of socialization. From birth, males and females are treated differently. Men are expected to be active and task-oriented, whereas women are expected to be nurturing and people-oriented. Socialization for these roles occurs in every aspect of American society, from children's storybooks to the mass media. From this socialization, children learn what is expected of themselves and others.

Socialization continues throughout life. Resocialization may be necessary when a person's life changes dramatically and abruptly, such as going to prison or entering retirement.

Goffman compared interaction to a drama on stage. We present ourselves as we want other people to define us and as we assume they expect us to behave. Once we have presented ourselves, everyone involved in the interaction is expected to maintain that presentation. We may have to justify our behavior by making excuses or disclaimers. If we cannot maintain our presentations, we will respond to our failure with emotion, often embarrassment or anger. Interaction is a very creative process based on what we have learned about self, others, and the situation in which we find ourselves.

Key Terms

behavior modification
behaviorism
classical conditioning
developmental theories
disclaimers
dramaturgical approach
ego
expressive role
Freudian theory
generalized other
id
instrumental role
looking-glass self
mass media
mortification of self
nature-nurture debate
operant conditioning
peer group
Piagetian theory
play
presentation of self
resocialization
role taking
"roleless" role
significant others
socialization
sociobiology
superego
symbolic interaction

Suggested Readings

Campbell, Ernest Q. **Socialization: Culture and Personality.** *Dubuque, Iowa: Wm. C. Brown, 1975.* This is a very brief book, but it summarizes well the topic discussed in this chapter.

Derber, Charles. **The Pursuit of Attention. Power and Individualism in Everyday Life.** *Cambridge, Mass. Schenkman, 1979.* An important book, delightful to read, and full of insights into how society shapes individual conversations.

Elkin, Frederick and Gerald Handel. **The Child and Society: The Process of Socialization. 4th ed.** *New York: Random House, 1984.* A coherent sociological perspective of how children are socialized in modern society.

Goffman, Erving. **The Presentation of Self in Everyday Life.** *Garden City, N.Y.: Doubleday, 1959.* This book describes the dramaturgical approach to the study of social interaction and analyzes interaction in great detail.

Goslin, David (ed.). **Handbook of Socialization Theory and Research.** *Chicago: Rand McNally, 1969.* This is an encyclopedia rather than a reading book, but it is highly respected in this area of study, and you may enjoy browsing through it to see the depth of study undertaken in socialization.

Hewitt, John P. **Self and Society: A Symbolic Interactionist Social Psychology, 2d ed.** *Boston: Allyn & Bacon, 1979.* This very readable text discusses symbolic interaction and expands on some of the topics discussed in this chapter.

Money, John. **Love and Love Sickness. The Science of Sex, Gender Difference and Pair-Bonding.** *Baltimore: Johns Hopkins University Press, 1980.* A discussion of the development of sex differences by a leading researcher in the field.

Pleck, Joseph H. and Jack Sawyer (eds.). **Men and Masculinity.** *Englewood Cliffs, N.J.: Prentice-Hall, 1974.* A collection of readings on male socialization.

Schur, Edwin. **The Awareness Trap.** *New York: McGraw-Hill, 1976.* Schur convincingly argues that we cannot change our emotional lives, the way we feel about ourselves, by analyzing the self alone but that we must understand our place in society and how society has shaped our behavior.

Shattuck, Roger. **The Forbidden Experiment: The Story of the Wild Boy of Aveyron.** *New York: Farrar, Straus, Giroux, 1980.* This is a recent description of the wild boy found in 1800 in France. It provides insights into the behavior of a child who knew no language.

Tallman, Irving, Ramona Marotz-Baden, and Pablo Pindas. **Adolescent Socialization in Cross-Cultural Perspective.** *New York: Academic Press, 1983.* A theory of socialization and an empirical examination of how families and adolescents in Mexico and the United States deal with change.

Weitzman, Lenore J. **Sex Role Socialization.** *Palo Alto, Calif.: Mayfield Publishing, 1979.* A brief overview of socialization with an emphasis on feminine behavior.

CHAPTER 7

Deviance and Social Control

The problem of building a human society is always the difficulty of establishing a relation between individual and communal happiness.

— Dora Russell

Deviance is universal. It exists in all societies, wherever people interact and live in groups. It is found in complex, industrialized, urban areas as well as in tribal, folk, and agrarian regions. Although it is sometimes claimed that people in certain societies cooperate in complete harmony and peace, anthropologists claim that no society or culture, large or small, rural or urban, has complete behavioral conformity and a total absence of deviance.

What Is Deviance?

Deviance means different things to different people. The definition we use influences our explanations of its causes and our attempts to control it. Does deviance reside in the individual? Is it a particular type of act or behavior? Is it defined socially? Are certain groups immune from being labeled deviants? Our answers to questions such as these will influence how we analyze deviance and whether we ultimately understand it.

We will define *deviance* as variation from a set of norms or shared social expectations. It involves a social audience that defines certain people and behaviors as going beyond the tolerance limits of social norms. Social norms, rules, and expectations about appropriate and inappropriate behavior exist in all societies. People everywhere have social controls to enforce the rules and punish those who do not conform.

Norms rarely state exactly which behaviors are acceptable and which are unacceptable, and universal adherence to norms is unknown. All societies permit variations in the behavior demanded by the norms. Where variations are possible, people will test their range, and some will inevitably exceed the boundaries of permissible

In the U.S., prostitution is viewed as deviant behavior, but in Amsterdam (above), Hamburg, and other cities in Europe, prostitutes can operate openly in certain areas. This view of prostitution as nondeviant may be due to its positive functions: income for women, sexual gratification for men, a safety valve for marriages, and an impersonal, commitment-free relationship.

and approved behavior. Deviance consists of these norm violations; the norm violators are the deviants. People's perceptions of deviance rarely correspond to its reality, however, as we will see in the following discussion of certain traditional views of deviance and deviants.

Traditional Views of Deviance and Deviants

There are many approaches to the study of deviance. Different explanations focus variously on people, behavior, or the social context of people and behavior. Other theories describe the socialization of deviance and its causes, support, and transmission. In addition, theorists have described how such social conditions as conflict, anomie, and labeling contribute to deviance and how it is formally and informally controlled. As you might guess, there are also biological, psychological, and sociological theories, to say nothing of explanations by lawyers, the clergy, and others who counsel, treat, punish, or work with those defined as deviant. Four of the more common traditional views of deviance are discussed below.

The Absolutist View

Until the middle of this century, most social scientists assumed that social rules were clear and obvious to most members of society. Certain behaviors were considered deviant regardless of the social context in which they occurred. This perspective, known as the *absolutist view*, was based on the assumption that everyone agreed on certain norms and that certain behaviors are clearly deviant regardless of the social context in which they occur. Thus prostitution, homosexuality, and the use of drugs might be assumed to be deviant at all times and in all cultures, and chastity, heterosexuality, and abstinence from drugs might be regarded as nondeviant. This view, however, fails to take into account variations in social norms and people's perceptions of them. In some cultures, homosexuality, certain types of prostitution, and the use of drugs are considered perfectly acceptable. The absolutist perspective has been rejected by most sociologists, but many nonprofessionals continue to assess deviance in these terms.

The Moral View

A second perspective, the *moral view*, is that deviance is immoral and antisocial. As in the absolutist perspective, certain behaviors are regarded as being deviant in all situations, but it is also assumed that deviance is bad or evil and that people who commit deviant acts lack morals and are depraved and antisocial. Like the absolutist, the moralist assumes that there are just two kinds of people and two kinds of behavior: the moral nondeviant and the immoral deviant. Deviant people are regarded as inherently different from others, that is, deviant by nature. They are considered innately antisocial and evil, and their behavior is considered harmful to others and to society. Today, many groups or categories of people in the United States are viewed as inherently deviant. Many people define atheists, homosexuals, and political liberals as innately evil and consider their behavior antisocial and harmful to U.S. interests. Likewise, shoplifters, unwed mothers, and marijuana smokers are sometimes viewed as different from others and lacking in moral judgment and moral behavior.

This view has also been rejected by social scientists. As we shall discuss later in this chapter, deviance is not inherent in persons or in acts. Even if it were, it is not necessarily antisocial, evil, or immoral. In fact, deviance has positive functions and desirable consequences for society.

The Medical and Social Pathological Views

A third approach is the *medical view* of deviance, in which deviance is assumed to be es-

sentially pathological, evidence that a society is unhealthy. Just as healthy humans function efficiently without pain or discomfort, healthy societies are thought to function smoothly without problems. The prevalence of child abuse, rape, robbery, mental disorders, and alcoholism are thought to indicate that a society has a sickness. This perspective closely parallels the social pathological view of the early 1900s.

Like the moral view, the medical view is absolutist. It assumes that people are either deviant or not deviant — there is no grey area — but this polarity is expressed in terms of health or illness. Today, it is not uncommon to hear references to a "sick" society, but few people agree on how to cure the sickness or on what constitutes a healthy society. Psychiatrists and doctors even have trouble distinguishing who is healthy and who is not.

The Statistical View

A fourth view of deviance relies on statistics. Any behavior that is atypical, that varies from the average or mode, is considered deviant. This view is not absolutist: deviance is assumed to be a variable characteristic that increases the further a behavior is removed from the average. Deviants are viewed not as sick people, as in the medical view, but simply as being different. According to the *statistical view*, any variation from a statistical norm is deviant. Thus a person who is left-handed, who has red hair, or who belongs to a minority group is defined as a deviant. (See Table 7-1 for additional examples.) Everyone fails to conform to the average in some respect, however, so according to this definition, we are all deviants.

Although this view avoids absolutism, judgments about morality, and analogies with medicine, it fails on several counts. It does not take into account the meanings people attach to behaviors, and it ignores situations in which deviance is defined by a powerful group that is a

Table 7-1

Statistical deviants in the United States, based on variation from the median or the most common characteristic, 1982

CHARACTERISTIC	MEDIAN OR MOST COMMON	STATISTICAL DEVIANTS, PERCENT	
1. Age	Median = 30.6	Under age 5	7.5
		Age 65 and over	11.6
2. Years of school completed	Median = 12.6	Less than 5 years	3.0
		4 years or more of college	17.7
3. Marital status	Married 64.5%	Single	20.9
		Widowed and divorced	14.7
4. Persons in household	1–3 = 72.4%	6 or more	4.9
5. Household income	Median = $20,171	Less than $5,000	9.6
		$50,000 and over	8.9

SOURCE: U.S. Bureau of the Census, *Statistical Abstract of the United States: 1984* (104th ed., U.S. Government Printing Office), Washington, D.C., 1983 (1) No. 33, p. 33; (2) No. 225, p. 146; (3) No. 50, p. 43; (4) No. 62, p. 48; (5) No. 754, p. 459.

numerical minority. Variations in the enforcement of rules are not considered, nor are interpersonal interactions, societal standards, or public awareness of or response to the deviance. Although much socially defined deviance falls outside of the average, the degree of variation may be less significant than the social definitions and social judgments attached to the variation.

The Relative Nature of Deviance

More recently, sociologists have begun to advocate a relativistic model. As we stated in Chapter 4, cultural relativism is the assumption that behaviors, ideas, and products can be understood or evaluated only within the context of the culture and society of which they are a part. In the same way, a *relativistic view* suggests that deviance can be interpreted only in the sociocultural con-

text in which it happens. Is a person 7 feet tall a deviant in the context of professional basketball? Is a person without a bathing suit a deviant at a nudist beach? Is killing deviant in the context of war? Context influences all of these determinations.

By assessing deviance in a particular social context, the relativistic model avoids the problems of the absolute, moral, medical, and statistical models. If deviance is relative rather than absolute, an act that is deviant in one context may not be deviant in another. A behavior considered "sick" in one society could be thought of as healthy in a different society. A certain act might be statistically deviant in one culture but not in another. As is generally true of cultural relativism, however, the fact that an act is defined as nondeviant in one situation does not mean that it is nondeviant everywhere. By the same token, acts that are defined as deviant in some places are not defined as such everywhere. Thus deviance does not consist merely of acts or behaviors, but of group responses, definitions, and the meanings attached to behaviors and therefore we can expect definitions of deviance to vary with circumstances. Some of the most important variations that affect these definitions concern time, place, situation, and social status.

Variation by Time

An act considered deviant in one time period may be considered nondeviant in another. Cigarette smoking, for example, has a long history of changing normative definitions. Nuehring and Markle (1974) note that in the United States between 1895 and 1921, fourteen states completely banned cigarette smoking and all other states except Texas passed laws regulating the sale of cigarettes to minors. In the early years of this century, stop-smoking clinics were opened in several cities and antismoking campaigns were widespread. Following World War I, however, cigarette sales increased and public attitudes toward smoking changed. Through the mass media, the tobacco industry appealed to women, weightwatchers, and even to health seekers.

States began to realize that tobacco could be a rich source of revenue, and by 1927 the fourteen states that banned cigarettes had repealed their laws. By the end of World War II, smoking had become acceptable, and in many contexts it was thought socially desirable.

In the 1950s, scientists found that smoking could cause a variety of diseases, including lung cancer and heart disease. In 1964 the Surgeon General published a landmark report on smoking and health, and soon thereafter some states began passing anticigarette legislation again. Laws were passed requiring a health warning on cigarette packages, and in 1973 the National Association of Broadcasters agreed to phase out cigarette advertising. Since then, airlines, restaurants, and other public places have begun to designate segregated sections for smokers and nonsmokers, and in many states smoking is completely prohibited in such places as elevators, concert halls, museums, and physicians' offices (Markle and Troyer, 1979), which suggests that smoking is again increasingly considered a deviant behavior. Early in 1984, however, the tobacco industry made an effort to discredit the negative research findings on cigarette smoking

Is this little girl deviant? The answer is yes, if "deviant" means atypical, in the minority, or different from the average. Children under age five comprise only about 7 percent of the total U.S. population and female children under five comprise only 3.5 percent of the total U.S. population.

in an attempt to increase sales. Many other examples could be given of how behaviors defined as deviant at one time may be ignored or even encouraged at another time.

Variation by Place

Behaviors viewed as deviant in one location, society, or culture may be considered nondeviant in others. In many cultures, having more than one wife is a sign of wealth, prestige, and high status. In the United States, however, having more than one wife at once is a punishable offense. Certain sexual acts that are deemed immoral, criminal, or delinquent in American society are accepted in Scandinavian countries. Bullfighting in Spain and Mexico and cockfighting in the Philippines are festive, legal gambling activities that produce income, but they are forbidden in the United States. On the other hand, American dating practices, divorce rates, and bathing attire are thought shocking by much of the non-Western world. Table 7-2 provides the result of research in six countries where the people were asked how they felt about the legal prohibition of specific acts. Note the extent to which the people in the United States differed from other countries in their response to the issues, particularly in regard to incest, homosexuality, and public protest.

There are variations in definitions of deviance within cultures as well as among them. Vast differences exist among regions of the United States in the approval granted to interracial dating, among states in the approval of teenage smoking, and among rural and urban areas in the acceptance of theaters showing pornographic films. Different subcultures often have norms that are viewed as deviant by other subcultures in the same society.

Variation by Situation

Behavior defined as deviant in one situation may not be in another, even in the same time period and geographical area. A man who dresses in women's clothes to act in a play would be considered normal, but a man who dressed in women's clothes in the audience would not. Sex between husband and wife in the home is granted social approval, but sex by the same husband and wife at a public beach or on the church altar might land them in jail or a mental hospital.

Variations in the acceptance of marijuana and alcohol use by college students were studied by Orcutt (1975). Their degree of acceptance varied widely, depending on such factors as (1) the social goals of the drug use, (2) the regularity of use in certain situations, and (3) the user's motivation for using drugs. Most students, for example, accepted marijuana or alcohol use at small parties with friends who were also using them. They tended not to accept a person's use of drugs or alcohol every day before going to a job to help cope with work, however (see Table 7-3 for student response in more detail). The social relativity of deviance reminds us that we must carefully select the time, place, and situation in which we behave in certain ways.

Variation by Social Status

Deviance also varies with social status, the position in society that one occupies. As described in Chapter 2, ascribed statuses are those acquired at birth: age, sex, race, and so on. Achieved statuses are those that people gain on their own: marital status, educational status, occupational status, and so on. Prince Charles of England's social status, for example, is ascribed — he was born into royalty. Sandra Day O'Connor's status has been achieved by her appointment to the Supreme Court. Until recently, a woman or a black person who aspired to be a bank president might have been considered deviant, but such an aspiration might have been encouraged in a white male. Similarly, members of a country club might try to encourage a rich

Table 7-2

Legal prohibition of various acts: views in six countries

"DO YOU THINK THIS ACT SHOULD BE PROHIBITED BY THE LAW?"
(PERCENT DISTRIBUTION: "DON'T KNOW" CATEGORY EXCLUDED)

	INDIA (N = 509)		INDONESIA (N = 500)		IRAN (N = 475)		ITALY (SARDINIA) (N = 200)		U.S.A. (N = 169)		YUGOSLAVIA (N = 500)	
	YES	NO	YES	NO	YES	NO	YES	NO	YES	NO	YES	NO
Incest	94.3	5.7	98.0	0.6	98.1	1.9	97.5	2.0	71.0	20.7	95.0	0.8
Robbery	97.3	2.7	99.2	0.0	97.9	2.1	100.0	0.0	100.0	0.0	98.4	0.4
Appropriation[a]	96.6	1.2	99.8	0.2	97.1	2.9	100.0	0.0	92.3	7.1	98.0	0.0
Homosexuality	74.1	25.0	85.9	7.2	90.3	9.7	86.5	12.5	18.3	66.9	71.6	13.6
Abortion	40.9	58.7	95.3	3.0	83.9	16.1	76.5	21.5	21.9	74.5	24.8	63.2
Taking drugs	74.9	24.6	93.3	2.4	89.8	10.2	92.0	3.0	89.6	11.8	89.2	4.2
Factory pollution	98.8	1.2	94.9	1.0	97.7	2.3	96.0	3.5	96.4	3.0	92.8	1.6
Public protest	33.3	65.8	72.3	20.9	77.0	23.0	34.5	64.5	5.9	91.1	46.2	38.4
Not helping	44.5	53.9	67.7	24.4	56.4	43.6	79.5	20.0	27.8	52.7	76.6	12.2

[a] Taking over someone else's property for your own use.

SOURCE: Graeme Newman, *Comparative Deviance: Perception and Law in Six Cultures*, Elsevier, New York, 1976, p. 116. Copyright 1976 by Elsevier Science Publishing Co., Inc. Reprinted by permission.

Deviance does not reside in acts or behavior per se, but in the meanings attached to them. In U.S. society, most people define nudity in public places as deviant. In a culture that stresses cleanliness, to cover oneself with mud is considered deviant as well. But what is viewed as deviant may depend on the stituation: identical behavior among two-year-olds would be seen in a different light.

Mafia member to join but treat the drug dealers and prostitutes who made the Mafia's money with contempt. The status associated with a person's sex, race, age, and income will influence which of his or her behaviors are considered deviant.

We can examine how deviance varies by social status by noting differences in appropriate behaviors for males and females. There are variations by time, place, and situation, but certain behaviors are generally given greater approval for women than men, whereas others are given greater approval for men than women. It is generally considered acceptable for women to wear high heels, panty hose, and earrings, but in our society such behaviors in men would be considered deviant. Men can go topless to any beach,

but women who do so would be considered deviant.

In the past, men and women differed greatly in types and degree of deviant behavior, although there is evidence that this is changing. A review of forty-four studies (Smith and Visher, 1980) dealing with the relationship between sex and deviance or criminality indicates that women are becoming more involved in personal offenses (e.g., drug and alcohol violations), youth offenses (e.g., truancy, school problems), and property offenses (e.g., theft, embezzlement, fraud) but differ considerably in involvement with violent offenses. This general narrowing of female-male differences seems consistent with the view that women may be experiencing greater structural opportunities to engage in de-

Table 7-3

Percentages accepting or indifferent to marijuana and alcohol use by situational item variations

SITUATIONAL ITEMS	% ACCEPTING OR INDIFFERENT	
	MARIJUANA	ALCOHOL
1 — A college student smokes marijuana (drinks alcohol) at a small party with his friends who are also using marijuana (alcohol).	82.8	97.0
2 — A college student working as a salesman smokes marijuana (drinks alcohol) with one of his clients who has offered it to him.	39.0	81.0
3 — A college student smokes marijuana (drinks alcohol) two or three times a week when he gets together with friends in the evening.	70.9	79.0
4 — During a boring party, a college student withdraws to a quiet corner to get high on marijuana (alcohol) to help him feel better.	41.7	34.9
5 — A college student uses marijuana (alcohol) to ease his anxieties about meeting others before going to any kind of a party.	39.6	48.5
6 — A college student working in an office regularly smokes marijuana (drinks alcohol) with his co-workers during their lunch break.	29.6	31.5
7 — On a particularly trying day at his part-time job, a college student smokes marijuana (drinks alcohol) during his lunch break to help him face the rest of his work.	26.5	20.9
8 — Every day before going to his job, a college student smokes marijuana (drinks alcohol) to help him cope with his work situation.	9.3	4.9

SOURCE: James D. Orcutt, "Deviance as a Simulated Phenomenon: Variations in the Social Interpretation of Marijuana and Alcohol Use," *Social Problems* 22 (February 1975):351. An adaptation of Table 1. Reprinted by permission.

viant behaviors because the social roles of men and women are changing. If and when total sexual equality is obtained, variation in deviance by sexual status may disappear.

The relativistic perspective acknowledges the diversity of behaviors, convictions, and sanctions that can be found in society, and also the variety of meanings and definitions attributed to behaviors and sanctions. This view also recognizes the potential for conflict in a society or a single person in attempting to conform to the norms of different groups. A teenager may be encouraged to smoke marijuana by peers but not by parents. A Catholic couple may wish to

use only "natural" contraceptive methods to conform to church norms, yet want to use "artificial" methods to conform to their own norms and those of their friends and society.

From the relativistic perspective, deviance is not assumed to reside exclusively in either people or actions. It is, rather, an interactive process involving people's behavior, an audience, norms and definitions, and society as a whole. To understand deviance, we must focus not only on people or acts but also on the conditions in which deviance occurs and how others react to it. Many factors must be taken into account: the social setting; the society's structure, definitions, and labels; the way people learn norms and the variation from norms that society permits; and the means by which behaviors within the range of variability are controlled and behaviors outside of this range are punished.

Theories of Deviance

As we have illustrated, deviance varies by time, place, situation, and social status. Given the wide variations in deviance, how can it be explained? What causes deviance? Why do people violate social norms? Equally important, why do people conform and obey social norms? Most people do conform, and conformity is granted greater social approval in most circumstances, so theories have tended to focus more on the deviant than the nondeviant. The two are not easily separated, however, and explanations of one are equally applicable to the other.

Scientists have developed a variety of theories to explain deviance, but the fact that many theories exist does not mean that one is correct and the others incorrect. Theories often reflect the discipline from which they developed. Biological theories tend to focus on genetic, anatomical, or physiological factors. Psychological theories tend to emphasize personality, motives, aggression, frustration, or ego strength. Sociologists usually emphasize sociocultural, organizational, environmental, or group factors. Although some theories have more empirical support than others, all can increase our understanding of the complexities of human behavior, whether deviant or nondeviant, and the social order.

Biological Theories of Deviance

Several of the traditional views discussed earlier in this chapter involved biological factors. The view that deviance is a sickness adhered to a medical model, which assumed not just a social pathology or mental illness but an unhealthy bi-

ological organism as well. Similarly, the moral model implied that certain people possess a biologically based resistance to conformity. These views share the assumption that certain defects or weaknesses in an individual's physical constitution produce deviant behaviors.

Biological theories of deviance are often traced back to the Italian physician-psychiatrist Cesare Lombroso (1835–1909). Lombroso, sometimes referred to as the father of modern criminology, was interested in the scientific study of crime. He believed that attention should be shifted from the criminal act to the criminal — specifically, to the physical characteristics of the criminal. He was convinced that the major determinants of crime (or deviance) were biological — that there was a "born criminal type." These conclusions were based on a comparison of four hundred prison inmates with a group of Italian soldiers. Lombroso found that the prisoners displayed physical abnormalities such as deviations in head size and shape, eye defects, receding chins, and excessively long arms, which led him to believe that criminal tendencies are hereditary and that potential criminals could be recognized by certain physical characteristics or body types. Several years after Lombroso published his work, an English research team headed by Charles Goring published the results of a study comparing prisoners with a group of non-prisoners that included undergraduate students at Oxford and Cambridge. This study revealed practically no physical differences between the two groups. Goring's group concluded that "there is no such thing as a physical type." Nevertheless, Lombroso's findings were influential for many years.

Other research on biological factors followed. In the 1930s, the American anthropologist Ernest Hooton claimed that criminals were organically inferior to "normal" people (Vold, 1958). In the 1940s, William Sheldon attempted to link body type to behavior. He classified people into three categories — endomorphs, who are soft, round, and usually fat; mesomorphs, who are muscular, stocky, and athletic; and ectomorphs, who are skinny and fragile. A disproportionate percentage of criminals were found to be mesomorphs, but the reasons for this remained unclear.

More recently, considerable excitement has been generated by claims that a specific genetic condition may be associated with crimes of physical violence (Suchar, 1978). Some violent criminals have been found to have an extra Y chromosome: they have XYY chromosomes rather than the usual XY. Other findings, however, indicate that the great majority of XYY males have never been convicted of any crime, which suggests that the XYY factor is not a cause of deviance.

As you may have guessed, there are many problems with biological theories of crime, delinquency, and deviance, but the recent interest in the new science of sociobiology testifies to the continuing appeal of biological approaches. There are theories suggesting that sexual behaviors, both deviant and nondeviant, are biologically rooted, and that alcohol and drug abuse are caused by some chromosome component or genetic deficiency. Most of these explanations fail to explain, however, why others with a similar biological makeup do not exhibit the same forms of behaviors. In other words, biological explanations do not clearly differentiate the deviant from the nondeviant, and they fail to explain the tremendous variation in deviance as well as its relative nature. Today, most sociologists reject the notion that biology, heredity, or constitutional factors cause deviance.

Psychological Theories of Deviance

Like biological explanations, psychological theories tend to focus on the person who engages in deviant behavior. Some psychological

Some theories of deviance focus on biological explanations such as a chromosome component or genetic deficiency; others focus on psychological explanations such as personality traits, unconscious needs, or stress. For adults, joblessness may be defined as deviant, and collecting unemployment compensation may produce intense frustration and stress. Sociologists would claim that factors such as unemployment or stress must take into account the societal context and social processes both in defining what is deviant and in explaining it.

theories share with biological approaches the notion that the causes of behavior are rooted in a person's physiological or genetic makeup: instincts, needs, drives, and impulses. In psychological theories, however, the emphasis is on the mind rather than the body. These theories focus on such factors as personality structure, learning, goals, interests, motivations, willpower, frustration, anxiety, guilt, and other psychic conditions and responses. Social psychologists often consider the social context of behavior in addition to these factors.

Psychological theories often associate deviance with a sickness, arguing that deviance results from a psychological abnormality, a psychopathic personality, or a mental illness. This explanation, following the medical model described earlier, assumes that deviant behaviors such as alcoholism, child abuse, and crime are the consequences of mental illness. It is certainly true that mentally ill people may commit deviant acts, but this theory does not account for deviance among people who are not mentally ill, nor does it explain why some mentally ill people are not deviant.

Some psychological explanations suggest that deviance results from *frustration* and *aggression*. When needs are not fulfilled, frustration results, which in turn leads to aggression and often to antisocial, deviant behaviors. The greater the frustration, the more extreme the aggression. Frustration over the lack of money, the loss of a job, or a failure in love can lead to aggressive acts: speeding, child abuse, robbery, or even murder. One difficulty with this explanation is that frustration is defined so broadly that it includes almost any behavior. Another problem is that it does not account for people who are frustrated but do not act deviantly.

Other psychological explanations exist as well. Freudian theorists linked deviance with defects of the superego or conscience. People with weak egos were said to be unable to control their impulses, defer gratification, or adhere to planned, rational courses of action. Other theorists have associated deviance with such factors as motivation, intelligence, stress, unconscious needs, and personality traits.

In general, these psychological explanations are not very useful, because theories involving instinct and unconscious needs are extremely difficult if not impossible to test empirically. Explanations based on frustration and aggression or illness fail to differentiate the deviant from the nondeviant. Another major difficulty with most biological and psychological theories is that they ignore the relative nature of deviance: the influence of social context, variations in rates of deviance, and social responses to deviance. Several sociological theories, some of which incorporate psychological components, consider factors other than acts and actors.

Sociological Theories of Deviance

Sociological theories attempt to explain deviance by looking at sociocultural processes and organizational structures, although acts and actors are considered as well. Anomie theory, a structural-functional theory, focuses on value conflicts between culturally prescribed goals and socially approved ways of achieving them. Conflict theory contends that groups in power define the acts of the weaker groups as deviant in order to exploit them. Sociocultural learning theories are concerned with how people interact and learn deviance. Labeling theory regards deviance as a process of symbolic interaction and focuses on the meanings, definitions, and interpretations applied to people and acts. Control theories concentrate more on conformity than on deviance and deal with internal and external social controls that inhibit people's involvement in deviance.

Anomie Theory

In Chapter 2 we discussed Durkheim's conclusion that suicide is a social phenomenon related to a person's involvement in group life and membership in a cohesive social unit. Anomic suicide, he said, happens because of social and personal disorganization. People feel lost when the values of a society or group are confused or norms break down. Under most conditions, norms are clear and most people adhere to them, but during times of social turmoil people find themselves in unfamiliar situations. Making distinctions between the possible and the impossible, between desires and the fulfillment of those desires, becomes impossible. This condition of social normlessness is termed "anomie."

Merton (1957) extended Durkheim's explanation of anomie. His *anomie theory* suggests that deviance arises from the incongruence between a society's emphasis on attaining certain goals and the availability of legitimate, institutionalized means of reaching these goals. Such groups as the poor, teenagers, racial minorities, and blue-collar workers are constantly informed through education, the media, and friends that material success is an important goal, but legitimate means for achieving it are often unavailable. Thus, deviance is the result of a strain between a society's culture and its social structure, between culturally prescribed goals and the socially approved ways of achieving them.

Merton listed five ways that people adapt to the goals of a culture and the institutionalized means of achieving them (see Table 7-4). Only conformity to both the goals and the means is nondeviant. The other four methods of adaptations are all varieties of deviant behavior.

A second mode of adaptation is innovation. Innovators accept social goals but reject the nor-

Table 7-4

Merton's typology of modes of individual adaptation

MODES OF ADAPTATION	CULTURE GOALS	INSTITUTIONALIZED MEANS
I. *Conformity*	+	+
II. *Innovation*	+	−
III. *Ritualism*	−	+
IV. *Retreatism*	−	−
V. *Rebellion*	±	±

NOTE: In this typology Merton used the symbol + to signify "acceptance," − to signify "rejection," and ± to signify "rejection of prevailing values and substitution of new values."

SOURCE: Robert K. Merton, *Social Theory and Structure*, revised and enlarged ed. Copyright 1957, by The Free Press, a Corporation. Reprinted with permission of Macmillan Publishing Co., Inc.

matively prescribed means of achieving them. Students who want to get good grades are adhering to widely held values, but if they cheat, they are violating a norm.

A third mode of adaptation is ritualism. Ritualists follow rules rigidly without regard for the ends for which they were designed. The office manager who spends all his or her time making sure employees come to work on time, don't drink coffee at their desks, and don't make personal phone calls is a ritualist. By focusing on petty rules, he or she loses sight of the real goal of the office. Ritualists conform to traditions and never take chances. Merton suggests that lower-middle-class Americans are likely to be ritualists, because parents in this group pressure their children to compulsively abide by the moral mandates and mores of society. This form of adaptation is not generally considered a serious form of deviant behavior. People cling to safe routines and institutional norms, thereby avoiding dangers and frustrations that they feel are in-

Robert Merton explained deviance as the result of the strain that arises from an incongruence between the goals of a culture and the legitimate means of attaining them. Bag ladies, tramps, alcoholics, and psychotics are examples of deviants who neither conform to socially approved cultural goals nor have or use legitimate means for achieving them. These people are aliens in society and are viewed as social liabilities.

herent in the competition for major cultural goals.

Retreatism is a more drastic mode of adaptation. Retreatists such as tramps, psychotics, alcoholics, and drug addicts reject both the cultural goals and the institutional means. These people are truly aliens: they are in the society but not of it. They are members of their society only in that they live in the same place. Retreatism is probably the least common form of adaptation, and it is heartily condemned by conventional representatives of society. Retreatist deviants are widely regarded as a social liability. According to Merton (1957), this fourth mode of adaptation "is that of the socially disinherited who if they have none of the rewards held out by society also have few of the frustrations attendant upon continuing to seek these rewards" (p. 155).

The fifth and final mode of adaptation is rebellion. Rebels such as members of revolutionary movements withdraw their allegiance to a society they feel is unjust and seek to bring into being a new, greatly modified social structure. Most social movements such as the gay rights or women's liberation movements fall short of what Merton considered rebellion since these activists do not reject most societal goals. These movements do advocate substituting new values in certain parts of society, however. Merton suggests it is typically members of a rising class rather than the most depressed strata who organize the resentful and the rebellious into a revolutionary group.

Merton's theory has been criticized on a number of different grounds (Schur, 1979; Thio, 1978). Critics argue that it erroneously assumes that a single system of "cultural goals" is shared by the entire society. It has also been faulted for failing to explain why some people choose one response while others choose a different one. Another weakness is that certain types of deviance — rape, the behavior of hippies in the 1960s — do not neatly fall into any of his five modes of adaptation. Other critics argue that Merton's theory ignores the influence of societal reactions in the shaping of deviance and the fact that much perceived deviance involves collective rather than individual action. Finally, much criticism has been leveled at Merton's underlying assumption that deviance is disproportionately concentrated in the lower socioeconomic levels.

Anomic theory does have some strengths. It provides a framework for examining a wide range of social behavior, it has stimulated many research studies, and it has raised the social consciousness of deviance analysts. This last-mentioned point is particularly true of some members of the new generation of sociologists. These theorists have devised conflict theories of deviance that emphasize the widespread social oppression and basic contradictions found at the heart of our socioeconomic system.

Conflict Theory

Conflict theorists are the major critics of the assumption of the functionalist and anomie theories that a society shares a single set of values. *Conflict theory* contends that most societies contain many groups which have different, often conflicting, values and that the strongest groups in a society have the power to define the values of weaker groups as deviant. Conflict theorists emphasize the repression of the weak by the powerful, the exploitation of the masses by strong interest groups, and the influential and often wealthy groups who use laws, courts, and other agencies to oppose the interests and activities of lower socioeconomic groups and minorities. Most businesses exist to make a profit, and if in making a profit they (intentionally or nonintentionally) provide jobs, raise the level of personal gratification, and improve the community as well, little conflict may result. If, however, high taxes, high wages, fringe benefits, safety requirements, or pollution controls disrupt profits, then lobbying groups, political contributions, and media campaigns are used to influence legislation, taxation, and controls. Part-time workers may be used extensively to eliminate fringe ben-

efits. Women and blacks may be hired at lower wages than those paid to men and whites. Community tax incentives may be granted to sustain businesses or industries at the expense of the individual. The powerful exploit those with less power, and this exploitation by the elite produces racism, sexism, inequality, and institutionalized violence. The conflict between the powerful and the weak, therefore, influences both the creation of deviance and our response to it.

Chambliss (1969) contends that many legal scholars and social scientists are not even aware of this class domination. Most assume that the law is based on the consensus of its citizens, that it represents the public interest, and that it treats citizens as equal and serves the best interests of society. Conflict theorists, however, argue that the law means just that legal authorities *ought* to be fair and just. Chambliss and Seidman (1971) found that they are actually unfair and unjust, favoring the rich and powerful over the poor and weak. This condition exists, they say, not because law enforcement officials are cruel or evil but because they would antagonize members of the middle and upper classes if they arrested them for their white-collar offenses. These classes might then withdraw their support from law enforcement agencies, thus leading to loss of jobs.

Quinney (1979) and Spitzer (1975), who agree that deviance and deviants are defined and controlled by the powerful, go a step further and blame the lack of justice directly on the capitalist system. Drawing heavily from Marx, Spitzer contends that populations are considered deviant by capitalists when they disturb, hinder, or question any of the following: (1) capitalist modes of appropriating the products of human labor, (2) the social conditions under which capitalist production takes place, (3) patterns of distribution and consumption in capitalist society, (4) the socialization of productive and nonpro-

Conflict theorists contend that the legal authorities are controlled by the rich and powerful. The "A Team" is a television series that dipicts a Robin-Hood-type band who help those who are not powerful enough to be protected by traditional legal authorities.

ductive roles, or (5) the ideology that supports capitalist society.

According to the conflict perspective, definitions of deviance are determined largely by the dominant class, rates of deviance are determined primarily by the extent to which certain behaviors threaten dominant class interests, and control of deviance is in large part determined by the extent to which the powerful can socialize and reward those who follow their demands. Many conflict theorists perceive their theory as a call for political action to raise a revolutionary consciousness and end the oppression of the powerless by the powerful.

Like other theories, conflict theory has its critics, who fault it for not searching for the causes of deviant behavior. They also say it does not explain the crimes and deviances that are basically nonpolitical (vices, trivial deviations).

In addition, conflict theorists have been criticized for assuming that in the utopian Communist society murder, robbery, rape, and other crimes will disappear after the power to criminalize them is abolished.

Sociocultural Learning Theories

Sociocultural learning theories deal with the processes through which deviant acts are learned and the conditions under which learning takes place. Deviant behaviors are learned through essentially the same processes as other behaviors (see Chapter 6). Unlike anomie and conflict theories, sociocultural learning theories emphasize the groups people belong to and how they learn the norms prescribed by those groups. Three of these theories focus specifically on deviance: cultural transmission theory, differential association theory, and social learning theory.

Cultural transmission theory, sometimes called subculture theory, stems from the Chicago School of sociology described in Chapter 2. This theory suggests that when deviance is part of a subculture's cultural pattern, it is transmitted to newcomers through socialization. Shaw and McKay (1929) noted that high crime rates persisted in certain Chicago neighborhoods over several decades even though the areas changed in ethnic composition and other ways. When there is a tradition of deviance in a subculture, they suggested, the norms of that subculture are passed on by the gang, peer group, or play group during interaction with newcomers. As a result, they too become deviant, not by violating norms but by conforming to the norms of the subculture.

Other sociologists quickly picked up on the idea that deviance is transmitted culturally through learning and socialization. These scientists extended the theory, suggesting that people learn not only from gangs or peer groups but also from other agents of socialization: parents, teachers, church leaders, business colleagues, and others. A person could learn deviant attitudes by observing that people throw away parking tickets, keep incorrect change in a supermarket, or find ways to avoid paying taxes. One primary source of learning about deviance may be institutions designed to correct deviance, such as juvenile homes, detention centers, reformatories, prisons, and mental hospitals. Even people within these subcultures, however, are exposed to and learn conforming behaviors, so why are some people attracted to deviant behaviors while others are not?

Differential association theory was devised by Sutherland (1939; Sutherland and Cressey, 1970) to answer this question and explain how deviance and crime are culturally transmitted.

Sutherland attempted to determine why crime rates vary among different groups of people. Why is the crime rate higher in the city than the country, in impoverished areas than other areas? Why do more males than females, more young people than older people, commit crimes? Sutherland also wanted to explain why some individuals become criminals and others do not.

Differential association theory suggests that deviance results when individuals have more contact with groups that define deviance favorably than with groups that define it unfavorably. Sutherland contended that criminal behavior is learned rather than inherited or invented and that it takes place through verbal and nonverbal communications, primarily in intimate groups. Learning a criminal behavior involves acquiring a set of motives, drives, rationalizations, and attitudes, as well as specific techniques for committing the act itself. Sutherland did not believe that contact with criminals was necessary for a person to become deviant — exposure to definitions favoring deviance was sufficient, and the influence and frequency of these exposures vary from person to person. According to this theory, deviance is a learned behavior, a set of behaviors transmitted to people through their interactions with others.

Social learning theory is a revision of Sutherland's differential association theory in accordance with the principles of behavioral theory (Akers, 1977; Akers et al., 1979). Social learning theory suggests that deviant and conforming behavior are determined by the consequences — rewards or punishment — that follow them. This is known as operant or instrumental conditioning, whereby behavior is acquired through direct conditioning, through imitation, or through modeling the behavior of others. A behavior is strengthened by rewards (positive reinforcement) or the avoidance of punishment (negative reinforcement) and weakened by aversive stimuli (positive punishment) or loss of rewards (negative punishment). Akers et al. (1979) state that the acquisition and persistence of either deviant or conforming behavior are a function of what particular behaviors have been rewarded or punished, which is known as *differential reinforcement*. The norms and attitudes people learn from others, especially peers and family, are also influential.

Suppose, for example, that a fifteen-year-old, John, has just moved to a new neighborhood. Initially, he has no friends. One day, unhappy and lonely, he defies a teacher and gets into a violent argument with him. After class, several of his peers comment admiringly on the way he told the teacher off. The attention serves as positive reinforcement: John needs friends. He tells his mother what happened, but she says only that she wishes she could tell her boss to go to hell once in a while, which encourages John to think that his behavior is acceptable. He begins to deliberately provoke arguments with teachers, and gradually he gets a reputation as a rebel.

Girls begin to pay attention to him (positive reinforcement). Eventually, however, he is suspended from school for two weeks, which then deprives him of the attention of his friends (negative punishment). When he returns, he finds that his teachers have collectively decided to ask him to leave the room whenever he acts up, so he learns to be more cautious (negative reinforcement). He is also required to clean the bathrooms after school every time he gets into trouble (positive punishment). The positive reinforcement encouraged him to act in a mildly deviant fashion, but the negative punishment, negative reinforcement, and positive reinforcement encouraged him to conform to school standards. Eventually, he finds a level of disruption that maintains his reputation without forcing his teachers to try to change his behavior. Akers et al. (1979) assessed their social learning theory of deviant behavior with data on factors that influenced the drinking and drug use of three thousand adolescents. They found that alcohol and drug use were both positively correlated

Sutherland, in his differential association theory of deviance, suggested that criminal and deviant behaviors are learned in group interaction. Members of gangs, for example, socialize one another as to what type of behaviors are appropriate or inappropriate and what norms and laws can be violated.

with exposure to users and association with users. They also found that drug and alcohol use increased when it was reinforced more than punished and when use was defined positively or neutrally. Although differential association accounted for most of the adolescents' variations in drug and alcohol use, differential reinforcement, definitions, and imitation were also influential.

Sociocultural learning theories focus on how deviance is learned. Critics argue that these theories do not explain how deviance originated or how certain behaviors came to be defined as deviant. It has also been argued that they do not deal adequately with those who commit deviant acts in isolation rather than as part of a group. Furthermore, these theories are often difficult to test empirically without engaging in circular reasoning: deviance is caused by a tradition of deviance caused by earlier deviance. Another weakness is that it is very difficult to determine precisely what stimuli or learning experiences cause a person to initially commit a deviant instead of a conforming act. Nevertheless, sociocultural learning theories have contributed to our understanding of the nature of deviance.

Labeling Theory

The theories of deviance discussed so far have focused on deviant people, deviant acts, the process of learning deviance, and the causes of deviance. *Labeling theory* is concerned primarily with how certain behaviors are labeled "deviant" and how being given such a label influences a person's behavior.

Most labeling theorists interpret deviance in terms of symbolic interaction processes (see Chapter 2). Like other behaviors, deviant behavior is not regarded as a certain type of act undertaken by a person in isolation. It is, rather, a result of human interactions, people's interpretations and definitions of their own actions and those of others. As Kitsuse (1962) stated it,

"Forms of behavior *per se* do not differentiate deviants from non-deviants; it is the responses of the conventional and conforming members of the society who identify and interpret behavior as deviant which sociologically transform persons into deviants" (p. 253).

Note that, according to this perspective, deviance is a relative condition. It is not a certain type of act, it is the consequence of applying a certain label. As Becker (1963) noted, "Social groups create deviance by making the rules whose infraction constitutes deviance and by applying those rules to particular people and labeling them as outsiders" (p. 9). Thus if two people commit the same act, one might be labeled a deviant and the other might not, depending on the meaning given to the act by their social groups.

Edwin Lemert (1951), one of the first labeling theorists, identified two categories of deviance. Primary deviance involves behavior that violates social norms but is temporary and sporadic. Individuals who are involved in primary deviance do not regard themselves as deviant, nor are they regarded as such by those around them. Secondary deviance involves habitual violation of norms by individuals who not only consider themselves deviant but also are labeled deviant by others. Secondary deviance becomes a routine resulting in a label that leads to further deviance. Thus we have the development of a deviant career and a label that becomes a master status: cheat, prostitute, liar, and so on. Getting so labeled leads others to view you in terms of that deviant status, overlooking other qualities or statuses, and then other "career" options may become closed and you may have little choice but to live up to the label and behave accordingly. The behavior, for example, of a student who buys one term paper to turn in to his history professor might be primary deviance. If this student consistently cheated on tests and turned in papers that he had not written himself, his behavior would be considered deviant by his peers, his professors, and himself, and would therefore constitute secondary deviance.

Who labels whom? Speaking from the conflict perspective, Becker (1974) says: "A major element in every aspect of the drama of deviance is the imposition of definitions — of situations, acts, and people — by those powerful enough or legitimated to be able to do so" (p. 62). The labelers, therefore, would include such social control agents as police, judges, prison guards, and psychiatrists, whereas the labeled would include criminals, delinquents, drug addicts, prostitutes, mental patients, and others. Generally, rich, white, or powerful people are more likely to apply labels and the poor, blacks, and the powerless are more likely to be labeled. A poor or black person is more apt to be arrested, prosecuted, and convicted than a rich or a white person for committing the same act. Data from the U.S. Bureau of the Census, for example, showed that approximately 10.1 million arrests took place in 1982. While blacks constituted 11.9 percent of the population, they were involved in approximately 28 percent of the arrests (*Statistical Abstract: 1984*, no. 302, p. 183). Of the total number of jail inmates, 41 percent were black (no. 324, p. 194). Of the prisoners under sentence of death, 42.5 percent were nonwhite (no. 331, p. 196). Similar statistics show a higher arrest, prosecution, and conviction rate among men, the young, the less educated, and the poor. In 1978, for example, 94 percent of all jail inmates were male, 72 percent were under thirty years of age, 61 percent had less than twelve years of schooling, 49 percent had no prearrest income or a prearrest income of under $3,000, and 87 percent had a prearrest income of under $10,000 (no. 324, p. 194).

What are the consequences of labeling? According to theorists, being labeled deviant has negative consequences because labeled people

Sociologists indicate that certain groups or categories of persons are more likely to be defined as deviant than others. Males, teenagers, the poor, blacks and other minority persons are disproportionately represented in arrests, convictions, and imprisonment.

tend to see themselves as deviant, which leads them to continue their so-called deviant behavior (Thio, 1978, p. 58). The application of a label may therefore play a part in originating and continuing deviant behavior. Ridicule, humiliation, harassment, or imprisonment may also result from labeling. Labeled people may no longer be treated as respectable parents, teachers, or community members; they may lose their jobs, be rejected by friends, or be sent to a prison or mental hospital. Responses of this sort often push labeled people further into the deviant activity. Ex-convicts who cannot get jobs may return to robbery or drug dealing. Those labeled as mentally ill lose many of the social supports necessary for mental health. Drug addicts, alcoholics, and prostitutes may turn to others who share the same label for support and companionship, which leads them to organize their lives around their deviance.

Although it is accepted by many sociologists, labeling theory has its critics. It does not explain the causes of deviance, nor can it be used to predict who will be labeled and in what contexts. Like other symbolic interaction theories, labeling theory is difficult to test empirically. Another criticism is one that also applies to conflict theory: If the powerful create and impose the deviant label, how is it possible that powerful people are also labeled deviant? Critics have also questioned the extent to which deviance encourages rather than deters deviant behavior. Finally, are all persons in prisons or mental hospitals there simply because someone chose to label them, or are some behaviors so disruptive that severe sanctions such as institutionalization must be imposed to maintain social order? Other social consequences of deviance are discussed in the next section.

The Social Consequences of Deviance

As we stated in our discussion of structural-functional theory in Chapter 2, social systems are composed of many parts, which exist because they perform some function in the maintenance of the system. Any part of a social system may be dysfunctional in some respects, but the part continues to exist because it performs a function that leads to the maintenance and stability of the system. Also, as we stated earlier in this chapter, deviance is universal — it exists in all societies and therefore it seems logical to assume that deviance continues to exist because it serves certain functions in the maintenance of societies.

Social Functions of Deviance

The notion that deviance may have positive effects runs counter to the traditional views described earlier. According to these views, deviance is harmful, immoral, antisocial, a sickness in society. Deviance is not merely a sickness, however; it is part of the nature of all social systems. It has also been traditionally regarded as evidence of social disorganization, but many deviant subcultures such as gangs, organized crime, prostitution, or police corruption may be found in highly organized societies and be highly organized themselves. Durkheim pointed out as early as 1894 that deviations should be regarded as a normal part of a society (Kelly, 1979). It appears that deviance performs various social functions, some of which are described below.

Deviance helps define the limits of social tolerance. By indicating the extent to which norms can be violated without provoking a reaction, it helps clarify the boundaries of social norms and the limits of behavioral diversity. Methods of social control such as arrests, psychiatric counseling, criminal trials, and social ostracism help define these limits. Arrests and trials indicate to the public the seriousness of certain deviations and the extent to which violations of norms are tolerated. Driving 57 miles per hour when the speed limit is 55, for example, is tolerated by police, and driving 60 usually is tolerated, but driving 80 or 100 is likely to lead to punishment. Spanking a child may be acceptable, but a parent who injures a child can be arrested. By observing societal reactions to deviance, members learn the limits of acceptable variation from norms.

Deviance can increase the solidarity and integration of a group. Such a label can unite the people who share it. Certain deviants find emotional support and a sense of community among others who share their values and behavior patterns. Student protesters, homosexuals, and members of religious cults and other subcultures tend to defend and protect one another and derive their identities from their deviant group. By the same token, highly integrated groups may form in an attempt to defeat or eliminate deviants — having a common enemy tends to unite group members.

Deviance can serve as a "safety valve" for social discontent. When people desire things that the social norms do not permit them to have, they may become frustrated and angry and attack norms or even attempt to destroy the social system. Certain types of deviance permit people to escape from conventional norms and rid themselves of frustration without disrupting the social system as a whole. Cheating on one's income tax may be an outlet for frustration with government spending on wasteful projects or with being underpaid. The use of illegal drugs may be a safety valve against job frustrations or a poor marriage. Income tax cheating and drug use involve risk to individuals, but they may prevent expressions of frustration more injurious to society. Thus they tend to indirectly support such basic institutions as marriage, the economy, and the government. By funneling off anger and discontent, deviance may remove some of the strain produced by social mores.

Deviance can indicate defects or inadequacies in the existing social organization and bring about changes. High rates of certain kinds of deviance may expose problems in the social order. Large numbers of parking violations may indi-cate that there is not enough parking space. Outbreaks of violence in prison serve as a warning that the system is inadequate. Activities such as freedom marches by blacks in the South, the burning of draft cards by young men in the 1960s, and the hunger strikes of IRA members in Ireland were organized acts of defiance (and deviance) intended to force leaders and the public to address perceived problems in the social system. Another functional aspect of deviance, therefore, is that it can set in motion steps that lead to social change, and these changes can occur in many different forms. They can involve modifications in the existing structure, modifications in behavior, or changes in the definitions of deviance. Until the early 1960s, a black person who tried to sit in the front of a bus in Alabama was regarded as deviant. Following court cases and rulings against segregation, this behavior is no longer considered deviant. As social norms change, so do their definitions, and folkways and mores may be modified as a consequence of deviant acts.

Social Dysfunctions of Deviance

Some consequences of deviance are dysfunctional: they can disrupt, destabilize, or lead to the complete breakdown of a social system. Given the range of tolerance of norm violations, isolated instances of deviance generally have little effect on the stability of systems. Widespread, long-term, and more extreme norm violations can impair the functioning of groups or entire systems.

Deviance can disrupt the social order. Violations of norms can disturb the status quo, make social life unpredictable, and create tension and conflict. Teachers who refuse to teach, parents who ignore their children, or workers who fail to do their appointed tasks can keep the system from functioning smoothly. The effect of an alcoholic father on a family system is a good example. The family's income may decrease, the wife may have to assume full responsibility for raising the children, and the children may be ashamed to bring friends home. All routines are subject to being disturbed by him. Deviance is often dysfunctional because it disrupts the order and predictability of life.

Deviance can disrupt the will of others to conform. If norm violations are unpunished or if members of society refuse to obey established rules, the desire to conform is decreased. Studying for an exam may seem pointless if you know other students are going to cheat. Obeying the speed limit can be frustrating if other drivers blow their horns to get you out of the way so they can speed by. To work hard when others are lazy, to be honest when others are dishonest, or to obey the rules when others ignore them can make one's efforts seem pointless. When deviance and conformity are not differentiated, deviance disappears. If they receive the same response or reward, what is the motivation to conform? Conformity to a given norm, rule, or law makes sense only if (1) others conform as well, (2) those who conform are differentiated from those who do not in some way, or (3) norm violators receive some type of punishment. Deviance that erodes the desire to follow rules and conform to social norms is dysfunctional.

Deviance can destroy trust. Social life is based in part on the assumption that other people are honest and trustworthy. When interpersonal trust decreases, people become more dependent on the legal system to define, interpret, support, and enforce the law. If all car dealers (or car buyers) were honest, written contracts would not be necessary and a few judges and lawyers would be out of work. In this sense, deviance is functional for the legal system, but it is dysfunctional to the society as a whole. Widespread deviance, just as it disrupts the will to conform, destroys our confidence and trust in others.

Deviance diverts resources that could be used elsewhere into social rehabilitation and control efforts. It may be functional in that it provides thousands of jobs for those who rehabilitate and control criminals, drug addicts, the mentally ill, and others, but it is dysfunctional in that the money used to deal with deviance cannot be used for other constructive and productive purposes. Criminal activities alone cost billions of dollars every year. Most would agree that these funds could be used more profitably elsewhere.

Clearly, deviance is neither all good nor all bad. Some of its consequences lead to the stability and maintenance of the system, others tend to disrupt it. Whatever the case, it is here to stay, an inevitable part of every society.

Deviance and Crime

We have defined deviance as variations from a set of norms or shared social expectations. A *crime* is a violation of criminal statutory law, and a specific punishment applied by some governmental authority generally accompanies the violation. Many types of deviance, such as rape, robbery, murder, and prostitution, are criminal acts; other types of deviance, such as mental disorders, wearing unusual clothes, or swallowing goldfish are not. Just as definitions of deviance vary from group to group, crime rates and criminal activities vary in different legal jurisdictions and with different rates of enforcement. A decade ago, for example, it was legally impossible for a man to rape his wife. Today, many states have amended their rape laws to make the relationship between the rapist and the victim irrelevant.

Accurate estimates of crime rates are difficult to make because a high percentage of most

Private Violence

What might be called public violence is as American as assassinations, mob wars and mass murders, the stuff of screaming headlines and periodic national soul searching. What might be called private violence, what people who know each other, even profess to love each other, do to each other, is a nightmarish realm only beginning to be forthrightly explored. Its particular horror stems from its violations of the trust upon which all intimate human relations depend: it is cruelty exercised on those nearest, most vulnerable, least able or inclined to defend themselves from their attackers.

Public violence, at least, can be neatly tallied. The FBI is aware of exactly 22,516 murders committed in the U.S. in 1981, a fifth of them killings of loved ones, and that is very close to the true total. Even the Government accounting of motor-vehicle thefts, 1,073,998 for 1981, is almost right, since victims cannot get their insurance money unless they file a police report. But when statisticians turn to private violence, the numbers become iffy, approximate in the extreme. Are there 650,000 cases of child abuse annually, or a million? Or 6 million? Bona fide experts, extrapolating and just guessing, variously cite all those figures and others. It

is said that every year 2 million women are beaten by their husbands, and it is also said that nearly 6 million are. Pick your figure. A Justice Department survey counted 178,000 rapes during 1981, but for every woman who reported a rape to the police, perhaps nine or maybe 25 did not. It is beyond dispute, however, that extraordinary numbers of women and children are being brutalized by those closest to them.

The uncertainty about the scope of private violence is a function of shame, of hushing up. Such crimes, unlike slashings or shootings on sidewalks and in taverns, often leave a victim more hurt and humiliated than outraged. Historically, beatings by one's husband, like rapes, were bad enough to suffer but more shameful still to reveal publicly. Childrearing, no matter how harshly executed, was an entirely private matter.

Today, the dirty secrets are no longer being kept. Victims of private violence are talking — to police, prosecutors, counselors, friends, one another — and U.S. society is trying to help. Private violence is becoming less private. Thus, while reports of child abuse in Florida, for example, rose from 35,301 in 1981 to 45,704 last year, such apparent increases may be due mostly to authorities' finding

out about more of the violence. Betty Friedan, the feminist author, believes that attacks on women are not necessarily on the rise, just coming out of the shameful murk: "Women don't tolerate it any more because they know it's all right to speak up."

There is no place so violent as home. About half of all rapes occur there. It is in the privacy of the home, both in cramped flats and in grand neocolonials, that women are pummeled by husbands and boyfriends. It was in his home in Houston a few years ago, for instance, that Second-Grader Daniel Brownell, whose stepfather's attacks had left him paralyzed and permanently senseless, was found branded with cigarette burns that spelled I CRY. One remarkable Connecticut woman named Carol,* 38, who is a volunteer counselor of imprisoned rapists, knows freakishly well that home is not necessarily a haven: it was in her childhood home in the early 1950s that she was the victim of incest, at a friend's home that a half-dozen men gang-raped her, in her very own home that her second husband beat the living daylights out of her again and again.

Out on the street, at least, one's guard is up. Muggers who demand money are, in a sense, just conducting a cutthroat business. Most of the time they do not lay claims on their victims' humanity. Home is meant to be life's one warm, safe place. Violence committed there, especially by somebody understood to be a guardian (husband, father, mother, uncle, babysitter), is a special betrayal. And once brawling becomes routine in a household, or primal taboos are cracked, there is often no stopping the spread of viciousness. Richard Gelles, a sociologist at the University of Rhode Island, describes the grim ecology of a violent family: "The husband will beat the wife. The wife may then learn to beat the children. The bigger siblings learn it's O.K. to hit the little ones, and the family pet may be the ultimate recipient of violence."

The worst thing about family violence is its natural reproduction of itself, like a poisonous plant sending out spores. Most rapists were preyed upon sexually as children, and most violent criminals were raised in violent homes. Children of punched-out women, accustomed to seeing family business transacted with fists, are prone to become battered wives and battering husbands themselves. Worse, battered children grow up predisposed to batter their own offspring. Sexually abused boys often become pedophiles and rapists, while sexually victimized girls, perennial targets, are likelier to become battered wives. Bruce Ritter, a Roman Catholic priest, runs a shelter for teen-age runaways and castoffs in the neon squalor of Manhattan's Times Square. "The girls who walk in off the streets with babies abuse them," Father Ritter says. "If a two-week-old baby is crying, the mother will slap the baby. We try to teach her not to do that."

Yet there are important distinctions between and within the three main genres of private violence. Slapping a spouse is different from shaking a child — an adult can more easily understand, fight back or flee — and both are very unlike rape. Of the three, rape is most unequivocally a statutory crime, and probably every rapist ought to be locked up for some time. They are real criminals. Of course, a parent who willfully scalds a child's arm is a criminal. Of course, a man who stomps his pregnant wife is a criminal. These cases are, ironically, the easiest ones to think about: when the violence is so ugly and utterly inexcusable, you just throw the book at the sick bastards.

But most cases of private violence are closer calls. What to do about a man who rapes his wife? What about the fights between spouses that are not pat, villain-and-victim episodes? What about Darrel Trueblood of Terre Haute, Ind., whose son Travis was taken from him for three months in 1980 because the father had punished him with the thwack of a ruler? Greg Dixon, a Baptist minister and head of Indiana's Moral Majority, says Trueblood was "just giving a normal whipping." Says he: "Reasonable people can detect whether it's assault and battery or not."

In most of the rest of the world, private violence is not considered a high-priority social problem. Not that punch-ups at home are any less prevalent. Rather, as a Thai social worker says, "it's so common that no one thinks it's a problem." If anything, victims abroad are more explicitly shamed into silence, with the legal and medical systems often oblivious. In most countries a man's home is practically his personal free-fire zone, off limits to busybodies. And the U.S. has far and away more shelters and programs where victims can find solace and help. But the vast array of American services is to meet a vast terror: a woman's chances of being raped in the U.S., for instance, are five or ten times as great as in Western Europe.

The U.S. cannot afford to get smug. Not all American victims are getting help, or even sympathy. "As a society," says sociologist Gelles of private violence, "we laugh at this behavior." We should not. But indeed, such behavior is not so completely unthinkable that decent folks do not chuckle when Jackie Gleason's Ralph Kramden angrily threatens to sock his ever-loving wife. "I'm gonna send you to the moon," he barks on *The Honeymooners*, his clenched fist waving. "To the *moon*, Alice."

* Those referred to by only their first names have been given pseudonyms at their request.

SOURCE: Kurt Anderson, *Time* magazine, Sept. 5, 1983, copyright 1983 Time Inc. All rights reserved. Reprinted by permission from *Time*.

Figure 7-1.
Crime clock, 1982

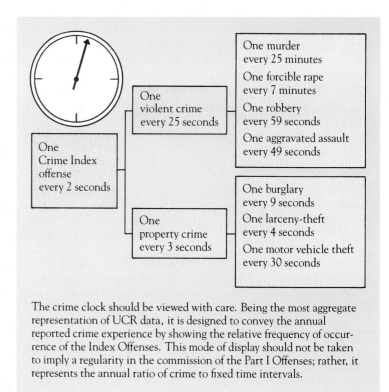

One Crime Index offense every 2 seconds

One violent crime every 25 seconds

One property crime every 3 seconds

One murder every 25 minutes

One forcible rape every 7 minutes

One robbery every 59 seconds

One aggravated assault every 49 seconds

One burglary every 9 seconds

One larceny-theft every 4 seconds

One motor vehicle theft every 30 seconds

The crime clock should be viewed with care. Being the most aggregate representation of UCR data, it is designed to convey the annual reported crime experience by showing the relative frequency of occurrence of the Index Offenses. This mode of display should not be taken to imply a regularity in the commission of the Part I Offenses; rather, it represents the annual ratio of crime to fixed time intervals.

crimes go undetected and unreported. Even crimes like murder in which the body of a victim can serve as evidence present classification problems. Official data on crime in the United States are collected by the Federal Bureau of Investigation and reported in a yearly volume entitled *Uniform Crime Reports*. The statistics are gathered from over 15,000 city, county, and state law enforcement agencies that voluntarily report data on criminal offenses. The crimes recorded in the FBI Reports are divided into two categories. One includes violent crimes such as murder, forcible rape, robbery and aggravated assault. The other category includes property crimes such as burglary, larceny of $50 and over, motor

vehicle theft, and arson. Nearly 13 million of these crimes were known to be committed in 1982. The famous FBI "Crime Clock" for 1982 shown in Figure 7-1 is one dramatic way of illustrating how frequently certain offenses are committed.

It is estimated that more than half of all serious crimes do not show up in official statistics, and a much higher percentage of the less serious ones go both undetected and unreported. Surveys asking people if they have been victims of crimes or asking them if they have committed various criminal acts show the incidence of crime to be much higher than that officially reported. These surveys also reveal a discriminatory bias in the legal system: certain groups of people are far more likely to be caught and punished for their crimes than others. Young people, blacks, persons from a lower socioeconomic status, and disadvantaged groups in general are more likely to be picked up by police, have their cases reported, be arrested, and be punished.

Biases in the legal system are also evident in the way the legal system handles certain types of crime. The term "white-collar crime" was coined by Edwin H. Sutherland (1940), who noted that certain crimes are committed by persons of "respectability" and high social status in the course of their occupations and daily business activities. Embezzlement by bankers, illegal sales and use of narcotics by physicians, and defrauding clients of securities by lawyers are crimes of this sort. Recently, white-collar crime has come to include offenses by businesses and corporations as well as individuals. Crimes of this nature include consumer fraud, stock manipulation, income tax evasion, misrepresentation in advertising, and bribery. These types of offenses, while costing billions of dollars yearly, are usually dealt with by federal and state regulatory agencies rather than criminal courts, and the offenders are more likely to receive fines than prison sentences.

Organized crime consists of groups expressly organized to carry out illegal activities: the distribution of drugs, the operation of a gambling business, or loan sharking (lending money at excessively high rates), for example. Some consider organized crime to be the tightly knit national organization variously called the Mafia, Cosa Nostra, the syndicate, or the mob; others use the term more loosely to cover any group of organized professional criminals who maintain control of a large-scale illegal business enterprise. In either case, the organization has a strict hierarchy, ranging from the "lords of the underworld" who make the important decisions and direct the activities to those at the lower levels who follow

John DeLorean, who was aquitted in the fall of 1984, had been accused of trafficking in cocaine. A former executive of General Motors, he was owner of a sports car manufacturing company in Ireland when he was charged by the FBI. Because of his social status, his trial attracted considerable attention in the media.

SOCIOLOGISTS AT WORK
Redirecting Juvenile Offenders

Linda Myers is a juvenile probation officer with the Geauga County Juvenile Court in Chardon, Ohio. "According to my job description," says Myers, "I see to it that juvenile offenders placed on probation follow the orders of the court. In fact, my job involves much more than that." Myers works with not only her probationers but also their families and teachers to gain insights into how the probationers interact with those around them — from authority figures to peers — and to formulate the most effective programs for helping the offenders overcome their deviant behavior.

After completing her bachelor's degree at Lake Erie College with a concentration in sociology and psychology, Myers was hired as an intake officer with the Geauga County Juvenile Court. As intake officer she screened incoming complaints against juveniles, conducted home and school investigations, and provided the judge with a social history of the juvenile as well as a recommendation on the handling of the case. Myers' sociological background in family systems and relationships helped her objectively assess home environments and their effect on the adolescents brought to court.

Although Myers' bachelor's degree also qualified her for her next job — the county typically hires bachelor's-level sociologists as probation officers — she decided to pursue a master's degree in applied sociology at Kent State University. She credits the program with giving her a greater understanding of social systems and social agencies, how they work and interact. At Kent she explored the "diversity of programs offered by the human services along with the organizational framework of such institutions and the numerous roles available to sociologists within the social services." This training is particularly useful to her in directing her probationers to the community services and agencies that she feels best fit their needs.

As part of her master's program, Myers also undertook an internship in which she investigated one of her main concerns — the relationship between substance abuse and the variety of offenses for which juveniles are brought to court. Geauga County's high recidivism rate — 48 per-

the orders. Those at the lower levels, who deal directly with the public, are the ones who get caught, but they often get released through the leader's connections with the police, judges, or relevant professionals. Organized crime groups maintain control through threats, intimidation, bribery, and, when necessary, violence. Most deviance is not controlled by such severe means, however. It should also be noted that certain types of control exist in all societies in order to encourage people to conform to social norms.

Deviance and Social Control

The fact that deviance is universal and sometimes has positive social functions does not eliminate the need to control it. If societies are to survive, they must have ways of making people

cent of juvenile offenders end up in court two or more times — convinced her that treatment was often misdirected toward an obvious offense like truancy while ignoring a more serious cause — drug abuse. Her study revealed that indeed 69 percent of juvenile offenses were drug-related. One thirteen-year-old girl, for example, was found guilty of unruliness, as charged by her parents who could not control her, and placed on probation. According to her social history, she had been involved in increasingly serious offenses since the age of ten — running away, truancy, shoplifting, and assault and battery. No one before Myers recognized the possibility of drug abuse as the problem. The girl had denied it vehemently and her parents agreed, pointing out that she didn't even smoke cigarettes. At one point, however, the girl asked Myers, "Do you think I'm insane?" "No," was Myers' response, "but I'm convinced you're on drugs." Shocked by Myers' detection of the problem, the girl admitted she'd been taking drugs for three years. Subsequent testing revealed that she was chemically addicted and only then did she begin receiving treatment.

Myers currently has a caseload of fifty-three female offenders, who are expected to obey a set of standardized rules, such as observing a curfew, making restitution in cases of vandalism, and not associating with others on probation. In addition, Myers and her probationers formulate an individualized set of goals and agree to the terms of a behavior contract that might include regular school attendance, involvement in at least one extracurricular activity, or doing chores at home. Myers also strongly believes in clearly defining the consequences of violating the agreement — from a warning to a return to court and possible incarceration.

Myers maintains close contact with her probationers through weekly meetings. At least half of each day she visits homes and schools, talking to parents, teachers, and friends to gain ongoing insights into her probationers' environment, progress, and needs. As she points out, however, "Crises have a way of not occurring between 8:30 and 4:30, and I spend many evening and weekend hours on the phone trying to defuse explosive situations." The long hours, however, are a price Myers is willing to pay to develop the close, supportive relationship through which she can best help her probationers and that often lasts long after the official relationship has ended.

Myers feels she will continue to work within the court system for some time. Her future may involve a private practice or involvement in preventive approaches to delinquency. Whatever she chooses, she is convinced her sociological training will continue to serve her well.

conform to social norms. Control is maintained by encouraging conformity, not by directly discouraging deviance; the absence of motivation to conform results in deviance.

Conformity to social norms is generally explained in terms of two social control processes. *Internal controls* cause members of society themselves to want to conform to the norms of society. *External controls* are pressures or sanctions that are applied to members by others. The two types of control tend to operate simultaneously.

Internal Controls of Deviance

Internal controls are those that exist within the particular individual's moral and social codes of behavior. They include a wide range of factors: positive self-image, self-control, ego strength, high frustration tolerance, and a sense of social responsibility, among others. The workings of internal controls can be explained in part by the socialization theories discussed in Chapter 6. These theories explained how we internalize norms, learn the expectations of others, and develop a desire to conform to them. Some types of deviance, such as criminality and mental illness, are widely believed to be caused by inadequate socialization, especially in the years of early childhood.

Most social control is directly related to a person's social self — our definitions of who we are in relation to the society we live in. Internal motivations to conformity result not from a fear of being caught or fear of punishment but because people have been socialized to see themselves in a certain way and to believe that stealing, cheating, murder, and certain other behaviors are wrong. In a study of deterrents to shoplifting, for example, Kraut (1976) concluded as follows: "People's definitions of themselves and of deviant behavior seem to act as internal constraints on shoplifting. When respondents explained why they hadn't stolen the last time they bought an item in a store, the two most important reasons they gave were their own honesty and their belief that shoplifting was unacceptable behavior" (p. 365).

Our feelings about right and wrong are sometimes referred to as our conscience. The saying "Let your conscience be your guide" assumes that you have internalized certain notions about deviant and nondeviant behavior. For most people, the conscience develops as a direct result of socialization experiences in early childhood and later in one's life. Social institutions such as the family and religion are significant in internalizing social norms. Once social norms are internalized, deviations produce feelings of guilt, remorse, or conflict. The relatively high prevalence of conformity in comparison to deviance is due largely to internal controls.

External Controls of Deviance

External controls are those that come from outside an individual. They can be either informal or formal. *Informal external controls* involve peers, friends, parents, or the other people one associates with regularly, who apply pressure to encourage one to obey the rules and conform to social expectations. The same techniques can be used to encourage conformity to deviant norms. In the shoplifting study just mentioned, Kraut (1976) found that external constraints are also very important and that informal sanctions are a stronger deterrent than formal sanctions. Shoplifting was strongly correlated with the subjects' perception of their friends' involvement in and approval of shoplifting. In other words, subjects whose friends shoplifted or approved of it were more apt to shoplift than subjects whose friends disapproved of it, which suggests that friends have a powerful influence on the acceptance or rejection of deviant behavior.

Informal social controls have been found to be the major cause of the low rates of alcoholism found among Jews. Glassner and Berg (1980) found that American Jews avoid alcohol problems through four protective social processes: (1) they associate alcohol abuse with non-Jews; (2) they learn moderate drinking norms, practices, and symbolism during childhood through religious and secular rituals; (3) they form adult relationships primarily with other moderate drinkers; and (4) they use a repertoire of techniques to avoid excessive drinking under social pressure. These techniques included reprimands by the spouse, developing reputations as nondrinkers by making jokes, avoiding many drinking situations, and finding rationalizations for not drinking. Alcoholism is a common form of deviance, but the low rate of alcoholism among Jews indicates that informal social controls can exert a powerful influence in controlling it.

Formal external controls, the systems created by society specifically to control deviance, are probably the least influential. Courts, police officers, and prisons are formal external controls. Unlike internal controls and informal external controls, formal controls are supposed to be impersonal and just. In actuality, however, the legal system tends to favor certain groups of people, as conflict theory suggests. Even in prisons, guards tend to overlook rule violations by certain prisoners and enforce rules with others. The discretionary power of police officers, prosecutors, judges, and other officials in arresting, prosecuting, and convicting people is often used arbitrarily. It may be highly dependent on factors other than deviance per se. Age, race, sex, social status, prior deviations, and other factors have all been shown to affect the nature and outcome of formal control mechanisms.

Summary

Deviance is universal, and every society has people who commit acts defined as exceeding the tolerance limits of social norms. There are several traditional views of deviance. The absolutist view assumes that certain acts or people are deviant in all contexts and at all times. Deviance has also been seen as immoral, evil, and antisocial. According to the medical model, deviance is evidence that a society is unhealthy. A statistical model defines deviance as any behavior that varies from the average or mode.

The relativistic view, a more sociological perspective, assumes that deviance can be defined only in the context of the society or group in which it takes place. Deviance is not thought to be a certain type of act. It is, rather, a relative condition that varies according to time, place, situation, and social status. This view takes into account the great diversity of meanings that can

be associated with people or acts in different situations.

Many theories have been developed to explain who is deviant, the causes of deviance, and how it can be controlled or modified. Biological theories have attempted to associate it with body type, physical abnormalities, and chromosome aberrations. Psychological theories emphasize such factors as personality, motivation, willpower, frustration, aggression, and ego strength. Sociological theorists do not ignore biological and psychological factors, but they tend to view theories based on these factors as insufficient. Sociological theories focus on the interactional, organizational, and social normative factors through which people learn definitions of deviance. These factors also determine people's behavior, which a social audience labels as either deviant or nondeviant.

Anomie theory links deviance to conflicts between culturally valued goals and institutionalized means of achieving them. Innovation, ritualism, retreatism, and rebellion are deviant modes of adaptation.

Conflict theorists say that definitions of deviance are devised by the powerful to repress and exploit the weak. An influential, wealthy elite is assumed to oppose and control the powerless, the poor, and minorities.

Sociocultural learning theories, which are basically both social and psychological in nature, emphasize the processes through which deviant acts are learned and the types of conditions under which they are learned. Cultural transmission theory, sometimes called subculture theory, explains the continuity of crime and deviance in certain geographical areas as the result of the transmission of deviant norms from one generation to the next. Differential association theory contends that deviance is learned through verbal and nonverbal communication. According to this theory, we learn either deviant or nondeviant attitudes and behaviors by associating differentially with deviant or nondeviant individuals and groups. The social learning theory of deviance, which draws heavily on differential association theory, suggests that operant (instrumental) conditioning and imitation play important roles in the learning of behaviors. Differential rewards and punishments and exposure to conforming or deviant models greatly influence whether we develop deviant or conforming attitudes and behaviors.

Labeling theory, rather than emphasizing acts or individuals in isolation, focuses on why certain people and acts are singled out as deviant and also on the effects of being labeled deviant. This approach, which is based on the principles of symbolic interaction, assumes that defining deviance and other behaviors is a collective process. People in social contexts define and interpret their own behavior and that of others and apply labels on the basis of their definitions. These labels have a significant effect on the continuation of deviant behavior for both those defined as deviant and the audience who labels them.

Deviance can influence social systems in several different ways. Some of the consequences are functional: they can help define the limits of social tolerance, increase the solidarity and integration of groups, indicate inadequacies in the system, and bring about constructive change. Other consequences are dysfunctional: deviance can disrupt the social order, decrease the will of others to conform, destroy trust, and divert resources that could be used elsewhere into social rehabilitation and control efforts.

Deviance differs from crimes in that crimes are violations of criminal statutory law. Rates of criminal activity are published annually by the Federal Bureau of Investigation in its *Uniform Crime Reports*, but offenses are widely underreported. Two types of crime that are generally not reported are white-collar crime and organized crime. The former is committed by higher-status persons or by businesses and organizations in the course of their daily activities. The latter involves a group organized with the expressed intent of carrying out illegal activities.

The control of deviance is generally explained in terms of two factors, internal controls and external controls. Internal controls, which are exerted by individuals on themselves, involve such factors as self-concept, ego strength, high frustration tolerance, and conscience. These controls are believed to be acquired through socialization. External controls include both informal interactions with people, such as family and friends, and formal controls, which are carried out by the agencies designated by society to maintain law and order.

Key Terms

absolutist view
anomie theory
conflict theory
crime
cultural transmission theory
deviance
differential association theory
differential reinforcement
external controls
formal external controls
frustration, aggression
informal external controls
internal controls
labeling theory
medical view
moral view
organized crime
relativistic view
social learning theory
sociocultural learning theories
statistical view

Suggested Readings

Becker, Howard S. **Outsiders: Studies in the Sociology of Deviance.** *New York: The Free Press, 1963.* This is one of the pioneering works of labeling theory applied specifically to marijuana use and the careers of dance musicians.

Douglas, Jack D. and Frances Chopert Waksler. **The Sociology of Deviance: An Introduction.** *Boston: Little, Brown, 1982.* An examination of a broad range of sociological theories that have been developed to explain deviance and the application of these theories to selected varieties of deviance.

Ferrell, Ronald A. and Victoria L. Swigert. **Deviance and Social Control.** *Glenview, Ill.: Scott, Foresman, 1982.* An interpretation of the major classic and contemporary theories of deviance and social control, emphasizing structural, interactional, and social-psychological influences.

Goode, Erich. **Deviant Behavior: An Interactional Approach.** *Englewood Cliffs, N.J.: Prentice-Hall, 1978.* A textbook covering deviance from an interactionist-labeling perspective.

Reid, Sue Titus. **Crime and Criminology, 3d ed.** *New York: Holt, Rinehart and Winston, 1982.* A textbook on crime including explanations of criminal behavior, the criminal justice system, and corrections.

Rosenberg, M. Michael, Robert A. Stebbins, and Alan Turowetz (eds.). **The Sociology of Deviance.** *New York: St. Martin's Press, 1982.* Eleven essays covering deviant careers, subcultures, power, conflict, social control, social change, and trends in deviance research.

Rubington, Earl and Martin S. Weinberg. **Deviance: The Interactionist Perspective, 4th ed.** *New York: Macmillan, 1981.* A collection of forty readings on the interactionist approach to deviance.

Schur, Edwin M. **Interpreting Deviance: A Sociological Introduction.** *New York: Harper & Row, 1979.* A systematic, comprehensive textbook on the interpretation of deviance.

Schur, Edwin M. **Labeling Women Deviant: Gender, Stigma, and Social Control.** *New York: Random House, 1984.* A sociological perspective of deviance, emphasizing the labeling process as applied to women.

Shoemaker, Donald J. **Theories of Delinquency.** *New York: Oxford University Press, 1984.* An integrative and comparative discussion of several theories of delinquency, individualistic as well as sociological.

Thio, Alex. **Deviant Behavior, 2d ed.** *Boston: Houghton Mifflin, 1983.* A textbook covering theories of deviance with a substantive analysis of murder, rape, robbery, prostitution, homosexuality, suicide, swinging, drug use, alcoholism, and various types of organized and white-collar crime.

Part II Readings

Boot Camp

Peter Rose, Myron Glazer,
and Penina Migdal Glazer

Resocialization is one of the most disrupting processes that a person can go through. In this article, the authors describe a marine recruit's experience.

Becoming a Soldier

The armed forces prepare men (and some women) to endure hardship, obey orders, achieve group solidarity, and acquire the skills and attitudes necessary for military service. To do this, authorities demand that recruits leave behind their families, possessions, ideas — indeed, their whole civilian selves — and forge new identities as military personnel.

Life in a Marine Boot Camp

How resocialization in the military occurs is well described by Steven Warner, a conscientious objector drafted in 1972 by the marine corps. (At this stage of the Vietnam War, the draft was still operating, though bitterly opposed by many Americans.) Warner, like the other recruits, found that many of his previous beliefs were challenged as the corps attempted to turn him from a citizen who hated war into a soldier who would obey on command. The experience made a strong impression.

> Our Greyhound drove onto Parris Island at ten that night. A few seconds after we stopped, a staff sergeant wearing the Smokey Bear hat all drill instructors wear came on the bus and said: "You're on Parris Island. There are two ways to leave here: on a bus like this in eight or nine weeks or in a

box.... If you have any cigarettes, put them out. If you have any gum, swallow it.... You have ten seconds to get into that building.... Move!...

> A staff sergeant began ... telling us how we were to behave from that moment on....

> Recruits must stand at attention at all times. Recruits will not eyeball. Recruits will doubletime everywhere. Recruits will do nothing without permission: they will not speak or swat bugs or wipe off sweat or faint without permission. Recruits will call everyone, except other recruits, "Sir." Recruits will never use the word "you" because "you" is a female sheep and there are no ewes on Parris Island. Recruits will never use the word "I" because "I" is what a recruit sees with, not what he calls himself.

An initial part of the resocialization process began with **depersonalization** — depriving people of their individuality. The young men were no longer called by their names. Their personal possessions were taken away, and a hundred rules (that is, new norms) were thrown at them. Merging with the group was stressed. A recruit had to speak, look, and act like every other recruit — or else. Uniforms and haircuts were important components of that transformation. Former roles and identities did not count. It no longer mattered whether a recruit had been a high school football captain, the owner of a custom sports car, or a promising writer. The sooner the past was forgotten, the better the recruit would get along.

The resocialization process included another crucial component made clear right at the beginning. The drill instructor (DI) immediately became the recruits' most important significant other. His welcoming speech not only set out a whole series of new norms but also established

194

that he controlled rewards and punishments. If the recruit did not live up to his role obligations, he would be observed and quickly reprimanded. The DI's opinion and reactions were what counted now. He and his fellow DIs were in control.

The subjugation of the recruits was immediately reinforced when the men were ordered to pick up their gear and follow their DI after the initial speech. Those recruits who couldn't keep the double-time pace were cajoled, cursed, and punished. The message was clear. Tough days were ahead. The DIs had the difficult task of turning soft individual civilians into a disciplined fighting unit. It may not have been a task they relished, but it was necessary, and they did it in a relentless manner.

The DIs' definition of their own roles reflected their sensitivity to the process of resocialization. The recruits brought with them a vast baggage of previous roles and cultural definitions. The armed forces assumed that all of these had to be broken down and discarded if the recruits were to become military men capable of responding to orders, working as a group, and living together. New norms had to be repeated continually and appropriate behavior demanded. There could be no exceptions. The DIs had to be constantly alert for infractions of the rules and ready to "chew out" (or "ream") offenders. The DIs' vigilance and consistency in playing their roles were important defenses against letting the recruits slide into former patterns of civilian behavior.

The controlled environment began to have its effect on Warner. The recruits were constantly warned about the cunning and toughness of North Vietnamese soldiers. Although Warner had come to boot camp unafraid of the "enemy" in Southeast Asia, the training sessions instilled fear in him. Other things were also happening. A sense of group solidarity was beginning to take shape. The men reached out to help one another

in time of trouble. As in actual combat, recruits acted out the belief that they could depend on their buddies. Primary group relations were developing under the supervision of the authorities.

Since the first days of boot camp, we had been warned about the PRT {Physical Readiness Test} we would take during the last week. This would be our initiation into the Marine Corps. . . .

We climbed some ropes in full gear, carried one another over our shoulders for a while, crawled a lot. . . . Then came the last hurdle: a three-mile run in full gear — steel helmet, boots, pack rifle.

Everyone was grim. Our commanding officer, also in full gear, ran in front of the company. Gordon {the DI} was in front of our platoon. . . . We ran silently for a while. The only sounds were heavy breathing and boots hitting the ground. Then Gordon started us on our chants: "Here we go-o! HERE WE GO-O! Long Road! LONG ROAD! Hard Road! HARD ROAD! Won't Stop! WON'T STOP! Gimme More! GIMME MORE! Marine Corps! MARINE CORPS!"

Two or three recruits were having a hard time. They had run the distance many times before, but now they gasped for air and stumbled trying to keep up. Other recruits took turns, carrying their rifles, their packs, and even their helmets. If the stragglers continued to fade, they were held up by the arms, even carried. . . . The point was, the platoon kept on running, and no one was left behind. We had learned our lesson.

When it was over, everybody was grins and backslapping. Gordon, sweating more than I had ever seen before, came into the barracks and gave us a small smile and said: "MARINES . . . take a shower." It was the first time he had ever called us that.

This episode includes some telling points about the process of resocialization. The men's new status required more than putting aside previous statuses. It required them to forge a new identity as marines. This included the belief that the recruit could overcome difficult physical challenges, that he must and could make sure that his buddies handled them too, and that success would be achieved under the leadership of competent authorities. The reward was a shared satisfaction that the unit had succeeded and that each member could be proud of his part in the achievement. Thus, while former statuses had been suppressed, the new one — marine — made all the sacrifices easier to bear.

In this effort, the peer group played a central part. Feelings of interdependence — that "We're in it together" — reinforced the authorities' value that the unit was more important than the individual. In a controlled environment, resocialization of participants is more effective if the peer group supports the values of the authorities.

How do the characteristics of a controlled environment described earlier apply to military basic training? All aspects of the recruit's life are conducted at one particular place — the military base — and under the control of one authority — the DI. Every aspect of the recruit's life takes place in the company of other recruits who are in the same circumstances and playing the same role. All daily activities are scheduled by the authorities without the consent of the recruits. Finally, all these activities fulfill the main purpose of the military — to prepare men to fight in wars. This means socializing them to respond to authority even when their lives are at stake. Behavior that had been acceptable in civilian life was now defined as deviant and subject to punishment. Even a conscientious objector like Steven Warner found his previous beliefs undermined. In a particularly revealing final statement, he wrote that if his own son ever had to be in the armed forces, he hoped the boy would serve in the marines.

Warner's experiences reveal other characteristics of controlled environments. For one thing, depersonalization is central to resocialization. It forces the recruit to leave behind former statuses and the roles and identities associated with them. Warner's experience also shows that unlearning former role behavior is a painful procedure that people are likely to resist. Significant others are crucial in the unlearning process. They in turn succeed best when they set out their expectations clearly and consistently and when they have the resources to reward conformity and punish deviance. And an individual is more willing to play a new role if it is shown to have some positive relation to past definitions of the self. In other words, recruits may vehemently dislike obeying orders, but they are more likely to do so if they can be convinced that this shows they "can take it" and are now fit to be called "marine." Resocialization occurs more easily if conformity to the rules of the new position is perceived as competence rather than subservience. Finally, resocialization proceeds more smoothly if the individual finds new groups with which to identify within the controlled environment.

SOURCE: From P. I. Rose, M. Glazer, and P. M. Glazer, *Sociology: Inquiring into Society*, 2d ed. Copyright © 1982 by St. Martin's Press and reprinted by permission of the publisher. Excerpted material from Steven Warner, "A Conscientious Objector at Parris Island." *The Atlantic Monthly*, June 1972. Reprinted by permission of Paul R. Reynolds, Inc.

The Managed Heart: Commercialization of Human Feeling

by Arlie Russell Hochschild

Human feelings have become a product, advertised by those who market good times. Employees are expected to project the feelings the company advertises. Hochschild describes how airline stewardesses sell feelings.

Even before an applicant for a flight attendant's job is interviewed, she is introduced to the rules of the game. Success will depend in part on whether she has a knack for perceiving the rules and taking them seriously. Applicants are urged to read a pre-interview pamphlet before coming in. In the 1979–1980 *Airline Guide to Stewardess and Steward Careers*, there is a section called "The Interview." Under the subheading "Appearance," the manual suggests that facial expressions should be "sincere" and "unaffected." One should have a "modest but friendly smile" and be "generally alert, attentive, not overly aggressive, but not reticent either." Under "Mannerisms," subheading "Friendliness," it is suggested that a successful candidate must be "outgoing but not effusive," "enthusiastic with calm and poise," and "vivacious but not effervescent." As the manual continues: "Maintaining eye contact with the interviewer demonstrates sincerity and confidence, but don't overdo it. Avoid cold or continuous staring." Training, it seems, begins even before recruitment.

Like company manuals, recruiters sometimes offer advice on how to appear. Usually they presume that an applicant is planning to put on a front; the question is which one. In offering tips for success, recruiters often talked in a matter-of-fact way about acting, as though assuming that it is permissable if not quite honorable to feign. As one recruiter put it, "I had to advise a lot of people who were looking for jobs, and not just at Pan Am. . . . And I'd tell them the secret to getting a job is to imagine the kind of person the company wants to hire and then become that person during the interview. The hell with your theories of what you believe in, and what your integrity is, and all that other stuff. You can project all that when you've got the job."

In most companies, after the applicant passes the initial screening (for weight, figure, straight teeth, complexion, facial regularity, age) he or she is invited to a group interview where an "animation test" takes place.

At one interview session at Pan American, the recruiter (a woman) called in a group of six applicants, three men and three women. She smiled at all of them and then said: "While I'm looking over your files here, I'd like to ask you to turn to your neighbor and get to know him or her. We'll take about three or four minutes, and then I'll get back to you." Immediately there was bubbly conversation, nodding of heads, expansions of posture, and overlapping ripples of laughter. ("Is that right? My sister-in-law lives in Des Moines, too!" "Oh wow, how did you get into scuba diving?") Although the recruiter had simply asked each applicant to turn to a neighbor, in fact each woman turned to her nearest man "to bring him out." (Here, what would be an advantage at other times — being the object of conversational attention — became a disadvantage for the men because the task was to show skill in "bringing out" others.) After three minutes, the recruiter put down her files and called the group to order. There was immediate total silence. All six looked expectantly at the recruiter: how had they done on their animation test?

The recruits are screened for a certain type of outgoing middle-class sociability. Sometimes the recruitment literature explicitly addresses friendliness as an *act*. Allegheny Airlines, for example, says that applicants are expected to "*project a warm personality* during their interview in order to be eligible for employment." Continental Airlines, in its own words, is "seeking people who convey a spirit of enthusiasm." Delta Airlines calls simply for applicants who "*have a friendly personality and high moral character.*"

Different companies favor different variations of the ideal type of sociability. Veteran employees talk about differences in company personality as matter-of-factly as they talk about differences in uniform or shoe style. United Airlines, the consensus has it, is "the girl-next-door," the neighborhood babysitter grown up. Pan Am is upper class, sophisticated, and slightly reserved in its graciousness. PSA is brassy, fun-loving, and sexy. Some flight attendants could see a connection between the personality they were supposed to project and the market segment the company wants to attract. One United worker explained: "United wants to appeal to Ma and Pa Kettle. So it wants Caucasian girls — not so beautiful that Ma feels fat, and not so plain that Pa feels unsatisfied. It's the Ma and Pa Kettel market that's growing, so that's why they use the girl-next-door image to appeal to that market. You know, the Friendly Skies. They offer reduced rates for wives and kids. They weed out busty women because they don't fit the image, as they see it."

Recruiters understood that they were looking for "a certain Delta personality," or "a Pan Am type." The general prerequisites were a capacity to work with a team ("we don't look for chiefs, we want Indians"), interest in people, sensitivity, and emotional stamina. Trainers spoke somewhat remotely of studies that indicate that successful applicants often come from large families, had a father who enjoyed his work, and had done social volunteer work in school. Basically, however, recruiters look for someone who is smart but can also cope with being considered dumb, someone who is capable of giving emer-

gency safety commands but can also handle people who can't take orders from a woman, and someone who is naturally empathetic but can also resist the numbing effect of having that empathy engineered and continuously used by a company for its own purposes. The trainees, on the other hand, thought they had been selected because they were adventurous and ambitious. ("We're not satisfied with just being secretaries," as one fairly typical trainee said. "All my girlfriends back in Memphis are married and having babies. They think I'm real liberated to be here.")

The trainees, it seemed to me, were also chosen for their ability to take stage directions about how to "project" an image. They were selected for being able to act well — that is, without showing the effort involved. They had to be able to appear at home on stage.

The training at Delta was arduous, to a degree that surprised the trainees and inspired their respect. Most days they sat at desks from 8:30 to 4:30 listening to lectures. They studied for daily exams in the evenings and went on practice flights on weekends. There were also morning speakers to be heard before classes began. One morning at 7:45 I was with 123 trainees in the Delta Stewardess Training Center to hear a talk from the Employee Representative, a flight attendant whose regular job was to communicate rank-and-file grievances to management and report back. Her role in the training process was different, however, and her talk concerned responsibilities to the company:

> Delta does not believe in meddling in the flight attendant's personal life. But it does want the flight attendant to uphold certain Delta standards of conduct. It asks of you first that you keep your finances in order. Don't let your checks bounce. Don't spend more than you have. Second, don't drink while in uniform or enter a bar. No drinking twenty-four hours before flight time. {If you break this rule} appropriate disci-

plinary action, up to and including dismissal, will be taken. While on line we don't want you to engage in personal pastimes such as knitting, reading, or sleeping. Do not accept gifts. Smoking is allowed if it is done while you are seated.

The speaker paused and an expectant hush fell across the room. Then, as if in reply to it, she concluded, looking around, "That's all." There was a general ripple of relieved laughter from the trainees: so that was *all* the company was going to say about their private lives.

Of course, it was by no means all the company was going to say. The training would soon stake out a series of company claims on private territories of self. First, however, the training prepared the trainees to accept these claims. It established their vulnerability to being fired and their dependence on the company. Recruits were reminded day after day that eager competitors could easily replace them. I heard trainers refer to their "someone-else-can-fill-your-seat" talk. As one trainee put it, "They stress that there are 5,000 girls out there wanting *your* job. If you don't measure up, you're out."

Adding to the sense of dispensability was a sense of fragile placement vis-à-vis the outside world. Recruits were housed at the airport, and during the four-week training period they were not allowed to go home or to sleep anywhere but in the dormitory. At the same time they were asked to adjust to the fact that for them, home was an idea without an immediate referent. Where would the recruit be living during the next months and years? Houston? Dallas? New Orleans? Chicago? New York? As one pilot advised: "Don't put down roots. You may be moved and then moved again until your seniority is established. Make sure you get along with your roommates in your apartment."

Somewhat humbled and displaced, the worker was now prepared to identify with Delta. Delta was described as a brilliant financial success (which it is), an airline known for fine treat-

ment of its personnel (also true, for the most part), a company with a history of the "personal touch." Orientation talks described the company's beginnings as a family enterprise in the 1920s, when the founder, Collett Woolman, personally pinned an orchid on each new flight attendant. It was the flight attendant's job to represent the company proudly, and actually identifying with the company would make that easier to do.

Training seemed to foster the sense that it was safe to feel dependent on the company. Temporarily rootless, the worker was encouraged to believe that this company of 36,000 employees operated as a "family." The head of the training center, a gentle, wise, authoritative figure in her fifties, appeared each morning in the auditorium; she was "mommy," the real authority on day-to-day problems. Her company superior, a slightly younger man, seemed to be "daddy." Other supervisors were introduced as concerned extensions of these initial training parents. (The vast majority of trainees were between nineteen and twenty-two years old.) As one speaker told the recruits: "Your supervisor is your friend. You can go to her and talk about anything, and I mean *anything*." The trainees were divided up into small groups; one class of 123 students (which included three males and nine blacks) was divided into four subgroups, each yielding the more intimate ties of solidarity that were to be the prototype of later bonds at work.

The imagery of family, with mommies and daddies and sisters and brothers, did not obscure for most trainees the reminders that Delta was a business. It suggested, rather, that despite its size Delta aspired to maintain itself in the spirit of an old-fashioned family business, in which hierarchy was never oppressive and one could always air a gripe. And so the recruit, feeling dispensable and rootless, was taken in by this kindly new family. Gratitude lays the foundation for loyalty.

The purpose of training is to instill acceptance of the company's claims, and recruits naturally wonder what parts of their feeling and behavior will be subject to company control. The head of in-flight training answered their implicit question in this way:

> Well, we have some very firm rules. Excessive use of alcohol, use of drugs of any kind, and you're asked to leave. We have a dormitory rule, and that is that you'll spend the night in the dormitory. There's no curfew, but you will spend the night in the dormitory. If you're out all night, you're asked to leave. We have weight standards for our flight attendants. Break those weight standards, and the individual is asked to resign. We have a required test average of 90 percent; if you don't attain that average, you're asked to resign. And then we get into the intangibles. That's where the judgment comes in.

From the recruit's point of view, this answer simply established what the *company* conceived of as "company control." In fact, this degree of control presupposed many other unmentioned acts of obedience — such as the weigh-in. Near the scales in the training office one could hear laughter at "oh-my-god-what-I-ate-for-dinner" jokes. But the weigh-in itself was conducted as a matter of routine, just something one did. The need for it was not explained, and there was no mention of the history of heated court battles over the weight requirement (most of them so far lost by the unions). One flight attendant commented, "Passengers aren't weighed, pilots aren't weighed, in-flight service supervisors aren't weighed. We're the only ones they weigh. You can't tell me it's not because most of us are women." Obviously, discussions of this issue might weaken the company's claim to control over a worker's weight. The trainers offered only matter-of-fact explanations of what happens to the weight gainer. If a flight attendant is one pound over the maximum allowable weight, the fact is "written up" in her personnel file. Three

months later, if the offender is still one pound over, there is a letter of reprimand; if another three months pass without change, there is suspension without pay. People may in fact be fired for being one pound overweight. Outside the classroom, of course, there was a rich underground lore about starving oneself before flights, angrily overeating after flights, deliberately staying a fraction over the weight limit to test the system, or claiming "big bones" or "big breasts" as an excuse for overweight. (One wit, legend has it, suggested that breasts be weighed separately.) Officially, however, the weigh-in was only a company routine.

The company's presumption was supported by several circumstances. It was difficult to find *any* good job in 1981, let alone a job as a flight attendant. There was also the fact that Delta's grooming regulations did not seem particularly rigid compared with those of other airlines, past and present. Flight attendants were not required to wear a girdle and submit to the "girdle check" that Pan American flight attendants recall. There was no mention of a rule, once established at United, that one had to wear white underwear. There was a rule about the length of hair, but no mention of "wig checks" (to determine whether a worker had regulation hair under her wig), which were used by several companies in the 1960s. There was no regulation, such as Pan Am had, that required wearing eyeshadow the same shade of blue as the uniform. There were no periodic thigh measurements, which PSA flight attendants still undergo, and no bust-waist-hips-thighs measurements that formed part of an earlier PSA routine. In an occupation known for its standardization of personal appearance, Delta's claims could seem reasonable. The company could say, in effect, "You're lucky our appearance code isn't a lot tighter." Under a more stringent code, those who could be judged a little too fat or a little too short, a little too tall or a little too plain, could feel pressured to make up for their physical deviations by working harder and being nicer than others. Some veteran workers ventured a thought (not generally shared) that companies deliberately tried to recruit women who were decidedly plainer than the official ideal so as to encourage workers to "make up for" not being prettier.

The claim to control over a worker's physical appearance was backed by continuous reference to the need to be "professional." In its original sense, a profession is an occupational grouping that has sole authority to recruit, train, and supervise its own members. Historically, only medicine, law, and the academic disciplines have fit this description. Certainly flight attendants do not yet fit it. Like workers in many other occupations, they call themselves "professional" because they have mastered a body of

knowledge and want respect for that. Companies also use "professional" to refer to this knowledge, but they refer to something else as well. For them a "professional" flight attendant is one who has completely accepted the rules of standardization. The flight attendant who most nearly meets the appearance code ideal is therefore "the most professional" in this regard. By linking standardization to honor and the suggestion of autonomy, the company can seem to say to the public, we control *this* much of the appearance and personality of *that* many people — which is a selling point that most companies strive for.

SOURCE: Arlie Russell Hochschild. *The Managed Heart: Commercialization of Human Feeling.* © 1983 by the Regents of the University of California. Used by permission of the University of California Press.

PART III

Social Inequality

We are not all equal. Some people are rich and some are poor. Some are respected and others are despised. Some are powerful and others are powerless. Being born into a rich family, a poor family, a respected family, or a powerful family makes a difference in the way we live our lives. This is true even in the United States where equality is valued.

Inequality is found in most societies and persists from generation to generation. Is it good for society? Does it serve any useful purpose? Or does it continue in spite of the conflicts and suffering it causes? This section on social inequality explores the view of inequality, how it develops, and how it persists. We look at how the structure of society maintains social differences, sometimes by force but usually because we are socialized to believe that things are as they should be. In Chapter 9, 10, and 11 we describe specific groups who are differentiated on the basis of wealth, status, and power — members of certain racial and ethnic groups, women, and the elderly. Through a variety of events in history, all these groups are held in positions in the lower strata of our society.

CHAPTER 8

Social Differentiation and Stratification

All animals are equal, but some animals are more equal than others.

— George Orwell

Social Stratification

Americans emphasize a commitment to equality and a belief in the American middle-class lifestyle. We tend to believe that we are all basically equal and that almost all of us are middle-class. We believe that a few people are rich because they worked extra hard to develop a particularly clever idea, such as building a better mousetrap or transistor or cooking a better hamburger. On the other hand, we tend to believe that only a few of us are poor, mostly as a result of not taking advantage of the opportunities this country has to offer.

What we Americans seldom realize is how incredibly wealthy a few of us are and how extremely poor others are. The Rockefellers and the Kennedys, for example, control great wealth and power. They live in luxury in summer and winter mansions. Nelson Rockefeller became a vice-president and John Kennedy became a president of the United States. Meanwhile, thousands of Americans eat in soup kitchens, have no homes at all, and without a home are not qualified to vote. In reality, we are not all equal.

Inequality — the unequal distribution of scarce goods or resources — is found in many different types of cultures. Certain goods and resources are hard to come by in every society. In some countries meat is scarce; in others it is plentiful. Land is a scarce resource in some areas of the world, but in others it is so plentiful that no one even bothers to claim ownership. There are not enough workers in some societies, which makes children a valuable resource. They work on the family farm and provide for their parents in old age, so a man who has many children may be a rich man. Some commodities are scarce in

Regardless of social class, students pass free time in conversation with one another like the prep school youths and the ghetto youths in these photos. The wealth of the prep school students, however, increases their life chances—they are more likely to get an advanced education and to meet influential people. They will therefore have a better opportunity to develop their talents and sell themselves in the job market.

many cultures; for example, mansions and luxury cars are scarce commodities everywhere.

We rank people according to the scarce resources they control. Money and property are two types of scarce resources. Other scarce resources are social position in the community, professional prestige, and high ranks in a political or philanthropic organization. The ranking of people according to their wealth, prestige, or social position is known as *social stratification*. Stratification separates the rich from the poor, the powerful from the powerless. Those who possess scarce resources have a high rank, and those who do not possess them have a low rank.

Our place in the stratification system influences every part of our lives: where we live, go to school, and work; what we eat; how we vote; and whom we marry. Our sexual behavior, sports, hobbies, and health are all affected by the rank society gives us.

Sources of Power

According to Weber (1946), the scarce resources used to rank people are the sources of power in society. *Power* is the ability to achieve one's desires, even when others resist. People who can grow food, raise armies, or win the respect of others have power over those who cannot.

Weber identified three scarce resources that are sources of power: social class, status, and party.

Social Class

Social class is based on several closely related factors: wealth, the power derived from wealth, and "life chances" to acquire wealth. *Life chances* are the opportunities people have to improve their income. A woman from the upper–middle class, for example, has a better opportunity to get a good education and thus a good job than a woman from the lower classes. A man who inherits an income from a rich uncle has a better chance to invest in the stock market than one who has no such source of income. A person who associates with educated people in the suburbs has a better chance to become well spoken and well dressed than a person who lives in an urban ghetto. One's use of language and style of dress increases one's chances of being successful in business. Weber wanted to point out that class was determined not only by wealth but also by whether one has all the opportunities to gain wealth. In a later section in this chapter we will discuss how occupation, housing, education, and medical care are related to life chances to earn wealth and power.

Marx and Engels, in *The Communist Manifesto* (1848), argued that social class was based entirely on wealth. The bourgeoisie, the rich, formed a class because they were the exclusive owners of the means of production — the farms and factories that produced needed food and supplies. The poor, the proletariat, formed a class because they had no land to produce food and no means to manufacture the supplies they needed. They could only sell their labor to the owners of the factories.

Because the rich had control of the means of production, they had power. They could hire the poor when it was profitable and fire them when they were no longer needed. The rich could make a profit on the labor of the poor. The poor, by contrast, had no power to claim the profits of their labor.

Max Weber (1946) agreed that social class is based on wealth, but he argued that a chance to acquire wealth is just as important as wealth itself. He said that a "life-chance" to acquire wealth is dependent on the possibility of making a profit in the marketplace. People who have a scarce resource other than wealth, such as an advanced education, a special skill, or a talent or service to sell, have power in the marketplace. They can sell when the price is right or sell to the highest bidder, and they can refuse to sell when the price is too low. Social class, then, is determined by life chances to acquire wealth as well as wealth itself.

Social Status

Social status, according to Weber, is the amount of honor and prestige a person receives from others in the community. Prestige is acquired by being born into a highly respected family, living in a high-status neighborhood, attending the right schools, or joining high-status groups or clubs. People also gain prestige by being able to buy consumer goods that others admire, such as expensive houses, yachts, or airplanes. In short, status is acquired by doing things and buying things that others admire. People who have status have power because they can influence those who respect them. They can use this influence to get a better job or increase their chances of marrying into wealthy or high-status families and thus use their power to increase their wealth.

Parties

Parties are organizations in which decisions are made to reach certain goals, the achievement of which affects a society. A person can gain power in the community by being politically active in national, state, or local parties, in special interest groups, in influential clubs, or in any other type of organization in which decisions are made to reach certain goals. By developing power in parties, people can increase their status through winning respect and increase their social class through reaching goals that are profitable to them.

Class, status, and party are often closely interrelated. Status and party can be used to increase wealth. Wealth can be used to buy consumer goods and increase status or to join prestigious clubs and increase political power. These three sources of power do not always go together, however. Wealthy people who are criminals, who live reclusive lives, or who are otherwise atypical have low status if no one respects them. Priests, ministers, college professors, and community leaders may be poor but still have a high status. Party leaders who use their position to increase their wealth sometimes do so in such a way that they lose status and the respect of others.

You may better understand characteristics of stratification — class, social status, party — if you think back to high school days and the ways that students could gain recognition. Some students gained recognition in dimensions of class, others gained recognition in dimensions of status, and still others, in dimensions of political activities. Table 8-1 provides examples of these dimensions of stratification.

Table 8-1
Dimensions of stratification in a high school elite

CLASS (WEALTH OR SKILLS FOR THE MARKETPLACE)	
Wealthy students	Most likely to succeed
Valedictorian	Best athletes
Honor Society members	Best actors and actresses

STATUS (HONOR AND RESPECT)	
Most popular	Best dressed
Best looking	Members of sororities and
Most poised	fraternities
	Prom queens

PARTIES (POLITICAL ACTIVITY)	
Student body officers and	Club officers
delegates	Newspaper editors
Class officers	
Sorority and fraternity	
officers	

Socioeconomic Status

It is difficult to place individuals in a particular social stratum because class, status, and party affiliations can all influence where they might be placed. Is the widower of a distinguished scholar who lives on a small retirement income in the same class as a mail carrier or a shoplifter who has the same income? Does a rural doctor who serves the poor and receives a small income have the same class position as a suburban doctor who serves the rich and has a large income? Does a prostitute have the same class position as the owner of a small employment agency? As you can see, class boundaries can be difficult to determine. A person who has a high position in one category may have a low position in a different category. Where, then, should that person be placed?

To resolve this problem, sociologists have developed the concept of *socioeconomic status* (SES). This measure considers income, education, and occupation when assessing a person's status. Someone who earns $50,000 will be ranked higher than a person earning $10,000, a college graduate will be ranked higher than a high school graduate, and anybody in a professional or management occupation will be ranked higher than a laborer. Usually there is a consistent pattern among these three rankings of status. People with many years of education hold occupations that afford high status and high incomes. One of the more interesting problems sociologists study is how to categorize people who have "status inconsistency" — an advanced education but a very low income, for example.

Theories of Social Stratification

Why are societies stratified? Why do some people acquire more of the scarce resources society has to offer? This question was widely debated

One example of status inconsistency is the Ph.D. who, because of social/economic conditions, is unable to find employment in his or her field. Many such graduates have been forced to take low-income or low-status jobs such as waiting on tables or driving cabs.

by early sociologists. As you will remember from Chapter 2, Spencer believed that superior people would educate themselves and become leaders, whereas inferior people would remain in the bottom ranks of society. Society, he said, developed through an evolutionary process, and those who profited from natural selection — "survival of the fittest" — came out on top. This process of natural selection was good for social progress, he argued, and society should not interfere with it.

The opposing view was formulated by Marx, who argued that stratification would eventually create revolution. The upper class in industrial society hired the proletariat to work in their factories, exploited them for profit, and drove them into poverty. As the proletariat became poorer, Marx contended, they would become aware of their plight and would revolt.

The theories of these early writers have had a strong influence on modern theories of stratification. Theoretical views of stratification were slow to develop, however. Like other Americans at the beginning of this century, sociologists believed that the very poor were misfits and that in time most people would rise to positions of high wealth and status if they worked hard and developed their talents. It was only when the Great Depression brought so much poverty to so many people that sociologists became aware of the importance of social stratification. It was then that two theories were developed to explain this phenomenon: structural functionalism and conflict theory.

Structural-Functional Theory

Structural functionalists have refined Spencer's notion that society, like any other organism, is self-regulating and self-maintaining. It consists of interrelated parts that serve a function in maintaining the system as a whole. When they recognized that stratification was a persis-

tent force in society, they assumed it must be functional. They hypothesized that because modern society is so complex, people with strong leadership skills are needed to organize and run the complex businesses and industries. People with strong leadership abilities must have advanced training and they must be willing to work very hard and assume a great deal of responsibility. Society must encourage these efforts by rewarding leaders with wealth and status, scarce resources that in turn can be used to gain power.

Thus, inequality is created by the needs of the society, not by the desires and needs of individuals (Davis and Moore, 1945). In terms of inherent worth as a human being, an artist or a teacher is certainly equal to a corporate executive. The talents of artists and teachers, however, are not as valuable to the society. Corporate executives who have the talent to lead business and industry must be more highly rewarded, not because they are more worthwhile human beings but because they are more valuable to the society. This theoretical perspective permits a belief in human equality at the same time that it explains inequality. If society had an equal need for all types of work, then all its members would be equal.

Conflict Theory

Conflict theorists reject the functional viewpoint (Duberman, 1976), arguing that inequality develops as a result of people's desire for power and that close-knit groups compete with one another to gain possession of the scarce resources that are a source of power. According to this view, resources are not rewards for talent or for assuming difficult tasks but are acquired through inheritance, coercion, or exploitation. Inequality results when one group acquires more resources than other groups.

Once the dominant group gets power, it tries to make its power appear legitimate by using propaganda to appeal to the masses through education, the mass media, religion, and politics. It tries to convince the masses to support the leadership of the dominant group for the good of the country, promising to protect the country from enemies such as capitalists in a communist country or communists in a capitalist country. The dominant group may also base its appeals for support on religious or moral grounds, claiming the divine right of kings or the moral right of the electoral system.

If the masses are influenced by thé propaganda of the upper class, they are said to have what Marx called *false consciousness,* a lack of awareness of class differences and an acceptance of upper-class rule. If, on the other hand, the masses are aware that different classes exist and that people's fates are tied to the fate of their whole class, they are said to have class consciousness. Regardless of their consciousness, there is little conflict if the masses have jobs and can live lives they find satisfactory. Serious conflicts develop only when the masses are severely exploited and class consciousness exists.

Attempts at Synthesis

Some sociologists have tried to reconcile the functional and conflict theories of stratification (Dahrendorf, 1951; Lenski, 1966; Tumin, 1963). Accumulating research suggests that stratification has a wide variety of causes, some based on conflict, some on cooperation. A stratification system based on religion, for example, may stress feelings of community and selflessness. Others, based on land ownership or accumulation of money, may emphasize competition and the efforts of individuals. As our understanding of the nature and development of stratification improves, it is becoming increasingly apparent that stratification is influenced by a great many different factors: how food is grown, how supplies are manufactured and distributed, how much

© 1984 G. B. Trudeau/Universal Press Syndicate

wealth accumulates, and how people use their leisure time, to name a few. Neither functional nor conflict theory offers us a full understanding of how stratification systems develop.

There is, however, widespread agreement that all stratification systems are based on the consensus among members of the society that inequality is good, fair, and just. People may accept stratification because they value the achievements of the wealthy or because they have been misled by the media. Whatever the reason, acceptance of the stratification system confers power on those of high rank.

There is also widespread agreement that all stratification systems have developed when there is an accumulation of wealth. Wealth creates leisure time, time to do something besides work. It also encourages division of labor — people spend their leisure time in diverse ways and develop special skills that enable them to do certain jobs better than others. Lenski (1966), who has classified societies into five types on the basis of their complexity, has shown that wealth, division of labor, and stratification increase as societies grow more complex. These five types of society are discussed next.

Types of Societies and Social Differentiation

Very simple societies have simple divisions of labor, and all people have about the same tasks and possessions; as a result there is little social differentiation. Societies grow more complex as their wealth increases, however, since there are many different jobs to be done. In a complex society such as our own there is a wide division of labor, which creates a wide array of social positions. Stratification develops as we rank these positions in order of importance. Lenski (1966) has shown that stratification increases as societies grow more complex and wealthy. He discerned five basic types of societies.

Hunting and gathering societies consist of about fifty people, or even less, who live on what they can find to eat. They are often nomadic, moving from place to place in search of food. They are usually very poor and must share what they find to eat in order to survive. No one can be excused from work. Surpluses of food or supplies are not accumulated, so no one can become wealthy. Some people may gain special respect because of their age, wisdom, skill in hunting, or magical abilities, but they do not derive any power from their status because there is no area

to exercise their authority and little to do except work. With so little differentiation in these societies, there is little stratification.

In *simple horticultural societies,* the people farm using a digging stick as their basic tool. They have a fairly reliable source of food and may even have a surplus from time to time. Thus, they can remain in one location, build shelters, and make tools. A surplus of food and supplies allows them some leisure time, which they use in sports and ceremonial activities. They also occasionally fight wars to protect their land. Certain specialized occupations develop: warriors and ceremonial and political leaders. Ceremonial leaders are sometimes paid for performing ceremonies, especially those involving healing, and they may become wealthy. Political leaders, with the assistance of warriors, can capture slaves and enforce their edicts. As labor is divided among different groups and wealth and status accumulate, a stratification system develops.

Advanced horticultural societies farm with irrigation, terracing, and fertilization. These techniques increase the food supply, so the size of the population can grow. Societies at this level have learned how to work metals, which increases the variety of material goods and also the variety of occupations. As the size and wealth of the population increase and a greater variety of occupations develops, stratification increases. The king becomes a very powerful person. He has a larger army and can capture more slaves and force them to do whatever he chooses. Social differentiation and stratification are much greater in these societies than in simple horticultural societies.

Agrarian societies, such as those found in Europe in the Middle Ages, have far more sophisticated technology than horticultural societies. This advanced technology increases the development of centralized power in two ways. As defenses and weapons are improved, arming a war-

A Gathering Society: The Tasaday

Sometime during the 1960s, a Filipino hunter named Dafal discovered three naked men digging roots deep in a rain forest. Dafal made friends with the men, exchanged some food, and parted. Dafal mentioned this meeting to Philippine officials, who asked to meet the forest people, and the Tasaday Cave-Dwellers became known to modern society.

The Tasaday numbered about two dozen people, living in three caves in the side of a mountain overlooking a large stream. They survived by foraging in the forest. Their basic food was a root they called *biking*, which was dug

and eaten either raw or cooked. They also gathered fruits and wild yams, and from the stream they gathered frogs, tadpoles, crabs, fish, and grubs. All food was shared among the members of the group.

Their tools were sticks and stones, their clothing was grass. They had no healing ceremonies, no elaborate marriage ceremonies, no burial ceremonies, apparently no ceremonies of any kind. They had no known magical or religious traditions.

The only division of labor observed among the Tasaday was that women swept the caves and

men gathered firewood. Men, women, and children searched for food. Men and women were equally responsible for the children. Decision making was a group process based on discussion, and all men and women expressed their opinions. They did not argue.

One woman appeared to exert more influence over the group than any other person. Her opinions were highly regarded, and her recommendations were followed more often than anyone else's. She usually divided up the supply of food. While she had influence, she did not have any power. She could not make anyone do anything they did not wish to do. The Tasaday were highly egalitarian.

SOURCE: Frank Robert Vivilo, *Cultural Anthropology Handbook: A Basic Introduction*, New York: McGraw-Hill, 1978.

A Tasaday family rest in their cave. From left are Lubo, Ivet (the mother), a baby who has not yet been named, Lolo sitting in the rear, Natek lying down, and Bilangen (the father). The Tasaday hunt and gather food using the simplest stone age tools. They have no wealth and therefore no class distinctions, although some members of the society may be considered more able and talented at the work of gathering food.

rior with the materials needed to win battles becomes an expensive proposition. By supplying the weapons, the rich are able to develop armies, which they use to conquer land and slaves and to control farmers, who become the serfs of the society. Second, as the variety of goods grows, a merchant class develops to trade them. The more powerful rulers tax the wealth accumulated by the merchant class and become extremely rich.

As wealth and power become concentrated in the hands of very few people, society becomes severely stratified. The ruler and governing classes probably received from a quarter to a half of the national income in the agrarian societies of the Middle Ages (Lenski, 1966).

Industrial societies such as the United States have the greatest division of labor and the most wealth and hence the most stratification. Industrialization, structured as it is on the factory system of production and the assembly line, requires workers to perform very specialized tasks. They specialize in operating a particular piece of equipment, packing a manufactured product, driving a truck to market, advertising the product, selling the product, and so on. Workers do not produce goods for personal consumption. Instead, they do a specific job in exchange for money and then buy personal goods with that money.

Durkheim (1947) believed that the division of labor created *organic solidarity*. As each person specializes in one phase of production, he or she becomes dependent on others to produce other products. As a result, Durkheim believed, society becomes more integrated. This interdependence does not, however, create a system of equality. The variety of specialized jobs in an industrial society, when ranked in a complex hierarchy of differing statuses and great differences in salaries, creates a very complex stratification system.

Industrial societies also have a wide gap between those at the top and those at the bottom because of the great production of wealth in these systems. The surplus of goods produced,

In a caste society, a person cannot move from one caste to another. In this photograph, we see evidence of the stratification system in India as a wealthy man driving a car ignores another who is poor begging in the street.

when accumulated in the hands of a few people, will make those people very wealthy compared with others. There is a huge gap between the American families who have enormous fortunes and the poor who have accumulated no wealth.

Types of Stratification

There are three basic types of stratification: estate, caste, and class. These are ideal types that do not exist in pure form in any society, but, rather, are found in combination.

The *estate system*, practiced in Europe during the Middle Ages, was based on a family's relation to the land. People were born to a certain rank — noble, serf, or slave — but there was some opportunity for rank to change. A commoner could be knighted; a serf could be freed or sold into slavery.

In a *caste system*, class is ascribed at birth. An individual's worth is judged on the basis of religious or traditional beliefs about the person or the person's family. The caste system is very rigid: no one can move into another caste.

This system is found in India and South Africa. In India, there are some three thousand castes. People must marry within their own caste, and their caste determines their status, identity, education, occupation, and trade union. It affects what kind of food they eat, where they live, what kind of medical care they receive, how they are supported in old age, and how they are buried. While economic or social success does not change an individual's caste, the caste as a whole can raise its status by changing its customs to imitate a higher caste. This process takes several generations, however.

In the *class system*, which is found only in industrial societies, social level is defined in terms of wealth or status. This system allows movement among classes. Although wealth and life chances to acquire wealth are often inherited, it

is also possible to acquire wealth or status through one's own achievements.

While the United States is predominantly a class system, the position of women and blacks has some of the characteristics of a caste system. These minority groups have rarely been able to achieve wealth by entering the prestigious professions, and they have rarely been accepted for top positions in business or government because of the ascribed statuses of the groups into which they were born. Even in those instances when an individual woman or black did gain a position that would ordinarily bring wealth or status, women and blacks have not received the income and status associated with such achievement. As with castes, the advancement of individual women and blacks will depend to a great extent on raising the status of the entire group.

The fact that some groups in the United States have castelike characteristics demonstrates that the typologies of caste and class are ideal types. Some systems are *open systems*, allowing a great deal of mobility, and some are *closed systems*, allowing little or no mobility. Sociologists use the ideal types to compare and contrast different social systems, recognizing that every system has variations within it.

Inequality in the United States

Social inequality in the United States is based on family background, wealth, education, occupation, and a variety of other characteristics. As a result, there is no widely accepted system for describing class in this country. The best way to understand the class system is to look at its various dimensions separately.

The Distribution of Income

In 1982, the median income in the United States for people with full-time jobs was $21,655 for men and $13,663 for women (U.S. Bureau of

Table 8-2

Distribution of families and unrelated individuals by income, 1982

INCOME	FAMILIES IN EACH CATEGORY, PERCENT	UNRELATED INDIVIDUALS IN EACH CATEGORY, PERCENT
$50,000 and over	10.9 ⎫	
$35,000–$49,999	16.0 ⎬	13.6
$25,000–$34,999	19.5 ⎭	
$20,000–$24,999	12.3	7.6
$15,000–$19,999	12.1	10.5
$10,000–$14,999	12.4	15.6
Under $10,000	16.6	52.9

SOURCE: U.S. Department of Commerce, Bureau of the Census, *Current Population Reports*, Series P-60, U.S. Government Printing Office, Washington, D.C., 1983.

Table 8-3

Percent of income and percent of wealth for each fifth of population, 1980

TOTAL POPULATION	TOTAL AVAILABLE INCOME	TOTAL AVAILABLE WEALTH[a]
Highest fifth	41.6%	76%
Second highest fifth	24.3% ⎫	
Middle fifth	17.5% ⎪	
Second lowest fifth	11.6% ⎬	24%
Lowest fifth	5.1% ⎭	

[a] Assets such as property, including stocks, bonds, and real estate.

SOURCE: U.S. Department of Commerce, Bureau of the Census, *Current Population Reports*, Series P-60, U.S. Government Printing Office, Washington, D.C., 1981; Daniel W. Rossides, *The American Class System: An Introduction to Social Stratification*, Houghton Mifflin, Boston, 1976.

the Census, 1983e). As you will remember, the median is the amount at which half of a given population falls above and half falls below. Table 8-2 shows that the distribution of this income was very unequal. Over half of the individuals who did not live with relatives made less than $10,000. The table also shows that families had an advantage over unrelated individuals in earning power, but even so, 16.6 percent of all families earned less than $10,000.

In 1982, the median income of families was $23,430. In one-parent families headed by a man, the median income was $20,140. In one-parent families headed by a woman, however, the median income was only $11,480 (U.S. Bureau of the Census, 1983e).

Some wealthy people arrive in their Rolls Royce to watch the Americas' Cup Race in Newport, Rhode Island. Perhaps they will view the race from their private yacht. Those of lesser means park in a distant lot and ride the free shuttle bus. The poor do not attend boat races at all. They have no opportunity to develop an interest in sailing.

Another way to look at income distribution is to consider the share of income received by each 20 percent of the population. Table 8-3 shows that the poorest 20 percent of the population received only 5.1 percent of the total available income in 1980, whereas the richest 20 percent of the population received 41.6 percent of the available income. This distribution of income has remained very stable over the past forty years.

The Distribution of Wealth

Wealth consists of personal property as well as income. Personal property includes liquid assets (cash in bank accounts), real estate, stocks, bonds, and other owned assets. In a study done in the early 1960s, it was found that families in the top 20 percent income bracket possessed 76 percent of the wealth in this country (Rossides, 1976; Vanfossen, 1979). Even in this group of high earners, however, the wealth was not distributed evenly. Families whose income was in

the top 1 percent earned 19 percent of the total income. They owned 60 percent of all corporate bonds and 57 percent of all corporate stocks.

Many people believe the concentration of wealth at the top has increased in recent years. Moreover, the very wealthy actually control even more money than they possess. By owning many shares of the major corporations, they influence not just their own fortunes but those of many others. The Rockefeller family, one of the wealthiest families in the United States, has estimated assets of at least one billion dollars. Because the family dominates key banks and corporations, they control assets of more than fifteen times their personal wealth (Szymanski, 1978).

Social Status in American Society

The earliest studies of stratification in America were based on the concept of status, people's opinions of other people. Status, re-

America's Richest People

Estimated Worth

$3 Billion to $5 Billion
du Ponts, Wilmington, Del. *Chemicals.*
Mellons, Pittsburgh, Pa. *Mellon National Bank.*

$2 Billion to $3 Billion
Gettys, Los Angeles, Cal. *Getty Oil.*
Daniel K. Ludwig, N.Y., N.Y. *Shipping, real estate.*

$1 Billion to $2 Billion
Rockefellers, N.Y., N.Y. *Standard Oil.*

$600 Million to $1 Billion
Fords, Detroit, Mich. *Ford Motor Company.*
Hunts, Dallas, Tx. *Oil.*

Pews, Philadelphia, Pa. *Sun Oil.*
Pritzkers, Chicago, Ill. *Hyatt Hotels, real estate.*

$400 Million to $600 Million
Bechtels, San Francisco, Cal. *Engineering and construction management.*
Henry Crown, Chicago, Ill. *General Dynamics.*
Marvin Davis, Col. *Colorado Oil.*
Michel Fribourg, N.Y., N.Y. *Continental Grain.*
William R. Hewlett, Palo Alto, Cal. *Hewlett-Packard.*
Keibergs, Kingsville, Tx. *King Ranch, real estate.*

SOURCE: From Dan Rottenberg in *Town and Country*, May 1978. © 1978. Reprinted by permission.

member, can be conferred on others for any reason a person chooses — mystical or religious powers, athletic ability, youth or beauty, good works — whatever seems appropriate to the person doing the ranking. It was found that in this country status was conferred on others on the basis of their wealth. In a study of a New England town called Yankee City (Warner and Lunt, 1942), for example, the local citizens placed people into six categories, all based on wealth:

1. *The upper-upper.* People who had inherited family wealth and high status.
2. *The lower-upper.* People who had income comparable to that of the upper class but who had acquired wealth recently and lacked a distinguished family background.
3. *Upper-middle.* Moderately successful business and professional people.
4. *Lower-middle.* People who were respectable, who lived in nice homes, and worked as low-ranking white-collar workers, foremen, or craftsmen.
5. *Upper-lower.* People who were factory and service workers; some low-ranking white-collar workers.
6. *Lower-lower.* Intermittent workers, families on welfare, and transients.

The Warner studies found that people at

different status levels had different lifestyles. They belonged to different churches, read different magazines, and had different leisure-time activities.

A study done during the depression of "Middletown" (Lynd and Lynd, 1929, 1937) found differences between the business class and the working class. When the study was originally done the business class lived in larger and better quality housing than did the working class. The very wealthy had elaborate mansions with indoor plumbing and central heating, while working-class homes were much smaller and often lacked indoor plumbing; water had to be carried in from an outdoor well. Heating was by a wood or coal stove.

A more recent study of Middletown (Caplow, et al., 1982) found that it had become more difficult to identify classes among the population. Now the working class lives in houses that are only slightly smaller than those of the business class, and they contain all of the amenities that modern society provides — not only indoor plumbing and central heating but also self-cleaning ovens, trash compactors, and other labor-saving devices. The wealthy, while living modestly in town, spend more of their money less conspicuously out of town, buying condominiums and yachts in Florida, for example. Today, then, it may be more difficult to tell who belongs to what class.

Class Consciousness

Class consciousness, you will recall, refers to the awareness that different classes exist in society and that people's fates are tied to the fate of

The tedium of office work has been compared to assembly-line work— moving a steady flow of paper from work station to work station, rather than moving a product along an assembly line. Notice the paraphernalia for caffeine—coffee cups and pots, cans of soft drinks—used to stimulate people.

their whole class. The sociologists who have done community studies in Yankee City, Middletown, and elsewhere found an awareness of different classes in the community, but descriptions of classes varied from community to community. Some communities named more classes than others, and there was not complete agreement about who belonged in what class.

Traditionally, most Americans identify themselves as middle class (Centers, 1949) but do not feel any allegiance to other members of the middle class or believe their fate is tied to what happens to their class. Even working-class people who belong to unions feel no allegiance to other union members. Middle-class people are aware of the rich and big businessmen and believe those groups have a great deal of power. They also believe more of that power should reside in the middle class (Form and Huber, 1969), but this has not created a strong class identity in the middle class.

On the other hand, the rich and big businessmen have more class consciousness. They are very aware of others in their class and feel a great deal of allegiance to the class. The rich, whom Domhoff (1971) estimates to be 0.5 percent of the population, know the other members of their class in all parts of the country. They summer and winter together in the same resorts, they sit on the same boards of directors, and their children marry each other.

Most people in the United States do not consciously make class distinctions. The feelings of allegiance that have developed have occurred along racial and gender lines rather than class lines. Blacks and women have been aware of themselves as classes and have felt allegiance to others in their own group. If any group has class consciousness, it is the rich rather than the middle class. Although they may not discriminate overtly, neither the rich nor the middle class has much awareness of those living in poverty.

Poverty

The U.S. government has developed a measure of poverty that takes into account the size of the family, the number of children, and whether the family lives on a farm. The income level considered impoverished varies with these factors. For a family of four not living on a farm, the poverty line in 1982 was $9,862, much less than the lower budget figure given in Table 8-4. The government reports that in 1982, 34.4 million people were living in poverty, an increase of 2.6 million over 1981.

Most poor people either work at low-paying jobs or cannot find jobs. Some are too ill to work, and others are single mothers who cannot earn enough to support their children. The poor cannot get loans to buy cars, and lacking transportation they cannot seek employment where work is available.

The poor also pay more for most of what they buy (Caplovitz, 1963). A larger percentage of their income is spent on food, and the food they purchase is often bought in more expensive inner-city locations. Without cars, they do not have the transportation to shop at more economical stores.

The hand-to-mouth existence of the poor requires only one emergency to create a downward spiral of trouble. If a mother cannot find adequate care for her child, even for a brief period, she has to stay home. If she loses her job, her utilities may be turned off, there may be no money for food, and she may be evicted from her apartment. The poor have no assets to protect themselves from the collapse of their precarious financial situation. They suffer a disadvantage in every arena of American life. They are handicapped at every turn. Compare their life chances with those of the rich and middle class in occupations, housing, education, and medical care, for example.

Table 8-4

Urban budgets for a four-person family, 1981

	LOWER BUDGET	INTERMEDIATE BUDGET	HIGHER BUDGET
Food	4,545	5,843	7,366
Housing	2,817	5,546	8,423
Transportation	1,311	2,372	3,075
Clothing and personal care	1,316	1,841	2,666
Medical care	1,436	1,443	1,505
Other consumption	644	1,196	1,972
Other costs (gifts, occupational expense)	621	1,021	1,718
Social Security	1,036	1,703	1,993
Income tax	1,696	4,443	9,340
Total cost (autumn 1981)	15,323	25,407	38,060

SOURCE: U.S. Department of Commerce, Bureau of the Census, *Statistical Abstract of the United States: 1982–83,* 103d ed., U.S. Government Printing Office, Washington, D.C., 1982, no. 763, p. 471.

Inequality and Life Chances

Occupations

For most people, the most important life chance in a society such as the United States is the opportunity to have a successful and dignified occupation or career that provides an adequate income. This is not true, however, for the upper classes; they receive the major portion of their wealth through assets and inheritance, not through occupational income. When members of the upper class hold jobs it is in order to gain power and prestige; they often become governor of a state, president of a bank, or a key figure in national politics, such as Secretary of State or Vice-President of the United States.

The majority of professional positions, including doctors, lawyers, business managers and other high ranking workers in large organiza-tions, are held by the upper-middle class. Many people think of the professional person as the typical American worker — educated, earning a comfortable living, owning a home, and sending children to college. Most people in the ordinary ranks of business management, however, would need a second worker in the family to afford this higher standard of living.

The majority of people in the United States are working class — craftsmen, foremen and laborers in industry, or service workers who provide cleaning, maintenance, and other services to those industries. Some sociologists argue that clerical workers, most of whom are women with routine jobs and low pay, should also be considered part of the working class. Strictly speaking, they are not blue-collar workers, because they don't wear work clothes and spend their days in a shop or plant. They wear white shirts and work in an office, but they have much in common with working-class people — low wages and strict supervision.

Other working-class occupations pay considerably less than either manufacturing or clerical positions. These workers make less than the median income even when there are no layoffs. Many blue-collar workers, especially construction workers, typically are laid off at some point during the year, which reduces their total annual income (Levinson, 1974). Many low-paid, working-class people fall below the poverty line and enter the class that has come to be called the "working poor." Most of these people work at jobs that do not pay enough money to bring them out of poverty. The minimum wage in the United States provides income below the poverty line for a family of four people.

Housing and Lifestyle

The rich often own several homes: a family estate, an estate in an exclusive resort area, and a large apartment in an exclusive apartment building in the center of a major city. They spend their leisure time with their wealthy friends and neighbors, and they work together on the boards of banks and corporations. They manage their business affairs with much mutual respect and close cooperation. Their children usually marry the children of other wealthy families, so rich families are usually related to one another, and their wealth remains in the same group. Their housing provides a lifestyle that enables them to know all the "right people," thereby giving them numerous opportunities to increase their wealth.

Upper-middle-class managers and professionals, who are near the top 20 percent of earners, are more likely to own homes in the suburbs. In addition to having a nice place to live, owning a home has proved to be a good investment because homes increase in value with inflation. They also provide income tax deductions.

Managers, who are often transferred, prefer to buy very conventional suburban homes since they are easier to sell (Margolis, 1979).

Working-class people are also likely to live in the suburbs, but they are less apt to own their own homes. Those who rent houses or apartments do not benefit from inflation or tax deductions. Instead, as prices go up, their rents go up, and they may find it very difficult to improve their standard of living. Some working-class people who cannot afford homes buy trailers and move to trailer parks to escape rising rents. In general, their life chance to improve their financial standing on the resale of a home is limited.

Poor people find it very difficult to get adequate housing. They may live in substandard housing in rural areas or in urban slums and often pay high rents for it. Sometimes two or more families share the same apartment, which may be very overcrowded, in order to meet the rent payments. The poor spend more money for roach killers than any other class of people. They must pay for expensive, inadequate heating systems and purchase goods in overpriced urban stores, which further reduces their life chances to improve their situations.

The poorest people in the United States do not even have homes or apartments. They live on the street. The number of street people is not known, but it is estimated that there are four thousand homeless women and a considerably larger number of homeless men in New York City. In Washington, D.C., approximately ten thousand women came to a shelter for homeless women during one year. The homeless have either lost contact with their families or they have no families. They also have no income — a person must have an address to receive welfare. They sleep in subways, doorways, or on park benches. They are often raped or assaulted, and in winter they sometimes freeze to death.

Education

The children of the rich are the group most likely to go to private preparatory schools and elite colleges, regardless of their grades. Not only do they earn credentials that are useful in business but also they make some valuable contacts with influential people who can help them get high-paying positions. Middle-class children ordinarily graduate from public or parochial high schools, and they have an excellent chance of going to college, if their grades are satisfactory. They can then earn degrees, but unless they can get into an elite school, they will not meet the influential people who can help them increase their life chances. Working-class children usually complete high school, but only those who achieve very high grades are likely to attend college. Even those who go to college are encouraged to enter technical occupations, which limits their chances to earn great wealth. Poor children tend to drop out of high school and often live in neighborhoods with poor schools, at which they may not even learn to read and write. Moreover, when they see that high school graduates often have trouble getting jobs, they become discouraged and quit as soon as they are old enough. Education is thus a life chance very closely associated with family wealth.

Medical Care

Good health is essential if one is to have a chance to earn a good living, but medical care is not distributed equally. The rich and the middle classes who are regularly employed are usually covered by medical insurance through their employers. Insurance covers most medical expenses, and members of these classes generally receive good medical care. They can afford to go to private doctors and private hospitals. They can comfortably discuss their health problems with doctors, and they understand the medical advice they receive. Most doctors are from the middle and upper classes themselves and they understand best the problems of people from the same background.

The poor have major health problems but they do not acquire the same medical care as the rich. They usually suffer from nutritional problems because they cannot afford meat and vegetables, substituting such starchy foods as beans, bread, and macaroni. They suffer from assaults, rat and dog bites, inadequate housing, and other hazards of living in poverty, and they are more likely to commit suicide.

In the middle 1960s, the U.S. government developed Medicaid, a health insurance program for the poor, and Medicare, a health insurance program for the elderly. Since these programs began, the poor have visited doctors more frequently and some are receiving better medical care. In poor neighborhoods, however, public clinics and hospitals are usually overcrowded, understaffed, and poorly equipped, and those who go to these facilities may have to wait four to six hours for treatment. They see whatever doctor is on duty, not necessarily the one they have dealt with before. In addition, they often have trouble communicating with doctors about their symptoms and problems, and they may have difficulty understanding the medical advice they receive. Doctors who work in public hospitals and clinics are often foreign born, and some speak English poorly. Those who were born in this country rarely come from working-class or impoverished backgrounds.

The very poor and homeless see doctors only when they are picked up by the police and brought to public hospitals. Among the most unfortunate cases seen in emergency rooms are homeless people who are frostbite victims. They may have to have a toe or a foot amputated, only to return to the streets to suffer frostbite again.

A woman rests on a city street next to her bundle of possessions. She is one of the thousands of people in the United States too poor to have a home. Many homeless people were once members of the middle class but have become widowed or divorced, have no family to support them, and are unable to find work to support themselves.

Social Mobility in the United States

Social mobility — changing one's social position — can occur in a variety of ways. *Geographic mobility* involves moving from one location to another. A move from one job to another job of equal rank is *horizontal mobility*. A change to a job of higher rank is *upward mobility*, and a movement to a job of lower rank is *downward mobility*. Upward and downward mobility are examples of *vertical mobility*. Mobility between generations is traditionally measured by comparing the social positions of fathers and sons (daughters are usually not studied). If a son has a higher position than his father had, the son is upwardly mobile; if the son's position is lower, he is downwardly mobile. Both the social structure and individual characteristics influence upward and downward mobility.

In the United States in the twentieth century, many structural changes have increased the wealth of the nation, and the standard of living has improved. Many sons have achieved a higher standard of living than their fathers as a result of these structural changes. Most children, however, have remained in the same social class as their fathers. It is only occasionally that a son has been able to achieve a position in a higher social status than his father.

Structural Characteristics of Mobility in the United States

Mobility in this country is influenced by (1) increased technology, (2) the growth of large corporations, (3) an increased standard of living, (4) the growth of urban areas, and (5) the maintenance of a split labor market.

Increased technology has eliminated some jobs involving manual labor and increased the number of white-collar clerical and service jobs. Should a move from a boring, low-paying assembly-line job to a boring, low-paying desk job be considered upward mobility, or is it, rather, horizontal mobility, movement that does not bring with it any real advantages? Some sociologists argue that white-collar work has a higher status, but others contend that this shift merely changes the nature of work, not the class or status of the worker.

The growth of large corporations has influenced the wages people are paid. Those who work in large organizations often earn more than those who work in small firms. People in supervisory positions earn a percentage more than the people they supervise, and their earnings generally increase as the number of people they supervise increases. Thus, as corporations grow larger, supervisors earn more. Many qualified people in large organizations never have the opportunity to be supervisors, however, and despite their high qualifications, they will never be able to earn the income of the supervisor. In a smaller organization they would more likely be promoted.

The increasing standard of living over the past century has improved the lives of most workers in the United States, even though their relative class or status remains unchanged. This improvement is especially true of factory workers, whose wages and living conditions have improved dramatically since the turn of the century.

The growth of urban areas, in which the cost of living is higher, has led to higher wages for city dwellers. Equally qualified people doing the same work are apt to earn more money in the city than in the country. Doctors, for example, earn considerably more in large metropolitan areas than in rural areas.

A *split labor market* is one in which some jobs afford upward mobility and others do not. A management trainee job may lead to management jobs of higher and higher rank and ultimately to the presidency of a company. A secretarial position, however, is much less likely to lead to an administrative job. The development of split labor markets is a great obstacle to higher earnings for women and minorities, who fill most of the jobs that have no career lines.

Individual Characteristics and Upward Mobility

A basic assumption of structural-functional theory is that society rewards people who develop leadership skills through education and hard work. Researchers have conducted many studies in order to learn about the characteristics of individuals who succeed. These studies, most of which were concerned with men, have examined the influence of such factors as family background, grades in school, years of education, and personality. Blau and Duncan (1967) studied upward mobility of American men using United States Census Bureau data. They used seventeen occupational categories and showed that many of the men moved up from one category to the next. There was a great deal of upward mobility, then, but only for a very short distance. If only a few categories had been used, however, there would have been no appreciable movement from one class to another.

The attitudes of young men from Wisconsin were thoroughly studied by William Sewell (Sewell, Hauser, et al., 1975). The research showed that Wisconsin boys whose attitudes were ambitious (i.e., who desired an occupation of a higher status than their fathers') often found it necessary to change their attitudes when they did not have the opportunity to reach their goals. In most cases people get discouraged when they cannot obtain the training required for a particular occupation and then adjust their attitudes to suit what they can attain.

Other studies (Jencks, 1979) show that family background is the factor that most accurately predicts the future earnings of men. Anywhere from 15 to 50 percent of the variation in men's earnings appears to be related to family background. Men from families with high incomes generally make more money than those from families with low incomes. The studies do not,

SOCIOLOGISTS AT WORK
Co-hosting on National Public Radio

Susan Stamberg is the co-host of *All Things Considered*, a nightly news and public affairs program broadcast on the National Public Radio network. She has been with the program since it was born in 1971, except for an eight-month break in 1981 to write her first book, *Every Night at Five: Susan Stamberg's "All Things Considered" Book* (Pantheon). She was the first woman to host a nationally broadcast nightly news program. The road that led Stamberg to *All Things Considered* includes along the way a bachelor's degree from Barnard College, with a double major — in English and sociology.

Why sociology? "I found it extremely absorbing, a way to make some sense out of my experience," says Stamberg. "I was intrigued with the idea of trying to sort out a lot of apparently disparate and incoherent information, of trying to create a framework for that information. That's sociology's greatest strength, but also its greatest weakness. Bernard Barber, who headed Barnard's excellent sociology department when I

was there, would create these lovely charts and try to pull *everything* into one of three columns. It was a brilliant attempt to impose order on life, even though sometimes large chunks of experience were left dangling."

Has Stamberg's study of sociology helped her in her work on *All Things Considered?* "It's funny," she says. "I split my major, but I would bury the sociology half of it, in college conversations. I'd say I majored in English and then I'd mumble the other part, largely because I couldn't stand the twitting I'd get — especially from the Columbia boys who had little respect for social sciences. They'd say, 'Sociology? Nothing but a command of the obvious. An aggressive obscuring of perfectly obvious facts.' But it was as important as the English in teaching me to deal with ideas. I felt it at the time, and I feel it even more strongly today. Just knowing that there are such things as social institutions, that actions are rarely random or entirely isolated, helps in my radio work. It was always clear, for instance, that every-

however, explain why family income is related to a son's future earnings. Structural functionalists argue that sons from families with high incomes usually have all of the advantages believed to contribute to future money-making ability. Their parents can teach their sons important skills, and they live in neighborhoods where their friends have the same advantages. Because of family advantages, they are likely to do well in high school and attend college.

Structural functionalists believe that the best way to increase upward mobility in this

country is to increase the opportunities available to children from poor families. Such a move would involve providing better preschool education, better public school education (including the opportunity to attend schools with young people from wealthier backgrounds), and the opportunity to go on to college or technical schools.

Conflict theorists criticize the notion that sons from high-income families succeed because they are more qualified. They argue that social class in the United States is an ascribed status

one has a family, but I was never aware of the *family* as an institution until I looked at it the way a sociologist looks at it. I can't really be specific about how that knowledge helps me in the course of asking questions" — Stamberg is renowned among her listeners as an insightful and thought-provoking interviewer — "but it does." It also helps her bring a fresh viewpoint to specific stories. "Reading Emile Durkheim was important. In my senior thesis at Barnard I took his concept of *anomie*, that feeling of public rolelessness and alienation from social institutions, and applied it to the works of some modern authors — André Gide, Albert Camus, and others. That concept was helpful in approaching contemporary stories about suicide, especially teenage suicide. It also helped with Watergate and the subsequent public apathy toward politics."

Stamberg's first job after graduation was as an editorial assistant at *Daedalus*, the journal of the American Academy of Arts and Sciences. Then she got married and moved to Washington, where she took a similar job at the *New Republic*. After a short while she moved over to radio — "I fell into radio" is the way she puts it — as the producer of a weekly news and public affairs program at a local public radio station. It was there she got her first air time, as a last-minute substitute when the weather girl got sick. She reflects on the experience of going on the air: "I couldn't just go out and say, 'All right, I'm about to talk to millions of people.' I would have got lockjaw. Instead, I concentrated on talking to one person — my husband. He was a perfect audience: he's intelligent, he's interested in a lot of things, he likes to laugh." This practice helped her when she moved to the national network and *All Things Considered*. "Most of our listeners are as curious and information-hungry as I am. They also follow the demographic profile of the country. People have a stereotype of public radio listeners as PhD, pipe-smoking professors. The average American is a high-school graduate. Our average listener is a high-school graduate. We reach everyone — blue-collar workers, white-collar workers, pink-collar workers, black-collar workers, you name it."

The impulse that drew Susan Stamberg to her work in radio is the same one that drew her to sociology. "It was interesting to me because it dealt with real people and what they were doing. It dealt with *today*." That interest makes millions of listeners tune in to *All Things Considered* every night at five.

and maintain that the poor cannot enter the upper class through increased education. Women and blacks have demonstrated that advanced education does not guarantee upward mobility. Members of minority groups may find it difficult to spend the time and money required to receive a higher education if they believe they will not be rewarded for their efforts. Conflict theorists contend that opportunity and equality for the poor will be brought about only through changes in the stratification system and in the distribution of wealth.

Summary

People's differing ranks in society are based on class and status. Class rankings are based on wealth, income, and life chances to acquire wealth and income. Status comes from the honor and respect people receive from others. Class and status are sources of power, and they are the criteria used to rank people in a system of stratification.

Structural functionalists believe that systems of stratification develop because societies need scarce leadership skills and reward those who are willing to assume the responsibility of leadership. Conflict theorists contend that stratification develops because certain groups gain a monopoly of the scarce resources through inheritance or conflict and use those resources to maintain their high positions.

Research indicates that stratification becomes more pronounced as wealth and the division of labor increase. Very simple societies have little division of labor and little stratification. Agrarian and industrial societies have more wealth, greater division of labor, and more stratification.

There are several types of stratification systems. In a caste system, positions are assigned at birth according to the position of the caste, and a person's caste is fixed for life. The class system is found only in industrial societies and allows movement into higher or lower strata through the accumulation or loss of wealth and status.

Inequality in the United States stems from wealth, income, education, and status — especially occupational status. Although most people identify themselves as middle class, the lifestyles of Americans vary widely. The differences are especially profound between the rich and the poor; the most important differences occur in occupation, housing, health care, and educational opportunity. It is these variations that affect life chances.

The American class system has been quite stable for at least fifty years. Those born into wealthy families remain wealthy, and those born in poverty usually remain poor. The most important determinant of one's class position in this country is family background.

Key Terms

caste system
class consciousness
class system
closed systems
downward mobility
estate system
false consciousness
geographic mobility
horizontal mobility
inequality
life chances
open systems
organic solidarity
parties
power
split labor market
social class
social status
social stratification
socioeconomic status (SES)
upward mobility
vertical mobility

Suggested Readings

Caplow, Theodore and Howard M. Bahr, Bruce A. Chadwick, Reuben Hill, and Margaret Holmes Williamson. **Middletown Families: Fifty Years of Change and Continuity.** *Minneapolis: University of Minnesota Press, 1982.* This study updates the classic Middletown studies and shows how (or how little) class and status have changed over the past fifty years.

Domhoff, G. William. **Who Rules America Now? A View for the Eighties.** *Englewood Cliffs, N.J.: Prentice-Hall, 1983.* An excellent description of the upper class in American society.

Duberman, Lucile. **Social Inequality: Class and Caste in America.** *Philadelphia: Lippincott, 1976.* A good basic text on stratification, including excellent sections on minority groups and women.

George, Susan. **How the Other Half Dies: The Real Reasons for World Hunger.** *Montclair, N.J.: Allanheld, Osmun, 1977.* This book discusses the exploitation of the world's poor by large international banks and businesses.

Howell, Joseph T. **Hard Living on Clay Street: Portraits of Blue Collar Families.** *Garden City, N.Y.: Doubleday/Anchor, 1973.* Howell, who lived in a neighborhood of southern working-class people, tells the moving, sometimes funny, sometimes sad story of their lives.

Margolis, Diane Rothbard. **The Managers: Corporate Life in America.** *New York: Morrow, 1979.* This study of eighty managers reveals how the corporation has shaped their professional and personal lives.

Piven, Frances Fox and Richard A. Cloward. **The New Class War: Reagan's Attack on the Welfare State and Its Consequences.** *N.Y.: Pantheon Books, 1982.* Piven and Cloward discuss recent political decisions that have changed the nature of poverty.

Rossides, Daniel W. **The American Class System: An Introduction to Social Stratification.** *Boston:*

Houghton Mifflin, 1976. A thorough text with good references for the student desiring further study in stratification.

Sexton, Patricia Cayo and Brendan Sexton. **Blue Collars and Hard Hats: The Working Class and the Future of American Politics.** *New York: Vintage, 1971.* A sympathetic discussion of the problems of the working class, this book argues for policies promoting downward mobility rather than upward mobility in order to reduce inequality.

Vanfossen, Beth E. **The Social Structure of Inequality.** *Boston: Little, Brown, 1979.* A more recent text discussing stratification for those who are interested in advanced study.

CHAPTER 9

Racial
and Ethnic
Differentiation

After all there is but one race —
humanity.

— George Moore

The United States is aptly called "a nation of nations." The diversity of the country's social and cultural life is a result of the many different groups who have migrated here. Can you imagine how monotonous life would be if people were all the same? Almost everyone enjoys the exotic sights, sounds, and smells of Chinatown. Greek, Italian, or Japanese cuisine is a welcome change from the usual American diet of hamburger or steak. We also benefit from our diverse cultural heritage in many more important ways as well.

Race and ethnic relations in the United States, however, are far from smooth. Our history has been marked by conflict, competition, prejudice, and discrimination. In this chapter we will identify the major minority groups in North America and discuss some of the causes and consequences of stereotyping, racism, prejudice, discrimination, and racial inequality. We will also consider two approaches, the pluralistic and integrationist perspectives, which may help reduce racial and ethnic inequality.

Racial, Ethnic, and Minority Groups

The terms "racial" and "ethnic" are often used rather loosely. Although they may be treated as equivalent or overlapping concepts, it is important to differentiate these terms before we discuss the more substantive issues of race and ethnic relations.

Racial Groups

The concept of race is extremely unclear. Anthropologists and biologists remain deadlocked over the issue of whether race is a meaningful biological concept. The essential question is whether there are significant variations in the traits of different populations of humans. The focus of investigation has ranged from obvious characteristics such as skin and hair coloring to less obvious traits such as blood type and genetically transmitted diseases (Newman, 1973). In pursuing their research, scientists have measured heads, examined eye color, and even examined ear wax. A wet type of ear wax was found to be common among East Asian groups, especially among the Chinese and Japanese, whereas a drier type was found among European and black populations.

Classification of peoples by skin color has been complicated by the effects of climate. It has been found that variations in skin shading are caused by varying degrees of exposure to sunlight. Asians and Africans have darker coloring because they live in tropical climates. Classification by skin color is further complicated by intermarriage. Many populations are the result of biological mixing — for example, the Creoles of Alabama and Mississippi, the Red Bones of Louisiana, the Croatians of North Carolina, and the Mestizos of South America. Whether members of these groups have Indian or black ancestors is a matter of dispute.

In reality, a social definition of racial groups takes precedence over biological criteria. From the biological standpoint, only those who had more than 50 percent black ancestry would be considered black. There was a time when Georgia and a number of other southern states classified as "colored" any individuals who had a known black ancestor, regardless of whether they were 60 percent black or 6 percent black.

Even the U.S. Bureau of Census used the concept of race loosely in its 1980 census in which race was equated with national origin. Hence, "Filipino," "Korean," and "Vietnamese" were treated as racial classifications. Moreover, classification by race was a matter of self-identification. There was no scientific definition to use

in determining which category to check on the census form.

In sum, social definitions far outweigh biological definitions of race, but these social definitions are based on some combination of certain inherited physical traits. Some physical traits such as hair color, height, and size of feet may be inherited, but these are rarely used to differentiate people into one racial category or another, while other physical traits such as skin color may be used. Taking these considerations into account, biological differences per se do not constitute racial differences. Rather, a *racial group* is a socially defined group distinguished by selected inherited physical characteristics.

Ethnic Groups

The word "ethnic" is derived from the Greek word *ethnikos*, which translates to "nations" in English. The word was initially equated with national origin and applied to European immigrants such as the Italians, Germans, Poles, and other national groups who came to the United States in large numbers, especially between 1900 and 1925. Today, ethnicity is given a wider definition and may also refer to group membership based on religion, language, or region. Using the word in this sense, Jews, Mormons, Latinos, and white Southerners can be considered as ethnic groups.

Whereas race is based on selected physical characteristics such as skin color, hair texture, or eye shape, ethnicity is based on cultural traits that reflect national origin, religion, and language. Cultural traits may be apparent in the manner of dress, speech patterns, and modes of emotional expression. Other cultural traits are less obvious but still vital to the group's heritage — such characteristics as ethical values, folklore, and literature.

Some authors prefer to focus on "sense of peoplehood" or "consciousness of kind" as the defining characteristic of ethnicity. Defined in

The diversity of ethnic groups in the United States today is ample evidence of the great numbers of immigrants who left their native lands to come to America. Between 1850 and 1920, from two to eight million immigrants arrived in the United States each decade. With the exception of Africans brought here enslaved, most European immigrants came voluntarily in search of higher standards of living as well as to escape persecution or hardship in their native lands.

this way, ethnicity may encompass both biological and cultural characteristics. Patterson (1975) defined ethnicity as a condition in a society in which certain members choose and emphasize a cultural, racial, or national tie as their primary identity outside the family. We take as our definition of ethnicity that of Milton M. Gordon, who likewise focused on the "sense of peoplehood" criterion. According to Gordon (1964), an *ethnic group* is

> any group which is defined or set off by race, religion, or national origin, or some combination of these categories. . . . All of these categories have a common social-psychological referent, in that all of them serve to create, through historical circumstances, a sense of peoplehood. (p. 27)

Minority Groups

Describing racial and ethnic relations in terms of minorities and majorities can be mis-

leading. A *minority group* is a group that is subordinate to the majority in terms of power and privilege; such groups are usually but not always smaller than the dominant group. Women, for example, are a numerical majority in American society, yet they have a minority status. In the Republic of South Africa, whites comprise less than one-fifth of the total population but they are in a position of dominance.

In the United States, Newman (1973) observed, the most highly valued norms or archetypes (standard patterns of behavior) are those of the white, Anglo-Saxon Protestant (WASP) middle classes (see Chapter 4). WASP norms, values, cultural patterns, and laws are widely observed and enforced. Minority groups are distinguished on the basis of the extent of their departure from these norms. They are also set apart on the basis of power and size. Using all three criteria — social norms, power, and size —

Newman (1973) defined minority groups as those

> that vary from the social norms or archetypes in some manner, are subordinate with regard to the distribution of social power, and rarely constitute more than one-half of the population of the society in which they are found. (p. 20)

According to this definition, the aged poor, poor people in Appalachia, southern whites, the handicapped, and homosexuals are minority groups. The minorities discussed in this chapter, however, were selected on the basis of racial and ethnic criteria.

Major Minority Groups in the United States

The black population is the largest minority group in the United States (see Table 9-1), constituting nearly 12 percent of the total population. The Spanish-speaking population is second to the black community in size, constituting approximately 6.4 percent of the population. The

Spanish classification, however, overlaps with other racial categories.

The third largest group, the Asian community, increased phenomenally during the past ten years. Twice as many Asian ethnics were counted in 1980 as in 1970. Following this group in size are the Native Americans, categorized in the U.S. Census as American Indians and grouped with the Eskimos and Aleuts (native Eskimoan tribes from the Aleutian Islands, which is a chain of volcanic islands extending some 1,100 miles from the tip of the Alaska Peninsula). These Native American groups included about one and a half million people in 1980, slightly more than one-half of 1 percent of the U.S. population. Unfortunately, comparable figures for white ethnics are not available. As a racial group, they are considered white and lumped together with the white native born.

Black Americans

As noted, black Americans comprise the largest racial minority in the United States. Because of such unique historical experiences as

Table 9-1

Distribution of the various minority groups in the United States for 1970 and 1980

RACE	1970 NUMBER	1970 PERCENTAGE	1980 NUMBER	1980 PERCENTAGE
Total	203,211,926	100.0	226,504,825	100.0
White	177,748,975	87.4	188,340,790	83.2
Black	22,580,289	11.1	26,488,218	11.7
Asian and Pacific Islander	1,538,721	0.8	3,500,636	1.5
American Indian, Eskimo, and Aleut	827,268	0.4	1,418,195	0.6
Other	516,673	0.3	6,756,986	3.0
Spanish origin (may be of any race)	9,072,602	4.5	14,605,883	6.4

SOURCE: U.S. Bureau of the Census, *Current Population Reports*, Series P-20, no. 363, *Population Profile of the United States: 1980*, U.S. Government Printing Office, Washington, D.C., 1981, Table 3, p. 9.

Black Americans comprise the largest racial minority in the United States. Most blacks share the aspirations and values of the dominant culture—home ownership, regular employment, pride in one's achievements—and an increasing number are moving into positions of leadership in government, business, and the professions. Pictured here is a station manager in Chicago conferring with one of her newscasters.

slavery, legal and social segregation, and economic discrimination, many blacks have lifestyles and value patterns that differ from those of the white majority. The relations between whites and blacks have been the source of a number of major social issues in the past several decades: busing, segregation, job discrimination, and interracial marriage, to mention a few.

In an examination of black families, Eshleman (1985), expanding on the work of Billingsley (1968), identified six major social transitions that have affected or will affect black Americans. The first transition was the movement from Africa to America, which is significant because of three factors: color, cultural discontinuity, and slavery. Color is the most obvious characteristic that sets whites and blacks apart. Cultural discontinuity was the abrupt shift from the culture learned and accepted in Africa to the cultural system of America. Rarely has any ethnic or racial group faced such a severe disruption

of cultural patterns. Slavery was the unique circumstance that brought many blacks to America. Unlike almost all other groups, Africans did not come to this country by choice. Most were brought as slaves to work on southern plantations. Unlike many free blacks in the North, slaves in the southern states had few legal rights. Southern blacks were considered the property of their white owners, who had complete control over every aspect of their lives.

A second major transition was from slavery to emancipation. In 1863, a proclamation issued by President Lincoln freed the slaves in all territories still at war with the Union. Although the slaves were legally free, emancipation presented a major crisis for many blacks because most were faced with the difficult choice of either remaining on the plantations as tenants with low wages or none at all for their labor or searching beyond the plantation for jobs, food, and housing. Many men left to search for jobs, so women became the major source of family stability. The shift to emancipation from slavery contributed to the third and fourth transitions.

The third transition was from rural to urban areas. For many blacks this shift had both good and bad effects. Cities were much more impersonal than the rural areas most blacks moved from, but they also provided more jobs, better schools, improved health facilities, a greater tolerance of racial minorities, and a chance for vertical social mobility. As of 1980, 81 percent of America's black population lived inside a Metropolitan Statistical Area (MSA), and 60 percent lived within a central city (*Statistical Abstract: 1984*: no. 21).

A closely related shift was the fourth transition, from southern to northern communities. The job opportunities created by World War I and World War II were the major impetus for the exodus of southern blacks to the North, a trend that continued through the 1960s. In 1900, 90 percent of all blacks lived in the South. By 1980, this figure had dropped to 53 percent (*Statistical Abstract: 1984*, no. 37). Today, there are more blacks in New York City and Chicago than in any other cities in the world, including African cities, and these cities have retained their top rankings for thirty years. In 1980, Detroit displaced Philadelphia as the city with the third largest black population.

The fifth transition was from negative to positive social status. The black middle class has been growing in recent years and resembles the white middle class in terms of education, job level, and other factors. A high proportion of blacks remain in the lower income brackets, however, because of the prejudice, segregation, and discriminatory practices endured by blacks throughout most of their time in this country. Only in the past twenty-five years have they achieved a measure of equality. Previously, they were routinely denied equal protection under the law, equal access to schools and housing, and equal wages. Discrimination has by no means been eradicated, but few would deny today that substantial progress has been made. Many social reform movements have been led by black leaders, perhaps because blacks have had the strongest grievances of any American ethnic group.

The final transition was from negative to positive self-image. A basic tenet of the symbolic interaction approach is that we develop ourselves, our identities, and our feelings of self-worth through our interactions with others. Throughout most of our history, blacks have been the last to be hired and the first to be fired. As shown in Chapter 1, however, blacks' self-evaluations are equal to or higher than those of whites and their rate of suicide is about one-half that of whites (see Table 1-2). Unfortunately, one major consequence of cuts in social programs under the Reagan Administration is that the cuts may have conveyed a message to all minority groups in the United States that they are of little importance compared with the interests of the dominant white middle and upper classes.

Spanish Americans

There are over fourteen and a half million people in the United States today who claim Spanish origins. This category includes those who classify themselves as Mexican, Puerto Rican, or Cuban and those from Spain or the Spanish-speaking countries of Central and South America. It also includes those who simply identify themselves as Spanish American, Hispanic, or Latino. Our discussion will focus on Mexican Americans, who constitute approximately 60 percent of this group.

Mexican Americans are also identified as Chicanos, a contraction of Mexicano. Over one million Mexican Americans are descendants of the Mexicans who lived in the Southwest before it became part of the United States. They became Americans in 1848, when Texas, California, New Mexico, and most of Arizona became U.S. territory. These four states plus Colorado contain the largest concentrations of this group today. Most urban Mexican Americans live in California, especially in Los Angeles.

Other Mexican Americans came from Mexico. They can be classified into three types: (1) legal immigrants; (2) braceros, or temporary workers; and (3) illegal aliens. Large-scale migration in the early 1900s was caused by the revolution and unsettled economic conditions in Mexico and by the demand for labor on cotton farms and railroads in California. Before the minimum wage law was passed, agricultural employers preferred braceros to local workers because they could be paid less, and the braceros were not a burden to the federal government inasmuch as they returned to Mexico when their services were no longer needed. Referring to the braceros,

one grower remarked, "We used to own slaves but now we rent them from the government" (Dinnerstein and Reimers, 1975, p. 101).

The number of illegal aliens from Mexico is not known; estimates range from one to ten million. Immigration policy concerning legal and illegal Mexican immigrants generally varies with the need for labor, which in turn depends on economic conditions. When the demand for Mexican labor was high, immigration was encouraged. When times were bad, illegal aliens were tracked down, rounded up, and deported. They were scapegoats in the depression of the 1930s, and they were again in the recession of the early 1980s.

Traditional Mexican-American culture is characterized by strong family ties, large families, *machismo*, and a practice known as *compadrazgo*. The extended family is the most important institution in the Chicano community. The theme of family honor and unity occurs throughout Mex-

Most Spanish-Americans in the United States today come from Mexico—legal immigrants, temporary workers, and illegal aliens. One of their cultural characteristics is an emphasis on strong family ties and the extended family—the most important institution in their subculture. Ties between extended families often take the form of co-parenthood, where godparents, or compadres, *are chosen from outside the kin network as a source of assistance and support.*

ican-American society irrespective of social class or geographical location. Madsen (1964) says that the upper-class rancher and the lower-class crop picker both think of themselves first as family members and second as individuals. This familism extends beyond the nuclear family unit of husband, wife, and children to relatives on both sides and persists even when the dominance of the male becomes weakened. It is a primary source of emotional and economic support and the primary focus of obligations.

Large families are a second major characteristic of traditional Mexican-American culture. Most American families have two or three children, but it is not unusual for Mexican-American families to have five or more. Families of this size, when linked with minimal skills and low levels of income, make it difficult for the Mexican American to enjoy life at a level equal to the dominant groups in American society.

Machismo is an exaggerated sense of masculinity. Some Mexican males and husbands assert their *machismo* by being the aloof, authoritarian head of the family, directing its activities, arbitrating disputes, and representing the family to community and society. Queen and Habenstein (1974) state that

> the husband, having long been socialized in the tradition of the sexual conquest of "bad" girls and the ascetic veneration of the "good," finds it difficult to assimilate sexual intercourse with the wife as an act of mutuality involving gratification and fulfillment equally shared; the wife, aware from earliest socialization that as a weaker female she cannot trust herself in sexual matters, denies herself or makes no sexual advances toward the spouse. The husband, free to continue the social activities enjoyed before marriage, finds conquests of other females ego building, and, as he makes no effort to deny such activities to his friends, they become just another means of demonstrating *machismo*. (p. 435)

One consequence of *machismo* is that it takes the husband out of the home and forces upon the wife an early and permanent role of motherhood. In contrast to the father, the mother continues to be the nurturing, warm parent even when her children are adults with children of their own.

Compadrazgo (godparenthood) is a social system that promotes ties between extended families. Its most common form is co-parenthood, linking two families through the baptismal ritual. The godparents, *compadres*, are chosen with care from outside the immediate kinship network. The male, the most important *compadre*, will hopefully be a man of influence, status, and respect in the community. *Compadres* are expected to develop close relationships and in times of trouble have the right to call on one another for assistance. *Compadrazgo* is most common among rural families.

Urban Chicanos conform more closely to the Anglo-Saxon nuclear family and egalitarian norms. The extended family and the *compadrazgo* system are considered less important, and the *machismo* syndrome has given way to more egalitarian husband-wife relationships.

A vigorous Mexican-American political movement emerged around 1966. Since then, the Chicanos have achieved a number of goals such as having bilingual instruction introduced at the elementary level. Cesar Chavez, one of the best-known Chicano leaders, organized Mexican farm workers in 1962 and started a lettuce boycott in 1972 that received nationwide publicity. A primary goal of Chicano political movements is to restore pride in Mexican-American heritage.

Asian Americans

The Asian community in the United States is a highly diverse group. The most numerous groups within it are the Chinese and Japanese. Also included in the Asian category are Fili-

Table 9-2

Top ten countries outside of North and South America sending immigrants to the United States: 1970, 1975, and 1980

1970		1975		1980	
Philippines	31,200	Philippines	31,800	Vietnam	43,500
Italy	25,000	Korea	28,400	Philippines	42,300
Greece	16,500	China	18,500	China	27,700
United Kingdom	14,200	India	15,800	Korea	32,300
China	14,100	Portugal	11,800	India	22,600
Portugal	13,200	Italy	11,600	United Kingdom	15,500
India	10,100	United Kingdom	10,800	Soviet Union	10,500
Germany	9,700	Greece	10,000	Iran	10,400
Korea	9,300	Germany	5,200	Portugal	8,400
Yugoslavia	8,600	Soviet Union	5,100	Germany	6,600

NOTES: All immigrants are listed by country of birth. China includes both mainland China and Taiwan.
SOURCE: U.S. Bureau of the Census, *Statistical Abstract of the United States: 1984*, 104th ed., U.S. Government Printing Office, Washington, D.C., 1983, no. 126, p. 92.

pinos, Asian Indians, Koreans, Hawaiians, and Guamanians. In the past decade, more immigrants have come from the Philippines, Korea, and Vietnam than from any country outside of North and South America (see Table 9-2). Many Taiwanese have also immigrated.

The Chinese were the first Asians to enter this country in large numbers. Unlike the Japanese, the Chinese resist assimilation and tend to uphold traditional values such as filial duty, veneration of the aged and deceased ancestors, and arranged marriages. Chinese-American families tend to be male-dominated, and an extended family pattern is the rule. The traditional family structure is difficult to maintain in the United States, however, in part because of political legislation. In early migrations, married Chinese males usually came alone with the intention of having their wives and children follow. The Immigration Act of 1904 made it impossible for them to send for their families, however, which resulted in what Betty Sung (1967) called the "mutilated family."

Today, most Chinese live in large urban enclaves in Hawaii, San Francisco, Los Angeles, and New York. A tourist visiting a Chinatown is likely to notice only the exotic sights, smells, and sounds; the problems prevalent in Chinatowns are less evident. There is often overcrowding, poverty, poor health, rundown housing, and inadequate care for the elderly. Not all Chinese live in Chinatowns, however. Those who have "made it" live in the suburbs.

At present, the Chinese have no national organizations. Their local organizations, which are often based on previous village ties or common family name, wield little power outside their communities.

Like the Chinese, most early Japanese immigrants were males imported for their labor, but important differences between these two groups resulted in different experiences (Kitano, 1980):

1. The Japanese came from a developing, industrial nation, the Chinese came from a primarily agricultural one.

In the second World War, the federal government placed more than 110,000 people of Japanese ancestry in relocation camps. Here, members of the Moshida family are shown awaiting the evacuation bus.

2. The Japanese used their embassy and consular officials as resources. The Chinese relied on informal organizations.

3. The Japanese started families almost immediately after they arrived. For the sake of their children, the Japanese had to accept American norms. The "split family syndrome" experienced by the Chinese precluded their beginning families, however. (p. 255)

As a result of these factors, Japanese Americans are today more fully integrated into American culture and have higher incomes than the Chinese or other Asian groups.

The traditional family system of the Japanese resembles that of the Chinese. It is characterized by male dominance, reverence for the aged, preference for male offspring, and strong family ties.

During World War II, fearing that there might be Japanese Americans working against the American war effort, the federal government moved most of them to "relocation camps." Regardless of their political views or how long they had been in this country, families were forced to pack up and move to camps in Utah, Arizona, California, Idaho, Wyoming, Colorado, and Arkansas, which severely disrupted their lives. Many were incensed at the suggestion that they were not loyal Americans capable of making valuable contributions to the American war effort. Some of the relocated families had sons serving in the armed forces. Altogether, more than 110,000 people of Japanese ancestry, 70,000 of them U.S. citizens by birth, were moved. After the war, the Japanese were allowed to return to their homes, but they were never compensated adequately for the time, businesses, or property that they lost.

Native Americans

The Native-American population is actually a varied group of tribes having different languages, cultures, and levels of civilization. At the time of the European invasion they could be divided into seven major geographical areas (Feagin, 1984, p. 177):

1. the Eastern tribes who hunted, farmed, and fished
2. the Great Plains hunters and agriculturists
3. the fishing societies of the Pacific Northwest
4. the seed gatherers of California and neighboring areas
5. the Navaho shepherd and pueblo farmers of the Arizona and New Mexico area
6. the desert societies of Southern Arizona and New Mexico
7. the Alaskan groups, including the Eskimos

Estimates of the number of Native Americans in the United States at the time of the European settlement range from one to 10 million. By 1800, the population had declined to 600,000, and by 1850 it had dwindled to 250,000 as a result of disease, starvation, and deliberate massacre. Since the turn of the century, however, their numbers have increased dramatically. In the 1970s, the Native-American population exceeded the one million mark for the first time since the period of European expansion, reaching approximately 1.4 million, according to U.S. Census Bureau data.

By the 1960s, Native Americans were no longer regarded as nations to be dealt with through treaties. Most tribes were treated as wards of the U.S. government and lived isolated lives on reservations. Today, about half of all Native Americans live on or near reservations administered fully or partly by the Bureau of Indian Affairs (BIA). Many other Native Americans have moved to urban areas or been relocated there by the BIA to help in their search for jobs and improved living conditions.

Native Americans are among the most deprived of American minority groups. Their unemployment rate is twice that of whites (Feagin, 1984). Most hold jobs at lower occupational levels and have incomes far below the median

Pictured here are two members of the Apache Tribal Council. Few opportunities exist for minority groups to gain power, and they are underrepresented in positions of leadership. Many Native Americans, for example, have relocated from reservations to urban areas in search of work only to find high unemployment or menial, low-paying jobs.

for American families. Housing is often severely crowded, and two-thirds of the houses in rural areas have no plumbing facilities. The life expectancy is about two-thirds the national average. Studies suggest that Native Americans have the lowest school enrollment rates of any racial or ethnic group in the United States, with high rates of drop-outs or "push-outs," in which "students {are} driven out of school because of white-oriented school regulations conflicting with the norms of their own Native American peer groups" (Feagin, 1984, p. 200). Children are often pressured not to speak their native language or practice their native traditions, which are quite different from the mainstream American traditions.

One area in which Native Americans differ from the mainstream culture is in family structure. The Indian equivalent to the family is the band, which includes a number of related families who live in close proximity. The band is composed of kinspeople who share property, jointly organize rituals and festivals, and provide mutual support and assistance. Bands are egalitarian and arrive at decisions collectively.

In the 1960s and 1970s, many Native-American tribes united and formed organized collectives to demand a better life for their people. Several tribes have banded together to bargain more effectively with the federal government, and they have sometimes used militant tactics to get results. But Native Americans, the only group that did not immigrate to the United States, remain a subordinate group. Stereotyped as bloodthirsty, savage, and inferior, they have suffered exploitation and discrimination in all of our basic social institutions.

White Ethnics

Most white ethnics in the United States today emigrated as a result of the European expansionist policy of the last 350 years. Earlier immigrants came mainly from northern and western European countries such as Britain, Ireland, Germany, France, and Switzerland. More recent immigrants came largely from southern and eastern European countries: Italy, Greece, the U.S.S.R., Yugoslavia, and Portugal (refer back to Table 9-2).

The majority of these immigrants discarded their roots and adopted American norms and values. Many dropped their European names in favor of names that sounded more "American," and most white ethnics have successfully assimilated. Michael Novak (1975), who is of Slovak ancestry, wrote the following about his experiences.

> Under challenge in grammar school concerning my nationality, I had been instructed by my father to announce proudly: "American." When my family moved from the Slovak ghetto of Johnston to the WASP suburb on the hill, my mother impressed upon us how well we must be dressed, and show good manners, and behave — people think of us as "different" and we mustn't give them any cause. (p. 593)

The emerging assertiveness of blacks and other nonwhites in the 1960s induced many white ethnics to reexamine their positions. John Goering (1971) found in interviews with Irish and Italian Catholics that ethnicity was more important to members of the third generation than it was to the migrants themselves. Novak (1975), a third-generation ethnic American, expressed the feeling of being deprived of his roots, his history:

> Odd that I should have such shallow knowledge of my roots. Amazing to me that I do not know what my family suffered, endured, learned, hoped these past six or seven generations. . . . As if history, in some way, began with my father and with me. (p. 592)

Today, many American ethnic communities

Jewish Americans are a predominant white ethnic group in the United States. Cultural and religious celebrations serve as binding and solidifying events for the Jewish people and other ethnic minorities. One such event is Sukkoth, a Jewish harvest festival that commemorates the wandering of the Jews in the desert after their expulsion from Egypt (circa 1200 B.C.). During this holiday the Jewish people build and eat in sukkas — booths with roofs of branches and leaves that recall the temporary shelters used by their forebears in the wilderness.

emphasize more than their folk culture, native food, dance, costume, and religious traditions in establishing their ethnic identities. They have sought a more structured means of expressing, preserving, and expanding their cultures, and many have formed fraternal organizations, museums, and native-language newspapers in an effort to preserve their heritage (Lopata, 1976).

One of the predominant white ethnic groups is the Jewish American. America has the largest Jewish population in the world, its estimated six million exceeding the approximately three and a half million Jews in Israel. They are heavily concentrated in New York City and its surrounding areas.

Jewish Americans are basically ethnic in nature in that they share cultural traits to a greater extent than physical features or religious beliefs. As a minority group they have a strong sense of group solidarity, tend to marry one another, and experience unequal treatment from non-Jews in the form of prejudice, discrimination, and segregation. While Jews are generally perceived to be affiliated with one of the three religious groups, the Orthodox, the Reform, or the Conservative, many, if not the majority of Jews, do not participate as adults in religious services or belong to a temple or synagogue. Yet they do not cease to think of themselves as Jews. The trend in the United States seems to be the substitution of cultural traditions for religion as the binding and solidifying force among Jewish Americans.

Injustices to Jewish people have continued for centuries all over the world. The most tragic example of anti-Semitism was during World War II, when Adolf Hitler ordered the extermination of 6 million Jewish civilians — the terrifying event that has become known as the Holocaust. While anti-Semitism in the United States never reached the extreme of Germany, it did exist. As early as the 1870s certain colleges excluded Jewish Americans. In the 1920s and 1930s a myth of international Jewry emerged that suggested Jews were going to conquer all governments throughout the world by using the vehicle of communism, which was believed by anti-Semites to be a Jewish movement. At that time, Henry Ford, the Catholic priest Charles E. Coughlin, and groups like the Ku Klux Klan published, preached, and spoke about a Jewish conspiracy as if it were fact. Unlike Europe, however, the United States government never publicly promoted anti-Semitism and Jewish Americans were more likely to face questions concerning whether to assimilate than how to survive.

Concern about anti-Semitism seemed to decrease drastically following World War II through the 1960s, but in the 1970s and continuing today, anti-Semitic sentiments and behaviors appear to be on the increase. The extent to which this is due to the Middle East conflict, black power activists, the rise of religious fundamentalist preachings, or some other reason is a subject for debate. Whatever the cause, racial or ethnic hostility tends to unify the victims against the attacker and Jewish Americans are no exception. Attitudes and their influence and some theories of prejudice and discrimination are discussed in the section that follows.

Attitudes and Their Influence

One of the most serious problems faced by most ethnic groups in America concerns how they are perceived by others. For a number of reasons, people tend to treat those they perceive to be different in ways that they would not treat members of their own group. Not infrequently, this has led to inequalities and increased the strains that society must deal with. To pursue the American ideal of equality, we must understand how the attitudes underlying unfair practices are formed.

Prejudice

A *prejudice* is a preconceived judgment, either good or bad, about another group. More specifically, it is "an attitude that predisposes a person to think, perceive, feel, and act in favorable or unfavorable ways towards a group or its individual members" (Secord and Backman, 1964, p. 165). We are concerned here chiefly with the negative connotation of the word — ethnic relations in this country are characterized more by antipathy than by empathy, as witnessed by the fact that a number of ethnic slurs such as "wetback" and "nigger" exist, but there are few ethnic nicknames that express positive feelings.

A variety of theories have been offered to explain prejudice. Early theories were often based on the premise that prejudiced attitudes are innate or biological, but more recent explanations tend to attribute the development of prejudices to the social environment.

Economic theories of prejudice are based on the supposition that competition and conflict among groups are inevitable when different groups desire commodities that are in short supply. These theories explain why racial prejudice is most salient during periods of depression and economic turmoil. In California, for example, from the 1840s through the depression of the 1930s, economic relations between whites and Chinese Americans were tolerant and amiable as long as the Chinese confined themselves to occupations such as laundry and curio shops. When they began to compete with whites in gold mining and other business enterprises, however, violent racial conflicts erupted. Japanese Americans had a similar experience.

The "exploitation" variant of economic theory argues that prejudice is used to stigmatize a group as inferior to put its members in a subordinate position and justify their exploitation. The exploitation theme explains how capitalists have traditionally justified exploiting recent immigrants who had little money, few skills, and difficulties with English.

Psychological theories of prejudice suggest that prejudice satisfies psychic needs or compensates for some defect in the personality. *Scapegoating* involves blaming another person or group for one's own problems. Another psychological view, *projection*, involves attributing one's own unacceptable traits or behaviors to another person. This perspective suggests that people transfer responsibility for their own failures to a vulnerable group, often a racial or ethnic group. *Frustration-aggression theory* involves a form of projection (Dollard et al., 1939). In this view, groups who strive repeatedly to achieve certain goals become frustrated after failing a number of times. When the frustration reaches a high intensity, the group seeks an outlet for their frustration by displacing their aggressive behavior to a socially approved target, a racial or ethnic group. Thus the Germans, frustrated by runaway inflation and the failure of their nationalist ambitions, vented their aggressive feelings by persecuting the Jews. Poor whites, frustrated by their unproductive lands and financial problems, drained off their hostilities through antiblack prejudices.

The *authoritarian personality theory* argues that some people are more inclined to prejudice than others due to differences in personality. According to the authors of the theory (Adorno et al., 1950), prejudiced individuals are characterized by rigidity of outlook, intolerance, suggestibility, dislike for ambiguity, and irrational

Stereotypes are widely held beliefs about the character and behavior of members of a group. In movies and on television, conformity to stereotypes perpetuates viewers' beliefs. The black mammy portrayed in the Jerome Kern musical Show Boat *is the stereotypical overweight happy servant.*

attitudes. They tend to be authoritarian, preferring stability and orderliness to the indefiniteness that accompanies social change. Simpson and Yinger (1972) questioned whether these traits cause prejudice and suggested that they may in fact be an effect of prejudice or completely unrelated to it.

Regardless of what theory one accepts, prejudice is sustained through *stereotypes*, which are widely held beliefs about the character and behavior of all members of a group. They are usually based on readily discernible characteristics such as physical appearance and are oversimplifications that seldom correspond to the facts. A prejudiced person might say of one group, "They breed like rabbits," of another, "They are a bunch of hoodlums," overlooking the great range of individual differences found in every group. They tend "to think of people in bunches as though they were bananas" (Berry and Tischler, 1978, p. 236).

Stereotypes of the majority are usually more favorable than those of minorities. Whites may be portrayed as industrious, intelligent, ambitious, and progressive, while blacks may be described as lazy, happy-go-lucky, and ignorant. There are several stereotypes associated with Native Americans. One image often projected to the public by the movies and television advertising is of the Native American who is strong and stoical, who has a special relationship to nature. A stereotype more common in the past was of the ruthless, bloodthirsty savage cruelly murdering innocent (white) settlers. A third suggests that all Native Americans are alcoholics who live in self-induced poverty. Needless to say, none of these stereotypes even begins to reflect the great diversity of behavior that exists now and has always existed among Native Americans, as among other groups.

Stereotyping is not entirely dysfunctional. Albrecht et al. (1980) have argued that "stereotypes afford us the comfort of recognition and

save us the time and effort of interpreting masses of new stimuli hourly" (p. 254). They help us mentally sort people into predictable categories, making social interaction easier and minimizing social errors. Most of our encounters are dominated by stereotyped conceptions of how we should act and how others should respond, whether we are dealing with bank tellers, employers, or family members.

Most would agree, however, that the dysfunctional aspects of stereotyping far outweigh the functional aspects. In addition to pointing out how stereotyping is functional, Albrecht et al. (1980) cited several harmful consequences. First, stereotypes are often based on inaccurate information, and distorting reality could very well interfere with a person's adjustment to his or her social environment. Second, they are used to justify discrimination against members of various ethnic and racial groups. The stereotype that blacks are lazy and unintelligent, for example, could be used as a basis for categorically barring blacks from highly paid executive and managerial positions.

A third damaging effect of stereotyping is that it may contribute to the development of an inferior self-concept. The symbolic interaction viewpoint tells us that self-perceptions are created through internalizing the attitudes, responses, and definitions one believes are held by others. An inferior self-concept may be developed because stereotyped predictions about behavior influence behavior in such a way that those predictions come true. The outcome is then used to confirm the original prediction. Robert Merton called this process the *self-fulfilling prophecy*.

Radke and Trager's (1950) early studies of black children support the idea that members of a stereotyped minority tend to internalize the definitions attached to them. In these studies, the children were asked to evaluate black and white dolls and to tell stories about black and white persons in photographs. The children overwhelmingly preferred the white dolls to the black. The white dolls were described as good, the black dolls as bad. The black individuals in the photographs were given inferior roles as servants, maids, or gardeners.

More recent studies of self-esteem found little or no difference between blacks and whites. Zirkel (1971) reviewed over a dozen studies of black and white students attending grammar and secondary schools and concluded that black and white children now have similar levels of self-esteem. Simmons et al. (1978) found that minority students have even stronger self-concepts than majority students. This change in attitudes can be linked to the civil rights movements of the late 1960s and early 1970s, when emerging ethnic pride began to be expressed in such slogans as "Red Power" and "Black is beautiful."

Discrimination

Prejudice is a judgment, an attitude. *Discrimination,* on the other hand, is overt behavior or actions. It is the categorical exclusion of "all members of a group from certain rights, opportunities, or privileges" (Schaefer, 1984, p. 55). According to the conflict perspective, the dominant group in a society practices discrimination to protect its advantages, privileges, and interests.

A number of authors (e.g., Allport, 1954; Kinloch, 1974) have argued that discrimination is a possible but not inevitable outcome of prejudice; that is, prejudiced people are likely to be discriminatory, but exceptions do occur. Recognizing the possible independence of these two concepts, Robert Merton (1976) classified people into four categories.

1. The unprejudiced nondiscriminator: all-weather liberal
2. The unprejudiced discriminator: reluctant liberal

3. The prejudiced nondiscriminator: timid bigot
4. The prejudiced discriminator: all-weather bigot (pp. 189–216)

People in categories 1 and 2 believe in the American creed of equality, human rights, human dignity, freedom, and justice. The all-weather liberals practice what they believe in and are likely to urge others to abide by the same American ideals. Reluctant liberals, although holding the same beliefs as the all-weather liberals, are prone to social pressure. Reluctant liberals are silent in the presence of articulate bigots and exercise discrimination in order "not to hurt the business." The overture "I don't have anything against you personally, but . . ." is familiar to many of us.

Like reluctant liberals, the timid bigots are susceptible to situational factors and will not discriminate when in the company of nonbigots. Also, bigoted employers are now deterred from discriminatory hiring practices by Affirmative Action laws. All-weather bigots are blatant bigots through and through. They do not believe that members of certain racial and ethnic groups are their equals, and they do not bother to conceal the antagonism they feel for these groups. They express their intolerance freely in their speech and their actions.

Discrimination does not operate solely at the individual level, however; institutional discrimination occurs as well. *Institutional discrimination* is the continuing exclusion or oppression of a group as a result of criteria established by an institution. In this form of discrimination, individual prejudice is not a factor, and laws or rules are not applied with the intent of preventing people of a certain race or ethnic group from belonging. Suppose, for example, that a school requires a certain minimum score on a standardized national exam for admission, or that a certain club requires a $10,000 annual membership fee. In such cases, no bias against any particular racial or

Black Women Who Made History: A Quiz to Test Your Knowledge

Black women have made contributions to American life in many areas: government, sports, the performing arts, business. Here is a 20-question quiz focusing on black women.

1. She was born in Africa and when she was a child she was sold as a slave on the docks of Boston in 1761. She achieved international fame as a poet and in 1773 her poems on various subjects were published in London.
   a. Phillis Wheatley
   b. Harriet Tubman
   c. Elizabeth Prophet

2. She was born in 1797 in Hurley, N.Y., and was a pioneer abolitionist.
   a. Sadie Latimore
   b. Nancy Burroughs
   c. Sojourner Truth

3. Born in Dorchester County, Md., in 1820, she became one of the chief engineers of the Underground Railroad, which helped runaway slaves escape to freedom.
   a. Ida B. Wells
   b. Jeanne Lea
   c. Harriet Tubman

4. She was born in 1868 and was a leading cosmetic manufacturer, a highly successful businesswoman and one of the first American women millionaires. She contributed generously to educational and charitable organizations.
   a. Madame C.J. Walker
   b. Lillie K. Edwards
   c. Velma A. Strayhorne

5. She was the first black woman lawyer in the United States. She was graduated from Howard University Law School in 1872, less than 10 years after the Emancipation Proclamation.
   a. Constance B. Motley
   b. Charlotte E. Ray
   c. Edith S. Sampson

6. She was an educator, social worker and a founder of a well-known college in Florida.
   a. Lorraine Ann Spellman
   b. Mary McLeod Bethune
   c. Gloria Mae Bennett

7. On July 22, 1939, she was appointed the first black woman judge in the United States.
   a. Geraldine Ford Bledsoe
   b. Jane Matilda Bolin
   c. Constance Baker Motley

8. In 1941 she was the first black person to sing with the Metropolitan Opera. Later she became a delegate to the United Nations. On Jan. 7, 1955, she became the first black singer to be signed by the Metropolitan Opera for a leading role.
   a. Dorothy Maynor
   b. Marian Anderson
   c. Violette Johnson

9. In 1950, she became the first black US delegate to the United Nations.
   a. Sadie T. Mosseli
   b. Frances A. W. Harper
   c. Edith S. Sampson

10. She was a black American singer born and educated in New Orleans. Having shown remarkable talent at an early age, she became a concert singer and recording artist. She is known

ethnic group may be intended — anyone who meets the criteria can be admitted. But the result is the same as it would be if the discrimination were by design. Few members of minority or ethnic groups could meet the requirements for admittance to the school or club, and the benefits of belonging would accrue only to groups that already belonged. This would tend to continue existing patterns of educational and occupational deprivation from one generation to the next.

A similar process operates in our criminal justice system. Suppose that individuals from

especially for her renditions of spirituals.

    a. Alberta Hunter
    b. Hilda Simms
    c. Mahalia Jackson

11. The first black woman to win the Wimbledon tennis championship (in July 1957) was . . .

    a. Althea Gibson
    b. Ora Washington
    c. Cheryl Roberts

12. She is a senior vice president of the Motown Corp., which was founded by her brother, Berry Gordy Jr.

    a. Esther Edwards
    b. Minnie Gaston
    c. Rose Morgan

13. She is regarded as the fastest female sprinter of all time. She won three gold medals in the 1960 Olympics.

    a. Althea Gibson
    b. Wilma Rudolph
    c. Susan McKinney

14. She is the first black writer to win a Pulitzer Prize in literature, for *Annie Allen*. Her other books include *Bronzeville Boys and Girls, Selected Poems* and *Riot*.

    a. Virginia Josey
    b. Gwendolyn Brooks
    c. Lorraine Hansberry

15. She became the first black female ambassador in US history when she was appointed ambassador to Luxembourg in 1966.

    a. Edmonia J. Davidson
    b. Patricia R. Harris
    c. Elizabeth Hartman

16. On Nov. 5, 1963 she became the first black woman elected to Congress.

    a. Shirley Chisholm
    b. Cardiss Collins
    c. Barbara Jordan

17. She is known as the "Voice of the Century" and was the first black operatic star to sing a leading role on television.

    a. Marian Anderson
    b. Hildred Roach
    c. Leontyne Price

18. Gladys Knight and Della Reese are best known as:

    a. Educators
    b. Fashion designers
    c. Pop vocalists

19. She is a distinguished educator and is currently president of the largest organization in the nation, the National Education Assn.

    a. Lorraine Williams
    b. Dorothy Height
    c. Mary Futrell

20. She won the Miss America Contest in 1983.

    a. Tawny Grodin
    b. Suzette Charles
    c. Vanessa Williams

Black history quiz answers

  1. a. Phillis Wheatley
  2. c. Sojourner Truth
  3. c. Harriet Tubman
  4. a. Madame C. J. Walker
  5. b. Charlotte E. Ray
  6. b. Mary McLeod Bethune
  7. b. Jane Matilda Bolin
  8. b. Marian Anderson
  9. c. Edith S. Sampson
10. c. Mahalia Jackson
11. a. Althea Gibson
12. a. Esther Edwards
13. b. Wilma Rudolph
14. b. Gwendolyn Brooks
15. b. Patricia R. Harris
16. a. Shirley Chisholm
17. c. Leontyne Price
18. c. Pop vocalists
19. c. Mary Futrell
20. c. Vanessa Williams

Scoring

16 to 20 correct: *Excellent.* 11 to 15: *Good.* 6 to 10: *Fair.* 0 to 5: *Poor.*

SOURCE: *The Boston Globe*, 1 Feb. 1984. Reprinted by permission of the author, Clarence N. Blake, Ed.D., Professor of Education, University of the District of Columbia.

two different ethnic groups are arrested for identical offenses and given the same fine. If one can pay the fine but the other can't, their fates may be quite different. The one who cannot pay will go to jail while the other one goes home. The result is institutional discrimination against the poor. Once a person has been imprisoned, that individual may find that jobs are harder to find. Research indicates that blacks and other minority groups do spend more time in jail, which disrupts family and work life and can continue the cycle of poverty.

Racism

Whereas prejudice is an attitude, racism is a system of beliefs and actions based on those beliefs. The distinction is sometimes difficult to grasp. Essentially, *racism* is discrimination based on racial characteristics. It can be regarded as having three major components. First, it is the belief that one's own race is superior to other racial groups. This component may involve racial prejudice, but it is not synonymous with it. Racial prejudice is an attitude, usually negative, toward the members of other racial groups. The belief in the superiority of one's own group may also involve ethnocentrism, which was defined in Chapter 4 as a belief in the superiority of one's own group on the basis of cultural criteria. A person's own group may be an ethnic group, but it need not be. Thus racial prejudice and ethnocentrism can be regarded as properties of racism, not synonyms for it.

The second property of racism is that it has an ideology, or set of beliefs, that justifies the subjugation and exploitation of another group. According to Rothman (1978), a racist ideology serves five functions:

1. It provides a moral rationale for systematic deprivation.
2. It allows the dominant group to reconcile values and behavior.
3. It discourages the subordinate group from challenging the system.
4. It rallies adherence in support of a "just" cause.
5. It defends the existing division of labor. (p. 51)

Perpetuators of racist ideologies claim that they are based on scientific evidence. One pseudoscientific theory, for example, held that the various races evolved at different times. Blacks, who presumably evolved first, were regarded as the most primitive race. As such, they were be-lieved to be incapable of creating a superior culture or carrying on the culture of the higher, white races, but the theory also argued that some benefits could accrue to the blacks by serving members of the white race. This theory is obviously self-serving and completely without scientific foundation.

The third element in racism is that the beliefs are acted upon. Many examples of racist actions in this country could be given. The lynching of blacks in the South and the destruction of entire tribes of Native Americans who were regarded as little more than animals are two of the more extreme instances.

Racism, like discrimination, can be of two types. Individual racism originates in the racist beliefs of a single person. Racist store owners, for example, might refuse to hire black employees because they regard them as inferior beings. *Institutional racism* occurs when racist ideas and practices are embodied in the folkways, mores, or legal structures of various institutions. The policy of apartheid in the Republic of South Africa (described by Berry and Tischler, 1978, pp. 7–8) is one of the most notorious examples of institutional racism. The policy of apartheid, reminiscent of Jim Crow legislation in the United States, calls for biological, territorial, social, educational, economic, and political separation of the various racial groups that compose the Republic of South Africa.

Racism can take many different forms — separatism, segregation, subjugation, exploitation, expulsion, and others. We will focus on two forms considered the most extreme: genocide and mass expulsion.

Genocide is the practice of deliberately destroying a whole race or ethnic group. The term was coined by Raphael Lemkin to describe the heinous crimes committed by the Nazis during World War II against the Jewish people, which is the supreme example of racism. Of the 9,600,000 Jews who lived in Nazi-dominated Europe between 1933 and 1945, 60 percent died in concentration camps (Berry and Tischler, 1978). The British also solved race problems through annihilation during their colonization campaigns overseas. Between 1803 and 1876, for example, they practically wiped out the native population of Tasmania. The aborigines were believed to be a degenerate race, wild beasts to be hunted and killed. One colonist regularly hunted natives to feed his dogs. But we don't have to go to Australia for illustrations. As early as 1717, the U.S. government was giving incentives to private citizens for exterminating the "troublesome" native Indians, and Americans were paid generous bounties for Indian scalps.

The Convention on Genocide of the United Nations formulated international legislation in the 1970s declaring genocide a punishable crime. More than seventy nations ratified the convention, but the United States, surprisingly, was not one of them. This country did not sign the genocide convention primarily because of the legal objections raised by American lawyers and the American Bar Association. The objections were based on technical questions about the definitions of such concepts as "group," "mental harm," and "physical harm."

Mass expulsion is the practice of expelling racial or ethnic groups from their homeland. The United States routinely used expulsion to solve conflicts with the Indians. In an incident known as "the trail of tears," the Cherokees were forced out of their homeland in the region where Georgia meets Tennessee and North Carolina. The re-

Institutionalized racism is embodied in the norms of a culture. The policy of apartheid in the Republic of South Africa has government support for racial segregation and discrimination against nonwhites. Overt indications of these practices can be seen in the signs of rest rooms for non-Europeans, that is, blacks, coloreds, and Asians.

Mass expulsion was forced on the Cherokee Indians as seen in this illustration of the "Trail of Tears." President Jackson saw the Indians as a nuisance and an impediment to growth and progress. In 1817, he began to force them to give up large tribal tracts and move west to areas that were seen as remote and of little interest to white settlers.

moval was triggered by the discovery of gold in the Georgia mountains and the determination of whites to take possession of it. The exodus went to the Ohio River and then to the Mississippi, ending in what is now Oklahoma. Of the ten thousand Cherokees rounded up, about four thousand perished during the exodus.

Racist thinking and racist doctrine were rampant between 1850 and 1950, which is aptly called "the century of racism." Since 1950, it has declined in many parts of the world, but there is no question that it still exists.

Patterns of Group Interaction

When different racial and ethnic groups live in the same area, widespread and continuous contact among groups is inevitable, but it rarely results in equality. Generally, one group seizes power and dominates the other groups. In some cases, the group in power attempts mass expulsion or genocide, but integration, assimilation, and pluralism are more common. Whatever the form of group interaction, relations among groups are strongly influenced by their stratification rankings and status.

Ethnic Stratification: Inequality and Interaction

As we saw in Chapter 8, stratification in a society takes a variety of forms. Sometimes it is based on rank, as in an estate system; sometimes it is based on a status ascribed at birth, as in a caste system; and sometimes it is based on an acquired status such as income or occupation, as in many industrialized countries. Some societies, including our own, stratify people on the basis of ascribed statuses like race and ethnic heritage in addition to the achieved statuses of education and income.

In America, the predominant norms, values, beliefs, ideas, and character traits are those of the majority — the white, Anglo-Saxon, Protestant middle class. The more a group diverges from the norms of the majority, the lower its rank in the social hierarchy. Thus it may be less desirable to be Chinese or Mexican than to be German or Irish, and less desirable to be German or Irish than to be a white Anglo-Saxon Protestant.

The consequences of allocating status on the basis of ethnic or racial membership are most evident in the different lifestyles, life chances, and opportunities of different groups. When social inequality is based on racial lines, the majority gets the more desirable positions and minorities get the less desirable ones.

Donald L. Noel (1975) contends that three conditions are necessary for ethnic stratification to occur in a society: ethnocentrism, competition

for resources, and inequalities in power. The inevitable outcome of ethnocentrism is that other groups are disparaged to a greater or lesser degree, depending on the extent of their difference from the majority. Competition among groups occurs when they must vie for the same scarce resources or goals, but it need not lead to ethnic stratification if values concerning freedom and equality are held and enforced. According to Noel, it is the third condition, inequality in power, that enables one group to impose its will upon the others. Power permits the dominant group to render the subordinate groups ineffectual as competitors and to institutionalize the distribution of rewards and opportunities to consolidate their position.

This view of inequality is central to the conflict perspective on racial and ethnic relations. Conflict theories assume that the relative powerlessness of minority groups provides a basis for exploitation and a pool of cheap labor for the ruling class. It is argued that racial or ethnic minorities who are willing to accept jobs at very low wages restrict the wages of *all* workers because workers from majority groups who demand higher wages can be replaced by low-status, relatively powerless minority members. This idea is described more fully in the upcoming sections on ethnic antagonism and the split labor market.

What positions do ethnic and racial groups occupy in the stratification system of the United States? Table 9-3 lists the income, education, and labor force status of selected groupings of racial and ethnic groups in America. Unfortunately, complete statistics on Native Americans are not available and groups such as Japanese Americans, Chinese Americans, Filipino Americans, Hawaiians, and Samoans are all grouped together under "Asian and Pacific Islanders." Nevertheless, major differences remain.

In our society, income and education are important indicators of a group's place in the strati-

Table 9-3

Income, education, and labor force status of whites, blacks, Asians, and persons of Spanish origin, 1980

CHARACTERISTICS	RACE				
	WHITE	BLACK	ASIAN AND PACIFIC ISLANDERS	AMERICAN INDIANS, ESKIMO, ALEUTIAN ISLANDERS*	SPANISH ORIGIN
Median Family Income (1979)	$20,840	$12,618	$26,456	$16,672	$14,711
Less than $10,000	17.5%	40.4%	18.1%	36.4%	32.7%
More than $25,000	37.8%	19.3%	44.6%	20.4%	21.7%
Years of School Completed					
Elementary: 0–8 years	16.6%	27.7%	16.4%	25.0%	40.8%
High school: 1–4 years	50.2%	50.5%	33.5%	50.8%	39.8%
College: 1–4 years or more	33.2%	21.8%	50.1%	24.2%	19.4%
Labor Force Status					
Persons in labor force, age 16 or over	62.2%	59.2%	66.3%	58.6%	63.4%
Males in labor force	76.0%	66.7%	76.3%	—	78.4%
Females in labor force	49.6%	62.9%	57.1%	—	48.9%
Males Unemployed	5.9%	12.8%	4.4%	—	8.7%
Females Unemployed	5.8%	11.2%	5.4%	—	10.1%

SOURCE: U.S. Bureau of the Census, *Statistical Abstract of the United States: 1982–83,* 103d ed., U.S. Government Printing Office, Washington, D.C., 1982, no. 41, p. 35.

* *Statistical Abstract: 1984,* 104th ed., nos. 42 and 43, p. 39.

fication system. As the table indicates, blacks, American Indians, and persons of Spanish origin had the lowest median family incomes and lowest levels of education in 1980. Nearly twice as high a percentage of whites and Asian Americans had median family incomes of more than $25,000. One-half of all Asian Americans had attended or completed college compared with one-third of the white population, one-fourth of the American Indian and Eskimo population, and one-fifth of the black and Spanish-origin populations. While the percentages of persons in

the labor force did not differ dramatically, the percentage of those unemployed did. Black and Spanish-origin males and females had about twice the rate of unemployment as white and Asian Americans.

The high income and education levels of Asian Americans reflect the emphasis placed on education by those groups. It probably also reflects the changes in immigration policy in the mid-1960s that gave priority to highly skilled and professional immigrants. The low incomes of black and Spanish families reflect their overrepresentation in certain less prestigious, less skilled, and lower-paying occupational categories. Native Americans would be in similar lower-level occupational groupings. One common consequence of these income, education, and employment differentials is antagonism among ethnic groups and between the less powerful and those with more power.

Ethnic Antagonism

Ethnic antagonism is mutual opposition, conflict, or hostility among different ethnic groups. In the broadest sense, the term encompasses all levels of intergroup conflict — ideologies and beliefs such as racism and prejudice, behaviors such as discrimination and riots, and institutions such as the legal and economic systems. Ethnic antagonism is closely linked to the racial and ethnic stratification system. The best-known theory of ethnic antagonism is that of the *split labor market* as formulated by Edna Bonacich in a series of articles in the 1970s (1972, 1975, and 1976).

The split labor market was discussed briefly in Chapter 8. The central tenet of split labor market theory is that when the price of labor for the same work differs by ethnic group, a three-way conflict develops among business, higher-priced labor, and cheaper labor. Business — that is, the employer — aims at having as cheap and docile a labor force as possible. Higher-priced labor may include current employees or a dominant ethnic group that demands higher wages, a share of the profits, or fringe benefits that increase the employer's costs. Cheaper labor refers to any ethnic group that can do the work done by the higher-priced laborers at a lower cost to the employer.

Antagonism results when the higher-paid labor group, who want to keep both their jobs and their wages (including benefits), are threatened by the introduction of cheaper labor into the market. The fear is that the cheaper labor group will either replace them or force them to lower their wage level. This basic class conflict then turns into an ethnic and racial conflict. If the higher-paid labor group is strong enough, they may try to exclude the lower-paid group. *Exclusion* is the attempt to keep out the cheaper labor (or the product they produce). Thus, laws may be passed that make it illegal for Mexicans, Cubans, Chinese, Filipinos, or refugees to enter the country; or taxes may be imposed on Japanese automobiles, foreign steel, or clothes made in Taiwan. Another technique used by higher-paid labor is the imposition of a *caste system*, in which the cheaper labor can get jobs only in certain low-paying, low-prestige occupations. As a result, the higher-paid group controls the prestigious jobs that pay well. In one sense it can be argued that a sort of caste system exists today for women and blacks. Both groups hold jobs of lower status and power and receive lower wages.

Bonacich (1975) claims that another process, *displacement*, is also likely to arise in split labor markets. Capitalists who want to reduce labor costs may simply displace the higher-paid employees with cheaper labor. They can replace workers at their present location or move their factories and businesses to states or countries where the costs are lower. The early 1980s witnessed many examples of strikebreaking by powerful business managers and government officials, who replaced union and higher-paid workers with nonunion and lower-paid employees. The steel, airline, and automobile industries are three cases in point.

An alternative to the split labor market is what Bonacich terms *radicalism* (1975), in which labor groups join together in a coalition against the capitalist class and present a united front. When this occurs, Bonacich claims, no one is displaced or excluded and no caste system is established. Anyone who gets hired comes in under the conditions of the higher-priced labor. Bonacich believes that as long as there is "cheap labor" anywhere in the world, there may not be a solution within a capitalist system (1976).

Integration and Assimilation

Integration occurs when ethnicity becomes insignificant and everyone can freely and fully participate in the social, economic, and political mainstream. *Assimilation* occurs when individuals and groups forsake their own cultural tradition to become part of a different group and tradition. To accomplish these goals, the removal of legal barriers must be complemented by the elimination of the prejudiced attitudes and social pressures that maintain ethnic and racial barriers. (Many Americans feel that assimilation should be the basis for an integrated society.) There are two variants of assimilation in the United States: the *melting pot* and *Anglo-conformity*. The formulations (Newman, 1973) below differentiate these two terms.

$$\text{Melting pot: } A + B + C = D$$
$$\text{Anglo-conformity: } A + B + C = A$$

In melting pot assimilation, each group contributes a bit of its own culture and absorbs aspects of other cultures such that the whole is a combination of all the groups. Anglo-conformity is equated with "Americanization," whereby the minority loses its identity completely to the dominant WASP culture. This approach has been the more prevalent integrationist policy in America during recent decades.

Integration is a two-way process: the immigrants must want to assimilate and the host society must be willing to have them assimilate. The immigrant must undergo cultural assimilation, learning the day-to-day norms of the WASP culture pertaining to dress, language, food, and sports. This process also involves internalizing the more critical aspects of the culture such as values, ideas, beliefs, and attitudes. *Structural assimilation* involves developing patterns of intimate contact between the "guest" and "host" groups in the clubs, organizations, and institutions of the host society. Cultural assimilation generally precedes structural assimilation, although the two sometimes happen simultaneously.

Gordon (1964) has observed that cultural assimilation has occurred on a large scale in American society, although the various minorities differ in the pace at which they are assimilating. With white ethnics of European origin, cultural assimilation went hand in hand with amalgamation (biological mixing through large-scale intermarriage). Among Asian ethnics, Japanese Americans seem to have assimilated most completely and are being rewarded with high socioeconomic status. In contrast, Chinese Americans, particularly first-generation migrants, have resisted assimilation and retained strong ties to their cultural traditions. The existence of Chinatowns in many cities reflects this desire for cultural continuity.

But assimilation involves more than just culture borrowing because immigrants want access to the host's institutional privileges. The issue of integration is particularly relevant in three areas: housing, schooling, and employment.

Members of most ethnic groups live in segregated housing. *Segregation* is the act of separating a group from the main body; it results in ethnic enclaves such as little Italies, black ghettos, and Hispanic barrios. The most significant division, however, is between the whites in the suburbs and the blacks and other minorities in the inner cities. At the institutional level, segregation can be attributed to discriminatory practices and policies of the federal housing agencies and mortgage-lending institutions. Suburban zoning patterns that tend to keep out poorer families are also influential. At the individual level, segregation is the result of some whites' refusal to sell their houses to nonwhites or the desire of minorities themselves to live in ethnic communities.

The city-suburb polarization of blacks and whites declined during the mid-1970s, however, partly because of the antisegregation efforts of the U.S. government. Since 1965, federal law has prohibited discrimination in the rental, sale, or financing of suburban housing. In Chicago, all banks and savings and loan associations bidding for deposits of federal funds were requested to sign anti–red lining pledges. "Red lining" is the practice among mortgage-lending institutions of imposing artificial restrictions on housing loans for areas where minorities have started to buy (Vitarello, 1975). Despite these and other advances American society has a long way to go in desegregating housing patterns.

Busing legislation is designed to eliminate racial segregation in schools. Defenders of the legislation argue that minority students who are exposed to high-achieving white middle-class students will do better academically (Coleman et al., 1966). They also contend that desegregation by busing is a way for whites and minority groups to learn about each other, which may diminish stereotypes and racist attitudes.

Opinion surveys indicate that opposition to integration is not the major concern of many people who oppose busing. A 1975 Harris survey found that 56 percent of adults were in favor of desegregating public schools and 35 percent were opposed. On the issue of busing, however, the overwhelming majority were opposed, 74 percent to 20 percent. Even among blacks, 40 percent were in favor of busing but 47 percent were opposed to it.

Concerning jobs, Hogan and Featherman (1977) and Featherman and Hauser (1976) believe that blacks will eventually be integrated into the stratification system of the majority, but prior to the early 1970s, ethnic group membership was a much more influential factor in determining what sort of jobs blacks could get. As Hogan and Featherman observed, "Black men have experienced a perverse sort of egalitarianism — neither the disadvantages of lower socio-

Integration occurs when ethnicity becomes insignificant and everyone can freely and fully participate in the social, economic, and political mainstream. Indications of the extent of racial integration can be witnessed in neighborhoods, jobs, churches, and the general community. In the field of education, busing, which was a heated political issue, brought a greater number of black and white students together.

economic origins nor the advantages of high social origins and education weigh as heavily in the
status attainments of Blacks as they do in those
of Whites" (p. 101).

In the 1970s, particularly among young
workers, patterns of socioeconomic stratification
varied less by race than they did in previous
years. The economic integration of blacks began
first and has proceeded furthest among blacks
born in the North. Internal differentiation of the
black population and the development of more
distinct socioeconomic strata also indicate that
blacks have made gains in socioeconomic integration.

Pluralism

Cultural pluralism can be defined as a situation in which the various ethnic groups in a society maintain their distinctive cultural patterns,
subsystems, and institutions (Newman, 1973).
Whereas an integrationist seeks to eliminate ethnic boundaries, a pluralist wants to retain them.
Pluralists argue that groups can coexist by accepting their differences. Basic to cultural pluralism are beliefs that individuals never forget or
escape their social origin, that all groups bring
positive contributions that enrich the larger society, and that groups have the right to be different but equal.

Two types of cultural pluralism may be distinguished on the basis of the nature of the contact among groups (Gordon, 1978). Cultural pluralism at the tolerance level is primarily
characterized by secondary contact across ethnic
lines involving formal, nonintimate associations.
This form of pluralism was found among blacks
and whites in the old South. At the good group
relations level, there is considerably more contact among groups. At this level, Gordon (1978)
argues, pluralism and some forms of integration
can coexist. This type of pluralism would involve
"employment integration, common use of public

accommodations, inter-ethnic composition of
civic organizations and frequent symbolic demonstrations of inter-group harmony which emphasize common goals and values" (p. 161).

Several authorities believe that assimilation
and pluralism are happening simultaneously in
American society. Glazer and Moynihan (1970)
perceive the process of becoming "hyphenated"
Americans as involving cultural assimilation.
Thus a Russian American is different from a
Russian in Russia and a black American is not
the same as a black in Africa. On the other hand,
they perceive the emergence of minority groups
as political interest groups as a pluralistic trend.
Gordon (1978) contends that assimilation of
minorities is the prevailing trend in economic,
political, and educational institutions, whereas
cultural pluralism prevails in religion, the family,
and recreation.

Cultural pluralism results in separate ethnic
communities, many of which are characterized
by a high degree of institutional completeness;
that is, they include institutions and services that
meet the needs of the group such as ethnic
churches, newspapers, mutual aid societies, and
recreational groups. These ethnic enclaves are
particularly attractive to recent immigrants who
have language problems and few skills. Schaefer
(1984) compared ethnic communities to decom-
pression chambers. "Just as divers use the
chambers to adjust to the rapid change in water
pressure, immigrants use the communities to adjust to cultural change they are forced to make
upon arriving in a new country" (p. 48).

Today, we are witnessing a resurgence of interest by various ethnic groups in almost forgotten languages, customs, and traditions. Greeley
(1971) calls this resurgence of ethnicity "a new
tribalism," characterized by increased interest in
the "high culture" of one's ethnic group, visits to
ancestral homes, the increased use of ethnic
names, and renewed interest in the native language of one's group (pp. 148–151).

The general rule has been for American minorities to assimilate, however. Most ethnic groups are oriented toward the future, not toward the past. American ethnics are far more interested in shaping their future within the American structure than in maintaining cultural ties with the past.

What of the future of ethnic groups and integration in the United States? Most observers agree that serious problems remain to be overcome. Racism continues to have a powerful influence on individual lives and the interactions of different ethnic groups, and each step in the process presents new problems. One recent twist, for example, involves allegations of reverse discrimination, in which members of the majority claim to be victims of racial discrimination. Where resources, positions, or memberships are limited, the inclusion of minority members may lead to the exclusion of qualified members of the majority or dominant group. In the most celebrated of these cases, Alan Bakke brought suit against the state of California for denying him admission to medical school while accepting members of minorities with lower scores on admissions tests. The busing controversy of the past decade is another well-known example of a shift in the nature of race relations.

Despite the new problems that crop up, there is reason for optimism. Just as few would argue that race relations are not everything they should be in this country, few would refute the fact that progress has been made during the past three decades. A number of barriers to equality have been eliminated. Civil rights activism during the 1960s and 1970s brought about reforms in laws and government policies. In 1963 Affirmative Action was established, and President Kennedy issued an executive order calling for the disregard of race, creed, color, or national origin in hiring procedures as well as in the treatment of employees. Affirmative Action has since become a principal government instrument in eradicating institutional racism (Feagin, 1984); its laws were later amended to include women so that today the laws prohibit discrimination on the basis of sex.

The reduction of institutional racism has had indirect as well as direct effects. According to the "contact hypothesis," interracial contact leads to reductions in prejudice under the following conditions: (1) when the parties involved are of equal status and (2) when the situation in which the contact occurs is pleasant (Schaefer, 1984). Rokeach, Smith, and Evans (1960) take a similar position, arguing that prejudiced people do not reject others because of their ethnic membership per se but because they perceive others as having different values and beliefs. These authors hypothesize that if people of different races encounter one another under conditions favoring the perception of similar beliefs, racial prejudice will be substantially reduced. Both these theories stress that contacts must be amiable to reduce prejudice.

Changes in the way minorities are portrayed in the mass media have also influenced levels of prejudice. During the 1950s and 1960s, when blacks and other minorities were portrayed at all, it was usually in stereotyped roles as servants or other low-status workers. Today, although it could be argued that portrayals of minorities in the media still tend to reflect stereotypes, the situation has improved considerably.

Another cause for optimism is the frequent finding of research studies that more educated people are more likely to express liking for groups other than their own. It may be that the educated have a more cosmopolitan outlook and are more likely to question the accuracy of racial stereotypes. It is to be hoped that the trend in this country toward a more educated population, along with the other advances that have been made, will contribute to a reduction in prejudice and the more complete realization of the American ideals of freedom and equal opportunity.

SOCIOLOGISTS AT WORK

Assessing Services for the Hispanic Population

JoAnne Willette is a senior research specialist for Development Associates, Inc., an international management and government consulting firm in the Washington, D.C. area. She does survey research, program evaluation, and policy analysis, mostly for the federal government. In her work she applies the theoretical, methodological, and statistical training in sociology she received as an undergraduate at George Washington University and a graduate student at the University of Maryland.

What tasks does Willette bring this training to bear on? In the area of policy analysis, she has worked on a study for the U.S. Department of Health and Human Services (HHS) to improve services to the Hispanic population in this country. One of the first tasks in the study was to review all the major programs in HHS, including Social Security, Medicare, Medicaid, Aid to Families with Dependent Children, Adolescent Pregnancy Prevention, Family Planning, Programs for the Aging, Head Start, Migrant Health, Child Welfare Services, and seven HHS block grants to the states.

For each of these programs she reviewed the legislation, guidelines, and funding. She also interviewed federal, state, and local program administrators, and people in the target populations. She did further interviewing on the block grants, funds that are given to the states with relatively few strings attached. In these interviews she tried to find the different ways states were planning to spend the funds, the criteria they were using to distribute the funds, and the amount of input the target population for these programs had in the decision.

Summary

A race is a socially defined group or category of people distinguished by selected inherited physical characteristics. An ethnic group is a number of individuals who feel they are one people because they have a common race, religion, national origin, or language. Racial and ethnic groups are considered minorities when they are subordinate to another group in terms of power, social status, and privilege and when their norms, values, and other characteristics differ from those that prevail in a society.

The major ethnic groups in the United States are blacks, Hispanics, Asians, Native Americans, and European ethnics. The black and Spanish-speaking populations are the largest. Due to changes in immigration policies in the mid-1960s, most immigrants today come from Asian countries, and the population of Asian Americans has increased dramatically.

A prejudice is a preconceived judgment about another group. A variety of theories have been offered to explain prejudice, including economic and psychological ones. Prejudice often involves acceptance of ethnic stereotypes, widely

Another part of this project was an in-depth study of the demographic and socioeconomic characteristics of the Hispanic population in the United States from 1950 to 1980. Trends in the Hispanic population were compared to those in the black, white, and total populations. Trends among the various Hispanic ethnic groups (Mexican-Americans, Puerto Ricans, Cubans, and those of other Spanish origins) were also compared to each other.

The analysis was based on census reports and other national statistics collected by the federal government. Tracing trends in the population was a challenge: methods of collecting data and defining variables change over time, and this affects the comparability of the data. For example, even the definition of Hispanic was changed between 1950 and 1980. In a statistical sense, the concept *Hispanic* is relatively new; the 1970 census was the first to ask people to classify themselves as Hispanic or non-Hispanic. Before this, Mexican-Americans in five southwestern states were identified using a manual coding system and a list of Spanish surnames. Puerto Ricans in New York City were identified by birth and parentage questions during coding procedures. Other Hispanics were not counted at all. The result was an undercount of unknown proportions.

A third part of this study was annual projections of Hispanic population from 1980 to 1990, derived from 1980 census data by some of Willette's demographer colleagues at Development Associates.

How did her training prepare her for this work? "I entered sociology with the intention of using it as an applied rather than an academic discipline," she says. "My sociological background has been useful in studying government programs whose effects can be seen in social changes. We ask such questions as: What needs to be done in a particular area or for a particular population? What is being done or what programs are in place? How effective are these programs? Sociology showed me how to move from the conceptual to the operational level, so you can measure things reliably and validly. My knowledge of sociological theory, research methods, statistics, and computer programming are very useful."

held beliefs about the character and behavior of all members of a group. Whereas prejudice is an attitude, discrimination is overt behavior on the part of individuals or institutions.

Racism is a system of beliefs and actions based on those beliefs. It has three distinguishing characteristics: (1) the idea that one's own race is superior to any other race, (2) an ideology, and (3) actions based on racist beliefs. Genocide and mass expulsion are consequences of extreme forms of racism.

Stratification in the United States runs to a large extent along racial and ethnic lines and is found only when three conditions are present: ethnocentrism, competition, and, most important, inequalities in power. This inequality may lead to ethnic antagonism. A leading theory of ethnic antagonism is that of the split labor market, which suggests that conflict results among business, higher-priced labor, and lower-priced labor. The basic fear of those in higher-priced labor is of being displaced by the lower-priced labor that business views as one way of reducing costs.

Racial and ethnic inequalities can be resolved through either integration or pluralism.

Integration involves assimilation, acceptance of the norms, values, and customs of the majority. Pluralism is the assumption that separate-but-equal coexistence is possible. Various ethnic groups have attempted different means and ways to participate in the mainstream of American society, but some have not adapted as completely as others. Several authorities believe that integration and pluralism are occurring simultaneously in American society today. In the past twenty years, American ethnic groups have experienced a renewed interest in their heritage.

Although relations among ethnic groups are far from perfect in this country, some progress has been made in the last few decades. Recent government regulations make it more likely that members of different groups will interact as equals, which several authorities suggest will lower levels of prejudice. Changes in the portrayal of minorities in the media and the trend toward a better-educated population may lead to further progress in this area.

Key Terms

Anglo-conformity
assimilation
authoritarian personality theory
caste system
cultural pluralism
discrimination
displacement
ethnic antagonism
ethnic group
exclusion
frustration-aggression theory
genocide
institutional discrimination
institutional racism
integration
mass expulsion
melting pot

minority group
prejudice
projection
racial group
racism
radicalism
scapegoating
segregation
self-fulfilling prophecy
split labor market
stereotypes
structural assimilation

Suggested Readings

Burstein, Paul. **"Equal Employment Opportunity Legislation and the Income of Women and NonWhites,"** American Sociological Review 44 (June 1979):367–391. Based on census, labor, and survey data, this study assesses the impact of federal Equal Employment Opportunity (EEO) laws passed in the 1960s and 1970s on the income of minorities and women.

Feagin, Joe R. **Racial and Ethnic Relations, 2d ed.** Englewood Cliffs, N.J.: Prentice-Hall, 1984. Focuses on major racial and ethnic groups in the United States: the English, Irish, Italians, Jews, Native Americans, blacks, Japanese Americans, and Puerto Ricans.

Gordon, Milton M. **Human Nature, Class, and Ethnicity.** New York: Oxford University Press, 1978. This book covers the author's general theory of racial and ethnic relations. It includes a collection of essays on social stratification, the nature of pluralistic group life, and assimilation in American society.

Killian, Lewis M. **The Impossible Revolution: Phase II.** New York: Random House, 1975. A powerful book relating black protest to four areas of concern to blacks: psychological well-being, political recognition, economic security, and social status.

Kitano, Harry H. L. **Race Relations.** Englewood Cliffs, N.J.: Prentice-Hall, 1980. A textbook considering race relations from the viewpoint of a minority-group member. It includes excellent accounts of the history and current statuses of the various Asian-American groups in the United States.

Newman, William M. **American Pluralism: A Study of Minority Groups and Social Theory.** *New York: Harper & Row, 1973.* A look at the United States as a pluralistic society.

Schaefer, Richard T. **Racial and Ethnic Groups, 2d ed.** *Boston: Little, Brown, 1984.* A textbook on race and ethnic relations that assesses recent development in the context of a historical framework and existing theoretical orientations.

Schermerhorn, R. A. **Comparative Ethnic Relations: A Framework for Theory and Research.** *Chicago: The University of Chicago Press, 1978.* A book ex-amining intergroup relations at a macrosociological level from the functionalist and conflict perspectives.

Vander Zanden, James W. **American Minority Relations, 4th ed.** *New York: Alfred A. Knopf, 1983.* A text examining the sources of racism, intergroup relations, and minority reactions to dominance and social change.

Wolf, Eleanor P. **Trial and Error: The Detroit School Segregation Case.** *Detroit: Wayne State University Press, 1981.* An extensive study of the Detroit busing case, this book examines courtroom testimony on residential segregation, education, and the use of social science evidence in judicial proceedings.

CHAPTER 10
Gender Differentiation

Equality of rights under the law shall not be denied or abridged by the United States or any state on account of sex.

— Equal Rights Amendment

Gender Differentiation

Although women bear children and often assume most of the responsibility for rearing them — buying food and clothes, making meals, and caring for the home — the role of housewife has a low status. Many women who work outside the home also find that their work is valued less than that of men. Waiters have a higher status than waitresses. Bricklayers are considered skilled workers, but typists are not. Doctors, who are mostly male, have much higher status than nurses, who are mostly female. In the Soviet Union, the majority of doctors are women, but they do not have the high status of doctors in the United States. On the other hand, many Americans would not vote for a woman for president.

Why does society tend to devalue women and the work they do? Why do so many women hold low-status jobs that pay poorly? Why are they often respected and rewarded less highly than men? Are there basic differences between the sexes that justify this situation?

Biological Bases of Gender Differences

Males and females differ from the moment of conception, when sex is determined. The ovum of the mother always carries an X chromosome, which bears the genetic material to develop a female. The father's sperm may carry either an X or a Y chromosome. If the sperm carries an X chromosome, the fetus will develop into a female. If the sperm carries a Y chromosome, testes develop that secrete a hormone that causes the embryo to develop as a male. The question physiologists and psychologists have struggled with is whether the sex hormones in the fetus affect the central nervous system and therefore influence how males and females behave.

We do know that children who are biologically of one sex can be socialized to behave as normal children of the opposite sex. One such case involved identical twin boys, one of whom lost his entire penis during a circumcision operation. He was brought to Johns Hopkins Hospital for treatment, where it was recommended that he be raised as a girl. Through surgery, it was possible to build him a vagina so that he could function as a female. Biologically, however, he was still a male and would never be able to bear children. The child was raised as a girl while her twin brother was raised as a boy. Money and Ehrhardt (1972) describe the process of change as follows:

> The first items of change were clothes and hairdo. The mother reported: "I started dressing her not in dresses but, you know, in little pink slacks and frilly blouses ... and letting her hair grow." A year and six months later, the mother wrote that she had made a special effort at keeping her girl in dresses, almost exclusively, changing any item of clothing into something that was clearly feminine. "I even made all her nightwear into granny gowns and she wears bracelets and hair ribbons." (p. 124)

The little girl later came to prefer dresses to slacks, and she took pride in her hair. She loved to have her hair set and she would sit under the dryer "all day long." She became very neat and clean and, unlike her brother, she loved to have her face washed.

According to the Money and Ehrhardt (1972) study, the mother reported that she hoped both children would go to college and "have some kind of career. That's what I would like for both of them. . . . As long as they get their high school, at least my daughter. My son, it's almost essential, since he will be earning a liv-

ing for the rest of his life" (p. 127). The son chose very masculine career goals, such as a policeman or fireman. He wanted to do what his father did, work where his father worked, carry a lunch kit, and drive a car. The daughter assumed she would get married and wanted to be a doctor, which her mother thought was a nice feminine occupation.

At birth, the girl had been the dominant twin, but by age three she was less rough than her brother, and her dominance took the form of being "a mother hen" to her brother. The boy, however, protected his sister if anyone threatened her. Money and Ehrhardt also reported that the mother wanted to "teach her to be polite and quiet. I always wanted those virtues. I never did manage, but I'm going to try to teach my daughter to be more quiet and ladylike" (p. 128).

Sociological Bases of Gender Differences

The twins in the study described above were both genetically male, and they received normal male hormones during the fetal period. (Hormonal treatment did not begin until puberty.) This study and others like it indicate that sex hormones do not affect the human nervous system in such a way that either masculine or feminine behavior is inevitable. This child's feminine behavior was clearly the result of socialization, some of it intentional, some of it unconscious.

These findings are corroborated by certain crosscultural studies. The influence of hormones on the nervous system is presumably the same in all humans, but in some cultures men and women occupy roles in ways very unlike those typically found in the United States. In the Chambri (formerly *Tchambuli*) society of New Guinea, for example, the women are the workers. They do the fishing, weaving, planting, harvesting, and cooking, carrying and caring for their children all the while. They are generally

Chambri women do most of the work necessary for survival in their society. Some of this work is considered by other societies to be appropriate for men. Chambri women grow and harvest crops, cook the food, care for the children, and do it all with good-natured confidence. In this picture Chambri women are shown going to market.

confident, laughing, brisk, good-natured, and efficient. They have a jolly comradeship that involves much rough joking. The men, on the other hand, are more involved in producing arts and crafts and planning ceremonies. They tend to be more emotional than the women and also more responsive to the needs of others. The women typically have an attitude of kindly toleration toward the men, enjoying the men's games and parties but remaining rather remote emotionally (Mead, 1935).

In many African societies, the women have traditionally owned much of the land. Europeans have often tried to impose their own system of ownership on these tribes, sometimes with dire consequences. When Europeans introduced modern farming methods to the Ibo tribe of Nigeria, they took the land from the women and gave it to the men. The men raised cash crops, which they sold, and the women were left without their traditional means of subsistence. In 1923, the Ibo women rioted. Ten thousand women looted shops and released prisoners from jail. In two days of intense rioting, fifty people were killed and another fifty were injured. Later, the women became more organized and continued their revolt against land reforms and taxation with more riots, strikes, cursing, and ridicule (Leavitt, 1971). In certain other societies, men and women both share what we would consider a traditional feminine role or a traditional masculine role. The point is that the *gender roles* — the cultural concepts of masculinity and femininity that society creates around gender — vary enormously in different societies, so much so that the existence of a powerful hereditary predisposition among men and women for certain gender roles seems unlikely.

The gender-role socialization of members of a society seems to vary with the type of society. In hunting and gathering societies in which survival depends on the constant search for food, both males and females are socialized to be assertive and independent, even though women must stay near their infants to nurse them, while men assume the tasks of hunting and fighting, probably because they are stronger. Yet as societies grow wealthier and more complex, as the division of labor increases and hunting is no longer necessary to provide food for people, gender-role differentiation increases. If both men and women are capable of meeting the demands of almost all positions or statuses without being constrained by biological factors, why does role differentiation increase? Why do women have lower status in modern society than men? Sociologists have explored these questions from several theoretical perspectives, including structural functionalism and conflict theory.

Theories of Gender Differentiation

Structural-Functional Theory

Structural functionalists, you will recall, believe that society consists of interrelated parts, each of which performs a function in maintaining the whole system. They assume, accordingly, that women have traditionally made important contributions to society. They raised children, maintained the home, and provided food, clean clothing, and other necessities of daily living. They have also played an expressive role, nurturing and providing emotional support for husbands and children returning home from work

Michael Keaton in the 1983 movie Mr. Mom *carries out a theme that has been in movies for years: It is not the function of men to stay home and cook; they make a mess of it. Conflict theorists would more likely argue that movies, and the men who make movies, are not very interested in changing the status of men and women in society.*

or school. The woman in the family created the atmosphere of close interpersonal relationships necessary to a worthwhile human existence, relationships lacking in the competitive workplace (Parsons and Bales, 1955). Although these skills are vital to society, they do not command a price and they are outside of the marketplace.

According to this perspective, the traditional function of the male was to protect and provide for his wife and children. He was the head of the household, controlling where the family lived, how money was spent, and making other decisions important to the survival of the family. He also made the political and economic decisions in the community by serving in powerful decision-making positions.

Structural functionalists believe that technological advances have reduced the workload of women in the household, making it possible for them to enter the work force outside of the home. They also believe that technology has reduced the number of hours that men have to work, so they can spend more time with their children and in other activities. As a result, they believe the family has become more egalitarian (Goode, 1970). Both men and women can spend time at home caring for children, and both can share in the role of provider. Because women have only recently entered the work force, they tend to be in low-paying jobs, but structural-functional theorists believe women should make rapid gains in earning power as they gain experience and skills.

Some functional theorists and others are concerned about changes in traditional family roles, fearing that equality between men and women will cause the disintegration of the family. They foresee increases in adultery and divorce, declining birth rates, increased juvenile delinquency, neglect of aging parents, and a host of other family-linked problems. Most functionalists, however, believe the family will survive as equality increases between men and women, al-though it may assume a different form than it had in the past.

Conflict Theory

Conflict theorists believe that women have low status because they have been exploited by more powerful men (Hartmann, 1977). Very early in the development of societies, military force was used to protect land and other valuable private property and also to capture women from other tribes. Women were prized possessions who could work for their captors to increase wealth and provide children who would grow into future workers. At the same time, they could increase the prestige of the men who owned them, especially if they were beautiful and desired by other men.

It was not just as future workers that children were important. Men needed children to look after the property when they grew old and to inherit it when they died. To know who his children were, a man needed to isolate his women from other men. Thus women became the protected property of men so that men could accumulate wealth and have children to inherit it. According to this perspective, women were from earliest times exploited by men for the work they did and the children they bore.

The process of industrialization removed work from the family, but, conflict theorists argue, men were not willing to lose their control over the labor of women. They tried to either keep women out of the work force entirely or allowed them to hold only the lowest-paying jobs. They passed laws regulating the kind of work women could do and the hours they could work. They also passed laws regulating women's rights to income, property ownership, and birth control, and made them exclusively responsible for domestic tasks. Men forbade women from joining unions and entering professions. Legally and by tradition, they prevented them from gaining high positions in the work force.

Less powerful men were also hurt by the practice of keeping women in positions with low pay. The existence of a labor force of poorly paid women meant that men who asked for higher wages could easily be replaced by lower-paid women. Conflict theorists believe that powerful men will have to be forced to give up their dominant position in the labor force and at home if women are to progress toward equality.

Gender Differentiation and the Workplace

Sociologists study gender differentiation in order to understand which theoretical perspective of society is more accurate. If the structural-functional perspective is correct, then as industrial society develops women should move into the work force and attain equality with men. If conflict theory is right, then as industrial society creates more wealth and power for men, they will use the wealth and power to improve their own position and women will lag farther and farther behind.

Women in the Workplace

The status of women in the workplace is often treated as if it were a new issue, but women have always played an important economic role in society. During the Middle Ages, they produced much of what was needed in the home and also made items for sale in the marketplace. With the growth of large cities at the end of this period, new options became available to them (Bernard, 1981). They became traders and innkeepers and occasionally ran breweries and blacksmith shops. They often joined guilds, which were a type of medieval trade union. Those who didn't wish to marry could join *Beguines*, urban communes of seven or eight women who pursued such occupations as sewing, baking, spinning, and weaving. Women from the upper class could join convents and become nuns. At that time, some convents had great scholarly reputations and were political forces to be reckoned with. Other women worked as maids or servants for very low wages. For most women, however, family life was the most secure option.

But the goods traditionally produced by women in the home were the first to be manufactured in factories at the beginning of the industrial revolution. The most important goods were textiles. Poor, young, single women went to work in the mills under terrible working conditions and for very little pay. Married women could not leave the home for the twelve-hour work days required in the mills and still maintain their homes, so they lost their ability to earn income. As industry and the population grew, good farm land became scarce, so men also became available for factory work. Protective labor laws were passed that limited the number of hours women and children could work and the types of work they could do. By the nineteenth century, then, women had lost the few work options that had existed for them in earlier centuries. The only source of economic well-being was marriage.

At the beginning of the twentieth century, many upper-class women received an education, and some worked in the professions. Poor women who worked were usually employed as servants. The vast majority of women, however, were married and worked in the home to meet the needs of their families. They produced few goods for the marketplace and had little income. By 1982, however, 53 percent of women in the United States were in the labor force. They comprised 43 percent of workers (World Almanac, 1984:125).

The major reason women today take jobs is, like men, for economic necessity. Nearly two-thirds of all women workers are either single, separated, or divorced. They must support themselves and sometimes their families. About

By the 1920s the American garment
industry had grown large and employed many women to operate
sewing machines. The fine needlework
skills used in the home to make
clothing, quilts, and other domestic
articles were no longer in demand.
Instead, women who needed to earn
money worked in factories that were
hot, crowded and unsafe, doing
tedious work for poor wages, but it
was one of the few ways a woman
could earn money. Most women
preferred to stay out of the labor force.

50 percent of all married women are now in the
work force, but research indicates that they too
work for economic reasons and not just to escape
boredom.

Income

The median income for women working full
time in 1982 was $13,663, 63 percent of the men's
median of $21,655. (The gap between men and
women varied from state to state, as shown in
Table 10-1.) During the 1960s and 1970s the gap
between men and women widened, until by the
late 1970s women made only 59 percent of what
men made. This wage differential now appears to
be narrowing, but it has not yet returned to the
level of 1958, when women earned 64 percent of
what men earned. There are three major reasons
for this gap in earnings.

1. Women are entering the work force in low-
   paying occupations. More women than men
   work in low-paying clerical service or blue-
   collar work. Often these jobs have no career
   lines, so women cannot advance to higher
   positions.
2. People with low salaries receive smaller
   raises. A 10 percent raise on $10,000 is
   smaller than a 10 percent raise on $20,000.
3. Women are sometimes paid less than men
   even though they hold equivalent jobs.

The percentage of women making low and high
salaries can be seen in Figure 10-1.

During the 1960s, the federal government
made a considerable effort to create equal opportunity for men and women. President Kennedy
established affirmative action in the federal service, and President Johnson continued the effort
with his Great Society programs. Despite these
efforts, men entering the federal service during
this period received salaries $800 to $1,300
higher than women entering equivalent positions
with equal qualifications and experience. In a
careful study (Grandjean, 1981) tracing the ca-

Table 10-1

The wage gap by state

WOMEN'S EARNINGS AS PERCENT OF MEN'S					
Washington, D.C.	78.4	Oklahoma	58.6	Rhode Island	56.6
New Jersey	66.1	California	58.4	Missouri	56.5
Vermont	65.4	Kentucky	58.4	North Dakota	56.0
New York	64.9	Minnesota	58.2	Iowa	55.7
Tennessee	63.8	Nevada	58.2	Idaho	55.4
Maryland	62.2	New Mexico	58.0	Montana	55.3
North Carolina	61.1	Ohio	57.9	Oregon	55.3
Michigan	61.1	Colorado	57.9	Alaska	55.2
South Carolina	60.9	Kansas	57.8	Delaware	55.1
Arkansas	60.7	Hawaii	57.7	West Virginia	55.0
Massachusetts	60.7	Arizona	57.6	Washington	54.7
Florida	60.0	Connecticut	57.5	Indiana	53.8
Mississippi	60.0	Illinois	57.5	Wyoming	53.7
Virginia	59.8	Wisconsin	57.5	Utah	53.3
Pennsylvania	59.7	Nebraska	57.2	Louisiana	49.8
New Hampshire	59.3	South Dakota	57.1		
Alabama	59.2	Texas	57.0		
Maine	59.1				

SOURCE: *What Women Earn.* Copyright © 1981 by Thelma Kandel. Reprinted by permission of the Linden Press, a division of Simon & Schuster, Inc.

reers of these men and women from the time they entered federal service until 1977, it was found that at each stage of their careers, the gap between men and women widened by an additional $600 to $2,000.

Occupation

While more and more women have been entering the labor force, the vast majority have taken low-paying jobs involving typing or filing, or they have entered service occupations and become waitresses, beauticians, or cleaning women. The number of women in all fields has grown, but the proportion of women in the more highly paid occupations is very low.

In 1940, 4 percent of all executives were women. In 1980, 5.6 percent were women. Why are there so few women moving into management jobs in corporations? Conflict theorists argue that one reason women are not advancing is the *split labor market.* As discussed in Chapter 9, in a split labor market there are two distinct and unequal groups of workers (Bonacich, 1972). The *primary labor market* is reserved for elites, people who will advance to high-level positions. Primary labor market jobs offer job security, on-the-job training, high wages, and frequent promotions. Corporate managers, professionals, and engineers belong to this labor market, and beginning positions are often management trainee positions.

In the *secondary labor market* jobs pay poorly and there is little job security. There are many lay-offs but few promotions or salary increases.

Figure 10-1

Percentage of persons fourteen years and older with income in each category, 1982

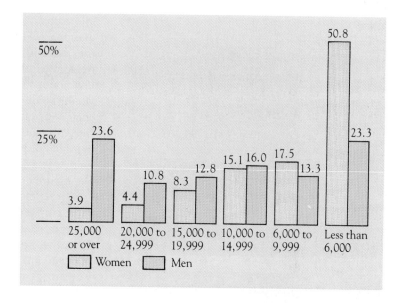

	25,000 or over	20,000 to 24,999	15,000 to 19,999	10,000 to 14,999	6,000 to 9,999	Less than 6,000
Women	3.9	4.4	8.3	15.1	17.5	50.8
Men	23.6	10.8	12.8	16.0	13.3	23.3

☐ Women   ☐ Men

Most women work in the secondary labor force in secretarial, typing and clerical jobs, or as sales clerks, waitresses, or other service personnel.

When we speak of upward mobility for women, we assume that women will be promoted into the primary labor force, but this is not likely to happen. After a person has been in the secondary labor force for a few years, it becomes more and more difficult to enter the primary labor force. There is no on-the-job training; knowledge and skills quickly become outdated; and the employee can no longer compete with those in the primary labor force. Also, those in the secondary labor force will be earning much less money than those who have spent several years in the primary work force. Corporation personnel offices assume that someone at a low wage level cannot move into the higher-paying positions in the primary work force. Employment offices want to know the previous salary of an applicant, and will not pay management level wages to someone who previously earned a low salary. The assumption is that low earners are

less capable than high earners. Conflict theorists argue that because most women are hired into the secondary labor force, upward mobility is impossible for the vast majority.

Structural-functional theorists believe that women will advance in the work force once their experience is equivalent to men's, but roles in the corporation have developed along traditional gender-role lines where men make the decisions and women help men (Kanter, 1979). Other gender-related factors may also impede the promotion of women. Married women may not be promoted because their bosses fear they will get pregnant and quit. Those who already have children may not be promoted because their employers fear they will leave work to care for them. Studies show that women are not absent more than men, however, and Roos (1983) found that divorced and single women are not promoted either. Apparently marital status and the possibility that a woman might bear children are not the reasons women are not promoted.

Attempts to determine why women work in

Today women work in a variety of occupations. Professional women, such as the architect (top) have more decision-making responsibilities and earn more money than most women, but few architects are women. The waitress works in a low-income field dominated by women and one that reflects typical gender role behavior— women serving other people.

low-status, low-paying jobs raise an important question. Do women receive low pay because they hold low-status jobs? Or are the jobs held predominantly by women considered to have low status because women work in them? It would be discriminatory to pay women less for their low-status jobs if the low status was conferred because of the sex of the worker. It is not considered discriminatory, however, to pay the worker less if the job has low prestige because of the nature of the work.

Bose and Rossi (1983) attempted to determine why certain jobs have low status by asking subjects to rank the prestige of jobs. In some cases they were told that the job was held by a man and in some cases that the job was held by a woman. They found that both men and women judged the occupation without paying too much attention to the sex of the jobholder, although the sex of the respondent did make some difference in the ratings. Unlike older respondents, college students of both sexes were not at all influenced by the sex of the jobholder when they ranked the prestige of the job. The study suggests, therefore, that women receive low pay because they hold low-status jobs.

Judging the status of an occupation seems to be a way of ranking the status of the person who works in the occupation. Men's status is certainly judged by the prestige of their occupations. The status of women is more difficult to judge, however.

The Status of Women

Judging the status of women presents many problems to sociologists. Women are often assumed to have the same status as their husbands, and to some extent this is a useful assumption. Certainly a company president's wife has higher status than a company vice-president's wife, and both rank higher than the wife of a businessman or blue-collar worker. But does the president's

The Cocktail Waitress

A study of cocktail waitresses found that while their work was devalued, their work was more difficult than the bartender's and designed to make his job easier. The cocktail waitress takes drink orders from the customer, then she goes to the bar and orders the drinks from the bartender, not as the customer named them, but naming them as the bartender recognizes them. She orders them, not in the order she receives them, but in the order the bartender will mix them, such as giving him brandy drinks together and beer orders together. While he makes the drinks, she puts fruits and straws in the drinks as required, stirs them and adds up the bill in her head, even though he could do it on the cash register. Then she must put the drinks on the tray, not in the order they were mixed, but in the order placed by the customers.

If the bartender wants a drink during working hours, he has one, but the waitresses are not allowed to drink. If the bartender wants a break, he can ask a waitress to fill in behind the bar, but he would never be expected to fill in for a waitress. When she helps him, she feels honored and thanks him for the opportunity. If he should on occasion help her, she thanks him for helping her. Spradley and Mann found that whenever there is an exchange of roles, the woman must show her appreciation to the man. Just as when a man "lets a woman drive" she thanks him, but when he helps her cook, she thanks him. The work and status of the cocktail waitress in many ways reflect the work and status of women in society.

SOURCE: James P. Spradley and Brenda J. Mann, *The Cocktail Waitress. Woman's Work in a Man's World.* New York: Wiley, 1975.

---

wife rank higher than the vice-president, businessman, or blue-collar worker? Assuming that a wife has the same status as her husband may indicate her relationship to other married women, but it does not indicate her relationship to men.

A second problem with this system of ranking women is that it does not indicate the women's relative power. Class and status are important because they are means of achieving power and influence, but what are the powers of the president's wife? Can she make decisions about the organization or its members? Can she decide how money will be spent or invested? Does she have money at her disposal, or must she get money and permission to spend it from her husband? A president's wife may have far less power and influence than the ordinary worker in the organization.

Third, how does one rank the working wife? If her occupation has a different status than her husband's, does she have her own occupational status or that of her husband?

And finally, how does one rank an unmarried woman? She is often ranked according to her occupation and education, but this also creates problems. A woman executive may be of the same rank as a male executive, but because she is a woman she may not receive the honor and prestige he receives. And how does she rank compared with other women? Is she of the same rank as the nonworking wife of another executive?

Jessie Bernard (1981) contends that the status of women cannot be compared with the status of men and suggests an alternative system. At the top of this system she places society women, who determine which individuals will be accepted into the elite. Beneath this stratum she places celebrities, famous actresses, sports stars, and others who have a great deal of money and

A woman who is the only member of a management team often may be mistaken for the secretary or expected to serve coffee. If she speaks softly, she will be ignored, because it is assumed she is not saying anything important. If she makes her point strongly, she will be considered aggressive, and men will often become defensive. A similar number of men and women on a management team generally promotes more comfortable interaction.

power. Intellectuals, the next level, are those who originate and disseminate ideas, such as writers, professors, lawyers, artists, judges, business people, and civil servants. Housewives are placed in fourth place because they play a vital role in society. White- and blue-collar women are placed in the same class below housewives because they generally have comparable income and educational status, although some would consider their position higher than that of housewives. Below working women, Bernard places two groups: welfare recipients and outcasts such as bag ladies and beggars. This system does not, of course, resolve the problems of the relative rank of men and women, but it may be a useful system for analyzing the status of women compared with other women.

Women and Political Power

In 1984, for the first time, a woman was named vice-presidential candidate on a major political party ticket. Presidential candidate Walter Mondale chose as his running mate Representative Geraldine Ferraro (NY). Mondale and Ferraro won the nomination at the National Democratic Convention in San Francisco.

Efforts by women to gain political and economic power — known collectively as the *women's movement* — have been taking place since the Civil War. Women finally gained the right to vote in the 1920s, and the women's movement began a resurgence in the 1960s.

Most of the women who have been active in these movements are from the upper-middle class. Educated women have the organizational skills and the economic security to pressure government and corporations for legal and economic gains. They have fought for the *Equal Rights Amendment* (ERA), a proposed amendment to the Constitution that would have guaranteed women equal rights. They have also fought for the right to enter jobs and the professions, for unbiased hiring practices, for equal pay, and for the right to abortions. They have worked to fight poverty, to make day care centers available for the children of working mothers, and to make marriage and divorce laws more equitable. Although working-class women generally support most of the goals of the women's movement, they have been less active in pursuing them. Their economic security is so precarious and so dependent on the family that conflicts are extremely threatening to their position.

As a result of their struggles, women did succeed in gaining many rights. They won the right to vote. They can now hold many jobs that in the past were barred to them. Today there are female bartenders, construction workers, and bus drivers, to mention just a few. In all these occupations, however, they are greatly outnumbered by men.

Many states continue to limit the amount of weight women can lift and restrict their work in other ways, but laws have been passed guaranteeing them equal pay for equal work, and they have gained the right to practice birth control and obtain abortions. Except for the right to vote, however, these rights are not guaranteed under the Constitution, and the laws that grant these rights could be changed at any time by Congress.

In 1972, the Equal Rights Amendment was approved by Congress. The ERA states that "Equality of rights under the law shall not be denied or abridged by the United States or any state on account of sex." Although the majority of Americans supported the ERA, it was not ratified by the required number of states to become a part of the U.S. Constitution. Arguments in favor of the ERA emphasized the necessity of giving women equality under the law. Arguments against it emphasized the need to protect women and their traditional family role.

The Consequences of Inequality

The most obvious result of gender inequality is the high level of poverty among women, but the stratification system results in other notable gender differences in our society as well. In this section we will discuss the problems of poverty, women's self-perception, stress and depression, sexual harassment in the workplace, family violence, and rape.

Women Below the Poverty Line

Given the many problems women face in the workplace, it's not surprising that many of those who are heads of families have incomes below the poverty line. (Women are said to be heads of families if they have children to support and if there is no man in the family.) Also, the number of women with families in poverty is increasing dramatically. Between 1969 and 1978 there was an annual net increase of 100,000 women with families living in poverty. Between 1978 and 1980 the net increase each year was 150,000 (Pearce, 1983).

Many women living in poverty receive welfare, but many more work full time for a living. One-third of the female labor force is employed in the lowest-paying jobs in the secondary labor force — household labor (maids), agriculture (field workers), retail sales, and service jobs (women who clean offices, do shampoos in a beauty shop, etc.). Many of these jobs are not covered by minimum wage laws, pay very low salaries, and do not provide fringe benefits such as overtime pay, sick leave, unemployment insurance, paid vacations, and medical plans, which add another 20 to 30 percent to the salaries of other workers (Shortridge, 1975). Most women are now eligible for Social Security if they work in one job steadily, but many employers do not pay Social Security, partly because they do not want to make the necessary contribution and partly because they do not want to deduct the necessary contribution from their workers' very small paychecks.

Why do women remain in these low-paying occupations? There are a number of reasons. Many women do not have the education or skills necessary to move to other occupations, and the jobs they have do not provide experience that permits them to eventually move to a better-paying position. The experience of a day worker or a migrant farm worker cannot be transferred to other occupations. Another reason is discrimination. Many women are simply not hired for better-paying jobs because of their sex, age, or race, and those in low-paying jobs are apt to be laid off from time to time rather than be given promotions or fringe benefits. As a result, they must reenter the work force at beginning salaries.

Shortridge (1975) suggests four alternatives for women who have to work at low pay: welfare, marriage, government regulation, and organization. None of these alternatives is very satisfactory. Welfare is sometimes difficult to qualify for, and in some rural areas, welfare payments are extremely low and available only in the winter. When spring planting jobs become available, welfare payments are cut off and the women must return to the fields and work for very low wages. Even if welfare continues to be available, it may be so degrading that the worst jobs are preferable.

Marriage is not an alternative for all women and becomes progressively less likely as women grow older. There are more women than men in the older age brackets, and five million more women than men in the United States. Also, older men often prefer to marry younger women.

Government regulations are of little help to these women. Some are not protected by minimum wage laws, and there is little government support for programs that would pay them supplementary wages. During the 1960s, the Johnson Administration began the Job Corps to train men for better-paying jobs, but this program specifically excluded women until women in Congress protested this discrimination.

Organizing women for better pay and improved working conditions is very difficult, especially among day workers who do not work for the same employer. Unions have sometimes resisted organizing women and allowing them to join existing unions. In some cases employers have fired women for attempting to form unions. Nevertheless, the number of unions for women is increasing, and more women are joining them all the time.

Women's Self-Perception

Many women are, sooner or later, housewives and mothers, at least for a time. Since our society gives so little respect and esteem to these roles, it is not surprising that women tend to give themselves little respect for accomplishments in these areas. Women are also unlikely to define themselves or other women as independent achievers equal to men (Hoffman and Nye, 1974), especially in the areas of science and technology. They continue to believe that they cannot do math, in spite of a great deal of evidence that they are quite capable of doing math (Tobias, 1976). Women are less likely than men to develop an interest in or pursue technical and engineering training, which further limits their opportunities.

Women also tend to be critical of their appearance. They are expected to be thin and beautiful. Women spend more time, energy, and money than men do on cosmetic, diet, and exercise products. Even in high school they may be extremely critical of their bodies and may diet to the point of malnutrition. In extreme cases, excessive dieting results in anorexia, an illness most often seen in women, which sometimes results in death from starvation.

Women are socialized to be more dependent than men (Hunt & Hunt, 1977; Lueptow, 1980). They use their appearance to attract the love of men and then depend on men for support. Given the extent of poverty in families headed by women, dependency is practical for women. Nevertheless, it leads to the habit of giving men more credit for being capable, clever, or knowledge-

Many women pay far more attention to their appearance than they do to their health. They are willing to spend money on various chemical concoctions for appetite control, even though some experts believe some of these products cause strokes and seizures. These same women often ignore the nutritional needs of their bodies.

able. This pattern of response tends to lower self-esteem and creates in some women a feeling of powerlessness and helplessness, which can lead to depression.

Stress and Depression

Stress and depression have long been known to be associated with feelings of powerlessness and helplessness. Studies show that rates of mental illness, and especially depression, are higher for women than for men (Dohrenwend and Dohrenwend, 1976; Gove and Tudor, 1973; Srole, 1975; Weitz, 1982). The rates of mental illness are decreasing in women, however, probably because women are entering the work force in larger numbers (Kessler and McRae, 1983). Married women have higher rates of depression than single women, but the highest rates are found among married women who do not work outside the home. Rates of depression are lower in married women who work outside the home, especially when they work because they want to.

Depression is also less common among women whose husbands help with the housework (Ross et al., 1983a). There is no indication that depression in men increases when they help with the housework.

Gove and Geerken (1977), in trying to develop a theory to explain stress, argued that married women experience high rates of stress because the role of a married woman is not respected in American society. To test this theory, a study was conducted comparing Anglo-American women with Mexican women (Ross et al., 1983b). Because the family is more highly valued in Mexico than it is in the United States, the research hypothesized that Mexican women would feel less stressful since they were more valued as family members. It was found that Mexican women did in fact suffer less stress and receive more support for their role in the family.

The cure for stress and depression in both women and men might be a society that provided better financial opportunities and more

A counselor welcomes a mother and her child to a family shelter. Here for a short period of time they will be protected from abuse in the home and helped to make better living arrangements. If a lack of funds makes other arrangements impossible, however, the mother and child may return home to suffer further abuse.

respect for family-related roles. In actuality, the cure for stress and depression in women has been drug therapy. When men go to their physician with complaints, they are likely to receive a very thorough physical. When women go to their physician with complaints, they are likely to receive a prescription for tranquilizers or antidepressants instead of a physical (Ehrenreich and English, 1979). These drugs are highly addictive and have serious side effects. As a result, the rate of prescription drug addiction among women is believed to be very high.

Sexual Harassment

Women in all types of jobs suffer from *sexual harassment*, sexual advances made by coworkers or superiors at work. Women who reject sexual advances may be denied a job, intimidated, given poor work evaluations, denied raises or promotions, or fired.

Sexual harassment is much more widespread than is generally realized. The first questionnaire ever devoted solely to this topic surveyed working women in 1975 (Farley, 1978). The results were startling: 92 percent of respondents cited sexual harassment as a serious problem, and 70 percent reported that they had personally experienced some form of harassment. Other studies indicate that sexual harassment is also a major problem in colleges and universities, in offices of the United Nations, in the United States military, in civil service jobs, and in private industry.

In deciding how to respond to sexual harassment, the victim must consider the economic necessity of keeping the job, opportunities for getting another job, the likelihood of achieving decent work evaluations and future promotions, the possibility of being fired, and the attitudes of family and friends to her situation. The victim usually decides to quit, transfer to another job within the organization, or do nothing and suffer in silence because probably no one will believe her if she makes a complaint.

Family Violence

Family violence is a widespread problem in the United States. Family disputes account for 30 percent of the aggravated assaults and 33 percent of homicides. More police officers are killed handling domestic disputes than in any other activity (Gelles, 1979). We often assume that such violence is carried on by people who are mentally deranged, but research has found that this is not true. Normal people in all walks of life and at all economic levels fall victim to family violence.

When a wife or child is being abused, the wife often does not leave the home or remove the child from the home. Sometimes the wife believes she deserves to be beaten, but women frequently have no money of their own and no place to go. It is likewise difficult for a woman to take her children out of her home when she has no means of support, no food, and no shelter. Thus, while the reasons for family violence are complex, one of the major reasons it continues is that women are unable to support themselves and their children and are therefore unwilling to leave home.

Rape

Rape is another form of violence that results in part from gender inequality. The FBI's Uniform Crime Reports for 1982 show that forcible rape was reported to authorities 72,000 times in 1982. Estimates of the actual occurrence of rape, however, are two to three times higher than the number reported because most rapes are never reported to authorities. Of the rapes that are reported to authorities, few end in an arrest, and even when an arrest is made, it is estimated that 40 percent of the defendants are either acquitted or the cases are dismissed (Manis, 1984).

Men often rape women to demonstrate their power and aggressiveness, their higher ranking in the stratification system. Sexuality plays a much lesser role in causing rape. But society often believes that women must have done something wrong to invite rape (Thornton et al., 1981), that rape is caused by women wearing enticing clothing, appearing in public at late hours, or not resisting the advances of men. While women get blamed for not resisting the advances of men, most programs dealing with rape prevention suggest that women should not use force to prevent rape, that cooperation is the safer course of action to survive attack. Research on rape, however, has found that women are safer if they do forcefully resist an attack (Bart, 1979).

The assumption that women are somehow to blame for rape makes it difficult for them to report a rape. If a woman calls the police to report a prowler whom she fears will rape her, little action is taken because as yet no crime has been committed. If a woman reports that she has been raped, she must submit to medical examinations and long hours of questioning to prove she was raped. In no other crime is it necessary to prove that the crime has been committed. If jewelry is stolen, for example, the victim does not have to prove that he or she did own the jewelry reported missing.

Efforts are being made to reduce the tendency to blame the victim of the rape for her victimization. Nevertheless, should the rapist be caught and brought to trial, the reputation of the victim will come under scrutiny. It will be assumed that if she is sexually active, the rapist may have interpreted her behavior as an invitation to him to attack her (Feldman-Summers and Palmer, 1980; Rose and Randall, 1982).

Some feminists have argued that rape and other forms of violence are the end result of the norms of aggressiveness that men learn to display toward women. Pornography has been severely criticized, not because it is sexual but because most pornography depicts women as passive victims of violent men. The message to readers of pornographic literature is that the violent abuse of women is both masculine and normal (Le-

SOCIOLOGISTS AT WORK
Advising Social Issues

Cathy Shine is a legislative assistant for Senator Bob Packwood of Oregon. In the four years since she graduated from Denison University with a B.A. in sociology and anthropology, she has also worked as a compensation specialist for a management consulting firm and as an organizer and lobbyist with the National Organization for Women. Her job with Senator Packwood reflects her interest in women's issues. She advises the senator on the civil, constitutional, and women's rights bills that come before the Senate.

"I have to research and understand the pros and cons of every pending bill in my area," she says. "A recent bill on school prayer involved a number of legal and constitutional questions, so I spent lots of time reading Supreme Court decisions to understand why the Court has ruled that school prayer is unconstitutional. I probably sent the senator twenty memos on that bill. On most issues he has discussions with staff members as well. I also talk with constituents and deal with lobbyists. We can actually draft bills, too; this entails working with many specialists including outside attorneys who practice in the area the bill is concerned with.

"Sociology helps you understand how people's political views are shaped by social structures. The school prayer amendment is a good example of how people's attitudes are shaped by religion. I learned from talking to constituents, some favored it for religious reasons and others opposed it for religious reasons. In the Senate, Senator Danforth (an ordained minister) said, "The debate on school prayer is not between the godly and the ungodly. For strongly held religious reasons, people have arrived at opposite conclusions on the pending amendment." The sociological perspective is useful in understanding how attitudes are shaped by a social structure like religion. Whatever theory you look at, whether it's Weber, Durkheim, or Marx, they all recognize the importance of religious institutions in shaping attitudes.

"My statistical skills are important because so much of what I do is based on numbers. The Congressional Budget Office (CBO) computes the costs of every bill that comes before Congress. I study their figures closely to see what factors they've taken into account. For example, Senator Packwood wrote one of the amendments

derer, 1980). A society that differentiates between the sexes, gives one sex a lower status than the other, and provides little opportunity for mutual respect between the sexes, is likely to continue to see violence against one sex by the other.

The Future of Gender Inequality

Will gender differentiation decrease? Will women become economically and occupationally equal to men? If the structural functionalists are correct, women will gradually win promotions and pay increases that will move them into the upper echelons of the bureaucratic work world and win them equality with men. If the conflict theorists are correct, women will be trapped in the secondary labor market, losing out on pay increases and promotions and falling farther and farther behind men.

A third alternative is also possible, one that combines aspects of the functionalist and conflict views. Upper-class women may use a college education as a steppingstone into the primary labor market. Their educational credentials and

to the Child Support Enforcement Bill that would strengthen a spouse's ability to get court-ordered child support payments. Packwood's amendment allows the IRS to intercept a federal tax refund from a delinquent spouse who hasn't paid child support. The CBO estimated the costs of the amendment, but they didn't take some factors into account. I reviewed their numbers and gave the senator alternative factors to use in his arguments in support of the amendment."

Some of Shine's most demanding work involves drafting bills. One flurry of activity began in 1984 when the Supreme Court narrowed a law, Title IX of the Education Amendments of 1972, that protected women from sex discrimination in education. Before Title IX, only about 300,000 girls participated in high school athletics. By 1979, 2 million girls were participating. Under the 1984 decision, many school athletic departments will no longer have to comply with Title IX. With Senator Kennedy, Senator Packwood filed a bill to overturn the decision, and Shine served as one of Packwood's representatives in drafting the bill.

"It's easy to say we'll submit a bill that will overturn a Supreme Court ruling," Shine says, "but how do we actually do it? We brought together Senate and House staff attorneys as well as a number of outside attorneys who practice in this area. Imagine trying to get forty lawyers to agree on anything! It took a long time, but we finally got a bill. It was also my job to get cosponsors — the more cosponsors you have, the better your chances of passing the bill. We got sixty-three cosponsors in the Republican-controlled Senate, including 25 Republicans, which is a record for the number of Republican senators sponsoring a piece of civil rights legislation at introduction."

Shine's work on social issues actually began when she was a student at Denison with her thesis, "A Case Study: Patterns of Campus Violence among Students." "Its value as a learning experience was incalculable," Shine says. "At the time, I was cochair of the student judicial system, so I had access to all of these cases. What I did was document what everyone knew, that the great majority of the offenses were committed by men belonging to fraternities during their freshman year. I concluded that the Greek system and the macho attitudes it fostered were responsible for most of the problems that came before the judicial system. After I graduated, my report was used in setting up a commission to deal with the problem. It's an example of work in sociology actually being used to generate social change."

their family background will help them get good positions, where, like upper-class men, they will be groomed for greater responsibility and achieve higher and higher positions. Working-class women, without family connections and educational opportunity, are likely to remain in the secondary labor market and fall farther and farther behind. In such a scenario, gender differentiation could diminish considerably even while class differences remained great. Complete equality between men and women requires an end to class as well as gender differentiation.

Summary

Modern society differentiates people on the basis of gender. The work that women do is devalued — even the work of raising the next generation. Evidence shows that our behavior is shaped by socialization rather than our biological inheritance, and men and women in other societies do not follow the same role behaviors that they do in Western society.

Structural-functional theorists believe that the roles of women in our society are changing.

Until quite recently, women were required to stay at home to maintain the house and care for the children, but recently labor-saving devices have made it possible for women to enter the work force. They are presently concentrated in low-level occupations but in time should gain the skills and experience to rise to levels equal to men.

Conflict theorists believe that women have low status because they are exploited by men. Men keep women in inferior positions in a variety of ways both at home and in the work force. According to this theory, women will never win equal status with men.

Women have always worked for economic gain, but until industrialization, this work was done in the home, in nunneries, or in Beguines. When society became industrialized, women were without economic opportunities unless they entered factory work. In 1982 women earned approximately 63 percent of what men earned. Most working women work in poor-paying clerical, industrial, or service jobs in the secondary labor market and play traditional feminine roles helping men.

It is difficult to measure women's status. While their own occupations may be low in status, women often gain status from their husband's occupation. Status based on someone else provides no power to make decisions, however. Women have less political power than men. The Equal Rights Amendment, which would have given women equality under the law, was not ratified; women have legal protection only when they can get specific laws passed, and these laws can be repealed at any time.

Inequality has serious consequences. Many women and the children they support live in poverty, and women often have poor self-images. They have learned that society does not consider them to be equal, especially in technical areas, and that society values them chiefly for their physical characteristics.

Women suffer from a great deal of stress and depression. Their role in the family is not respected, and many women must deal with both family and work roles. They suffer from sexual harassment in the workplace and family violence at home. They often cannot escape such violence because they have no economic alternatives other than the job or the marriage that supports them. Women suffer from rape because males sometimes choose rape to demonstrate their power and dominance.

In the future, inequality may decrease as women gain skills and experience in the workplace. If they are in fact relegated to the secondary labor market and not allowed to advance into the higher levels of the workplace, however, inequality may remain at today's levels. It is likely that women from families at higher economic levels will advance. Women who lack the support of an advantageous family background may remain in the secondary labor market, and gender differences would then follow class lines.

Key Terms

Beguines
Equal Rights Amendment (ERA)
gender roles
primary labor market
secondary labor market
sexual harassment
split labor market
women's movement

Suggested Readings

Bernard, Jessie. **The Female World.** *New York: The Free Press, 1981.* This book treats women as living in a world very different from the world of men and emphasizes the assets women can offer to make a more human world for everyone.

Boserup, Ester. **Woman's Role in Economic Development.** *London: Allen and Unwin, 1970.* This is an excellent discussion of how women suffer as a result of economic development in modernizing countries.

Kanter, Rosabeth M. **Men and Women of the Corporation.** *New York: Basic Books, 1979.* This book is an excellent discussion of the pressures and problems of work in a large corporation for both men and women.

Kinzer, Nora Scott. **Stress and the American Woman.** *Garden City, New York: Anchor Press/Doubleday, 1979.* A discussion of stress and problems related to stress based on a study of the women in the first class to allow women at West Point.

Kreps, Juanita M. **Women and the American Economy, a Look to the 1980s.** *Englewood Cliffs, N.J.: Prentice-Hall, 1976.* Written by an economist, this book concisely discusses the class position of women today.

Rosseau, Ann Marie. **Shopping Bag Ladies: Homeless Women Speak About Their Lives.** *New York: The Pilgrim Press, 1981.* A moving collection of photographs depicting homeless women in the United States.

Spadley, James P. and Brenda J. Mann. **The Cocktail Waitress, Women's Work in a Man's World.** *New York: Wiley, 1975.* Good reading, especially for anyone who thinks this is an easy job. It will make cocktail waitresses aware of their job in a new way.

Sayre, Anne. **Rosalind Franklin and DNA.** *New York: Norton, 1975.* An excellent book on one woman's experiences in scientific research.

CHAPTER 11

Age Differentiation

Youth is a gift of nature, but age is a work of art.

— Garson Kanin

People in all societies expect different behaviors from the young and the old. In many countries people are living longer than ever before, and an aging population creates new concerns for both individuals and societies. Many individuals do not look forward to growing old because they associate attractiveness, health, and productivity with the young. For the society as a whole, an increasing aged population arouses concerns about financial support, health care, housing, productivity, and other issues.

The systematic study of the aging process is known as *gerontology*. It is an interdisciplinary field of study that draws heavily on the biological and social sciences. One biological branch of gerontology, for example, is *geriatrics*, the medical care of the aged. *Social gerontology*, another branch of gerontology, focuses on the social and cultural factors related to age and the aging process.

Age is an ascribed status. As such, we have different social expectations about the behavior of different age groups. We expect babies to suck their thumbs and crawl on the floor, but we don't expect adults to do these things. We expect children to skip down the sidewalk, teenagers to attend school, and middle-age executives to wear suits. Expectations about the behavior considered appropriate for people of a given age are called *age norms*. Since these particular expected behaviors are associated with particular ages, we ask people, according to their age, if they have finished high school, are married, have children or grandchildren, or are retired. These social timetables tell people if their lives are on schedule. There seems to be wide agreement among adults about age norms within societies, but age norms vary widely among different societies.

One society may agree that the aged should be accorded deference, respect, and reverence; another may agree that they should retire and become less productive. One society may expect old people to live with and be cared for by their families; another may expect them to join other elderly persons in retirement communities or be cared for by the government.

Many age norms, particularly those concerning the aged in the United States, are inaccurate and tend to restrict the lifestyles and limit the personal fulfillment of elderly persons. Many definitions and perceptions of old people or the aging process are stereotypes — conventional mental images applied universally to all old people. Although widely held, many of these stereotypes are not supported by empirical evidence. Unfortunately, these misinformed, negative stereotypes can lead to *ageism:* prejudice and discrimination based on age. Like racism and sexism, ageism involves beliefs about the inherent inferiority of a group that are used to justify individual or institutionalized discrimination. We examine a few of these prejudices, stereotypes, and myths in the next section of this chapter.

Myths About Old Age

The development of gerontology as a field of study and our increasing body of research on the aging process show that many traditional beliefs about the aged are inaccurate. Kart (1981) lists ten misconceptions about old people and the aging process:

1. Old age is inevitably accompanied by *senility*, a mental infirmity associated with the aging process.
2. In general, old people are miserable.
3. Most old people are lonely.
4. The majority of old people have health problems.
5. Old people are more likely than younger people to be victimized by crime.
6. The majority of old people live in poverty.
7. Most old people are unable to manage a household.
8. Old people who retire usually suffer a decline in health.
9. Most old people have no interest in, or capacity for, sexual relations.
10. Most old people end up in nursing homes and other long-term care institutions. (p. 4)

Some of these myths are discussed later in this chapter. At this point we will briefly summarize why each of these statements is false. The first statement suggests that senility inevitably accompanies old age, but many people, including a number of the world's leaders and other famous figures, make significant contributions in their seventh and eighth decade of life. In the absence of disease, age-related changes in learning ability appear to be small, even after the keenness of the senses has begun to decline.

The second and third statements say that most old people are miserable and lonely. Yet the evidence consistently indicates that old people are satisfied with their lives. Many are alone, but this does not necessarily mean they are lonely. The meaning of loneliness appears to change with age, and except for widows who miss their husbands and express higher degrees of loneliness, other groups of older people do not find loneliness to be problematic.

The fourth myth is that most of the elderly have health problems. While many old people do have health problems, the majority of those over sixty-five do not have problems that limit their ability to work, keep house, or engage in routine daily activities.

The fifth statement focuses on victimization. Crime against older people is an area of increasing study, and surveys show that the elderly are more fearful of crime than the young. But the popular belief that elderly persons are victimized more often is false. The victimization rate of old people for assault and robbery, for example, is

The need for and interest in intimacy and affection has no age boundary. The significance of a kiss, hug, or tender gesture, comment, or the feeling of the warmth of another person is often undervalued for older persons. For many, noncoital sensual arousal and response is especially cherished. The capacity to share empathic affection may actually improve with age.

much lower than it is for others. The one exception may be personal larceny such as purse- and wallet-snatchings, in which the victimization rates are about equal.

The sixth stereotype, that most old people live in poverty, is false as well. Admittedly, many of the elderly are poor. But taking into account Society Security benefits, private pension plans, tax relief laws, and income from sources such as rents, annuities, retirement plans, savings, dividends, and so on, plus the high percentage of older people who own their own homes and automobiles, the vast majority are not at the poverty level. In 1982, 8.0 percent of all male householders and 14.8 percent of all female householders age sixty-five and over were below the poverty level (*Statistical Abstract: 1984*, Table 36). The same was true for about one-fourth of all males and one-third of all female unrelated individuals over sixty-five. A "household" is a group consisting of related family members and all unrelated persons who occupy a housing unit. "Unrelated individuals" are people not living with any relatives.

The seventh stereotype is that most old people can't manage a household. Yet, in 1982, 92 percent of men over sixty-five and 80 percent of women lived alone or with their spouse in their own household (see Table 11–3 later in this chapter). Most aged people prefer to live close to their adult children but in separate households from them.

The eighth myth is that when old people retire they suffer a decline in health. People do re-

Highlights of the Aged Population in America

One of the most significant demographic facts affecting American society is the aging of its population. The number of elderly persons has grown and, for the next fifty years, will continue to grow more rapidly than the total population. In 1982, 11 percent of all Americans were elderly (sixty-five and older); by the year 2025, a projected 19 percent of the total population will be elderly.

Other statistics reveal that:

The sixty-five and over population grew twice as fast as the rest of the population in the last two decades.

The eighty-five and over group is growing especially rapidly, up one hundred sixty-five percent from 1960 to 1982.

The death rates of the elderly population, especially women, fell considerably over the last forty years.

The ratio of elderly to those under sixty-five will probably be one to five in 1990 and one to three in 2025.

In fifty years, the ratio of people over sixty-five to people eighteen to sixty-four will be almost three times as great as it was in 1950.

The median income of elderly persons had a higher percentage increase over the last two decades than the median income of the younger adult population.

About one of every seven Americans over the age of sixty-five lives in poverty.

Elderly women are almost twice as likely as elderly men to be poor; half of elderly widowed black women live in poverty.

About eight in ten persons sixty-five and over now describe their health as "good" or "excellent," compared with others of their own age.

Elderly men are most likely to be married while elderly women are most likely to be widowed.

The number of elderly women living alone has doubled in the last fifteen years.

During the last decade, the number of elderly persons living in central cities has declined, while the number living in the suburbs and small towns has increased.

Half of those sixty-five and over who work now do so on a part-time basis as compared with a third twenty years ago.

In the 1980 election, one-third of Americans who voted were fifty-five or older; 70 percent of those aged fifty-five to seventy-four voted.

SOURCE: U.S. Bureau of the Census, *Current Population Reports,* Series P-23, no. 128, "America in Transition: An Aging Society," U.S. Government Printing Office, Washington, D.C., 1983, p. 1.

tire because of health problems, but the widespread tale of the individual who retired and "went downhill fast" appears to have little empirical support.

The ninth statement concerns interest in or capacity for sexual relations. Although sexual interests, capacities, and functions do change with age, detailed clinical studies of sexuality in late life have demonstrated the lifelong potential for sexual response and the reversibility of sexual disorders occurring later in life (Masters and Johnson 1966, 1970). Weiler (1981) contends that patterns of sexual activity tend to remain stable in middle and late life and that the notion of declining sexuality is a myth. It is clear that sexual expression continues late in life and that sexual intimacy, including but not restricted to intercourse, is important to older persons.

The tenth stereotype suggests that most old people are in nursing homes and other long-term care institutions, but Census Bureau data indicate that only about 5 percent of the elderly are in old-age institutions of one kind or another. The vast majority of them live alone or with their spouse in their own household.

Demographic Aspects of Aging

As you will learn in Chapter 19, the study of population is a central concern of sociologists. A number of questions tend to arise in examining any population: How many people are there? Has the number of people changed in the past? How is it likely to change in the future? What are the characteristics of the population? How do these numbers compare with other groups in society and with the numbers of similar groups in other societies? The answers to questions such as these alert us to the increasing significance of aging in most industrialized nations, because the number of elderly people is unprecedented in world history. Never have so many people lived so long.

One key question in investigations of an aged population concerns the age at which people are considered elderly. Most of us know of men and women over seventy who look, think,

and act young and others who seem old at thirty-five or forty-five. Nevertheless, social policy and much of the available data in the United States define the elderly population as those sixty-five years of age and over. While this cut-off point is somewhat arbitrary, it is widely used by gerontologists and we will follow it in this chapter. It is not universal, however, and today many gerontologists distinguish between the "young-old" (those fifty-five to seventy-four) and the "old-old" (those seventy-five and over). You should recognize that numbers such as these are statistical generalizations and that wide variations exist in people's life expectancy, income, activity, and so forth.

Numbers of the Elderly: The Graying of America

As Table 11-1 and Figure 11-1 indicate, the elderly population in the United States has been growing since 1900, and it is expected to keep growing for decades to come. In 1900, the population of those sixty-five and over was about 3.1 million, comprising about 4.0 percent of the pop-

The life span, the age beyond which persons cannot expect to live, is slightly over 100 years. On occasion, reports or pictures are issued of persons believed to have lived well in excess of that figure. The age of Temyr Vanachia, pictured here, has been reported to be 118 years. Never has a group or subculture been known to achieve that length of life.

Table 11-1

Growth of the older population, actual and projected:
1900–2050 (numbers in thousands)

| YEAR | 65 YEARS AND OVER | |
	NUMBER	PERCENT
1900	3,084	4.0
1910	3,950	4.3
1920	4,933	4.7
1930	6,634	5.4
1940	9,019	6.8
1950	12,270	8.1
1960	16,560	9.2
1970	19,980	9.8
1980	25,544	11.3
1990	31,799	12.7
2000	35,036	13.1
2010	39,269	13.9
2020	51,386	17.3
2030	64,345	21.1
2040	66,643	21.6
2050	67,061	21.7

SOURCE: U.S. Bureau of the Census, *Current Population Reports*, Series P-23, no. 128, "America in Transition: An Aging Society," U.S. Government Printing Office, Washington, D.C., 1983, p. 3.

ulation or one person in twenty-five. Today, the elderly number between 25 and 30 million and comprise about 12 percent of the population, or about one person in eight. It is projected that in fifty years there will be more than 60 million elderly people in America, about one person in five. These numbers are not wild speculation, since these people have already been born, and barring any major wars or diseases, nearly three-fourths of those currently living can expect to reach old age. These numbers can of course be influenced by migrations of people into or out of the United States in addition to the unexpected death factor.

This pattern of growth raises many questions relating to work, leisure, health, housing, family life, and other matters. One approach gerontologists have taken in considering how changes in these areas will affect society involves examining the relationship between the elderly and the rest of the population.

The Dependency Ratio. One way to examine the relationship between the old and the young is by calculating the *dependency ratio*, the ratio between the number of persons in the de-

Figure 11-1

Population 65 years and over by age: 1900–2050

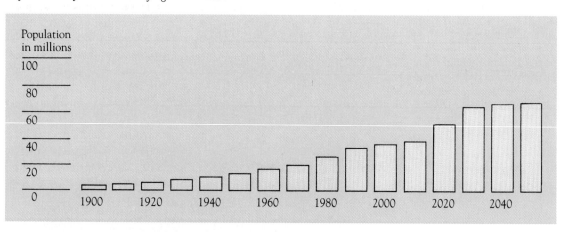

The labor force participation of the elderly has decreased over the past several decades. Many persons continue to use their skills however, in self-employed activities, in volunteer services or in part-time employment. Employed white and male workers are most likely to be in white-collar and professional occupations; black and female workers are most likely to be in blue-collar and service type jobs.

pendent population and the number of people in the supportive or working population. The dependent population includes both the aged and children, but an old-age dependency ratio can be determined by dividing the number of persons over sixty-five by the number of those in the supportive or working population, generally ages eighteen to sixty-four. Another form of the dependency ratio involves noting the number of persons sixty-five or over per one hundred persons eighteen to sixty-four years old. In 1982, this figure was nineteen (*Statistical Abstract: 1984,* Table 617); that is, there were nineteen persons sixty-five and over for every one hundred people between eighteen and sixty-four, a ratio of one to five. Clearly not all those between eighteen and sixty-four are working or supportive, nor are all persons over sixty-five dependent, but this ratio still provides a useful index of the relationship between these two segments of the population.

An old-age dependency ratio can be used in several ways. First, it tells how many people under sixty-five there are to support those over sixty-five. A figure of nineteen people over sixty-five per one hundred people eighteen to sixty-four tells us that there is one dependent person over sixty-five for every five persons working to support him or her. The Census Bureau provides another, more precise dependency ratio — the number of *nonworkers* sixty years old and over per one hundred *workers* age twenty to fifty-nine. In 1982, this figure was thirty (*Statistical Abstract: 1984,* Table 617), meaning that there were about three workers under sixty to support each nonworker sixty or over.

A dependency ratio can also be used to note changes in the age distribution of the population. In 1930, there were only nine people over sixty-five per hundred workers. By 1960, this figure had increased to thirteen, by 1970 to seventeen, and by 1982 to nineteen, as mentioned above. Since the baby boom of the 1940s and 1950s put more persons in the eighteen-to-sixty-four work group, a relatively stable dependency ratio is expected for the next thirty years. But as this group reaches retirement age, today's lower birth rate will result in a projected dependency ratio in 2030 of twenty-nine dependents per hundred workers, or three to four working persons to support each elderly person. Given the increasing number of elderly and the decreasing number of workers to support each nonworker, we can expect issues such as Social Security, health care costs, and support services to become serious concerns. These shifts in dependency ratios will create problems of familial and societal support of the aged throughout this century, and such problems will become even more serious after the turn of the century at about the time most of you will be considering retirement.

Life Expectancy

Life expectancy is the average years of life remaining for people who attain a given age. The most commonly cited life expectancy figure is based on birth. In other words, how many years, on average, can infants born in a given year ex-

pect to live? The expectation of life for Americans born in 1982 was 74.5 years, but this figure varies considerably by sex and race. White females had a life expectancy of 78.7, compared with 71.4 for white males. Black females had a life expectancy of 75.2, compared with 66.5 for black males (*Statistical Abstract: 1984*, Table 101).

Figure 11-2 illustrates how these figures have changed since 1900. Note that (1) regardless of sex or race, the expectation of life at birth has increased considerably in this century; (2) the life expectancy difference between males and females has widened continually for both blacks and whites; and (3) the life expectancy of black females has surpassed that of white males in the past twenty years. These changes and differences are a result of declining mortality rates, improved health and nutrition, and changing socioeconomic conditions. The consequence is that more people are living to reach old age, with women increasingly outnumbering men in the older-age categories. As of 1982 there were an estimated 10.3 million men and 15.0 million women in the United States who were sixty-five years old and over. This translates into a sex ratio of sixty-nine males per one hundred females.

Figure 11-2

Expectation of life at birth by race and sex: 1900–1980

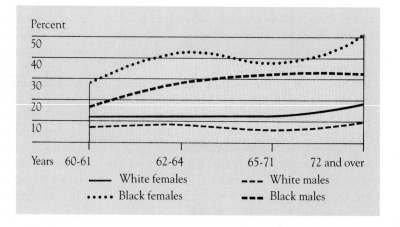

Table 11-2

Marital status of men and women, aged sixty-five and over, March 1982 (percentage distribution)

MARITAL STATUS	MEN		WOMEN	
	AGED 65–74	AGED 75 AND OVER	AGED 65–74	AGED 75 AND OVER
Single	4.9%	3.3%	5.3%	6.1%
Married	81.5	70.3	49.3	22.4
Separated	2.5	2.3	2.0	1.2
Widowed	7.5	21.7	38.3	68.5
Divorced	3.6	2.4	5.1	1.8
Total	100.0	100.0	100.0	100.0

SOURCE: U.S. Bureau of the Census, *Current Population Reports*, Series P-20, no. 380, "Marital Status and Living Arrangements, March 1982," U.S. Government Printing Office, Washington, D.C., 1983, Table 1, p. 8.

What about the life expectancy of older persons? Suppose we consider life expectancy at age sixty-five rather than life expectancy at birth. In 1980, the life expectancy at sixty-five was 16.4 (*Statistical Abstract: 1984*, Table 103), which means that those who lived to age sixty-five could expect on average to live to age 81.4. Surprisingly, in 1900 the life expectancy of those who reached sixty-five was 11.9, which means they could expect to live until age 76.9. Thus, although many more people are living longer, there has been relatively little increase (4.5 years) in the life expectancy of older persons since the turn of the century.

This finding is related to the notion of *life span*, the biological age limit beyond which no one can expect to live. Gerontologists estimate the life span to be slightly over a hundred years, and many believe it has remained basically unchanged throughout recorded history. Therefore, while life expectancy has increased dramatically and more people are reaching old age than ever before, the life span is virtually unchanged.

Despite frequent efforts to find a "fountain of youth," most biologists see no major scientific breakthrough in the near future that will extend the life span. Furthermore, according to the Russian gerontologist Medvedev (1974, 1975), reports of groups who live to be 130 and individuals who live to be 150 are without scientific foundation.

Social Characteristics of the Elderly

The elderly population, like the rest of the population, varies by sex, marital status, living arrangements, geographical distribution, labor force participation, and other characteristics. Many characteristics are related in some way to the fact that women greatly outnumber men. The sex ratio is about sixty-nine men per hundred women age sixty-five and over. This factor has a major impact on conditions such as marital status and living arrangements.

Elderly men and women differ sharply in their marital status (see Table 11-2). More than

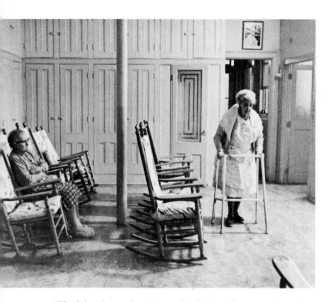

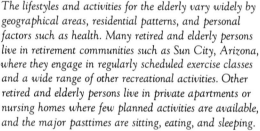

The lifestyles and activities for the elderly vary widely by geographical areas, residential patterns, and personal factors such as health. Many retired and elderly persons live in retirement communities such as Sun City, Arizona, where they engage in regularly scheduled exercise classes and a wide range of other recreational activities. Other retired and elderly persons live in private apartments or nursing homes where few planned activities are available, and the major pasttimes are sitting, eating, and sleeping.

three-fourths of all older men are married and living with their spouse, compared with less than half of the women. The most dramatic difference in marital status between the sexes is shown under the category "Widowed." In 1982, of those age sixty-five to seventy-four, 7.5 percent of the men and 38.3 percent of the women were widowed. Of those age seventy-five and over, 21.7 percent of the men and 68.5 percent of the women were widowed. These differences are due to the fact that men tend to marry younger women and die at younger ages. Also, elderly widowed men have remarriage rates about seven times higher than those of women.

Living arrangements differ as well. Most elderly men are married, and 77.6 percent live in their own household with their spouse, while only 38.5 percent of the women have this arrangement (see Table 11-3). More than 40 percent of the women live alone, compared with 14 percent of the men. And as we noted earlier, the notion that most old people end up in nursing homes and other long-term care institutions is a myth. Only about 5 percent, or one in twenty, is institutionalized.

Geographically, the elderly are heavily concentrated in metropolitan areas and in a few states. Compared with those under age sixty-

Table 11-3

Characteristics of persons sixty-five years and over, by sex, 1970 and 1982

	1970		1982	
CHARACTERISTICS	MALE	FEMALE	MALE	FEMALE
Total (in millions)	8.3	11.5	10.3	14.9
Percent of population	8.5	11.1	9.4	12.7
Median income (in dollars)				
Family householders	$4,779	$4,986	$14,553	$12,429
Unrelated individuals	2,101	1,777	6,627	5,607
Percent below poverty level (by percent)				
Family householders	16.6	23.5	8.0	14.8
Unrelated individuals	40.0	49.9	23.4	31.4
Family status (by percent)				
In families	79.2	58.5	83.6	56.7
Primary individuals	14.9	35.2	15.4	42.4
Secondary individuals	2.4	1.9	1.0	.8
Residents of institutions	3.6	4.4	(N/A)[a]	(N/A)
Labor force participation (by percent)				
Employed	26.2	10.0	17.1	7.6
Not in labor force	73.8	90.0	82.9	92.4
Living arrangements (by percent)				
Living in household	95.5	95.0	99.9	99.9
Living alone	14.1	33.8	14.5	41.4
Spouse present	69.9	33.9	77.6	38.5
Living with someone else	11.5	27.4	7.7	19.9
Not in household	4.5	5.0	.1	.1

[a]N/A indicates that figures are not available.

SOURCE: U.S. Bureau of the Census, *Statistical Abstract of the United States: 1984*, 104th ed., U.S. Government Printing Washington, D.C., 1983, no. 36, p. 35.

five, elderly persons are less likely to live in the suburbs. In 1981, as was true a decade earlier, about two-thirds lived in metropolitan areas. Black and Hispanic elderly are especially concentrated in central cities, whereas whites are more likely to live outside the central city. In 1980, there were seven states with more than one million people sixty-five and over: California (2.4 million), New York (2.2 million), Florida (1.7 million), Pennsylvania (1.5 million), Texas (1.4 million), Illinois (1.3 million), and Ohio (1.2 million). If Michigan's elderly population of more than 900,000 is included, nearly half of the total elderly population of the United States is found in eight states. Alaska had the smallest number of elderly persons — only 11,500, less than 3 percent of its population. Florida is the state with the highest proportion over sixty-five — 17.3 percent. During the past decade the largest increases in the elderly population were in the South and West.

The labor force participation of older men has dropped rapidly over the last thirty years. In 1950, almost half were employed in the labor force, but by 1970 the figure was one in four, and by 1982 it was approaching one in six (see Table 11-3). The decreases are partly due to an increase in voluntary early retirement and a drop in self-employment. For elderly women, the labor force participation has varied little. In 1950 about 10 percent of elderly women were employed, with the percentage dropping to less than 8 percent in 1982. This is a sharp contrast to the female labor force in general, in which the proportion of working women rose from 31 percent in 1950 to 52.4 percent in 1982. Among the more than 3 million elderly workers, over half were in white-collar occupations. Sex and race are also important determinants of the occupations of the employed elderly. White and male workers were most likely to be in white-collar and professional occupations, while black and female workers were more likely to be in blue-collar and service jobs.

Theories of Aging and of Age Differentiation

In Chapter 6 we discussed certain aspects of socialization and social interaction. While tremendous emphasis is given to children and youth in the literature, the socialization and resocialization needs of the elderly are largely ignored. The socialization of young people involves families, schools, peers, jobs, and the community. But what socialization agents exist to direct the aging process, to train people for retirement, widowhood, illness, or death? How can we explain differences among age groups in income, status, prestige, usefulness, and similar characteristics?

Aging is a biological process, and many theories of aging focus on genetic or physiological changes. As we age, our skin wrinkles, our posture becomes stooped, our muscle reflexes become less efficient, and our responses to sexual stimuli are slower. These biological changes are important to note. They do not, however, explain what happens to humans socially as they grow older. For these explanations we turn to social-psychological and sociological theories.

Structural-Functional Theory

Structural-functional theories assess aging in terms of social changes such as population shifts and industrialization, attempting to determine how they influence social organization. According to the functionalist perspective, societies should be able to provide rewards and meaningful lives for all their citizens, including the elderly. Yet some observers argue that changes in the extended family structure have stripped the elderly of their respected positions as leaders and authorities. With today's rapid changes in industry and high technology, the elderly often lack the skills and training needed to fulfill beneficial economic roles. Today, there are more old people and fewer productive roles for them to fulfill. One could say that there is an imbalance between the age structures and the role-performance structures of our basic social institutions. This view is reflected in two structural-functional perspectives, modernization theory and disengagement theory.

Modernization theory (Cowgill, 1974; Cowgill and Homes, 1972) states that with increasing modernization the status of older people declines, which is reflected in diminished power and influence for the elderly and fewer leadership roles in community life. This lower status is a consequence of the processes of modernization: scientific technology, urbanization, literacy and mass education, and health technology. Scientific technology leads to new occupations and reduces opportunities for retraining. Urban life, unlike

A Japanese grandmother plays a shamisen for her grandchildren. The Japanese have a great deal of respect for the wisdom and talents of the elderly, as shown by the rapt attention these children give their grandmother. In the United States, grandparents would more likely be the listeners and their grandchildren the performers.

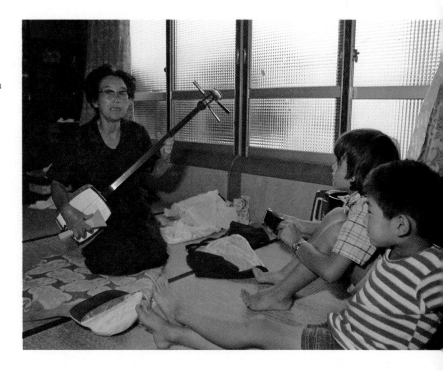

farm life, involves a good deal of mobility, especially among the young, and this mobility tends to separate the youthful generation from the older generation. Mass education is targeted at the young, so younger people rapidly gain a higher level of literacy and greater skills than their parents. Health technology has led to declining birth rates and longer lives. Together, these factors encourage early retirement and deny the elderly a chance to participate in the labor market, which reduces their income, prestige, honor, and status.

Critics of modernization theory say that "modernization" is a vague term often used to describe development, progress, and, more specifically, Westernization. They note that whatever modernization may be, it is not necessarily a linear process, and the elderly and other age groups may be affected differently by different stages in the process. They also note exceptions such as Japan, where a decline in status of the elderly did not accompany modernization. In Japan, respect for the elderly still remains.

Disengagement theory (Cumming and Henry, 1961) states that as people grow older, they and the younger people around them go through a period of mutual disengagement or mutual withdrawal. This theory has been widely discussed since the 1960s, but the available evidence lends it little support. Consistent with aspects of structural functionalism, disengagement theory suggests that gradual withdrawal or disengagement of the elderly from jobs and certain other roles is functional for both the elderly and for society. It prepares them for the end of life and also opens up opportunities for the younger generations, whereas a sudden withdrawal of the elderly would lead to social disruption.

Clara Peller, pictured here, gained national fame with Wendy's 1984 commercial that asks of its competition, "Where's the Beef?" Seldom are elderly or retired persons given positive recognition in advertising or by the mass media in general. They generally are shown encouraging the purchase of vitamins, pain killers, or ways to reduce irregularity.

Implicit in this theory is the idea that society should help older people disengage themselves from their accustomed roles by separating them residentially (having them retire to the Sunbelt or retirement communities), educating them about new activities designed for the elderly, and providing recreational alternatives such as social centers for senior citizens. These steps, which are often initiated by aging individuals themselves, are believed to help the old surrender their roles to a younger segment of the population. This disengagement process also prepares people for death with minimal disruption to society.

Disengagement theory did contribute to the view that old age is a normal stage of life. It differentiated this stage of life from middle age and emphasized that a lower level of social involvement and activity can still be highly rewarding. Critics, however, argue that elderly people do not want to be disengaged, do not want to be "put away," and do not want to withdraw from the mainstream of society. Robert Atchley (1980) states that although disengagement is not what most older people want, it is what they get.

Symbolic Interaction Theory

Symbolic interaction theory focuses on how people define themselves and others, what meanings they give to events, and how they relate to their reference groups. When applied to the elderly, the theory emphasizes how people define the aging process and the status of the aged. Interaction patterns that bring satisfaction to the elderly are also noted. For many older persons, marital and family relationships are primary sources of social involvement, companionship, fulfillment, and happiness. Lee (1978), for example, found that marital satisfaction has a positive effect on morale, which supports the basic tenet of symbolic interaction theory: that interactions with significant others in primary types of group relationships are crucial to personal satisfaction and psychological well-being.

Symbolic interaction theory provides the context for what Lemon and his colleagues (1972) have termed the activity theory of aging. In contrast to disengagement theory, which suggests that aging people go through a process of mutual withdrawal and a severance of relationships, *activity theory* argues that the best-adjusted elderly persons are those who remain active. While many older people may not have the desire or the ability to perform the roles they performed at age thirty or forty, they have essentially the same need for social interaction that they had years earlier. Activity theory contends that in order to achieve a satisfying adjustment to the aging process, avocations, part-time jobs, and hobbies should replace full-time employment and friends or loved ones who move away or die should be replaced by new friends and associates.

In an attempt to test activity theory, Lemon and his colleagues investigated a sample of more than four hundred potential joiners of a retirement community in southern California. His findings were mixed. He discovered that informal activity such as interaction with friends, relatives, and neighbors was significantly related to life satisfaction, whereas solitary activities such as housework and formal activities such as involvement in voluntary organizations were not. Other evidence, for example, Knapp's study (1977) of elderly people residing in England, tends to support activity theory. This study found a strong positive relationship between life satisfaction and time spent with friends and relatives in informal activities.

This theory, however, presents problems as well. While the basic idea of involvement in activities with primary networks of people has merit, it is not safe to assume that elderly persons have full control over their social lives and ready

In the United States, certain groups of persons are exempt from mandatory retirement. One of those groups is the United States Congress. Claude Pepper of Florida through his 70s and into his 80s remains an active member of the House of Representatives and serves as one of the chief congressional advocates for legislation that relates to the interests of senior citizens.

access to intimate relationships. Widows who lose loved ones or retirees who have too much leisure time and lower incomes may find it extremely difficult to replace loved ones and fill time with meaningful activities. Furthermore, the economic resources needed to reconstruct their lives may be lacking. Another questionable assumption is whether activity of any kind can always substitute for the loss of a spouse, job, child, friend, or of one's health. Psychologists and sociologists alike would agree that merely knowing a large number of people and being involved in many activities is not enough for a satisfactory life. Moreover, it is not easy to find substitutes for life-long relationships.

Social Exchange Theory

Social exchange theory, as discussed in Chapter 2 and elsewhere in this book, assumes that people try to maximize rewards and reduce costs. It suggests that voluntary social interactions are contingent on rewarding reactions from others. Each person receives in the exchange something perceived as equivalent to that which is given. If the reciprocal exchanges are not fair, one person is at a disadvantage and the other controls the relationship.

Dowd (1975, 1980) drew on exchange theory to offer an alternative to the disengagement and activity theories of aging. He believes that the problems of the aged in twentieth-century industrial societies are really problems of decreasing power. The low status of the elderly relative to younger people limits their bargaining power. Their economic and social dependence means they have less power than the rest of society, and with the gradual loss of power comes the need to comply. The elderly, who once could exchange their labor and skills for wages, must now exchange compliance for a Social Security pension or health care benefits. According to Dowd, the withdrawal from social roles that disengagement theorists view as satisfying to the elderly is the result of a series of exchange relationships in which the aged lose power.

Even those who have financial resources, skills, and good health are often at a disadvantage in an exchange relationship. Their ability to attain new skills, more resources, or better health is limited. Stereotypes about the aged, rules forcing them to retire at a specific age, and declining physical capacities all hinder their ability to compete with their younger counterparts. Conflict theorists might suggest that the elderly form coalitions to increase their power, but for the majority this has not taken place because the aged lack a shared awareness of common social and economic circumstances.

Conflict Theory

The conflict theory of the aged emphasizes the inequality and discrimination that occur among all subordinate groups that have little power. According to this view, the aged are a minority group in a youth-oriented society. Because they are less powerful than the younger group, they are treated unfairly, especially in the job market. The corporate elite prefers to hire younger people, who are stronger, healthier, and work for less pay than older, more experienced employees. Younger workers, concerned about the scarcity of jobs, support laws that force the elderly to vacate jobs the younger workers need. Faced with the opposition of these two powerful groups, the elderly are forced to retire. Since younger workers do not want to pay high taxes to support large numbers of older people, the elderly are often left with no work and little or no income.

Without income, conflict theorists contend, the elderly have little power. As a result, they are unable to combat the negative stereotypes assigned to them. The aged may often be perceived as unattractive, poor, neglected, sickly, depressed, and senile, and these perceptions are used in turn to justify denying them an equitable share of society's resources. Like other minority groups, they are discriminated against in jobs, wages, housing, and many other areas.

According to conflict theorists, the controversies that result from this inequality are beneficial insofar as they emphasize aging as a social problem and alert increasing numbers of people to the plight of the elderly. Recognizing the problem is the first step toward organizing for political action. Just as the National Organization for Women (NOW) was established to fight for equal rights for women, the Gray Panthers was founded in 1971 by Margaret Kuhn, a retired church worker, to promote the rights of the elderly. Conflict theorists suggest that groups of this type are essential to bring inequalities to public awareness, to campaign for social reform, and to force social policy changes.

Problems of the Aged

The problems faced by the elderly in the United States resemble those that some other groups face, but they are compounded by old age. These problems are often magnified among ethnic and minority group members such as black Americans, Spanish Americans, Native Americans, and Chinese Americans (see Gelfand, 1982; McNeely and Colen, 1983). Here we will discuss just four of these areas of concern: retirement, lifestyles and income, health, and abuse.

Retirement

Retirement is basically a phenomenon of modern industrialized nations. In agrarian societies, there is little paid employment from which to retire. In many areas of the world the life expectancy is such that too few people live to old age to make retirement an issue of social concern. In Japan, on the other hand, people commonly retire as early as age fifty-five.

Retirement is likely to be problematic when it is nonvoluntary or when it is associated with loss of status, productivity, usefulness, income, or life itself. Voluntary retirement, which appears to be increasing, is often viewed as an opportunity to travel, enjoy one's freedom, and work at what one enjoys. When retirement is mandatory, on the other hand, the person involved does not have control over the decision. Retirement of both types involves resocialization

to accommodate new roles, definitions of self, and a modified lifestyle.

Mandatory retirement has been the subject of a long and heated debate. According to Harris and Cole (1980), the issue goes back to 1777 when the first American mandatory retirement laws were enacted in New York. By 1820, six other states had passed laws requiring the mandatory retirement of judges at ages ranging from sixty to seventy. The decision to begin retirement at age sixty-five dates back to the Social Security Act of 1935. This cut-off point was the standard mandatory retirement age until 1978, when Congress raised it to seventy, and the issue is still not settled today. It is argued that mandatory retirement is discriminatory, fails to take the abilities of older people into account, and leads to resentment among those who want to keep working. Others argue that mandatory retirement is not discriminatory because it ensures that everyone is treated equally and serves as a face-saving device when it is necessary to ease out ineffective workers. It also opens up job and promotional opportunities for younger workers.

Having a set retirement age places the emphasis on retirement as an event rather than a process. As an event, we note the age, the year, or the date at which we leave work. There may be an announcement in the company or community newspaper and a ceremony with a token gift and speech making. The *process* of retirement, however, may cover a span of many years.

Robert Atchley (1982) believes that the retirement process involves three major periods: preretirement, the retirement transition, and postretirement. Preretirement is the period of looking ahead to retirement: determining when to retire, wondering what to expect, and the like. The retirement transition requires leaving one's job and taking up the role of a retired person. The postretirement period involves life without the job that was a major focus of time and attention in the preceding years.

To investigate the retirement process, Atchley mailed questionnaires to men and women in a small town near a large metropolitan area in 1975, 1977, 1979, and 1981. Of the 1,100 respondents, about 350 were in the preretirement period and employed full time. About fifty of the respondents did not plan to retire because they were self-employed and in good health or were unmarried women too poor to retire. The mean planned retirement age for those who planned to retire was sixty-four. Women were much more likely than men to plan to retire before sixty or after seventy. The early retirees tended to have high social status and to be married, while the late retirees tended to have low social status and to be unmarried. Thus, there appear to be important class differences in retirement, but general statements about women's retirement should be viewed with caution. Less than 1 percent of either sex in this preretirement period had negative attitudes toward retirement.

One hundred and seventy persons went through the retirement transition between 1975 and 1979. Those who had a negative attitude toward retirement (17 percent of the women and 11 percent of the men) were more apt to have poorer health, lower social status, and incomes they regarded as inadequate. Retirement turned out better than they expected, however, and attitude scores went up significantly following retirement. For both men and women in the total sample, retirement tended to improve life satisfaction slightly, regardless of marital status, health, income adequacy, social status, or living arrangements. It also reduced the activity level for both sexes, but the reduction was much greater for women than for men because their level of activity was much higher before retirement. These activities included visiting with friends, being with children or grandchildren, going for walks, attending church, and so on.

About three hundred respondents were in the postretirement period in 1975. This group had very positive attitudes toward their retirement, relatively high activity levels, and positive life satisfaction scores for both sexes. Activity level was a strong predictor of morale among retired men; health was more important among retired women. Interestingly, the older the women, the more positive their attitudes toward retirement were likely to be. It should be noted that the findings in this study were for generally healthy people in one small community who had many opportunities for participation. In this context, people look forward to retirement, go through the transition smoothly, and find life in retirement satisfying.

Lifestyles and Income

The lifestyles of the elderly resemble those of other adult age groups (see Figure 11-3). The very wealthy are often exempt from mandatory retirement laws, which cover white-collar and blue-collar workers but not top executives, people running their own businesses, members of Congress, or those in other elite positions. The wealthy are better able than others to live with their families and continue the activities they previously enjoyed.

The middle classes usually leave their suburban homes when they retire because their income is reduced to the point where they cannot continue to maintain a house. They may move from urban to rural areas, where the cost of living is lower, or to the warmer climates of the South. Many have enough money to move to retirement villages where they can enjoy a variety of activities and the companionship of other elderly people. Others do not like the age segregation and retire to small towns or rural areas.

People who have always been poor usually continue to live in the same poor areas when they grow old. They may live in subsidized housing for the elderly, in cheap hotels or rooming houses in the city, or in rural housing. The rural poor occasionally migrate to the city because of the shortage of affordable housing and adequate services in rural areas. The elderly poor in gen-

Figure 11-3

The lifestyles of older people by social class

	Vacation	Place for social life	Recreation	Rejuven-ation aids	Retirement rite	Retirement residence	Gifts to grand-children under 18	Gifts to grand-children over 18
Upper class	Mediter-ranean cruise	Country club	Golf	Spas in Switzerland and Romania	Guest of honor at banquet	Condo-miniums or age-segregated apartment buildings	Money	Checking accounts and cars
Middle class	Group bus tours	Senior citizens center	Shuffle-board	Vitamins	Gold watch and group dinner	Retirement commu-nities	Toys	Clothes
Lower class	Visit sister Dora in Detroit	Park bench	Checkers	Patent medicines	Handshake and a beer with the boys	Public housing or living with children	Cookies and pies	Cookies and pies

eral are most likely to suffer from social isola-tion. They often have no network of friends for socializing and no money to spend on activities. They frequently live in crime-ridden areas and are afraid to venture out into the streets. Their nutrition may be inadequate, so they are more apt to be ill than wealthier people. The elderly poor suffer from poverty in much the same way younger groups suffer from poverty.

The aged comprise one of the largest groups of the nation's poor. In 1982, the median income of all families with a householder age sixty-five or over was $16,118 compared with a total me-dian income of $23,433 for all families and $30,727 for householders age forty-five to fifty-four. People who did not live with their families

had a median income of $6,424. Those sixty-five and over comprised 14.6 percent of the popula-tion below the poverty level (U.S. Bureau of the Census, *Current Population Reports*, 1983e, pp. 4, 12). As can be seen in Figure 11-4, the poverty rate varies dramatically by race and sex. Black females have a rate nearly four times that of white males or white females in the sixty-to-sev-enty age category and show the largest increase in poverty after seventy.

Despite these figures and the sharp decline in income among the elderly, David Cheal (1983) reminds us that, overall, old people in North America are not as poor as stereotypes may suggest. While average incomes decline sharply, so do average expenditures. The owner-

Figure 11-4

Poverty rate in 1981 of persons sixty years and over by age, race and sex

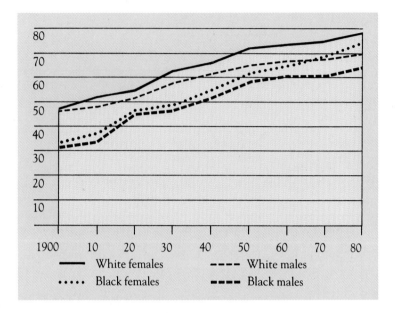

ship of domestic assets such as the family home makes it possible to enjoy a certain standard of living with a lower income than would otherwise be required. In fact, Cheal says that gift giving by old people is more significant than might be expected and that the elderly give financial aid to relatives more often than they receive it.

The most common source of income for the aged is *Social Security*. In 1982, the average monthly benefit was $470 for men and $362 for women (*Statistical Abstract: 1984*, no. 624). If people work to earn additional income, their Social Security may be reduced or eliminated. If retirees are not eligible for Social Security and have no other income, they are eligible for Supplemental Security Income (SSI), which in 1982 paid a single person an average of $196 a month (*Statistical Abstract: 1984*, no. 651).

The United States began the Social Security program during the depression of the 1930s, when millions of people were out of work and unable to support themselves. It was designed such that working citizens covered by the program paid a part of their wages into the program

and at sixty-five became eligible to receive income based on the amount they had contributed. It was not intended to provide an adequate income, however. It was assumed that savings or pensions accumulated during the working years would also be used during retirement and that Social Security would just provide a secure base on which to build a retirement income. As stated earlier, the mandatory retirement age of sixty-five was raised to seventy in 1978 for all workers except government workers, who are not required to retire.

Social Security benefits have increased steadily since the program began in order to reduce the number of people living in poverty. Whether these benefits will continue to increase is a serious concern to the elderly. As the number of older people increases, the costs of paying benefits may put pressure on the Social Security system, and many expect to see benefits reduced.

Millions of workers in the lowest-paying jobs were never even covered by Social Security. Either they were employed by companies that did not have pensions or they lost their pensions when they were laid off. The meager wages earned during their working years did not permit them to save money. Today, many of these people live in poverty even when they are assisted by the small Supplemental Security Income payments.

A married woman who did not work receives half of her husband's Social Security benefits after he dies, and the pensions of husbands are often stopped when the husband dies. Working women often receive low benefits or none at all because they earned low wages or worked in occupations not covered by Social Security. Thus, on the average, women collect much lower benefits than men.

Health

As you will recall, one of the myths discussed earlier in this chapter is that most old people have health problems. No one denies that organs deteriorate and gradually diminish in function over time, but diminishing function alone is not a real threat to the health of most older people. As the U.S. Census Special Report on Aging states (U.S. Bureau of the Census, *Current Population Reports*, 1983d, p. 15), the older population is healthier than is commonly assumed. In 1980, nine out of ten elderly persons described their own health as fair, good, or excellent compared with others of their own age. Only 8 percent said their health was poor. About 40 percent reported that, for health reasons, a major activity had been limited (compared with 20 percent between ages forty-five and sixty-four), but 54 percent reported no limitations of any kind in their activities. It is not until age eighty-five and older that about half of the population report being unable to carry on a major activity because of a chronic illness. Good health among the elderly is highly associated with higher income levels, which probably reflects different opportunities for leisure activities and different eating and nutritional habits.

Health is one area in which differentiating the old-old from the young-old reveals significant differences. The very old need more assistance in eating (4 percent of those over eighty-five compared with 1 percent under), in toileting (7 percent versus 2 percent), in dressing (11 percent), and bathing (18 percent). The report indicates that, on the basis of these types of activities, more than 80 percent of the noninstitutionalized very old can take care of their own daily needs.

Why, then, is there so much concern about health as a social problem among the elderly? There are several reasons. One is chronic disease. The principal diagnoses made by doctors for the elderly in 1980 and 1981 were for hypertension, diabetes, chronic heart disease, cataracts, and osteoarthritis. The diseases predominant among older men are likely to cause death, while those that predominate among older women are causes of illness.

A second major concern is medical care. The census report on aging indicates that persons sixty-five and over average only six doctor visits for every five made by the general population. But the elderly are hospitalized approximately twice as often, stay twice as long, and use twice as many prescription drugs, all of which are very expensive. At the same time, the cost of drugs, hospital care, and physicians has increased at a rate far exceeding that of inflation. Medicaid and Medicare, although widely believed to cover these bills, actually pay for only about half. In addition, both medical programs totally exclude such items as hearing aids, eyeglasses, and certain dental services. The problem is compounded by the fact that (1) the American medical profession has a general lack of interest in the problems of the elderly, who are less likely to be cured; (2) the income of the elderly decreases after retirement and becomes fixed, which means they cannot keep pace with increasing costs; and (3) qualifying for Medicaid requires "pauperization" — people are eligible only after they have drained their resources and literally joined the aged poor.

A third problem, one that is often over-looked, is mental health. A destructive stereo-type suggests that senility is inevitable in old age and that aged individuals who are not in some state of mental deterioration are rare. But senil-ity, mental infirmity due to old age, is not inevi-table. It is estimated that 15 to 25 percent of the elderly have significant symptoms of mental ill-ness with about 10 percent due to depression and 5 to 6 percent to senile dementia (U.S. Bureau of the Census, *Current Population Reports*, 1983d, p. 16). Psychiatrists and gerontologists are increas-ingly reporting that even patients who have se-nile dementia can be helped if the disability is deemphasized and the general quality of their life is improved.

Abuse

One problem that has only recently received major research and policy attention is the abuse, exploitation, and neglect of the elderly by the people upon whom they depend. This is one of our newest social problems, and little informa-tion was available until the late 1970s. Since then a number of investigations have been conducted, and they show that a substantial problem exists, with between 500,000 and 2.5 million cases of abuse per year (Douglas, 1983).

The severity of mistreatment of older people ranges from reasonably benign neglect to severe emotional and physical abuse. The most com-mon form of neglect is passive, such as when an elderly dependent is left alone without essential medical care, food, or clothing. Passive neglect may also happen because a caretaker is inept or unable to provide for the needs of the elderly person. Active neglect, which is less common, occurs when needed goods or services are inten-tionally withheld and social contacts are forbid-den. Caretakers have been known to tie older people to a bed or chair or lock them in a room while they go out, give them alcohol or excessive

medication to make them more manageable, threaten violence to force them to sign over a Social Security check, and deceive them into changing their wills. A commonly cited "cause" of such abuses is that the caretaker is being overtaxed by the requirements of looking after a dependent adult. This burden may lead to de-spair, anger, resentment, and violence. In some instances the abuse is clearly malicious and in-tentional, while other cases involve caretakers with serious emotional problems.

Physical abuse may involve beating, hitting, pushing, burning, cutting, mugging, sexually molesting, or otherwise injuring an elderly per-son. This type of abuse, more than neglect, is likely to come to the attention of police, physi-cians, community social service workers (case-workers), or clergy. The professionals involved in such instances are also likely to observe var-ious other forms of emotional abuse such as threats, fraud or financial exploitation, and in-timidation.

With all types of abuse, women are victims more often than men. Victims also tend to be the older elderly (seventy-five or older), people who are frail and mentally or physically disabled. The abuser is usually a son or daughter of the victim and is often experiencing great stress brought about by alcoholism, drug addiction, marital problems, or chronic financial difficulties in ad-dition to the burden of caring for an aging parent.

Parallels can be drawn between the abuse and neglect of the elderly and the abuse and ne-glect of children. In both cases the victims are heavily if not totally dependent on others for basic survival needs. They both lack resources such as strength, speed, and finances to protect themselves. The family or intimate group net-work is the source of abuse far more often than strangers are. In both cases, the abuse generally occurs in the home. In fact, for all citizens, young or old, rich or poor, the most dangerous place is the home.

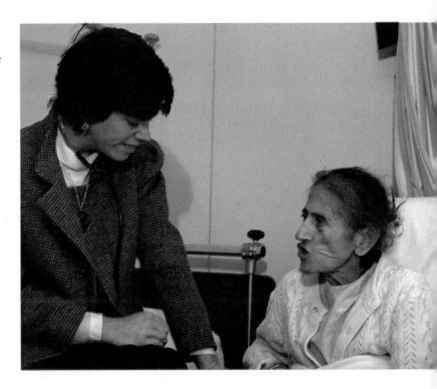

A hospice is a therapeutic environment for the terminally ill that is designed from the patients' perspective and welcomes family and friends. The attempt is to combine good medical care with emotional and psychological care.

It is unlikely that major government-supported programs at a federal, state, or local level will be created to combat neglect and abuse of the elderly, even though governments have taken action to prevent child and spouse abuse. Today's political climate, economic support for social programs, and conservative orientation toward social concerns all tend to place the emphasis on voluntary responses to human needs. Some local and voluntary agencies have joined together to organize reporting and referral systems and temporary shelters for elderly victims. Other services are needed, however — mandatory abuse reporting laws, free or low-cost legal service systems, and increased support services such as transportation, meal preparation, and chore and homemaker services. Many of these services now exist at a minimal level, but the need is too great, and voluntary services alone cannot solve the problem.

Death and Dying

The aged must confront two difficult facts — their own death and the death of their friends and loved ones. Surprising though it may seem, socialization also plays a role in preparing people for death. As with other types of social behavior, our social institutions, norms, and practices largely determine how we think about dying. Symbolic interaction theory, for example, would suggest that the definitions and meanings we attach to illness and death greatly influence our ability to cope with it. An understanding of reference groups may help us understand the functioning of the church, friends, or a kin network as support systems in facing death. How we mourn, what we do with the physical remains of the dead, how we behave after the death of a family member, how we prepare for our own

SOCIOLOGISTS AT WORK
Evaluating Programs for the Elderly

Francis G. Caro is the director of the Institute for Social Welfare Research at the Community Service Society of New York. He also serves as principal investigator on several of the institute's research projects. He joined the institute in 1974 after teaching sociology at Brandeis University and the University of Colorado and working as a community researcher in New Haven, Connecticut and Kansas City, Missouri.

Frank Caro has long been interested in the study of age groupings. In his student days (at Marquette as an undergraduate, at the University of Minnesota as a graduate student) he studied the way teenage boys approached educational and occupational decisions. More recently he has been involved in studying the special problems of

the elderly, and in particular the disabled elderly. "I got involved in this area while I was at Brandeis," he says. "When I came to New York City, I came to a setting where there was a substantial commitment to providing home care for functionally disabled older people. In the rest of the country this is being done on a small scale, in demonstration programs. Here, without a lot of visibility, the city's Human Resources Administration just went out and did it. They started with a program created for disabled younger adults, but then they opened the program to the elderly and it has grown rapidly. The city's program now has 30,000 clients and spends upwards of $200 million a year. We want to know how it's working."

death — all are influenced by cultural, class, and other social factors.

In the United States and most other cultures, the family and kin network is the major social support in times of illness. Among the elderly, the presence of relatives may make it possible for bedridden persons to live outside of institutions. Immediate family and other kin not only supply the housebound and ambulatory aged with care, but their face-to-face visits also provide the major ties to the community (Shanas, 1979). Elderly people turn first to their families for help, then to neighbors, and finally and only as a last resort to bureaucratic replacements for families. This sequence is consistent with survey findings that show that most people

would like to die at home. Nevertheless, medical attention, nursing care, and social wokers for the dying are hospital-based. While four people wish to die at home for every one who would like to die in a hospital, in actual practice the ratio is reversed (Hine, 1979–1980, p. 175).

The hospice movement is intended to make family interaction with the terminally ill or dying patient easier. A *hospice* (see Koff, 1980) is a therapeutic environment designed from the patients' point of view. Unlike a regular hospital with its emphasis on privacy, a hospice provides space for interaction with staff, family, and friends. Instead of subordinating the patient to the needs of the institution, hospice programs are designed to provide as much care in the patient's home as

The Community Service Society is an old private social welfare agency, founded in the middle of the nineteenth century. As more and more direct services were taken over by government agencies, CSS shifted its aims to trying to exert a constructive influence on government programs, conducting or studying pioneer programs. "We have a great deal of credibility in the city," Caro says, "so we have access to a lot of information, and we get an attentive audience when we publish our results."

Caro is serving as principal investigator in CSS's study of the city's program for the disabled elderly. "We are dealing with a group that has serious self-care limitations. They have trouble with the problems of daily living — walking, eating, toilet functions — and with using the telephone, paying bills, taking medicine. These are especially serious problems among the disabled elderly, who are faced with the illnesses, weakness, and loss of mental capacity that often accompany aging. The city provides homemakers and home attendants to help these clients manage the tasks of daily living. They do shopping, cleaning, and cooking; they make beds, provide companionship, serve as escorts. All are nonprofessional services."

"One area we're studying is the way family members, if they are available, work with the public service agency. We're concerned with the intergenerational relationship. Throughout the life cycle, intergenerational family relations tend to be quite strong. There is a great deal of reciprocity over the years, but until very late in their lives, parents tend to give more help to their adult children than they receive in return. When parents are very old, they often can't manage on their own, and need help. To what extent do they get it? Do they get it from spouses? Adult children? Other informal supports? Organized services? What is the division of labor between the family and the service agency, and what should it be? We draw on sociological insights regarding intergenerational patterns of family bonds. A sociological perspective helps us understand what family members are committed to doing on behalf of a disabled relative and the circumstances under which they seek outside assistance."

possible; when medical facilities are required, they include a team of medical, nursing, psychiatric, religious, and social workers as needed, plus family members. The concern is on increasing the quality of the last days of life and on providing humane care. The family of the institutionalized patient is encouraged to be involved: they can bring in "home cooking," bathe the patient, supply medication, or bring along the family dog. Hours for visits are unlimited, and patients are allowed to interact with young children or grandchildren. The program is innovative, but it is very expensive as well and few hospices care for chronically ill people who are expected to live for a year or more.

A controversial issue concerning the terminally ill is euthanasia. *Euthanasia*, sometimes called mercy killing, is deliberately ending a person's life to spare him or her from the suffering that goes with an incurable and agonizing disease. Should someone's life be ended when there is no hope of recovery? Even the strongest proponents of euthanasia support its use only for patients whose death is imminent. There are no serious proposals for using euthanasia to end the lives of patients expected to live for many months or even years.

Although only 5 percent of the elderly live in institutions, most people believe this is not a suitable way to live out one's life, but society has provided no satisfactory alternative social structure for these people. As the population lives longer and more and more people reach old age, one of our great challenges will be to devise social structures that will allow the elderly to lead active lives for as long as possible and to live graciously and with dignity even when they can no longer be active.

Summary

All societies differentiate behavior by age. The systematic study of the aging process is known as gerontology. Social gerontology, a subfield of gerontology, focuses on the social and cultural aspects of age and the aging process.

Expectations about the behavior considered appropriate for people of a given age are called age norms. Many such norms reflect inaccurate stereotypes and may lead to ageism, which is prejudice and discrimination based on age.

Myths about the aged suggest that they are senile, miserable, lonely, unhealthy, frequent victims of crime, poor, unable to manage households, incapable of and disinterested in sexual relations, and that most live in nursing homes. All of these stereotypes are basically false.

The elderly are considered to be those age sixty-five and over. Some gerontologists differentiate between the young-old (fifty-five to seventy-four) and the old-old (seventy-five and over). Demographically, the percentage of elderly people in the total population is increasing, as is life expectancy, although there are considerable variations due to sex and race. Interestingly, the life expectancy of those who reach old age has increased very little and the life span is basically unchanged. The proportion of older people who don't work is increasing in comparison to the younger working population; this proportion is known as the dependency ratio.

The social characteristics of the elderly vary widely according to sex, marital status, living arrangements, geographical distribution, labor force participation, and other factors. Women greatly outnumber men, and many women are widows, but most of the elderly live in their own homes or with their families. Geographically, they tend to live in metropolitan areas, and they are heavily concentrated in certain states. The proportion of the elderly in the labor force has dropped considerably over the past several decades.

There are a number of theories on aging and age differentiation. Theories based on the structural-functional perspective include modernization and disengagement theory. Modernization theory assumes that the status of old people declines with increasing modernization. Disengagement theory, which is less widely accepted, contends that as people grow older they go through a period of mutual disengagement or withdrawal from the rest of society. A symbolic interaction perspective, activity theory, states that those who remain active, particularly with avocations, part-time jobs, and interaction in primary networks, will be best adjusted. Social exchange theory suggests that both withdrawal and activity can be best explained in terms of the decreasing power of the elderly. Having less to exchange and a greater dependency on others forces the elderly into social compliance. Finally, conflict theory, drawing on exchange theory, assumes that inequalities in areas such as jobs, wages, and housing permit the elderly to be exploited. Today, a small proportion of elderly people are organizing into groups such as the Gray Panthers to fight for political action.

The aged share many of the problems of the rest of society, but their problems are often compounded because they have fewer resources and less power. Retirement problems are more common when retirement is mandatory. In general, most people look forward to retirement as a period of leisure.

The lifestyles of the elderly vary greatly, depending on their social class and income. Women and blacks are the groups most likely to live in poverty. The most common source of income for the aged is Social Security. A minimal income is available to those not on Social Security through the Supplemental Security Income program. Income and class level greatly influence the health of the elderly. While most say their health is fair, good, or excellent, those whose health is poor often face chronic disease, high medical costs, and prolonged hospitalization. A relatively small proportion of the aged suffer from senility.

The abuse of the elderly has come to be recognized recently as a widespread problem. Like dependent children, the elderly are often neglected or physically abused. They have few resources to protect themselves. In most cases, they are abused in their homes by their caretakers.

A hospice is a therapeutic environment for terminally ill patients designed to permit interaction with family and friends and to combine good medical care with humane treatment. Euthanasia, sometimes called mercy killing, is a controversial issue concerning the elderly who have terminal illnesses.

Key Terms

activity theory
age norms
ageism
dependency ratio
disengagement theory
euthanasia
geriatrics
gerontology
hospice
life expectancy
life span
modernization theory
senility
social gerontology
Social Security

Suggested Readings

Blau, Zena Smith. **Aging in a Changing Society, 2d ed.** *New York: Franklin Watts, 1981.* A book on aging that focuses on identity, friendship, work and illness alienation, patterns of response, and new roles for later life.

Dowd, James J. **Stratification Among the Aged.** *Monterey, Calif.: Brooks/Cole, 1980.* A summary of various theories in social gerontology, with an emphasis on the relationship of the aging process to the social-class membership of the aged person.

Gelfand, Donald E. **Aging: The Ethnic Factor.** *Boston: Little, Brown, 1982.* Part of the Little, Brown series on gerontology, this book provides a succinct and readable overview of ethnicity and aging.

Kart, Cary S. **The Realities of Aging: An Introduction to Gerontology.** *Boston: Allyn & Bacon, 1981.* An introductory textbook on aging that covers various myths of aging; biological, psychological, and sociological aspects of the aging process; and special issues in aging, including the minority aged, institutionalization, and death and dying.

Keith, Jennie. **Old People as People: Social and Cultural Influences on Aging and Old Age.** *Boston: Little, Brown, 1982.* Part of the Little, Brown series on gerontology, this book covers aging from a cross-cultural perspective with an emphasis on age norms and formal and informal interactions.

McNeeley, R. L. and John L. Colen (eds.). **Aging in Minority Groups.** *Beverly Hills, Calif.: Sage Publications, 1983.* A collection of papers and essays on issues relating to the minority elderly: housing, crime, health, income, political involvement, and other matters.

U.S. Bureau of the Census. **Current Population Reports, Series P-20, no. 128, "America in Transition: An Aging Society."** *Washington, D.C.: U.S. Government Printing Office, 1983.* This special, highly readable report on aging provides an excellent overview of the demographic aspects of aging.

Woodruff, Diana S. and James E. Birren. **Aging: Scientific Perspectives and Social Issues, 2d ed.** *Monterey, Calif.: Brooks/Cole, 1983.* A multidisciplinary text with a focus on the processes and problems of aging and on providing services to the elderly.

Part III Readings

The Elderly Poor: An Example of What Happens to the Unproductive in Capitalist Society

by Harold Freeman

The golden years? Sociologist Harold Freeman discusses the tragic circumstances that make the golden years a nightmare for the 50 percent of America's elderly who live in poverty.

Consider a single group of damaged participants, the elderly poor. Of the 26 million Americans below the federal poverty line, approximately 5 million are over 65; 50 percent of all elderly Americans, 33 percent of all rural elderly and 60 percent of all elderly blacks live in poverty.

The urban elderly poor find it hard to get around; in many smaller communities bus service during the middle hours of the day is infrequent. So, for food, they shop in nearer, smaller, and more expensive stores. If hot food is served at a center few can get to it. They are particularly vulnerable to assault and theft; to the dissident young, as Dr. Marvin Wolfgang has explained, the elderly poor are attractive targets. In the view of the elderly themselves, their most serious concern is fear of crime against them — more serious than concern over money, health, or loneliness. They fear to leave their homes and they fear to stay in them. And they have reason for fear. In a recent study financed by the Law Enforcement Assistance Administration and the Department of Housing and Urban Development, elderly poor living in multiple housing occupied also by young adults are 3½ times more vulnerable to crime by the young than are other residents. In a period of one year, 1973 to 1974, Americans 65 and older experienced a 46 percent increase in assault. In 1975, 35 percent of New York City's elderly lived in its 26 poorest neighborhoods; of the sample interviewed 40 percent had been criminally victimized. These are among the scores of grim facts documented in the subcommittee inquiry, directed by Congressmen Edward Roybal and John Hammerschmidt, for the House Select Committee on Aging.

Occupational opportunities are few, though a surprising part of their small current income does come from whatever work they can get — often as part-time janitors, watchmen, house- and babysitters. The work-at-home offers to which some are drawn are often fraudulent. They cannot read the fine print, they have slender legal recourse against misrepresentation. They are many among the 15 million who come annually to the bar of justice with anxious complaints but without funds, and now even the limited capacity of the legal remainder of the Office of Economic Opportunity to provide help for them has been reduced by the elimination of its vital back-up research funds. In the United States, one lawyer is available to 9,570 poor, a ratio one-twelfth of that holding for the general population. In some States the ratio is even lower — in North Carolina one lawyer to 67,000 poor. These figures need to be considered alongside (a) 23 percent of the poor have at least one legal problem per year; (b) public funding for such problems is $2.16 per poor person.

315

Medical burdens are particularly heavy on the elderly poor. According to the Senate Special Committee on Aging, up to 2.5 million elderly Americans in need of mental care have been pushed out of budget-minded state mental hospitals — saving in 1978 an average of $21,000 per patient — into federally supported profit-making boarding houses and nursing homes; in some instances, state officials have received up to $100 per head from the homes. There the elderly live without needed therapy and without follow-up by state health officials. In no way is this exodus the consequence of progressive anti-institutional thinking; the Senate Committee uses the term "wholesale dumping."

Eighty-six percent of persons over 65 have one or more chronic diseases. With their physical infirmities the elderly are easy victims of medical quacks, and steady users of useless and unsafe drugs. By 1973 medical fraud in the United States had reached the $10 billion level; the scandals of 1978 suggest a higher figure now. The largest subset of victims are always the elderly poor.

The elderly poor cannot readily reach a clinic and when they do the hours they face in outpatient corridors are exhausting. In some areas the long clinic lines now have an added feature — for the elderly poor among the 25 million Americans who have no Medicare, Medicaid, or private health insurance, up to $21 a visit payable in advance. Similar though costlier is private medicine. Twenty-five percent of all American doctors now demand on-the-spot payment for all visits, and over 30 percent demand immediate payment for at least the first visit. By 1977, the average per capita health cost for persons over 65 had climbed to $1,738 per annum; on the average, Medicare covers 38 percent.

In New York City, only 23 percent of doctors accept Medicaid patients, and 4 percent to 7 percent of the city's doctors — many of them practicing in its infamous "Medicaid mills" —

collect up to 85 percent of all Medicaid fees; one doctor, William Triebel, received $451,156 in 1974 and $785,114 in 1975. Ninety-five percent of New York City's Medicaid dental services are provided by 5 percent of the city's dentists. In Chicago, 73 of Cook County's 6,000 private doctors (another study puts these figures at 100 of 9,000) see over half of the county's 285,000 Medicaid recipients. This amounts to one doctor per 2,000 persons on Medicaid, and the ratio gets worse as these doctors, with their increased income from Medicaid fees, leave the poorer sections of the county. In New York City there are 280 doctors per 100,000 population, but in the impoverished South Bronx area the number has fallen to 10. In the nation's capital about 20 persons, most of them elderly poor, die each year in the process of transfer from private hospital *emergency* rooms, where they are not wanted, to the District of Columbia General Hospital. In 1970 in Chicago, 18,000 persons, again with a disproportion of elderly poor, were turned away from private hospital emergency rooms, and more than 50 of them died in the process of dismissal or transfer to Cook County Hospital, an overloaded facility which cares for half of Chicago's Medicaid patients (and half of the county's blacks). The turnaway, known in medical circles as patient dumping, generally consists of suggested use of a car or taxi, or simply pointing out the nearest bus stop.

Some of the elderly poor are still involved in the consequences of earlier unwise installment buying; harassment is common and repossession is more than occasional. Some have discovered that not only can an item on which one default has occurred be repossessed, but other items sold on prior contracts by the same merchant and completely paid for can also be repossessed. They have learned that dealers sometimes sell the notes of cheated buyers to finance houses, thereby nullifying complaints of fraud against the dealers. The few loans available to the elderly poor are seldom from banks and always at high interest rates; up to 1,000 percent per year in the experience of Justice William Douglas. With their too-small last-ditch savings (40 percent have assets under $1,000), they are the vulnerable prey of flim-flam specialists. They are exploited in smaller stores skilled at offering inferior merchandise to the elderly and to welfare recipients and careful not to show prices; side-street merchants have discovered the optimal way to deal with the elderly poor — get all you can now.

Five and one-tenth million women — a number rapidly increasing — and 1.3 million men over 65 live alone. One-third of all elderly poor women, a very high percentage of them widows, live alone; their median income is $2,600. Many are found in declining residential hotels and tenements. With minimal experience one can describe, confidently, a typical room before seeing it — the rust-locked window, artificial flowers, slow plumbing, framed family pictures and the inevitable two-burner hot plate. Thirty percent of the residences of the elderly poor have no inside flush toilets, 40 percent no hot water bath, 54 percent have minimal winter heat. Except in seven states the tenant's obligation to pay rent is absolute (while the landlord's obligation to maintain the premises is unmentioned), and the consequence for some is eviction. Contrary to a few dramatic situations noted by the press, most rental evictions are quiet; for different reasons neither the landlord nor the tenant is eager for publicity.

Arrests of the elderly poor for shoplifting food are up sharply in the United States. A fair number of the elderly poor have discovered the greater protein value of dog food, that it is edible though bland (ketchup and onions are a standard addition), that the health hazard is probably small, that it is somewhat cheaper than the food previously bought, and they have quietly made the change. The Washington Post estimates

that the elderly poor purchase more dog food than do dog owners. Dr. Edward Peeples, Jr. estimates that pet food forms a significant part of the diet of at least 225,000 American households — up to 1 million persons. The Senate Nutrition Committee estimates that one-third of all pet food purchased in depressed areas is for human consumption.

Except for burial policies, insurance is either not available or is outside their means; a furniture fire insurance policy is uncommon. Against even more primitive menaces like hunger, prolonged illness, and eviction, protection is slight. Protection could come from savings or income, but the savings are modest and the principal source of lifetime income — typically small earnings — have often come to an end. For the elderly poor, with their small inflation-damaged income from federal and state sources and their improved life span, insecurity is even more threatening than poverty; it saps much of their remaining vitality. As they age, we watch them draw on their children's resources, then move or be moved to the lower strata of rest and nursing homes. The latter, over 23,000 in all and three-quarters of them profit-making, have been described in detail in numerous studies, among them the report by Val Halamandaris to the Senate Special Committee and Robert Butler's *Why Survive?* These studies find the nursing home industry to be, on average, one of America's most destructive. Edith Stern describes many of these homes, housing 900,000 persons, under the title "Buried Alive."

Even final dignity is denied the elderly poor; they are cheated on funeral and cemetery arrangements.

Among these people you find no general absence of character, not even irremediable loss of initiative. Their strength is diminished but it is not negligible; it has been paralyzed by forces against which they cannot, acting separately as the elderly poor do, prevail. Researches by Dr.

David Blau and others have shown the alacrity with which, given some support, the elderly poor can recover mental and physical strength. But in the common absence of such support, degradation sets in. Seeing those who are better off express by indifference their doubt of the value to the community of the elderly poor, so finally the elderly poor themselves doubt their value. For many the consequence is to turn inward, to protect what little they still have, not reaching out at all. Watching such a person, who wanted no help, get a solid block of ice out of a toilet in an apartment on Western Avenue — a street in Cambridge halfway between Harvard University and the Massachusetts Institute of Technology — one learns to respect the characteristic reaction of the elderly poor to all indignities, silence.

The tragedy of the elderly poor is unmistakable. Yet it would be difficult to find Americans in ordinary walks of life who would decline to support measures ensuring a better deal for these people; in a Harris poll in 1975, 76 percent of Americans questioned stated that a person should be able to live comfortably during retirement no matter how much was earned during his or her worklife. But nothing like this prevails and the situation improves minimally. Why? The reason is uncomplicated. In the logic of capitalism the elderly poor are a problem simply because they are unproductive. In a society which rewards according to contribution they have no proper place. Like the sick and disabled, like all who can produce but little, the elderly poor are an externality to the theory of capitalism; they are found, if at all, in a chapter toward the end of the textbook. They have no solution within the system; Duncan Foley writes,

Capitalism offers no systematic support to these people so that more or less effective devices outside the capitalist distribution system become necessary. Charity, welfare, public housing, socialized medicine . . . exist to support or help support persons of low productivity but they are all unnatural in a capitalist society, conflict with its basic principles, and as a result tend automatically to be controversial, badly run, inadequate and ineffective.

In his study of poverty Ben Seligman writes, "The aged are simply an embarrassment. They are poor, unable to provide medical care for themselves, they violate the canon of self-help, so we dishonor them." Seligman continues, "Perhaps in *our* society . . . give the aged poor money and let them stand aside, silent and unseen."

Liberals believe that the elderly poor may somehow, someday enjoy political influence commeasurable with their numbers; the 1978 heavy election turnout of the elderly in seven states in successful support of limits on taxation offers some credence in such an expectation. But the economics of capitalism is heavily stacked against the elderly poor. Most of these millions of men and women worked hard; they were energetic and productive for years. But not at a level which enabled them to save much for their old age. Capitalism rewards according to assets, not effort; on this scale the elderly poor do not measure up.

SOURCE: Harold Freeman, *Toward Socialism in America*. Copyright © 1979 Schenkman Publishing, Cambridge, Mass. Reprinted by permission.

The Doctor-Nurse Game

by Leonard I. Stein

Social inequality and stratification influence every phase of our lives, although often we are not aware of it. Most of us tend to relax in the company of our equals but treat with deference those of higher social status. Even in matters of life and death, physicians and nurses behave according to their social rank, as the following reading describes.

The relationship between the doctor and the nurse is a very special one. There are few professions where the degree of mutual respect and co-operation between co-workers is as intense as that between the doctor and nurse. Superficially, the stereotype of this relationship has been dramatized in many novels and television serials. When, however, it is observed carefully in an interactional framework, the relationship takes on a new dimension and has a special quality which fits a game model. The underlying attitudes which demand that this game be played are unfortunate. These attitudes create serious obstacles in the path of meaningful communications between physicians and nonmedical professional groups.

The physician traditionally and appropriately has total responsibility for making the decisions regarding the management of his patients' treatment. To guide his decisions he considers data gleaned from several sources. He acquires a complete medical history, performs a thorough physical examination, interprets laboratory findings, and at times, obtains recommendations from physician-consultants. Another important factor in his decision making is the recommendations he receives from the nurse. The interaction between doctor and nurse through which these recommendations are communicated and received is unique and interesting.

The Game

One rarely hears a nurse say, "Doctor, I would recommend that you order a retention enema for Mrs. Brown." A physician, upon hearing a recommendation of that nature, would gape in amazement at the effrontery of the nurse. The nurse, upon hearing the statement, would look over her shoulder to see who said it, hardly believing the words actually came from her own mouth. Nevertheless, if one observes closely, nurses make recommendations of more import every hour and physicians willingly and respectfully consider them. If the nurse is to make a suggestion without appearing insolent and the doctor is to seriously consider that suggestion, their interaction must not violate the rules of the game.

Object of the game. The object of the game is as follows: the nurse is to be bold, have initiative, and be responsible for making significant recommendations, while at the same time she must appear passive. This must be done in such a manner so as to make her recommendations appear to be initiated by the physician.

Both participants must be acutely sensitive to each other's nonverbal and cryptic verbal communications. A slight lowering of the head, a minor shifting of position in the chair, or a seemingly nonrelevant comment concerning an event which occurred eight months ago must be interpreted as a powerful message. The game requires the nimbleness of a high wire acrobat, and if either participant slips the game can be shattered; the penalties for frequent failure are apt to be severe.

Rules of the game. The cardinal rule of the game is that open disagreement between the players must be avoided at all costs. Thus, the nurse must communicate her recommendations without appearing to be making a recommendation statement. The physician, in requesting a recommendation from a nurse, must do so without appearing to be asking for it. Utilization of this technique keeps anyone from committing themselves to a position before a sub rosa agreement on that position has already been established. In that way open disagreement is avoided. The greater the significance of the recommendation, the more subtly the game must be played.

To convey a subtle example of the game with all its nuances would require the talents of a literary artist. Lacking these talents, let me give you the following example which is unsubtle, but happens frequently. The medical resident on hospital call is awakened by telephone at 1:00 A.M. because a patient on a ward, not his own, has not been able to fall asleep. Dr. Jones answers the telephone and the dialogue goes like this:

This is Dr. Jones.
(An open and direct communication.)
Dr. Jones, this is Miss Smith on 2W — Mrs. Brown, who learned today of her father's death, is unable to fall asleep.
(This message has two levels. Openly, it describes a set of circumstances, a woman who is unable to sleep and who that morning received word of her father's death. Less openly, but just as directly, it is a diagnostic and recommendation statement; i.e., Mrs. Brown is unable to sleep because of her grief, and she should be given a sedative. Dr. Jones, accepting the diagnostic statement and replying to the recommendation statement, answers.)
What sleeping medication has been helpful to Mrs. Brown in the past?
(Dr. Jones, not knowing the patient, is asking for a recommendation from the nurse, who does know the patient, about what sleeping medication should be prescribed. Note, however, his question does not appear to be asking her for a recommendation. Miss Smith replies.)
Pentobarbital mg 100 was quite effective night before last.
(A disguised recommendation statement. Dr. Jones replies with a note of authority in his voice.)

Pentobarbital mg 100 before bedtime as needed for sleep; got it?
(Miss Smith ends the conversation with the tone of a grateful supplicant.)
Yes, I have, and thank you very much, doctor.

The above is an example of a successfully played doctor-nurse game. The nurse made appropriate recommendations which were accepted by the physician and were helpful to the patient. The game was successful because the cardinal rule was not violated. The nurse was able to make her recommendation without appearing to, and the physician was able to ask for recommendations without conspicuously asking for them.

The scoring system. Inherent in any game are penalties and rewards for the players. In game theory, the doctor-nurse game fits the nonzero sum game model. It is not like chess, where the players compete with each other and whatever one player loses the other wins. Rather, it is the kind of game in which the rewards and punishments are shared by both players. If they play the game successfully they both win rewards, and if they are unskilled and the game is played badly, they both suffer the penalty.

The most obvious reward from the well-played game is a doctor-nurse team that operates efficiently. The physician is able to utilize the nurse as a valuable consultant, and the nurse gains self-esteem and professional satisfaction from her job. The less obvious rewards are no less important. A successful game creates a doctor-nurse alliance; through this alliance the physician gains the respect and admiration of the nursing service. He can be confident that his nursing staff will smooth the path for getting his work done. His charts will be organized and waiting for him when he arrives, the ruffled feathers of patients and relatives will have been smoothed down, and his pet routines will be happily followed, and he will be helped in a thousand and one other ways.

The doctor-nurse alliance sheds its light on the nurse as well. She gains a reputation for being a "damn good nurse." She is respected by everyone and appropriately enjoys her position. When physicians discuss the nursing staff it would not be unusual for her name to be mentioned with respect and admiration. Their esteem for a good nurse is no less than their esteem for a good doctor.

The penalties for a game failure, on the other hand, can be severe. The physician who is an unskilled gamesman and fails to recognize the nurses' subtle recommendation messages is tolerated as a "clod." If, however, he interprets these messages as insolence and strongly indicates he does not wish to tolerate suggestions from nurses, he creates a rocky path for his travels. The old truism "If the nurse is your ally you've got it made, and if she has it in for you, be prepared for misery" takes on life-sized proportions. He receives three times as many phone calls after midnight as his colleagues. Nurses will not accept his telephone orders because "telephone orders are against the rules." Somehow, this rule gets suspended for the skilled players. Soon he becomes like Joe Bfstplk in the "Li'l Abner" comic strip. No matter where he goes, a black cloud constantly hovers over his head.

The unskilled gamesman nurse also pays heavily. The nurse who does not view her role as that of consultant, and therefore does not attempt to communicate recommendations, is perceived as a dullard and is mercifully allowed to fade into the woodwork.

The nurse who does see herself as a consultant but refuses to follow the rules of the game in making her recommendations has hell to pay. The outspoken nurse is labeled a "bitch" by the surgeon. The psychiatrist describes her as unconsciously suffering from penis envy and her behavior is the acting out of her hostility towards men. Loosely translated, the psychiatrist is saying she is a bitch. The employment of the unbright outspoken nurse is soon terminated. The outspoken bright nurse whose recommendations are worthwhile remains employed. She is, however, constantly reminded in a hundred ways that she is not loved.

Genesis of the Game

To understand how the game evolved, we must comprehend the nature of the doctors' and nurses' training which shaped the attitudes necessary for the game.

Medical student training. The medical student in his freshman year studies as if possessed. In the anatomy class he learns every groove and prominence of the bones of the skeleton as if life depended on it. As a matter of fact, he literally believes just that. He not infrequently says, "I've got to learn it exactly; a life may depend on me knowing that." A consequence of this attitude, which is carefully nurtured throughout medical school, is the development of a phobia: the over-determined fear of making a mistake. The development of this fear is quite understandable. The burden the physician must carry is at times almost unbearable. He feels responsible in a very personal way for the lives of his patients. When a man dies leaving young children and a widow, the doctor carries some of her grief and despair inside himself; and when a child dies, some of him dies too. He sees himself as a warrior against death and disease. When he loses a battle, through no fault of his own, he nevertheless feels pangs of guilt, and he relentlessly searches himself to see if there might have been a way to alter the outcome. For the physician a mistake leading to a serious consequence is intolerable, and any mistake reminds him of his vulnerability. There is little wonder that he becomes phobic. The classical way in which phobias are managed is to avoid the source of the fear. Since it is impossible to avoid making some mistakes in an active practice of medicine, a substitute defensive maneuver is employed. The physician develops the belief that he is omnipotent and omniscient, and therefore incapable of making mistakes. This belief allows the phobic physician to actively engage in his practice rather than avoid it. The fear of committing an error in a critical field like medicine is unavoidable and appropriately realistic. The physician, however, must learn to live with the fear rather than handle it defensively through a posture of omnipotence. This defense markedly interferes with his interpersonal professional relationships.

Physicians, of course, deny feelings of omnipotence. The evidence, however, renders their denials to whispers in the wind. The slightest mistake inflicts a large narcissistic wound. Depending on his underlying personality structure the physician may be obsessed for days about it, quickly rationalize it away, or deny it. The guilt produced is unusually exaggerated and the incident is handled defensively. The ways in which physicians enhance and support each other's defenses when an error is made could be the topic of another paper. The feeling of omnipotence becomes generalized to other areas of his life. A report of the Federal Aviation Agency (FAA), as quoted in *Time Magazine* (August 5, 1966), states that in 1964 and 1965 physicians had a fatal-accident rate four times as high as the average for all other private pilots. Major causes of the high death rate were risk-taking attitudes and judgments. Almost all of the accidents occurred on pleasure trips, and were therefore not necessary risks to get to a patient needing emergency care. The trouble, suggested an FAA official, is that too many doctors fly with "the feeling that they are omnipotent." Thus, the extremes to which the physician may go in preserving his self-concept of omnipotence may threaten his own life. This overdetermined preservation of omnipotence is indicative of its brittleness and its underlying foundation of fear of failure.

The physician finds himself trapped in a paradox. He fervently wants to give his patient the best possible medical care, and being open to the nurses' recommendations helps him accomplish this. On the other hand, accepting advice from nonphysicians is highly threatening to his omnipotence. The solution for the paradox is to receive sub rosa recommendations and make them appear to be initiated by himself. In short, he must learn to play the doctor-nurse game.

Some physicians never learn to play the game. Most learn in their internship, and a perceptive few learn during their clerkships in medical school. Medical students frequently complain that the nursing staff treats them as if they had just completed a junior Red Cross first-aid class instead of two years of intensive medical training. Interviewing nurses in a training hospital sheds considerable light on this phenomenon. In their words they said,

> A few students just seem to be with it, they are able to understand what you are trying to tell them, and they are a pleasure to work with; most, however, pretend to know everything and refuse to listen to anything we have to say and I guess we do give them a rough time.

In essence, they are saying that those students who quickly learn the game are rewarded, and those that do not are punished.

Most physicians learn to play the game after they have weathered a few experiences like the one described below. On the first day of his internship, the physician and nurse were making rounds. They stopped at the bed of a fifty-two-year-old woman who, after complimenting the young doctor on his appearance, complained to him of her problem with constipation. After several minutes of listening to her detailed description of peculiar diets, family home remedies, and special exercises that have helped her constipation in the past, the nurse politely interrupted the patient. She told her the doctor would take care of the problem and that he had to move on because there were other patients waiting to see him. The young doctor gave the nurse a stern look, turned toward the patient, and kindly told her he would order an enema for her that very afternoon. As they left the bedside, the nurse told him the patient has had a normal bowel movement every day for the past week and that in the twenty-three days the patient has been in the hospital she has never once passed up an opportunity to complain of her constipation. She quickly added that *if* the doctor wanted to order an enema, the patient would certainly receive one. After hearing this report the intern's mouth fell open and the wheels began turning in his head. He remembered the nurse's comment to the patient that "the doctor had to move on," and it occurred to him that perhaps she was really giving him a message. This experience and a few more like it, and the young doctor learns to listen for the subtle recommendations the nurses make.

Nursing student training. Unlike the medical student who usually learns to play the game after he finishes medical school, the nursing student begins to learn it early in her training. Throughout her education she is trained to play the doctor-nurse game.

Student nurses are taught how to relate to physicians. They are told he has infinitely more knowledge than they, and thus he should be shown the utmost respect. In addition, it was not many years ago when nurses were instructed to stand whenever a physician entered a room. When he would come in for a conference the nurse was expected to offer him her chair, and when both entered a room the nurse would open the door for him and allow him to enter first. Although these practices are no longer rigidly adhered to, the premise upon which they were based is still promulgated. One nurse described that premise as, "He's God almighty and your job is to wait on him."

To inculcate subservience and inhibit deviancy, nursing schools, for the most part, are tightly run, disciplined institutions. Certainly there is great variation among nursing schools, and there is little question that the trend is toward giving students more autonomy. However, in too many schools this trend has not gone far enough, and the climate remains restrictive. The student's schedule is firmly controlled and there is very little free time. Classroom hours, study hours, mealtime, and bedtime with lights out are rigidly enforced. In some schools meaningless chores are assigned, such as cleaning bedsprings with cotton applicators. The relationship between student and instructor continues this military flavor. Often their relationship is more like that between recruit and drill sergeant than between student and teacher. Open dialogue is inhibited by attitudes of strict black and white, with few, if any, shades of gray. Straying from the rigidly outlined path is sure to result in disciplinary action.

The inevitable result of these practices is to instill in the student nurse a fear of independent action. This inhibition of independent action is most marked when relating to physicians. One of the students' greatest fears is making a blunder while assisting a physician and being publicly ridiculed by him. This is really more a reflection of the nature of their training than the prevalence of abusive physicians. The fear of being humiliated for a blunder while assisting in a procedure is generalized to the fear of humiliation for making any independent act in relating to a physician, especially the act of making a direct recommendation. Every nurse interviewed felt that making a suggestion to a physician was equivalent to insulting and belittling him. It was tantamount to questioning his medical knowledge and insinuating he did not know his business. In light of her image of the physician as an omniscient and punitive figure, the questioning of his knowledge would be unthinkable.

The student, however, is also given messages quite contrary to the ones described above. She is continually told that she is an invaluable aid to the physician in the treatment of the patient. She is told that she must help him in every way possible, and she is imbued with a strong sense of responsibility for the care of her patient. Thus she, like the physician, is caught in a paradox. The first set of messages implies that the physician is omniscient and that any recommendation she might make would be insulting to him and leave her open to ridicule. The second set of messages implies that she is an important asset to him, has much to contribute, and is duty-bound to make those contributions. Thus, when her good sense tells her a recommendation would be helpful to him she is not allowed to communicate it directly, nor is she allowed not to communicate it. The way out of the bind is to use the doctor-nurse game and communicate the recommendation without appearing to do so.

Forces Preserving the Game

Upon observing the indirect interactional system which is the heart of the doctor-nurse game, one must ask the question, "Why does this inefficient mode of communication continue to exist?" The forces mitigating against change are powerful.

Rewards and punishments. The doctor-nurse game has a powerful innate self-perpetuating force — its system of rewards and punishments. One potent method of shaping behavior is to reward one set of behavioral patterns and to punish patterns which deviate from it. As described earlier, the rewards given for a well-played game and the punishments meted out to unskilled players are impressive. This system alone would be sufficient to keep the game flourishing. The game, however, has additional forces.

The strength of the set. It is well recognized that sets are hard to break. A powerful attitudinal set is the nurse's perception that making a suggestion to a physician is equivalent to insulting and belittling him. An example of where attempts are regularly made to break this set is seen on psychiatric treatment wards operating on a therapeutic community model. This model requires open and direct communication between members of the team. Psychiatrists working in these settings expend a great deal of energy in urging for and rewarding openness before direct patterns of communication become established. The rigidity of the resistance to break this set is impressive. If the physician himself is a prisoner of a set and therefore does not actively try to destroy it, change is near impossible.

The need for leadership. Lack of leadership and structure in any organization produces anxiety in its members. As the importance of the organization's mission increases, the demand by its members for leadership commensurately increases. In our culture human life is near the top of our hierarchy of values, and organizations which deal with human lives, such as law and medicine, are very rigidly structured. Certainly some of this is necessary for the systematic management of the task. The excessive degree of rigidity, however, is demanded by its members for their own psychic comfort rather than for its utility in efficiently carrying out its mission. The game lends support to this thesis. Indirect communication is an inefficient mode of transmitting information. However, it effectively supports and protects a rigid organizational structure with the physician in clear authority. Maintaining an omnipotent leader provides the other members with a great sense of security.

Sexual roles. Another influence perpetuating the doctor-nurse game is the sexual identity of the players. Doctors are predominately men and nurses are almost exclusively women. There are elements of the game which reinforce the stereotyped roles of male dominance and female passivity. Some nursing instructors explicitly tell their students that their femininity is an important asset to be used when relating to physicians.

The Community

The doctor and nurse have a shared history and thus have been able to work out their game so that it operates more efficiently than one would expect in an indirect system. Major difficulty arises, however, when the physician works closely with other disciplines which are not normally considered part of the medical sphere. With expanding medical horizons encompassing cooperation with sociologists, engineers, anthropologists, computer analysts, etc., continued expectation of a doctor-nurselike interaction by the physician is disastrous. The sociologist, for example, is not willing to play that kind of game. When his direct communications are rebuffed the relationship breaks down.

The major disadvantage of a doctor-nurselike game is its inhibitory effect on open dialogue which is stifling and anti-intellectual. The game is basically a transactional neurosis, and both professions would enhance themselves by taking steps to change the attitudes which breed the game. . . .

SOURCE: From "The Doctor-Nurse Game," *Archives of General Psychiatry* 16 (June 1967):699–703. Copyright 1967, American Medical Association. Reprinted by permission of the author and the publisher.

PART IV
Social
Institutions

Social institutions are systems of norms, values, positions, and activities that develop around a societal goal. They are the basic foundation of society. In Part IV we look at six institutions and discuss how they are organized and how they function.

The chapter on families deals with how families are organized in order to care for children. The chapter on religion shows how various types of religious systems affect the beliefs of the public. We discuss how educational systems are organized to socialize children, and how political systems maintain order, make decisions, and distribute the resources of a society. We then examine how economic systems control production goods and services we need. Finally, we look at various health care systems and how they meet the needs of society.

CHAPTER 12

Family Groups and Systems

The family is the nucleus of civilization.
— Will and Ariel Durant

If we want to understand society and social life, it is impossible to ignore the family. Most of us spend a major portion of our lives in one form of family or another. It is unlikely that any society has ever existed without some social arrangement that could be termed family, and we cannot overestimate its importance to the individual and society as a whole.

In this chapter, we will consider the family as a group, a social system, and a social institution. For most of us, the family serves as a primary social group. It is the first agency of socialization (see Chapter 6). Sociologists consider the family a social system because it is composed of interdependent parts, it has a characteristic organization and pattern of functioning, and it has subsystems that are part of the larger system. The family is considered a social institution because it is an area of social life that is organized in discernible patterns and because it helps meet crucial societal goals.

Families do not exist in isolation, of course. They are an interdependent unit of the larger society. If families have many children, for example, schools may become crowded and unemployment may become a problem. If, on the other hand, they have few children over several generations, Social Security, the care of the aged, and an adequate work force may become important issues. It also makes a difference whether one spouse is employed or both are. Do newlyweds live with one set of parents or establish independent residences? Is divorce frequent or infrequent? Do people select their own mates or have them selected for them? Family practices have a profound influence on many aspects of social life.

We begin our discussion by clarifying what

we mean by "family." Although the answer may appear quite obvious, this issue raised a major controversy at the 1980 White House Conference on Families. The definition of "family" influences who is eligible for various benefits. Certain definitions could result in informal stigmatization and discrimination against families who did not meet the qualifications, such as a mother and her child, two men, or an unmarried man and woman.

What Is a Family?

There is usually little confusion about what we mean by "family" when we talk with friends about our own family life because we generally associate with people from our own social class and culture who share our values and norms about families. In other cultures around the world, however, there is tremendous variation in family structure.

The smallest units are called *conjugal families*, which must include a husband and wife but may or may not include children. *Nuclear families* may or may not include a husband and wife — they consist of any two or more persons related to one another by blood, marriage, or adoption who share a common residence. Thus, a brother and sister or a single parent and child would be nuclear families but not conjugal families. These terms are sometimes used interchangeably, and some families fall under both categories.

The definition used in census reporting in the United States is the nuclear family. In 1982, there were 61.0 million family households in this country. Of these, 49.6 million were husband-and-wife family households, 1.9 million were male households with no wife present, and 9.4 million were female households with no husband present (U.S. Bureau of the Census, 1983c, p. 2).

Approximately 95 percent of all Americans marry at some time in their lives. In so doing, they become members of two different but over-lapping nuclear families. The nuclear family in which one is born and reared (consisting of oneself, brothers, sisters, and parents) is termed the *family of orientation*. This is the family in which most basic early childhood socialization occurs. When a person marries, a new nuclear (and conjugal) family is formed, which is called the *family of procreation*. This family consists of oneself and one's spouse and children. These relations are diagrammed in Figure 12-1.

In the world as a whole, conjugal and nuclear families as isolated and independent units are rare. In most societies, the norm is the *extended family*, which goes beyond the nuclear family to include other nuclear families and relatives such as grandparents, aunts, uncles, and cousins.

Is the typical family in the United States nuclear or extended? Actually, it is both. American families typically have what is called a *modified-extended family structure*, in which individual nuclear families retain considerable autonomy and yet maintain connections with other nuclear families to exchange goods and services. This type of family differs from the extended family in that its members may live in different parts of the country and choose their occupations independently rather than following the parent's occupation.

Generally, we may define the *family* as a group of kin united by blood, marriage, or adoption who share a common residence for some part of their lives and assume reciprocal rights and obligations with regard to one another. The family is the principal source of socialization, especially of the infant, and factors such as those in the definition tend to differentiate the family from other social groups.

Family groups and systems are only one type of kinship association. *Kinship* is the web of relationships among people linked by common ancestry, adoption, or marriage. All societies have general norms for defining family and kin groups and how these relationships are organized. These norms concern such matters as who lives to-

Figure 12-1
Families of orientation and procreation

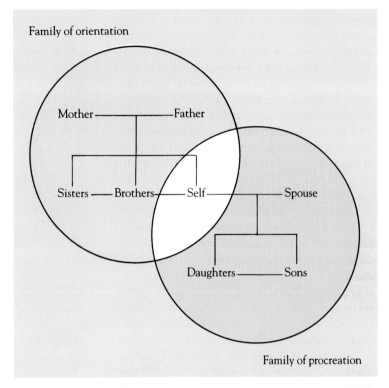

Family of orientation

Family of procreation

gether, who is the head of the group, who marries whom, how mates are selected, which relatives in family and kin groups are most important, and how and by whom children are to be raised. Although certain general norms tend to determine the statuses and roles of family members, other norms and the kinship systems they govern vary greatly. These variations are discussed in the next section.

Variations in Kinship and Family Organization

Each society defines certain patterns of marriage, family, and kinship as correct and proper. Because we tend to be ethnocentric and favor the family structure found in our own society, we may overlook the wide range of variations that

exist. We may also tend to assume that if our current family forms change too drastically, the institution of the family will collapse. It is important to recognize that a tremendous variety of marriage, family, and kinship patterns exist and that any of these patterns may be both appropriate and workable in a particular social context. One fundamental variation concerns marriage and the number of spouses considered acceptable.

Marriage and Number of Spouses

Marital status (single, married, separated, widowed, divorced) and number of spouses (none, one, more than one) are two major variations in family organization. Every society permits some form of marriage, although certain groups believe that the single life is the ultimate form of perfection. Nuns in the Catholic church, for example, are regarded as being symbolically married to God. In the United States today, it seems that remaining single may be emerging as an acceptable lifestyle. It is unclear, however, whether this is a permanent alternative to marriage or just a delay in marriage.

To most Americans, the most "proper" form of marriage is *monogamy*, in which one man is married to one woman at a time. Throughout the world, this form of marriage is the only one universally recognized; it is the predominant form even in societies where other forms exist. However, only about 20 percent of the world's societies are strictly monogamous, considering monogamy the only acceptable form of marriage.

Although the United States is considered strictly monogamous, it is possible to have more than one husband or one wife. An increasing number of married people end their relationship with one spouse and remarry another. This pattern of marrying is called *serial* or *sequential monogamy*. It is both legally and socially approved to have more than one wife or husband as long as it is done sequentially and not simultaneously.

There are a variety of alternatives to monogamy. Murdock (1957) investigated the frequency of *polygamy*, marriage to more than one spouse, in a sample of 554 societies from around the world. He found that *polygyny*, in which a man has more than one wife, was the norm in 77 percent of these societies, whereas *polyandry*, in which a woman has more than one husband, was culturally favored in less than 1 percent. *Group marriage*, in which several or many men are married to several or many woman, is practiced in some societies, but it is nowhere the dominant marriage form.

In discussing polygamy, several words of caution are in order. First, a distinction must be made between ideology and actual occurrence. The fact that a society permits one to have sev-

Many societies include norms of polygyny, the practice of having more than one wife. Frequently, this is a mark of high prestige, distinction, and status. This Iranian family consists of a Bakhtiari chief with his three wives and many children. The eldest wife is probably his first wife and is likely to occupy a privileged position among the women of the family.

eral spouses does not necessarily mean that a large proportion of all marriages are polygamous. Second, except for group marriage, multiple spouses are possible on a large scale only when the ratio of the sexes is unbalanced. Third, when polygamy is practiced, it is controlled by societal norms like any other form of marriage. Rather than resulting from strictly personal or psychological motives, it is supported by the values and norms of both sexes and is closely linked to the economic conditions and belief systems of the wider society. Fourth, polygamy itself may take a variety of forms. The multiple husbands may all be brothers or the multiple wives may all be sisters, for example.

The most common form of polygamy is polygyny. In many societies, having several wives is a mark of prestige and high status. The wealthy, the leaders, and the best hunters may get a second or third wife. Multiple wives may also be desired as a source of children, especially sons. Polygyny is very common in Africa, among Muslim groups in the Middle East and Asia, and in many tribal groups in South America and throughout the world. In Ibadan, Nigeria, for example, a study of more than 6,600 women (Ware, 1979) found that nearly one wife in two was living in a polygynous marriage; the proportion rose to two out of three for wives aged forty and above. The Muslim religion permits men to have up to four wives. In the United States, despite its illegality, polygyny is practiced by certain Mormon fundamentalists living in Utah and neighboring states.

Polyandry is quite rare. Where it is practiced, the co-husbands are usually brothers, either blood brothers or clan brothers who belong to the same clan and are of the same generation. Among the Todas, for example, a non-Hindu tribe in India, it is understood that when a woman marries a man she becomes the wife of his brothers at the same time.

Norms of Residence

When people marry, they must decide where to live. Decisions about place of residence are typically dictated by societal norms and conform to one of three patterns.

In Western societies, the residence norm is *neolocal* — the couple lives alone wherever they wish — but this pattern is rare in the rest of the world. Of the societies Murdock (1949) exam-

ined, only about 10 percent considered it appropriate for newlywed couples to move to a place of residence separate from both the husband's and the wife's families. This type of residence pattern seems to be linked with norms of monogamy and individualism. Nearly three-fourths of the societies studied by Murdock were *patrilocal* — the newlywed couple lived not just in the groom's community, but usually in his parents' home or compound. This type of residence is most common in polygynous hunting and gathering societies throughout Asia, Africa, and Latin America. In the United States, the Amish communities represent one example of a patrilocal system. A *matrilocal* residence pattern, in which the newly married couple lives with the wife's family, was the norm in about 15 percent of the societies Murdock studied and was generally found where women held title to the land.

Norms of Descent and Inheritance

Children inherit two separate bloodlines at birth, the mother's and the father's. Most societies place more importance on one lineage or the other. In much of the Western world, particularly in the United States, lineage is of small importance. It determines surname but little else. In most societies, however, explicit rules indicate that one blood line is more important than the other. These rules are known as the norms of descent and inheritance.

The most common norms of descent are *patrilineal*, in which kinship is traced through the male kin, the father's lineage. In this type of descent system, offspring owe a special allegiance and loyalty to the father and his kin, who in turn protect and socialize the children and eventually pass to the sons their authority, property, and wealth. Under this system, the key ties are those among father, sons, and grandsons. The wife may maintain ties to her kin, and she contributes her genes to her children, but she and her chil-

The Trobriand Islanders, about 200 miles off the northeast coast of New Guinea, have a matrilineal descent system. While some powers and functions, such as that of village chief, are vested in the male, these hereditary offices or social positions are passed on exclusively through the mother line. The Trobriand Islanders do not consider a child to be biologically related to its father, for they believe the father has no procreative function. Thus the important males for children are not their fathers but their mothers' brothers.

dren are considered members of her husband's family.

In a *matrilineal* system of descent, descent and inheritance are traced through the mother's line. The mother's kin assume the important role among offspring. Matrilineal norms of descent are uncommon, but they do exist. Among the Trobriand Islanders, for example, kinship, wealth, and responsibility for support are traced through the female line.

In the United States, the norm is to assign influence, wealth, and power to both sides of the family. This system is referred to as *bilateral.* Kinship lines are traced equally through the biological relatives of both the mother and the father and inheritance is passed on in equal proportions to all children regardless of sex. One consequence of this descent system is that, although the kin of both parents are equally recognized and respected, neither kin group exerts much power and influence over the children, which has a significant effect on social change: a newlywed couple coming from families with different values and lifestyles may choose to conform to neither and establish a lifestyle of their own. In addition, the likelihood of marrying someone with different values increases, since the parents and kin groups in bilateral systems have relatively little influence over who their sons or daughters marry.

Norms of Authority

All families and kinship systems have norms concerning who makes important decisions. These norms follow the pattern of other norm variations in that they are aligned with gender. Most societies are *patriarchal* — the men have the power and authority and are dominant. In Iran, Thailand, and Japan, the male position of dominance is even reflected in the law. In *matriarchal* societies, the authority rests with the females, especially wives and mothers. Matriarchal systems are rare, even among matrilineal societies such as that of the Trobriand Islanders, where the wives do not have authority over their husbands.

It is important to recognize that although authority in most families rests with the males, other family members have a strong influence on the decision-making process. Male family members are generally most influential, but wives and mothers often have a strong impact on decisions as well.

The least common pattern of authority is the *egalitarian* model, in which decisions are equally divided between husband and wife. Some have argued that the United States is egal-

itarian because husbands and wives either make decisions jointly or assume responsibility for different areas of concern. The husband might make decisions related to his job, the automobile, or home repairs, whereas the wife might make decisions related to her job, the home, food, clothing, or the children. Many would argue that the family system in the United States is more patriarchal than egalitarian, however, since males generally control income and other family resources.

Norms for Choice of Marriage Partner

Every society, including the United States, has norms concerning the appropriateness or unacceptability of certain types of marriage partners. These norms can be divided into two categories: *exogamy*, in which people must marry outside of their own group, and *endogamy*, which requires that people considering marriage share certain group characteristics.

Certain exogamous norms are almost universal. *Incest*, sexual relations or marriage with close relatives, is forbidden in almost every society. One cannot marry one's mother, father, brother, sister, son, or daughter. Isolated exceptions to this taboo are said to have existed among Egyptian and Inca royalty. Most societies also forbid marriage between first cousins and between members of the same sex.

Endogamous norms of one sort or another are also very widespread, although they vary greatly from one society to another. In this country, for example, marriages between members of different racial groups were considered improper or even forbidden by law at different times.

Why have norms concerning endogamy and exogamy evolved? It seems clear from their universality that they perform an important social function, but the nature of that function is widely debated. A number of authorities have suggested that the incest taboo, for instance, is a result of the dangers of inbreeding. Others contend that the taboo is instinctive, that prolonged associations with people during childhood precludes viewing them as a marriage partner, or that marriage within a kinship group would lead to intense conflicts and jealousy. Each of these explanations has its shortcomings, however. Murdock (1949) suggests that a complete explanation of the incest taboo must synthesize theories from the different disciplines that deal with human behavior.

There are also a number of explanations for endogamy. It is widely believed that members of similar groups share similar values, role expectations, and attitudes, which result in fewer marital or kinship conflicts. Other explanations suggest that people from similar age groups share similar developmental tasks and interests or that marriage within one's own race maintains "pure" genetic traits. It has also been suggested that marriages between people of the same socioeconomic status keep the wealth and power within the social class and that those of the same religious orientation are likely to agree on childrearing practices, family rituals, and beliefs relating to the sacred. Although the norms of endogamy vary among and within societies such as the United States, all societies foster suspicion and dislike of groups whose values, behaviors, and customs are unfamiliar or seem strange. Both exogamy and endogamy, therefore, restrict the eligibility of available marriage partners for both sexes.

A Functionalist Perspective on the Family

The functionalist perspective, which was introduced in Chapter 2, emphasizes the structures of social systems and the functions of these parts in maintaining the society. Despite the many variations that exist in family structure around the world, families everywhere perform many of the same functions. Among the more important are

socialization, affection and emotional support, sexual regulation, reproduction, and social placement.

Socialization

As discussed in Chapter 6, the family is one of the most important agents of socialization because it teaches its members the rules and expectations for behavior in the society. Reiss (1965) argues that although families perform many functions, only the function of nurturant socialization of children is universal. It is doubtful whether infants could even survive, much less develop into mentally, physically, and socially healthy human beings, outside of the intimate network of the family. The family is not only more permanent than other social institutions but also provides the care, protection, and love best suited to teaching children the knowledge, skills, values, and norms of the society and subculture. However excellent hospitals, day care centers, and nursery or elementary schools may be, none seems to perform the socialization and learning functions as well as the family (Elkin and Handel, 1984; Spitz, 1945). This emphasis on the infant and young child should not cause us to overlook the socialization function of the family on adults, however. Parents learn from each other, from their children, and from other kin as they interact in the intimate network bound by blood and marriage ties. This affective support is a second function provided by the family.

Affection and Emotional Support

Thirty years ago, Parsons and Bales (1955) suggested that the family has two essential functions: (1) the primary socialization of children so that they can become true members of the society they were born in and (2) the stabilization of the adult personalities of the society. This second function, while often ignored, seems to be just as important as the first. Although some individuals enjoy living alone, most people need others who care, show affection, share joys and

A universal function of families is that of nuturant socialization. The primary group interaction between parent and child has proven to be indispensable to the development of mentally and physically healthy human beings. The role of the father is important in this process, and it appears that an increasing number of fathers are becoming more involved in performing nontraditional child rearing tasks.

sorrows, and give support in times of need. Humans are social animals who depend on their families at every stage of the life cycle, and while social support is also provided by friends, neighbors, coworkers, and government agencies, none is as effective as the family at providing warm, supportive relationships.

The importance of this family function is evidenced in many different ways. Aging persons, as you saw in Chapter 11, often indicated that good relationships with their children are a major source of gratification. In fact, people who have a network of family connections live longer than those who are single, widowed, or divorced.

Sexual Regulation

All societies approve of some sexual behaviors and disapprove of others. As mentioned earlier there is an almost universal taboo against incest, whereas marriage is the most universally approved outlet for sexual behavior. Both are linked to the family system.

Societies control sexual activity in a number of ways. The chief means is by socializing sexual norms and attempting to enforce them. The norm of chastity, for example, might be enforced by secluding single women. Society also differentiates sexual rights in accordance with various roles and statuses (male, female, single, married, priest, teacher) and places taboos on intercourse at certain times in the reproductive cycle such as during menstruation, pregnancy, or following childbirth. The norms of most societies discourage practices such as rape, child molesting, voyeurism, and the like. Sexual norms are concerned with more than just sexual intercourse; they also cover such behaviors as kissing and touching as well as appropriate attitudes and values.

In the United States, the most pervasive socially approved sexual interest is heterosexual. Sexual relationships are generally defined in terms of the family and marriage, as premarital or extramarital relationships, for example. Other institutions — religion, education, economics, or politics — may also regulate sexual behaviors and attitudes, but it is not one of their primary tasks. Families have the chief responsibility in this area, and since they regulate sexual activity, it seems logical that they also control the function of reproduction.

Reproduction

The family is the most widely approved social context for having children. Children are sometimes born outside the family, of course, but if it is common it is considered a social problem. According to the functionalist perspective, a society's reproductive practices should conform to institutional patterns and be integrated with other societal functions such as sexual regulation, physical and emotional support, and socialization. This view reflects the *principle of legitimacy* formulated by Bronislaw Malinowski (1930) more than fifty years ago. The principle states that every society has a rule that every child should have a legitimate father to act as the child's protector, guardian, and representative in the society.

Those who are not functionalists may be disturbed at this explanation of the role of the family. It suggests that children born outside of the family are stigmatized in some way, that they are illegitimate. Even functionalists would concede that there are functional alternatives to a biological father; father substitutes can fulfill the essential social tasks and roles of a father. Interactionists would also argue that the biological link between parent and child is less significant than the social links — what is important to the child are role models, social support, and patterns of interaction that will enable the child to develop adequately and function effectively in society. Although it is true that children born outside the family can develop into functioning members of society, it is undeniably the family that universally fulfills the function of giving legal status and social approval to parenthood and reproduction. This function is related to another family function, that of social placement.

Social Placement

The social placement of children is a family function closely associated with socialization and reproduction. Social placement involves determining what roles and statuses the child will occupy in society. As discussed in Chapter 2, some of the statuses that a person will occupy are ascribed at birth, such as age, sex, and social class position. Children generally assume the legal, re-

One function of the family is social placement: influencing and determining the many roles and statuses children will occupy in society. Here, young children, most likely as a result of their parents' influence and Catholic religious status, prepare to receive their first Communion.

ligious, and political status of their family as well. Even statuses that are achieved such as marriage, occupation, and education are greatly influenced by one's membership in a particular family or kin network.

The family performs functions other than

the five mentioned. It fulfills basic economic, protective, educational, recreational, and religious functions as well.

A Conflict Perspective on the Family

Conflict theorists, like functionalists, recognize variations in family structure and accept the idea that the family provides basic social needs and goals. The two approaches are fundamentally very different, however. Conflict theorists contend that social systems, including the family, are not static structures that maintain equilibrium and harmony among the parts. They argue, rather, that social systems are constantly in a state of conflict and change. They contend that conflict is natural and inevitable in all human interactions including those between male and female, husband and wife, and parent and child, and that these conflicts are the result of a continual struggle for power and control. Marriage is one of many contexts in which each person seeks his or her rights. The struggles of parenthood involve not just rivalries between siblings but between parents and children as well.

Conflict stems from the unequal distribution of scarce resources. In all systems, some have more resources than others, which gives them dominance and power over others. These inequalities exist not only in the economic and occupational realm but also in the family. Friedrich Engels (1902) claimed that the family, the basic unit in a capitalist society, serves as the chief means of oppressing women. The husband is the bourgeois and the wife the proletariat. As general Marxist theory suggests, when woman become aware of their collective interests, they will question the legitimacy of the existing patterns of inequality and join together against men to bring about changes and the redistribution of resources: power, money, education, job opportunities, and the like. Conflict is as inevitable in the family as it is in society, and it leads to change.

As indicated in Chapters 2 and 8, conflict theory assumes that economic organization, especially the ownership of property, generates revolutionary class conflict. In families, property ownership involves not just one's home and possessions but people as well. Collins (1971) argues that basic to the institution of sexual stratification is the notion of sexual property, the belief that one has permanent exclusive sexual rights to a particular person. In societies dominated by males, the principal form of sexual property is male ownership of females, husband ownership of wives. This pattern of male ownership and male dominance has a long history, stemming from laws in ancient Hebrew society and continuing through the twentieth century. The Hebrew laws stated, among other things, that if a man had sexual intercourse with an unbetrothed (not contracted for marriage) virgin, he was required to marry her and pay her father the bride price. In many societies, women are closely guarded so they will not attract other men and lose their market value. These practices are reflected in such customs as wearing a veil and strict chaperonage. Even in the United States, women could not legally make contracts or obtain credit until recently, and women are still not guaranteed equal rights under the Constitution. The status of women is also evident in wedding ceremonies, in which the father "gives away" some of his property — the bride — and the bride vows not just to love but to honor and obey her new owner (the groom).

How can this inequality and the prevalence of male domination be explained? The most common theory relates power and domination to available resources. Men gain power over women by their physical strength and their freedom from the biological limitations of childbirth. The traditional resource of women, on the other hand, is their sexuality. Before and during mar-

Muslim women are often identified by the chador, *or veil. At approximately age nine, according to Islamic belief, women become adults and must wear this type of garb in public. Departing from past tradition, many women today do not cover the entire face or all the hair. Thus the* chador *is less likely to provide anonymity, but, nevertheless, serves as modest and nonprovocative dress, as a source of status identification, and as religious-political symbolism.*

riage, women traditionally control men by with-holding sexual "favors."

Conflict theory suggests that the structure of domination shifts as resources shift. Thus women today have a better bargaining position because they hold jobs and are economically independent and because they are free from unwanted pregnancies and childbirth. As Collins (1971) states, "Women become at least potentially free to negotiate their own sexual relationships" (p. 13). The changes involve much more than just sexual relationships, however. There seems to be a major trend, at least in the more industrialized nations, toward greater equality between the sexes both within and outside of marriage and the family.

Conflict in families also occurs over issues other than inequality between men and women. It can arise over a variety of issues: place of residence, inheritance rights, decision making, selection of mates, violence (especially rape), sexual relationships, and marital adjustment, to mention a few. In every instance, the issue is likely to involve an inequality of power, authority, or resources, which will lead to conflict.

Other Perspectives on the Family

An Exchange Perspective

All human interactions, including those between husbands and wives or parents and children, can be viewed in terms of social exchange. Social exchange theory assumes that people weigh rewards and costs in their social interactions. If the exchange is unequal or perceived as unequal, one person will be at a disadvantage and the other will control the relationship. In this regard, exchange theory parallels the conflict perspective. If people in a relationship give a great deal and receive little in return, they will perceive the relationship as unsatisfactory. These ideas can be illustrated with mate selection.

Everywhere in the world, selecting a mate involves trying to get the best spouse for what one has to offer. As you know from our earlier discussion of the endogamous and exogamous rules of marriage, selecting a mate is never a matter of completely free and independent choice. One must conform to societal norms.

Marriages may be arranged in several ways. At one extreme, they may be organized by the families of the people to be married; the prospective spouses may have no say in the matter at all. When this practice is followed, the criteria of the exchange involve such factors as money, prestige, family position, or power. When, on the other hand, the people to be married choose their mates themselves, the exchange criteria involve factors like love, beauty, fulfillment of needs, prestige, or personality. The latter procedure is rare in the world as a whole, the United States being one of the few countries that practices it.

One of the most widely researched exchange theories of mate selection is the theory of *complementary needs*. Robert Winch (1954, 1958) believed that although mates tend to resemble each other in such social characteristics as age, race, religion, ethnic origin, socioeconomic status, and education, they are usually complementary rather than similar in respect to needs, psychic fulfillment, and individual motivation. Rather than seeking a mate with a similar personality, one seeks a person who will satisfy one's needs. If both people are dominant, for example, the relationship won't succeed, but if one is dominant and the other submissive, the relationship is complementary and the needs of both parties are met. A great deal of research was instigated by this theory of complementary needs, but the results did not provide empirical support for the notion that people choose mates whose needs complement their own.

An earlier exchange theory of mate selection was Willard Waller's (1938) analysis of courtship conduct as a process of bargaining, exploitation, or both. In his words, "When one marries he makes a number of different bargains. Everyone knows this and this knowledge affects the sentiment of love and the process of falling in love" (p. 239). While it is doubtful that "everyone knows this," the fact that bargaining and exchanges take place in the mate selection process is today widely recognized and accepted. Good looks, athletic stardom, a sense of humor, clothes, or money are resources commonly perceived as valuable in the exchange process. In mate selection as in other interaction processes, people rarely get something for nothing although each person, either consciously or unconsciously, tries to maximize gains and minimize costs. Over the long run, however, actual exchanges tend to be about equal, and if they are not the relationship is likely to end.

An Interactionist Perspective

An interactionist perspective on the family uses a social-psychological approach to examine interaction patterns, socialization processes, role expectations and behaviors, and the definitions or meanings given to various family issues. As noted in earlier chapters, this approach considers not just structural variations but the interactional patterns and covert definitions associated with structural arrangements.

Few relationships are more enduring or more intense than marriage, and few reflect the principles of interactionism so comprehensively. Marriage exemplifies all the ideas central to symbolic interaction: shared meanings, significant others, role expectations, role taking, definitions of situations, symbolic communication, and so on.

Marriage is dynamic — the needs of the married individuals and their role relationships change frequently. According to the interactionist perspective, husband and wife have a reciprocal influence on each other. Each partner continually affects the other, so adjustment is a process, not an end result. Good adjustment means that "the individual or the pair has a good

working arrangement with reality, adulthood, and expectations of others" (Waller and Hill, 1951, p. 362).

Everyone brings to a marriage certain ideas about what is proper behavior for oneself and one's spouse. Inevitably, people find as they interact that some behaviors do not fit their preconceived definitions. Unless the definitions or the behaviors change, one spouse or both may be frustrated in attempting to fulfill their roles. Some argue that these frustrations are increasing, since the roles of husband and wife are more flexible and diverse than they were in the past. Others maintain that today's increased flexibility and diversity decrease marital strain by allowing partners a greater range of options. In either case, what the interactionist considers important is that the couple share definitions, perceptions, and meanings. Also, disagreements may not lead to conflict if they involve issues considered unimportant. Suppose, for example, that a husband likes football but his wife does not. The situation will not lead to conflict if the wife defines football as important to her husband and accepts his behavior. In the same way, a wife's desire for full-time employment or her wish to avoid cooking is a source of conflict only if the husband has different expectations. Adjustment is a result of shared expectations.

To maintain a satisfactory relationship, married couples must continually redefine themselves in relation to each other, which is often an unconscious process. When problems arise, marriage counseling may help by bringing unconscious definitions into consciousness, thus allowing the couple to examine how they influence the relationship.

The interactionist perspective stresses the importance of analyzing marriages and other relationships in the context in which they occur. A definition, role expectation, or behavior that is appropriate in one setting may be inappropriate in another. This perspective also emphasizes the notion that a successful marriage involves a process of adjustment, or continual adaptation to shifts in shared meaning.

A Developmental Perspective

The developmental perspective on the family suggests that families pass through a *family life cycle*, a series of different responsibilities and tasks. This perspective suggests that successful achievement at one point in the developmental process is essential to effectively accomplish later tasks, while failure in earlier tasks leads to increased difficulty with later tasks. Just as individuals must learn to crawl and walk before they can run, new families must be able to perform various financial, sexual, and interpersonal tasks to maintain the family unit and meet later developmental goals.

During its life cycle, the family passes through a sequence of stages that require different interaction patterns, roles, and responsibilities. The number of stages identified depends on the intent of the researcher. There may be as few as two, but the most typical division is of seven stages. The transition points between stages most often center around the age of the oldest child.

The first stage typically begins with marriage and extends to the birth of the first child. For most couples this stage involves defining the marital relationship, learning to communicate effectively and resolve conflicts, working out mutually satisfying and realistic systems for getting and spending the family income, and deciding about parenthood. Obviously, not all newlyweds face the same tasks. If the woman is pregnant before the marriage, if it is a teenage, interracial, or second marriage, or if the couple lived together before marriage, their concerns may differ. Nevertheless, the first stage of the family life cycle typically focuses on the married couple and their adjustment to life as a married pair.

Stage two may include families with a preschool child or be subdivided into families with an infant (birth to age two or three) and families with an older preschool child (ages two or three

An interactionist perspective of marriage alerts us to the importance of each spouse fulfilling the expectations of the other. An increasing expectation of wives is that housework should be a mutually shared activity. While evidence suggests that expectations still exceed behaviors, many husbands are assuming or assisting in a variety of tasks that were traditionally assumed to be the responsibility of the wife.

to six). During this stage, the couple changes from a dyad of husband and wife to a triad of parents and offspring. The central tasks are adjusting to parenthood, dealing with the needs and development of the infant and young children, relating to parents and in-laws who are grandparents to the child, assuming and managing the additional housing and space needs, and continuing the communicative, sexual, and financial responsibilities described in stage one.

Stage three may extend from the time the oldest child begins school until he or she reaches the teens. When children enter school, both parents and children face new relationships and responsibilities. In this stage, the family focuses on the education and socialization of children. The increasing significance of peer relationships, children's changing interests and activities, and the management of parent-child conflicts are added to the ongoing marital, work, and other responsibilities. A second or third child, the loss of a job, or the dissolution of the marriage modifies the responsibilities generally associated with this stage.

Stage four is the family with adolescents or teenagers. Data suggest that at the adolescent stage, the family often undergoes economic problems. Medical and dental costs, food, clothing, transportation, entertainment, education, and other expenses often place a strain on the budget. For many families such issues as drinking, drugs, and sex become additional sources of strain. New types of adolescent dance, music, dress, and jargon also must be accommodated. In addition, families in this stage begin to prepare their teenager to be launched from the home.

Stage five begins when the oldest child leaves home and is frequently called the launching stage. The young person's departure — to marry, to attend college, or to take a full-time job — creates a significant transition for both parent and child. This stage may be very brief, as with a one-child family in which the child marries upon graduation from high school, or it may extend

over many years, as happens when there are several children or when an unmarried child remains in the home for many years, dependent on parents for support. When the children have been launched, the family returns to the original two-person conjugal unit; at the same time, however, it may expand to include sons- or daughters-in-law and grandchildren.

Stage six is the period when all the children have left home; this is called the empty-nest stage. It starts with the departure of the last child from the home and continues until the retirement or death of one spouse. Again, it may be very brief because of one or more children who remain in the home through their twenties or because of an early death of a parent, or it may cover many years as when the last child departs when the parents are in their late thirties or early forties and when the parents remain employed until age seventy or later. At this stage, the interpersonal focus is on the married couple yet intergenerational family responsibilities can arise. The husband and wife in the middle years may have some responsibility for their retired and elderly parents and also for their married children and grandchildren, who may seek emotional and financial support from the middle generation from time to time.

The seventh and final stage generally begins with retirement and extends until the marriage ends with the death of one spouse. Because women live longer than men and are usually younger than their husbands, they are widowed more often than men. (The needs and responsibilities of elderly persons were described in the previous chapter and need not be repeated here.) With the death of both spouses the family life span for that family has ended, and the cycle continues with each successive generation.

Family life-cycle stages can be used to analyze a wide range of behaviors and interaction patterns. Frequency of sexual relations, income patterns, recreational activities, and interactions with children have been found to differ by the stage of the family life cycle. Olson et al. (1983), for example, used a seven-stage family life-cycle model to study how 1,140 families managed their lives and why they succeeded in some areas better than in others. One finding consistent with other studies was that adults' satisfaction with marriage and family tends to decline between the birth of the first child and adolescence and rise as the children are launched from the nest. One explanation for the dramatic increase in satisfaction following the launching stage concerns the relaxation of sex roles between the parents. Women see themselves as more free to look for work and organizational roles outside the home, and men find themselves with decreased financial responsibilities and allow themselves to be more passive and dependent.

The American Family System

As indicated earlier in the chapter, the American family system emphasizes monogamy, neolocal residence, a modified-extended kinship linkage, bilateral descent and inheritance, egalitarian decision making, endogamous marriage, and relatively free choice of mate. A number of other structural characteristics have also been described: American families tend to be small and, compared with other countries, rather isolated; marital and family roles for women and men are becoming increasingly ambiguous; we tend to emphasize love in mate selection; we are often sexually permissive prior to or outside of marriage; and divorce is granted easily.

Table 12-1 shows the marital status of the population by sex and age. You can see that as of 1982, the population of the United States included 78.1 million males and 86.6 million females age eighteen and over. Approximately 67 percent of the men and 62 percent of the women were married. Nearly one-fourth (24.5 percent) of the men and one-sixth (17.6 percent) of the women were single. A relatively small percentage (2.4 percent) of the men were widowers compared with 12.5 percent of the women who were widows. While much publicity is given to the frequency of divorce, less than 6 percent of the men and 8 percent of the women were divorced. Note how these figures vary by age. Very few older people are single and very few young and middle-aged people are widowed. The divorced population is concentrated most heavily in the thirty to fifty age group.

Broad profiles of the sort given in the two previous paragraphs, however, do not indicate the frequency or range of specific trends in the evolution of the family. In the following sections, we will examine some of these trends in more detail.

Marriage Rates and Age at Marriage

Rates of marriage are influenced by a variety of factors. The rate characteristically falls during periods of economic recession and rises during periods of prosperity. The rate also tends to rise at the beginning of a war and after a war has ended. Variations in the age of the population are also influential.

In the United States prior to 1900, the rate was relatively stable, varying between 8.6 and 9.6 marriages per 1,000 population per year. Shortly after the turn of the century, the rate rose until the depression of the early 1930s, when it dropped to a low of 7.9. As can be seen in Figure 12-2, it rose dramatically at the outset of World War II as young men sought to avail themselves of the deferred status granted to married men or simply wanted to marry before going overseas. The end of the war and the return of men to civilian life precipitated another upsurge in marriages. In 1946, the marriage rate reached 16.4, an unprecedented and to date unsurpassed peak. Subsequently, it dropped. Over the past thirty years, the rate has fluctuated between 8.5 and 11.0 per thousand (see Figure 12-2).

In the United States, marriage rates have

Table 12-1
Marital status of the population, by sex and age: 1982

SEX AND AGE	NUMBER OF PERSONS (1,000)					PERCENT DISTRIBUTION				
	TOTAL	SINGLE	MARRIED	WIDOWED	DIVORCED	TOTAL	SINGLE	MARRIED	WIDOWED	DIVORCED
Male	**78,132**	**19,125**	**52,543**	**1,860**	**4,605**	**100.0**	**24.5**	**67.2**	**2.4**	**5.9**
18–19 years	4,005	3,801	198	—	5	100.0	94.9	4.9	—	.1
20–24 years	10,363	7,458	2,769	1	134	100.0	72.0	26.7	—	1.3
25–29 years	9,968	3,594	5,769	3	603	100.0	36.1	57.9	—	6.0
30–34 years	9,122	1,581	6,692	11	838	100.0	17.3	73.4	.1	9.2
35–44 years	13,404	1,186	10,911	44	1,264	100.0	8.8	81.4	.3	9.4
45–54 years	10,761	584	9,132	166	878	100.0	5.4	84.9	1.5	8.2
55–64 years	10,198	472	8,819	355	553	100.0	4.6	86.5	3.5	5.4
65–74 years	6,770	331	5,686	510	244	100.0	4.9	84.0	7.5	3.6
75 years and over	3,540	118	2,566	770	86	100.0	3.3	72.5	21.8	2.4
Female	**86,576**	**15,262**	**53,625**	**10,795**	**6,895**	**100.0**	**17.6**	**61.9**	**12.5**	**8.0**
18–19 years	4,099	3,480	592	—	27	100.0	84.9	14.4	—	.7
20–24 years	10,716	5,725	4,600	14	375	100.0	53.4	42.9	.1	3.5
25–29 years	10,224	2,392	6,886	50	897	100.0	23.4	67.4	.5	8.8
30–34 years	9,390	1,087	7,100	69	1,135	100.0	11.6	75.6	.7	12.1
35–44 years	13,995	788	11,113	331	1,765	100.0	5.6	79.4	2.4	12.6
45–54 years	11,561	471	9,070	789	1,230	100.0	4.1	78.5	6.8	10.6
55–64 years	11,672	484	8,271	2,019	898	100.0	4.2	70.9	17.3	7.7
65–74 years	8,927	469	4,580	3,419	458	100.0	5.3	51.3	38.3	5.1
75 years and over	5,993	365	1,414	4,104	110	100.0	6.1	23.6	68.5	1.8

— Represents zero or rounds to zero.

Note: In thousands of persons eighteen years old and over, except percent. As of March. Based on Current Population Survey, which includes members of Armed Forces living off post or with their families on post, but excludes all other members of the Armed Forces.

SOURCE: U.S. Bureau of the Census, *Statistical Abstract of the United States: 1984*, 104th ed., U.S. Government Printing Office, Washington, D.C., 1983, no. 51, p. 44.

distinct seasonal and geographic variations. More marriages take place in June than in any other month, followed by August and September. The fewest marriages are in January, February, and March. Interestingly, the favorite month for marriage varies by age group: teenage brides and grooms prefer June; brides aged thirty to thirty-four and grooms aged forty-five to fifty-four most often choose December; and brides thirty-five to fifty-four and grooms fifty-five to sixty-four tend to select July. Most marriages take place on Saturday. Friday is next in popularity, and Tuesdays, Wednesdays, and Thursdays are the least popular. Marriage rates also vary from state to state. The extremes in 1980 were 143 per 1,000 population in Nevada and 7.5 per 1,000 in Delaware and New Jersey (*Statistical Abstract: 1984*, no. 121).

Most marriages in the United States are between people of roughly the same age, although people are free to marry someone considerably older or younger within the legal limits determined by each state. *Current Population Reports* (1983b, p. 2), published by the U.S. Bureau of the Census, shows the median age at first marriage in 1982 to be 25.2 for men and 22.5 for women, a difference of 2.7 years.

The median age at first marriage and the age difference between males and females have changed considerably since the turn of the century. In 1900, these figures were 25.9 for males and 21.9 for females, a difference of four years. Recently, people have been postponing marriage until they are older, which reflects a decision on the part of young people to live independently as they pursue higher education or job opportuni-

Figure 12-2
Marriage rate: United States, 1925–1982

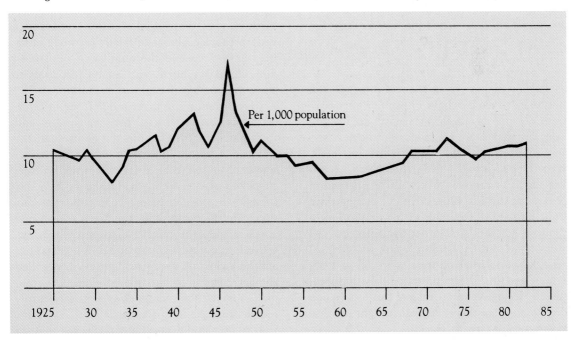

Per 1,000 population

ties. In the past ten years, there has been a rapid increase in the percentage of men and women who have never married. In 1970, one in every ten women (10.5 percent) aged twenty-five to twenty-nine years had never married, but by 1982 this proportion had more than doubled to nearly one in four (23.4 percent). For men it was more than one in three in 1982, a 90 percent increase over the one-in-five rate of singlehood in 1970 (U.S. Bureau of the Census, 1983b, p. 2).

Teenage marriages are an issue of special concern in the United States. Married teenagers have an increased high school dropout rate and a high unemployment rate. The divorce rate for teenagers is estimated to be from two to four times the rate for marriages that begin after age twenty. Many teenage marriages involve a pregnancy at the time of marriage, and data consistently show a higher divorce rate among marriages begun with a pregnancy (Teachman, 1983). Studies indicate that people who marry young are unprepared for the process of selecting a mate and assuming a marital role and are disproportionately represented in divorce statistics.

Family Size

In this country, as in the rest of the world, most married couples have or want to have children. Voluntarily childless marriages are uncommon, although as we will discuss in the next section, a pattern of childless marriages does exist. In the United States in 1982, there were 3.7 million births, a rate of 16 per 1,000 population (*Statistical Abstract: 1984*, no. 83). Like marriage rates, birth rates fluctuate with wars, socioeconomic conditions, and other variables. At the turn of the century, the birth rate was over 30 per 1,000 population. Decreasing to 18.7 in 1935, it increased to 25 by the mid-1950s. It subsequently declined until it reached a rate of 14.6 in 1975. Since then there has been a slight increase to the current rate of 16.

The "baby boom" period of the late 1940s and 1950s produced an unanticipated but significant rise in the United States birth rate. It may have been caused by increases in the normative pressures on women to have children, the end of the disruption brought about by war, postwar economic prosperity, or the long-term psychological effects of growing up during the Great Depression. Bean (1983) states that while social and cultural conditions during the era supported having families, increased costs tended to discourage having *large* families. Thus, only a minor part of the baby boom can be attributed to families deciding to have three or more children.

Since the baby boom the average number of expected lifetime births (including the number of actual births) has declined for currently married women. In 1981, the average number of births expected was 2.19, a decline from a 2.64 average in 1971 and a 3.05 average in 1967 (U.S. Bureau of the Census, 1983a, p. 7). In 1982, only 3.5 percent of all families had four or more children compared with 9.8 percent in 1970 (*Statistical Abstract: 1984*, no. 69). Improved methods of birth control, liberalized abortion laws, and a widespread acceptance of family planning measures have decreased the number of unplanned and unwanted births and enabled couples to have the number of children they want.

Does family size make a difference in interactions between siblings or between children and their parents? Since families are groups and the number of people in a group influences the behavior of its members, the answer is yes. But specifically how does family size make a difference? Perhaps the greatest difference in family interaction patterns comes with the birth of the first child because the transition to parenthood involves a major shift in parental role expectations and behaviors. A number of writers have called the early stages of parenthood a crisis, a traumatic change that forces couples to drastically reorganize their lives (Hobbs, 1965; LeMasters, 1957). Later studies concluded, however, that for most couples, beginning parenthood is a period

Throughout the world, most couples have or want to have children. Childbirth classes help prepare women (and men) for labor and birth. A French obstetrician, Fernand Lamaze, suggested that because the woman, not the physician, is the principle actor in pregnancy and birth scripts, she should go through a series of general conditioning exercises. Women are encouraged to bring their husband or another companion to the classes to learn the relaxation and breathing techniques as well and coach them at the time of childbirth.

of transition but not a period of change so dramatic that a crisis results.

With the birth of the first child, the expectation exists that a second and third child should follow. One-child families have generally been viewed as unhealthy for parents and child alike. The "only child" has been described as spoiled, selfish, overly dependent, maladjusted, and lonely, and the parents of a single child have been described as selfish, self-centered, immature, cold, and abnormal (Hawke and Knox, 1977).

In sharp contrast are the findings of Blake (1981a and 1981b), who claims that single children are intellectually superior, have no obvious personality defects, tend to consider themselves happy, and are satisfied with the important aspects of life, notably jobs and health. In fact, Blake's research supports the "dilution model," which predicts that, on average, the more children a family has the lower each child will achieve in such areas as educational and occupational attainment.

While people may agree that a one-child family is small, there is less agreement about the number of children required to make a family "large." Perceptions of a family as small or large are relative. A family with four children in the United States at the turn of the century would not have been perceived as large. However, today it generally would be. The more central issue in reference to family size, however, concerns the consequences of having more children in a given family.

It is known that family size increases with factors such as younger ages at marriage, lower educational and socioeconomic levels, and rural residence. Certain religious groups, such as the Amish and Mormons, place a major value on children and tend to have large families. It is known that as families increase in size, the chances increase that some children will be unplanned and unwanted. And finally, an increased family size appears to have a negative effect on the level of health of its members. In a review of studies concerning the relationship between family size and factors relevant to health, Wray (1971) found no evidence of significant health benefits associated with large families. It is not family size per se, however, that creates health problems or family difficulties. Large families heighten the complexity of intragroup relations, pose problems in fulfilling family needs, and influence how much money and attention can be devoted to each child.

Divorce

Whenever two people interact, conflicts may arise and one person or both may want to end the relationship. This is true not only of marriage but of other relationships as well. Unlike most relationships, however, marriage involves civil, legal, or religious ties that specify if and how the relationship can end. In countries such as Spain, Brazil, and Peru, in conformity with the doctrine of the Roman Catholic church, marriage is indissoluble except by death. In Switzerland, the Scandinavian countries, the U.S.S.R., and Poland, a divorce is granted if it is shown that the marriage has failed. The laws of Islam and Judaism give a husband the power to terminate his marriage by simply renouncing his wife or wives. In this country most states, traditionally at least, grant a divorce if it is shown that one party has gravely violated his or her marital obligations. Since 1970, however, many states have moved to a no-fault divorce system in which marriages can be ended on the basis of "irreconcilable differences."

The United States has one of the highest divorce rates in the world. According to the United Nations, *Demographic Yearbook* (1983), the U.S. rate of divorce per 1,000 persons per year in 1981 was 5.3, compared with 3.5 in the U.S.S.R., 2.9 in Cuba and Germany, 2.4 in Sweden, 1.3 in Japan, 1.2 in Israel, 1.1 in Poland, 0.3 in Mexico, and 0.2 in Italy. This high divorce rate can be misleading. It means that only ten people get divorced per 1,000 population.

Why, then, do we so often hear that one marriage in two ends in divorce? Because the divorce rate is figured by dividing the number of divorces in a given year by the number of marriages in the same year. Thus if your state had fifty divorces and one hundred marriages in 1984, the divorce rate would be 50 percent. This is the rate used to illustrate the "breakdown in the American family." It does not, however, mean that half of all marriages end in divorce, any more than the finding that a given state had one hundred marriages and one hundred divorces in a certain year would mean that every marriage ended in divorce. There is, nevertheless, a great deal of concern about the frequency of divorce in the United States.

In 1982, there were approximately 1,180,000 divorces in this country, a rate of 5.1 divorces per 1,000 population, about half the rate of 10.8 marriages per 1,000 population. This figure decreased slightly from the 1981 figure of 1,219,000 and the rate of 5.3, the highest ever for the United States (see Figure 12-3).

Like marriage rates, divorce rates tend to decline in times of economic depression and rise during periods of prosperity. They also vary by geographic and social characteristics. Geographically, the general trend in the United States is for divorce rates to increase as one moves from east to west. Demographic figures show that approximately one-half of all divorces are among persons in their twenties, and the rate is exceptionally high among teenagers. Divorce is also most frequent in the first three years after marriage, and the incidence is higher among the lower socioeconomic levels. Whether education, occupation, or income is used as an index of socioeconomic level, the divorce rate goes up as the socioeconomic level goes down.

These variations in rate of divorce give us clues about its causes. The fact that rates are higher in the West indicates that divorce may be related to the liberality of the laws and the degree of cultural mixing. Financial problems and

Figure 12-3

Divorce rates in the United States: 1920–1980

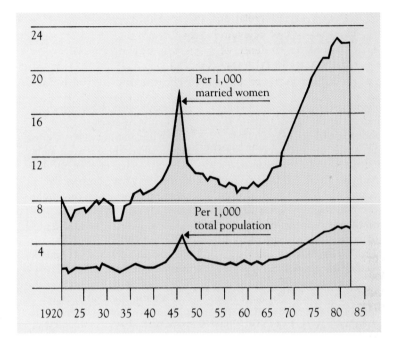

emotional immaturity may be factors in the high rates found among teenagers. Difficulties in adjusting to new relationships or discrepancies in role expectations may contribute to the divorce rates in the first three years after marriage. Money problems, lack of education, and working at a low-status job may account for the rates found in the lower socioeconomic levels. Although other factors are involved and some exceptions exist to these general patterns, divorce is not merely a result of personal characteristics. These variations illustrate how social and cultural factors can influence the chances that a marriage will end in divorce.

Nontraditional Marital and Family Lifestyles

In the United States today, many people are choosing alternatives to the traditional family. This family consisted of a husband, a wife, and two or more children. The husband was the authority and primary if not sole wage earner, while the wife was submissive to the husband and served as primary child caretaker and homemaker. But now the diversity of families in this country is greater than ever before, and changes are occurring rapidly. Consider the following statistics derived from 1982 census data (U.S. Bureau of the Census, 1983a and 1983b):

- More than 1.8 million unmarried couples were living together, more than triple the 523,000 in 1970.
- The median age of first marriage had advanced about two years since 1974, from 23.1 to 25.2 for men and 21.1 to 22.5 for women.
- More than one-half of all women and nearly three-fourths of all men aged 20 to 24 in 1982 had not yet married for the first time, as compared with 36 percent of the women and 55 percent of the men in 1970.

Working Families in Sweden and U.S.

The majority of mothers of children under the age of 6 are in the labor force in both the United States and Sweden, but it is more difficult for American women to combine careers and motherhood because of a lack of support from government and business. That was the message delivered to a conference of the Coalition of Labor Union Women and the Swedish Information Service.

Statistics presented at the conference showed that more than 60 percent of American mothers of children under 6 work outside the home. In Sweden, 80 percent do. Juggling a career with family responsibility is not easy in either country, experts from both nations said. Stress is high because of the need for child care, the high cost of raising children and emergencies such as a child's illness.

"Sweden leads the world in tackling these problems," said Dana Friedman, a senior research fellow of the Conference Board, a nonprofit business research center based in New York City. "It is

well established in Sweden that steps must be taken to foster family life, but not in the United States, where there is great ambivalence because most of our decision makers have no personal experience with child care problems."

Varied Representation

Mrs. Friedman made her remarks at the conference, called "The Working Family: Perspectives and Prospects in the United States and Sweden." It was attended by 75 representatives of universities, corporations and governmental agencies in the United States and Sweden, who convened for one day at the United Engineering Center, 345 East 47th Street.

Mrs. Friedman, who estimated that about 100 United States corporations offer child care services for employees, also cited several other reasons why the United States lags behind Sweden in helping dual career families:

Poor economic conditions in recent years have discouraged

United States workers from requesting the establishment of day-care centers, flexible work schedules and maternity leaves. "It is hard to raise the banner of motherhood when there is 11 percent unemployment," Mrs. Friedman said.

American managers are not trained to consider the positive effect of day-care centers on employee productivity.

Since the 1970s civil rights leaders have argued that an employee's sex, marital status, number of children and other factors should be disregarded in hiring, promotion and other personnel practices. Thus it is not easy now to persuade employers to start considering these factors in designing the work place.

Sweden has had a governmental policy to foster family life for working parents since 1968, according to Berit Rollen, under secretary of the Swedish Ministry of Labor.

"The policy states that the government wants to make it possible for both men and women to achieve economic independence and to maintain family life," she said. "The surprising thing is that the campaign for this policy has been conducted through trade

☐ More than one of every five children (22 percent) under 18 years old lived with just one parent, compared with one in nine (11.9 percent) in 1970. One in two (49.2 percent) black children lived with just one parent.

☐ The ratio of divorced to married persons

was higher for black women (265 per 1,000) than for any other race or sex group, as compared with 176 for black men, 155 for Spanish women, 79 for Spanish men, 128 for white women, and 86 for white men.

☐ The number of persons living alone in-

unions and through women's associations within the political parties because Sweden has not had a women's movement as vigorous as that of the U.S."

Soren Kindlund, secretary of the Commission of Children and Youth of the Swedish Ministry of Social Affairs, discussed the financial benefits Sweden offers the one million families who have two million children under 18 living at home. He said that Sweden adopted these incentives because of concern over the low birthrate. Financial incentives range from an annual living allowance for all children under 16 to a special housing allowance for poor children.

Sweden also grants parents a nine-month leave and the right to return to one's job after a child is born (the leave can be divided between the parents), up to 60 days' leave each year to care for a sick child, and extra leave for two weeks when a child enters school or a day-care center.

"Less than 25 percent of the fathers eligible for paternity leave for childbirth have taken advantage of it since 1983," said Mr. Kindlund, "but we think this will increase in the future as the idea of men taking time off to take care of children in the early months of life becomes more acceptable. About 200,000 fathers stayed at home to care for sick children during this period, almost as many as mothers."

Sweden also maintains an extensive system of state-supported child care, ranging from nurseries for 6-month-old babies to after-school programs for 12-year-olds.

One of the biggest differences between dual career families in the United States and Sweden is that Swedish parents have the right to a six-hour working day, instead of eight, with a cut in pay, until their children are 8 years old. A majority of Swedish women work part time when their children are young and then assume full-time jobs when their children enter school.

The higher the job status of Swedish women, the more likely they are to work full time when their children are young. When asked whether there was any correlation between part-time work and the fact that there are fewer Swedish women who are executives than American women, Miss Rollen said no. She said she thought the difference was that American women worked in a broader range of industries and thus had more opportunities.

Making Managers Aware

A common thread running through the conference was the belief in the importance of making managers, especially men, aware of family problems. Another participant, Ellen Galinsky, who is director of a project on work and family life at the Bank Street College of Education in New York, said that studies have shown that managers are more understanding of men who have family problems than they are of women.

"Managers are generally aware of the issues in only extreme cases," she said. "They don't realize the toll the everyday issues, such as picking up the kids from school, take on employees."

Most of the participants agreed with a representative of a United States governmental agency who said: "I wish that more than four men had attended this conference. After all, responsibility for raising the future generation is something that affects all of us, not just working mothers."

SOURCE: *The New York Times*, 25 May 1984. Copyright © 1984 by the New York Times Company. Reprinted by permission.

---

creased from 10.6 million in 1970 to 19.4 million in 1982.

□ The number of families below the poverty level in 1982 was 7.5 million, or 12.2 percent of all families. This figure includes 9.6 percent of white families, 33.0 percent of black families, and 27.2 percent of families of Spanish origin.

These figures illustrate a few of the dramatic shifts taking place in the lifestyle of American families. Four nontraditional approaches to family life are discussed in more detail below.

Nonmarital Heterosexual Cohabitation

As stated above, more than 1.5 million unmarried couples lived together in 1982, more than triple the number in 1970. *Nonmarital heterosexual cohabitation,* or living together, occurs when a man and a woman who are not married to each other occupy the same dwelling. Contrary to a widely held assumption, nonmarital heterosexual cohabitation is not just a college student phenomenon, nor is it confined to the generation under age twenty-five. In fact, close to one-third (29.3 percent) of all unmarried couples living together in 1982 were between twenty-five and thirty-four years old, and an additional 16 percent were forty-five and over. Of this latter group, 5.5 percent or 103,000 people were sixty-five years of age and over (U.S. Bureau of the Census, 1983a, p. 6).

Despite these findings, most research on cohabitation has involved college student populations. In a review of this research, Macklin (1983) found that nonmarried cohabitants are significantly less committed to each other than married couples. With regard to the division of labor, cohabiting couples tended to mirror the society around them and accept gender roles characteristic of other couples their age. The same was true for sexual exclusivity. Most believed in sexual freedom within their nonmarried relationship, but most voluntarily restrained their sexual activity with outsiders.

Nonmarital heterosexual cohabitation does not appear to be a substitute for marriage, a cure-all for marital problems, or a solution to the problem of frequent divorce. Most cohabitating relationships are short-term and last only a few months, but the longer couples cohabit, the more likely they are to eventually marry. Unmarried couples experience problems quite similar to those of married couples: concern over financial matters, the division of labor, and relationships with extended family members. In cohabiting couples, as in married couples, women do most of the housework. Although unmarried cohabitation does not fall within acceptable value limits for everyone, it does appear to have functional value for an increasing number of adults of all ages. For many couples, it provides a financially practical situation (two together can live more cheaply than two separately), a warm, homelike atmosphere, ready access to a sexual partner, an intimate interpersonal relationship, a nonlegal, nonbinding union, and a form of trial marriage.

Childless Marriage

Most unmarried couples are childless. Among these couples, a desire for children, a pregnancy, or the birth of a child often leads to marriage. But what of the legally married couples who have no children and desire none? In recent years, the subject of the voluntarily childless marriage as an acceptable marital lifestyle has gained increased attention for a number of reasons. First, it is inconsistent with myths about the existence of a maternal instinct, the notion that all women want to have, love, and care for a child or children. Second, it changes the functions of marriage and the family that deal with reproduction, nurturant socialization, and social placement. Third, the availability and reliability of contraceptives and abortion make it possible for women and couples to have no children if they so choose.

Census data show that in 1982, 7.6 percent of all married or previously married women aged forty to forty-four were childless (*Statistical Abstract: 1984,* no. 93). This figure increases to 27.5 percent among twenty-five to twenty-nine-year-old married women, 42.9 among those twenty to twenty-four, and 52.8 among those fifteen to nineteen years of age. These younger age groups had not completed their childbearing years, however, and most expected to have children at some time in their lives. Approximately 11 percent of all women aged eighteen to thirty-four

did not expect to have any children in their lifetime. This figure was highest (19.5 percent) for women with five or more years of college and lowest (7 percent) for women who were not high school graduates (U.S. Bureau of the Census, 1983a, p. 26).

Veevers (1975) conducted in-depth interviews with childless wives living with their husbands and found that they held a number of unusual beliefs about parenting. Most of these women were married to husbands who agreed that children were not desirable. The wives defined parenthood in negative rather than positive terms and denied the existence of a maternal instinct. They dismissed the accusation that childlessness was abnormal. Pregnancy and childbirth were perceived to be at best unpleasant and at worst difficult and dangerous. They regarded child care as excessively burdensome and unrewarding and as having a deleterious effect on a woman's life chances. Finally, they defined parenthood as a trap that interfered with personal happiness.

The child-free alternative may be an acceptable family form and lifestyle for a small proportion of families (6 to 8 percent). Under certain conditions, as in the dual-career marriages discussed later, childlessness may be conducive to both personal and marital satisfaction and adjustment.

One-Parent Families

One-parent families are those in which the mother or more commonly the father does not share the household with the children and the remaining parent. As shown in Table 12-2, 80.8 percent of white and 42.4 percent of black children under age eighteen were living with both parents in 1982. In the traditional view, this is the way families "should be," the most appropriate family structure for the socialization of children. However, 15 percent of white children and 47 percent of black children were living with the mother only, an additional 2 percent of all

children were living with the father only, and another 2 percent of white children and more than 8 percent of black children were living with neither parent. As the table shows, the percentage of fatherless families has increased considerably since 1970 (8 to 15 percent for whites and 29 to 47 percent for blacks).

These figures are rendered more dramatic by the fact that more than one-third (36.3 percent) of all fatherless families were below the poverty level (U.S. Bureau of the Census, 1983e, p. 19). This group included 27.9 percent of whites, 56.2 percent of blacks, and 55.4 percent of Spanish origin. The families below the poverty level — particularly one-parent families — are those that receive Medicare, school lunches, food stamps, and live in subsidized housing. These are the families affected most harshly by middle-class efforts to cut welfare, religious group efforts to forbid abortion, and government policies that demand "workfare." Members of such families often have disproportionate school drop-out rates, few skills, high unemployment rates, irregular incomes, little dental or health care, and little control over their own fate.

In a cross-cultural study, Bilge and Kaufman (1983) contend that one-parent families are neither pathological nor inferior. Stigmatizing them in this way, they claim, is a refusal to recognize the economic inequalities of our society. They say that in combination with an extended network of concerned kin (grandparents, siblings, uncles, aunts, etc.) single-parent families can offer emotional support and that they are a suitable alternative to the traditional family. Bilge and Kaufman also note that around the world, one-parent female-headed families are able to bring up children and provide emotional support.

What happens to children in female-headed families? Cashion (1982) reviewed the social-psychological research pertaining to female-headed families published between 1970 and 1980. She concluded that children in these families are

Table 12-2
Children under eighteen years old, by presence of parents and whether living with mother only, by marital status of mother, for the United States, 1970, and 1982. (Percentages, except for all persons under age eighteen.)

PRESENCE OF PARENTS AND MARITAL STATUS OF MOTHER	1970 WHITE	1970 BLACK	1982 WHITE	1982 BLACK
All persons under age 18				
Thousands	59,026	9,483	51,086	9,377
Percent	100.0	100.0	100.0	100.0
Living with both parents	89.2	58.1	80.8	42.4
Living with mother only	7.8	29.3	15.3	47.2
Married (spouse absent)	2.8	16.2	4.3	13.6
Widowed	1.7	4.2	1.5	3.3
Divorced	3.1	4.6	8.0	9.6
Single (never married)	0.2	4.4	1.6	20.8
Living with father only	0.9	2.2	1.9	2.0
Living with neither parent	2.2	10.3	2.0	8.4

SOURCE: U.S. Bureau of the Census, *Current Population Reports*, Series P-20, no. 380, "Marital Status and Living Arrangements: March 1982," U.S. Government Printing Office, Washington, D.C., 1983, Table E, p. 5.

likely to have good emotional adjustment, good self-esteem except when they are stigmatized, intellectual development comparable to others in the same socioeconomic status, and also rates of juvenile delinquency comparable to other children of the same socioeconomic standing. The major problems in these families stem from poverty and stigmatization. Poverty is associated with problems in school and juvenile delinquency. It also contributes to poor attitudes among mothers about their situations and impairs a mother's sense of being in control. Stigmatization is associated with low self-esteem in children. It results in defining children as problems even when they don't have problems. Cashion's general conclusion is that the majority of female-headed families, when not plagued by poverty, have children who are as successful and well adjusted as those of two-parent families.

Dual-Career Marriages

One of the important social changes since World War II has been the increase of women in the labor force. In 1940, despite a sharp increase in the number of working wives during the depression of the 1930s, only 15 percent of all married women living with their husbands held an outside job. By 1960, the proportion had risen to 32 percent and by 1982 to 52 percent. Today, more than half of all married women aged thirty-five years or younger hold jobs.

Women who have children are less likely to hold jobs than those who do not, although with each decade, the presence of children decreases in importance as a factor in whether women are employed. The proportion of married women in the labor force is highest among those who have no small children to take care of at home.

Among these women under age thirty-five, 80 percent hold jobs. Even among the women who have one or more children under the age of six, 40 percent are employed. Most of these employed women are in clerical or service work with earnings well below those of their male counterparts. Arrangements of this type are called dual-employed marriages. (It is assumed, sometimes incorrectly, that the husband is also employed.)

Although women have been taking jobs in increasing numbers, the "dual-career" marriage is a relatively recent development. The word "career" is used to designate jobs taken, not primarily to produce additional income, but for the satisfaction involved. Careers typically involve a higher level of commitment than "paid employment," and they progress through a developmental sequence of increasing responsibility. One study (Burke and Weir, 1976) of one- and two-career families found that women in two-career families reported fewer pressures and worries, more communication with husbands, more happiness with their marriages, and better physical and mental health. In contrast, the men in the two-career families were in poorer health and less content with marriage, work, and life in general. It seems that the husband of a career wife loses part of his support system when his wife no longer functions as a servant, homemaker, and mother. Wives who have careers, on the other hand, are able to expand into roles that have a more positive value for them.

Most studies of dual-career marriages suggest that they involve certain strains. One of these strains, particularly for women, is brought on by what Fox and Nichols (1983) call a "time crunch." Wives are often expected to perform the majority of household tasks whether they have careers outside the home or not. In addition, wives usually accommodate more to the husband's career than vice versa, and husbands and wives have differential gains and losses when both have a career. Although the professional

Dual-career marriages have received growing attention over the past decade. In the United States, day care for infants and young children is an issue of major financial and social concern for both unmarried working mothers and dual-career couples. Although a couple may perceive equality as an ideal, when a husband in a dual-career marriage gets a job transfer, the wife frequently is expected to give up her job and resume primary responsibility for housework and childcare.

employment of women is gaining increasing acceptance, sexual equality in marriage has not yet been achieved. Wives are generally expected to give up their own jobs for the sake of their husbands and to consider their families their first duty.

Summary

The family serves a number of different purposes. It is the primary social group, a system of interdependent statuses and structures, and a social institution organized to meet certain essential societal goals. The smallest family units, the

SOCIOLOGISTS AT WORK
Family Counseling

Marie Witkin Kargman is a family disputes mediator in Boston. In addition, she practices marriage counseling, divorce counseling, and family counseling. She brings unique qualifications to this work: She is both a lawyer and a sociologist.

How do these different backgrounds and trainings fit together in her work? Kargman tells of a realization that she came to early in her career. "Before I trained in sociology at graduate school (Department of Social Relations, Harvard University), I was a practicing lawyer in the juvenile and family courts of Chicago. I discovered that the law is in a very real sense applied sociology: It deals with institutionalized patterns of behavior legitimized by the legal system, and with the sanctions applied when people deviate. I felt I needed to know more about the family, its structure, and its functions to be a better lawyer. Most lawyers rearrange the family, writing divorce and separation agreements that create new family structures, without knowing much about the sociology of the family. I was not comfortable rearranging family relationships when I knew so little about the theory in the field. But by the time I got my sociology degree I knew that I wanted to be a marriage counselor who worked with lawyers, helping them do a better job."

She explains how she is able to apply the sociological theory she has learned: "In my family disputes mediation, and particularly in child custody disputes, I am apt to say to the divorced parents who have a child custody problem, 'What we are trying to do here is to get two parents and their children to come together to carry out family functions without the foundation of living in a joint household. Each household is a family group with a political system, an economic system, and a kinship system. The child must now

nuclear and conjugal families, consist of persons related by blood, marriage, or adoption who share a common residence. Sociologists also distinguish families of orientation, families of procreation, extended families, and modified-extended families.

Families throughout the world vary in many different ways. First, they may vary in number of spouses. A person may have one spouse (monogamy) or two or more (polygamy). In group marriages, there are several people of each sex. Sequential monogamy involves having several wives or husbands in succession but just one at any given time. Polygyny, in which one man is married to more than one woman, is the most common form of polygamy; polyandry, in which one woman has several husbands, is very rare.

Second, families vary in their norms of residence. Most cultures adhere to one of three patterns: neolocal, in which the couple is free to choose its own place of residence; patrilocal, in which the couple lives in the groom's community; and matrilocal, in which the couple lives in the bride's community. Worldwide, the patrilocal pattern is the most common.

Third, families have different norms of descent and inheritance. The patrilineal pattern, in which lineage is traced through the father's kin, is the most common, but there are also matrilineal and bilateral patterns.

Fourth, there are variations in the norms of authority and decision making. Sociologists rec-

live in two households, juggle two different sets of systems, integrate them, or deal with them as unrelated parts of his or her life.' We then look at the similarities of expectation of the child's two separate households, and try to decide what is in the best interests of the child."

Marie Kargman offers the following example of a case where she has relied on her sociological training. "The judge in a child custody dispute appointed me guardian ad litem." (*Ad litem* is Latin for, "for the course of the suit." The mother and the father could arrange for their own representation and choose their own lawyers; it was Kargman's job to see that the third party in the dispute — the child — was fairly represented.) "When I read the record, I discovered that two different psychiatrists and one social worker had been appointed guardians ad litem before me. When I asked the judge why he appointed me, all he said was, 'Please come up with a decision!' In this particular case, the mother had asked the court for permission to take the child out of Massachusetts. She had remarried in Massachusetts, and there were two children by the

second marriage. The mother and stepfather wanted to relocate to the Midwest, where both had good job offers. After a delay of one year, the judge permitted the mother to move. Her husband had gone ahead, and she stayed behind with the children, fighting the court battle. Now the question of reasonable visitation was in dispute.

"Before I got into the dispute, the only persons discussed by the lawyers were the natural father, the natural mother, and the child. That the child was part of many different family relationships was never discussed. From a legal point of view the family before the court was the original family of procreation. But this child was a member of his original family and an additional two families, the step-family and the family of his half-sisters. The child wanted to spend holidays with 'his family' and the natural father wanted the holidays on a strict two-parent division. All of the child's social systems were described in my report to the judge, whose decision was made based on the child's multifamily expectations."

ognize systems of three types: patriarchal, matriarchal, and egalitarian. The patriarchal pattern of male dominance, power, and authority is the most widespread.

Fifth, norms vary with regard to the marriage partner considered appropriate. Endogamous rules state that a marriage partner should be from a similar group. Exogamous rules state that marriage partners should be from a different group. Incest and same-sex marriages are almost universally forbidden, whereas marriage to a person of the same race, religion, and socioeconomic status is widely encouraged.

Several theoretical perspectives are widely used to explain family structures, interaction patterns, and behaviors. Functionalists examine

variations in family structures such as those just described in terms of the functions they perform. According to this perspective, the family has many major functions: socialization, affection and emotional support, sexual regulation, reproduction, and social placement. Socialization, especially of young infants, is one of the few universal family functions. Affection and emotional support from families are important not just for infants and children but for adults as well. In its capacity as a sexual regulator the family defines socially approved and disapproved sexual outlets while its reproductive function assures that children will be born and raised in a context in which their needs will be met. Finally, the social placement function helps family members make the transition from the family to the wider society.

According to the conflict perspective, family members continually struggle for power and control. Conflict, which stems from the unequal distribution of scarce resources, is a major force behind social change. The exchange perspective assumes that there are rewards and costs in all relationships, including those in marriage and the family. This view suggests that when selecting a spouse, people try to get the best they can with what they have to offer. The complementary needs theory proposes that people seek mates who will meet their needs without causing conflicts. The interactionist perspective emphasizes the influence of role expectations and how people define situations. In this view, marriage, like other relationships, is a dynamic process of reciprocal interactions. The developmental perspective focuses on the time dimension. Change is analyzed in terms of the family life cycle, a series of stages that families go through from their inception at marriage through their dissolution by death or divorce.

The American family system emphasizes norms of monogamy, neolocal residence, modified-extended kinship, bilateral descent and inheritance, egalitarian decision making, endogamous marriage, and relatively free choice of mate. In a number of respects, however, the American family is quite variable. Rates of marriage vary widely in terms of time period, geographical location, economic conditions, and other factors. The number of marriages also vary by season and day of the week. The age at marriage in the United States, which declined from the turn of the century until the mid-1950s, has since increased, and teenage marriages are unlikely to last. Norms concerning family size and parent-child relations are influenced by such variables as socioeconomic status, religion, education, urbanization, and female participation in the labor force. Although most married couples have or want to have children, younger women today generally plan to have small families compared with earlier generations. The United States has one of the highest divorce rates in the world. Like birth rates, rates of divorce vary with time period, geographical location, and socioeconomic level, and differing techniques of computing the divorce rate yield different figures about the rate of divorce. Variations in these rates illustrate how social and cultural factors influence the chances of marital dissolution.

Many marital and family lifestyles exist today that don't conform to the traditional model of two parents, two or more children, with the husband and wife performing fixed roles. For example, the number of unmarried couples of all ages who live together is increasing dramatically. Childless marriages are increasingly common, in part because of the availability and reliability of contraceptives and abortion. The number of one-parent families is increasing sharply, and many of these families are below the poverty level. Marriages in which both spouses work have been common for a long time, but the dual-career marriage is a relatively recent development. There are many strains in these marriages, but women who have careers report fewer life pressures and worries and more happiness in their marriages. The men involved in two-career marriages tend to be relatively discontent, however.

Key Terms

bilateral
conjugal families
egalitarian
endogamy
exogamy
extended family
family
family life cycle
family of orientation
family of procreation
group marriage

incest
kinship
matriarchal
matrilineal
matrilocal
modified-extended family structure
monogamy
neolocal
nuclear families
patriarchal
patrilineal
patrilocal
polyandry
polygamy
polygyny
principle of legitimacy
serial or sequential monogamy

Suggested Readings

Burr, Wesley R., Reuben Hill, Ivan F. Nye, and Ira L. Reiss. **Contemporary Theories About the Family, vols. I and II.** *New York: The Free Press, 1979.* A two-volume work that attempts to systematically develop interrelated propositions on a wide variety of family topics. Volume II has chapters dealing with exchange theory, symbolic interaction theory, general systems theory, conflict theory, and phenomenological approaches to the family.

Caplow, Theodore, Howard M. Bahr, Bruce A. Chadwick, Reuben Hill, and Margaret Holmes Williamson. **Middletown Families: Fifty Years of Change and Continuity.** *New York: Bantam Books, 1982.* A team of sociologists returns to "Middletown" (Muncie, Indiana), the community investigated in two classic studies by Robert and Helen Lynd in 1929 and 1937, and examine changes that have taken place in family life since the original studies.

Eshleman, J. Ross. **The Family: An Introduc-**tion, **4th ed.** *Boston: Allyn & Bacon, 1985.* A sociological examination of families in the United States and around the world, this book discusses changes in the family, structural and subcultural variations, patterns of interaction throughout the life cycle, marital crises, and divorce.

Goode, William J. **The Family, 2d ed.** *Englewood Cliffs, N.J.: Prentice-Hall, 1982.* A brief but intense sociological examination of the family system and its relationship to the larger social structure.

Macklin, Eleanor D. and Roger H. Rubin. **Contemporary Families and Alternative Lifestyles.** *Beverly Hills, Calif.: Sage Publications, 1983.* A collection of articles covering a wide range of nontraditional family life-styles, including childlessness, stepfamilies, and commuter marriages.

Mindle, Charles H. and Robert W. Habenstein. **Ethnic Families in America: Patterns and Variations, 2d ed.** *New York: Elsevier, 1981.* An excellent overview of the family lifestyles of sixteen ethnic minorities in America.

Scanzoni, John. **Sexual Bargaining: Power Politics in the American Marriage, 2d ed.** *Chicago: University of Chicago Press, 1982.* Sexual bargaining, an exchange approach, deals with motivations to marry, marital conflict as a positive force, and marital change.

Skolnick, Arlene S. and Jerome H. Skolnick (eds.). **Families in Transition, 4th ed.** *Boston: Little, Brown and Company, 1983.* A popular collection of readings dealing with the changing family, gender and sex, couples, parents and children, and other issues.

Straus, Murray A., Richard J. Gelles, and Suzanne K. Steinmetz. **Behind Closed Doors: Violence in the American Family.** *New York: Anchor Books, 1980.* A report on the extent and meaning of violence in 2,143 families in the United States.

Willie, Charles V. **A New Look at Black Families, 2d ed.** *Bayside, N.Y.: General Hall, 1981.* The stories of eighteen black families, combining a descriptive analysis and a theoretical explanation of behavior patterns.

CHAPTER 13

Religious Groups and Systems

Religion is a candle inside a multicolored lantern. Everyone looks through a particular color, but the candle is always there.

— Mohammed Naguib

Young American students of college age have a bewildering array of belief systems and religious groups to choose from. James takes a class in Tai Chi offered by the local Tai Chi club. His roommate, Sara, takes yoga classes at the local branch of the Sikhs. A friend of theirs seldom makes a decision without consulting the I Ching. Another can never attend Friday night ball games because that is when her prayer group meets. James and Sara themselves decided in high school to join a commune rather than attend college. The members of the commune rise at 3 A.M. every morning and meditate for two hours before going to work in the vegetarian restaurant they run.

Throughout the world, people meditate, pray, join communes, worry about "being saved," partake in rituals, bow to statues, burn incense, chant, offer sacrifices, torture themselves, and proclaim their allegiance to many gods or to a particular god. Anthropologists suggest that events, acts, and beliefs such as these are part of every society, both today and throughout history. Together, these behaviors comprise a society's religious system.

Religion has always been the anchor of identity for human beings. Religious beliefs give meaning to life, and the experiences associated with them provide personal gratification as well as a release from the frustrations and anxieties of daily life. Ceremonies, formal acts, or rituals are essential for both personal identity and social cohesion. We have ceremonies to rejoice about the birth of an infant, to initiate a young person into adult society, to celebrate a new marriage, to bury the dead, and to fortify our belief that life goes on. Most of these ceremonies are linked to religion.

It may make you uneasy to examine these events and rituals objectively, but the goal of sociological investigations of religion is not to criticize anyone's faith or compare the validity of different religions. Sociologists are interested, rather, in studying how religion is organized and how it affects the members of a given society. They study how people organize in groups around religious beliefs and how these belief systems affect their behavior in other areas such as family life and economic achievement. Sociologists also examine the kinds of belief systems developed by people in different circumstances and how religious beliefs change over time as external circumstances change.

A Sociological Approach to Religion

What Is Religion?

One of the earliest writers on the sociology of religion was the French sociologist, Emile Durkheim. In *The Elementary Forms of the Religious Life* (1926) Durkheim defined religion as "a unified system of beliefs and practices relative to sacred things, that is to say, things set apart and forbidden — beliefs and practices which unite into one single moral community called a Church, all those who adhere to them" (p. 47).

In this definition, Durkheim identified several elements that he believed to be common to all religions. The first element, a system of beliefs and practices, he saw as the cultural component of religion. The beliefs are states of opinion and the practices, which Durkheim termed rites, are modes of action. These beliefs and practices exist within a social context, consistent with the values and norms of the culture.

The second element, a community or church, he saw as the social organizational component. A church in this sense is not a building or even a local group that gathers together to worship. Rather it is a collective of persons who share similar beliefs and practices. He claimed that in all history, we do not find a single religion without a community of believers. Sometimes this community is strictly national, sometimes it is directed by a corps of priests, and sometimes it lacks any official directing body, but it always has a definite group at its foundation. Even the so-called cults satisfy this condition, for they are always celebrated by a group, the family, or a corporation. What the community does is translate the beliefs and practices into something shared, which led Durkheim to think of these first two elements — the cultural and social components of religion — as being linked. Contemporary sociologists of religion do recognize a functional difference between the two, in that a person may accept a set of religious beliefs without being affiliated with a particular church.

The third element, sacred things, he saw as existing only in relation to the profane. The *profane* is the realm of the everyday world: food, clothes, work, play, or anything generally considered mundane and unspiritual. In contrast, the *sacred* consists of objects or ideas that are treated with reverence and awe: an altar, bible, prayer, or rosary is sacred. A hamburger, rock song, football, or sociology text is profane. However, Durkheim believed that anything could become sacred. Sacredness is not a property inherent in an object. It exists in the mind of the beholder. Thus a tree, a spring, a pebble, a piece of wood, or a house may be considered sacred.

Durkheim hypothesized that religion developed out of group experiences as primitive tribes came to believe that feelings about sacredness were derived from some supernatural power. As people perform certain rituals, they develop feelings of awe, which reinforce the moral norms of society. When they no longer feel in awe of moral norms, society is in a state of anomie or normlessness. Informal social control is possible largely because people have strong feelings that they should or should not do certain things. When they no longer have such feelings, social control breaks down. We see an example of this in some of our cities, where church doors are locked to prevent robberies. In many societies, nobody steals from churches because they believe they will be punished or suffer some form of retribution.

Other sociologists present somewhat different views of religion, but most would agree that a *religion* has the following elements:

1. *Things considered sacred* such as gods, spirits, special persons, or any object or thought defined as sacred.

2. A *group or community of believers* who make religion a social as well as a personal experience, since members of a religion share goals, norms, and beliefs.

3. A *set of rituals, ceremonies, or behaviors* that take on religious meaning when they express a relationship to the sacred. In Christian ceremo-

Religious practices and beliefs take many forms. Here, members of a cargo cult in the South Pacific worship a cross in the belief that it will bring a return of the ancestors and give members access to the material goods of Western civilization. Cargo cults are so named because their adherents believe that European goods or cargo are made by their ancestors, but intercepted by Europeans for their own selfish purposes. In the future the Europeans will be destroyed, the ancestors will return, and the cargo will arrive. To prepare for this cargo, some cults build docks, runways, and warehouses.

nies, for example, wine is considered a sacred symbol of the blood of Christ.

4. A *set of beliefs* such as a creed, doctrine, or holy book. These beliefs may define what is to be emphasized, how people should relate to society, or what life after death is like.

5. A *form of organization* that reinforces the sacred, unites the community of believers, carries out the rituals, teaches the creeds and doctrines, recruits new members, and so on.

The Organization of Religion

People have tried to understand the world around them throughout history, but we do not know exactly how or why they began to believe in supernatural beings or powers. Societies such as the Tasaday of the Philippines or the Bushmen of Africa, who rely on hunting and gathering as their primary means of subsistence, often explain things in naturalistic terms. This type of religion is known as *animism,* which is the belief that spirits inhabit virtually everything in nature: rocks, trees, lakes, animals, and humans alike, and that these spirits influence all aspects of life and destiny. Sometimes they help, perhaps causing an arrow to strike and kill a wild pig for food. At other times, they are harmful, as when they make a child get sick and die. These spirits can sometimes be influenced by specific rituals or behaviors, however, and pleasing them results in favorable treatment.

Some tribal societies practice a form of religion known as *shamanism,* which revolves around the belief that certain individuals, called shamans, have special skill or knowledge in influencing spirits. Shamans, most of whom are men, are called upon to heal the sick and wounded, to make hunting expeditions successful, to protect the group against evil spirits, and to generally ensure the group's well-being. Shamans receive their power through ecstatic experiences, which might originate from a psychotic

episode, the use of a hallucinogen, or deprivation such as fasting or lack of sleep. The American Indians of the northwestern United States hold that ancestral spirits work for the good or ill of the tribe solely through shamans.

A third form of religion among primitive peoples is totemism. *Totemism* is the worship of plants, animals, and other natural objects both as gods and ancestors. The totem itself is the plant or animal believed to be ancestrally related to a person, tribe, or clan. Totems usually represent something important to the community such as a food source or dangerous predator, and the people often wear costumes and perform dances to mimic the totem object. Most readers are probably familiar with the totem pole used by North American Indians. This tall post, carved or painted with totemic symbols, was erected as a memorial to the dead. Totemism is still practiced today by some New Guinea tribes and by Australian aborigines. Durkheim believed that totemism was one of the earliest forms of religion and that other forms of religious organization evolved from it.

Religions may be organized in terms of the number of gods their adherents worship. *Polytheism* is the belief in and worship of more than one god. Hinduism, which is practiced mainly in India, has a special god for each village and caste. People believe that these gods have special powers or control a significant life event such as harvest or childbirth. *Monotheism,* on the other hand, is the belief in only one god. Monotheism is familiar to most Americans because the three major religious groups in this country, Protestants, Catholics, and Jews, all believe in one god.

Most Westerners are less familiar with such major religions as Buddhism, Confucianism, Shintoism, and Taoism. These religions are neither monotheistic nor polytheistic, because they do not involve a god figure. They are based, rather, on sets of moral, ethical, or philosophical principles. Most are dedicated to achieving some

Religion is believed to be a cultural universal, yet it is extremely diverse in beliefs and behaviors. Among the Libinza Tribe in Zaire, Africa, for example, medicine men are believed to have special powers and abilities to influence the spirits. Particularly during times of a sickness within the tribe, they are called upon to use their charm and skill in warding off evil spirits or pleasing the good ones. This is often done through chants, dances, and a variety of rituals that serve both the sick persons and the entire family, group, or tribe.

form of moral or spiritual excellence. Some groups, such as the Confucianists, have no priesthood. Shintoism and Confucianism both place heavy emphasis on honoring one's ancestors, particularly one's parents, who gave the greatest of all gifts, life itself.

Churches, Sects, and Cults

Religious systems differ in many ways, and sociologists have devised numerous ways for classifying them. We have already seen how Durkheim divided the world into the sacred and the profane. We have noted how the religious practices of hunting and tribal societies were described in terms of animism, shamanism, and totemism. But can Christianity be understood in terms of the profane or of shamanism? Most contemporary religious scholars think not. Thus, another scheme of classification is used, that of churches, sects, and cults. This scheme focuses

directly on the relationship between the type of religious organization and the world surrounding it.

Max Weber (1905) was one of the first sociologists to clarify the interrelationships between people's beliefs and their surroundings. In his classic essay, *The Protestant Ethic and the Spirit of Capitalism*, he argued that capitalism would not have been possible without Protestantism because Protestantism stressed the importance of work as an end in itself, personal frugality, and worldly success as a means of earning salvation and as evidence of God's favor. In dealing with this relationship between religion and the economy, he identified two major types of religious leaders. One, the *priest*, owes authority to the power of the office. By contrast, the *prophet* holds authority on the basis of charismatic qualities. Priestly and prophetic leaders are often in conflict, for the priest defends and represents the institution or society in question and supports the status quo. The prophet, not bound to a given institution, is more likely to criticize both the institutions and the general society.

This contrast led Weber to suggest that different sectors of society would develop different types of organizations to accompany their different belief systems. The ruling class or leaders, the better educated, and the more wealthy would need a more formalized type of religion that accepts modern science and the existing social world. The laboring class, the less educated, and the poor would need a type of religion that em-

phasizes another world or life and an emotional, spontaneous experience to console them for the deprivation in this life.

A German theologian and student of Weber, Ernst Troeltsch (1931), continued this line of thinking. Troeltsch divided religions into three categories: mysticism, churches, and sects. *Mysticism* is the belief that spiritual or divine truths come to us through intuition and meditation, not through the use of reason or the ordinary range of human experience and senses. Mystics, persons who believe in mysticism, are outside organized religion. They often pose

Different religious organizations and symbolisms evolve to accommodate different belief systems. Many Protestant churches tend to minimize the formality of services, the extent of ritualistic behavior, and the presence of religious symbolism in dress and church objects. Other groups, such as the Russian Orthodox Church, have a highly formal bureaucratic organization and elaborate religious garb, ceremonies, and artifacts.

problems for other religious groups because they purport to be in direct contact with divine power.

The church and the sect are differentiated by their relationships with the world around them. A *church* is an institutionalized organization of people who share common religious beliefs. The membership of churches is fairly stable. Most have formal bureaucratic structures with trained clergy and other officials, and they are closely linked to the larger society and seek to work within it. The majority of the religious organizations in the United States would be considered churches. The Roman Catholic church is the largest religious group in the United States with 50.4 million members as of 1980. More than half of all church members in this country are Protestants, however. Protestants belong to such churches as the National and Southern Baptist conventions, the Assemblies of God, the United Methodist church, and the Lutheran church, to mention just a few. The Church of Jesus Christ of Latter-Day Saints (Mormons) with 2.81 million members, the Greek Orthodox church with 1.95 million members, and the Jewish congregations with 5.92 million members are the largest non-Protestant churches.

Two categories of churches that are sometimes differentiated are the ecclesia and the denomination. An *ecclesia* is an official state religion that includes all or most of the members of society. As a state church, it accepts state support and sanctions the basic cultural values and norms of the society. Sometimes it administers the educational system as well. The Church of England in Great Britain and the Lutheran churches in the Scandinavian countries are two contemporary examples of national churches. The power of these churches, however, is not as great as the power of the Roman Catholic church in Western Europe in the Middle Ages and today in Spain, Italy, and many Latin-American countries.

Churches in the United States are termed *denominations*. They are not officially linked to state or national governments. In fact, various denominations may be at odds with state positions on war, abortion, taxes, pornography, alcohol, equal rights, and other issues, and no nation has more denominations than the United States. The U.S. Bureau of the Census lists approximately eighty-five denominations with memberships of 50,000 or more (*Statistical Abstract:* 1984, no. 79), but the list would be considerably longer if all of the small or independent denominations were added.

Whereas churches (ecclesia and denominations) are well established and highly institutionalized, *sects* are small groups that have broken away from a parent church and call for a return to the old ways. They follow rigid doctrines and emphasize fundamentalist teachings. Fundamentalism is the belief that the Bible is the divine word of God and all statements in it are to be taken literally. The creation controversy, for example, stems from the fundamentalist position that the world was literally created in six days. Sect groups follow this type of literal interpretation of the Bible, although different groups focus their attention on different scriptures. Their religious services often involve extensive member participation with an emphasis on emotional expression. The clergy of sects, who frequently preach part time, often have little professional training and no seminary degrees. Members of sects tend to emphasize "otherworldly" rewards and are more likely to be of lower occupational and educational status than members of churches. Most of them are dissatisfied with their position in life and believe the world is evil and sinful. As a result, their degree of commitment to the sect is often far greater than the commitment found among church members. Unwilling to compromise their beliefs, they are often in conflict with the government, the schools, and other social institutions. Al-

When Prophecy Fails: Cult Behavior

During the week before Christmas, 1954, in a midwestern college town, a small band of students were waiting for a flying saucer to pick them up and take them to the planet Clarion, on the other side of the moon, where they would be safe from an anticipated cataclysm on earth.

Originating as a study group of students interested in flying saucers, the cult met every Sunday evening under the leadership of a physician, Dr. Armstrong, who was employed by the university health service. After six months of meeting, the belief system developed by this group became increasingly exotic, borrowing heav-ily from the belief system of the so-called "flying saucer cult." These people believe that flying saucers or UFOs from outer space visit earth and that some humans have gone for rides in a flying saucer.

Early in the fall of 1954, Dr. Armstrong met a woman named Mrs. Keech at a convention on flying saucers. Mrs. Keech was a medium who believed she could conduct power from a higher plane. During that fall, the Arm-strongs visited Mrs. Keech in her home in Chicago, and she visited the Armstrongs in Collegeville. Messages written by Mrs. Keech were studied at the Sunday eve-ning prayer meetings. One message said that Jesus had lived on earth in many incarnations, and that one of his names was Sananda. The study group believed that Sananda had visited them one Sunday afternoon in the form of a hummingbird hovering near the patio of the Armstrongs' house. By this time, the more skeptical members had stopped attending the study group, and only the most devout believers re-mained.

In October, Mrs. Keech began receiving messages about an impending cataclysm. It was pre-dicted that Atlantis would rise from the floor of the Atlantic, and Mu from the Pacific, thereby flooding the continent of North America. She also wrote that the faithful would be transported by flying saucer to Clarion for lead-ership training. The night before the cataclysm, this "mother ship" would hover over the earth while

though most sects are short-lived, some acquire a stable membership and a formal organizational structure and gradually become denominations. There are many sects in the United States today, including the Jehovah's Witnesses, Jews for Jesus, and a number of fundamentalist, evangelical, and Pentecostal groups. While evangelical groups, like fundamentalist groups, maintain that the Bible is the only rule of faith, they focus their attention on preaching that salvation comes through faith as described in the four New Testament Gospels: Matthew, Mark, Luke, and John. Pentecostal groups, though usually both evangelical and fundamentalist, are Chris-tian sects with a highly emotional form of wor-ship experience.

Another form of religious organization is the *cult*, the most loosely organized and most temporary of all religious groups. Unlike sects, cults call for a totally new and unique lifestyle, often under the direction of a charismatic leader. Jim Jones and Father Divine, for example, be-lieved that they were divinely chosen to lead hu-manity, as does the Reverend Sun Myung Moon today. In cults, the emphasis is on the individual rather than society. Because cults operate outside the mainstream of society and are focused around one leader or prophet, their existence depends on the life and health of their leader. In some cases, they have given up their more radi-cal teachings and, accepting more mainstream beliefs, have become churches. The Seventh-

little "peapod saucers" would pick up the believers. After the flooding and physical devastation had subsided following the cataclysm, the faithful would be returned to earth to repopulate it.

On the night of the expected cataclysm, Dr. and Mrs. Armstrong and their older daughter drove to Chicago with several student group members to join Mrs. Keech and her group there. The peapod saucer was due to arrive at midnight. Midnight came and went, but no peapod saucer arrived. The group waited as minute after minute, then hour after hour passed. At long last, at 4 A.M., Mrs. Keech received a message. The cataclysm had been averted. God, in his infinite mercy, had spared the earth because the group had met and prayed.

As a consequence of the nationwide publicity about the end of the world, Dr. Armstrong was asked to resign his job with the university. He moved to Arizona, followed by some members of the faithful. Three years later they emigrated to Peru, where they proposed to found a model farm.

The cult that formed around Mrs. Keech and her beliefs was studied by some social psychologists who joined the group as participant observers. The social psychologists were testing the hypothesis that cults and sects grow as a consequence of failed prophecy. Many cults and sects are built around a belief system which includes a prophecy that the world is coming to an end; such groups are called messianic or millenarian movements. The researchers wondered what happens to these groups when the prophecied end of the world never comes.

Research into cults shows that the prophet develops a rationalization about why the world did not end. Sometimes he or she changes the date. Eventually, the group develops a new belief system. To reinforce their belief in this new system, cult members become evangelical and go forth to convert others to the new belief: if others can be persuaded to believe, the belief must have some truth in it.

Another example of this phenomenon is the Unification Church of Rev. Sun Myung Moon. This group was studied in the early 1960s when it contained forty-five members who believed that the world would end in 1969. After this prophecy failed, and perhaps because it failed, the group grew by the thousands.

SOURCE: Leon Festinger, Stanley Schachter, and Henry W. Reicken, *When Prophecy Fails: A Social and Psychological Study of a Modern Group that Predicted the Destruction of the World*, New York, Harper, 1956.

Day Adventists, for example, began as a cult group that proclaimed the end of the world on a specific date, but when that date passed, it maintained many of its other beliefs. Today, it is a church with a trained clergy, a stable membership, and a formal organizational structure.

Theories of Religion

A Functionalist Approach

The universality of religion suggests to the functionalist that religion is a requirement of group life and that it serves both manifest and latent functions. Durkheim's (1915) classic study of religion, *The Elementary Forms of the Religious Life*, posed two basic questions: What is religion? and What are the functions of religion for human society? In answering the first question, he noted that religion is a unified system of beliefs and practices relative to sacred things. He answered the second question by focusing on religion's social function of promoting solidarity within a society.

Unlike most people today, who view religion as primarily a private and personal experience, Durkheim believed that the primary function of religion was to *preserve and solidify society*. Noting that worship, God, and society are inseparable, he paid little attention to the other functions of religion.

This perspective assumes that religion is the central focus for integrating the social system. By developing the awe that members of society feel for moral norms, religion functions to hold society together. This social solidarity is developed through rituals such as church or synagogue services, baptisms, bar mitzvahs, Christmas caroling and gift giving, and the multitude of observances and ceremonies practiced by specific religious groups.

Another function, one related to promoting social solidarity, is that of creating a *community of believers*. A religion provides a system of beliefs around which people may gather to belong to something greater than themselves and to have their personal beliefs reinforced by the group and its rituals. Those who share a common ideology develop a collective identity and a sense of fellowship.

A third function is *social control*. Religion reinforces social norms, providing sanctions for violations of norms and reinforcing basic values such as property rights and respect for others. Society's existence depends on its members' willingness to abide by folkways and mores and to interact with one another in a spirit of cooperation and trust.

Religion also serves the function of *providing answers to ultimate questions*. Why are we here? Is there a Supreme Being? What happens after death? Religions provide systems of belief based on the faith that life has a purpose, that someone or something is in control of the universe. They make the world seem comprehensible, often by attributing familiar, human motives to supernatural forces.

According to Weber (in Fischoff, 1963), one of the questions that religions must address is *theodicy*: Why does God allow evil to exist? In attempting to answer this question, theologians develop complex systems to explain the meaning of life, which among other things deal with values — what is good and what is evil? These values provide the basis for ethical systems, rules of behavior by which people may find favor in the sight of God. Buddhism and some other religions involve no belief in a supernatural power because they have developed into an ethical system altogether.

Religion also provides us with rites of passage, ceremonies and rituals designed to give sacred meaning and a social significance to birth, the attainment of adulthood, marriage, death, and other momentous events.

Religion helps reconcile people to hardship. All societies have inequality, poverty, and oppression, and everyone experiences pain, crises, prejudice, and sorrow. By belonging to a religion, people may come to feel that they are special in some way, that they will be rewarded in the future. Many religions call for caring, mercy, charity, kindness, and other prosocial behaviors. They may provide moral, ethical, social, and even financial support to those in need.

Religion can cultivate social change. Many religious groups criticize social injustice, existing social morality, and community or government actions. Some take action to change unfavorable conditions. The churches have been a major force in the civil rights movement, for example Many protests against the Vietnam war were a result of religious teachings about love and peace. Other major protests have been mounted by religious groups against the right to have an abortion, equal rights for homosexuals, and the women's rights movement.

This list of manifest functions performed by religion could be continued. Some latent functions of religion concern mate selection, experience in public speaking, and psychic reward for donating funds or labor to worthy causes. While other groups and systems may be able to fulfill some of these manifest or latent functions, many social scientists argue that the functions provided by religion cannot be adequately met by other means.

A functionalist approach to religion reminds us that while it performs many basic functions

Religion performs many functions. Some religious groups advocate social justice and specific government action. During the Vietnam war, for example, Quakers demonstrated in front of the White House for peace in Vietnam. The Quakers (Friends), the Church of the Brethren, and the Mennonites are three of the historic peace churches in the United States.

for society and individuals, it is likely to have dysfunctions as well. If it serves to preserve and solidify society, to create a community of believers, to reinforce social norms, and to reconcile people to hardship, it also can serve to divide society, create bias against the nonbeliever, exclude nongroup members, and maintain the status quo. Religion can be dysfunctional in forcing people to accept inequities and in inhibiting its members from acting to change them. It can be dysfunctional in convincing its followers to reject this world for a future life in which rewards are guaranteed, and it can often inhibit the search for new truths, new ideas, and additional knowledge.

Examples of religion as both a source of integration and conflict are evident throughout the world. In Iran, the religious teachings of Islam form the basis for convincing youth that it is honorable to die for their country in their war with Iraq. In Northern Ireland, protests abound

between Catholics and Protestants. In the Middle East, the conflicts between Jews and Moslems are intense. In India and Pakistan, caste and class conflicts linked to religious traditions cause death and destruction. In many countries, Jews are persecuted. Overpopulation and wars can be justified in the name of religion. As seen in Chapter 5, to have in-groups is to have outgroups. To believe that there is only one Truth is to reject all ideas that challenge one's prejudices.

A Conflict Approach

As discussed in previous chapters, the conflict approach focuses on the exploitation of the poor by the elite. The classical Marxist perspective suggests that religion, like other social structures, can be understood only in the context of its role in the economic system.

In sharp contrast to the functionalist approach, conflict theorists view religion as a tool the elite uses to get the poor to obey authority and follow the rules established by the privileged. Religion counsels the masses to be humble and accept their condition. In the words of Karl Marx, religion "is the opium of the people" because it distracts them from finding practical political solutions to their problems. The powerless find an illusion of happiness through religion and look forward to future life after death where the streets will be paved with gold and life will be joyful and everlasting. Marx urged revolution to bring, during life, the joy and freedom that religion postpones until after death.

Most theorists today would agree that religion serves interests other than those of the ruling class, but it is unquestionably true that there are strong relationships between religion and social class. Churches are highly segregated along racial and economic lines. There are a number of denominations that are largely or wholly black in the United States. Within the white population different religious groups tend to attract people of similar educational and occupational levels. For example, very few factory workers are Episcopalians and very few professional people and company executives are Baptists or members of pentecostal groups. While some groups, such as the Roman Catholic church, have working-class as well as wealthy members, the data generally show that occupation and income vary with religious affiliation.

Is religion related to class conflict? In a general way, yes. Religious affiliation is related to class, and many social controversies result from perceptions that differ according to one's social class. Opinions on such issues as prayer in the schools, the teaching of creationism, abortion, women as clergy, the Equal Rights Amendment, and homosexuality vary both by class and religion. The conservative positions are generally supported both by fundamentalist and pentecostal churches and by people who have lower incomes and less education.

Religions of the World

It is difficult to obtain accurate counts of the number of adherents to the world's religions. The procedures used by different countries and groups to measure religious membership vary widely. Some assessments include only adults, others include everyone who attends services. Some people may be included in several different religious groups, such as Confucianism, Taoism, and Shintoism. Some religions forbid counts of their members. In countries where a certain religion has prevailed for many centuries (such as Christianity in Europe and Hinduism in India), the entire population may be reported as adherents.

Because of these and other variables, the figures in *Table 13-1* are only rough estimates. According to the table, the world population is 4.680 billion and the total membership of all religious groups is 2.532 billion. Simple subtraction shows that 2.148 billion people are not included, either because they did not belong to one of the major religions or because they were not included in the tallying procedure.

Christianity and Judaism

There are approximately one billion Christians and more than 16.8 million Jews in the world today (see Table 13-1). *Christians* profess faith in the teachings of Jesus Christ, as found in the New Testament of the Bible, while adherents to *Judaism* find the source of their beliefs in the Hebrew Bible (called the Old Testament by Christians), especially in its first five books, which are called the Torah. The Torah was traditionally regarded as the primary revelation of God, originally passed on orally and eventually written.

Judaism is the oldest religion in the Western world. It comprises both a religious and an ethnic community (see Chapter 9). It was the first religion to teach monotheism, which was based

Table 13-1
Estimated membership of the principal religions of the world

RELIGIONS	NORTH AMERICA[1]	SOUTH AMERICA	EUROPE[2]	ASIA[3]	AFRICA	OCEANIA[4]	WORLD
Total Christian	240,745,200	191,046,100	336,868,700	100,975,700	140,013,900	18,520,700	1,028,170,300
Roman Catholic	134,411,300	180,251,200	176,039,500	55,979,100	54,921,400	5,191,300	606,793,800
Eastern Orthodox	5,185,500	408,000	49,946,900	2,784,500	9,131,800[5]	406,600	67,863,300
Protestant[6]	101,148,400	10,386,900	110,882,300	42,212,100	75,960,700[7]	12,922,800	353,513,200
Jewish	7,266,900	699,950	4,470,800	4,096,870	213,530	72,800	16,820,850
Muslim[8]	1,326,200	405,400	20,959,600	375,105,400	150,192,200	86,700	548,075,500
Zoroastrian	2,750	2,600	14,000	236,200	900	1,000	257,450
Shinto[9]	60,000	75,000	—	38,000,000	—	—	38,135,000
Taoist	—	—	—	25,000,000	—	—	25,000,000
Confucian	107,600	69,700	507,000	167,907,800	3,500	19,400	168,615,000
Buddhist[10]	214,100	290,100	188,600	248,833,900	16,600	26,100	249,569,400
Hindu[11]	254,600	673,700	392,500	454,955,800	1,263,800	340,700	457,881,100
Totals	249,977,350	193,262,550	363,401,200	1,415,111,670	291,704,430	19,067,400	2,532,524,600
Population[12]	381,818,000	257,798,000	758,889,000	2,760,514,000	498,080,000	23,427,000	4,680,526,000

[1]Includes Central America and the West Indies.

[2]Includes the U.S.S.R. and other countries with established Marxist ideology where continuing religious adherence is difficult to estimate.

[3]Includes areas in which persons have traditionally enrolled in several religions, as well as mainland China with a Marxist establishment.

[4]Includes Australia and New Zealand as well as islands of the South Pacific.

[5]Includes Coptic Christians, of restricted status in Egypt and precariously situated under the military junta in Ethiopia.

[6]Protestant statistics vary widely in style of reckoning affiliation. See *World Church Membership*.

[7]Including a great proliferation of new churches, sects, and cults among African Christians.

[8]The chief base of Islam is still ethnic, although missionary work is now carried on in Europe and America. In countries where Islam is established, minority religions are frequently persecuted and accurate statistics are rare.

[9]A Japanese ethnic religion, Shinto declined rapidly after the Japanese emperor surrendered his claim to divinity (1947); a revival of cultic participation in the homeland had chiefly literary significance. Shinto does not survive well outside the homeland.

[10]Buddhism has produced several renewal movements in the last century which have gained adherents in Europe and America. Although persecuted in Tibet and sometimes elsewhere in Asia, it has shown greater staying power than other religions of the East. It also transplants better.

[11]Hinduism's strength in India has been enhanced by its connection with the national movement, a phenomenon also observable in the world of Islam. Modern Hinduism has developed several renewal movements that have won adherents in Europe and America.

[12]United Nations, Department of International Economic and Social Affairs; data refer to midyear 1982.

SOURCE: Reprinted with permission from the *1983 Britannica Book of the Year*. Copyright © 1983 by Encyclopaedia Britannica, Inc., Chicago, Ill., p. 600.

on the Old Testament verse "Hear O Israel, the Lord our God, the Lord is one" (Deut. 6:4). Jews, the people who identify with and practice Judaism, believe that God's providence extends into a special covenant with the ancient Israelites: to bring God's message to humanity by their example. As a result, the emphasis is on conduct rather than on doctrinal correctness. Adherents to Judaism have a considerable measure of latitude in matters of belief since their beliefs have never been formulated in an official creed. This lack of an official creed also meant that Judaism did not stop developing after the Bible was completed. One result of this development was the traditional Jewish prayer book, which reflects the basic beliefs of Judaism as well as changes in emphasis in response to changing conditions.

Judaism has a system of law that regulates civil and criminal justice, family relationships, personal ethics and manners, and social responsibilities to the community, as well as worship and other religious observances. Individual practice of these laws varies widely. Some widely observed practices concern strict adherence to Kosher foods, daily prayer and study, the marital relationship, and the meaning of the Yarmulka (skull cap) and Tefillin (worn on the forehead and left arm during morning prayers).

The Jewish religious calendar, which is of Babylonian origin, consists of twelve lunar months amounting to approximately 354 days. Six times over a nineteen-year cycle a thirteenth month is added to adjust the calendar to the solar year. The Sabbath is from sunset Friday to sunset Saturday.

Male children are circumcised on the eighth day after birth as a sign of the covenant with Abraham. At age thirteen, a bar mitzvah is given to Jewish boys to signify adult status and a responsibility for performing the commandments. A similar ceremony for girls, the bat mitzvah, is a more recent innovation.

Christianity diverged from Judaism in ancient Israel. Christians considered Jesus to be the Jewish savior, or Messiah, and incorporated the Hebrew writings of Christ's followers into the canon of their faith, the Bible. After his death (and, as Christians believe, his resurrection), Christ's teachings spread to Rome and many other centers of the Roman Empire. When the Roman Empire split in 1054 A.D., so did the Christian church; it came to be called the Orthodox church in the East and the Roman Catholic church in the West. The Roman Catholic church was united under popes until the sixteenth century. Today, of the estimated one billion Christians nearly sixty percent are Roman Catholic. Slightly more than one-third are Protestant and the rest are Eastern Orthodox.

Christians, like Jews, believe in one god (monotheism), but their God takes the form of a Holy Trinity: Father, Son, and Holy Spirit. Christians experience God as the Father, Jesus Christ as the son of God, and the Holy Spirit as the continuing presence of God. Most Christians worship on Sunday instead of Saturday, which is the Jewish Sabbath. They also practice baptism by water when they become adherents or give a public testimony of their acceptance of Christ. Christians also take the Eucharist, a sacred meal recalling the last supper that Jesus had with his disciples. The breaking of bread, symbolizing the body of Christ, and the drinking of wine, symbolizing the blood of Christ, are sacred acts (sacraments) to most Christians. Prayer and preaching are also important Christian functions.

Islam

There are more than half a billion Islamic adherents in the world. Followers of *Islam* follow the teachings of the Koran and of Muhammad, a prophet. *Islam* means "surrender," "resignation," and "submission." A person who submits to the will of Allah, the one and only God, is called a Muslim (sometimes spelled Moslem). This surrender involves a total commitment in

Muslim women are bound by rules of behavior set down in the Koran. These rules support the subordination of women and the dominance of men. While the men may marry outside the Muslim faith, may have up to four wives, and may divorce easily, the women have no such freedom. Traditionally, the women covered their hair and faces in public, although this practice is not followed as strictly today. The primary roles of Muslim women were those of housekeeper and bearer of children — preferably male children.

faith, obedience, and trust to this one God. The insistence that no one but God be worshipped has led many Muslims to object to the term "Muhammadanism," a designation widely used in the West but thought to suggest that Muhammad, a great prophet to the Muslim, is worshipped in a manner that parallels the worship of Christ by Christians.

It is sometimes assumed that Islam originated during the lifetime of Muhammad (570–630), specifically during the years in which he received the divine revelations recorded in the Muslim sacred book, the Koran. Many Muslims, however, believe that the prophet Muhammad simply restored the original religion of Abraham.

Islam encompasses a code of ethics, a distinctive culture, a system of laws, and guidelines and rules for other aspects of life. The Muslim place of worship is the mosque, and the chief gathering of the congregation takes place on Fridays. Muslims profess their faith by repeating that "there is no God but God, and Muhammad is the messenger of God." The Muslims also have a deep awareness of the importance of a fellowship of faith and a community of believers.

The Koran includes rules for ordering social relationships. It is especially explicit about matters pertaining to the family, marriage, divorce, and inheritance. The family is basically authoritarian, patriarchal, polygamous, patrilineal, and largely patrilocal. Women are clearly subordinate to men and receive only half the inheritance that male heirs receive. Muslim males may marry non-Muslim women, but except in countries where the holy law has been abolished, Muslim women may not marry outside their faith. A Muslim male may take up to four wives (polygyny) and traditionally can divorce a wife by simple pronouncement and dowry repayment. Children, especially sons, are perceived as desirable.

Although laws are changing in many Islamic countries and the education of women has increased dramatically, fewer females than males attend school and even fewer women receive a higher education. Marriage and housekeeping are considered the proper occupations of women. It is not surprising, therefore, that Islam is finding it difficult to come to terms with the scientific ideas and the technology of the Western world.

Hinduism

The great majority of the 457 million Hindus in the world live in India and Pakistan. In India, approximately 85 percent of the population is Hindu. *Hinduism* has evolved over about 4,000 years and comprises an enormous variety of beliefs and practices. It hardly corresponds to most Western conceptions of religion since organization is minimal and there is no religious hierarchy.

Hinduism is so closely intertwined with other aspects of the society that it is difficult to describe it clearly, especially in the case of castes (described in Chapter 8). Hindus sometimes refer to the ideal way of life as fulfilling the duties of one's class and station, which means obeying the rules of the four great castes of India: the Brahmins, or priests; the Ksatriyas, warriors and rulers; the Vaisyas, merchants and farmers; and the Sudras, peasants and laborers. A fifth class, the Untouchables, includes those whose occupations require them to handle "unclean" objects.

These classes encompass males only. The position of women is ambiguous. In some respects they are treated as symbols of the divine, yet in other ways they are considered inferior beings. Traditionally, women have been expected to serve their husbands and to have no independent interests, but this is rapidly changing.

Although caste is a powerful influence in Hindu religious behavior, one's village community and family are important as well. Every village has gods and goddesses who ward off epidemics and drought. Hindu belief holds that the universe is populated by a multitude of gods (polytheism) who behave much as humans do, and worship of these gods takes many forms. Some are thought to require sacrifices, others are worshipped at shrines or temples, and shrines devoted to several gods associated with a family deity are often erected in private homes.

To Hindus, the word "dharma" means the cosmos, or the social order. Hindus practice rituals that uphold the great cosmic order. They believe that, to be righteous, one must strive to behave in accordance with the way things are. In a sense, the Hindu sees life as a ritual. The world is regarded as a great dance determined by one's Karma, or personal destiny, and the final goal of the believer is liberation from this cosmic dance. Hindus also believe in transmigration of souls. After one dies one is born again in another form, as either a higher or lower being, depending on whether the person was righteous or evil in the previous life. If one becomes righteous enough, one will cease to be reborn.

A fundamental principle of Hinduism is that our perceptions of the external world are limitations. When we think about one thing, we are cut off from the infinite number of things we are not thinking about but could be. If we think of nothing, we become in tune with the universe and freed of limitations. One means of doing this is through meditation.

The actual belief systems of India are extremely confusing to Westerners, because so many different tribal religions have been assimilated into Hinduism, but the basic nature of polytheism in general and Hinduism in particular permits new gods to be admitted.

Buddhism

Buddhism has about 250 million adherents. It is impossible to precisely determine the number of Buddhists because many people accept Buddhist beliefs and engage in Buddhist rites while practicing other religions such as Shintoism, Confucianism, Taoism, or Hinduism.

Buddhism is thought to have originated as a reaction against the Brahminic tradition of Hinduism in the fifth century B.C. At this time, a prince named Siddhartha Gautama was born in northern India to a prosperous ruling family. As he grew older, he was distressed by the suffering he witnessed among the people. At the age of twenty-nine, he left his wife and family to go on a religious quest. One day, sitting under a giant fig tree, he passed through several stages of awareness and became the Buddha, the enlightened one. He decided to share his experience with others and became a wandering teacher, preaching his doctrine of the "Four Noble Truths": (1) this life is suffering and pain; (2) the source of suffering is desire and craving; (3) suffering can cease; and (4) the practice of an "eightfold path" can end suffering. The eightfold path consisted of right views, right intentions, right speech, right conduct, right livelihood, right effort, right mindfulness, and right concentration. It combined ethical and disciplinary practices, training in concentration and meditation, and the development of enlightened wisdom. This doctrine was Buddha's message until the age of eighty,

Buddhism is practiced throughout most of East and Southeast Asia. Many of the Buddhist clergy live in monastic communities. Others serve, as pastors in Christian communities, offering prayers, counseling, and instruction, and maintaining close contact with the people.

when he passed into final Nirvana, a state of transcendence forever free from the cycle of suffering and rebirth.

After Buddha's death, legends of his great deeds and supernatural powers emerged. Stories were told of his heroism in past lives, and speculations arose about his true nature. Some groups viewed him as a historical figure while others placed him in a succession of several Buddhas of the past and a Buddha yet to come. Differing views eventually led to a diversity of Buddhist sects in different countries. Some remained householders who set up Buddha images and established many holy sites that became centers of pilgrimage. Others became monks, living in monastic communities and depending on the laity for food and material support. Many monks became beggars, and in several Southeast Asian countries, they still go on daily alms rounds. They spend their days in rituals, devotions, meditation, study, and preaching. Flowers, incense, and praise are offered to the image of the Buddha. These acts are thought to ensure that the monks will be reborn in one of the heavens or in a better place in life from which they may be able to attain the goal of enlightenment.

In every society where Buddhism is widespread, people combine Buddhist thought with a native religion, supporting the monks and paying for rituals in the temples. These societies are organized around other religions, however.

Today, Buddhism is divided into two major traditions, but its integration into many cultures has resulted in many different interpretations of the way to Buddhahood. Yet we can all achieve Nirvana by seeing with complete detachment, by seeing things as they really are without being attached to any theoretical concept or doctrine.

Confucianism

Confucianism, which has about 170 million adherents, is associated primarily with China, but it has influenced the civilizations of Korea, Japan, and Vietnam as well. Confucianism is the philosophical and religious system based on the teachings of Confucius. Confucius, born to a poor family in 551 B.C. in what is today Shantung Province in China, was orphaned at an early age. As a young man, he held several minor government positions, but he became best known as a teacher, philosopher, and scholar. Distressed by the misery and oppression that surrounded him, he dedicated his life to attempting to relieve the suffering of the people.

By talking with younger men about his ideas to reform government to serve the people rather than the rulers, Confucius attracted many disciples. He emphasized the total person, sincerity, ethics, and the right of individuals to make decisions for themselves. Although Confucius was not a religious leader in the usual sense of the word, he believed that there was a righteous force in the universe, and yet his philosophy was founded not on supernaturalism but on humanity. Virtue, he said, is to love people, and wisdom is to understand them.

The basic philosophy of Confucius is found in his many sayings. All people are brothers. Sincerity and reciprocity should be one's guiding principles. The truly virtuous person, desiring to be established personally, seeks to establish others; desiring success for oneself can help others to succeed. The superior person stands in awe of three things: the ordinances of Heaven, great persons, and the words of sages. The ideals of Confucius were motivated not by the desire for rewards or an afterlife but simply by the satisfaction of acting in accordance with the divine order.

Confucius had a pervasive influence on all aspects of Chinese life, so much so that every county in China built a temple to him. Everyone tried to live in accordance with the Confucian code of conduct. His values guided human relations at all levels — among individuals, communities, and nations. His thought guided one's conduct in work and in the family. Even today, the Chinese who profess to be Taoists, Buddhists, or Christians generally act in accordance with Confucian ideals.

One of the books in the classical literature of Confucius is the *Book of Change,* or the I Ching. This book is familiar to many Americans and is used to guide a person's behavior and attitude toward the future.

Religion in the United States

The United States, which has no state church, has more than two hundred denominations and is greatly influenced by a variety of religious groups and belief systems. In addition to churches and denominations, revivalists preach on TV and radio and religious leaders such as Billy Graham give spiritual advice. Bumper stickers tell us that "Jesus Saves" or to "Honk if you love Jesus."

Williams (1980) conceptualizes American religion as an interplay between two forces, the structured and the unstructured, the major religious communities and the informal groups that he calls "popular religions." These two trends developed, he says, in response to the demands of life in a new country. Faced with a diverse population, a new political system, and rapid technological change, Americans sometimes found organized religions too limited, and in response to the demands of a new nation, they developed new religious movements.

The Development of Religious Movements

Religion in American society has become increasingly rationalized and centralized. Some "liberal" religious groups have downplayed the supernatural aspects of Christianity and emphasized neoorthodoxy, which is a theological

movement emphasizing the importance of ethical conduct and a remote, depersonalized God. Others worship a personal god and express their beliefs emotionally. Those who worship in this way seek signs of divine intervention in their daily lives.

Another religious movement is the development of sect groups. The proliferation of these groups accompanied the breakdown of the feudal structure and the development of industrialization. One wave of groups known as the pietist sects rejected worldliness in favor of pacifism, communal living, and aspiration toward perfection. The Amish and the Hutterites are American groups descended from these sects.

One of the pietist sects is the Quakers, who came to Pennsylvania from England. Quakers believe in an "Inner Light," that people mystically partake of the nature of God. Thus they see no need for a religious structure interceding between God and human beings.

Another persistent theme in American religious life is *millennialism,* the belief that a dramatic transformation of the earth will occur and that Christ will rule the world for a thousand years of prosperity and happiness. One millennial movement took place among the Millerites in the 1830s. William Miller, the founder, was convinced that the Second Coming of Christ would happen in 1843. When it did not, he changed the date to 1844. Again nothing happened. Some of his followers, who believed that the Second Coming had occurred invisibly and spiritually, founded the Seventh-Day Adventists.

Other religious movements have been based on divine revelation. One American prophet who received a divine revelation was Joseph Smith, who founded the Church of Jesus Christ of Latter-Day Saints (Mormons) in 1830. His following was recruited from the rural people of upstate New York. About thirty years later, Mary Baker Eddy began a movement in the

The Church of Jesus Christ of Latter-Day Saints (Mormons) had its beginnings in an atmosphere of supernaturalism, millenialism, and religious revivalism during the early part of the 19th century. Today it has a membership of approximately three-and-one-half million people. The main temple and tabernacle are located in Salt Lake City, and its membership is heavily concentrated in Utah and surrounding western states.

urban middle class known as the Christian Science movement. Mrs. Eddy's revelation was that illness could be controlled by the mind. This sect developed into a denomination when people of wealth and status became adherents.

Pentecostalism involves a practice similar to divine revelation. Pentecostal Christians hold highly emotional services that resemble revivals, and they "speak in tongues." Participants go into an ecstatic seizure during which they utter a rapid flow of meaningless syllables.

An offshoot of pentecostalism is faith healing, which experienced a rapid growth after World War II. In faith healing, the fundamentalist preacher asks members of the congregation who are sick or disabled to come forward. The preacher asks the disabled person and the rest of the congregation to call upon the power of the Lord to heal: "In the name of Jesus, Heal." If their faith in Christ is strong enough, the blind will see, the lame can throw away their crutches, and so on. The clientele of faith healers comes primarily from the poor who do not have the resources for adequate medical treatment.

A recent manifestation of the interplay between churches or denominations and fundamentalist groups of the sect type concerns the teaching of evolution in the public schools. Most educated people in the United States accept Darwin's theory of biological evolution. Many fundamentalist Christians, however, interpret the Bible literally and believe that God created heaven and earth in six days. The highly vocal creationists are urging that creationism be given "equal time" with evolution in school science classes. The basic assumptions of scientists and religious fundamentalists are in direct conflict: science is based on deductions drawn from empirical reality, whereas creationism is based on divine revelation. The issue of whether creationism should be taught in the public schools was temporarily muted in January of 1982 when Federal District Judge William Overton of Little

Rock, Arkansas, ruled that the two-model approach of the creationists is simply a contrived dualism that has no scientific factual basis or legitimate educational purpose. The ruling contended that since creation is not science, the conclusion is inescapable that the only real effect of teaching creation theory is the advancement of religion. What the creation law does, in effect, is make the teaching of creationism in the public schools unconstitutional.

Current Trends in Religion

The use of computers and sophisticated statistical techniques have brought about significant changes in social science research in general and the scientific study of religion in particular. Researchers can now deal efficiently with large samples of the population and test some of the theories developed by Durkheim and Weber.

One such study was published in 1961 by Gerhard Lenski, whose book, *The Religious Factor,* is now considered a pioneering quantitative study of religion. Using survey techniques on a probability sample of males in the Detroit area, Lenski tried to test Weber's notions about the Protestant ethic. Lenski reasoned that if Protestants were more oriented toward the Protestant ethic than Catholics, they should show more upward mobility. He found that more white Protestant men than Catholic men rose into the upper middle class or retained that status and that Catholic men were more likely to move into or remain in the lower half of the working class.

Subsequent studies (reviewed by Riccio, 1979) have contradicted Lenski's findings and show no direct relationship between Protestant or Catholic religious beliefs and socioeconomic status. Nevertheless, quantitative research on religion became much more popular following Lenski's publication. We now have a profile of American religious beliefs and their relation to social class, race, age, and other factors. One important finding of this research has been that a

sizable part of the population has no conventional religious commitment, although they are concerned with religious belief. This movement away from the church is known as secularization.

Secularization

It is widely accepted by social scientists that the dominant trend in modern religion is secularization. *Secularization* is the trend toward the declining influence of religion in the lives of people and in the institutions of society. Today, for example, marriages are assumed to be decided between humans, not foreordained by a god. Tragedies such as automobile accidents are explained in terms of human interactions and the laws of science, not as manifestations of divine will.

Two factors suggesting the move toward secularization relate to church attendance and supernaturalism. Not only are fewer people attending church, but the churches themselves are moving away from supernaturalism. Stark and Bainbridge (1981), however, dispute the dominant view that secularization is an irreversible trend that will eventually bring about the end of religion and its influence.

Although Stark and Bainbridge agree that liberal Protestantism is in a state of decline, they note several signs that human commitment to supernaturalism will remain. One is that those who claim no religious affiliation are likely to accept a whole range of supernaturalism — from astrology to Zen. A second sign is the fact that most Americans who grew up in an irreligious home enter a Christian denomination as adults. Third, the evangelical denominations are growing. Fourth, they claim it is myopic to note the weakening of once potent religious organizations but dismiss the significance of the formation of new religions.

For these reasons, Stark and Bainbridge argue that secularization is a self-limiting process that prompts religious revival and innovation. In other words, the secularization of the long-dominant religions is a source of the energy pouring into new religious channels. Their central thesis is that cults will flourish where the conventional churches are weakest. They provide evidence that in America there are very robust *negative* correlations between church membership rates and cult activity rates. The states and cities that have low church membership rates have the highest rates of membership in cults. Centuries ago, Christianity, Judaism, Islam, and Buddhism began as cults that rose to power because of the weaknesses in the dominant religions of their time. Stark and Bainbridge argue that the same process is happening today.

Religiosity and Church Attendance

Is religion important to Americans? *Religiosity*, intensity of religious feeling, is a qualitative factor that is difficult to accurately assess. Church attendance figures may provide some in-

dication of religiosity, however. Beginning in the late 1950s, weekly church attendance declined steadily for fifteen years (see Figure 13-1), but since the early 1970s it has remained stable at about 40 percent (Jacquet, 1979). Yet church attendance may not be an accurate measure of religiosity because people go to church for many reasons: to worship God, see friends, enjoy music, meet social expectations, and so on. Public opinion polls consistently indicate that a high percentage of people believe in God (more than 90 percent) and a life after death (about 75 percent) and overwhelmingly want their children to have religious training. The discrepancy between church attendance figures and religious beliefs indicates that factors other than formal religious organizations influence religious thought.

The Electronic Church

Through the medium of television many people in the United States "attend church" without ever leaving their homes. Although the

Today television brings religious services into the homes of millions of people around the world. The names and faces of Billy Graham, Robert Schuller, Rex Humbard, Oral Roberts, Jerry Falwell, and others have gained widespread familiarity through this electronic media. Jimmy Swaggart, shown here conducting one of his services for television viewing, invites persons to publicly come forth to give their lives to Christ and their financial resources to his ministry.

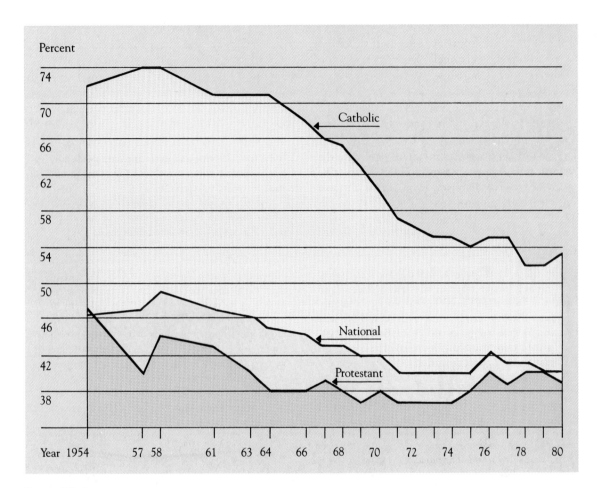

Figure 13–1
Church attendance: 1954–1980

impact of religious programming is not fully understood, its influence should not be underestimated. The electronic church, as it has been called, apparently fulfills some religious functions. It may provide answers to ultimate questions, reconcile people to hardship, and promote social change. The extent to which it facilitates social integration, creates a community of believers, and provides rituals is questionable, however. It is unlikely that many people kneel for prayer or join hands with others in front of a TV set. On the other hand, the millions of dollars sent to television preachers, most of whom are conservative, fundamentalist, and anticommunist, indicate that they are important to many Americans.

SOCIOLOGISTS AT WORK

Helping Religious Refugees Adjust

Baila Miller is assistant director of research at the Jewish Federation of Metropolitan Chicago. She joined the federation in 1982 after two years as a program consultant with the United Way of Metropolitan Chicago. Before that she spent six years lecturing, researching, and completing a doctorate in sociology at the University of Illinois at Chicago Circle.

How does Baila Miller use her sociological training in her work at the Jewish Federation? "The federation raises charitable funds and allocates them to Jewish causes in Israel and overseas and to local Jewish social welfare, health, and educational institutions. The office of research and planning is a small department — just three people. We are responsible for analyzing the budgets of some of the agencies we support, for preparing service statistics for submission to the United

Way, for collecting and analyzing data needed by our volunteer committees, and for carrying out special research projects."

It is in these special research projects that Miller finds the fullest application of her training. "We recently completed a survey of the Jewish population of greater Chicago," she says — a survey that presents unique problems among population studies because the U.S. Bureau of the Census does not collect data on religious affiliations in its decennial census. "We did a lot of random-digit dialing," she admits. "We were trying to determine many things about the Jewish community: How many people are there? Where do they live? How are they maintaining their Jewish identify? Are they participating in religious observances and in Jewish education? What are their service needs and how can a Jewish agency

Ecumenism

One response to the current trend toward secularization has been for different denominations to join together in pursuit of common interests. This trend, known as *ecumenism* or the ecumenical movement, calls for worldwide Christian unity. Interdenominational organizations such as the National Council of Churches are attempting to reconcile the beliefs and practices of different religious groups.

A New Religious Consciousness

A number of new religious groups have sprung up in the United States over the last few decades. Many of them emphasize the personal

religious experience rather than a rational, bureaucratic religious organization. The ideas of many of these new groups, such as the Moral Majority, Jews for Jesus, and the Christian World Liberation Front, are rooted in the Christian tradition. Others, like Synanon, EST, and Silva Mind Control, grew out of the "human potential" movement of the 1960s and 1970s. Still others are rooted in Eastern religions such as Buddhism, Hinduism, and Confucianism.

Why have these groups and religious movements arisen? A number of factors may be responsible. Durkheim believed that as societies become more complex and diversified, so do the forms of religious belief and practice. Hans Mol (1976) suggests that the new religious conscious-

meet them? Should we be concentrating on services for the elderly or on day care for two-career families? Where are the Jewish poor?"

Another research project that Miller will be involved in at the Jewish Federation of Chicago is a study of the adjustment of Soviet Jewish emigrés to life in various communities in the United States. "We will be working with a data set collected at the University of Illinois, where Rita and Julian Simon, a sociologist and an economist, have done pioneering research in this field. We will approach the data four ways. On an individual level, we will study four adjustment outcomes: occupational achievement, language acquisition, social and cultural involvement in the Jewish community, and maintenance of Jewish identity. We'll be looking for the relative effects of *background characteristics* — social and economic status and place of origin in the Soviet Union — and of *mediating factors* — the type of early resettlement services that are offered in various communities in this country. Then we will analyze our data on a community level, looking for *aggregate measures* of differences in adjust-

ment in various cities in the United States. We will be looking at comparable studies that have been done or are being done in thirteen cities, including Denver, Houston, and New York. We will do a cross-cultural analysis, looking for similarities and differences in adjustment in other large refugee or emigré groups — Indochinese and Mexican, for example. Then we plan to do a policy analysis, with implications for Jewish agencies and national refugee organizations. We will examine the relative advantages and disadvantages of different service patterns: Is it better to provide many services intensively for the new immigrant, at greater short-term cost, or sequential services, such as language training, then vocational training and job placement? We will try to determine the relative effectiveness of different approaches."

"Gathering information like this on the characteristics of a religious group is a challenging task," Baila Miller says. "I use my sociological background in many ways. Research methodology, statistics, and organizational theory — I hope to put all of these to use in my projects at the Jewish Federation of Chicago."

ness is a search for identity and meaning. Some see these movements as a reaction against the militaristic and capitalistic values that are emphasized by contemporary American society. Others contend that the new religions have arisen in response to the climate of moral ambiguity in the United States. The decline of the established churches has undoubtedly been influential as well. In all probability, each of these factors has had an effect.

Religion and Other Institutions

The relationship between the church and other institutions is a complex one. The institutions and the functions they perform are not always easy to differentiate. Durkheim made this

point clearly when he stated that anything can be made sacred. Political rituals such as those that accompany the election of a president, family behaviors such as dinner together, economic goods such as automobiles, or educational events such as a graduation can all be considered sacred. These interrelationships and religious influences extend beyond the basic institutions. Note, for example, how religious principles have served as the foundation for opposition to war, restrictions on alcohol, or exclusion from taxes. In today's society, while the church as a social institution has come under attack, religion and religious values continue to exert a major influence on societies and on the lives of individuals throughout the world.

Summary

A religion is a ritualized system of beliefs and practices related to things defined as sacred by an organized community of believers. People have believed in supernatural powers throughout history. Some societies have believed that supernatural powers inhabit objects such as rocks and trees, which is known as animism. Others have assumed that supernatural powers reside in a medicine man or shaman who could be called upon to protect the group or to bring success. A third form of belief is totemism, in which a plant or animal is thought to be ancestrally related to a person or tribe. There are monotheistic religions that believe in one god and polytheistic religions that believe in a number of gods.

Religion may take a variety of forms. Mysticism is based on the belief in powers that are mysterious, secret, and hidden from human understanding. Churches are institutional organizations with formal bureaucratic structures. They are sometimes differentiated into ecclesia, which are official state religions, and denominations, which are independent of the state. Sects are small separatist groups that follow rigid doctrines and emphasize fundamentalist teachings. Cults are loosely organized religious organizations whose members adopt a new and unique lifestyle. Rather than attempting to change society, cults generally focus on the spiritual lives of the individual participants.

There are a number of theories about religion. The functionalist perspective examines what religion does for society. Religion is generally perceived as fulfilling social functions such as preserving and solidifying society, creating a community of believers, cultivating social change, and providing a means of social control. It also fulfills personal functions such as answering ultimate questions, providing rites of passage, and reconciling people to hardship. The conflict perspective views religion as a tool used by the dominant forces to justify their position and to keep the less privileged in subordinate positions.

More than 2.5 billion people are believed to have an affiliation with one of the world's major religions. About one billion are Christians, who profess faith in the teachings of Jesus Christ. Another half billion believe in Islam, surrendering their wills to Allah and following the teachings of the prophet Muhammad. The third largest group, followers of Hinduism, is closely linked to the traditional caste system of India. Hindus have a vast array of religious practices and beliefs. Followers of Buddhism believe that they can avoid human suffering by following an eightfold path of appropriate behavior. Confucianism, based on the life and teachings of Confucius, is both a philosophy and a religion and is closely linked to Taoism and Shintoism.

The United States has no state church, but a wide variety of religious groups exist in this country. There are two contrasting trends in contemporary religious practice. One type of group emphasizes formal religious organization, whereas the other emphasizes an informal, personalized, emotional belief system. Throughout our history, religious life has been influenced by folk religions, sects, pentecostal groups, and groups that believe in millennialism, divine revelation, and faith healing.

Currently, religion is being studied in new ways as a result of developments in qualitative and quantitative research techniques and computer technology. The use of these and other techniques has revealed a trend toward secularization, which is believed to contribute to the emergence of cult activities. While church attendance has leveled off at an estimated 40 percent, a large majority of the population profess a belief in God and life after death, and televised religious programs reach millions of persons in their homes. Along with these developments have come increased ecumenicalism and a new religious consciousness. This new consciousness is professed by many new religious sects and movements, some derived from the Christian tradition, others from the human potential movement and Eastern religions. Several explanations for the creation of these groups have been offered. It has been suggested that they have arisen in response to our diverse culture, our search for identity, our need for precise, simplistic answers, or as a protest against secularization and materialism. The religious system in America and around the world is closely linked with the family as well as economic, political, and educational institutions.

Key Terms

animism
Buddhism
Christians
church
Confucianism
cult
denominations
ecclesia
ecumenism
Hinduism
Islam
Judaism
millennialism
monotheism
mysticism
polytheism
priest
profane
prophets
religion
religiosity
sacred
sects
secularization
shamanism
theodicy
totemism

Suggested Readings

Berger, Peter L. **A Rumor of Angels: Modern Society and the Rediscovery of the Supernatural.** *Garden City, N.Y.: Doubleday, 1970.* A sociologist's explanation of the role of religion in the modern world.

Greeley, Andrew. **Unsecular Man. The Persistence of Religion.** *New York: Schocken Books, 1972.* A Catholic priest's declaration that because human needs are timeless, people need religion.

Lofland, John. **Doomsday Cult.** *Englewood Cliffs, N.J.: Prentice-Hall, 1966.* A study of the beginning of a millenarian movement.

McGuire, Meredith B. **Religion: The Social Context.** *Belmont, Calif.: Wadsworth Publishing Co., 1981.* A sociology of religion text focused on key issues: systems of meaning, the individual's religion, religious collectivities, change, and secularization.

Mol, Hans. **Identity and the Sacred.** *New York: The Free Press, 1976.* An attempt to integrate anthropological, historical, psychological, and sociological approaches to religion into a general social-scientific theory of religion.

Roberts, Keith A. **Religion in Sociological Perspective.** *Homewood, Ill.: The Dorsey Press, 1984.* A text on the sociology of religion covering major aspects of religious life and religion as a social institution.

Williams, Peter. **Popular Religion in America.** *Englewood Cliffs, N.J.: Prentice-Hall, 1980.* A fresh approach to religion in America. The author describes the varied religious activities practiced by Americans.

Wilson, Bryan. **Religion in Sociological Perspective.** *New York: Oxford University Press, 1982.* A discussion of the sociology of religion as a science, the functions of religion, culture and religion in the East and West, sects, new religious movements, and secularization.

Wilson, John. **Religion in American Society: The Effective Presence.** *Englewood Cliffs, N.J.: Prentice-Hall, 1978.* A text providing comprehensive coverage of recent literature on the sociology of religion.

Wuthnow, Robert (ed.). **The Religious Dimension: New Directions in Quantitative Research.** *New York: Academic Press, 1979.* The application of systematic, quantitative research techniques to the study of modern religion.

CHAPTER 14

Educational Groups and Systems

The aim of education is the knowledge not of fact, but of values.

— Dean William R. Inge

Children in the United States are required to go to school. They sometimes begin at age two or three, long before the required age of six or seven, and often stay in school long past age sixteen, when they could legally drop out. While education dominates the lives of children, it also plays an important role in adult life, as adult students, parents, taxpayers, school employees, government officials, and voters participate in the school system.

Why is education so important? We all know some of the reasons we believe in education. We learn science, the arts, skills for employment, and we learn to make informed judgments about our leisure activities, our political involvement, and our everyday lives.

But is this all that we get from education? What else does it accomplish for society? What part does our education system play in creating a literate population and selecting people for occupations that match their talents? What part does it play in maintaining the stratification system and justifying the unequal distribution of wealth in society? Much of the debate about whether schools are doing the job they are supposed to do is really a debate about the proper function of schools. The goal of this chapter is to help you understand how education functions in society today.

Structural-Functional Theory of Education

Structural-functional theory recognizes the family as an important agency of socialization. It is in the family that the child learns the culture's values, norms, and language — how to be a social person. By the age of five or six, the child has developed a unique social personality, and in a properly functioning family the child is socialized to adjust to the routines and disciplines of the school system. How does education in the schools differ from education in the home?

The Manifest Functions of Schools

The manifest, or intended, function of the educational system, according to structural functionalists, is to supplement family socialization. The schools use experts (teachers) to teach children the knowledge, skills, and values necessary to function in the world outside the family (Parsons, 1959).

The most obvious teaching in school is the teaching of skills. Students today are expected to learn to read, write, and do arithmetic, which are taught by specially trained experts. Schools also teach students about the larger world through such courses as history, geography, and science. In addition, students learn the values of the larger society, including those that pertain to large organizations. They learn to tell time and be punctual, to cooperate with others to achieve group goals, and to obey the rules necessary for a smooth-running organization.

Another function of education is to select and develop, through evaluation and testing, those young people who have especially useful talents so that each individual will be as productive as his or her abilities permit. Schools give I.Q. tests to determine how capable the students are, and they give grades and achievement tests to find out how much students have learned. They also give psychological tests to help determine which occupations suit the students so that they can then guide them into vocational lines appropriate to their abilities. Some students are guided into vocational courses and the work force; others go to academic high schools and then into junior or four-year colleges. A few of the most talented go to elite colleges and then on to the professions.

A third function of the education system is to transmit new behaviors, skills, ideas, discoveries, and inventions resulting from research. Today, for example, schools teach typing and place less emphasis on penmanship. In some school systems, elementary school students are taught to use a computer terminal before they've mastered their multiplication tables.

The creation of new knowledge is another function of education. Our medical technology is one outstanding example of the knowledge developed in universities. Attempts have also been made to use the educational system to decrease poverty. Education develops the skills necessary to earn income, and special programs have been devised to help the poor develop these skills. Some high schools and colleges, for example, offer students training in specific skills such as car repair, computer programming, or restaurant management. Programs like Head Start are designed to teach disadvantaged children the skills they need to keep up with their peers.

The Latent Functions of Education

The functions so far discussed are the manifest functions, but the educational system also operates in ways that are latent, or unintentional, and these functions are also influential. Two latent functions are prolonged adolescence and age segregation.

Prolonged adolescence is a unique feature of modern industrial society. In other societies, the transition from childhood to adulthood is clearly marked. The Kpelle of Liberia in West Africa, for example, mark the passage of boy to man by a circumcision ritual. After this ceremony, the young man is regarded as having the same responsibilities as the other men of his tribe. In our society, children have been relieved of work roles for increasingly longer periods so they can acquire an education. The age of mandatory school attendance was raised from twelve to fourteen and then to sixteen, so students

Our educational system segregates adolescents by age and postpones their entry into adulthood well beyond the age when they mature physically. These students have free time to play with each other, and as they do so they create their own games, their own jokes, and their own set of values. In the process, they create a peer culture different from the expectations of family and school.

today have to remain in school for a longer time than they once did. Another factor that has increased the number of years they spend in school is that many jobs require a high school or college diploma. Students stay in school longer when unemployment rates are high and jobs are not available, and parents have to continue to support and assume responsibility for their children during this extended education. As a result, childhood and adolescence sometimes continue for almost two decades in the United States, and maybe even longer for upper-middle-class children.

Age segregation is the separation of certain age groups from the larger population. Children in schools spend their time with children of the same age, their peers, and as discussed in Chapter 6 the peer group is an important agency of socialization. Peer groups sometimes develop into distinct subcultures, whose members dress alike, listen to the same music, eat the same foods, wear similar hairstyles and makeup, and develop code words and slang — a language of their own. One such age-segregated subculture evolved in the late 1960s. During that decade, adolescents and college students were often in conflict with families, schools, and businesses. Fathers and sons stopped speaking over the length of the sons' hair, and students were expelled from schools and colleges and denied jobs because they wore long hair and blue jeans. Signs appeared on storefronts announcing "Shirts and shoes required." Students in the late 1960s learned values of equality and individual worth in school but found that the larger society did not reflect these values.

Our education system has also developed other latent functions, such as baby-sitting. This function has become increasingly important in American society because in many families both parents must work simply to make ends meet. Although the hours that children are in school

— 9 A.M. to 3 P.M. — are often not convenient for working parents, they could not even consider working if their children weren't in school. Some school systems are so attuned to their baby-sitting function that they offer afterschool play-groups — at a nominal fee — to take care of children until a parent gets off work and can bring the child home.

In sum, structural functionalists believe the educational system fulfills both manifest and latent functions. It reinforces the socialization process that started with the family, prepares children for work in a complex industrial society, and guides them into the occupations most appropriate to their abilities and society's needs. Certain latent functions of education, the segregation of age groups and the extension of adolescence, give peer groups an important role in society.

Conflict Theory of Education

Conflict theorists believe that the educational system is used by the elite to maintain their social position (Bowles and Gintis, 1976; Collins, 1979). The "elite" is the group that controls the wealth and power and has the kinds of jobs that afford wealth and prestige to those who hold them. Since such jobs are scarce and since so many people want them and compete for them, the people who control the jobs can require qualifications of their applicants that have little to do with the skills needed for the job but serve to weed out the nonelite. The school system is controlled by the elite, who use their control to select elite children for elite jobs.

The Hidden Curriculum

The elite requires students to learn, albeit subtly, how to behave appropriately for their position in society. This learning is not a part of the stated curriculum, unlike such subjects as

reading, writing or arithmetic. It is a part of a hidden curriculum, in which students learn such things as obedience, competition, and patriotism. No one ever announces that these qualities are being taught. Nevertheless, if students are to be educated for a job they must learn to obey rules, to do whatever a superior orders them to do, to work as hard as they can or at least harder than their coworkers, and to be loyal to the superior, the organization, and the nation in which they work. Both the values and the norms of the elites are a part of the hidden curriculum.

Teaching Values

Conflict theorists believe that schools teach children the values of the group in power. Children are taught patriotism by saying the pledge of allegiance and by studying the history and geography of the United States and of their state and community. They learn that the United States is a great country founded by great leaders who believed in freedom for all. Students learn about the democratic system of government, the fairness of representation, and the importance of the vote. They are taught to value the capitalist system, in which everyone has the right to accumulate as much private property as possible and pass it on to one's children.

Not all youngsters are taught the same values, however. Children in upper-class schools, for example, are more apt to be taught a sense of civic duty (Litt, 1963). They learn to vote and otherwise participate in politics. They are also taught about the importance of group struggles in settling political issues. The civics courses in lower-class schools, on the other hand, are more likely to emphasize the smooth working of an invisible hand of government. Lower-class students were not taught the importance of power and group conflict in the political process.

The importance of teaching values can be appreciated by looking at the conflicts that sometimes arise in schools. Teachers may be fired if they teach high school students the advantages of communism or the disadvantages of capitalism. The topics omitted from school curricula also shed light on the teaching of values. Students are not instructed on the family systems or sexual practices of people in other cultures. They are not taught about great philosophers who have criticized the United States's political or economic systems, and they are not made aware of the people who have suffered under these systems. Students who reach a college sociology course that attempts to analyze both strengths and weaknesses of social systems are often shocked by what they learn.

Learning Norms

Students learn to conform to elite standards of behavior through the educational process. They are told when to stand in line, when to take turns, when to talk, when to be quiet, when to read, when to listen, when to hang up their coats — the list goes on and on. Rules are an important part of the complex organization of a school, and acceptance of rules is vital to the maintenance of the social order.

Students also learn to compete with other students in school. They are taught that they must do better than others to receive attention, good grades, and privileges. Those who do not compete, who pursue the activities they enjoy, may fail, be separated from their peer group, and be labeled slow, hyperactive, disabled, or otherwise deviant. In short, they are punished.

The competition, however, is unfair because it is based on the norms of the middle class, not those of working-class ethnics or inner-city blacks. Most teachers come from the middle class and teach students their own values and norms. They teach middle-class literature, not literature that might be more germane to their students. Stories about middle-class children in the suburbs with a house, a lawn, a pet dog, and a car are used to teach reading to young children.

Children are assumed to receive equal education and equal evaluation through testing, but education in American schools is based on the middle-class culture. Children from other racial, ethnic, or class groups do not have the same cultural background and often have a more difficult time achieving the expected performance levels in the middle-class environment.

They would be difficult for a five-year-old inner-city child to understand when the child has never had a house to live in, a lawn to play on, a pet dog, or a car to ride in. Even the sports are middle-class, not the jump-rope and "break-dancing" of the inner city.

Middle-class children will do better on tests

and be given a college-preparatory education. Working-class children are given working-class vocational training, and the poor, who do not know middle-class norms, will fail completely. Conflict theorists argue that the competitive school system is used to justify keeping the poor in poverty.

Credentialism

Conflict theorists argue that the credentials, diplomas, and degrees given by schools represent learning that is not essential to doing most jobs (Collins, 1979). *Credentialism* is the practice of requiring degrees for most high-paying jobs whether or not the degrees actually signify skills necessary to accomplish the jobs. Everyone from physicians to assembly-line workers learn much more than is necessary to do their work. Physicians must take four years of college, four years of medical school, and a one-year internship to become general practitioners. Those who want to specialize need an additional three or more years of training. Communist societies such as China and Cuba successfully train people in a much shorter time to take care of most of the health needs of the society. The system in the United States perpetuates the prestige of physicians by demanding credentials that can be obtained only by those who have the time and money to enter this elite profession. In addition, physicians come to form their own subculture of shared values and beliefs during their years of training.

Collins also argues that the jobs requiring a great deal of education do not necessarily require the skills people learn in school, but the jobs do require the cultural norms learned in school. When college-educated people enter management positions, the elite can rest assured that the managers will make decisions consistent with the cultural norms.

In sum, conflict theorists believe that the educational system is run by the group in power to legitimate their position. They teach values and norms useful in maintaining their position, use an unfair competitive system to legitimate upper-middle-class success, and insist on certification of skills beyond those necessary to do a job. The upper-middle class has the competitive advantage, but everyone learns the values and norms that maintain the system.

Historical Perspectives on Education

When sociologists study education, they ask whether it functions to teach a body of knowledge to students, to select the students most capable to perform work in society, or to generate new knowledge. They also ask if education reflects the conflicts in society by maintaining the stratification system. When we look at historical evidence to analyze how the system functions, we find that from the beginning education has been related to occupational training.

Occupational Training

The Puritans, who considered education important, founded Harvard College in Massachusetts in 1636 to educate ministers. Initially, only male students between the ages of twelve and twenty were accepted. The subject matter was morals and ethics, and learning was accomplished through rote memorization. William and Mary (1693), Yale (1701), and Princeton (1746) were founded in quick succession and for the same purpose as Harvard.

The University of Virginia, founded by Thomas Jefferson in 1819, had a somewhat broader goal than many earlier universities. Aware of the need to train national leaders, Jefferson wanted to form an institution to educate a "natural aristocracy" in a wide range of subjects including modern languages, science, and mathematics. This curriculum was widely adopted later in the century (Seely, 1970).

After about 1850 emphasis on occupational

Jefferson built the University of Virginia to educate gentlemen for the new nation. He designed the campus himself and built it in sight of his home, Monticello. Here we see the rotunda, which originally served as the library, with original classrooms and dormitory rooms facing the lawn. Jefferson's influence on education remains strong at this school and throughout American universities.

training increased. The federal government began to encourage states to begin colleges that would teach agriculture and mechanics. They were provided with land grants to build the colleges. These land-grant colleges developed into today's public state universities.

During the same period, universities such as Johns Hopkins (1876), which emphasized a scientific curriculum, were founded. Johns Hopkins was also one of the first to systematically support advanced research and the publishing of research findings. Prior to the founding of schools with advanced scientific programs, professions such as medicine, law, and dentistry were learned through the apprenticeship system or practiced without formal education. Once scientific programs were developed, professionals were required to go to school to be accepted into the profession.

Compulsory public education is education that is mandatory until a certain age and that is paid for with public funds. It developed during the eighteenth and nineteenth centuries to educate immigrants. The immigrant children who attended school learned English and were assimilated into American society, but some became ashamed of their parents, who often did not learn the new culture (Novak, 1972).

Public schooling met with resistance from a variety of groups. Some religious leaders believed that education should include training in morals and ethics. Catholic religious leaders were afraid that public education would be Protestant education. Landowners did not want to pay taxes for other people's education because they felt that this was socialism. Farmers did not want to lose the labor of their sons to the schoolroom. In spite of the objections of these groups, however, local educational systems were developed and run by local leaders, which reflected the strong commitment to local governance in the United States.

Beliefs About Children

The goals and structure of an education system shape and are shaped by the society's views of the nature and role of children. Are children good or evil, impulsive or rational? Are they fundamentally different from adults in some ways? Are they naturally curious or naturally passive and indolent? The answers a society provides to questions such as these are manifested in the structure of its education system.

During the Middle Ages, society was considered corrupt and children were believed to be innocent. Children were thought to need protection from the adult realm of sin and worldliness. Accordingly, the Jesuits who started the first schools for children were careful to guard them from influences considered immoral. Vestiges of this view can still be found in our education system today, in which children are gener-

ally forbidden access to books dealing with sex, different political systems, and other potentially "corrupting" influences.

The Puritans believed that children were basically evil, as if they were possessed by the devil. Their education involved memorizing parts of the Bible, catechisms, and other sources of moral wisdom until the evil nature of children was overcome. This process was hurried along by the schoolmaster's liberal use of the switch. Rather than being isolated from adults, children were encouraged to emulate their good example, since it was assumed that adults had already learned right from wrong.

Early in this century, it was thought that children were impulsive, controlled not by the devil but by their biological drives, and thus strict discipline was necessary. Children were required to sit in rows, memorize their spelling and mathematics, and raise their hands to recite.

Two centuries ago children of all ages attended school together, where reading, writing, and arithmetic were the subjects emphasized. Lessons were memorized and reciting for the teacher was an important part of classwork. Notice the absence of books in the classroom — children who are not reciting work on their slates. In spite of the strict discipline in these schools, children relaxed when the teacher's back was turned.

Since 1960, some important changes have taken place. The moral issue of whether children are good or evil has lost importance, but it has come to be believed that children have a natural curiosity — they want to learn. In schools based on this belief, discipline has decreased, rows of chairs have been rearranged to allow freedom of movement, and "learning centers" have been developed and placed around the room so that children can move from center to center as their interest dictates. This view has not been adopted by most parents, who think that children need to be controlled. They would like to see a return to an emphasis on basic skills and strict discipline. They believe that an education is necessary in order to acquire a good job, and they want to be sure their children learn the necessary skills rather than relying on their natural curiosity. While parents may not approve of the way schools are run, their power to bring about changes is limited.

Who Rules the Schools?

Most American education is public — the schools are open to everyone. They are funded by local and federal governments, so there are strong ties between the educational system and the political system. Education is paid for by tax dollars, and although it is controlled locally, it complies with all the laws of the land.

The Bureaucratic Structure of Public Schools

The bureaucracy of a local school system is headed by a school board, which adopts a budget, sets policies, and directs the supervisor of schools. The supervisor develops guidelines based on the policies of the school board and directs the principals of the schools in the area. The principals make rules for the local schools

based on the guidelines of the supervisor and direct the teachers to carry out the rules. The teacher establishes rules for the classroom in accordance with the principal's direction and teaches the students.

Although the United States emphasizes local control of schools, it is somewhat misleading to suggest that school boards operate independently because the federal government passes many laws that affect the educational system. Schools must respect the rights protected by the Constitution; they must allow religious freedom and offer equal opportunity. The federal government influences such issues as prayer in school, the teaching of evolution, equal opportunity for minorities, and the education of the handicapped. School boards must comply with federal laws regarding these and other concerns.

States also have constitutions, which cannot contradict federal law. Within the restrictions of federal law and the state constitution, the states pass laws that set standards for the schools. They certify teachers, set the number of days students must atend school, determine holidays, and establish minimum requirements for the curriculum and for graduation. Any school board policies, therefore, must comply with these laws.

Compare the bureaucratic system of modern schools to the informal organization of private tutors and craftsmen who taught in the Middle Ages. Boys and men sought out a tutor who agreed to teach or to take them on as an apprentice in a trade. There were no rules about who could teach, who could learn, what subject matter would be covered, what the fees would be, how often lessons would take place, or how long the teaching-learning relationship would continue. Unlike what is practiced in present-day school systems, decisions about each of these considerations were made by the individual pupil and teacher and therefore could be tailored to the individual's needs.

Financing the Schools

Public elementary and secondary schools are financed entirely by taxes. Local real estate taxes are the largest source of support for schools, but funds from federal and state governments have played an increasingly important role in funding schools, as shown in Table 14-1. Public colleges and universities likewise receive much of their support from taxes, but they also charge tuition to help pay the costs of running the colleges and raise money from alumni and charitable foundations. Private schools at every level rely on tuition and private donations for support. Donations come from alumni, charitable foundations, and sponsoring churches, but private schools also receive state and federal tax dollars to support special programs such as research projects, experimental programs, and the training of scarce professionals such as physicians or scientists. Wealthy private colleges rely heavily on endowments, the money the college has to invest. Income from these investments is used to help pay yearly expenses.

Stratification in the School System

Like other social systems, schools reflect stratification and can be a cause of it. The school that children attend can have an enormous influence on their life chances. Those who attend first-rate elementary and high schools usually go on to prestigious colleges and land high-paying jobs. Those who receive a poor education may become so frustrated that they quit without graduating. Some critics contend that schools are biased in favor of middle- and upper-class students at all levels, from the federal education bureaucracy to the local school board.

Table 14-1
Percent of public school revenue by source

	1920	1940	1960	1983
Local	83.2	68.0	52.8	38.1
State	16.5	30.3	31.1	43.3
Federal	.3	1.8	3.9	6.8

SOURCES: U.S. Bureau of the Census, *Statistical Abstract of the United States: 1984*, 104th ed., (U.S. Government Printing Office, Washington, D.C., 1984, no. 211, p. 138; *Historical Statistics of the United States*, Washington, D.C., 1984.

Elite School Boards

Local school boards are usually elected by the people of the school district, although in about 10 percent of the districts they are appointed by the mayor. They consist primarily of white, male business or professional people, even in predominantly black or working-class schools. Sometimes board members come into conflict with the minority groups in their school districts. Disagreements have ranged from hair styles to vocational training, from teaching the basics of reading, writing, and arithmetic to discipline.

Eighty-five percent of the college regents or trustees in the United States are male. One-third are in administrative or executive positions in business or industry and one-fourth are in a profession, but only one in seven is employed in education. Some critics argue that school boards would represent their communities better if they consisted of a greater variety of intelligent people, including members from minority groups, ethnic groups, labor, faculty, and the student body.

The Middle-Class Faculty

The majority of the faculty in elementary schools are women, 74 percent of whom are from the middle class. In high schools, there are more male faculty, many of whom are from the lower socioeconomic class. White males in the public school system often move rather rapidly into administration, normally to vice-principal and then on to more responsible positions in the hierarchy. Women and blacks move into administration much more slowly, and when they do, it is often in special assignments, such as in programs specifically for women and blacks. These moves out of the mainstream make future promotions even more difficult (Ortiz, 1982).

In colleges and universities, the majority of faculty members are white males, although the number of females has increased. Women are found mostly in the lower ranks and are often paid less than their male colleagues of equal rank, in spite of laws requiring equal pay for equal work. Women in some schools have filed complaints to raise their salaries to the level of the men on the faculty but to date full equality has not been achieved. Also significant is the fact that blacks are underrepresented in college and university teaching.

Segregated Students

Traditionally, schools have been segregated by socioeconomic class in the United States, be-cause children go to neighborhood schools and neighborhoods are segregated. Students of different races often attend different schools for the same reason. Many blacks and Hispanics live in inner-city neighborhoods and go to predominantly black and Hispanic schools. They also traditionally finish fewer years of school (see Table 14-2).

Achievement in school has been related to social class and to race. Compared with working-class students, upper-middle-class white students have higher grades and higher achievement and I.Q. test scores. They are more likely to go to college, they more frequently attend four-year colleges, and they complete more years of education. Working-class students, in turn, have higher achievement than blacks. Why have our schools so often failed to educate black students properly?

To answer this question, James Coleman and a team of sociologists (1966) compared the facilities of schools in black and white neighborhoods. He found that the schools were the same age, spent the same amount of money per pupil, and had equivalent library and laboratory facilities. Teacher qualifications and class size were also the same. He concluded the differences in achievement were related to the students' socio-

Table 14-2

Comparative levels of education of the population age twenty-five and over, March, 1982

	PERCENT SPANISH ORIGIN	PERCENT BLACK	PERCENT WHITE
Less than four years of high school	54.0	45.0	27.2
High school, four years	27.2	32.5	38.8
College, one to three years	10.9	13.6	15.4
College, four or more years	7.7	8.7	18.4

SOURCE: *The World Almanac and Book of Facts, 1984* edition. Copyright © Newspaper Enterprise Association, 1984, New York 10166. Reprinted by permission.

economic backgrounds, not to differences in the schools themselves. Coleman also found that black students performed better in white schools and recommended busing students to promote integration. Busing was carried out in many localities, but few people, black or white, liked busing children to schools in other neighborhoods. Many argued that it interfered with the concept of neighborhood schools and local control.

Bowles and Gintis (1976) have theorized that elites benefit from neighborhood school systems that segregate students. In segregated school systems, students learn their place in the stratification system. Upper-class students learn about the hierarchy and the need to follow the rules of a hierarchy. They learn to accept rules made by elites and they also learn that they too can someday take their rightful place among the elite. They are actively socialized into the social system.

Lower-class students also learn that the elites have a legitimate right to rule because of their superior talents. Lower-class students do not learn to read and write as well as elites, however. As a result, they may develop low self-esteem and come to believe they are not capable of joining the elite. This lowers their achievement motivation, and they become apathetic and alienated from the system that has educated them to feel inferior. Recent research (Oakes, 1982) has found evidence that supports the Bowles and Gintis hypothesis.

One tool used in schools that may be biased in favor of the middle class is the I.Q. test, which was designed by Lewis M. Terman in 1916 to test skills used in upper-middle-class occupations that involved manipulating numbers and words. The purpose of the test was to select students who might benefit from advanced training. Terman and others believed that it measured an inherited genetic trait called intelligence. They assumed that those who scored low on the test lacked intelligence and were less capable of learn-

ing than those who did well. It was argued that those who did poorly should be assigned to lower-class jobs.

Critics have argued that I.Q. tests measure not an inherited characteristic but a person's knowledge of upper-middle-class American culture, which is why immigrants, the working class, the poor, and blacks score low while upper-middle-class Americans score high. These critics say the test serves the stratification system by creating a myth that convinces the lower classes that their station in life is part of the natural order of things (Karier, 1976).

Can a low score on an I.Q. test hurt even a bright student in the classroom? Rosenthal and Jacobson (1968) believe it can. As discussed in Chapter 6, "Socialization and Social Interaction," these investigators found that students do not learn as well when their teachers believe they are not very bright. If teachers have learned that lower-class and minority students do not perform well on I.Q. and achievement tests, they will have lower expectations of them in class. Even if they do perform well, teachers may not recognize their talents, give them lower grades, and confuse and frustrate them.

In one study of pupil-teacher interaction, it was found that teachers asked black students simpler questions than they asked white students. If a black pupil could not answer a question the teacher asked somebody else. If a white pupil could not answer a question, however, the teacher gave an explanation. Teachers also praised and complimented white students more than black students when they gave correct answers (Weinberg, 1977, p. 232). Notice in Table 14-2 how much less education blacks and people of Spanish origin have than whites.

Is All This Education Necessary?

In spite of the unequal education received by various groups in the United States, most people have had great faith in education as a

Children from a black neighborhood in Boston are bused to another neighborhood where they will be able to attend school with white children. There is some evidence that children perform better in integrated schools, but black children must often face discrimination from teachers, from white children, and from educational and testing procedures that were not designed for children with their cultural background.

means to upward mobility. It is this faith that is largely responsible for the phenomenal growth of our educational institutions, especially public institutions. Community and junior colleges have been built, and loan programs have been established to assist those who could not otherwise afford a college education. The women's movement has stressed education as a means of upward mobility for women, and poverty programs have focused on training and educating the poor to help them rise out of poverty. Underlying all these steps is the assumption that education leads to upward mobility.

In the past, most sociologists supported this view. Blau and Duncan (1967), for example, argued that if children from large families could get as much education as children from small families, their existing occupational disadvantages would largely disappear. The belief among sociologists that education leads to upward mobility was so widespread that the presidential address of the annual meeting of the American Sociological Association in 1971 (Sewell, 1971) was

essentially a call for political action to increase opportunities for the less privileged to acquire an education so that they too might become upwardly mobile.

There is, however, reason to doubt that education has much impact on social mobility. Sociologists such as Randall Collins (1979) and Ivar Berg (1970) have argued that increasing educational opportunities for the disadvantaged creates a hardship for them. They are encouraged to spend more money on education, but when they complete their education, they do not have additional earning power. Berg refers to this low return on educational investment as "the great training robbery."

The fact that increased education does not necessarily lead to better jobs may come as a surprise. The truth is, however, that factors other than education have a powerful influence on what jobs people take and what salaries they earn. Family background, for example, is more closely related to future occupation than level of education (Jencks, 1979). A son from a working-

On Being a Steelworker's Daughter

My elite classmates don't grasp hard-working unionized lives

In 30 years as a millworker, my father can't remember a whole mill ever shutting down. Now Clairton Coke Works has been down since July. Other mills — Duquesne, Homestead, McKeesport — have been wholly or partly down even longer. So my father waits for the ax to fall and cut him down to another statistic in the morning papers. He comes home and says to my mother, "Well, I'm on the schedule again this week. For now, it looks like I still have a job."

"If you don't take academics, there ain't nothing," says my father, patting me on the head with one hand and, with the other, thrusting me into Carnegie-Mellon University, the school first built with Andrew Carnegie's steel wealth.

My father's own background is a Clairton High diploma, but my father wanted my sister and me to attend college, and he was strict with us during our childhood. "Do your best in whatever you choose to do," he'd say, offering us an extra dollar for every straight-A report card. But the best reward was the smile on his face when my sister was accepted to medical school, and I got the OK from CMU.

So I took the financial aid and enrolled in what my middle-class hometown calls a "good" school. The dorms didn't bother me — I'm used to living in a house that looks like everybody else's on the block. The difficulties I did not anticipate were conflicts with students from wealthier white-collar backgrounds.

Some conflicts are subtle, like watching the evening news with a friend who never had a father out of work. The unemployment rates are announced, but he doesn't understand: "There's got to be jobs out there; why don't they look for them?" At other times, the conflicts are not subtle, like sitting in class listening to disdainful descriptions of how typical blue-collar people spend leisure time: "They drink beer and watch football games, but they never go to the theater."

When I'm outnumbered, in class especially, I sink lower into my seat and pretend that all those nights I spent at the firehall or church bingos were really spent at the symphony or riding lessons.

---

class family is more likely to enter a working-class occupation than a son from a middle-class family, even if they have the same amount of education (Lipset and Bendix, 1967; Jencks, 1979). Children who grow up on welfare are hampered more by their poverty than their lack of education (Schiller, 1970). At the opposite end of the spectrum, an increasing proportion of business executives come from families of high economic status (Keller, 1968).

It seems that as the level of education for everyone in the society increases, members of the upper class get more education than others, go to the elite schools, and use their influential family and friends to help them find the best jobs. On the other hand, the children of the working class, although they get more education than their parents had, find that working-class jobs now require at least a high school diploma, and many jobs in corporations that used to require

But when I'm told by a white-collar girlfriend that her "daddy's company doesn't like unions," I don't hesitate to tell her that my "daddy" works in a part of the city where the air's so bad people drive with their car windows up. That my "daddy" has friends who have been crippled and killed by machinery accidents. And that my "daddy" belongs to a union.

It's even more difficult to explain a blue-collar world to an unsympathetic professor. When a professor confides, "My God, even steel workers make as much as I do," then I know to dress preppy for his class. Blend in. His wife doesn't worry about his getting lung cancer from pollution. Nor does she wait by a phone when a furnace blow-up is reported on the noon news.

Blend in. Professors of this type cannot or will not hear a blue-collar student's views.

"They tell you what they want," says my father, puffing his pipe. "Production is all management decisions. The workers have no input."

I ask him if the bosses make mistakes. "Oh, my God!" he laughs, "It's a wonder they ever make money. Like that new coke battery they built, millions of dollars. Now we're going over the work the contractors did because they didn't do it right the first time. Nobody has a handle on why it wasn't done right." Says my father, "A job that they can do once, they do twice."

My father is a millwright. That means he is a mechanic in charge of fixing and maintaining machinery. He can't go any higher without going into management. It took him 20 years to work up to that position from a broom and shovel.

As I go to classes, I realize I am leaving my father's blue-collar past for my professor's white-collar future. I worry about becoming what my father and I have always disliked.

I hate to mention things like the Robotics Institute when I go home for dinner. Robots don't cheer my father since he's seen his friends put out of work by automation.

"What's going on is the government's fault," he says, banging his fist on the kitchen table. "They know this new technology is coming up and they don't train. It's up to the government, through public schools, to train young people. Why should industry worry about me? If I don't have a job it's the government I'm going to turn to for relief."

"It's good to have robots," my father reasons, "but you have to take the human view into account. A robot may build a thousand cars in one day, but who's going to buy them?"

The houses on my street don't have two-car garages. And my father hasn't told me if he's on the schedule this week.

SOURCE: *The Washington Post*, Jan. 2, 1983. Article adapted from one in *Focus*, Carnegie-Mellon University's faculty and staff newspaper. Reprinted by permission.

---

only a high school diploma now require a college degree.

Another factor affecting upward mobility is that the size of the educated work force has been increasing faster than the need for educated workers. Berg (1970) estimated that between 1950 and 1960, the labor force gained one-half million more college graduates than it needed. This excess of graduates has been escalating ever since, and because of this increase, we now have a much more highly educated population than other countries. As a result, college graduates began to take white-collar jobs that had previously gone to high school graduates. High school graduates, no longer able to get white-collar jobs, moved into blue-collar work. Middle-class fathers with a high school education and a white-collar job who send a son through college often find that the son has to settle for a white-collar job at the same level of prestige as

A student who attends Eton, a prestigious British prep school, entertains his parents while other students look on. The opportunity to attend an elite school such as Eton assures these students of an education in one of Great Britain's finer universities and continued membership in the British upper class.

the father. The excess of college graduates has continued to increase, so the benefits of having a college degree are also decreasing. Surprisingly, one recent study (Burris, 1983) shows that most people, even when overeducated for their jobs, are quite satisfied with their work and their lives.

The excess of college graduates has also affected blue-collar workers. When it became apparent that blue-collar jobs were growing scarce, students from blue-collar families began finishing high school in increasing numbers, hoping to move into white-collar jobs. Today, however, many blue-collar jobs require a high school diploma, and much white-collar work requires at least some college. Thus, despite their increase in education, the sons and daughters of blue-collar families tend to remain in blue-collar work. The existence of this obstacle to upward mobility is substantiated by statistics: in 1960, 26 percent of all blue-collar workers were high school graduates; in 1970, the proportion was 41 percent.

The costs of remaining in school for long periods of time are enormous. Collins (1979) argues that long years of expensive training and educational credentials should not be used to determine who advances in jobs. Secretaries should be allowed to move into management jobs, as they did before the turn of the century when many secretaries were men. Medical professionals should all start as orderlies and work their way through the ranks of nurse to become physicians through a combination of work experience and special training. This system would make it possible for people who could not pay for long years of education to reach rewarding positions in society.

Imagine how different your education would be if it were not so oriented toward a career. If you were assured a place in the work force when you graduated regardless of how good your

Increasing years of education are necessary for people to achieve upward mobility in today's job market. These women look determined as they receive their Ph.D. degrees. Advancement into a good job, even at this level, is difficult, and women with Ph.D.'s earn lower incomes than men with the same education. At the Ph.D. level, white women earn less than black women.

grades were, you could relax and enjoy both your classwork and your free time. You could explore more subjects in new areas or in areas where you had little talent. You could write new and different term papers instead of conforming closely to a traditional format. You could relax and enjoy your education because you would be assured of a career position. Students in some societies are virtually guaranteed jobs upon graduation and so they can relax a bit more than American students can.

Contest and Sponsored Mobility

In the United States, students can get as much education as they are willing and able to pay for as long as they maintain the grades necessary for acceptance at the next higher level. This system has been labeled *contest mobility* (Turner, 1960), because students can continue as long as they meet the standards of each level. The high school graduate can apply to college, the junior college graduate can apply to a four-year institution, and the college graduate can apply to a graduate school.

By contrast, Japan and most European countries have a system known as *sponsored mobility*. In these countries, students must pass qualifying examinations to gain admittance into different types of high schools and colleges. They may receive a classical education leading to a university degree, a business education, or engineering and technical training. Once they enter a particular track, they rarely change to another type of education. A student in business school, for example, is unlikely to switch to a university.

Education in Britain is typical of the sponsored-mobility system. The British have a long tradition of formal education for the elite. Oxford and Cambridge, both founded in the Middle Ages, emphasized Latin and the classics. Members of the elite class were selected to attend the university and become educated gentlemen.

In time, private grammar schools (called public schools) developed to prepare the young of the upper classes for their university education. This system of upper-class education continues in Great Britain today.

Tax-supported schools for British working-class children were slow to develop. At the turn of the twentieth century, education for all children became mandatory until age twelve. This law, however, was resisted by farmers who would lose the help of their sons and country squires who would lose their source of cheap labor.

After World War II, the British realized that to keep up with advanced technology, they had to have technical education, so they gradually developed a system of secondary schools. Under this system, the grammar schools taught the traditional college preparatory subjects, technical schools taught engineering and sciences, and other schools were designed to provide a more general education. Children were selected for one of these types of schools at age thirteen on the basis of tests and teacher evaluations. Only 20 percent of the schools were grammar schools, and these were attended almost exclusively by members of the elite classes.

In the 1960s, publicly financed secondary schools were changed to offer a comprehensive education, so the elite fled to privately funded schools where they could continue to receive the grammar school preparatory education. At about the same time, a crash program was begun to build public colleges, but financing for the program ran out. The cost of building a system of higher education and class differences in access to higher education remain major problems in the British educational system.

Education and Change in the 1980s

Americans take great pride in education and the public school system. At the same time, we speak of a crisis in American education, which is re-

Students mark the closing of their high school in Alpena, Michigan, by draping the doorway with a black banner. There has been a decrease in the number of children in the school-age population in some areas, especially in neighborhoods where the children have grown up and moved away from home.

flected in lowering achievement test scores, discipline problems, the persistent lack of upward mobility for the poor, and the decreasing worth of a college degree. Although debates about these crises tend to focus on the schools, many of these problems are caused by changes in the larger society. One major change that has altered education in the past two decades and will continue to affect it is the size of the school-age population.

Decreasing Population

The number of young children in this country grew dramatically with the onset of the baby boom in the late 1940s. Many children were born to people who had postponed childbearing during the depression of the 1930s and during World War II. These babies were born in addition to those being born to people who were just reaching the age of marriage and childbearing. More will be said about the reasons for this population increase in a later chapter.

The baby boom children entered the public school system in the 1950s, and an enormous building program had to be undertaken to construct schools for them. Classrooms were crowded, children went to classes in shifts, and there was a shortage of teachers. When these

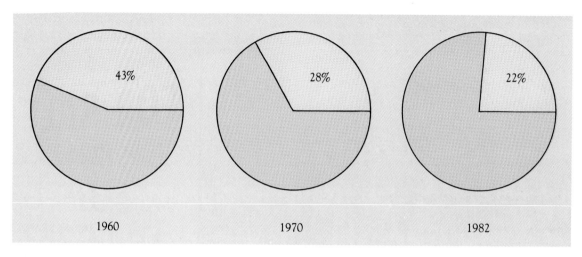

Figure 14-1
Enrollment in private institutions as a percentage of enrollment in all U.S.
institutions of higher education, 1960, 1970, and 1982.

same students went on to college in the affluent 1960s, public colleges grew rapidly, and new community and state colleges were built. Some classes in large universities were enormous, and there was a severe shortage of teachers at this level as well.

The baby boom children began to enter the job market in the 1970s. Just as there were not enough schools for them, there were not enough jobs for them. College graduates were absorbed into the job market, but high school graduates had to struggle for low-paying jobs, and the poor, especially black youths, often could not find any jobs. A college education seemed less worthwhile unless one studied for a career, and the number of students in the liberal arts decreased while the number in engineering and business increased.

By the beginning of the 1980s, the last of the baby boom generation had entered college — the baby boom was over. Today school enroll-

ments are decreasing. Elementary schools and secondary schools began closing in the 1970s, and there is an overabundance of teachers. The number of college-aged people is decreasing and by 1997, there will be 23 percent fewer eighteen- to twenty-four-year-olds than there were in 1977 (Stadtman, 1980). Public colleges, which grew so rapidly for two decades, may become smaller, but because they are financed by tax dollars and relatively inexpensive to attend, they should continue to recruit students. Private colleges, however, are in serious trouble. Since they must charge more tuition, they can't compete with the public colleges, and many are closing. In 1960, 43 percent of all students attended private colleges. In 1982, that figure had dropped to 22 percent (see Figure 14-1). There may be empty college buildings and unemployed professors unless a larger percentage of today's high school graduates go to college.

These figures suggest that, in the future, colleges will be less diverse. Most students will probably attend public institutions that emphasize education for careers. Public colleges have also been attempting to attract students with evening programs, work-study programs, weekend programs, and other options for working students. The diversity provided by small liberal arts colleges may all but disappear from the American scene.

Because there are fewer young people in the population, there are fewer young people entering the work force. Employers may be willing to start college-educated people in better jobs, and they may be more willing to hire high school graduates. If the high school diploma becomes more valuable, high school students may be more motivated to compete for jobs, and high school achievement scores and discipline may improve. Whatever the employment situation, working with computers will be a part of the job.

Computers in the School

Microcomputers, notwithstanding their usefulness in the modern world, have created a dilemma for the educational system. On the one hand, many people believe that every student should be able to use computers and that the only way to accomplish this is to teach computers in the schools. At the public school level, then, local tax dollars must buy enough computers to make them available to all students. This is much more likely to happen in schools in wealthy districts than it is in schools in poor areas, which threatens to increase the amount of inequality in American education. Students from the better-equipped schools will have a skill that students from poorer districts will not have. This means that once again students from wealthy suburban neighborhoods will have an advantage over those from poorer neighborhoods when they apply for jobs.

At the college level, the dilemma takes on added dimensions. Some colleges now require each student to purchase a personal computer, but as college costs rise, every added expense becomes a severe burden for some students, and some will not be able to attend college at all with such expensive requirements. If the college chooses to supply computers, however, it becomes an enormous expense to the college. Most colleges will not be able to buy endless supplies of computers and will therefore find it necessary to ration their use. Some colleges have already decided that word-processing is not an appropriate use of the computer and will not permit students to type term papers on computers. It somehow seems more appropriate to use computers for work involving numbers. Hence, computers are more likely to be used for scientific and technological work. Word-processing, however, is extremely useful for students. If computers were brought to class, legible notes could be taken effortlessly. Term papers could be automatically checked for spelling and indexed. Essay exams done with a computer in class could be far more coherent and legible.

The introduction of the computer means that new rules must be established for their use. May they be brought to class? May students write essay tests on their computers? Does this give them an advantage over students who do not have computers? If students have drafts of essays and bibliographies in the computer, does cheating become a problem? Many questions will need to be answered as the school system adjusts to this new technology. The nature of teaching, learning, test taking, and grading may change dramatically.

What people fear most about the computer, however, is its ability to store massive amounts of data. Many details about the student's college career can now be kept on the computer: grades, attendance, appointments with the dean, use of

SOCIOLOGISTS AT WORK
Selling College Textbooks

Kate Campbell is a college sales representative for Little, Brown and Company. Her job is to sell textbooks at about thirty campuses from Boston to Maine. Her interest in sociology began when she was a student at the University of Vermont. "When I was in school in the early 1970s, the social and political upheaval of the times was in the forefront of most student's minds," she says. "I wanted somehow to understand that upheaval. I had entered the university as a literature major, and after a couple of semesters, I began to feel that I was missing what was happening in the world around me. Sociology responds to what's happening in society, both historically and at the moment. I decided that a degree in sociology was the best avenue for becoming involved in and learning about the social phenomena of the times."

After receiving her B.A. in sociology, Campbell took a job as editor for a management consulting group. "Although I had an excellent job and a fabulous salary, I found the lack of in-terest in books and of intellectual curiosity among my coworkers quite disturbing. I found myself in a position where I was supposed to be working with the best and the brightest MBAs from Stanford and Berkeley, and when I began to see a certain lack of intellectual development, it became the most important thing in the world for me to find another niche." She has never regret-ted her decision to switch careers — or to switch her major in sociology.

"The college sales representative's job has many aspects, but the primary responsibility is to inform professors about new titles being pub-lished and to arrange for examination copies to be sent to the appropriate academics. The posi-tion is billed as a sales job, but it's really much more than that. I doubt that there are many aca-demics who can be really 'sold' on a book that isn't right for their course in the first place. The job, then, is to pinpoint exactly what the profes-sor or department is looking for in a new book and then show how that subject or concern is

the library and books checked out, and visits to counseling centers, medical clinics, and birth control and abortion clinics. This information could also be combined with high school records, police records, past medical history, and payroll and income tax records. Files could be kept on students that contained more informa-tion than the students know about themselves.

Computers and the misuse of information are not the biggest concern of those who play in-fluential roles in the educational system, how-ever. In the past few years, critics of what is hap-pening in education have been most concerned with mediocre achievement levels.

The New Wave of Criticism

In 1983 both the National Commission on Excellence in Education and The Twentieth Century Fund released reports that expressed concern over mediocrity in our educational sys-tem, noting particularly the declining SAT scores of high school students. Neither report attempted to explore reasons for the mediocrity in the schools.

Parents generally responded to the report with a cry for more discipline in the schools, perhaps something reminiscent of the Puritan approach, which suggests that children have to

treated in your book. Obviously, the only way to do this quickly is to know as much as possible about all the texts you're selling. The job provides a unique intellectual challenge in this regard, because most publishers will have at least a hundred new titles a year.

"Every year, college text publishers market hundreds of new texts written at every conceivable level and orientation. I like to think of my job as providing a valuable service to busy professors who have neither the time nor the inclination to review every new text that's published, but who want to give their students the best text available. In a matter of a few minutes, a publisher's 'rep' can answer important questions that may take the instructor an hour to find in the book if he sits down with it without any previous knowledge about it.

"My background in sociology has been invaluable in my job. First, the understanding I gained in sociology about institutions and the similarities among them has helped immensely. As we learn in sociology, there are similarities in all institutions — and universities are no exception. All schools have a logic that guides their procedures, where faculty departments are likely to be located, and where you may park your car. If you think it's tough figuring out the campus where you're a student, imagine trying to simply figure out thirty different campuses! An understanding of the underlying logic of universities as institutions saves a lot of time.

"Second, and more important, is the knowledge I gained as a sociology major about group dynamics — it's very important to try to ascertain the role each department member plays in the textbook decision. At some schools, the individual instructor chooses his or her own book, but at other schools, the department as a whole will decide on one book. Sometimes a committee is chosen to review new texts, sometimes each faculty member casts a vote. Always, there is a core group or a single 'leader' whose decision is most influential. The problem for the publisher's rep is discovering who that person or core is, who's for your book and who's against it. A background in sociology and particularly group dynamics has helped me very much in determining those situations where my books have the best chance and where I should spend the most time."

be *forced* to be good. Educators also made many proposals; most recommended more of what schools are currently doing, such as increasing requirements in high school English, mathematics, science, social studies, computer science, and foreign languages. They also proposed having children begin school at age four, increasing the length of the school day and the school year, and paying teachers on the basis of merit, which often translates into paying teachers on the basis of how well students perform. Recommendations were also made to involve business and industry more extensively in the educational system.

A wholesale increase in schooling is a risky proposition at best, however, when we do not know why students are not performing well. If schools, however subtly, are encouraging our lower classes and minority students to fail, increasing the school day, the school year, and the number of requirements might also increase the apathy and discouragement felt by these students. Likewise, if school is too occupation-oriented and therefore discouraging to people from the lower classes, might involving the business community in the schools make matters worse? Simple solutions to remedy our very complex problems in education and stratification will probably not work.

Summary

Why is education so important? Structural-functional theory argues that education in a complex industrial society supplements what families can teach their children, that it helps children acquire complex skills and the knowledge necessary to function in the world. The educational system also selects students on the basis of their talents and abilities to meet the needs of society, directing the most talented into advanced education and training for positions of leadership and directing those with less talent to the positions in which they will serve society best. Educational institutions also create new knowledge and new technology, which they teach to the next generation. They create innovation and change so that society can advance.

Conflict theory argues that education is a means by which powerful groups prevent change. The elites use the educational system to teach children elite values and norms so that everyone will believe that the position of the elites is justified. Elite groups promote children and give diplomas and degrees on the basis of how well students know the elite culture. Elite children usually receive high credentials and move into elite jobs, whereas those from the lower classes tend to remain in lower-class jobs.

The American educational system was begun by the Puritans and later developed into our modern system of elementary schools, secondary schools, colleges, and universities. These schools are complicated bureaucracies, directed and financed by local, state, and federal boards who determine curriculums, testing procedures, and other requirements for certification. Supervisors, principals, and teachers implement the various rules and standards, and students, upon meeting the standards, receive the appropriate diplomas and degrees.

Whether students are from the upper or lower classes, family background is the single most accurate predictor of the school attended, years of schooling, type of occupation, and income.

The British school system is similar to the American system, but the process of selecting who will receive a higher education and an advanced job and who will enter working-class vocational schools and jobs takes place much earlier, at age thirteen. Family background is an important predictor of which type of education a student will receive.

The baby boom of the late 1940s dramatically increased the number of students attending school during the 1950s and 1960s. This burst of population is over now, and the number of students is decreasing, which may lead to declining college enrollments, especially in private colleges. A larger proportion of students will probably attend local and state public colleges. Whether more working-class and poor students will attend college and whether a college education will become more or less valuable in the job market depends on the political decisions and economic hiring policies of the next decade.

The use of computers is being taught at all levels of our education system, but this development is controversial in some respects. There is currently a perceived widespread decline in our education system, and the problem is a complex one that defies easy solution.

Key Terms

compulsory public education
contest mobility
credentialism
sponsored mobility

Suggested Readings

Berg, Ivar. **Education and Jobs: The Great Training Robbery.** *New York: Praeger Publishers, 1970.* Berg provides extensive evidence that the amount of education people were expected to have was not necessary to perform the work they did. Jobs had not increased in difficulty and could have been performed with much less training.

Chesler, Mark A. and William M. Cave. **A Sociology of Education: Access to Power and Privilege.** *New York: Macmillan, 1981.* A basic text that emphasizes how the social structure influences education.

Clark, Burton R. **"The Cooling-Out Function in Higher Education," American Journal of Sociology** *(May 1960):569–576.* A discussion of the role of counseling in junior colleges in placing students in working-class jobs.

Collins, Randall. **The Credential Society: An Historical Sociology of Education and Stratification.** *New York: Academic Press, 1979.* This book argues strongly that education maintains the current stratification system and the status quo rather than encouraging upward mobility.

Jencks, Christopher and David Riesman. **The Academic Revolution.** *Garden City, N.Y.: Doubleday, 1968.* A classic sociological analysis of universities.

Mandell, Richard D. **The Professor Game.** *New York: Doubleday, 1977.* A good description, sometimes critical, sometimes sympathetic, often funny, of why professors act as they do.

Schrag, Peter and Diane Divoky. **The Myth of the Hyperactive Child.** *N.Y.: Pantheon Books, 1975.* This book argues that children are drugged to keep control in the classroom, not because the children are ill.

Stadtman, Verne A. **Academic Adaptations: Higher Education Prepares for the 1980s and 1990s.** *San Francisco: Jossey-Bass, 1980.* A Carnegie report on education containing articles on recent studies and statistics.

CHAPTER 15

Political Groups and Systems

Man by nature is a political animal.
— Aristotle

The United States is a nation of many laws. We register our births, go to school, marry, and often divorce according to the law. We paint our houses, mow our grass, shovel our sidewalks, take our driving tests, and park our cars when and where we are supposed to, and we refrain from spitting in public places. We may get a summons if we do not behave as the law states we should, but often we are not even aware that there are laws dictating these activities.

Some laws are not obeyed, however. Prohibition of liquor did not stop people from drinking, banning abortions did not stop people from having them, and making marijuana illegal did not stop people from smoking it.

In large, complex societies, many decisions must be made about the duties and responsibilities of citizens and also about their rights and privileges. If the society is to be orderly, people must obey the rules that are made.

Politics is the use of power to determine who gets what in society. The political institution establishes and enforces the laws and punishes those who disobey them. It can levy taxes, distribute scarce resources, sponsor education, plan the economy, encourage or ban religion, determine who can marry and who is responsible for children, and otherwise influence behavior. The study of political groups and systems, then, is the study of power.

Types of Power

Weber (1958) pointed out that there are several types of power. Physical force is one obvious type. An individual or an army can be captured and put in handcuffs or prison by a stronger individual or army. Often, however, sheer force accomplishes little. Although people can be physically restrained, they cannot be made to perform complicated tasks by force alone.

Latent force, or the threat of force, is more powerful than force alone. A kidnapper can get what he wants from a victim by demanding ransom in exchange for the victim's life. The kidnapper wants the money and hopes the threat of murder will produce it — a dead victim doesn't do the kidnapper any good. Similarly, a ruler can say, "Either perform your duty or you will go to jail," hoping that the threat of jail will make the citizen perform the desired duty. Putting the citizen in jail, however, does not really help the ruler. In fact, latent force can sometimes produce results in situations in which direct force would not.

Controlling a society through force, whether actual or latent, is expensive and inefficient. It does not bring about the cooperation necessary for society to function productively. A group that relies on force to maintain its power faces a constant threat of being overthrown by its citizens, whereas more reliable types of power do not rely on force for their effectiveness. Legitimate power, for example, is power that is accepted by the people in a society as being necessary and beneficial, such as the power to make and enforce rules beneficial to all.

Authority is power accepted as legitimate by those it affects. The people give the ruler the authority to rule, and they obey willingly without the need or threat of force.

Weber, who was a master at classifying the abstract concepts needed to understand society, identified three types of authority. In *traditional authority,* the leader of the group leads by tradition or custom. In a patriarchal society, the father is the ruler and is obeyed because it is the accepted practice. When the father dies, his eldest son becomes ruler and has authority based on the nation's customs. Rulers who have tradi-

tional authority are usually born into their positions and their competence to rule is not usually at issue. Also, the bounds of authority for traditional rulers are fairly broad — their power can range from settling minor disagreements to dictating who can marry whom.

The second type of authority is charismatic. *Charismatic authority* is based on the personal attributes of the leader. Sometimes a person can win the confidence, support, and trust of a group of people who then give the leader the authority to make decisions and set down rules. A charismatic leader attracts followers because they judge him or her to be particularly wise or capable.

Martin Luther King was this kind of leader. King gained followers because he was a moving speaker who addressed people with sincerity and a sense of mission and won their respect. With their support he was able to lead a political fight to improve the position of blacks in the United States.

Another charismatic leader is the Reverend Sun Myung Moon of the Unification Church. Moon has built a following on the basis of his own conviction that he was chosen by God to spread the word of Christianity throughout the world and to rebuild God's kingdom on earth. Moon, who has gained followers in his native Korea and in Japan, Europe, and America, instructs his people to work hard and live a simple life of poverty. When they join the church, they sacrifice their worldly goods and the pleasures they consider evil, such as alcohol, tobacco, and drugs.

The third type of authority, *legal authority,* is based on a system of rules and regulations that determine how the society will be governed. In the United States, the Constitution sets down the bases for the government's authority, the Congress enacts the laws, and the president carries them out. He directs the military when it is

Martin Luther King speaks to demonstrators who marched on Washington in August of 1963. King was leader of the Southern Christian Leadership Conference, a group with no legal power to rule in this country. King's charismatic leadership, however, enabled him to lead great masses of people in peaceful demonstrations and to press those with legal authority for equal treatment of blacks.

needed to enforce the law and brings before the courts or pardons those who break it. The courts interpret the laws and make judgments about whether they have been broken.

Weber was extremely concerned about certain characteristics of legal authority. As discussed in Chapter 5, the power granted in legal authority is based on the rules and regulations governing the office. The power of the individual officeholder is limited by those rules, and the individual has power only as long as he or she adheres to them. Legal authority rests in the organization, and the organization attempts to serve its own interests and meet its own goals. Thus power in the United States rests in organizations and not in the will of individual citizens. For example, the federal bureaucracy in the United States has grown so much in recent years that its size has become an issue in presidential elections. Candidates routinely promise to cut back on the number of federal employees. Once in office, however, they find that the bureaucracy has ways of resisting major cutbacks, and it is almost impossible to make substantial reductions — even in the president's own executive branch! Since a president cannot afford to antagonize the people he relies on to implement his policies, the bureaucracy serves its own interests, and the taxpayer ends up footing the bill.

The Development of Political Systems

As societies become wealthier and more complex, political systems grow more powerful. In Chapter 8, we discussed an example of a very primitive and simple society, the Tasaday, who had no ruler and made decisions as a group. As societies evolved from similar uncomplicated bands, they grew wealthier and their rulers were able to control larger areas with their armies. These rulers gained power by force, through charismatic leadership, or by inheriting leadership in accordance with group tradition. At first the controlled areas were small, but later cities and the surrounding areas came under the power of individual rulers. These territories were called *city-states*. Today most of the world is organized into *nation-states*, large territories ruled by a single institution. Nation-states developed in Europe several centuries ago, but they arose in Africa only during the last century.

When does a nation-state become a cohesive society? How does a country develop laws that will unite the population, create an orderly society, give authority to the governed, and eliminate the need for force? These are two of the oldest questions in political history, but the modern ideas of particular concern to sociologists fall within the basic theoretical approaches discussed throughout this text.

Structural-Functional Theory

Structural functionalists believe that a society is built on a common set of values. As discussed in Chapter 4, our society believes in work, achievement, equal opportunity, and the freedom to run our own lives, to name just a few of our predominant values. These values are learned by young children in the family and passed on to subsequent generations.

In a legal system of authority, a society's values shape its laws and political policies. If people value achievement, the law will protect the right to achieve. If people value freedom, the law will protect freedom and social policy will encourage freedom — no one will be forced to practice a particular religion, for example, and marriage will be a matter of personal choice. It is

the political institutions that pass laws and develop policies that reflect the values of the population. Often, the political institution must extend itself into international affairs to protect the society's values. It may limit imports of foreign goods to protect its own workers and negotiate with other nations to allow trade for the benefit of its own citizens. It protects its citizens from aggressive acts and maintains armed forces to carry out its international functions.

Sometimes, however, the values of a society are not mutually consistent. Our views about work and achievement may come into conflict with our view about the freedom to run our own lives: if some people do not want to work, forcing them to do so would impinge on their freedom. Even when values are shared, it is not always easy to determine which values should be translated into laws and which laws will be obeyed. The abortion issue involves two basically conflicting values, one involving the rights of the fetus and one involving the rights of the mother. Legislatures must decide which rights to protect and individuals must choose whether to abide by the law or act according to their own values if they conflict with the law. Predicting which laws will be obeyed becomes even more difficult when different subcultures have conflicting values. Youth groups who use drugs and religious groups who practice polygamy are subcultures whose values are in conflict with the dominant culture.

Structural functionalists believe that the political institution holds the values of the dominant society and arbitrates conflicts when they arise. One person may act on a value of freedom by marrying more than one spouse, or members of a subculture may feel free to use drugs. It is the political system that decides which values must be upheld and which must be limited to maintain social order. In the United States, where freedom is a value, constant arbitration is necessary to protect the freedoms of the individual without impinging on the other values of society.

Conflict Theory

Conflict theory differs radically from structural-functional theory. It assumes not that societies are based on a set of values but that they are drawn together by people's need for resources: food, shelter, and other necessities. Some groups get a larger share of the resources, and they use these resources to gain power. Just as they hire people to work for them in the economic sphere, they use their resources to hire people to protect their interests in the political sphere. They use their wealth to influence political leaders to support their economic interests and bring about the downfall of individuals or governments who do not support their interests.

The history of Europe provides many examples of how economic groups have used legal power to protect their own interests (Pirenne, 1914). European merchants in the Middle Ages at first sold their goods at strategic points along heavily traveled highways. Eventually, however, they built towns at those points and passed laws restricting others from trading, thus using their political power to create a monopoly of trade. These merchants dominated the cities of Europe for several centuries by passing laws to protect their interests.

In the fifteenth and sixteenth centuries, as worldwide shipping increased, nation-states became powerful and used their political power to protect their shippers. When machinery came into use and manufacturing grew, the manufacturers initially required no political support. They preferred a laissez-faire economy, a free, competitive market. Workers were plentiful and industry could hire them for very low wages and fire them at will. The workers, who suffered greatly under this system, eventually caused seri-

During the Middle Ages merchants settled in towns to carry on their trade, as shown in this French engraving of an apothecary, a barber, a furrier, and a tailor. Merchants developed their political power by forming organizations called guilds. Only members of a guild were permitted to trade in the town, and the merchants were able to reduce the competition from vagabond traders.

ous civil disturbances, and the industrialists had to develop a legal system to protect their interests. Conflict theorists believe that in every age, the wealthy have used both laws and force to protect their wealth.

Why, then, do the great majority of people

support the laws of the wealthy? According to conflict theorists, it is because the rich use their wealth and power to control the mass media. They teach their values to the majority of people by controlling the schools, the press, radio, television, and other means of communication. They try to convince the population that the rich have a right to their wealth and that they should have the power to restrict trade, hire and fire workers, and otherwise restrict the behavior of the majority to maintain their own position. Unlike the structural functionalists, who believe that the values of the society shape the political system, conflict theorists believe political systems shape the values of society.

Political Structures in Modern Societies

There are two types of legal political rule in modern societies. Neither type is found in a pure form, and many countries have a mixed power structure. In analyzing modern societies, however, it is useful to describe power structures in terms of their ideal types. The two types are democracy, in which the people control the government, and totalitarianism, in which the state rules the people.

The Democratic State

In its ideal form, a *democracy* is a power structure in which people govern themselves. Philosophers such as Jean Jacques Rousseau, John Locke, John Stuart Mill, and John Dewey believed that people knew what was in their own best interest and could learn how to protect these interests within the political system. They also believed that the experience of being politically involved would develop better citizens (Orum, 1978).

An early attempt to practice democracy was made by the Greek city-state of Athens. Leadership was rotated and all government responsibility was shared among the citizens. This system is evident in the Greek use of the term *citizen* to refer to those who were considered members of the city-state and who were entitled to the freedoms and privileges granted to members of the state. Only a small percentage of the population of Athens were citizens, and because there were so few, every citizen could participate directly in the political process. However, the great majority of the city's inhabitants — the slaves, women, and foreigners — were not considered citizens and had no political standing. Thus, although the Greeks called their system a democracy, it would more accurately be considered an *oligarchy*, government by a small elite group.

Changes in social attitudes have raised women, the lower classes, and other groups from the low status they occupied in ancient Greece to the status of citizens in modern Western civilization. But true democracy continues to be impossible because of the unwieldy size of modern political populations. As a result, modern democracies have chosen a system of representation by which the population elects officials to act as their agents. The elected officials in turn appoint the upper-level civil servants and justices of the court. Therefore, when we refer today to "democratic" power structures, we mean those in which people are allowed to vote for elected representatives. It is assumed that the elected representatives will be removed from office if they are not responsive to the desires of the people. Although representative governments of this sort have laws to limit the power of officials and protect the rights of individuals, especially their equality and their right to dissent, there is no question that the elected officials and the people they appoint have a great deal of power.

Democracies have typically developed in societies like the United States where there is an abundance of natural resources. Wealth gives people the freedom to be involved in politics, and the abundance of resources permits the economy to grow without regulation. Yet, some poor countries such as India have also developed democratic political systems despite their poverty.

The Totalitarian State

Totalitarianism is a system of rule in which the government has total control. The government dictates the society's values, ideology, and rules. It also controls the economic development, which is planned in advance, and production is based on the needs of the society as determined by the leaders.

Totalitarian societies do not permit dissent. Their goal is to develop a unified population, one that is not divided by differing religious loyalties or political views. They eliminate dissenters either through violence, imprisonment, or expulsion, especially when the societies are just developing.

Democratic and totalitarian societies have several characteristics in common, and they often have similar ideologies. Both types of government may believe in freedom and equality for their citizens, but inequalities exist under both systems. Another ideological similarity is that each considers its own system superior to the other. The most conspicuous similarity, however, is their bureaucratic organization. Both systems are run by bureaucracies of enormous complexity and power, and political parties play an important role in shaping and unifying their organizational structures.

Political Parties

Political parties are groups of citizens formed with the express intent of gaining control of the political body of the state. They exist in both democratic and totalitarian states. Parties nominate candidates to run for office, provide personnel for bureaucratic posts, and make public policy. Their goal is not just to influence government but to manage it.

Political party systems vary in structure, organization, and reasons for existence. Some parties form around a particular person, such as Charles de Gaulle's Gaullist party in France, which was a strong force in French politics even after the death of its founder. Other parties exist to promote a specific issue. The Green party of West Germany was created to support environmental and antinuclear legislation. The National Woman's party was founded at the beginning of this century in the United States to represent the interests of a particular minority. Most powerful parties, however, are not organized around a single issue. They concern themselves with managing the entire government.

A party's role in government is strongly influenced by the number of parties in a particular governmental system. Totalitarian states have only one party, so there is no competition for control of the government. Nevertheless, unless the party is run by the military and order is maintained by force, the political party must react to public opinion while at the same time encouraging support for the government. The party also selects candidates for public office, usually in an informal way, and then presents them to the general public. There are no competing candidates in one-party systems, however, so nomination ensures election. In addition, the party defines issues and must convince the electorate to support their stand on these issues. The issues not brought up by the party are not debated, but every effort is made to win support from the public for the activities the party does undertake.

The two-party system is found in democratic countries. It allows competition between candidates and debate over competing issues. However, to gain and maintain power, a party must gain a majority of the votes, so each party tries to attract the voters in the moderate center. Since they have to avoid taking any stand that would alienate this group, both parties have to be moderate and the voter has little real choice.

Governments with more than two political parties tend to be relatively unstable. In political systems of this sort, the parties do not seek moderation. Instead, they take a definite stand and try to satisfy a group of people who are committed to a particular issue — a labor issue, an antiwar issue, or an environmental issue. They then nominate a candidate who will take a strong stand on the chosen one or two issues. Because it is very difficult for such a candidate to get a majority of votes, parties compromise with each other and form coalitions even when they hold opposing positions on a variety of issues. Government policies can change dramatically with each election, depending on which party or coalition of parties gains power. Nevertheless, the voters have a clear choice on a variety of issues when they cast their ballots.

France: A Democratic State. France is a democracy. The government is headed by a president elected by popular vote. The president ap-

points a prime minister to be "in general charge of the work of the government" (Ridley, 1979, p. 75). Thus it is not clear whether the president or the prime minister runs the government. In practice, the president has been the more powerful official, although many presidential acts such as decrees, appointments of senior officials, pardons, and foreign treaties also require the signature of the prime minister. The prime minister selects the ministers of justice, defense, budget, education, and so on, and directs their activity, but the president must approve the prime minister's choices. The two legislative houses, the Parliament and the National Assembly, are elected, but the National Assembly can be dissolved by the president.

The French government is a strong, central government, but there are extensive conflicts among the various ministers, their staffs, and the legislative bodies. The state's stability rests in its huge civil service, especially the elite corps of bureaucrats, who have so much power that they have been called "a state within a state" (Ridley, 1979, p. 105).

To qualify for an elite position in the French civil service, candidates must pass through a special school that trains government officials, the Ecole National d'Administration (ENA). Selection for the ENA is based on a competitive examination, and students usually study for these exams after they have completed college. After completing the two-year ENA program, they must again take competitive examinations.

The civil servants selected through this process serve in the top jobs in government and industry. While serving in government posts, they are allowed to participate in labor or political organizations, and they can leave the civil service to run for an elected office. They head the government-owned industries: coal, gas, the railways, aviation, the largest banks, and the Renault car firm. They are recruited for key posts in private corporations and often move back and forth between the civil service and private industry. According to some critics, they are an elite ruling class that controls government and industry.

The Soviet Union: A Totalitarian State. The Soviet Union's political system is based on the ideas of Karl Marx and Friedrich Engels. Marx believed that a society's first responsibility is to meet the economic needs of its people. Communism, he argued, could meet those needs. He did not describe how a communist system would work, but after Marx's death Engels spoke of the "withering away of the state" (Hazard, 1980, p. 6), which would happen when the people were prosperous and knew the rules of social living necessary to maintain prosperity. At that time, there would be no need for a state or police to enforce laws. People would live cooperatively, and only administrators would be needed to achieve efficient production and direct the flow of goods to the people.

The Soviet Union's goal is very clear: a communist nation run by administrators. Communism is not yet possible, however, partly because the economy is not yet efficient enough and partly because the people have not yet learned how to live in a communist society. Until they learn to function in such a society, strong leadership will be necessary to reach the goals of communism.

This leadership is provided by the Communist party, which is open to any citizen who understands the goals of communism and is committed to work for them. Membership is gained when two members of the party recommend the applicant. Currently, about 10 percent of the population of the Soviet Union belong to the party.

Members meet in local groups called "primary party organizations." All members are al-

Delegates elected by Communists throughout the Soviet Union meet in Moscow under an image of Lenin to decide who will lead the Communist party. The party does not officially rule the Soviet Union, but it is the only political party in that country and extremely powerful in determining Soviet policy.

lowed to speak at meetings, but they are not allowed to create factions or rival groups. They may not discuss their views with other party members outside of meetings, nor may they try to win support from other members before they speak to the group as a whole. In short, they cannot organize coalitions (Hazard, 1980).

The primary party organization elects a secretary as a leader and delegates to represent the organization at local conferences. At these local conferences, the delegates elect a committee which, in turn, elects a secretary to run regional affairs. They also elect delegates to the larger provincial conferences. The process continues on a larger scale; ultimately, about 5,000 delegates meet in Moscow to elect the Central Committee, which elects the Political Bureau, a steering committee of thirteen members and nine alternates. This committee determines policy and elects the leader of the Communist party.

Because members are carefully selected and vote only at the local level and because factions cannot get started, there is little chance of great upheaval within the Communist party. The secretaries at each level normally place only their own names on the ballot to elect secretaries for higher-level posts, so it would take an enormous wave of discontent to disturb the election process.

The Communist party determines Soviet government policy, but it is not itself the government. The government is the Soviet, a system of committees begun in 1905 before the Russian Revolution. This system parallels the party system. The Supreme Soviet is the highest committee, dealing with the budget, foreign affairs, new legislation, and other important matters. The members of the Supreme Soviet and the various local Soviets do not have to belong to the Communist party, but party members are well represented in the Soviets, especially those at higher levels.

From time to time the Communist party has tried to ignore the Soviet committees, but they have been more successful when they work with them. Cooperation enables them to radiate party influence to citizens outside of the party, and they benefit from the expertise of members of Soviets who are not party members.

The state owns all industry, and most people work for the state. It is possible to have a private business, but taxes are very high, while pensions and payments for disability are very low. Consequently, career-minded people strive for a state position. The better positions are obtained by successfully completing a university education; students enter the university after the tenth grade. The vast majority of people, who are not selected to attend the university, never get management-level jobs. Those who do receive higher

education are assigned a job in their field for three years, after which they are free to seek employment where they wish.

The Soviet Union considers itself a democracy. All citizens are equal under the law regardless of race, sex, or nationality, and all have the right to vote, but these freedoms may be used only to further the socialist cause. Thus people may speak or publish statements to further the cause of communism, but they may not oppose it. The Communists control the press and censor statements that do not promote communism. They welcome letters to the editor, but they publish only those that support major policies or help promote efficiency in the lower echelons of the bureaucracy.

The Political System in the United States

The United States has a democratic political system. Citizens are expected to rule the country by participating in the political process — debating issues, joining one of the two political parties or remaining "independent," voting for officials, and then expressing their opinions to officeholders.

The elected officials serve in a diverse, decentralized system of federal, state, and local governments. Each level of government has a system of checks and balances: the legislative branches make the law, the executive branches carry out the law, and the judicial branches interpret the law. Our system of government is representative, but how representative is it in practice? Who holds the power? Which groups influence government the most? There are three major perspectives on power in America. The first is that big business holds all of the power, the second is that three powerful groups hold power, and the third viewpoint is that power is divided among a number of groups.

How Powerful Is the President?

Max Weber, the great German social scientist (some would say the greatest of the past century), defined power as the ability of an individual or group to win the subordination of others — if necessary, against *their* will. Not even from the White House is such subordination easily won.

The tendency to misjudge the power of the Presidency begins with what may be called the illusion of power. This, a matter of prime importance, takes several forms. A politician, and notably a President, goes before a thoughtfully chosen audience and makes a speech that is written, as a matter of course, to express what the audience already believes. The resulting applause is deafening. Everyone, and notably the reporters covering the scene, see this oratory as a decisive exercise of power. It is so described. At best, those addressed have been confirmed a little more deeply in their previously held beliefs — or prejudices.

Radio and television lend themselves further to the illusion of power. When at a loss as to what else to do, the President all but automatically takes his case to the public. Much toil goes into the speech; eventually, it emerges in acceptable English, and the President is said to have expressed himself extremely well. No one reflects that, in a day or two, most people will have forgotten what they heard. There is simply too much these days to remember. The presumption of power lies in the *act* of speaking, not the result. Let the reader try to recall a Presidential speech that changed his or her mind.

Next, there is what may be called the sycophancy of power. If the President is held to have power, a very large number of other people can believe that they have power too. This is highly agreeable, and they will be sought out and celebrated by those who are similarly misled. I speak here of the Presidential staff, the Cabi-

net members and, most important of all, the newspaper and television reporters who cover the White House. All are freeloaders on the presumed power of the Presidency. All, by enhancing the impression of Presidential power, enhance the impression of their own.

This impulse is especially the tendency of the media. All have seen it in the faces and manner of the television news commentators covering the White House. Here are men and women whose responsibility is a heavy burden. None allows himself or herself a trace of humor; there is that special gravity in those closing words: "Joseph Zilch *at the White House*." Joe is there sharing that power; not for him to do anything to minimize it. Someday, he will tell of his burdens and responsibilities and how he discharged them in a very serious book with a slightly offhand title, *The White House Beat*.

Then there is the question of how Presidential decisions are actually made — the matter of the large organization and the related role of what may be called the synthetic personality. This requires a word of explanation:

Big Business

Derived from Marx, the first view sees big business dominate America. G. W. Domhoff (1971, 1979) argues that power is held by a "governing class" made up of the highest social class, about one-half of 1 percent of the population.

These people have a disproportionate share of the wealth. They control most of the business and industry, share educational experiences in the same elite schools, socialize together in the same clubs, marry members of the same social group, and have similar economic concerns. They also hold most of the political offices.

We live in an age of very large organizations — large public bureaucracies (the Pentagon, Department of Health and Human Services), large corporate bureaucracies (Exxon, General Motors, General Dynamics). In each, the process of decision-making begins deep within the organization — with the shared knowledge of experts and specialists working in a hierarchy of committees and task forces from which comes the best or least bad course of action or, as often happens, the only available compromise. In such fashion, decisions emerge at the top from General Motors and similarly from the Pentagon, the State Department, the Department of Agriculture — and from the President's own large staff around the Oval Office.

In other words, the power in the great number of everyday Presidential decisions lies not with the President but with the organization. This is not publicly admitted; it is regularly concealed even from the President himself. Everyone with White House experience knows the design: The President is presented with alternative courses of action called options. One is possible; the others range from the politically disastrous to the overtly insane. The President chooses the only possible one; those seeking the decision express their agreement and nod with approval when he announces it to the press. The decision should, of course, be attributed to the organization. But there is no glamour in that. So wherever decision is by organization, personal power is emphasized — personality is synthesized. It is not the Presidential staff but the President.

How we attribute to individuals much that really belongs to organization is demonstrated by what happens to the Cabinet officer or corporation president when he leaves office. A curtain descends; nothing is heard of him again until the few fulsome paragraphs in the obituary columns. Past Presidents do better, but not much. Ford and Carter have passed largely from sight, although, perhaps with some effort, Richard Nixon does keep himself in the news. Calvin Coolidge was a considerable figure when in office; when word came of his death, the writer Dorothy Parker asked, "How can they tell?"

In considering the role of organization, we must reflect in a somber way on the possibility that such organization can, in our time, become stronger than the President himself. President Dwight D. Eisenhower, in his best-remembered speech, given in his last days in office, warned against the power, sought or unsought, of the military-industrial complex — of the hundreds of thousands of people, reinforced by hundreds of billions of dollars, that now comprise the civilian staff of the Pentagon, the armed services, the weapons industry, the serving scientists and engineers and the captive politicians. It will not be said, even by his most devout defenders, that President Reagan has been much motivated to control this complex; he has contributed notably to its power. But the greater question arises as to whether any President can control it. It is a question on which all should reflect and on which all Presidential candidates should be warned and pressed.

SOURCE: Excerpted from John Kenneth Galbraith "How Powerful is the President?" *Parade*, 13 May 1984. Reprinted by permission.

Given that members of this group have so much in common, it is not surprising that they support similar political policies. They argue for the protection of their national and foreign investments, and they favor income tax advantages for the wealthy. They support candidates who will represent their interests, regardless of political party affiliation. They send representatives to Washington to influence legislation, to lobby for special privileges, and to hold key positions in government. In other words, big business ensures that the friends of *big business* will be elected, and these friends promote legislation designed to meet the needs of big business.

The Power Elite

C. Wright Mills (1958) argued that the United States is run by a *power elite* consisting of leaders in the upper echelons of business, the military, and the government. These leaders, Mills contended, are likely to come from similar backgrounds and have similar beliefs and values. There is no actual conspiracy among these leaders to promote the interests of their own high social stratum, but they nevertheless tend to support the same policies.

One example of the operation of a power elite is what has come to be known as the military-industrial complex. This complex evolved during World War II, when some of the checks and balances regulating the defense department were dismantled. The absence of these checks and balances meant that the American defense industry was producing for a consumer, the American taxpayer, for whom price was not negotiable. As a result, unprecedented profits were made. In this way, United States military "police" actions in foreign countries such as Korea and Vietnam kept the defense industry employed, and the industry became a decisive force in governmental policy. In 1961, departing President Dwight D. Eisenhower, a career soldier prior to his presidency, asserted that the "conjunction of an immense military establishment and a large arms industry is new in the American experience.... We must guard against acquisition of unwarranted influence ... by the military industrial complex. The potential for the disastrous rise of misplaced power exists and will persist" (Galbraith, 1983). Since that time the bureaucracy has slowly shifted toward the wishes of the defense industry. The Office of Management and Budget has the last word on all budget requests — with the singular exception of those originating in the Department of Defense.

The United States has laws that essentially remove the risk of doing business for corporations that have government contracts and place that risk on the American taxpayer. Research and development costs, buildings, and equipment are government funded, and incredible cost overruns are absorbed by the buyer, the taxpayer. When Lockheed spent $1.1 billion more than anticipated on a government project, the American people covered almost all of their additional expense. With their tremendous legislative influence, one can only wonder how far into related fields these companies' influence reaches and whether other groups can compete with the military-industrial complex for power in the political system.

Political Pluralism

Many sociologists believe that numerous groups in the United States play a significant role in political decision making. David Riesman et al. (1953) described the power system of the United States as one of *political pluralism* — rule by many different groups. A variety of special interest groups try to influence legislation. They form lobbies that represent various industries, labor, religions, educational groups, and other special interests. These groups try to protect their own interests by pressuring politicians for favorable legislation and fighting against legislation they dislike. Thus, Riesman et al. believed, no single group had absolute power because different groups would balance one another's actions when they had competing interests.

There is little question that a variety of interest groups exist in the United States today. The issue for critics of pluralism is whether these various groups have any real power. Political pluralists believe many groups are equally powerful and balance the power of other groups. Those who believe that a governing class or a military-industrial complex is most powerful fear that other groups are not strong enough to coun-

Table 15-1

Top PAC contributors to congressional races in 1982

COMMITTEE	AMOUNT
Realtors PAC	$2,045,092
American Medical PAC	1,638,795
United Automobile Workers PAC	1,470,354
Machinists Non-Partisan Political League	1,252,209
National Education Assn. PAC	1,073,896
American Bankers Assn. PAC	870,110
National Assn. of Home Builders PAC	852,745
Associated Milk Producers PAC	842,450
Automobile and Truck Dealers Election Action Comm.	829,945
AFL-CIO COPE Political Contributions Comm.	823,125
Seafarers Political Activity Donation	802,261

SOURCE: *World Almanac and Book of Facts*, 1984 edition, copyright © Newspaper Enterprise Association, Inc., 1984, New York, NY 10166. By permission.

teract the power of the elite no matter how active and well organized they are.

Two types of groups are frequently in the news in American politics: Political Action Committees, who contribute money to political campaigns, and lobbies, who attempt to influence legislation. Both types clearly have more power than individuals who do not belong to such groups. Questions remain about whether either type of group has enough power to counteract the power of elites or whether these groups actually tend to represent and extend the power of elite groups.

Political Action Committees

Political Action Committees (PACs) are organizations formed to raise money for political campaigns. Candidates running for office need a great deal of money for political advertising, office overhead, transportation, and other needs. The expense can reach into millions of dollars. As a rule, the people who are elected to political office spend more money than their opponents, and PACs help to pay these election expenses.

PACs represent many special interest groups — often groups that are at variance with one another. Business groups, labor groups, and professional groups all sponsor PACs (see Table 15-1). Many of the most powerful favor the Republican party, but others favor the Democratic party. Those that have business interests often split their contributions, giving money to members of both parties. But although PACs support both parties and a variety of candidates, they do not represent a cross section of American voters. Only groups with moneyed connections can possibly raise the sums needed to be influential in funding candidates. An estimated $80,000,000 was contributed to candidates in the 1982 congressional elections (Leach, 1983).

A few PACs, particularly very conservative groups, have used PAC money to try to defeat incumbents, elected officials who already hold office and are trying to be re-elected. Most PAC money, however, goes to incumbents and therefore tends to maintain the power structure as it is.

Each PAC is allowed to contribute $5,000 to each politician per election unless it is a presidential campaign in which case $10,000 is allowed. PACs are not permitted to persuade politicians to take a particular stand, but they of course support only politicians who will support their cause. Oil and gas PACs, for example, supported congressional members who voted to authorize that $50 billion worth of the costs of the Alaskan natural gas pipeline be billed to consumers before construction was started.

Although PACs are not technically allowed to persuade politicians to take political stands, thousands of associations and groups are permitted to try to influence both politicians and civil servants. These groups are commonly called lobbies.

Lobbies

Lobbies are organizations of people who wish to influence the political process on specific issues. Unlike political parties, lobbies do not nominate candidates or hope to manage the government. Their goal, rather, is to persuade elected and appointed officials to vote for or against a particular regulation or piece of legislation. Groups of people with a common interest often form an association with the express purpose of influencing the legislative process. Thousands of such associations are based within blocks of the United States Capitol, where they monitor the legislation being considered. They maintain close contact with government officials and scrutinize the work of bureaucrats when budgets are being prepared or hearings are being held so that they can influence the government to their own best interest. Since most national associations are federations of state and local associations, they have influence at every level of

government, from the smallest town to the federal government.

Some of the largest and best-known associations are the National Association of Manufacturers (NAM), the Chamber of Commerce of the United States, the American Medical Association (AMA), and the AFL-CIO. Many smaller groups also represent their interests, such as the American Farm Bureau Association, the Chemical Specialties Manufacturers Association, the National Asphalt Pavement Association, the Evaporated Milk Association, the National Association of Retail Druggists, the National Cemetery Association, and the Undersea Medical Society. The list is endless.

While most of the wealth and power of lobbies are found in those associated with manufacturing, many lobbying groups are concerned with issues unrelated to business. They are supported by donations from the public and lobby on issues related to the public good. Such groups include Common Cause, the National Wildlife Federation, the Center for Science in the Public Interest, and the American Civil Liberties Union (ACLU).

The workings of the powerful automobile lobby show how much time, energy, and money are involved in influencing the political process. During the early 1960s, Ralph Nader, a public interest lobbyist, launched an attack on the faulty design of American automobiles in his book *Unsafe at Any Speed*. After the book was published, Nader continued to work for improved auto safety. Congress considered passing legislation to set safety standards for cars, but the auto lobby, led by Henry Ford, moved in to stop the legislation (Dowie, 1977). Ford went to Washington and spoke to the Business Council, an organization of one hundred executives of large organizations who come to Washington from time to time to advise government. He visited members of Congress, held press confer-

Ralph Nader is a lawyer who holds no legal position in government, but he lives in Washington, D.C. and lobbies for consumer protection legislation. His charisma stems from his commitment to his cause, and his followers have been nicknamed "Nader's Raiders." He and his group have lobbied for consumer protection in the sale of many products and services, but they are most noted for their fight for auto safety.

ences, and recruited business support, but he failed to stop the passage of the Motor Vehicle Safety Act, which was signed into law in 1966.

A regulatory agency was then made responsible for setting guidelines for auto safety, but the Ford Motor Company sent representatives to the agency to argue that poor drivers, unsafe guardrail designs, poor visibility, and a variety of other highway and driving hazards were responsible for accidents. Not only was the automobile safe, they contended, but regulations requiring improvements would increase the cost of cars while saving few lives.

Nevertheless, in 1968 the regulatory agency issued new safety standards designed to reduce the risk of fire in automobiles after a rear-end crash. As required by law, the agency scheduled hearings on the regulation. Ford responded with a report stating that automobile fires were not a problem. The agency then had to do several studies to determine if fire was a problem. It found that 400,000 cars burned up every year and that 3,000 people burned to death. It again proposed safety standards, and Ford again responded, arguing that although burning accidents do happen, rear-end collisions were not the cause. The agency researched this question and found that rear-end collisions were in fact the cause in most cases. Again regulations were proposed, again Ford responded, and again research was conducted. The total delay in developing regulations was eight years. The regulations eventually did pass, giving a victory to Ralph Nader and consumer groups and a defeat of sorts to the Ford Motor Company. During those eight years, however, the company killed regulations requiring other safety measures, and it cost taxpayers a great deal to finance the eight-year battle to improve automobiles. The improvements ultimately cost the auto manufacturers approximately $11 per car.

This account of one corporation's reluctance to comply with an auto safety regulation shows that big business has enormous but not absolute power over government. It also shows how time-consuming and expensive the business of lobbying is. It is a procedure that can be practiced only by organizations with much wealth and power, and bureaucratic organizations have much more power than any individual citizen.

The Role of the Individual

Special interest groups can use their power to try to influence political decisions, but what is the role of the individual? As stated earlier in this chapter, American citizens are expected to participate in the political process by voting, debat-

ing issues, joining one of the two political parties or remaining "independent," and expressing their views to their elected officials. People learn these and other responsibilities through the process of political socialization.

Political Socialization

In most American communities, many children watch the mayor lead the Fourth of July parade. The very young assume that the mayor is a good and benevolent leader. Most youngsters also learn that other leaders likewise give time and money to make the community a better place to live. During elections, children are often taught about political parties by their families, and frequently they identify with a political party on an emotional level long before they can understand political issues. To a child, the President of the United States is to the country what the father is to the family: a leader, provider, and protector.

Political socialization of this sort continues when children enter school. Through formal courses in history, literature, and government, they learn to respect society's norms and political system. From their relationships with teachers, they learn that leadership is acquired through achievement. The principal, they discover, has achieved more than the teacher, and team captains, class officers, and other school leaders have attained their posts through their achievements.

Not all children emerge from their family and school socialization with the idea that political leaders are benevolent, caring, achieving people, of course. They may accumulate contradictory evidence along the way, perhaps having experiences with parents, teachers, or other leaders that indicate leaders are not to be trusted. They may also acquire a distrust of the political system by listening to parental complaints about lack of jobs or other conditions

President Ronald Reagan was photographed teaching an English class in Farragut, Tennessee. We don't know what he discussed with this class of young people, but we can safely assume that the students were learning a good deal more about politics than they were about English.

that result from political decisions and cause family hardship. Schools teaching middle-class values may fail to convince a child living in poverty that the political system is fair and benevolent; realities in the child's environment may provide harsh evidence that not everyone can move from log cabin to president. Children from Appalachia and urban ghettos are much less apt to support the American political system than are middle-class Americans (Dowse and Hughes, 1972).

By the time children finish school, they have developed political attitudes that will shape their political behavior in adult life, but political socialization still continues, especially through the mass media, which reinforce childhood socialization. Much mass media socialization presents political issues in emotional terms. Slogans that promise a better America without of-

fering factual data about how this is to be done are seeking an emotional response from voters, a response resembling the one a child feels for the mayor leading the Fourth of July parade. Although these emotional appeals for voter support are routinely criticized as "flag waving," emotion is believed to play a very large role in voter choice.

The most effective way for the mass media to influence people is to present information in such a way that there is only one obvious conclusion (Goodin, 1980). The media often give only one side of an issue, and if the "obvious" solution is heard frequently enough, it will seem to make sense to most people. Often, for a year or two before an election, we hear a candidate mentioned as the "obvious" choice for the party. If people don't have jobs, it is "obviously" because they don't want them. If people don't vote, they are "obviously" not interested. These statements are not obvious at all, but unless information is provided they may seem obvious enough and will probably be accepted by the majority of the public.

In the United States, there is concern that the mass media express only the views of the large corporations that generally own them. Few newspapers, for example, are still locally owned and compete with other locally owned newspapers. In 1977, only thirty-seven cities had competing newspapers (Reasons and Perdue, 1981), and many of these were owned by large publishing syndicates that controlled the press in several cities. There are only three major television networks: ABC, NBC, and CBS. Thus information about politics may be severely limited, and the information presented may represent only the viewpoint of the mass media owners.

The federal government also provides information to its citizens on health, agriculture, education, labor, housing, and population statistics. This information is dispensed in a variety of ways, through county agricultural agents, public health centers, libraries, newspapers, radio, and television. Many of the statistics used by sociologists are collected and published by government agencies. Sociologists are well aware, however, that the government also attempts to shape public opinion, and sometimes reports provide information that presents a misleading description of a problem. Government unemployment figures, for example, count only those unemployed who are actively seeking work; they do not report the number of people who have given up the search for a job, which lowers the statistics on unemployment in the country.

Political Participation

Most voters in the United States tend to remain very loyal to either the Republican or Democratic party. This party loyalty seems to be based primarily on emotional ties formed during the earlier socialization process (Dowse and Hughes, 1972). Most people are not well informed about political issues and do not choose a party on the basis of political opinions. Rather, they support a party for traditional or emotional reasons — perhaps because their families have always supported that party — and they are then guided by the party's stand on the issues. In other words, voters are socialized by their political parties to view political issues in a certain way.

The so-called moral issues such as race, sexual behavior, and religion are an exception to this general rule. People usually have a strong opinion on moral issues, and they will leave their party and not vote or else vote for the other party if they disagree with their party's stand. As a result, political parties generally try to avoid moral issues altogether and take a middle-of-the-road stand on other issues to attract the largest number of voters.

Certain groups outside of the major political parties have attempted to bring moral issues into politics. They recognize that often a large minority of people can be easily influenced by emotional issues and have used these issues to attract followers. They cannot, however, attract the majority of voters. If the majority of the voters agreed, for example, that abortions should be outlawed, the major political parties would also express that belief and the issue would cease to exist.

The *right wing* in American politics is associated with the Republican party. It consists of conservative people who want to preserve the traditional ways of life. They often express views on moral issues because they fear the decay of traditional American values. Most conservatives come from middle-class families in which they or their parents were small shop owners, farmers, garage owners, small business owners, or members of middle management in larger organizations.

Ku Klux Klansmen march to a rally in Salisbury, North Carolina in 1957 to protest Supreme Court actions that aided black citizens. The Klan is an extreme right wing group, that protests changes in social policy that advance the cause of others. Protestors at Seabrook are typical of left wing groups, that desire change in the status quo.

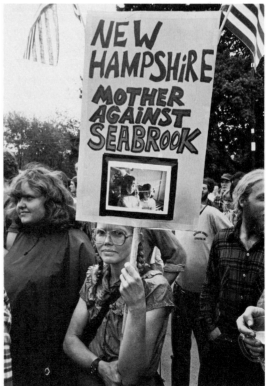

One hypothesis about the right suggests that its members are frustrated by their inability to acquire status, either in small communities or large ones. Due to social changes, it has become more difficult to succeed in small businesses and in small towns. In addition, the attainment of status is not easy to display when so many people live in large cities, work in large organizations, and are unknown to most of their neighbors. Under these conditions, people feel insecure about their status. They want recognizable success, theorists argue, and believe that they would achieve it if society would return to what it was in the past. The more extreme groups in the right wing are the Ku Klux Klan and the John Birch Society.

The *left wing* of American politics, which is associated with the Democratic party, is also motivated by political or religious moral issues, but its followers are more likely to be deprived economically. They want to change certain

438 PART IV SOCIAL INSTITUTIONS

Figure 15-1

Participation in elections for president, 1932–1980

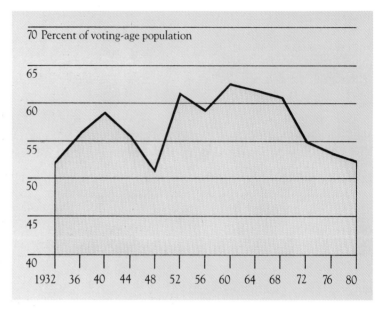

aspects of American life to create more equality and jobs, less poverty, better housing for all, and other improvements. To reach these goals, they argue, a radical redistribution of wealth and power is necessary. They are therefore sometimes considered enemies of the American political system.

One such group is the Black Muslim church, which has attracted poor blacks who have been utterly frustrated with their living conditions. They believe that American society will never integrate blacks, and they want to develop a separate and distinct culture within the nation so that blacks can have the self-respect and economic security not available to them in a racist society.

Voter Apathy

The United States has one of the lowest voter turnouts in the democratic world. Less than 54 percent of the eligible population voted in the presidential election of 1980, which was a low point in voting participation over the past several decades (see Figure 15-1). Low voter turnout hurts the Democratic party because the blocks of people who do not vote — the young, the poor, and blacks — are statistically more apt to be democratic. When voter turnout is low, the Republican party is more likely to win elections and social programs that help the poor and minority groups are more likely to be ignored.

A variety of explanations exist for this lack of voter participation. One explanation attributes it to voter apathy — voters lack knowledge and do not participate because they quite simply do not care. Those who adopt this perspective also tend to believe that if government is less than perfect the voters have no one to blame but themselves. If they seek change they should give politics more attention.

Another explanation for low voter participation is that voting in this country is burden-

A woman is urged to register as a voter and then will be urged to vote on election day. In any political system, power becomes legitimate authority only when the rulers have the consent of the ruled. If this woman votes, she will be expressing her willingness to participate in the political process, and people will assume she consents to be ruled by the outcome.

some. Registering to vote is often rather difficult. It sometimes requires traveling to the county seat or even the state capital. Once registered, there are too many elections, too many elected officials, and too many referenda, questions on the ballot concerning everything from building roads to changing the qualifications of elected officials. In some countries, registration is automatic when the voter reaches an eligible age. In other countries, voting is mandatory, and people who do not vote are fined.

Two other explanations for low voter partic-

Policymaking in City Government

Mel Ravitz is a member of Detroit's city council, the only sociologist ever to serve on that body. He is a graduate of Detroit's Wayne State University and has a doctorate in sociology from the University of Michigan. For thirty years he has been combining political activity and community organizing with a teaching career at Wayne State.

What insights can a sociologist bring to the role of urban policymaker? "The sociologist," Mel Ravitz says, "should be expected to contribute a comprehensive way of looking at social problems; to point out that nothing exists apart from other things and that, to be understood, a proposal, plan, or ordinance must be analyzed in relation to other proposals, plans, or ordinances; and to emphasize that any response to any issue must be seen in terms of its real consequences rather than in terms of its author's intentions." As a sociologist, he feels that he is especially well prepared to understand the social dimensions of community life — a welcome balance to the preoccupation of most people in government with things physical and fiscal. "Other policymakers," he says, "at both the legislative and the administrative levels are often people whose ex-

perience is in working with material things rather than with social or cultural ones." His city council colleagues during his first term were an accountant, a civil engineer, a former union leader, a former major league baseball player, and four lawyers. "Of course they were more familiar with, and therefore more trusting of, such things as neighborhood design, facility location, and budgeting than they were with the concepts of cultural difference, social stratification, social mobility, assimilation, and relative deprivation. There was only the barest beginning perception of the human effects of urban renewal."

In his first campaign, in 1961, Ravitz had his eyes opened to the power of various groups in the city politic. As he told a meeting of sociologists, "It should come as no surprise that there are countless groups meeting simultaneously around the city. The firsthand experience of visiting fifteen meetings in one day makes you realize that all these diverse groups — unions, church groups, house parties, block clubs, political associations — are functioning side by side around the city, busily and narrowly focused on their respective problems, each unaware of the existence of the

ipation involve the interpretation of voter satisfaction. Conservatives often believe that voters do not vote because they are satisfied with the way the government is run. Not voting is "passive consent" to the present system. Liberals argue that voters do not vote because they are alienated from a system where neither political

party supports their views and none of the elected representatives represent their viewpoints, interests, and concerns. If an actual survey of those who don't vote could be conducted, we would probably find that nonvoting is caused by all of these factors and some others as well.

others. One has a thrilling insight into the complex social organization of a vast urban community."

Ultimately, it was the strength of such groups that swept Ravitz into office in 1961. "In my role as a community organizer I had built a political constituency," he says, and that constituency — made up of, among others, well-organized groups of the elderly and teenagers — worked tirelessly on his campaign. Then an unforeseeable sequence of events mobilized other important groups. Several astonishing incidents of police brutality took place in the black community. An ordinance that would have increased the power of the city's Commission on Community Relations to deal with such incidents was defeated in the city council. After this, a coalition of black church and community groups, white liberals, and labor union members endorsed a slate of reform candidates, including Ravitz. All four of the incumbents endorsed by the coalition were re-elected, Ravitz and two other new council members were chosen, and the incumbent mayor was ousted. It was the biggest political upset in Detroit history.

After his election, Ravitz had to make adjustments in his way of looking at the world and at himself. The need for the first such adjustment became apparent immediately: "My change of status from professor to council member brought about a significant change in social perception and behavior. Before the election I was simply a liberal or even radical sociology professor. Only my friends paid any attention to what I said. After the election, the manager of the city's best hotel extended his best wishes; the police officers and fire fighters associations wired their congratulations and a dozen roses; and a large homeowners organization hoped I would be guided by 'good will' during my tenure in office. If ever one doubted the significance of status change, here was ample proof."

More important, he saw a need for change in his approach to his work. "The sociologist by academic preparation and professional experience is an analyst of and adviser on decisions rather than a decision-maker. I had to be willing to accept a shift of role. No longer could I afford the luxury of never-ending analysis; no longer was I able to qualify issues and categorize them into infinite shades of grey. Time is always short for legislators, and decisions are constantly demanded by both colleagues and constituents. Any one who cannot make decisions on the basis of available and always limited information cannot long survive in this public role."

Mel Ravitz was re-elected to four-year terms in 1965 and 1969. In 1973 he ran for mayor, lost, and became director of the Detroit-Wayne County Community Mental Health Board. But in 1981 the political bug bit him again, and he ran for and won his old seat on the city council. That's where you'll find him today, as he says, "legislating, advocating, serving as an ombudsman, performing a ministerial function, attending political events, speaking — and campaigning."

Summary

A society's political institution is the structure that has the power to rule in a society. Power is the ability to make others follow the rules or dictates set down by those in control. This can be done by force, but force is an inefficient way to control a society. Latent force, making people comply by threatening them with punishment, is more effective.

Authority is a still more powerful means of control and is considered legitimate because the people believe the ruler has a right to rule and they comply voluntarily. Traditional authority is derived from accepted practices or customs. Legal authority is based on a system of legislated rules and regulations. Charismatic authority comes from the personal traits of the leader.

Structural functionalists believe that political systems reflect societal values. If a society values freedom, monogamy, hard work, and achievement, laws will be passed to enforce these values, and members of the society will comply with the law because it reflects their own beliefs. Structural functionalists also believe that the political system must try to resolve conflicts in values. The value of freedom, for example, may come in conflict with the value of hard work, and the government must arbitrate to ensure that behavior does not infringe on either value. Some subcultures teach values that conflict with those of the larger society, but the government must protect the values of the dominant society.

Conflict theorists believe that certain groups gain power because they possess a large share of society's resources. They use these resources to acquire power and use the law and the political system to protect their own wealth. The rich teach the population through the schools and the mass media that their wealth, power, and laws are legitimate. In other words, they shape the values of the society to serve their own interests.

Modern societies have two types of legal power structures. Democratic systems allow citizens to participate in their own governance. Totalitarian systems provide a consistent form of government in which different groups do not cause dissent as they compete for power. Within these systems political parties are formed to attempt to gain control of the political process.

The French government is a democracy with elected officials and appointed civil servants. The French bureaucracy is very complex and powerful, and often the civil servants play very important roles in both government and business. The Soviet Union is a totalitarian society with a very powerful single political party. The members of the party play the most powerful roles in the government. Both power systems profess a belief in freedom and equality for their citizens and are organized bureaucratically. The bureaucracies may be the real seats of power in both countries.

Debate about how power is distributed in the United States has continued for many years. Theorists have argued variously that there are many powerful groups that all try to protect their own interests, that a power elite made up of business and government officials controls the power, and that big business runs the country. Regardless of the explanation one accepts, power clearly requires resources that many groups do not have.

In the United States, socialization legitimates legal authority, and political socialization begins early. Youngsters learn about political leaders and political parties at home and in the community. Socialization continues in school, and most children learn to respect the political system, although poor children are more likely to question government and its practices.

Most Americans remain loyal to one political party and permit it to guide them on important issues. On moral issues, however, voters tend to act more independently.

Key Terms

authority
big business
charismatic authority
citizen
city-states
democracy
left wing
legal authority
lobbies
nation-states
oligarchy

Political Action Committees
political parties
political pluralism
politics
power elite
right wing
totalitarianism
traditional authority

Suggested Readings

Adams, Gordon. **The Iron Triangle: The Politics of Defense Contracting.** *New York: Council on Economic Priorities, 1981.* Adams is a specialist in defense spending and the role of the military-industrial complex. He researches his topic thoroughly.

Baden, John and Richard L. Stroup (eds). **Bureaucracy vs. Environment: The Environmental Costs of Bureaucratic Governance.** *Ann Arbor: University of Michigan Press, 1981.* A collection of essays on how businessmen have influenced government to use or misuse natural resources at great cost to the taxpayer.

Ferguson, Thomas and Joel Rogers. **The Hidden Election: Politics and Economics in the 1980 Presidential Campaign.** *New York: Pantheon Books, 1981.* A variety of essays on how economic and social events shaped the political elections.

Goodin, Robert E. **Manipulatory Politics.** *New Haven: Yale University Press, 1980.* If you believe that

you are sometimes manipulated by politicians' use of the information they control, you should read this book.

Janeway, Elizabeth. **Powers of the Weak.** *New York: Knopf, 1980.* This book suggests that the weak in a stratified society — women, blacks, and the poor — have power because they do not have to meet the expectations of the powerful. They cannot be ruled if they do not consent to it.

Mills, C. Wright. **The Power Elite.** *New York: Oxford University Press, 1958.* This classic, which is still being debated, describes how supposedly diverse powerful people and groups are really interrelated to form one power elite.

Orum, Anthony M. **Introduction to Political Sociology: The Social Anatomy of the Body Politic.** *Englewood Cliffs, N.J.: Prentice-Hall, 1978.* A well-documented text that could serve as a handbook for anyone interested in pursuing the topic of political sociology.

Schiller, Herbert I. **Who Knows: Information in the Age of the Fortune 500.** *Norwood, N.J.: Ablex, 1981.* Company executives in the computer industry are convincing the U.S. government to contract to them the dissemination of government information and, as a result, are gaining control of much information formerly controlled by government.

Szymanski, Albert. **The Capitalist State and the Politics of Class.** *Cambridge, Mass.: Winthrop Publishers, 1978.* This basic text is especially useful for understanding how the elite control power.

CHAPTER 16

Economic Groups and Systems

The love of money is the root of all evil.
— I Timothy 6:10

Lack of money is the root of all evil.
— George Bernard Shaw

To survive, people need food, shelter, and health care. Except for those who live in the tropics, people also need clothing and a source of heat. To be accepted in modern American society, however, we need a great deal more — soap, deodorant, toothpaste, shoes, and various types of clothes for different occasions. We also like the luxuries our society provides: plates, knives, forks, furniture, cars, sporting equipment, radios, televisions, and so on. All these things, from the most basic necessities to the most expensive luxuries, are produced by our economic system.

The economic system is the social system that provides for the production, distribution, and consumption of goods and services. Sociologists study the economic system because it is a major social institution that influences every aspect of society. Sociologists are not economists, however. Economists study the internal workings of the economic system: supply and demand, how much industry is producing, how much consumers are buying, how much government is taxing, borrowing, and spending, and so on. Sociologists, on the other hand, study how the economic system interacts with other social institutions. They study types of economic systems, the size and power of corporations, the occupations in economic systems, how work affects the rest of our lives, and similar issues.

Although sociologists and economists do not study the economy in the same way, they actually cover much of the same material. Economists cannot understand the success or failure of an economic system without considering how it interacts with the rest of society. Sociologists cannot understand how systems interact unless they understand the internal functioning of each system. Nevertheless, the disciplines have different goals. Economists specialize in studying the economic system as one of society's important interacting parts. Sociologists study the whole of society, including the economic system.

Types of Economic Systems

To produce goods and services for a society, an economic system requires land on which to produce food and build factories. It also needs raw materials, tools and machinery to process them, and labor. Economic systems in modern societies vary according to who owns the land, the factories, the raw materials, and the equipment. These means of production may be privately owned, that is, owned by individuals, or they may be owned publicly by the state. *Capitalism* is a system based on private ownership. *Socialism* is a system based on state ownership of the means of production. Once again we are dealing with ideal types. In capitalist societies, some property is owned by the state, and in socialist societies, some property is privately owned, perhaps just small plots of land used to grow food. No society is purely capitalist or purely socialist. Mixed economies in which private and public ownership are both practiced extensively have a system called *welfare capitalism* or *democratic socialism*. A society's economic system has a powerful influence on how it produces and distributes goods.

Capitalism

The United States has a capitalist economic system. The means of production, the land and the factories, are owned by one or more individuals. Most large corporations are owned by the many groups and individuals who own stock, stock being shares of the corporation. Many small businesses are owned by one person, a family, or a few individuals.

Capitalism is a *market economy*. The goods sold and the price they are sold at are determined by the people who buy them and the people who sell them. Products no one wants to buy or sell are not traded. If everyone needs a product — fuel, for example — the product will be sold for as much money as people will pay for it. In a free market system, all people are theoretically free to buy, sell, and make a profit if they can, although there are prohibitions against selling sex or certain drugs. This type of market system is the reason capitalism is so strongly associated with freedom.

Socialism

Socialism differs from capitalism in that the means of production are owned by all the people through the state. Socialist systems are designed to ensure that all members of the society have some share of its wealth. Ownership is social rather than private. So-called communist systems such as the Soviet Union are actually socialist systems because the government owns all of the industries in the country.

Socialism also differs from capitalism in that it is not controlled by the marketplace. It has a *planned economy* — the government controls what will be produced and consumed, sets prices for goods, decides what goods the society needs, what are luxuries, and what can be done without altogether. Thus, there is no free market. The Soviet Union, for example, faced with a severe housing shortage after World War II, gave high priority to building low-cost housing for its population. Poland's government has large debts to other countries and makes decisions about how much to pay farmers for food, how much to allow the Polish people to buy, and how much to export in order to pay its international debts. The decisions to pay farmers low prices for food and to export food, which caused shortages within the country, created much of the unrest and worker strikes that began in 1981.

Welfare Capitalism

Welfare capitalism, sometimes called democratic socialism, is found in most West European countries. In Sweden and Great Britain, some industries are privately owned and others are state owned. Generally, the state owns the industries most vital to the country's well-being such as the railroads and communications industry. The most crucial needs — housing, medical care, education, and old age benefits — are paid for by the government with tax dollars. The taxes in welfare capitalist countries are quite high in order to pay for these benefits and to prevent a few people from accumulating all the wealth.

Whether a country is more or less capitalistic can sometimes be determined by comparing the taxes collected to the *Gross National Product* (GNP), the total value of the goods and services the country produces in a year. Often, the greater the proportion of the GNP that goes to taxes, the more social programs the country has. The GNP includes all necessities, luxuries, and military supplies produced for a price. It does not include anything not produced for profit. The worth of the work of housewives, for example, is the largest item not included in the GNP. As you can see from Table 16-1, taxes in the United States are low compared with those of most West European countries.

The GNP does not indicate what the various countries produce, nor does it show what tax

The British government has assumed responsibility for providing a good rail system. As a result, Britain has modern, rapid public transportation serving London and outlying areas. In contrast, the United States has resisted the idea that government should provide transportation services, and rail passenger service has deteriorated rapidly in the past few decades.

Table 16-1

Total tax revenues expressed as a percentage of gross national product

COUNTRY	PERCENT
Sweden	49.6
Norway	47.3
Netherlands	46.2
Luxembourg	45.8
Denmark	45.7
Britain	36.1
Canada	32.9
United States	30.7
Japan	26.1
Spain	24.5

SOURCE: Revenue statistics from the Organisation for Economic Co-operation and Development, Paris. Reprinted by permission.

dollars are spent for. The United States, which spends much of its tax money on the armed forces, includes military spending in its GNP. Sweden, on the other hand, spends little of its tax revenue on the military and a great deal on health, social planning, and the reduction of poverty. As a result, Sweden has the lowest infant mortality rate of all nations, the most hospital beds per capita, and the fifth highest life expectancy. The United States has an infant mortality rate almost twice that of Sweden, and United States citizens have a shorter life expectancy (Heilbroner, 1980). Sweden has clearly combined social programs with capitalism through taxation and government spending programs.

Theories of Economic Development

Historically, capitalism became the dominant economic system in Europe during the industrial revolution, although in the broadest sense capitalistic and socialistic systems have existed throughout recorded history. How did these systems develop and why do they persist? Theorists have been considering this question for several centuries. As in so many areas of sociological inquiry, two basic perspectives have evolved — structural functionalism and conflict theory.

Structural-Functional Theory

As you know, structural-functional theory suggests that social systems reflect the values of a society and work to meet basic social needs. According to this perspective, the capitalist economic system reflects the social values a society places on the freedom of the individual to accumulate and own private property. Especially in the United States, capitalism is highly valued and welfare programs are hotly debated. The capitalist system has evolved because immigrants coming to this country brought with them the desire to be free to determine their own economic welfare.

Functionalists argue that capitalism succeeds so well because it meets basic needs. Conservative economists have been describing capitalism as a vast cooperative system for centuries. In *The Wealth of Nations*, Adam Smith pointed out the beautiful balance that is achieved in the ideal functioning of the capitalist economy. This balance, which we know as the law of supply and demand, ensures that social needs will be met because it is profitable to meet them. When there is a demand, someone will profit from supplying it. People need food, clothing, and medical care, for example, and huge industries have developed to meet these needs. By tending to their self-interests, this theory suggests, everyone who produces a necessary product or service will profit and thereby benefit both themselves and society.

In recent years structural functionalists have been concerned about the large number of people who seem unable to find profitable means of supporting themselves. Most structural functionalists do not fault the capitalistic system, but they do recognize that certain dysfunctions make it difficult for some individuals and groups to have an equal opportunity in the marketplace. A child raised in an urban ghetto or impoverished Indian reservation is unlikely to get the good education that is needed to land jobs that pay well. Even when members of certain minority groups do manage to get a good education, racism and stereotyping may prevent them from finding a profitable occupation. As a result, the benefits of a capitalistic system are not equally available to all. Another dysfunction concerns the development of monopolies, which limit competition and thereby narrow the range of opportunities available in the marketplace.

Conflict Theory

In the *Communist Manifesto*, Marx described the development of both capitalism and communism as historical events. When most people produced needed goods directly from farming, there was an agricultural economic system. As industrialization developed and trading of manufactured articles increased, however, the economy came to be based on money, or capital. Marx realized that as some people increased their store of capital, they would be able to buy more and more factories and other means of production. Those who did not own any means of production would be forced to sell their only asset — their labor — to the factory owners. As the owners grew richer and more powerful, they would buy up more and more of the means of production and force more people to rely on their labor for subsistence. Eventually, Marx believed, the number of workers would grow so large that competition would reduce wages to the minimum needed for survival, and an entire class of impoverished workers would develop. He felt that conditions among the working class would ultimately deteriorate to the point that they would revolt, overthrow the owners, and develop a system in which the means of production would be owned communally and operated for the benefit of all.

Max Weber (1946) agreed with Marx's fundamental view of the economic order, but he differed slightly in his assessment of the means and outcome of oppression. Weber was concerned with the growth of bureaucracy. Bureaucracies operate in accordance with rational rules and procedures rather than humanitarian principles. With the compartmentalization of responsibility, it would be possible for a company to become extremely ruthless in the pursuit of profit, even if it meant that thousands of workers and the population at large would suffer. Those who made the decisions would be far removed from those who actually carried them out and who were in a position to observe their consequences. Weber was less optimistic than Marx, believing that eventually bureaucracies would grow so rich and powerful that no human effort could dislodge them. Even today, some conflict theorists contend that giant multinational corporations are too powerful to be controlled by individuals or even nations and that the world will come under progressively greater corporate control.

The American Economic System

Most American citizens are convinced that the capitalist system is good and cherish the freedom of the marketplace, the freedom to buy, sell, and earn a living any way one can. We value these freedoms as much as we value our religious freedom, and in fact the two systems arise out of the same tradition.

In *The Protestant Ethic and the Spirit of Capitalism* (1905), Weber discussed the Puritans' influence on the American desire for profit. He noted that capitalism, the exchange of goods for profit, has existed at one time or another in all societies. In the United States, however, profit became a major goal, desired not simply to provide for one's daily needs but to accumulate wealth.

The Puritans were Protestant Calvinists. Their doctrine stated that most people lived in sin but that a few had been predestined for everlasting life by the grace of God. No one on this earth could affect that predestination; people's fates were sealed by God. The chosen were on earth to build God's kingdom as God intended.

How did people know if they were among the elect? They couldn't know, but it was believed that those who were involved in the work of the world, who appeared to be building God's kingdom, must be among the elect. Those who spent their lives in idleness, carousing, drinking, and card playing were obviously not doing God's work and obviously not among the chosen. The Calvinists, fearing death, sought confirmation that they were among the chosen. They worked to produce goods, taking wealth as a sign that they were among the chosen. They did not spend time or money on comforts, play, or anything else that might indicate they were not chosen, nor did they associate with people believed to be outside the elect. They worked and they accumulated wealth, believing it to be an indication of self-worth. We now know this perspective as the *Protestant ethic.*

Although religious factors no longer play a strong role in justifying the accumulation of wealth, our religious heritage has had a strong influence on our economic values (Chesler and Cave, 1981). Several of these values are described below.

1. We value the individual rather than the group. We believe everyone should have an opportunity to accumulate wealth, and we will protect the individual's rights even if it makes the group suffer. Building office buildings for profit

is considered acceptable even when there is a housing shortage.

2. We value the economic well-being of the individual. The rich are considered successful, the poor are not. We do not judge people on the basis of how much they love or are loved by their family or friends, how much fun they have, how long they live, or whether they understand themselves and others. When we talk about success, we mean economic success.

3. We value private property. That people should own property seems natural, a God-given right. People who own and conquer the land, harvest timber, or drill for oil have a right to the profit, just as if they were the elect building God's kingdom. How different we are from the American Indians, who believe the land is not theirs to own or conquer but to live with in harmony.

4. We value growth, the ever-increasing accumulation of wealth. We do not make a profit to subsist or even to live comfortably. We value profit for the sake of profit, and the more the better.

The Growth of Large Corporations

The almost religious fervor with which we work for profit has contributed to the growth of large corporations. Building one car by hand is very expensive. Obviously, workers on an assembly line using machinery can assemble many identical parts and produce many cars in less time, at a lower cost per car. The cars can then be sold at a much greater profit than could be earned from building cars by hand one at a time. Factories and mass production have replaced the shoemaker, the spinner, the weaver, the dressmaker, the furniture maker, the cigar maker, the glass blower, the potter, the butcher, the baker, and the candlestick maker. Factories and the specialized division of labor were the basis of the industrial revolution. These innovations made it

A man works at a forge while his helper works behind him. Men in the eighteenth and nineteenth centuries manufactured products by hand, carrying out the various processes necessary to achieve the final product. Workers learned their skills by serving an apprenticeship until they had learned each stage of the manufacturing process. Production was slow and products lacked uniformity, but exceptional craftmanship was highly valued.

possible to mass produce goods that could be sold at low cost and still bring profit to the manufacturer.

More recently, profits have been increased by vertical expansion of businesses. If a business owns not only the factory that produces the goods but also the source of the raw materials purchased by the factory, the trucks that take the goods to market, and the stores that sell the products, the business can cut its costs at every step of the operation. It doesn't have to pay part of its profits to the owner of the raw material, the trucker, and the store owner. A business that owns all related businesses from the raw material to the retailer can increase its profits at every stage of its operation.

American corporations have expanded their operations to control the entire process from raw material to retail sales (Zwerdling, 1976). Safeway, for example, owns thousands of food stores and over a hundred manufacturing and processing plants, including bakeries, milk plants, ice cream plants, soft drink plants, meat processors, and coffee roasting plants. It manufactures its own soap, peanut butter, and salad oil, and owns a fleet of thousands of trucks to ship these products to its stores. Members of the board of directors of Safeway also sit on the boards of banks and corporations involved in agriculture, food production, food processing, food packaging, gas and electric power, and fuel oil. By owning or influencing every stage of production from the land food is grown on to retail sales, Safeway has become a very large corporation.

Another form of expansion that assures continued profits is *diversification,* entering a variety of businesses in an attempt to ensure a stable rate of profit. Investors might buy a variety of stocks so that if one went down, another might remain stable or go up and they would be protected from losing their entire investment. In the same way, corporations buy a variety of businesses so that those that are not highly profitable can be supported by those that are. Great Western United reportedly owns sugar companies, Shaky's Pizza, and large real estate holdings. The real estate is extremely valuable, but it does not provide income. By diversifying, Great Western United can support its real estate holdings with income from other sources.

Between 1950 and 1960, 20 percent of this country's largest 100 firms merged with other large, healthy firms because they could increase their profits by working together (Chesler and Cave, 1981). In 1980, another round of mergers by major corporations took place, and corporations grew larger still.

The size of corporations as they are legally structured tells only half the story of their tremendous power. Corporate links may join corporations that appear to be unrelated. A large bank or investment company, for example, may own controlling stock in a variety of corporations and control their business such that each will be able to maintain optimum profits. Family wealth is also used to control large corporations that are otherwise unrelated. Families such as the Fords, Gettys, Dows, DuPonts, Rockefellers, and Mellons hold large blocks of stock in many corporations. Firms and families from foreign countries also own large blocks of stock in United States corporations.

Multinational Corporations

As corporations grow, they do not confine their operations to their own country. They also own companies in foreign nations, where they employ workers and produce and sell their products. These companies are known as *multinational corporations.* One-third of the assets of Ford Motor Company are invested in foreign countries, and one-third of Ford's employees are foreigners working in these countries (Heilbroner, 1980).

Most multinational corporations are owned by Americans. These companies often become involved in political arrangements made between the United States and other countries. They affect the economies of this country and those in which they have holdings in several ways. They can buy foreign companies even when the United States would like to reduce overseas spending and have us "Buy American." They can also play one country against another, offering to build a plant in the one that gives them the greatest advantages in taxes, cheap labor, and freedom from regulation. By closing unprofitable plants, they can create unemployment problems. In a sense, multinational corporations are above the laws of any nation because they can use their vast wealth and power to dominate a nation's economy. The annual sales of either General Motors or Exxon are greater than the GNP of countries such as Austria, Denmark, Norway, Greece, Portugal, and the smaller nations of the world. Corporations can borrow vast amounts of money on the basis of their sales; countries can tax only their GNP. As corporations increase in size, they gain progressively more power to dominate the economies of entire nations.

The major increase in multinational business has been in the developed nations of the world. Canada has been affected especially strongly by multinational corporations. Canadians own only about 15 percent of their own industry. Almost half of Canadian industry is owned by United States corporations and individuals, and most of the rest is owned by Europeans, which makes it extremely difficult for the Canadian government to control its own economy.

Third World nations have also been powerfully influenced by multinationals. Large agricultural corporations, for example, have converted large tracts of farmland into huge plantations cultivated by modern machinery to produce cash crops for worldwide shipment. Ralston-Purina has built a large feedmill in Colombia to process corn for feed — corn that had previously been consumed by people (George, 1977). Del Monte and Dole grow pineapples in the Philippines and Thailand, where there is an abundance of cheap labor, and ship the pineapples to United States and Japanese markets. Gulf and Western controls land in the Dominican Republic, which is used to grow sugar for Gulf and Western's sugar mill. The large corporations often do not own the land but enter into agreements with local landowners to grow what they need for their processing plants, and the local landowners and governments cooperate even when the nutrition of the local people suffers.

American multinational corporations do business throughout the world, producing a great deal of food for export. Some products are for local consumption, however, and these are advertised widely to create a demand. This worker in Kenya earns his living working for an American multinational corporation familiar to us all.

Multinational corporations have such a great impact on the nations in which they do business and are so influential in international relations that some observers believe that nations as we know them today will eventually vanish and that affairs of state will come to be run by the boards of directors of huge corporations. Whether this will happen and whether it would create a more peaceful and orderly world or more poverty for workers is for now a matter of speculation. In any case, as corporations change and grow, the nature of work also changes.

The Changing Nature of Work

In simple agricultural societies, most people are *primary workers*. Those who grow food, fish, mine, or otherwise produce raw materials are referred to as primary workers because their work is so essential to their country. In an industrial society such as our own where most farming is done by machine, only a small portion of the population farms for a living. As Marx predicted, most of the population works to produce manufactured goods; these workers are called *secondary workers*. They are the wage earners, the people on the assembly line, the construction workers, the laborers in industry. The fastest growing segment of the labor force consists of *tertiary (or service) workers*. This group includes such people as police officers, doctors, lawyers, maids, and plumbers. In the following section we will describe the nature of secondary and tertiary work in modern society.

The Factory Worker and Alienation

In an earlier era, the cobbler or the candlestick maker developed a product from start to finish, sold it to the customer, took pride in the finished goods, and stood by his or her reputa-

tion as a skillful producer. The factory worker has none of these satisfactions, which has been a continuous problem for worker and management alike.

"Alienation" is a term Marx used in describing the working conditions of the factory worker. Factory workers are alienated from their work because they have no control over it and derive no satisfaction from it. Their work involves only a part of the finished product, and they see neither the beginning nor the end of the process. They have no satisfaction in creating a product and no pride in selling it to the customer. They perform one routine task over and over again, and in return they receive money, which may or may not be enough to provide them with a satisfactory lifestyle.

Factory workers have been studied extensively since the turn of the century. Initially, most studies were designed to improve worker efficiency through scientific management, and this remains an important focus of research in the workplace. More recently, the human relations school of management has gained prominence; this perspective suggests that increasing worker satisfaction and decreasing alienation could also increase production.

Scientific Management. *Scientific management*, a term coined by Frederick W. Taylor (1911), is management designed to improve worker efficiency. In an entrepreneurial setting, the workers own the business and are responsible for knowing the best way to do their own job. In companies that practice scientific management, the manager is assumed to know how to accomplish a task most efficiently. By keeping records and using a stopwatch, the manager determines rules for the most efficient work routine and then selects and trains workers to follow directions. The division of labor requires the manager to do the thinking and the worker to do the labor.

At Staley, Management Loves Worker Takeover

LAFAYETTE, IND. Out here on the prairie, almost within earshot of the consumptive rattles of the big steel and automobile centers, one view of the future of American industry is taking shape, and it is not without a sweeter side, no pun intended.

This future involves computers and people, but here at the A. E. Staley Manufacturing Co.'s plant, where corn is converted to high-powered syrup, the story really is about people.

Workers have taken over the Staley plant — not by force, but by management fiat, from the home offices in Decatur, Ill. To no one's real surprise, it's working like a charm.

The sudden rise of the high fructose corn syrup (HFCS) industry in itself is fascinating

enough, but there's more to it than that. Staley is pioneering management techniques that are as compelling as the automation making the plant one of the most modern in the sweetener industry. Some examples:

Since it opened in 1977, the $120-million plant has been expanded twice — in part because demand for HFCS has grown by quantum leaps, in part because workers keep exceeding production goals that Staley regularly sets for them.

All 240 employees, management or not, are on salary. There are no time clocks. Plant workers, set up as teams, decide who is hired, who is fired; who gets a raise, who

doesn't; who works when, who needs disciplining for not doing his or her share.

In keeping with their added responsibilities, the nonunion plant workers here are paid more and have heftier benefits than their brethren in other unionized Staley corn and soybean processing plants in the Midwest.

Involvement of workers in some of the basic decisions that rule their lives is not that revolutionary in American industry. Such household names as DuPont, Alcoa, Procter and Gamble, and Texas Instruments, among others, have moved in that direction.

But here in Lafayette, it is being taken farther, faster than elsewhere and the results — steadily increasing production, notable efficiency, pride in work and team spirit — are laden with implications for the troubled U.S. industrial machine.

SOURCE: *The Washington Post*, April 26, 1981, p. G1. ©1981 The Washington Post. Reprinted by permission.

Taylor developed his program at Bethlehem Steel Company to improve the efficiency of workers loading pig iron into railroad cars. A pig of iron weighed 92 pounds; workers lifted a pig, carried it up a plank, and dropped it into a car. Before Taylor designed his scientific management plan, each worker loaded an average of $12\frac{1}{2}$ tons of pig iron a day. By carefully controlling the pace at which the workers lifted, walked up the plank, rested, and lifted again, Taylor found that he could get the workers to load 47

tons of pig iron a day, almost four times as much as they had been loading. The workers were rewarded with a pay increase of 60 percent, and the profit to the company was enormous.

Taylor (1911) described the best type of worker to handle pig iron as follows: "He shall be so stupid and so phlegmatic that he more nearly resembles in his mental make-up the ox than any other type" (p. 51). A man who was alert and intelligent would quickly be dissatisfied and bored with routine labor and the way it was scientifically managed. Nevertheless, scientific management played an important role in increasing the efficient use of workers; the fact that most workers were not as dumb as an ox was overlooked. The intelligence of human workers, however, eventually had to be considered, and it was at that point that the human relations school of management developed.

The Human Relations School. The *human relations school* of management considers the psychological makeup of workers, their attitudes toward management, peer pressures, and similar factors in an attempt to promote worker efficiency. A scientific management study discovered the importance of human relations in the workplace by accident. In the now famous Hawthorne studies, experiments were done to improve the productivity of assembly line workers making telephone equipment. As you may recall from the discussion of the Hawthorne effect in Chapter 3, worker productivity did not increase as scientific management had expected — the workers responded to the attention they received from the researchers. More important, the study found that worker productivity depended on the informal group structure of the workers. When they were allowed to form their own working relationships and develop some of their own rules, they were much more cooperative with management, and their productivity increased. When they felt uneasy about changes handed down by management, they resisted these changes and productivity did not increase. The findings of the Hawthorne studies made management aware of the importance of informal groups, their attitudes toward management, and the effect these factors could have on productivity.

The human relations school of worker management developed to probe these issues further. Its researchers studied the formal organization of the workplace, company rules and working conditions, and informal organization among the workers themselves, including their customs, traditions, routines, values, and beliefs (Roethlisberger and Dickson, 1939). The goal of these studies was to find the best type of person for the job and the best type of environment for maintaining and improving worker attitudes.

A classic study of employee values and their effect on productivity was done in a gypsum factory by Gouldner (1954). Initially, the workers had been quite happy with their management and management had been flexible with the workers. They were occasionally allowed to leave early for personal reasons, and they were sometimes allowed to take supplies for their personal use. They were also encouraged to discuss work problems with management and make suggestions for improving working conditions. Managers and workers cooperated well together, and neither took advantage of the other.

Then, however, a new management team came to the company. To increase production, they adhered strictly to the rules. Workers were not allowed to leave early or take supplies, nor were they given a chance to discuss problems with management. The workers, who valued the flexibility of the earlier managers, resented the enforcement of the rules. They believed they were being treated with less respect, and they no longer cooperated with and supported the company.

After decades of research in human relations, workers in the United States are still frustrated in their jobs, and management continues to be frustrated with low productivity. In recent years, American managers have turned their attention to Japanese workers to try to understand why they are more productive than Americans.

Modern Trends in Management

The Japanese work force has proven itself to be exceptional in producing automobiles, and American employers have been studying their

Workers in a Nikon factory in Japan take a break from making cameras to exercise at their stations. The Japanese have developed a variety of practices to reduce workers' fatigue and increase efficiency and morale.

productivity with increasing interest (Ouchi, 1981). Their efficiency is attributed to two Japanese employee policies — lifetime jobs and quality control circles.

Lifetime jobs are held by only a third of Japanese men and no women, and they are held only until age fifty-five or sixty, which creates a hardship for workers when they are older. Nevertheless, a guarantee of even this short a "lifetime" job creates security for the Japanese man — a security most American workers do not have because they can be fired or laid off at any time. The Japanese man is also encouraged to have

close personal relationships with other workers, and to care about those in his work group just as he cares about his family. The group takes pride in its work and its members do not need to compete as individuals. They are paid a low base pay and then receive a bonus, often 50 percent of base pay, on the basis of their productivity. The arrangement of lifetime jobs, commitment to the group, and high productivity works to everyone's advantage.

Quality control circles are meetings held by the group to improve its productivity. Orders do not come down from the manager, as they do in

American bureaucracies; instead, the groups meet regularly to decide how their work can best be accomplished and then make recommendations to management. If management approves the recommendations, the work group is allowed to change its procedures.

Although these management techniques seem quite revolutionary to American managers, who still value scientific management, efficiency experts, and stopwatches, quality control groups are being tried in a few American companies with reported success.

Unionization

Workers have for years tried to improve their own working conditions and economic benefits through *unionization*, organizing workers to improve wages and working conditions. Unions can be traced back to the guilds of the Middle Ages, which protected skilled workers in the arts and crafts. As factories developed, workers formed unions to better their work environments. In the United States, skilled craftsmen were unionized before 1800, and women textile workers united in the early 1800s to protest working conditions in factories.

The latter part of the nineteenth century was a period of intense labor union struggle and conflict, and the results of this struggle continue to shape labor unions today. The more conservative unions of the period worked to protect their jobs through legislation. Tariff laws were passed to prevent competition from cheap imported goods, and immigration laws prevented cheap foreign labor from entering the country. Protective labor laws kept women and children out of the labor force, thereby eliminating another source of cheap labor. In addition, the unions maintained a cooperative relationship with their employers. They wanted work contracts and preferred to settle disputes by mediation and compromise. Strikes were used only as a last resort.

There was also a strong and popular socialist movement in the United States during this period, which was influenced by Marx's theory and his conception of alienation. Workers in various industries saw that they had much in common with one another and wanted to build a strong union covering all workers. They did not expect to cooperate with industry. They wanted, rather, to fight for collective ownership of industry so that they would own the companies they worked in and reap the profits of their own labor. Removing industry from private ownership and placing it in collective ownership would cause a radical redistribution of wealth, of course. The owners of American business, with the aid of federal, state, and local police and military power, forced these more radical labor unions out of existence, deported their foreign-born members, tried citizens for treason, and passed laws preventing such unions from forming in the future.

The more conservative type of union that accepts the private ownership of business is the kind representing labor in America today. Increasingly, this type of union covers the lower-paid workers in a newer set of occupations, the service workers.

Service Workers

The increase in the size of corporations has increased the number of tertiary, or service, workers, who are not directly involved in producing goods. These are the employees who answer the telephones, keep the records, file the papers, pay the taxes, clean the buildings, and do a host of other jobs necessary to keep large corporations functioning. Another class of service workers meets community rather than corporate needs, and this class has also been growing. As people have moved to urban areas to work, more police officers, firefighters, teachers, doctors, lawyers, and accountants have been needed to serve them.

Service workers are an expense to a corporation, part of its fixed overhead costs. They increase the costs of products, but they do not directly increase the production of products. Similarly, in a community they are a necessary expense to taxpayers, but they do not produce any tangible wealth. Service workers such as filing clerks, typists, police officers, and teachers typically have more education and training than blue-collar workers, but they do not necessarily receive more pay. Most lower-paid service workers are joining unions whereas the higher-paid ones are professionals who can control their work environment and demand high fees.

The professions are widely regarded as rewarding service occupations. Professional jobs share five characteristics that set them apart from other types of work:

1. *A body of knowledge.* The professions are based on knowledge not generally available to the public. Because only professionals fully understand this knowledge, they can control how it is applied.

2. *A code of ethics.* Professionals gain the confidence of the public by adhering to a code of ethics promising a certain level of service.

3. *Licensing.* Licensing demonstrates to the community that the licensed individuals have in fact mastered the body of knowledge associated with their profession.

4. *Peer control.* Because the body of knowledge is specialized, only professionals can judge one another's work. Outsiders do not have the knowledge necessary to make such judgments.

5. *A professional association.* The association devises and maintains the profession's educational standards, licensing requirements, peer review procedures, and code of ethics.

The most important professions in the United States are law and medicine. Professionals in these fields are not only well paid, but

they also have some autonomy in their work, which is protected by both legislation and the peers who review their work. The proportion of professionals employed by both profit and non-profit organizations — hospitals, pharmaceutical companies, medical and legal clinics, and large companies in other fields — has been increasing in recent years. Professionals may gradually lose some autonomy in these organizations.

Politics and the Distribution of Wealth

The economic system in our society produces wealth, but it has no responsibility to distribute wealth to all of the citizens. It is the political system that determines how the wealth is distributed. Although the government can levy taxes and use its funds to support programs for its citizens, there has been much debate in recent years on whether government should support corporations or the less privileged in society. Opponents in the debate tend to favor either supply-side or demand-side economic policies.

Demand-Side Economy

A *demand-side economy* is one in which political and economic policies are designed to put more money in the hands of consumers so they will be able to spur the economy by buying more goods and services. Such policies are associated with Franklin Roosevelt and the Great Depression, but the chain of events that led to them actually began in the previous decade.

During the 1920s, the rich became very rich and the poor became poorer. By 1929, the richest fifteen-thousand families in the United States made as much money as the 5 to 6 million families at the bottom of the pay scale combined (Heilbroner, 1980). These top-earning families did not spend all or even most of their money on consumer goods, however — they saved it. The 6 million people at the bottom of the pay scale could not buy consumer goods because they did not have enough money. When the Great Depression hit, millions of people lost their jobs. As a result, business could not find buyers for manufactured products because so many people were unemployed and the working people could barely make ends meet.

Roosevelt's New Deal programs were designed to put more spending money into the hands of millions of these poorer Americans. Income taxes were developed to tax the rich, and programs such as the Emergency Farm Mortgages Act and the Civilian Conservation Corps were initiated to put unemployed workers back to work. When the amount of money available to the poor increased, their purchasing power improved and demand was created in the marketplace.

World War II caused a demand for the goods needed to fight a war, and it was this demand that pulled the United States out of the Great Depression. After World War II, the returning military forces created a demand for homes, cars, furnishings, and other amenities of a middle-class lifestyle. That generation had large families whose needs continued to increase demand throughout the middle part of this century.

Supply-Side Economy

While the demand for goods and services was strong, American industries made large profits selling consumer products. At the same time, however, factories were growing old and the United States was falling behind other nations in its ability to produce such vital products as steel and automobiles. Products such as railroad passenger cars and ball bearings did not bring as much profit, and production of these items stopped. The United States was then no longer able to supply the manufactured goods consumers demanded as efficiently as other nations. Thus, while demand in the marketplace

remained strong, the supply-side of the economy had weakened.

Current *supply-side economics* suggests that the economy can be spurred by putting more money in the hands of the rich, who will invest in more competitive manufacturing systems — upgrading factories and machinery, for example. Accordingly, the Reagan Administration, which advocated supply-side economics, reduced the taxes of the rich so that they would have more money to invest in businesses. Reagan also reduced taxes on money made from investments as a further incentive for investment. As a result, the rich saved money on taxes, and the earnings they made if they invested their savings were taxed at a lower rate. The government, however, received fewer tax dollars and cut programs designed to aid the poor, such as welfare, Medicaid, food stamps, and the school lunch program.

Some critics of supply-side economics have argued that investment money is used to buy existing corporations that are already profitable rather than to develop additional manufacturing capability. They contend that the country must not drop programs that aid those unable to work because they are too young, too old, ill, or because no jobs are available. These critics argue that a fundamental change in the capitalist profit system is required. They believe that as long as the needs of society are met only when they provide profits to capitalists, the society will continue to have unemployment and poverty, and human needs will go unmet simply because it is not profitable to meet them. Whether profit is made by manufacturing consumer goods, building modern factories, or building military armaments, critics contend that today's profit system will maintain inequality and the problems associated with it. They argue that a more equitable redistribution of money would permit everyone to benefit from the wealth generated by society. They would also prefer an economy designed to meet the needs of society even when those needs

President Roosevelt practiced de-mand-side economics by supporting the Emergency Farm Mortgages Act to get money into the hands of poor farmers. He is shown here shaking hands with Georgia farmers during the depression. President Reagan, shown with Lee Iacocca and other Chrysler executives, practiced sup-ply-side economics by getting money into the hands of large corporations with government backed loans.

do not yield great profit. Today, the government's efforts to help those who cannot manage financially take the form of some type of welfare payment.

Welfare

Welfare consists of payments made by the govenment to people who have an inadequate income. Welfare programs include:

1. Aid to Families with Dependent Children (AFDC), the largest program, aids families with children under eighteen years of age if there is no adult capable of supporting them. This program does not provide payments when there is an able-bodied male in the household.
2. Medicaid is the medical insurance program for the poor.
3. Supplemental Security Income (SSI), part of the Social Security system, is designed to aid the poorest of the aged, blind, and disabled.
4. General Assistance is a program to help poor people not covered by other programs.

Because there are so many poor people in this country, the costs of programs are high but benefits are very meager. The program that provides support for children when parents cannot work (AFDC) cost over $12 billion but paid only an average of $102.80 per month per recipient in 1982 (*World Almanac*, 1984).

Critics of the present welfare system argue that it exploits poor people. Gans (1972) lists some advantages to the middle and upper classes of keeping people on welfare:

1. They are a source of cheap labor.
2. They can be sold goods of inferior quality that otherwise could not be sold at all.
3. They serve as examples of deviance, thereby motivating others to support the norms of the dominant group.

4. They make mobility easier for others, because they are out of the competition.
5. They do the most unpleasant jobs.
6. They absorb the costs of change, since they suffer the unemployment when technological advances are made by industry.
7. They create jobs in social work and related fields for the middle class.
8. They create distinctive cultural forms in music and art, which the middle class adopts.

Welfare payments also tend to keep the unemployed from expressing their discontentment. Piven and Cloward (1971) have shown that welfare payments increase when unemployment is high and discontent is widespread but decrease when workers are scarce and unemployment is low.

Other "Welfare" Programs

Welfare payments to the poor comprise only a small part of the federal government's efforts to improve living conditions. Actually there are many programs designed to assist classes other than the poor.

1. veterans benefits such as life insurance, health care, educational support, housing loans, and burial grounds
2. housing loans, available to higher-income groups, offering lower interest rates and reduced down payments
3. business loans on favorable terms, available to owners of both small and large businesses
4. farming subsidies to landowners who agree not to farm certain of their lands
5. social security, which is not available to the unemployed or to those who work in jobs the program does not cover
6. medical care in hospitals built with government funds, staffed by doctors educated with government support, who use treat-

ments developed with the help of government grants

7. college classrooms and dormitories built with government funds and financial assistance for college students

In fact, there are more government programs to help the middle and upper classes than the poor. Yet it is the programs for the poor that generally come under attack when the government tries to cut the domestic budget. Programs that benefit the middle class, especially veterans' and housing benefits, are considered "sacred cows" and are never reduced. As you will see in the next section, some societies place the welfare of their entire population at the top of the hierarchy of priorities.

The Chinese System: An Example of Socialism

Economic systems, whether capitalist or socialist, are strongly influenced by the societies of which they are a part. We cannot discuss adequately in this chapter all of the variations that exist in the world. We will, however, describe one socialist system, that of the Chinese, to provide a comparison with capitalism.

In 1920, China was a nation ruled by local warlords and populated by millions of poor peasants. More than half the peasants owned no land whatsoever, and many who did have land owned so little that they could not support themselves. Chinese workers in the cities were equally poor. Women and children who worked in the silk mills labored fifteen hours a day for 12¢. The average wage for male workers was $10 a month (Freeman, 1979).

Two groups of Chinese organized to fight the warlords and modernize the Chinese nation. One group, the Kuomintang, was made up of middle-class people, merchants, nationalists, and intellectuals. This group had the support of the United States in their efforts to organize labor and make China a modern industrial nation. The other group, the Chinese Communist party, developed around a small number of radicals from the middle class. This group had the support of the Soviet Union.

For almost thirty years, these two groups fought the warlords, Japanese invaders, and each other. The Japanese invasion of China did much to turn peasant support to the Communist party. The Kuomintang leaders treated the peasants cruelly, forcibly drafting them into their army and bringing them to training camps in chains. When the Kuomintang fought the Japanese in open battle, they generally lost and then they taxed the peasants heavily to rebuild their army. Inflation and corruption were rampant. When World War II ended, the Kuomintang controlled most of Chinese industry and had the support of most of the world's nations. The United States sent them $1.1 billion in aid in 1945 alone. They had no social programs; they specialized in graft and corruption and treated the peasants with contempt.

The peasants, unhappy under Kuomintang rule, turned to the Communist party, where they were well treated. The Communists gave the peasants guns, fought the Japanese in guerrilla warfare, and were better able to protect themselves and the peasants. They preached mutual love and assistance and instructed their army to behave as follows (Freeman, 1979, p. 210):

1. Obey orders in all your actions.
2. Do not take a single needle or piece of thread from the masses.
3. Turn in everything captured.
4. Speak politely.
5. Pay fairly for what you buy.
6. Return everything you borrow.
7. Pay for anything you damage.

SOCIOLOGISTS AT WORK
Societal Analysis in the Auto Industry

Carroll DeWeese is a staff research scientist in the Societal Analysis Department of General Motors Research Laboratories. The objectives of GM Research Laboratories are to generate new technical knowledge of commercial interest to GM, to evaluate outside technical advances for possible application to GM products and processes, to anticipate future technological needs and develop the expertise to meet those needs, and to assist in the analysis of corporate priorities, policies, and programs. About 1,500 people work at GM Research Laboratories. More than a third of them are research and development professionals; of this number, about thirty come from backgrounds in the social sciences, including four with doctorates in sociology.

The Societal Analysis Department is an interdisciplinary department whose mission is to study the impact of GM on society and vice versa. DeWeese leads a group with degrees in applied mathematics, economics, operations research, psychology, and sociology.

Research in the department is generally interdisciplinary, problem-oriented, and quantitative. Researchers have worked on a variety of topics, including air pollution, auto safety, auto service, customer satisfaction, energy, product quality, diesel odor, and other areas of public concern.

Carroll DeWeese studied sociology at the University of Houston and at Purdue. He joined GM Research Laboratories immediately on completing his work at Purdue. One of his first jobs there was to develop a computerized system for identifying and studying public concerns as they emerge and grow. This valuable information could then be put to good use by GM's management. After this solid start, he was soon put in charge of all the department's sociologists, and a few years later he was promoted to his current position as leader of an interdisciplinary research group.

The thing that most appeals to DeWeese about his work at GM Research Laboratories is his independence. "I have picked all the projects I work on. No one tells me what I have to do or how I have to do it. My superiors are primarily concerned with providing the resources for me to

8. Do not hit or swear at people.
9. Do not damage crops.
10. Do not take liberties with women.
11. Do not ill-treat captives.

The Communists gained the support of the peasants, two million in the army and ten million in village self-defense squads. They eventually won the civil war and created the People's Republic of China on October 1, 1949.

In a matter of months, the Communists made dramatic changes in support of their theme of mutual love and assistance. They outlawed opium growing, gambling, female infanticide (the killing of girl infants), dowries, arranged marriages, the selling of wives and concubines,

accomplish my objectives, and with helping me get my results across to others. Time and resources are made available for researchers to explore and test ideas at an early stage of development without having to justify them. I am not tied down to what management or my colleagues tell me I have to work on, although their suggestions are important inputs. I have more freedom to do research than the academic sociologists I know."

DeWeese has done a lot of thinking about what makes researchers successful in this challenging environment. He has been able to identify several characteristics: "They must be pragmatic, not ideological — interested in doing whatever is necessary to solve a problem. They are persons looking for tools to solve problems, not persons with some particular tool trying to find problems to solve. They must be able to communicate, to excite and convince others about their ideas. Brevity is a virtue here. After a year's work, they should be able to convince a decision-maker of the importance of the problem studied and the results found on a single sheet of paper or in five minutes of conversation. They must know how to identify critical problems — the more critical the problem, the more attention any actionable results will receive. They must know how to work as part of a team, to secure the cooperation and support of their colleagues. And they must have quantitative ability combined with qualitative

flexibility. That's where the interdisciplinary arrangement, the variety of perspectives, pays off.

"But perhaps most of all, successful people in this job are persistent. They can go a long time without positive feedback. They are self-starters who know how to keep a project alive until it bears fruit. Some of the most successful research projects I know of were only minimally supported by management at first and were kept alive by researchers who believed in their importance. These researchers knew how to overcome all obstacles until the usefulness of their ideas became clear to others. They took risks to provide what was really needed, not just what other people thought was needed."

It is no accident that DeWeese's list of characteristics of the successful researcher in his department does not include specific substantive knowledge. "People are expected to acquire whatever substantive knowledge is needed to solve the problem they are working on," he explains. "On the other hand, use of the sociological imagination is critical for identifying, studying, and solving problems. The strength of sociology is the perspective it gives a person. I am not saying substantive knowledge is unimportant. When we hire people, we have problem areas in mind and we look for people with substantive backgrounds in those problem areas. But that substantive knowledge is a given. It is not a characteristic of success."

and many other practices that had existed for centuries. The benefits were great to everyone except the wealthy landowners.

The primary workers were formed into thousands of agricultural communes. The communes of today average 15,000 members, each divided into brigades averaging 1,000 members each. Brigades are divided into teams of 150 persons. The peasants were slow to adapt to communes after centuries of working their own plots, but the Communists brought much new land under cultivation by terracing hillsides, digging wells for irrigation, improving the soil, and using new seed strains. They also introduced modern farming equipment such as machines for planting and transplanting rice. As improvements in

Chinese workers assemble parts in a small factory. These workers benefit from the development of industry in Communist China because it provides a way for them to earn a living. The small size of this factory also allows them to develop a sense of community with their fellow workers.

farming developed, crop yields increased enormously. The life of the peasants improved, and they have now adapted to communal living.

The Chinese Communists developed successful industries rather quickly. Industries such as iron, steel, machinery, coal, petroleum, electric power, and chemicals were developed in moderate-size factories and plants spread about the country. An effort was made to keep industry in small-scale plants so the secondary workers would not feel lost or alienated. In addition, workers were encouraged to feel pride in their individual contribution to the functioning of the plant and the commune it served.

The Communists also made remarkable strides in tertiary or service areas such as education and health care. To facilitate educating their people, the Chinese language was simplified, schools and colleges were opened, and teachers were trained. In the ten years after the Communist takeover, enrollment in middle schools, comparable to our junior high and high schools, jumped from one million to 12 million students. The schools emphasize the teaching of Communist doctrine, equality, mutual love and assistance, and pride in the ability to contribute to the good of society.

The Chinese system developed in a very poor nation that now has over one billion people. While China is still poor by U.S. standards, the planning and setting of priorities required by the socialist system allowed the Chinese to make the most use of their people and their resources. At the same time, it must be acknowledged that the average Chinese worker has sacrificed many of the freedoms that Americans take for granted. In China, people are expected to put the welfare of the group above their own interests; such cultural norms leave little room for individual self-expression or the accumulation of wealth.

Summary

A society's economic system provides for the production and distribution of the goods and services the society uses. Sociologists study economic systems to better understand how the production of goods influences social life.

There are currently two basic types of economic systems. One is capitalism, in which the property needed to produce resources and goods is privately owned. The United States is the most capitalistic of modern nations, but even in this country some property is not privately owned. In the other type of system, socialism, the property needed to produce goods and resources is owned by the state. In countries such as Great Britain and Sweden, which were originally capitalist, some property is private and some is owned by the state. This system is called welfare capitalism.

Capitalism is a market economy in which the emphasis is on products that provide a profit

to manufacturers. In contrast, socialism is a planned economy. The state decides what will be manufactured and sold, and at what price.

Structural-functional theorists point out that capitalism reflects social values favoring private property and the freedom to determine one's own economic course. Functionalists believe that capitalism persists because it functions well, providing profit to whoever supplies needed goods. Conflict theorists argue that capitalism creates a monopoly of wealth and alienates workers. The traditional Marxist view is that the workers will eventually be oppressed to the point where they will overthrow the capitalists and create a communist economic system.

The American economic system reflects values held by its people. These values were strongly influenced by the Puritans, who believed that those who accumulated wealth were chosen by God. Americans value the individual right to accumulate property and confer status on the rich. They also value growth and increasing profits.

American corporations have grown from large factories to giant corporations that control every step in the manufacturing process from raw materials to retail sales. Some corporations own a number of different types of businesses, and even unrelated businesses may be linked through being owned or controlled by the same bank or wealthy individual. Many very large corporations do business in many countries. These are called multinational corporations.

Marx believed that work in large factories was alienating, because employees who could not control their work or create a product from start to finish could take no pride in their work. A great deal of research has been done to increase productivity, but the scientific management and human relations perspectives offer different views on how to improve efficiency. The Japanese, who emphasize lifetime jobs and quality control circles, have been more successful than Americans in this respect.

Employees have formed unions to improve their working conditions. American unions have been conservative, cooperating with management and striking only as a last resort. More radical labor unions, which wanted workers to own the means of production, were outlawed in America.

Large corporations and urban areas need many service workers. Most of them are poorly paid, and many are joining unions. Professionals are an exception, however. They are highly trained workers familiar with certain specialized bodies of knowledge and have codes of ethics, licensing procedures, peer controls, and professional organizations. Through legislation, they can limit the practice of their profession and demand high fees. More and more professionals now work for large corporations.

China has a socialist economic system. Through their planned economy, the Chinese have been able to improve the standard of living of a very poor nation. The Chinese Communist party organized workers into communes, built industries, and provided for the country's other basic needs. Their economic system differs greatly from the American economic system, however.

Key Terms

capitalism
demand-side economy
democratic socialism
diversification
economics
Gross National Product (GNP)
human relations school
lifetime jobs
market economy
multinational corporations
planned economy

primary workers
Protestant ethic
quality control circles
scientific management
secondary workers
socialism
supply-side economics
tertiary workers
unionization
welfare capitalism

Suggested Readings

Anderson, Arthur L. **Divided We Stand.** *Dubuque, Iowa: Kendall/Hunt, 1978.* In this study of churches, Anderson argues that churches are more in agreement about our fundamental economic beliefs than they are about Christianity.

Anthony, P. D. **The Ideology of Work.** *London: Javistock Publications, 1977.* The work ethic is deeply ingrained in industrial society. Anthony philosophically analyzes why this is so and challenges managers of workers to take a realistic look at their own work.

Deal, Terrence E. and Allan A. Kennedy. **The Rites and Rituals of Corporate Life.** *Reading, Mass.: Addison-Wesley, 1982.* A short introduction to corporate cultures and how they are related to productivity.

Dixon, John. **The Chinese Welfare System, 1949–1979.** *New York: Praeger, 1981.* Mr. Dixon, an Australian, has carefully and objectively observed China's development over the past thirty years.

Freeman, Harold. **Toward Socialism in America.** *Cambridge, Mass.: Schenkman, 1979.* Freeman describes the strengths and weaknesses of both capitalism and socialism and suggests that this country make certain adjustments in its economy.

Gouldner, Alvin W. **Patterns of Industrial Bureaucracy.** *New York: The Free Press, 1954.* A classic case study in industrial sociology which shows that cooperation decreases when rules are strictly enforced.

Heilbroner, Robert L. **The Making of Economic Society.** *Englewood Cliffs, N.J.: Prentice-Hall, 1980.* This book, referred to several times throughout the chapter, is a good, brief, readable introduction to economics. It is written by an economist.

Page, Benjamin I. **Who Gets What from Government. *Berkeley: University of California Press, 1983.* A short, detailed book that demonstrates that the more you have, the more you are likely to benefit from government programs.

Skolnick, Jerome H. and Elliot Curie. **Crisis in American Institutions.** *Boston: Little, Brown, 1976.* A good collection of articles on the social problems caused by our economic system.

Weber, Max. **The Protestant Ethic and the Spirit of Capitalism.** *New York: Scribner's, 1958.* Weber's brilliant thinking is evident in his discussion of the relationship between religion and the economy. This is one of Weber's more readable works.

Yankelovich, Daniel. **New Rules: Searching for Self-Fulfillment in a World Turned Upside Down.** *New York: Random House, 1981.* Middle-class Americans discuss how they have tried to adapt to the changing economy, which has moved from affluence to inflation and conflict between the employed and the unemployed.

CHAPTER 17

Health Care Groups and Systems

The desire to take medicine is perhaps the greatest feature which distinguishes men from animals.

— Sir William Osler

Every society must give serious attention to the health of its population if it is to survive. Illness disrupts society inasmuch as members who are ill cannot fulfill their social roles, they use scarce resources such as medicines, and they require the time and attention of healthy persons to take care of them. Because of these factors, every society has developed ways of coping with illness.

We often think of health and illness in strictly biological terms and believe that the diagnosis and treatment of illness are based on a scientific analysis of a biological problem. Social factors, however, play a major role in defining who is well and who is ill, and they also influence how illness is treated. This chapter discusses health and illness from a sociological perspective.

The Social Nature of Health and Illness

Health, according to the World Health Organization (WHO), is "complete physical, mental and social well-being and not merely the absence of disease and infirmity" (Mechanic, 1978). One wonders how many people would be considered totally healthy according to this glowing definition. Does anyone ever have complete physical, mental, and social well-being all at the same time? Rather than use such an all-encompassing definition, others in the health field prefer to define health as the body in a state of equilibrium. Our biological systems should function in a particular way, and we are healthy when they function as they should.

Others prefer to define health as the absence of illness, but illness is an equally difficult term to define. *Pathological illnesses* are those in which the body is clearly diseased or malfunctioning in some way, as when viruses cause measles and chicken pox, cancer cells develop and grow, or an artery to the heart is blocked. These conditions are either obvious when examining the patient, or they are detected in laboratory tests involving X rays, microscopes, or the more advanced technology available today. Not all biological abnormalities are considered illnesses, however. Herpes, for example, was not considered an illness until venereal herpes became widespread and life-threatening to newborn infants.

Statistical illnesses are those in which one's health varies from the norm. High blood pressure is a statistical illness that exists when one's blood pressure is considerably higher than normal. The trouble with defining statistical illnesses is knowing if the norm is actually healthy. In the case of high blood pressure, the norm in the United States, 140/95, is probably too high for optimal health. A much lower blood pressure is probably desirable, say 100/60, but that level is so abnormally low in the United States that if it were used as a standard, everyone would be classified as ill. A tribe of Indians in South America has a similar problem. They have such a high incidence of a disease indicated by colored spots on the skin that anyone in the tribe who does not have such spots is considered abnormal (Dubos, 1965).

Iron-deficiency anemia is another example of a statistical disease. How much below the norm does one have to be before being considered anemic? When does one need to take iron? The answer is determined by the norm for the majority of the population.

The need for a tonsillectomy is also determined by how much tonsils differ from the norm. Few tonsils are perfect, but how bad do they have to be before they need to be removed? This varies with the times. In the 1940s and 1950s many children had their tonsils removed in the United States. Today fewer children have tonsillectomies, not because the tonsils are in better condition but because the standards for tonsillectomies have changed.

Hysterectomies, the surgical removal of the uterus, also go in and out of fashion. A surgeon could remove any uterus that is not in perfect condition or only those that cause life-threatening conditions. The tendency today is to perform hysterectomies for a wide range of conditions, not just for those in which a woman's life is threatened. As a result, hysterectomies are considered one of the most overused types of surgery.

Mental illnesses are even more difficult to define than physical ones. Manic depressives have more extreme mood swings than normal, but everyone has mood swings. How depressed must one be before one is assumed to have the illness called depression? We are all depressed sometimes. The diagnosis is made by comparing an individual's behavior to the norm. Similarly, people who drink more than the norm may be considered alcoholics, but norms on drinking vary. A person who would be considered a problem drinker in an American Baptist community might be considered normal in an Irish or French community.

Medical researchers are searching diligently for biological causes of depression, alcoholism, and other behavioral concerns, and they may in time find biological bases for some of these problems. Behavior is social, nevertheless, in that it is learned in social interaction, and whether our behavior is considered healthy or ill will continue to be determined by social criteria. Even the particular illnesses people suffer from and the causes of death are related to social circumstances.

The Change in Illness Over Time

Prior to industrialization in Europe, nutrition was poor and death rates from infectious diseases were high. Whenever crops failed, there was a food shortage. Transportation was not good enough to bring in large supplies of food, so the population became undernourished, weak, and increasingly susceptible to infection. Devastating plagues swept Europe from 1370 on. In some areas, one-third to one-half the population died. Often, when the plague hit a city, people fled to the countryside, dying on the way or carrying the plague deep into rural areas.

In the Middle Ages, the causes of the plague and other diseases were not understood. In the cities, human waste was thrown into the streets. People did not concern themselves with cleanliness and did not use soap and water. It was considered immoral to concern oneself with the flesh and immodest to wash below the waist (Thomlinson, 1976).

When it was discovered that rats carry the plague and that germs cause infections, urban sanitation systems were developed. Supplies of water were brought to cities and sewage systems were built. The improvement of sanitation may have added more to the average life expectancy than all modern medical advances.

Improvements in nutrition played an even more dramatic role in reducing the death rate. It is believed that nutrition improved in Europe when the potato came into widespread use in about the middle of the eighteenth century. The potato is rich in nutrients and easy to store and ship from place to place. Until the development of potato crops, infectious diseases were rampant and the average life expectancy was probably less than forty years.

Modern medicine may have helped reduce the death rate from infectious diseases in two important ways. Penicillin and other antibiotics were developed to cure infections and vaccines were developed to prevent diseases. While there is no question antibiotics save lives, researchers McKinlay and McKinlay (1981), argue that vaccines actually affected the death rate only

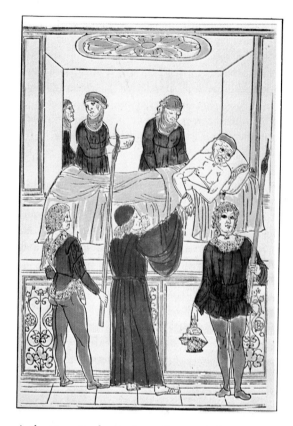

A physician attends a patient suffering from the plague while servants burn perfume. The plague and other infectious diseases killed so many people that the size of the population decreased markedly. When cities developed better sanitation and a better food supply, the number of deaths from infectious diseases went down and the size of the population began to increase rapidly.

slightly, reducing it by 3.5 percent at most. The infectious diseases that were the major causes of death in 1900 — influenza, pneumonia, tuberculosis, diphtheria, typhoid, scarlet fever, measles, and whooping cough — were declining steadily as causes of death long before modern vaccines were discovered. They continued to fall after the vaccines were introduced, but not appreciably. Poliomyelitis is an exception. It showed a very noticeable decline soon after the vaccine came into widespread use. Otherwise, the reduction in infectious diseases was a result of better nutrition, better sanitation, and better housing.

Current Causes of Death

Poor nutrition is still widespread among the poor of most nations, and starvation and infectious diseases are persistent problems. However, the causes of death in industrial societies are dramatically different. Since 1950, the major causes of death in the United States and most other industrial nations have been heart disease, cancer, and stroke (see Table 17-1). Heart disease and strokes have been declining, especially in younger people and women. The cancer rate is increasing. Cancer caused 129 deaths per 100,000 population in 1968 and 184 deaths per 100,000

in 1981 (U.S. Dept. of Health and Human Services, 1981).

It is estimated that 80 percent of all cancer cases are environmentally induced (Agran, 1975). The risk of carcinogens (cancer-causing products) in the environment has been known since 1942, when publications urged that measures be taken to minimize cancer hazards on the job, but no effective action has been taken. Rubber workers die of cancer of the stomach and prostate, leukemia, and other cancers of the blood and lymphatic systems. Steelworkers have excessive rates of lung cancer. Asbestos workers die of lung cancer at rates seven times higher than other groups. Workers who produce dyestuffs have high rates of bladder cancer. Miners have a wide range of cancers, and half of them die from some form of cancer. Dry cleaners, painters, printers, petroleum workers, and others who are exposed to benzene have high rates of leukemia. The 1.5 million workers who are exposed to insecticides, copper, lead, and arsenic

Table 17-1

Major causes of death in the United States

1900	1981
Influenza and pneumonia 11.8%	Heart disease 38.1%
Tuberculosis 11.3%	Cancer 21.4%
Gastroenteritis 8.3%	Stroke 8.3%
Heart disease 8.0%	Accidents 5.1%
Stroke 6.2%	Pulmonary diseases 3.0%
Kidney disease 4.7%	Influenza and pneumonia 3.0%
Accidents 4.2%	All other[a] 21.2%
Cancer 3.7%	
Infancy diseases 3.6%	
All other[a] 38.2%	

[a] No disease in this category represents more than 3 percent of all deaths.

SOURCE: Adapted from National Center for Health Statistics, U.S. Dept. of Health and Human Services, Washington, D.C., no date.

In 1955, school children received the first Salk polio vaccine. At the time, poliomyelitis was a dread disease that crippled children and was often fatal. Initially, people were afraid of the vaccine, but it seemed the lesser of two evils. The fear now is for those children who are not vaccinated.

have high rates of lung and lymphatic cancer. Machinists, chemical workers, woodworkers, roofers, and countless other suffer from cancer risks of one kind or another.

Cancer rates are also higher in neighborhoods where these industries are located, thereby shortening the lives of people who never even enter the plant. Since little or nothing is being done about these problems, increasing cancer rates may shorten life expectancy and cause genetic defects in the next generation.

Accidents, the fourth most common cause of death, are the leading cause of death for persons under age thirty-five. Motor vehicle accidents, which account for half of these deaths, have increased steadily since 1976, when the rate declined briefly as speed limits were reduced to 55 miles per hour. White males between the ages of fifteen and twenty-five have the highest death rate from automobile accidents.

Theoretical Perspectives on Illness

How does society handle illness? Who decides when we are ill and when we are well? Why is it that we can sometimes miss school or work while at other times when we feel just as bad we are not excused? Why do tonsillectomies and hysterectomies go in and out of style? Shouldn't illness be decided objectively on the basis of biological criteria? Sociologists do not believe that an objective view of illness can ever be achieved, because illness is social as well as biological.

A Functional Explanation of Illness

Talcott Parsons (1951) pointed out that people are not classified as ill on the basis of their physical condition but on the basis of how they are functioning in society. If people do not function well in their social roles, especially in family

*Portrait of a hypochondriac: Some
people are indeed overly concerned
about illness and tailor their lives to
accommodate imaginary physical
ailments.*

and work roles, they are considered deviant and disruptive to society. To maintain social order, such people are labeled "ill" and placed in a *sick role,* a set of expectations, privileges, and obligations related to their illness. The expectations of the sick role vary somewhat depending on the person and the illness, but they generally involve three assumptions.

First, people are expected to reduce their performance in other roles. Those with a serious case of the flu who have a high temperature and other symptoms may be excused from all other roles. Those suffering from a mild case of mononucleosis may be expected to perform work or student roles as usual, but they will be expected to reduce social and recreational roles. The sick role reflects a society's need to have members participate in the work of that society. The first roles relinquished are those that are for pleasure. The last ones relinquished are work roles.

Second, people in the sick role are expected to try to get better. They should do whatever they can to improve their health and not linger in their illness.

Third, they are expected to take the advice of others. Children must take the advice of parents, and adults must listen to their doctor or to the family members who are caring for them. Sometimes children take care of their parents, and while they would not usually tell their parents how to behave, in the event of illness they give extensive advice. Furthermore, if the advice is not accepted, the advice giver often becomes very hurt or angry.

Society places the power to declare who is sick in the hands of physicians. Only the physician has the legal right to diagnose and treat illness. The physician can excuse you from work or school, admit you to a hospital, or have you declared disabled or too ill to stand trial in a court of law. A person's self-diagnosis is not adequate. He or she must go to a doctor to be seriously considered ill. If the doctor does not agree with the patient's diagnosis, the individual is labeled "well." If the patient disagrees with the diagnosis as well, the individual may be called a *hypochondriac,* a well person who believes he or she is ill. If people believe they are healthy but a physician declares them ill, they can be declared mentally ill as well as physically ill. A person diagnosed as having cancer who refused to accept such a diagnosis might be sent for psychiatric evaluation, for example.

The sick role varies depending on a variety of social circumstances such as age, sex, and the influence of caretakers. Elderly people are expected to be ill and are easily placed in the sick role. It is also acceptable for women to be ill unless they have responsibility for young children — women are rarely excused from child-care duties. The caretaker also influences the sick role. If he or she accepts the illness, the sick person will play the role more fully, but if the caretaker is someone who carries on staunchly under all but the most dire circumstances, the sick person may be required to perform work roles. Some mothers are happy to bring soup and tender loving care to their children for long periods of time. Other mothers believe they should be up and about as soon as possible. Although its expectations may vary, the sick role does place a person in the social order with a set of both responsibilities and privileges to guide behavior so that the social order can be kept integrated and functioning.

The Conflict Perspective of Illness

Conflict theorists believe that society places deviant individuals in the sick role in order to control their behavior and maintain social order. However, conflict theorists point out that this is often done for the benefit of the social system rather than for the benefit of those who are ill. Doctors, who for the most part come from and represent the upper classes, have the power to excuse people from work or refuse to excuse them. Physicians can put business executives in a hospital for days or weeks of treatment for a painful back condition but give laborers pain killers for a similar back condition and send them back to work. Conflict theorists contend

that the system of giving birth in hospitals rather than at home or in birthing centers persists because it is convenient for doctors and profitable for hospitals. Deliveries are made by doctors rather than by midwives because it provides employment for doctors, not because it is necessary or better for women and babies. Physicians declare who is eligible for insurance payments for illness and disability and who must return to work. Insurance programs such as Medicare and the federal health insurance program for the elderly are structured such that wealthy people receive more benefits than the poor (Davis, 1975).

Conflict theorists also point out that doctors can declare criminals insane and unable to stand trial and that they more often declare elite criminals insane. Lower-class black criminals are more likely to stand trial and go to prison. Physicians are also more likely to commit poor black individuals to public mental hospitals, whereas wealthy people are treated outside the hospital.

Conflict theorists argue that much of the diagnosis and treatment of diseases benefits the large medical corporations more than the patients. Although drug companies sell drugs of questionable safety and effectiveness for the common cold, they do not manufacture "orphan" drugs that are valuable in the treatment of rare diseases but not profitable to the manufacturer. Manufacturers of medical equipment may sell unnecessary and unsafe devices to hospitals, which raises hospital costs by encouraging more testing and procedures that must be paid for by the patient. The conflict perspective maintains that the sick role and illness are used to perpetuate the existing social system.

Symbolic Interaction and Illness Behavior

Because illness is social, symbolic interaction has played a major role in the study of medical groups and systems. Patients are the first to recognize their own illness and decide to visit a doc-

Some Contingencies of the Moral Evaluation and Control of Clientele: The Case of the Hospital Emergency Service

The hospital emergency service is a setting where a minimum of information is available about the character of each patient and a long-term relationship with the patient is usually not contemplated. Even under these conditions, judgments about a patient's moral fitness and the appropriateness of his visit to an emergency service are constantly made, and staff action concerning the patient — including diagnosis, treatment, and disposition of the case — are, in part, affected by these judgments.

Take, for example, patients who are labeled as drunks. They are more consistently treated as undeserving than any other category of patient. They are frequently handled as if they were baggage when they are brought in by police; those with lacerations are often roughly treated by physicians; they are usually treated only for drunkenness and obvious surgical repair without being examined for other pathology; no one believes their stories; their statements are ridiculed; they are treated in an abusive or jocular manner; they are ignored for long periods of time; in one hospital they are placed in a room separate from most other patients. Emergency-ward personnel frequently comment on how they hate to take care of drunks.

Thus, it might seem that the staff is applying a simple moral syllogism: drunks do not deserve to be cared for, this patient is a drunk, therefore, he does not deserve good treatment. *But* how do we know that he is drunk? By the way he is treated. Police take him directly to the drunk room. If we ask why the police define him as drunk, they may answer that they smell alcohol on his breath. But not all people with alcohol on their breath are picked up by the police and taken to a hospital emergency room. The explanation must come in terms of some part of the patient's background — he was in a lower-class neighborhood, his style of dress was dirty and sloppy, he was unattended by any friend or family member, and so on. When he comes to the emergency room *he has already been defined as a drunk*. There is no reason for the emergency-room personnel to challenge this definition — it is routine procedure and it usually proves correct insofar as they know. There is nothing to do for drunks except to give them

tor, who then takes a medical history. How the patient describes symptoms influences the diagnosis, and patients describe their illness based on what society teaches them. They learn that nausea and dizziness are signs of illness (unless they are smoking their first cigarette, in which case they ignore it). They learn that headaches or stomach pains require a drugstore remedy but chest pains require a visit to the doctor. They learn that if they are tired at night they need to go to bed, but if they are tired in the morning they must ignore it and go to class or work as expected. These "facts" that we learn are not necessarily good diagnoses, however. Pains in the head or stomach, nausea, dizziness, and fatigue are symptoms that may indicate serious as well as mild diseases.

Children learn about the causes of disease as they grow up. They learn that if they don't wear a sweater, boots, or a coat, they will catch cold. If they don't eat right or get enough sleep, they will get sick. If they go outdoors for fresh air and ex-

routine medications and let them sleep it off. To avoid upsetting the rest of the emergency room, there is a room set aside for them. The police have a standard procedure of taking drunks to that room, and the clerks place them there if they come in on their own and are defined as drunk on the basis, not only of their breath odor (and occasionally there is no breath odor in someone defined as drunk), but in terms of their dress, manner, and absence of protectors. The physicians, having more pressing matters, tend to leave the drunks until last. Of course, they may miss some pathology which could cause unconsciousness or confusion because they believe the standard procedure proves correct in the great majority of cases. They really do not know *how* often it does not prove correct since they do not check up closely enough to uncover other forms of pathology in most cases, and the low social status of the patients and the fact that they are seldom accompanied

by anyone who will protect them means that complaints about inadequate examination will be rare. There *are* occasional challenges by doctors — "How do you know he's drunk?" — but in most cases the busy schedule of the house officer leaves little time for such luxuries as a careful examination of patients who have already been defined as drunks by others. Once the drunk label has been accepted by the emergency room staff, a more careful examination is not likely to be made unless some particularly arresting new information appears (for example, the patient has convulsions, a relative appears to tell them that he has diabetes, an examination of his wallet shows him to be a solid citizen), and the more subtle pathologies are not likely to be discovered.

Thus, it is just as true to say that the *label* of "drunk" is accepted by hospital personnel because of the way the patient is treated as it is to say that he is treated in a certain way because he

is drunk. Occasional cases show how persons with alcohol on their breath will not be treated as drunks. When an obviously middle-class man (obvious in terms of his dress, speech, and demands for service) was brought in after an automobile accident, he was not put in the drunk room, although he had a definite alcohol odor, but was given relatively quick treatment in one of the other examining rooms and addressed throughout in a polite manner.

From Julius A. Roth, *American Journal of Sociology*, 77 March 1972, pp. 839-56. © 1972 by the University of Chicago Press. All rights reserved. Reprinted with permission.

The study on which this paper is based was supported by National Institutes of Health grants HM-00437 and HM-00517, Division of Hospital and Medical Facilities. Dorothy J. Douglass, currently at the University of Connecticut Health Center, worked with me and made major contributions to this study.

ercise they will be healthier. Then, when they get sick they wonder what they did wrong. As adults, we tend to blame sick people when they develop heart disease or cancer. Did they eat too much or drink too much? Did they live stressful lives? Surely they must have done something wrong. We accept a great deal of guilt and blame for our health in this society, even though there is no evidence that we can prevent death, little evidence that we can even forestall death significantly, and a great deal of evidence that the envi-

ronment influences our health more than behavior influences our health.

We also learn medical theories of illness as we grow up. We learn that viruses, germs, or other enemies of the body attack us from outside and that we must ward off attack, if not with boots and sweaters, then with prayer, drugs, food, vitamin C, rest, exercise, or whatever else is fashionable at the time. The approach of the American Indians was more peaceful. They believed illness occurred when there was an imbal-

Pharmaceutical companies strive for extreme cleanliness and accuracy in their work environment, but are criticized, nonetheless, because they manufacture drugs for profit. The capitalistic economic system is reflected in the medical system in many profit-oriented businesses.

ance with nature, and treatments were designed to bring the ill person back into harmony with nature. These treatments were often successful.

Other societies, and our own in an earlier age, placed illness in a religious context. Lepers and alcoholics were sinners. The ill were disfavored by the gods or possessed by a devil that had to be exorcised. Exorcists, priests, shamans, or religious leaders of other types were called upon to treat the ill person. Ceremonies were performed, gods were called upon to remove the illness, and the shaman was well paid for his talents.

The American Health Care System

Historically the greatest strides in reducing illness have been changes in lifestyle, particularly in nutrition, sanitation, and shelter. The *social*

model of illness suggests that much disease is caused by social conditions and that it can be cured by changing those conditions. Some observers believe that death rates from modern causes such as heart disease, cancer, and automobile accidents could also be reduced by taking a social approach. For example, food supplies could be improved by having a more varied assortment of whole-grained food on the market, ones that did not contain sugar or excessive amounts of salt. Vegetables and fruits could be improved by practicing farming methods that put nutrients into the soil and keep pesticides out of the soil. More efficient water systems could reduce waste and provide pure drinking water. A modern transportation system could reduce air pollution and accidents. All of these improvements would need to be accomplished through social reorganization and social change, however.

Currently almost all of our research and health care are based on a *medical model of illness* in which sickness is viewed as an individual problem requiring individual treatment. Cures for heart attacks and cancer are applied after the patient is sick. People are taken to shock trauma centers after the automobile accident occurs. Even when preventive measures are considered, the responsibility rests with the individual. People must seek good food to eat and clean water to drink. They must find ways to get proper exercise. Health is viewed as an individual matter.

The American health care system is designed to maintain the medical model of illness with a full complement of physicians, nurses, and other staff, plus hospitals, the pharmaceutical industry, and modern medical technology. Ninety-three cents of every health care dollar is spent trying to cure people after they get sick.

The Profession of Medicine

The profession of medicine, for which an M.D. degree is required, is one of the most prestigious professions in the United States. But this has not always been true. In the early years of United States history, there were very few doctors. Women took care of the ill members of the family and community and also delivered babies. Older women often gained considerable experience in these activities and would be consulted whenever someone was particularly ill or when a baby was born. Many of the women of the community would gather for births, so younger women observed and understood the birthing process before they had their own children. A doctor was rarely needed.

There were only a few physicians in this country at the time of the American Revolution and they were trained in Europe, where they studied Latin or Greek. There was little science taught in universities in those days, and no medical science. Most physicians learned to practice medicine by being an apprentice to a physician, taking on more and more responsibility until they were able to venture out on their own, often

to the frontier to seek patients who needed their services. The medicine practiced was often *heroic medicine,* a dramatic intervention by the physician. Patients were bled, blistered, and given poisonous laxatives in an attempt to kill the disease. Often the treatment killed the patient. Most people went to doctors only when they were desperate. Doctors were often poor and had little work to do. They sometimes had to beg in the streets to survive (Rothstein, 1970).

By the early 1800s there were many physicians entering the profession, some trained in Europe, some trained in apprenticeships, and some not trained at all. There was also a populist health movement at this time, when many groups formed health clubs, started to eat health foods, and learned the best healing remedies from the women in the community. Some even set up medical schools to train and graduate physicians in one or another favorite type of remedy. This situation concerned the physicians who had been educated in Europe and who knew that in Europe the profession was held in high esteem. They felt it was necessary to create the same respect for medical authority here in the United States (Starr, 1982).

In about 1800, educated physicians were able to get state legislatures to pass laws forbidding healers without formal education from practicing medicine, but the laws were unpopular and were soon repealed. In 1847, physicians formed the American Medical Association (AMA) and adopted the Hippocratic Oath as a vow to promise good and ethical medicine. They lobbied states to ban abortion, which was widely practiced until that time and an important source of income to women healers who were not physicians. As noted earlier, these healers also cared for the sick and delivered babies. The AMA again succeeded in getting state legislatures to limit the practice of medicine to the educated, which was a major step in developing the profession.

In 1910, Abraham Flexner published the Flexner Report, which stated that most existing medical schools were inadequate. Congress responded to the Flexner Report by giving the AMA the right to determine which schools were qualified to train physicians, an important power in controlling the profession. All seven medical schools for women and most medical schools for blacks were closed, eliminating women and most blacks from the practice of medicine. Part-time schools were also closed, eliminating those who could not afford full-time study. The medical field remained open to white males of the upper classes, and a shortage of physicians developed, which made medicine a very lucrative profession.

Today, medical care has become a huge industry in the United States, with 450,000 doctors supported by the pharmaceutical industry, the medical technology industry, the health insurance industry, and over 7,000 hospitals. The AMA controls hospitals, medical education, prescription drugs, the use of medical technology, and the qualifications for receiving insurance payments.

The most common type of medical practice is private practice on a *fee-for-service* basis, in which the physician is paid for each visit and each service rendered. The doctor usually has privileges at a hospital that patients may be brought to under the physician's care. There the doctor performs surgery, delivers babies, runs tests, and provides other services. In this type of practice the physician is self-employed and must establish an office with expensive equipment. As the supply of doctors and the cost of setting up private practice both increase, there is a risk that some will not have enough patients to maintain a successful practice. More and more physicians are either going into group practices where office and equipment are shared or taking salaried jobs as an alternative to fee-for-service practice.

Nurses

In the early days of medicine, nurses were considered gentle and caring people who wiped fevered brows and otherwise tenderly cared for patients. Nurses played the roles of wife to the doctor and mother to the patient. In the days before advanced scientific knowledge, nursing duties were not very different from what was done at home. As medicine has changed, the role of the nurse has changed. However, the nursing profession has had difficulty changing its image, partly because of the way nurses are educated.

To be a nurse, one must get certification as a Registered Nurse (RN). The educational requirements for RNs vary. Originally they were trained in hospitals in a three-year program with some classroom work to supplement their on-the-job training. Hospitals gained their labor for three years, and they paid only room, board, and sometimes a modest fee for tuition. Most nurses were from the working class and the low-cost training gave them entrée to a profession that was far superior in salary and working conditions to the typical kind of factory job they might otherwise obtain.

Advances in medical technology brought changes to this educational system. As scientific knowledge accumulated in the 1950s and 1960s, nurses needed more time in the classroom. This was expensive for hospitals, however. During these same two decades, two-year community colleges, four-year colleges, and universities were expanding, and these schools wanted students to train for occupations. At that point, the needs of the schools matched the needs of hospitals, so the latter continued to train nurses in the hospital but turned the classroom education over to schools. The two-year colleges awarded the RN after two years of school and the four-year colleges awarded the RN after four years. Two-year colleges served the working classes and four-year colleges served upper-middle-class women. Some

A male nurse providing patient care is rather unusual because few men have entered the nursing profession. Today, the stigma associated with nursing as a "female profession" seems to be lessening somewhat.

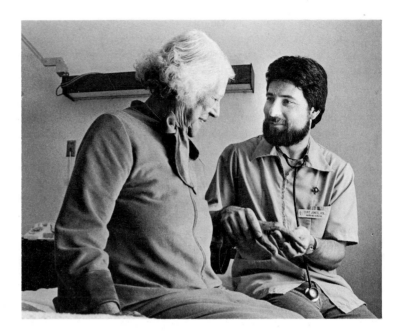

nurses were still trained entirely by hospitals.

As a result of this change in education, some nurses have two years of college training, some have four years, and some have no formal college training but more practical hospital training. The goals of the different groups vary. Nurses with four years of college training would like to change the image of nursing to an upper-class profession with more autonomy, more respect, and better salaries. The four-year nurses have not won the support of many less educated nurses because the new standards would require several more years of education. Nurses have not won the support of physicians either. Doctors now have authority over them and do not want to relinquish it. Even those who specialize in a field such as nurse midwifery have difficulty finding autonomous ways to practice their profession. Nurse midwives are trained to deliver babies, and they use methods that are, in the opinion of many, safer than the drugs and possi-

ble Caesarean surgery procedures used by physicians. Nurse midwives also have difficulty getting hospital privileges and must practice under the supervision of a doctor. By law only a physician can diagnose or treat illness.

The work of nurses is not easy. They work at inconvenient hours, evenings, nights, and weekends. They work under the strict supervision of the physician, and even though they spend more time than the doctor with patients, they must follow the physician's directions at all times. They are not paid as well as other professionals, and in spite of their efforts to improve their professional standing, hospitals, suffering under increasing budgetary pressures, resist these efforts.

Most doctors and nurses are *primary care givers*. They provide *primary medical care,* the first general, overall care the patient requires. Patients need to give a history, have a general checkup, and have their minor cuts, colds, and sore throats treated in the physician's office. Not all doctors and nurses are primary care givers, however. Some work in more specialized fields such as performing surgery in hospitals.

Hospitals

Hospitals provide *secondary medical care,* which is more specialized than the general practitioner provides, and *secondary care givers* are those who deliver the specialized care. Hospitals were once poorhouses or places where people went to die. When there was little specialized knowledge of complex treatment procedures, there was no advantage to putting people in the hospital for treatment. Babies were born at home and tonsils were removed using the kitchen table as an operating table. As medical knowledge increased and hospitals came to be better equipped and more convenient places for doctors to treat patients, hospitals with their specialized staff of physicians, nurses, and technicians drew large numbers of patients needing short-term specialized care.

There are now many types of hospitals. The most common is the community *voluntary hospital,* a nonprofit facility that treats patients who need short-term care. Most of these hospitals are in the suburbs, and money to build some of them was provided by the Hill-Burton Act of 1954. The only restriction made by Congress was that such hospitals should do some charity work. Otherwise, physicians had complete control over the new buildings and where they were built. As a result of the Hill-Burton Act, many more hospitals than necessary were built.

A second type is the *municipal hospital,* which is built by a city or county. These hospitals treat the urban poor and often have names like "City General." They are noted for their busy emergency rooms, which serve as primary care centers for the urban poor, who do not have private doctors.

A third type is the *proprietary hospital.* These are private property usually owned by physicians or hospital corporations. They are usually small and can treat patients at less cost than nonprofit hospitals. They specialize in less expensive short-term procedures, and they do not invest in the variety of equipment and services necessary to serve a whole community.

A fourth type of hospital, developed with federal funds after World War II, was the *medical center,* which trains new physicians, conducts research, and gives *tertiary medical care,* long-term care requiring complex technology. Tertiary health care is the most expensive. It uses specialized modern equipment — artificial kidneys, heart-lung machines, computerized axial tomography (CAT) scanners, coronary care units, electronic fetal-monitoring machines, radioisotopes, ultrasound, and fiber optics. This equipment may or may not be safe or effective and it is not regulated by the federal government. It is also extremely expensive. A CAT scanner can cost more than $1.5 million to buy and millions more to maintain since it requires special technicians around the clock. CAT scanners are being replaced by the far more expensive nuclear magnetic resonance (NMR) scanners, even though many believe these scanners have no advantage over the CAT.

In a well-planned medical system, the very expensive technology used in tertiary care is centrally located in medical centers to which patients would be referred from their community hospitals. In a free economy such as ours, corporations are eager to sell their very expensive equipment to all hospitals, and hospitals, competing to fill their beds, have bought high technology regardless of cost. Every hospital wants to have its own coronary care unit, CAT scanners, fetal monitors, and all of the other technology. Tertiary health care, which theoretically should be limited to a few medical centers, is hardly distinguishable from secondary health care.

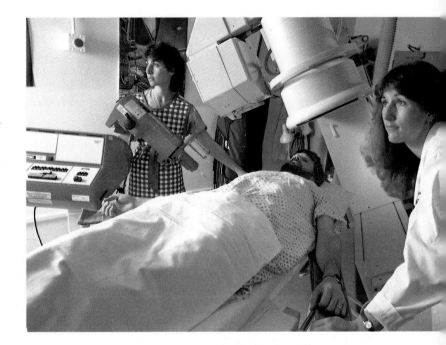

Technicians use a digital floroscope system to provide expensive, tertiary health care to a patient. The patient will probably never see these technicians again after treatment is completed. His primary care physician is the one responsible for guiding him through the highly technical world of tertiary health care and interpreting for him the results of each procedure.

This extension of the secondary health care system to provide tertiary services has the obvious disadvantage of being very costly. Forty cents of every medical care dollar is spent in hospitals, much of it to buy and operate equipment. Having spent so much on costly equipment, hospitals and doctors feel pressured to use it. Ordinary head injuries get CAT scans, and every baby being born is subject to fetal monitoring. *Fetal monitoring*, measuring the vital signs of the infant being born, is not an exact science. Changes in the patterns measured are often treated with unnecessary alarm, and the mother is subject to a Caesarean section, a procedure that involves opening the womb surgically. Caesarean sections have increased from less than 5 percent to more than 20 percent of all births since the introduction of fetal monitoring and the rate is even 25 percent in some areas. Technology, then, is expensive to buy and use, and its overuse adds further expense.

The High Cost of Medical Care

Because the government has been so generous in funding hospitals, there is an overabundance of hospitals in the United States and an estimated excess of 100,000 beds. Hospitals must have 70 to 80 percent of their beds occupied with paying patients just to break even financially. With 100,000 excess beds in the nation, hospitals are now competing with one another for patients, but it is harder and harder for them to remain financially solvent. In the past when patients were hospitalized, their insurance covered whatever tests and services they received. It was profitable for hospitals to have their patients admitted the night before treatment, stay an extra day after treatment, and receive a complete array of services. Now insurance companies are reluctant to pay all costs. Medicare, for example, has set fixed rates for each case. If the set rate is $3,000 for a particular case (this is the average cost of a hospital stay) and the hospital cannot treat the case for $3,000, the hospital loses money.

Under great pressure to get patients and cut costs, hospitals try to attract doctors who admit many patients by providing office space, use of equipment, and perhaps a car to favored doctors. Hospitals are also opening walk-in clinics, sometimes called "docs-in-a-box," and they are paying doctors to make house calls. Their hope is that such contacts with patients will result in more patients being admitted to the sponsoring hospitals.

At the same time, hospitals are beginning to monitor the number of expensive tests ordered by their physicians. The number of tests and services each doctor uses in each case is monitored by computer, and physicians are notified when they run up costs that are not profitable to the hospital. Doctors therefore often cut back so that hospitals can treat patients within the limits of their insurance. In addition to monitoring, many hospitals also must reduce their staffs significantly in order to maintain balanced budgets.

Paying for Medical Care

Medical care in the United States cost $322 billion in 1983 and accounts for 11 percent of the Gross National Product (GNP), the total dollar value of the goods and services our country produces in a year. The GNP is growing, but the cost of medical care is growing even faster. In 1970 medical care was only 8 percent of the GNP.

Only 29¢ of every dollar spent on medicine comes directly from the patient. Another 29¢ comes from private health insurance companies and the rest, 42¢ of every dollar, comes from federal, state, and local governments through such programs as Medicare and Medicaid as well as government support for county, city, and veterans' hospitals.

Some people have proposed that the federal government spend more on the health care system, but others warn that this might cause further increases in the use of technology and treatments of questionable value. Most Americans continue to have faith in our medical system, however, and currently show little inclination to change it, but new developments are occurring in the area of prepaid health care plans.

Prepaid Health Care

In the United States, the emphasis has been on fee-for-service care, in which the doctor charges a fee for each visit. But another type of health care provider, the *Health Maintenance Organization* (HMO) is growing rapidly. HMOs are prepaid plans in which a fee is paid in advance and all necessary health care is provided at no additional cost.

HMOs began during the depression in California, when a physician named Dr. Sidney Garfield noted that workers were not visiting him when they were ill because they did not want to pay the fee. He offered to meet all of their medical needs for a small fee paid in advance. Thus,

Figure 17-1

Where each dollar spent on medical care comes from

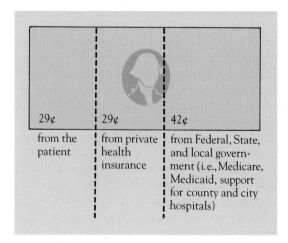

29¢	29¢	42¢
from the patient	from private health insurance	from Federal, State, and local government (i.e., Medicare, Medicaid, support for county and city hospitals)

he had an income and workers had medical care. When the industrialist Henry Kaiser learned of this system he enrolled his workers in a prepaid plan and sent physicians to his sites at the Grand Coulee dam and to his ship-building operations. The Kaiser Permanente HMO has since become the largest in the nation with over 4 million members. (There are now 280 HMOs with a total of 12.5 million members.)

HMOs have four goals: (1) to provide preventive medicine and early detection of disease; (2) to practice the best scientific medicine possible when a disease is detected; (3) to reduce hospitalization through the use of preventive medicine and early detection of disease; and (4) to reduce medical costs through better use of tests, procedures, and hospitalization.

Because their health care is prepaid, HMO members do not hesitate to have regular checkups and visit their doctor when illness occurs. Because physicians practice in groups, they can communicate with one another easily, they have access to all the necessary equipment and other services, and they have resources and schedules that allow ongoing educational programs. Medical testing can be done knowledgeably, reducing the use of unnecessary tests. Preventive medicine and good medical care reduce hospitalization and medical costs. HMOs also trim costs by using auxiliary medical personnel such as nurses and physicians' assistants whenever possible, reducing the need for doctors and giving those there are more time to see more patients. Physicians are motivated to keep costs down because HMOs share cost savings with them in the form of bonuses. Some HMOs even have their own hospitals and are motivated to run these efficiently for further cost savings.

HMOs attract members by their lower costs and by providing a complete array of services. They even provide prescription drugs and optical examinations in the prepayment plan. Researchers who study cost containment have re-cently found that HMO members do go to the hospital less often and spend less time there than people in other insurance programs, but they do not know why this is so. Supporters of HMO programs argue that they provide excellent medical care that keeps people out of the hospital. However, HMOs are large bureaucratic structures, and access to their facilities is through an appointments clerk. Researchers have not yet learned whether busy phone lines, lack of available appointment times, and other bureaucratic problems prevent people from getting adequate attention. If this is the case, the reduced costs would be the result of poorer rather than better health care.

HMOs provide a new way to structure medical care so that it is less costly than fee-for-service care. This system is compatible with American values and norms of independence and freedom to choose a health plan and a physician. HMOs, however, are very conservative organizations and will not dramatically change the nature of health care. Their emphasis is on preventive medicine, and the responsibility for prevention rests with the patient. HMO doctors, like fee-for-service doctors, treat patients when they are ill and do little work within the social model of illness, which emphasizes social factors as causes and cures of health problems.

Health Movements

In the past, lack of trust in physicians and reliance on home treatment meant that people took responsibility for their own health. Since health was linked to religious values, slovenliness, gluttony, and neglect of one's health were considered sinful. It is not surprising, then, that the most notable health movement was inspired by religion. It occurred in the United States during the Second Great Awakening, a popular religious movement that swept through the northeastern part of the country in the early part of the nineteenth century. A leader in this health

Dry cereals originated as a health food, but are now the focus of criticism. They contain excessive amounts of sugar and refined grains that lack a variety of vitamins and minerals found in whole grains. Kellogg's cereals (shown here) and Post cereals (not shown) still dominate the cereal industry, however.

movement was Sylvester Graham, a Presbyterian minister who believed that foods should be simple, not concocted from complicated recipes. He recommended eating fruits and vegetables, which were unpopular at the time, and although he did not know about vitamins or other scientific nutritional matters, he recommended eating the whole kernel of wheat (Root and de Rochemont, 1976). Graham developed a wheat cracker and traveled through the Northeast preaching his dietary religion and gaining many followers. Boarding houses were set up to serve the Graham crackers and other foods recommended by Graham. Oberlin College reserved part of its cafeteria for those following the Graham diet.

Food additives were already problematic. It quickly became difficult to get the Graham flour, which was simply whole wheat flour. Millers would take out much of the germ and bran, valuable parts of the wheat, and put in sawdust as a filler. It was recommended that one take one's own wheat to be milled to be sure of a pure product.

The health movement developed an ecumenical spirit when Seventh-Day Adventists became followers of Dr. Graham. Mother Ellen Harmon White, a Seventh-Day Adventist, founded the Western Health Reform Institute in Battle Creek, Michigan, a sanitarium to restore health to the ailing. She hired Dr. John Harvey Kellogg to manage it. Kellogg thought that chewing on dried, crispy foods would benefit the teeth and he added them to the menu. One patient, Charles Post, was treated for ulcers at the sanitarium for nine months. Although not cured of ulcers, he believed the food business might be profitable and developed a drink called Postum and later a cereal, Post Toasties. Kellogg soon followed suit, and the development of packaged foods began.

Today most health movements are not religiously oriented; they tend to come and go along with other movements. The student peace movement of the late 1960s was against pollution and rejected both chemically filled foods and packaging that added to litter and pollution. Health food stores sprang up to serve foods without chemicals, dyes, hormones, antibiotics, pesticides, and other nonfood ingredients. Foods were sold in bulk and used a minimum of packaging.

Food additives account for $1.5 billion in sales for American chemical companies, who assure us that they are safe, and most Americans are satisfied with that assurance. However, the current interest in food and diet is based on concerns about weight and appearance rather than concerns about health. The saying, "You can't be too rich or too thin" reflects today's emphasis on appearance, which may be so extreme that it is actually detrimental to health. Anorexia, a disease in which a person cannot or will not eat and gets excessively thin, has become widespread. This disease is most common among young women, but it occurs among young men as well. The desire to be thin also plays a major role in the current trend toward certain types of exercise.

This is probably the first time in history that exercise could be classified as a social movement. In the past, people got a good deal of exercise quite naturally. Everyone knows that Abraham Lincoln walked miles to school, and so did our grandparents and some of our parents. Walking was a common and reliable form of transportation.

Several changes made walking obsolete. There was a population shift from small communities to large urban areas. The automobile became widely available and people could drive. The pattern of neighborhoods changed. People once lived in the shadow of the factory where they worked and every neighborhood had a store, but zoning laws now separate homes from work and shopping districts. People live in one neighborhood, work in a second neighborhood, and shop at large shopping centers. The dis-

People in modern societies may work fewer hours than people did in the early industrial societies, but their work life is not physically invigorating. Today, many men and women use their leisure time for physical activity. It is hard to imagine a farmer or a construction worker using leisure hours for physical workout.

tances are too great to travel on foot, and a car has become a necessity.

The forms of exercise we hear most about are those related to products advertised in the media. Jogging has produced a surge in the shoe business. Health clubs with exercise equipment and aerobics classes are a high-growth industry. Exercise books, records, and videotapes have enormous sales. Swimming is considered an excellent form of exercise, but it is costly to provide swimming facilities and fewer swimming clubs are available. To date no one has been able to capitalize on walking as a form of exercise.

Only a small segment of the population regularly exercises. Perhaps a social approach to exercise would increase participation. Neighborhoods could be arranged so that people would find it both necessary and beneficial to walk each morning. Living areas could be built near work areas with green spaces and hiking and biking trails between home and work. As a disincentive to the automobile, parking could be restricted to distant lots so that walking would be necessary even if a car were used to get to work. Stores could also be returned to neighborhoods, and safe and efficient public transportation systems could be built to move people longer distances. Public transportation usually requires a healthy walk at each end of the line. Of course, if social planning were inadequate and people had to dodge traffic and breathe exhaust fumes in order to walk, walking would probably not improve the health of Americans.

Health Care in Other Countries

Most countries do not have the resources that are available to American citizens. If their populations are to receive modern health care, they must usually plan to use their scarce resources efficiently. The health care systems of Great Britain and China illustrate how planning can

work. Health care in underdeveloped regions, such as in Africa, is traditional and does not involve expensive technological medicine.

The British Health Care System

At the beginning of the industrial revolution, Great Britain had a *laissez-faire* economy, an economy with no government planning and intervention. Health care depended on *noblesse oblige*, the obligation of the rich to give to the poor and the suffering. Unfortunately, the economy produced a great many poor and suffering people who were not taken care of by the rich. The British economic system gradually progressed from laissez faire to welfare capitalism, in which the government takes a major responsibility for the welfare of its people within the capitalist system. The move to welfare capitalism was inspired in part by the need for an adequate health care system.

In the nineteenth century Great Britain was forced to use government money to provide some medical care for its people, and since 1911, Great Britain has had national health insurance, which covered the medical expenses of workers. Their wives and children were not insured, however, and they either did not go to doctors or else postponed treatment until it was too late. After World War II, the poor health of the people and the large number of elderly in the population created a serious problem, and the British developed the National Health Service (NHS), which is funded by tax revenue.

The NHS has three branches, which are patterned after the health care system that already existed in Great Britain. General practitioners deliver primary health care, treating the sick in their communities. Consultants, physician specialists in hospitals, provide secondary health care. The third sector is the public health sector, consisting of nursing homes, home nursing services, vaccination services, health inspections, and other community health services.

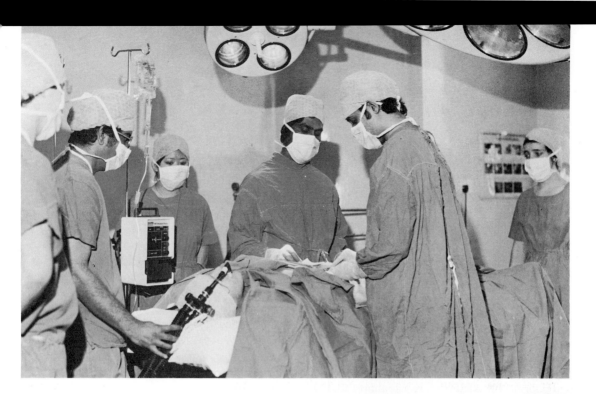

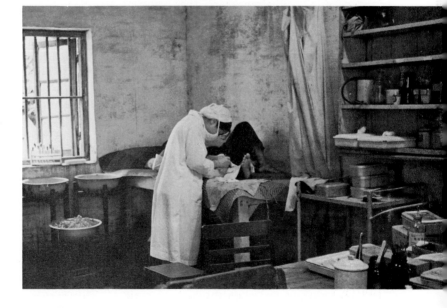

Compare here the modern British hospital with the rural Chinese commune hospital. The rural hospital is certainly crude, but the Chinese, like the British, have a system of socialized medicine. All Chinese citizens have access to health care in their own areas as well as access to modern medical centers in the cities if an illness requires more extensive treatment.

Physicians lost their autonomy when the government took control. General practitioners are now paid according to the number of patients they care for. This system does not provide the independence of a fee-for-service practice, but it does allow physicians more control over their income than working for straight salaries. Physicians are also allowed to see private patients and charge them whatever they are willing to pay. This dual setup has been criticized for creating a two-class medical system, but very few patients want private care.

The working class is especially pleased with the NHS. Any citizen can go to a general practitioner without paying a fee; if hospitalization is required, the general practitioner refers the patient to a hospital consultant, again without charge. To control the costs of such a system, patients who do not have serious problems may have to wait for weeks or months for a consultation. Those who do have serious problems are seen first. The citizens of Great Britain have been very happy with the system.

Health Care in Communist China

The most dramatic development of a health care system occurred in China after the Communist takeover in 1949. Before that time, the huge Chinese population suffered from malnutrition and poor health. Medical care was almost totally lacking. When the Communists came into power, disease and starvation were rampant (Denton, 1978). There was a shortage of doctors, and the few doctors available were divided between Eastern and Western medical practices. Since their resources were very scarce, the Communists had to make efficient use of what little they had.

They did not try to develop scientific medicine after the model set by Western physicians. They combined Western medicine with traditional Chinese medicine, using acupuncture and herbs along with Western drugs and technology. The Communists also trained enormous numbers of so-called *barefoot doctors* to serve as unpaid health workers. The barefoot doctors are selected by the peasants in the communes, not on the basis of their academic or intellectual achievements, but rather on the basis of their political attitudes and their attitudes toward people. They are required to support the political system as well as the communes they serve.

Barefoot doctors receive three to eighteen months of training in both Eastern and Western medical techniques. They then serve in their communes, emphasizing preventive medicine by developing sanitary systems and practices in the community, by teaching peasants proper hygiene and health care, and by vaccinating the population. As volunteers, they work at ordinary jobs side by side with the peasants they take care of and can easily recognize those who have poor health habits or illnesses. They treat simple illnesses and emergencies and direct the more seriously ill to better-trained doctors and nurses.

Not so well trained as the barefoot doctors are the Red Guard doctors, who work in urban areas, and the worker doctors, who work in factories. These doctors receive less training because highly trained full-time physicians and nurses are available in urban areas. The Red Guard and worker doctors serve the same grassroots function as the barefoot doctors, serving without pay, stressing preventive medicine such as sanitation and inoculations, and generally looking after the health of members of their communes.

When hospitalization is necessary for an illness, individuals must pay for it. A variety of insurance plans are available to cover the costs of hospital care, but the costs are not high. Open heart surgery, the most expensive procedure, costs about two weeks' wages, far less than in the United States.

The Chinese Communists emphasize equality. Although most doctors work in urban areas, they are transferred to rural areas if the need develops. They are not free to practice where they wish. They are expected to help nurses care for patients, and differentiating the various types of doctors and nurses along class lines is forbidden.

When the Communists began their health care system, the number of educated people needed to administer the large bureaucracy were in short supply. Since physicians were the most educated and capable people in the society, they became the leaders of the health care system regardless of their political leanings. As the Communists increased their power, they became concerned about the independence of the Ministry of Public Health and its practices. The group did not place enough emphasis on treating rural populations, the Communists said, and they focused on curative rather than preventive medicine (Maykovich, 1980). By 1955 the Communists had developed more political leaders to rule the Ministry of Public Health along with physicians. Conflicts developed and some errors were made because the politicians were not trained in medicine, but the conflicts generally broadened the work of the Ministry because the politicians insisted on emphasizing areas that do not ordinarily interest physicians. The conflict between the interests of physicians and political interests has continued. Currently the emphasis is on that which interests the physicians — developing better technology and more sophisticated procedures for treating complicated illnesses.

Along with their interest in technology, the Chinese are doing more than any other country to develop the ancient art of herbal medicine, the use of plants in natural health care systems (Ayensu, 1981). Peking has an Institute of Medi-

cal Materials, and Canton has the Provincial Institute of Botany for the study of herbal medicines. Thousands of medicinal plants are under cultivation for use in biological evaluations and chemical studies, and every year thousands of barefoot doctors are taught about the use of these herbs in health care. Medicinal plants have been used to treat venereal diseases, leukemia, high blood pressure, ulcers, poor digestion, skin cancer, and countless other diseases. They can be used as heart stimulants, diuretics, sedatives, and to induce abortion. The value of herbs is widely known throughout the world; for example, 25 percent of prescription drugs in the United States are based on flowering plants.

The Herbalist in Underdeveloped Nations

The World Health Organization estimates that between 75 and 90 percent of the world's rural populations have herbalists as their only

The Indian woman pictured here is selling medicinal herbs. Such herbs are valued in the United States as foods, teas, and ornamental plants as well as for their medicinal qualities. Chamomile, for example, has long been used as a sedative and is still available as an herbal tea, and aloe has recently gained renewed popularity in skin care.

SOCIOLOGISTS AT WORK
Helping Disabled Drug Addicts

Alexander Boros is the director of Addiction Intervention with the Disabled (AID) in Cleveland, Ohio. He started that program in 1974 when a group of deaf people in Cleveland asked him to do something about the lack of alcohol- and drug-abuse programs for the deaf community. Boros was the right person for the job: In more than twenty years as an applied sociologist at Kent State University, he has been involved in numerous applied projects in the area of rehabilitation of the physically disabled. And in 1969 he organized the first graduate program in applied sociology.

How does Alex Boros use his sociological perspective in his work at AID? "Human services people tend to have a very individualistic orientation," he says. "Whether they're doctors or therapists or counselors, they deal with the problem as an individual's problem. Sociologists try to understand the social and cultural conditions in which the problem arises. Most deaf people, for example, live out their lives as members of a closed community. They have their own language and their own culture. They read at, on the average, a third-grade level. The rate of intermarriage within the group is about 90 percent. Deaf people represent a different community with different needs. As a sociologist, I am able to see the social context in which members of this group act out their problems through alcohol and drug abuse."

The deaf leaders who approached Boros had one immediate short-term goal: They wanted sign-language interpreters at local meetings of Alcoholics Anonymous. AID organized a national

health care practitioners. Cultural tradition gives the herbalist an important role not only as a leading health practitioner but also as an influential spiritual leader who uses magic and religion as well as herbs to heal.

There are three types of healers in the African rural tradition, according to Ayensu (1981). The herbalists have the most prestige, but there are also divine healers who cure through religious ceremonies and witch doctors who intercede against the evil deeds of witches who have possessed a patient. These three types of doctors have kept the native population reasonably healthy throughout history.

Herbalists have a three-year educational

program. The first year consists of ritual training and ceremony, including abstinence from sex and a ritual bath in a cemetery to make contact with ancestors. Alcohol, quarreling, and cutting or combing the hair are forbidden. The first year's training serves to set the trainee apart from the rest of the community in order to develop a distinct personality.

The second year begins with practical training in the gathering, identification, and use of herbs. The herbalist is also trained to carefully observe the natural habitats of herbs. Animals have been known to use plants in a medicinal fashion, and they can provide clues to the herbalist in the various uses of plants. Herbalists also

conference on treating deaf alcoholics. It also conducted workshops for people already involved in the treatment of alcohol and drug addiction on the unique needs of the deaf. But Boros began to perceive a larger need. "About 16 percent of the population is disabled — deaf, blind, retarded, spinal cord-injured, and so on. We have been able to determine that the rate of alcohol and drug addiction among the deaf is about the same as among the general population. But the other disabled lack the kind of cohesive community the deaf have developed. They probably experience a much higher rate — some of us estimate twice as high. But in the standard treatment programs, the rate of participation by the disabled is about 1 percent. So it's not just that the need was being met badly. It wasn't being met at all."

The solution: Set up special services for the deaf and multidisabled, find the alcohol and drug abusers in that population, and refer them to those services. "The rehabilitation agencies for the disabled tend not to understand alcohol and drug addiction. They see it as a self-inflicted problem. They prefer to work with what they call the 'true disabled.' The people who work in alcohol addiction treatment, on the other hand, are people whose expertise is life experience: They tend to be recovering alcoholics themselves. Many do not have the time or the desire to learn about the special needs of the deaf or the disabled. So we needed something new."

Something new is what they got. Boros, his staff of three, and their volunteer assistants train alcohol- and drug-abuse counselors to work with the deaf and the disabled. They use publicity to create an awareness of their activities among the disabled, and they conduct educational programs. They get referrals from individuals and from rehabilitation agencies. Once they have located a disabled person with a problem, they help him or her obtain the necessary services. "We started out in Cleveland, and we are still based in Cleveland," Alex Boros says. "But we soon started getting referrals from other communities. By now we are getting referrals from six or seven states. Once the word got out, we started hearing from people all over."

learn to be sensitive to any spiritual messages that may increase their knowledge.

After the training program is completed at the end of the third year, herbalists pass through many ceremonies and rituals. They take an oath of allegiance to the trainer and have a graduation ceremony, much as physicians in the United States take an oath and are graduated so that the community will recognize their new status.

Many natives of Third World cultures who are trained in modern medicine in other countries resume using herbs for treatment when they return to their native cultures. The herbs are not only beneficial in themselves, but the tradition and ceremony involved in their use probably provides a *placebo effect* for the patient, a benefit arising from the belief that the medicine will work. It is widely known in our culture that if one believes a medicine will help, the medicine will in fact make the patient feel better.

However, some Third World physicians trained in modern medicine and the use of modern chemical pharmaceuticals do not use herbal medicines when they return to their native lands, probably because they are ignorant of their benefits. This is especially unfortunate because pharmaceutical companies often go to underdeveloped countries and export the very plants that modern physicians ignore. In fact, the export of medicinal plants to Western pharmaceutical companies is becoming so widespread that some plants — for example, a type of yam used as the foundation material in birth control pills — are becoming rare. After the plants are exported and manufactured into pharmaceuticals, they are then sold back to the country of origin at exorbitant prices.

Summary

Health and illness are of interest to sociologists because they are defined socially as well as biologically and because society needs a healthy population to survive. Pathological illnesses are those in which the body is diseased or malfunctioning. Statistical illnesses are those in which one's health varies from the norm. Sociologists are interested in both types of illnesses and in their variation from society to society and from time to time. In preindustrial days, when nutrition and sanitation were poor, infectious diseases were the greatest health hazard. Now the major health hazards are heart disease, cancer, stroke, and accidents. Changing social structures often cause changes in prevailing illnesses — for example, industrialization and its accompanying pollutants are a major cause of cancer.

Structural functionalists, who emphasize the integrative, functional characteristics of society, note that a sick role exists to integrate ill people into the social structure. This sick role involves certain expectations — for example, sick people are expected to get better and resume their major roles, thereby ensuring the smooth functioning of society. Conflict theorists contend that physicians share the viewpoint of elite classes in society and use their power over patients to maintain the social system. Symbolic interactionists study the learned meanings associated with illness. In many societies, illness was once associated with sin or demons, and treatment often had religious overtones.

In the American health care system the medical model of illness prevails. The individual is considered responsible for prevention; the health care system becomes involved only when a person is already sick. The social causes of illness receive little attention. The profession of medicine has great prestige in part because of political action of the AMA. Nursing is a comparatively low-paying profession that still reflects its origins as an occupation for working-class women. Different factions have arisen in nursing over the profession's educational requirements. Many nurses would like to raise the profession to a higher social and economic status.

Most doctors and nurses are primary health care workers, who provide basic medical care directly to patients. Secondary care is provided by hospitals, which have specialized equipment and staff. There are several kinds of hospitals: nonprofit voluntary hospitals, tax-supported municipal hospitals, and privately owned proprietary hospitals. Tertiary health care, the very highly specialized care developed with modern technology, is given in medical centers, which also conduct research and train physicians. Since specialized technology has been purchased by the other types of hospitals as well, the cost of medical care has greatly increased.

Hospitals have more beds available than are required to serve the population. To stay within their budgets, they are now advertising, opening clinics, and trying to attract patients in other ways. Their costs, especially for technology, have risen dramatically, however, and they are having a very difficult time staying within their budgets. Furthermore, insurance companies are no longer willing to pay the costs the hospitals demand.

The major departure in health care delivery from the fee-for-service system is the Health Maintenance Organization (HMO). By using resources more efficiently, HMOs may provide a better, less costly system. Their bureaucratic structure, however, could reduce the quality of care in some cases.

Americans seem satisfied with their medical system. While there have been some health movements calling for improved food, air, and water supplies, health movements today are concerned with appearance, notably thinness, and not health. The current emphasis on thinness rather than health has contributed to the dramatic rise in cases of anorexia.

Medical care in other countries reflects practices in their social systems. Great Britain's health care system has evolved from the laissez-faire economic system with its belief in noblesse oblige to a welfare system within the capitalist framework. The British National Health Service (NHS) now serves all the people with a system of general practitioners, consultants in hospitals, and a public health service. The British themselves are very satisfied with the NHS.

China has developed a health care system using both Eastern and Western medical knowledge. It has been able to integrate the system with its political system, and it has developed a corps of barefoot doctors who provide preventive health care in rural areas. China has also done research on the more sophisticated use of traditional medicines.

Underdeveloped nations continue to depend on herbalists, as they have for centuries. Herbalists go through an extensive training period, which both sets them apart from other members of their society and teaches them how to use herbs. Herbalists have been successful because their medicines do cure illness. Modern pharmaceutical industries know this and are doing research to further understand the healing power of natural medicine.

Key Terms

barefoot doctors
fee-for-service
fetal monitoring
Health Maintenance Organization (HMO)

heroic medicine
hypochondriac
laissez faire
medical center
medical model of illness
municipal hospital
noblesse oblige
pathological illness
placebo effect
primary care givers
primary medical care
proprietary hospital
secondary care givers
secondary medical care
sick role
social model of illness
statistical illness
tertiary medical care
voluntary hospital

Suggested Readings

Brown, E. Richard. **Rockefeller Medicine Men: Medicine and Capitalism in America.** *Berkeley: University of California Press, 1978.* An enlightening book about big business's motivation to get involved in health, including a discussion of their influence on the Flexner Report.

Grusky, Oscar and Melvin Pollner (eds.). **The Sociology of Mental Illness: Basic Studies.** *New York: Holt, Rinehart & Winston. 1981.* A collection of readings in an area that bridges the fields of sociology of medicine and social psychology.

Jaco, E. Gartly (ed.). **Patients, Physicians and Illness. A Sourcebook in Behavioral Science and Health, 3rd ed.** *New York: The Free Press, 1979.* A collection of readings covering a wide range of topics in the field, this book has become a classic among readers and is widely available in one or another of its editions.

Light, Donald. **Becoming Psychiatrists.** *New York: W. W. Norton, 1983.* A study of psychiatrists done by a sociologist, this book has broad appeal.

Logan, Michael H. and Edward E. Hunt, Jr. **Health and the Human Condition: Perspectives on**

Medical Anthropology. *North Scituate, Mass.: Duxbury Press, 1978.* A collection of readings in the sociology of medicine from a cross-cultural perspective, this book is interesting and helps us understand health and illness in our own society.

Marieskind, Helen I. **Women in the Health System. Patients, Providers and Programs.** *St. Louis: C. V. Mosby, 1980.* Marieskind presents a good survey of research done on issues of particular concern to women. Her discussion of fetal monitoring is excellent.

Mechanic, David. **Medical Sociology, 2d ed.** *New York: The Free Press, 1978.* A widely used text written by one of the best known researchers in the field.

Scully, Diana. **Men Who Control Women's Health: The Miseducation of Obstetrician-Gynecologists.** *Boston: Houghton Mifflin, 1980.* Scully studied training programs and wrote this critical evaluation of them. She discusses their emphasis on surgery and their neglect of the more routine care required by women.

Shapiro, Martin, M.D. **Getting Doctored: Critical Reflections on Becoming a Physician.** *Kitchener, Ontario: Between the Lines, 1978.* A frank discussion of medical education, written by a liberal man in a conservative institution. It would be funny if the issues were less serious.

The American Family in the Year 2000

*by Andrew Cherlin
and Frank F. Furstenberg, Jr.*

Social institutions evolve and change, as we are now witnessing in the structure of the American family. These changes are adaptations to a changing society. Nevertheless, they can be disruptive to the lives of many people. The authors of this reading attempt to predict where these changes will lead.

- At current rates, half of all American marriages begun in the early 1980s will end in divorce.
- The number of unmarried couples living together has more than tripled since 1970.
- One out of four children is not living with both parents.

The list could go on and on. Teenage pregnancies: up. Adolescent suicides: up. The birthrate: down. Over the past decade, popular and scholarly commentators have cited a seemingly endless wave of grim statistics about the shape of the American family. The trends have caused a number of concerned Americans to wonder if the family, as we know it, will survive the twentieth century.

And yet, other observers ask us to consider more positive developments:

- Seventy-eight percent of all adults in a recent national survey said they get "a great deal" of satisfaction from their family lives; only 3% said "a little" or "none."

- Two-thirds of the married adults in the same survey said they were "very happy" with their marriages; only 3% said "not too happy."
- In another recent survey of parents of children in their middle years, 88% said that if they had to do it over, they would choose to have children again.
- The vast majority of the children (71%) characterized their family life as "close and intimate."

Family ties are still important and strong, the optimists argue, and the predictions of the demise of the family are greatly exaggerated.

Neither the dire pessimists who believe that the family is falling apart nor the unbridled optimists who claim that the family has never been in better shape provide an accurate picture of family life in the near future. But these trends indicate that what we have come to view as the "traditional" family will no longer predominate.

Diverse Family Forms

In the future, we should expect to see a growing amount of diversity in family forms, with fewer Americans spending most of their life in a simple "nuclear" family consisting of husband, wife, and children. By the year 2000, three kinds of families will dominate the personal lives of most Americans: families of first marriages, single-parent families, and families of remarriages.

In first-marriage families, both spouses will be in a first marriage, frequently begun after living alone for a time or following a period of cohabitation. Most of these couples will have one, two, or, less frequently, three children.

A sizable minority, however, will remain childless. Demographer Charles F. Westoff predicts that about one-fourth of all women currently in the childbearing years will never bear children, a greater number of childless women than at any time in U.S. history.

One other important shift: in a large majority of these families, both the husband and the wife will be employed outside the home. In 1940, only about one out of seven married women worked outside the home; today the proportion is one out of two. We expect this proportion to continue to rise, although not as fast as it did in the past decade or two.

Single-Parent Families

The second major type of family can be formed in two ways. Most are formed by a marital separation, and the rest by births to unmarried women. About half of all marriages will end in divorce at current rates, and we doubt that the rates will fall substantially in the near future.

When the couple is childless, the formerly married partners are likely to set up independent households and resume life as singles. The high rate of divorce is one of the reasons why more men and women are living in single-person households than ever before.

But three-fifths of all divorces involve couples with children living at home. In at least nine out of ten cases, the wife retains custody of the children after a separation.

Although joint custody has received a lot of attention in the press and in legal circles, national data show that it is still uncommon. Moreover, it is likely to remain the exception rather than the rule because most ex-spouses can't get along well enough to manage raising their children together. In fact, a national survey of children aged eleven to sixteen conducted by one of the authors demonstrated that fathers have little contact with their children after a divorce. About

half of the children whose parents had divorced hadn't seen their father in the last year; only one out of six had managed to see their father an average of once a week. If the current rate of divorce persists, about half of all children will spend some time in a single-parent family before they reach eighteen.

Much has been written about the psychological effects on children of living with one parent, but the literature has not yet proven that any lasting negative effects occur. One effect, however, does occur with regularity: women who head single-parent families typically experience a sharp decline in their income relative to before their divorce. Husbands usually do not experience a decline. Many divorced women have difficulty reentering the job market after a long absence; others find that their low-paying clerical or service-worker jobs aren't adequate to support a family.

Of course, absent fathers are supposed to make child-support payments, but only a minority do. In a 1979 U.S. Bureau of the Census survey, 43% of all divorced and separated women with children present reported receiving child-support payments during the previous year, and the average annual payment was about $1,900. Thus, the most detrimental effect for children living in a single-parent family is not the lack of a male presence but the lack of a male income.

Families of Remarriages

The experience of living as a single parent is temporary for many divorced women, especially in the middle class. Three out of four divorced people remarry, and about half of these marriages occur within three years of the divorce.

Remarriage does much to solve the economic problems that many single-parent families face because it typically adds a male income. Remarriage also relieves a single parent of the multiple burdens of running and supporting a household by herself.

But remarriage also frequently involves

blending together two families into one, a difficult process that is complicated by the absence of clear-cut ground rules for how to accomplish the merger. Families formed by remarriages can become quite complex, with children from either spouse's previous marriage or from the new marriage and with numerous sets of grandparents, stepgrandparents, and other kin and quasi-kin.

The divorce rate for remarriages is modestly higher than for first marriages, but many couples and their children adjust successfully to their remarriage and, when asked, consider their new marriage to be a big improvement over their previous one.

The Life Course: A Scenario for the Next Two Decades

Because of the recent sharp changes in marriage and family life, the life course of children and young adults today is likely to be far different from what a person growing up earlier in this century experienced. It will not be uncommon, for instance, for children born in the 1980s to follow this sequence of living arrangements: live with both parents for several years, live with their mothers after their parents divorce, live with their mothers and stepfathers, live alone for a time when in their early twenties, live with someone of the opposite sex without marrying, get married, get divorced, live alone again, get remarried, and end up living alone once more following the death of their spouses.

Not everyone will have a family history this complex, but it is likely that a substantial minority of the population will. And many more will have family histories only slightly less complex.

Overall, we estimate that about half of the young children alive today will spend some time in a single-parent family before they reach 18; about nine out of ten will eventually marry; about one out of two will marry and then divorce; and about one out of three will marry, divorce, and then remarry. In contrast, only about one out of six women born in the period 1910 to 1914 married and divorced and only about one in eight married, divorced, and remarried.

Without doubt, Americans today are living in a much larger number of family settings during their lives than was the case a few generations ago.

The life-course changes have been even greater for women than for men because of the far greater likelihood of employment during the childbearing years for middle-class women today compared with their mothers and grandmothers. Moreover, the increase in life expectancy has increased the difference between men's and women's family lives. Women now tend to outlive men by a wide margin, a development that is new in this century. Consequently, many more women face a long period of living without a spouse at the end of their lives, either as a widow or as a divorced person who never remarried.

Long-lived men, in contrast, often find that their position in the marriage market is excellent, and they are much more likely to remain married (or remarried) until they die.

Convergence and Divergence

The family lives of Americans vary according to such factors as class, ethnicity, religion, and region. But recent evidence suggests a convergence among these groups in many features of family life. The clearest example is in childbearing, where the differences between Catholics and non-Catholics or between Southerners and Northerners are much smaller than they were twenty years ago. We expect this process of convergence to continue, although it will fall far short of eliminating all social class and subcultural differences.

The experiences of blacks and whites also have converged in many respects, such as in fertility and in patterns of premarital sexual behavior, over the past few decades. But with respect to marriage, blacks and whites have diverged markedly since about 1960.

Black families in the United States always

have had strong ties to a large network of extended kin. But in addition, blacks, like whites, relied on a relatively stable bond between husbands and wives. But over the past several decades — and especially since 1960 — the proportion of black families maintained by a woman has increased sharply; currently, the proportion exceeds four in ten. In addition, more young black women are having children out of wedlock; in the late 1970s, about two out of three black women who gave birth to a first child were unmarried.

These trends mean that we must qualify our previously stated conclusion that marriage will remain central to family life. This conclusion holds for Americans in general. For many low-income blacks, however, marriage is likely to be less important than the continuing ties to a larger network of kin.

Marriage is simply less attractive to a young black women from a low-income family because of the poor prospects many young black men have for steady employment and because of the availability of alternative sources of support from public-assistance payments and kin. Even though most black women eventually marry, their marriages have a very high probability of ending in separation or divorce. Moreover, they have a lower likelihood of remarrying.

Black single-parent families sometimes have been criticized as being "disorganized" or even "pathological." What the critics fail to note is that black single mothers usually are embedded in stable, functioning kin networks. These networks tend to center around female kin — mothers, grandmothers, aunts — but brothers, fathers, and other male kin also may be active. The members of these networks share and exchange goods and services, thus helping to share the burdens of poverty. The lower-class black extended family, then, is characterized by strong ties among a network of kin but fragile ties between husband and wife. The negative aspects of this family system have been exaggerated greatly;

yet it need not be romanticized, either. It can be difficult and risky for individuals to leave the network in order to try to make it on their own; thus, it may be hard for individuals to raise themselves out of poverty until the whole network is raised.

The Disintegrating Family?

By now, predictions of the demise of the family are familiar to everyone. Yet the family is a resilient institution that still retains more strength than its harshest critics maintain. There is, for example, no evidence of a large-scale rejection of marriage among Americans. To be sure, many young adults are living together outside of marriage, but the evidence we have about cohabitation suggests that it is not a lifelong alternative to marriage; rather, it appears to be either another stage in the process of courtship and marriage or a transition between first and second marriages.

The so-called "alternative lifestyles" that received so much attention in the late 1960s, such as communes and lifelong singlehood, are still very uncommon when we look at the nation as a whole.

Young adults today do marry at a somewhat older age, on average, than their parents did. But the average age at marriage today is very similar to what it was throughout the period from 1890 to 1940.

To be sure, many of these marriages will end in divorce, but three out of four people who divorce eventually remarry. Americans still seem to desire the intimacy and security that a marital relationship provides.

Much of the alarm about the family comes from reactions to the sheer speed at which the institution changed in the last two decades. Between the early 1960s and the mid-1970s, the divorce rate doubled, the marriage rate plunged, the birthrate dropped from a twentieth-century high to an all-time low, premarital sex became accepted, and married women poured into the labor force. But since the mid-1970s, the pace of change has slowed. The divorce rate has risen modestly and the birthrate even has increased a bit. We may have entered a period in which American families can adjust to the sharp changes that occurred in the 1960s and early 1970s. We think that, by and large, accommodations will be made as expectations change and institutions are redesigned to take account of changing family practices.

Despite the recent difficulties, family ties remain a central part of American life. Many of the changes in family life in the 1960s and 1970s were simply a continuation of long-term trends that have been with us for generations.

The birthrate has been declining since the 1820s, the divorce rate has been climbing since at least the Civil War, and over the last half century a growing number of married women have taken paying jobs. Employment outside the home has been gradually eroding the patriarchal system of values that was a part of our early history, replacing it with a more egalitarian set of values.

The only exception occurred during the late 1940s and the 1950s. After World War II, Americans raised during the austerity of depression and war entered adulthood at a time of sustained prosperity. The sudden turnabout in their fortunes led them to marry earlier and have more children than any generation before or since in this century. Because many of us were either parents or children in the baby-boom years following the war, we tend to think that the 1950s typify the way twentieth-century families used to be. But the patterns of marriage and childbearing in the 1950s were an aberration resulting from special historical circumstances; the patterns of the 1960s and 1970s better fit the long-term trends. Barring unforeseen major disruptions, small families, working wives, and impermanent marital ties are likely to remain with us indefinitely.

A range of possible developments could throw our forecasts off the mark. We do not know, for example, how the economy will behave over the next twenty years, or how the family will be affected by technological innovations still at the conception stage. But, we do not envision any dramatic changes in family life resulting solely from technological innovations in the next two decades.

Having sketched our view of the most probable future, we will consider three of the most important implications of the kind of future we see.

Growing Up in Changing Families

Children growing up in the past two decades have faced a maelstrom of social change. As we have pointed out, family life is likely to become even more complex, diverse, unpredictable, and uncertain in the next two decades.

Even children who grow up in stable family environments will probably have to get along with a lot less care from parents (mothers in particular) than children received early in this century. Ever since the 1950s, there has been a marked and continuous increase in the proportion of working mothers whose preschool children are cared for outside the home, rising from 31% in 1958 to 62% in 1977. The upward trend is likely to continue until it becomes standard practice for very young children to receive care either in someone else's home or in a group setting. There has been a distinct drop in the care of children by relatives, as fewer aunts, grandmothers, or adult children are available to supplement the care provided by parents. Increasingly, the government at all levels will be pressured to provide more support for out-of-home daycare.

How are children responding to the shifting circumstances of family life today? Are we raising a generation of young people who, by virtue of their own family experiences, lack the desire and skill to raise the next generation? As we indicated earlier, existing evidence has not demonstrated that marital disruption creates lasting personality damage or instills a distinctly different set of values about family life.

Similarly, a recent review on children of working mothers conducted by the National Research Council of the National Academy of Sciences concludes:

> If there is only one message that emerges from this study, it is that parental employment in and of itself — mothers' employment or fathers' or both parents' — is not necessarily good or bad for children.

The fact that both parents work *per se* does not adversely affect the well-being of children.

Currently, most fathers whose wives are employed do little childcare. Today, most working mothers have two jobs: they work for pay and then come home to do most of the childcare and housework. Pressure from a growing number of harried working wives could prod fathers to watch less television and change more diapers. But this change in fathers' roles is proceeding much more slowly than the recent spate of articles about the "new father" would lead one to expect. The strain that working while raising a family places on working couples, and especially on working mothers, will likely make childcare and a more equitable sharing of housework prominent issues in the 1980s and 1990s.

Family Obligations

Many of the one out of three Americans who, we estimate, will enter a second marriage will do so after having children in a first marriage. Others may enter into a first marriage with a partner who has a family from a previous marriage. It is not clear in these families what obligations remain after divorce or are created after remarriage. For one thing, no clear set of norms exists specifying how people in remarriages are supposed to act toward each other. Stepfathers don't know how much to discipline their step-

children; second wives don't know what they're supposed to say when they meet their husbands' first wives; stepchildren don't know what to call their absent father's new wife.

The ambiguity about family relations after divorce and remarriage also extends to economic support. There are no clear-cut guidelines to tell adults how to balance the claims of children from previous marriages versus children from their current marriages. Suppose a divorced man who has been making regular payments to support his two small children from a previous marriage marries a woman with children from her previous marriage. Suppose her husband isn't paying any child support. Suppose further that the remarried couple have a child of their own. Which children should have first claim on the husband's income? Legally, he is obligated to pay child support to his ex-wife, but in practice he is likely to feel that his primary obligation is to his stepchildren, whose father isn't helping, and to his own children from his remarriage.

Our guess, supported by some preliminary evidence from national studies, is that remarriage will tend to further reduce the amount of child support that a man pays, particularly if the man's new family includes children from his new wife's previous marriage or from the current marriage. What appears to be occurring in many cases is a form of "childswapping," with men exchanging an old set of children from a prior marriage for a new set from their new wife's prior marriage and from the remarriage.

Sociologist Lenore J. Weitzman provides a related example in her book *The Marriage Contract*. Suppose, she writes, a fifty-eight-year-old corporate vice president with two grown children divorces his wife to marry his young secretary. He agrees to adopt the secretary's two young children. If he dies of a heart attack the following year:

> In most states, a third to half of his estate would go to his new wife, with the remainder divided

among the four children (two from his last marriage, and his new wife's two children). His first wife will receive nothing — neither survivors' insurance nor a survivors' pension nor a share of the estate — and both she and his natural children are likely to feel that they have been treated unjustly.

Since the rate of mid-life divorce has been increasing nearly as rapidly as that of divorce at younger ages, this type of financial problem will become increasingly common. It would seem likely that there will be substantial pressure for changes in family law and in income security systems to provide more to the ex-wife and natural children in such circumstances.

Intergenerational Relations

A similar lack of clarity about who should support whom may affect an increasing number of elderly persons. Let us consider the case of an elderly man who long ago divorced his first wife and, as is fairly typical, retained only sporadic contact with his children. If his health deteriorates in old age and he needs help, will his children provide it? In many cases, the relationship would seem so distant that the children would not be willing to provide major assistance. To be sure, in most instances the elderly man would have remarried, possibly acquiring stepchildren, and it may be these stepchildren who feel the responsibility to provide assistance. Possibly the two sets of children may be called upon to cooperate in lending support, even when they have had little or no contact while growing up. Currently, there are no clear guidelines for assigning kinship responsibilities in this new type of extended family.

Even without considering divorce, the issue of support to the elderly is likely to bring problems that are new and widespread. As is well known, the low fertility in the United States, which we think will continue to be low, means that the population is becoming older. The difficulties that this change in age structure poses

for the Social Security system are so well known that we need not discuss them here. Let us merely note that any substantial weakening of the Social Security system would put the elderly at a great disadvantage with regard to their families, for older Americans increasingly rely on Social Security and other pensions and insurance plans to provide support. A collapse of Social Security would result in a large decrease in the standard of living among older Americans and a return to the situation prevailing a few decades ago in which the elderly were disproportionately poor.

The relations between older people and their children and grandchildren are typically close, intimate, and warm. Most people live apart from their children, but they generally live close by one or more of them. Both generations prefer the autonomy that the increased affluence of the older generation has recently made possible. Older people see family members quite often, and they report that family members are their major source of support. A survey by Louis Harris of older Americans revealed that more than half of those with children had seen them in the past day, and close to half had seen a grandchild. We expect close family ties between the elderly and their kin to continue to be widespread. If, however, the economic autonomy of the elderly is weakened, say, by a drop in Social Security, the kind of friendly equality that now characterizes intergenerational relations could be threatened.

One additional comment about the elderly: Almost everyone is aware that the declining birthrate means that the elderly will have fewer children in the future on whom they can rely for support. But although this is true in the long run, it will not be true in the next few decades. In fact, beginning soon, the elderly will have more children, on average, than they do today. The reason is the postwar baby boom of the late 1940s and 1950s. As the parents of these large families begin to reach retirement age near the end of this century, more children will be available to help their elderly parents. Once the next generation — the baby-boom children — begins to reach retirement age after about 2010, the long-term trend toward fewer available children will sharply reassert itself.

Were we to be transported suddenly to the year 2000, the families we would see would look very recognizable. There would be few unfamiliar forms — not many communes or group marriages, and probably not a large proportion of lifelong singles. Instead, families by and large would continue to center around the bonds between husbands and wives and between parents and children. One could say the same about today's families relative to the 1960s: the forms are not new. What is quite different, comparing the 1960s with the 1980s, or the 1980s with a hypothetical 2000, is the distribution of these forms.

In the early 1960s, there were far fewer sin-gle-parent families and families formed by remarriages after divorce than is the case today; and in the year 2000 there are likely to be far more single-parent families and families of remarriage than we see now. Moreover, in the early 1960s both spouses were employed in a much smaller percentage of two-parent families; in the year 2000, the percentage with two earners will be greater still. Cohabitation before marriage existed in the 1960s, but it was a frowned-upon, bohemian style of life. Today, it has become widely accepted; it will likely become more common in the future. Yet we have argued that cohabitation is less an alternative to marriage than a precursor to marriage, though we expect to see a modest rise in the number of people who never marry.

SOURCE: From *The Futurist*, June 1983; reprinted by permission. Published by the World Future Society, 4916 St. Elmo Avenue, Washington, D.C. 20014.

The Cult Boom

*by A. James Rudin
and Marcia R. Rudin*

In a changing society there are likely to be groups who do not conform to the expectations of established institutions. Religious cults are such groups. They attract those who have not found a comfortable niche in established institutions; however, cults frighten many people who prefer stability in society and who fear the power that cult leaders develop.

A brilliant Ivy League college graduate writes his parents a short cryptic note informing them he has found a new life with the Children of God. They never see their child again.

On Manhattan's West Side a former opera coach named Oric Bovar proclaims himself Jesus Christ and attracts followers from the entertainment world who contribute large sums of money to support his cult. When one of his young followers dies Bovar prays over the body for its resurrection in an apartment for three months. Finally health officials intervene and bury the body. On April 14, 1977, Oric Bovar jumps to his death from the window of his tenth-floor West-End Avenue apartment.

Dr. Joseph Jeffers builds a $200,000 pyramid called the Temple of Yahoshua, 100 miles southwest of St. Louis, Missouri. Jeffers, who claims he is the Son of God, is the founder and leader of a religion called Yahwism.

In November, 1978, 911 men, women, and children, members of the Reverend Jim Jones's Guyana jungle utopia, Jonestown, die by drinking a Kool-Aid and cyanide mixture or are shot to death by guards.

What Are the New Religious Cults?

What are these new religious cults? Are the cults a new phenomenon, or are they similar to religious cults that have always existed? How many new groups are there? How many members have they attracted? Are they a fad that will pass, or are they a permanent part of the world-wide religious scene? Are they dangerous, or are they a welcome addition to religious and to cultural pluralism?

Sociologists define cults as deviant groups which exist in a state of tension with society. They do not evolve or break away from other religions, as do religious sects, but, rather, offer something new and different. Although by definition cults conflict with "the establishment," there are degrees of conflict: the more total the commitment the cults demand from their followers, the more hostility they meet from society.

There have always been religious cults, particularly in unstable and troubled times such as ours. For example, the Roman Empire, which allowed great freedom of religion, was deluged with apocalyptic movements that sprang from the meeting of Eastern and Western cultures. Throughout history there have always been people, both young and old, who have sought personal fulfillment, peace, mystical experience, and religious salvation through such fringe groups.

Today's religious cults, however, are different from those of the past for several reasons. First of all, there has never in recorded history been such a proliferation of cults. The signs of this cult "boom" are everywhere. Bulletin boards on hundreds of college campuses advertise a smorgasbord of religious options. Both conventional newspapers and magazines and "alternative life-style" publications carry advertisements. Cult members recruit and solicit contributions in stores, on street corners, and in public parks, in tourist centers and airports. Everywhere one hears stories of children, brothers and sisters, nieces and nephews, older parents, or friends who become members of one of these groups. Ministers, priests, and rabbis hear desperate pleas for help, as do the major Jewish and Christian organizations.

How Many Cults Are There?

Although we do not know the precise number of these cults, we do know that it is large and that the numbers are growing. After an extensive study, Drs. Egon Mayer and Laura Kitch, sociologists at Brooklyn College, concluded that since 1965 more than thirteen hundred new religious groups have appeared in America. Other observers estimate that there are between one and three thousand such groups in the United States alone. Not all are large and well-known. Some last only a short time. Many of these cults are simply the personal creations of their founders and do not outlive them, such as that of Oric Bovar, which came to an end with his suicide.

Just as it is difficult to know how many cults there are, so, too, it is difficult to estimate the number of people involved in them. Accurate membership records are not available. The membership figures the cults release are usually highly inflated in order to appear larger and to give the impression that their growth is more rapid than may really be the case. Cult critics who overreact in their concern may inadvertently inflate the figures or may underestimate them. Cult members tend to float from one group to another with the consequence that one individual may be counted in membership figures several times. Dr. Marc Galanter, a psychiatrist at Yeshiva University's Albert Einstein Medical School in New York City who, along with Richard Rabkin and Judith Rabkin, studied the Unification Church in late 1978, discovered that 90 percent of its members had had a previous involvement with another cult, confirming that there is a good deal of "shopping around" within these groups. Some experts estimate there are three hundred thousand cult adherents. Flo Conway and Jim Siegelman, authors of *Snapping,* assert there are perhaps as many as 3 million past and present cult members in America alone. Dr. Margaret Thaler Singer, a psychiatrist on the staff of the Wright Institute at Berkeley, California, and the University of California in San Francisco and a cult expert, who counsels former cult members, agrees that there are 2 to 3 million people in these groups.

Never before have religious cults been so geographically widespread. They are in every area of the United States, in every major city and on college campuses throughout the nation. They have spread to Canada and to Western Europe — Great Britain, France, Holland, Denmark, Italy, and West Germany — where governments are alarmed about their rapid growth. There are cult centers also in Asia, Africa, South America, Israel, Australia, and New Zealand.

Today's cultists are trained in the latest methods of group dynamics and "Madison Avenue" public relations, advertising, and media-manipulation techniques. They bring great enthusiasm to their work and make certain that all members are highly visible and effective missionizers. This dedication heightens their efficiency well beyond their numbers.

Why Are Today's Cults Different?

One of the major factors which set the new religious cults off from those of the past is their use of new, specific, and highly sophisticated techniques which successfully manipulate thought and behavior of new cult members. Hundreds of former cult members testify this is so in court proceedings, public information hearings concerning the cults, magazine and newspaper interviews, and counseling sessions. Psychiatrists and other professionals who counsel former cultists confirm this. These techniques include constant repetition of doctrine, applica-

tion of intense peer pressure, manipulation of diet so that critical faculties are adversely affected, deprivation of sleep, lack of privacy and time for reflection, complete break with past life, reduction of outside stimulation and influences, the skillful use of ritual to heighten mystical experience, and the invention of new vocabulary and the manipulation of language to narrow down the range of experience and construct a new reality. Psychiatrists and counselors who treat former cult members say their emotional and intellectual responses have been severely curtailed. Dr. John G. Clark, Jr., Associate Clinical Professor of Psychiatry at Massachusetts General Hospital — Harvard Medical School, who has worked with former cult members for the past six and one-half years says:

> They appear to have become rather dull and their style and range of expression limited and stereotyped. They are animated only when discussing their group and its beliefs. They rapidly lose a knowledge of current events. When stressed even a little, they become defensive and inflexible and retreat into numbing cliches. Their written or spoken expression loses metaphor, irony, and the broad use of vocabulary. Their humor is without mirth.

Observers believe some cults use hypnosis and posthypnotic suggestion.

These methods can bring about a complete personality transformation. The cult leader can mold the recruit's new beliefs and personality according to his desires so the new adherent will have total commitment to the group. This can happen very quickly, sometimes within a period of weeks.

Authors Conway and Siegelman believe that in most cults there is "a single moment of conversion and transformation," which they term "snapping." This moment is "induced in the course of a cult ritual or therapeutic technique that is deftly orchestrated to create the experience of a momentous psychic breakthrough." After this experience the person is highly vulnerable to suggestion. The cults follow up the process by chanting, meditation, speaking in tongues, or other mental exercises which reinforce the effects of the sudden psychic experience and also act as mechanisms to stifle future doubts. The results of this expert thought manipulation can be neutralized only with great difficulty. In some cases these changes are permanent.

The Religious Cults Are Wealthy

Today's religious cults are unique also because of their great wealth. They charge high fees for classes or lectures and sometimes actually take over their members' financial assets. They own extensive property, operate lucrative and diversified businesses, and skillfully extract millions of dollars every year from the public by solicitations. Their incomes are tax-exempt. The People's Temple had over $10 million in various bank accounts at the time of the mass suicides and murders in Guyana. Ex-Unification Church official Allen Tate Wood estimates that movement's income is over $200 million per year.

Money buys power. Some cults can afford to hire the best legal minds to help them fight their opponents. They sue journalists who write about them and campaign against legislation that aims to curb their activities. The Unification Church hires top journalists and columnists to write for its newspaper, News World, which offers a widespread platform for its political viewpoint. Critics accuse the Unification Church of using its great wealth to influence United States Government policy.

Money can also purchase respectability. The cults are changing their tactics. They are less flamboyant and no longer hire Madison Square Garden or the Houston Astrodome for rallies. They are taking many adherents off the streets and putting them into "white collar" jobs. Cultists who are visible to the public dress in a better manner than they did in the past so that outsiders will think the group is less eccentric and therefore less dangerous. Many Hare Krishna members, for example, now wear wigs and conventional clothing when they solicit on the streets rather than their exotic Indian garb. The Unification Church employs renowned theologians to teach at its seminary and to lecture on the group's behalf. It "dialogues" with Evangelical Christians and desires conversations with other religious groups. It seeks the academic world's stamp of approval by inviting over four hundred fifty prominent academicians to annual conferences sponsored by a Unification Church organization, ICUS (International Conference on the Unity of Science), which pays for their travel expenses and large honoraria. Some academics are flattered by the invitations, while others refuse to attend the controversial meetings because of the Unification Church connection.

Because of their vast wealth and the power and respectability money can buy the contemporary cults are not merely a passing fad. They are not simply temporary way stations for those who may "be into" something else next year, as some hope. They are a permanent and rapidly growing part of the worldwide religious and cultural scene.

Guarding Against Complacency

Although the cults are a very real presence on the religious and cultural scene this does not mean that we must be complacent about them. They want people to get used to them, to become resigned to their existence, to tire of worrying and stop fighting against them. They want to be perceived as "new religious movements" rather than as "cults," a negative label which implies that they are at odds with society. They liken themselves to other religious movements which were previously considered radical and which are now, after the passage of time, old, established, and accepted groups. Unification Church officials often compare their legal difficulties and negative public image to the past harassment of the Mormon Church, implying that just as the Mormons were once considered outsiders and were eventually accepted by society, so too the Unification Church will eventually be accepted. They cite cases of extremism in the Roman Catholic Church, claiming that the treatment of their members is no worse, and that there are Catholic parents who are unhappy at their children's decision to join the cloistered nuns' or monks' orders just as parents of Unification Church members are unhappy that their children have renounced the world to dedicate themselves to a new life.

Characteristics of the Cults

All religions have at some point in their histories been guilty of excesses. Extremism, fanaticism, and irrationality are found in all religions and, one can argue, are perhaps an essential component of all religious or mystical experiences. However, these new religious cults are *not* like the Roman Catholic Church, the Mormon Church, or other past "new religious movements." The contemporary cults exhibit characteristics that set them apart from past religious cults and from established religions. These fundamental differences make them different in kind as well as degree, and make them a unique phenomenon.

What are these characteristics? (One must remember that the following characteristics are generalizations and do not apply equally to all of the groups.)

1. Members swear total allegiance to an all-powerful leader whom they may believe to be a Messiah. The leader determines the rules for daily life and proclaims doctrines or "Truths," but generally the leader and his or her "inner circle" are exempt from the rules or prohibitions. These rules, doctrines, or "Truths" cannot be questioned. The leader's word is the absolute and final authority.

2. Rational thought is discouraged or forbidden. The groups are anti-intellectual, placing all emphasis on intuition or emotional experience. "Knowledge" is redefined as those ideas and experiences dispensed by the group or its leader. One can only attain knowledge by joining the group and submitting to its doctrine. One cannot question this "knowledge."

If the follower shows signs of doubting he is made to feel that the fault lies within himself, not with the ideas, and he feels intensely guilty about this doubt. Says Rabbi Zalman Schacter, Professor of Religion and Jewish Mysticism at Temple University, "Any group which equates doubt with guilt is a cult."

3. The cult's recruitment techniques are often deceptive. The potential follower may not be told what he is getting into and what will be required of him. The Unification Church often does not mention its name or that of Reverend Moon for perhaps several weeks. By then the person is well indoctrinated into the movement. Most cult members probably would not join if they knew ahead of time what was involved. Says Jeannie Mills, who with her husband and five children spent six years in the People's Temple, "Your first encounter with a cult group is going to be a very pleasant experience. . . . How many people would join a church if the leader stood up in front of them and said, 'You'll never have sex anymore, you're not going to have enough food to satisfy your needs, you're going to sleep four to six hours a night, and you're going to have to be cut off entirely from all your family ties?'"

4. The cult weakens the follower psychologically and makes him believe that his problems can only be solved by the group. The cult undermines all of the follower's past psychological support systems; all help from other therapy methods, psychologists or psychiatrists, religious beliefs, or parents and friends is discredited and may actually be forbidden. Psychological problems as well as intellectual doubts are soothed away by denying the reality of the conflicting feelings, by keeping the adherent so busy and constantly on the move that he has no time to

think about them, and by assurances that faithful following of the cult's teachings will in time assuage them. The cult follower may reach a plateau of inner calm and appear to be free from anxiety. But this placidity may be only a mask for unresolved psychological turmoil which still presents a grave danger to the adherent.

The cult may make the follower feel helpless and dependent on the group by forcing him into childlike submission. Former Unification Church member Christopher Edwards relates in his book *Crazy for God* how childlike he felt during a confusing game played during his recruitment:

> During the entire game our team chanted loudly, "Bomb with Love," "Blast with Love," as the soft, round balls volleyed back and forth. Again I felt lost and confused, angry, remote and helpless, for the game had started without an explanation of the rules.

He described how he surrendered himself to the comfortable feeling of being a small child again:

> "Give in, Chris," urged a voice within me. "Just be a child and obey. It's fun. It's trusting. Isn't this the innocence, the purity of love you've been searching for?"

The cults offer total, unconditional love but actually extract a constantly higher and higher price for it — total submission to the group. Explains Edwards:

> Suddenly I understood what they wanted from me. Their role was to tease me with their love, dishing it out and withdrawing it as they saw fit. My role was not to question but to be their child, dependent on them for affection. The kiddie games, the raucous singing, the silly laughter, were all part of a scenario geared to help me assume my new identity.

5. The new cults expertly manipulate guilt. The devotee believes the group has the power to "dispense existence," to determine, according to psychologist Moshe Halevi Spero, "who has the

right to live or die, physically or metaphorically." Members may be forced to "confess" their inadequacies and past "sins" before the group or certain individuals. In their book *All God's Children* journalists Carroll Stoner and Jo Anne Parke report that "counter-cult activists claim that some religious cults keep dossiers on members and their families — the more secrets the better — in order to use the material as emotional blackmail if the members should decide to leave, and tell of cases where this has happened."

6. Cult members are isolated from the outside world, cut off from their pasts, from school, job, family, and friends as well as from information from newspapers, radio, and television. They may be prohibited from coming and going freely into the outside world, or are so psychologically weakened that they cannot cope with it. They are told that the outside world is evil, satanic, and doomed, and that salvation can come only by remaining in the group and giving up everything else.

7. The cult or its leader makes every career or life decision for the follower. The Hare Krishna group regulates every hour of activity for those members who dwell in the temples. The cults determine every aspect of the adherent's personal life, including sexual activities, diet, use of liquor, drugs and tobacco, perhaps the choice of marriage partners, and whether, when, and how to bear children. Even if one does not live within the group the cult comes to overpower all other aspects of life. Career and schooling may be abandoned and all other interests discouraged so that the cult becomes the follower's total world.

8. Some cults promise to improve society, raise money, and work to help the poor, etc., in order to attract idealistic members. However, their energies are channeled into promoting the well-being of the group rather than towards improving society. All energy and financial resources are devoted to the cult, in some cases to the benefit only of the leaders. Cults usually

exist solely for the purposes of self-survival and financial growth. While all religious organizations must be concerned with such practical affairs, these considerations are not their sole raison d'être.

9. Cult followers often work full time for the group. They work very long hours, for little or no pay, and in demeaning circumstances and conditions. They are made to feel guilty or unworthy if they protest. If they do work outside the group, salaries are usually turned over to the cult. The lower-echelon members may live in conditions of self-denial or extreme poverty while cult leaders live comfortably or even luxuriously.

10. The cults are antiwoman, antichild, and antifamily. Women perform the most menial tasks of cooking, cleaning, and street solicitations and are rarely elevated to high decision-making positions in the group. Birth control, abortion, and the physical circumstances of childbirth are often regulated by the group's leaders, who are usually men. The Unification Church teaches that Eve's sin of intercourse with Satan is the root of human estrangement from God. There are reports of sexual abuse of women in the Church of Armageddon. A fourteen-year-old was raped in the Children of God when she disobeyed a leader. Women in the Children of God are encouraged to use sex to recruit new members.

There are reports of child neglect and beatings. Children are often improperly cared for and inadequately educated. They are at times taken away from their parents and raised by others in the group or even geographically separated from them. Because some members have now been in a cult for many years, the consequences of the cult experience are affecting a second generation.

Family bonds must be subordinated to loyalties to the cult, which may speak of itself as a higher family. Children and parents may not form close relationships because this may threaten group loyalties. Families are often deliberately broken up, members forced to renounce spouses who do not approve of the group or who leave it. Cult leaders may order "marriages" with other partners even though the follower may be legally married to another either inside or outside of the cult.

The followers' ties with their families outside of the group are strained if their family disapproves of the cult, and adherents may be forced to sever connections with them. Families are often prevented by the cult from locating their member or from talking with him or her privately. The cult may tell the adherent that his family is satanic and warn him that it will try to trick him into leaving the group or may try to kidnap him.

11. Most cult members believe the world is coming to an end and they are elite members of an "elect" survival group. They believe in a Manichean dualistic conflict between Absolute Good and Absolute Evil. By joining the cult they believe they have affiliated themselves with the Good which will eventually triumph over Evil.

They shed their old identities and take on new ones in preparation for this "new age." They have a sense of rebirth, or a starting over, and so often adopt new names, new vocabulary, and new clothing in order to purify themselves for their new lives.

12. Many of these groups have the philosophy that the ends justify the means. Since the "ends" are so important — salvation of souls, salvation of the world, triumph of Good over Evil — any means required to carry them out are permitted and even encouraged by the cult. There may be a double standard of truth, one for cult members and another for the outside world. The cult member may be encouraged to lie to outsiders. The Unification Church practices what it calls "Heavenly Deception" and the

"Hare Krishna Transcendental Trickery." The Children of God believe that since the world is so corrupt they are not subject to its laws and teach their members to subvert the legal system. However, within the cult the members must be truthful to each other and to the cult leaders.

13. The cults are often shrouded in an aura of secrecy and mystery. They keep new members in the dark, promising more knowledge about the group as they become more involved in it. Some leaders are rarely, if ever, seen by the average member. The cults may hide financial information from the public.

14. There is frequently an aura of violence or potential violence. Two Unification Church recruitment centers are guarded. The Divine Light Mission premises and the Krishnas at their farm in West Virginia have their own security forces which they insist are necessary to protect the cult leaders or to protect themselves from hostile neighbors. Many Way International members take a weapons training course. There was a large arsenal of automatic rifles, shotguns, and handguns at Jonestown. People's Temple followers were closely guarded before Congressman Ryan and members of his party were slain and many adherents took poison or were shot by Jones's security forces.

Some cult members have been involved in incidents of beatings or shootings. In May, 1979, a Swiss court sentenced the head of a Divine Light Mission at Winterhur to fourteen years in prison on charges ranging from breach of the peace to attempted murder. In August, 1979, two Unification Church area directors were arrested and charged with shooting at the car of two former members. Christopher Edwards' parents had to hire private detectives to guard their home for several months after he was deprogrammed and had left the Unification Church. Since Edwards' book about his experiences with the Unification Church was published, he has received two death threats. Private investigator Galen Kelly was hospitalized with a concussion for a week in 1979 after, he alleges, a Unification Church member hit him on the head with a rock.

Are the New Cults Dangerous?

Observers of the religious scene are divided over the issue of what these new groups in our society mean. Some scholars see the new cults as the "cutting edge" of a healthy and growing spiritual awakening in the Western world. They maintain that the cults promote religious pluralism by ensuring freedom of choice and a variety of religious alternatives. But cult critics perceive them as wild and poisonous weeds invading religion's vineyard. They believe the new cults are actually antipluralistic because they claim to possess the one, only, and final truth. They discourage or forbid their members to discuss other ideas and alternatives and vow to triumph over other viewpoints. This attitude, critics maintain, hinders rather than promotes religious pluralism.

SOURCE: From A. James Rudin and Marcia R. Rudin, *Prison or Paradise? The New Religious Cults.* Philadelphia: Fortress Press, 1980, pp. 13–29. Reprinted by permission of Bernice Hoffman Literary Agency.

15,684
41,430

PART V

Human Ecology and Change

At this point in history societies are changing very rapidly. The size of the population is increasing dramatically, due, in part, to factors such as better health care and longer life expectancy. Many people, however, are not getting enough to eat, and problems such as pollution are destroying our natural resources. Because the ever-increasing numbers of people make our earth more crowded, many now live in congested urban areas, and our cities are straining under the weight of this population increase. All these issues are examined in the first three chapters of this section.

How can we possibly understand what our future will be like? The last chapter in this book summarizes theories of social change and analyzes the kinds of events that could have a great impact on modern societies. While we cannot know which events will occur in the future, we can better understand what impact certain types of events might have. As you read through these final chapters, we hope you find that you have gained a new perspective, a sociological perspective, that gives you a new understanding of the world about you. We trust this new perspective will be useful as you prepare for your own future in this rapidly changing world.

CHAPTER 18

Collective Behavior and Social Movements

Clapping with the right hand only will not produce a noise.

— Malay proverb

Most facets of social life follow patterns of rules and norms. People generally have a daily routine and conform to the roles expected of them. In the same way, such organizations as schools, churches, factories, and governments are highly structured institutions that tend to be stable and relatively static. In these organizations, decisions are made through some semblance of logical, rational discussion.

There is, however, another dimension of social life in which the activities are relatively spontaneous, unstructured, and unstable. This category includes such collective actions as panics, demonstrations, riots, fads and fashions, disasters, and social movements. These actions, which may also follow certain patterns and established norms and rules, are instances of what sociologists call collective behavior.

What Is Collective Behavior?

Sociologists use the term *collective behavior* to refer to spontaneous, unstructured, and transitory behavior of a group of people in response to a specific event. If the term were taken literally, it would incorporate all behaviors involving more than one person, that is, all of sociology, but sociologists use it in a more restrictive sense. The difference between the literal and the sociological definition can be clarified with an example. Take an event such as automobile crashes. To conduct safety tests, car manufacturers have a group of employees perform tests repeatedly and collect data in an organized fashion about what happens when a car moving 35 mph hits something. Compare this with the behavior of a group of people gathered at the site of a highway accident. Although both groups gathered to observe car crashes and are thus behaving collectively in the literal sense, only the second group is engaged in collective behavior in the sociological sense. The car company employees are reacting to a carefully controlled event in which the action is both expected and repeated. The group observing the highway accident reacts to a spontaneous, unstructured, unexpected, nonrecurring event. Panics, riots, crowds, fads, and fashions can all be viewed as spontaneous collective responses to transitory and loosely structured circumstances.

Collective behavior can be contrasted with *institutionalized behavior,* which is recurrent and follows an orderly pattern with a relatively stable set of goals, expectations, and values. In the example above, the auto workers are involved in institutionalized behavior. Other examples of routine, predictable behavior would be going to class, commuting on a train, and going to church. If some unusual event takes place — an earthquake, train wreck, or fire, for example — collective behavior takes over. When people are confronted with an unfamiliar event, for which no norms or rules have been established, they may behave in ways that differ radically from their normal conduct. People generally leave a theater in a calm, orderly fashion without pushing or shouting. But if a fire breaks out, their conventional behavior would change to screams, shoving, and a rush for the exits. The ordinary norms break down and are replaced by new ones. Such actions occur infrequently, however, and only under certain conditions.

Preconditions of Collective Behavior

Certain conditions in contemporary societies tend to increase the likelihood of collective behavior. Rapid social change creates tensions and conflicts that sometimes lead to collective actions and violence. Social diversity and the associated inequalities in the distribution of wealth and opportunities have produced many social movements — the women's movement, the Gray Panthers, the civil rights movement, and the labor movement. The mass media also play an important role in the dissemination of information of all types, from the cabbage patch doll and pet rock fads to prison riots. Some critics have suggested that the ghetto riots of the 1960s occurred in part because information on riots in other cities was transmitted through the media.

In addition to rapid social change, social diversity, and mass communications, certain other preconditions encourage collective behavior. Neil Smelser, in his *Theory of Collective Behavior* (1962), identified six factors that, when they exist simultaneously, will produce collective behavior: (1) structural conduciveness, (2) structural strain, (3) generalized belief, (4) precipitating factors, (5) mobilization for action, and (6) operation of social control.

Structural conduciveness, the most general precondition, is the extent to which a society's organizaton makes collective behavior possible. A society that has no stock market cannot have a stock market crash. A country that has only one race or religion will not have race or religious riots. Note that structural conduciveness — the existence of banks, stock markets, or different religious or racial groups, for example — does not cause collective behavior. Rather, it is a measure of the existence of conditions in which it can occur. The fact that some aspect of a society is structurally conducive does not mean that collective behavior *will* happen; it means that, given certain other conditions, it *can.*

A *structural strain* is any kind of conflict or ambiguity that causes frustration and stress. Structural strains may be caused by conflicts between real and ideal norms, by conflicts between goals and available means to reaching them (anomie), or by the gap between social ideals (full

Collective behavior is the spontaneous and unstructured response of a group of people to a specific event. Prior to the 1983 Christmas holiday season, stores throughout the country witnessed one form of spatially proximate collective behavior when they announced the availability of Cabbage Patch dolls. Customers shoved and pushed and even snatched dolls from the hands of other shoppers in their frenzy to purchase these prized objects before they were sold out.

employment, wealth, equality) and social realities (unemployment, poverty, and discrimination by age, race, and sex). Widespread unemployment among teenage blacks is an example of a structural strain.

A third determinant of collective behavior is *generalized belief*. Given structural conduciveness and structural strain, people must identify a problem and share a common interpretation of it for collective action to occur. People develop generalized beliefs about the conditions causing the strain. The women's movement, for example, began to grow only after the belief became widespread that women were discriminated against in employment, education, and other areas. Mobs form and riots take place only when people share a perception of some injustice or unfair treatment. Generalized beliefs may be based on known facts, shared attitudes, or a common ide-

ology. The truth or accuracy of the beliefs is unimportant — the important thing is that they are shared.

Precipitating factors are the fourth determinant. Structural conduciveness, structural strain, and generalized belief alone do not inevitably cause collective behavior. A precipitating event must trigger a collective response. The precipitating event itself is sometimes fairly insignificant. An unwarranted search may start a collective protest in an overcrowded prison. Commodity trading may proceed quietly until a rumor arises that frost has severely damaged the expected orange harvest. The precipitating event can also be a more serious incident, of course. News that a policeman has shot a black youth can inflame a tense racial situation. As was true of generalized beliefs, a precipitating event need not be true or accurately communicated to exert an influence. Even an unfounded rumor can lend focus and support to a belief and increase the likelihood of a collective response.

Mobilization for action is the fifth determinant of collective behavior. Once a precipitating event has taken place, people have to be persuaded to join the movement. Sometimes an event mobilizes a group spontaneously, as when the crowd boos the umpire for making a bad call or when a crowd panics if someone yells fire. Sometimes leaders emerge from within the group to encourage participation, which is what occurred during the formation of the Solidarity labor movement in Poland in 1980, when Lech Walesa, an unemployed electrician, quickly became the leader and spokesman for the group. In other cases, outside leadership steps in to organize the people and push them into action, which is what often happened during the era when labor unions were being formed in this country. Collective behavior begins when mobilization for action takes place.

The *operation of social control* is the sixth and final determinant of collective behavior. Social control consists of the actions of the mass media, government, and other groups when they try to suppress or influence collective behavior (Smelser, 1969). In the case of a potential strike, management might agree to listen to grievances, make a few changes, or raise wages slightly. If the strike takes place, it might fire striking workers and hire new ones. If social control cannot prevent collective action before it starts or halt it once it has begun, the collective behavior continues.

Smelser's approach, then, suggests that a series of six preconditions is necessary to produce collective action. The preconditions are closely interrelated — structural strains will not appear unless the society is structurally conducive to them, for example. This approach has been widely criticized, but it remains the most systematic and important theory of collective behavior.

Smelser's model was applied by Lewis (1972) in an attempt to explain events at Kent State University on May 4, 1970, when four students were killed and nine others wounded by National Guardsmen. The incident happened during a period of widespread student antiwar rallies and protests, and the Kent State rally was a reaction to President Nixon's announcement that troops had been sent into Cambodia. The situation was extremely tense, and ultimately the National Guard fired at the taunting students. In evaluating Smelser's general theory as applied to this incident, Lewis found that all six conditions were present: (1) the circumstances were structurally conducive to a hostile outburst; (2) structural strain was produced by the National Guard's presence on the students' turf, by illegal student rallies, and by the use of tear gas; (3) a generalized hostile belief about the Guard developed; (4) the use of force and the actions of the Guard in making a stand in front of a burned ROTC building served as precipitating events; (5) the events themselves as well as the announcement that the rally was illegal tended to mobilize the Guard as well as the students for action; (6) attempts to exert social control were made by the Guard, but these efforts were unsuccessful. The theory was found to be extremely useful in organizing the large body of information generated by the Kent State episode.

Now that we have considered preconditions to collective behavior, we will direct our attention to specific types of collective behavior.

Spatially Proximate Collective Behaviors: Crowds

A *spatially proximate collective* exists when people are geographically close and physically visible to one another. The most common type of spatially proximate collective is the crowd.

A *crowd* is a temporary group of people in face-to-face contact who share a common interest or focus of attention. This common interest may be unexpected and unusual but not necessarily. Although people in a crowd interact a good deal, the crowd as a whole is organized poorly if at all. According to Turner (1978), crowds have certain features that make them a unique area for study, including anonymity, suggestibility, contagion, and emotional arousability.

Most types of collective behavior involve anonymity. People who do not know those around them may behave in ways that they would consider unacceptable if they were alone or with their family or neighbors. During a riot, the anonymity of crowd members makes it easier for people to loot and steal. In a lynch mob, brutal acts can be committed without feelings of shame or responsibility. Whatever the type of crowd, the anonymity of the individuals involved shifts the responsibility to the crowd as a whole.

Because crowds are relatively unstructured and often unpredictable, crowd members are often highly suggestible. People who are seeking direction in an uncertain situation are highly responsive to the suggestions of others and become very willing to do what a leader or group of individuals suggests, especially given the crowd's anonymity.

The characteristic of contagion is closely linked to anonymity and suggestibility. Turner (1978) defines this aspect of crowd behavior as "interactional amplification" (p. 284). As people interact, the crowd's response to the common event or situation increases in intensity. If they are clapping or screaming, their behavior is likely to move others to clap or scream, and contagion increases when people are packed close together. An alert evangelist, comedian, or rock singer will try to get the audience to move close to one another to increase the likelihood of contagion and encourage the listeners to get caught up in the mood, spirit, and activity of the crowd.

All crowds share a common focus. Expressive crowd behavior is common among teenagers at concerts of popular rock groups such as the Police, The Rolling Stones, or Michael Jackson. The emotional expression generally includes screaming, shouting, clapping, and even attempts to touch or hug the performers. Perhaps the most famous performers of the past few decades who elicited this type of crowd response were The Beatles, shown here.

A fourth characteristic is emotional arousal. Anonymity, suggestibility, and contagion tend to arouse emotions. Inhibitions are forgotten, and people become "charged" to act. In some cases, their emotional involvement encourages them to act in uncharacteristic ways. During the Beatles concerts in the early 1960s, for example, teenage girls who were presumably quite conventional most of the time tried to rush on stage and had to be carried away by police. The combination of the four characteristics of crowds makes their behavior extremely volatile and frightening.

Although these four aspects of crowd behavior may be seen in almost any crowd, their intensity varies. Some crowds permit greater anonymity than others, some have higher levels of suggestibility and contagion, and yet one or more of these characteristics may not appear at all. The presence or absence of certain crowd features has been used to organize crowds into different categories.

Types of Crowds

All crowds are spatially proximate and temporary, and every crowd shares a common focus. The most complete classification, advanced more than forty years ago by Herbert Blumer (1939), identified crowds of four types: (1) casual, (2) conventional, (3) expressive, and (4) acting.

A *casual crowd* is high in anonymity but low in suggestibility, contagion, and emotional arousal. A group of people gathered to listen to a street musician, to observe a person who has fainted, or to look at an animated holiday display would be a casual crowd. Casual crowds have little unity and a very loose organization. The participants interact little with one another; they are drawn together to observe an event out of simple curiosity or a common interest. Blumer notes that although the chief mechanisms of crowd formation occur in the casual crowd, their influence is not very strong.

A *conventional crowd* resembles the casual crowd except that it is more highly structured and participants express themselves in established ways. The spectators at a baseball game, the audience at a concert, students listening to a lecture, or the passengers on an airplane are conventional crowds. Although the participants are generally unknown to one another (anonymous), they have a specific goal or common purpose. This type of crowd is conventional in that the members are expected to follow established social norms and rules. Running up and down the aisles and shouting, for example, would be disapproved behaviors in a theater or airplane.

Conventional crowds may not seem like crowds at all since they generally follow established rules and procedures. Concerts and baseball games are scheduled at preestablished times and places, and crowd members sit in designated areas. People applaud at the end of the music or when an outstanding play has been made. Nevertheless, a conventional crowd has all of the characteristics of our definition: it is spatially proximate, temporary, and focused on a single event.

The distinguishing feature of the *expressive crowd*, which Blumer also terms the "dancing" crowd, is the physical movement of its members as a form of release. Unlike the other types, the expressive crowd's attention is not directed toward an external object or goal. Rather, "It is introverted in that its impulses and feelings are spent in mere expressive actions, usually in unrestrained physical movements, which give release to tension without having any other purpose" (Blumer, 1939, p. 182). Expressive crowds can be found at street carnivals and festivals, at discos, at evangelical religious revivals, and elsewhere. The expressive activities may include singing, shouting, drinking, and competitive events as well as dancing. At events of this sort, people "let loose," become emotionally involved, and in extreme instances become completely uninhibited.

Crowds share a common focus, are spatially proximate, are temporary, and are of various types. One of these types, the expressive crowd, can be witnessed annually at the Mardi Gras in New Orleans. Here people "let loose" with costuming, street dancing, singing, and relatively uninhibited forms of behavior.

Although this expressive behavior may appear wild and unrestrained, social rules and norms are operating: people know what kinds of behavior are acceptable within the boundaries of the ceremony or festivity. For this reason, most expressive crowd events, including very large gatherings such as the Mardi Gras or rock festivals, are quite orderly and peaceful. Anthropologists point out that expressive events are especially important in cultures with a high level of emotional repression. The dances and festivals provide an outlet for tensions and emotions.

The *acting crowd* acts on the basis of aroused impulses and may be volatile, aggressive, and dangerous. It exhibits all the features of crowds mentioned earlier: anonymity, suggestibility, contagion, and emotional arousal. Like the casual or conventional crowd, the acting crowd focuses on some external goal or object, but it is not restrained by rules or the confines of a structured organization. Participants have rapport with other crowd members and are drawn into the excitement of the event. They respond immediately and directly to the remarks and actions of others without thinking about them or trying to weigh alternative courses of action. The two most dramatic forms of acting crowds are mobs and riots.

Mobs are groups that are emotionally aroused and ready to engage in violent behavior. They are generally short-lived and highly unstable. Their violent actions often stem from strong dissatisfaction with existing government policies or social circumstances, and extreme discontentment with prevailing conditions is used to justify immediate and direct action. Disdainful of regular institutional channels and legal approaches, mobs take matters into their own hands.

Most mobs are predisposed to violence before their actions are triggered by a specific event. When feelings of frustration and hostility are widespread, leaders can easily recruit and command members. With aggressive leadership, an angry, frustrated mob in an atmosphere of hostility can be readily motivated to riot, commit lynchings, throw firebombs, hang people in effigy, or engage in destructive orgies.

Mob violence has erupted in many different circumstances. During the French Revolution of the 1780s and 1790s, angry mobs stormed through Paris, breaking into the Bastille prison for arms and calling for the execution of Louis XVI. In nineteenth-century England, enraged workers burned the factories they worked in. Lynchings of blacks in the United States for real or imagined offenses continued into the twentieth century, often with little or no opposition from the formal agencies of control — police, courts, and public officials. Although lynch mobs are uncommon today, occasional instances of mob behavior take place over civil rights issues such as busing or housing, during political conventions and rallies, and among student or labor groups angry about perceived injustices.

Riots are collective actions involving mass violence and mob actions. The targets of their hostility and violence are less specific than those of mobs, and the groups involved are more diffuse. Most riots result from an intense hatred of a particular group with no specific person or property in mind. Destruction, burning, or looting may be indiscriminate, and unfocused anger can lead to violent acts against any object or person who happens to be in the wrong area at the wrong time. Like mobs, rioters take actions into their own hands when they feel that institutional reactions to their concerns about war, poverty, racial injustices, or other problems are inadequate.

The race riots of the 1960s in Watts in Los Angeles, Harlem in New York, and many other cities are the most commonly cited examples of rioting. These riots, which generally occurred in black ghettos, involved widespread destruction of property followed by extensive looting. The National Advisory Commission on Civil Disorders (Kerner, 1968) found that riots are associated with a number of factors, including discrimination, prejudice, disadvantaged living conditions, and frustration over the inability to bring about change. The incident that triggers a riot can be relatively trivial. In Detroit, for example, riots began after police raided social clubs suspected of permitting illegal gambling and the sale of liquor after hours. The riots of the 1960s, however, took place almost without exception in communities long frustrated by high unemployment, poverty, police harassment, and other factors. In the riots of the summer of 1967, tensions were increased by the sweltering weather.

These findings are highly consistent with those of Lieberson and Silverman (1965), who studied conditions underlying seventy-six race riots in the United States between 1913 and 1963. They found that only four of them started without a precipitating event such as a rape, murder, arrest, or holdup. They also found that riots are most probable in communities with a history of being unable to resolve racial. problems. The characteristics of crowd behavior — anonymity, suggestibility, contagion, and emotional arousal — were present in all the riots studied by Lieberson and Silverman.

Theories of Acting Crowd Behavior

Students of crowd behavior have historically focused on acting crowds. How do acting crowds diminish individualism and encourage people to accept the attitudes and behaviors of the group? We have already examined Smelser's theory about the preconditions of collective behavior. Four additional perspectives are representative of the various other interpretations prevalent today. These include Le Bon's classical perspective, Blumer's interactionist perspective, Turner and Killian's emergent norm perspective, and Berk's game perspective.

The Classical Perspective

The *classical perspective* on acting crowd behavior suggests that people in a crowd lose their conscious personalities and act impulsively on the basis of their instincts rather than reason. This perspective was articulated in what is prob-

ably the most influential single book ever written on collective behavior, *The Crowd: A Study of the Popular Mind* (1895), by the French sociologist Gustave Le Bon (1841–1931). During Le Bon's life, France was experiencing rapid social change, and, earlier, mobs and riots had brought about the French Revolution. Le Bon, who considered crowds pathological, violent, threatening groups, believed that their destructive potential stemmed from "the psychological law of the mental unity of the crowd." According to Le Bon (1968),

> The sentiments and ideas of all the persons in the gathering take one and the same direction, and their conscious personality vanishes. A collective mind is formed, doubtless transitory, but presenting very clearly defined characteristics. The gathering has thus become what, in the absence of a better expression, I will call an organised crowd, or, if the term is considered preferable, a psychological crowd. It forms a single being, and is subjected to the *law of the mental unity of crowds.* (p. 2)

Paintings such as the Prise de la Bastille *tended to convey to early scholars of collective behavior the image of a collective mind and the mental unity of crowds. Individuality and rationality were overcome by impulsive collective mob behavior.*

Myths About Disasters

The term *disaster* is used to refer both to events — earthquakes, floods, tornadoes, explosions — and to the social disruptions caused by these events. They are discussed here because they generally happen in a limited geographical area and involve a group of individuals in close association with one another — a spatially proximate collective.

Most of us have a number of misconceptions about disasters and their aftermath, which are often created and reinforced by the mass media. We have all seen movies of people fleeing in panic from a nuclear holocaust, fires, or flying saucers, for example, but studies indicate that panic flight following a disaster is rare. Even after a catastrophe as terrible as the bombing of Hiroshima, "the rate of extreme nonadaptive behavior . . . is generally very low" (Barton, 1970, p. 146). In the same way, we assume that looters descend on the sites of disasters and steal everything they can lay

their hands on from the homes and businesses of the victims. Once again, however, studies show that looting is uncommon following disasters. Victims themselves have been found to believe that looting is a widespread occurrence. The prevalence of this belief is probably due to the publicity given to looting during civil disturbances.

Below are listed some other common myths about disasters:

Martial law must be established following a disaster to control both the victims and the exploiters. In most situations, martial law is neither necessary nor desirable, and it has never been declared in a disaster area in the United States (Quarantelli and Dynes, 1972).

Crime rates rise during a disaster. Crime rates actually drop during disasters. The reduction in arrests, however, may be due more to changes in law enforcement than to lower rates of crime.

When residents are warned of an impending disaster they get out of

the disaster area. The evidence suggests that most inhabitants will not leave until forced to do so by the effects of the disaster or by legal authorities.

Disaster victims go into a state of shock and are unable to care for themselves. The few shock reactions that do occur are generally short-lived. The initial search and rescue activity, casualty care, and provision of essential services are usually undertaken by the victims themselves.

The Red Cross, the disaster relief organization, is on the scene immediately, and it is welcomed by the disaster victims. The Red Cross does provide valuable assistance to disaster victims, but many studies indicate that victims express resentment and hostility toward this agency, noting its tendency to overstate its accomplishments, its reliance on outsiders, its imperialistic stance, its failure to convey sympathy, and its insensitivity to local problems.

Most of those who evacuate their homes use shelters established by the authorities. Most people actually find shelter with their friends, relatives, or neighbors, or else they provide for their own lodging.

This quote mentions two key concepts in the classical view of crowds: "collective mind" and "mental unity." Le Bon, the originator of the "group mind" concept, believed that crowds cause people to regress. According to this view, crowds are guided by instinct, not by rational decisions. Under the influence of crowds, even conventional, law-abiding citizens may act impulsively and be guided by unconscious influences. Crowds do not reason, they respond instantly to the immediate situation. Why? (1) The anonymity of the collective gives each person in a crowd a feeling of power. (2) A contagion sweeps through the crowd like a virus passing from one person to another. (3) The participants become as suggestible as if they had been hypnotized. The result is the unquestioned acceptance of and obedience to the leaders.

The Interactionist Perspective

The *interactionist perspective* assumes that people in crowds reinforce and heighten one another's reactions. It was developed by Herbert Blumer (1939), who, like Le Bon believed that crowd behavior is often irrational and emotional. Blumer, however, rejected the idea that it stems from a group or collective mind. Rather, he believed that crowd behavior results from "circular reactions" operating in a situation of social unrest. In Blumer's words, a circular reaction is

> a type of interstimulation wherein the response of one individual reproduces the stimulation that has come from another individual and in being reflected back to this individual reinforces the stimulation. Thus the interstimulation assumes a circular form in which individuals reflect one another's states of feeling and in so doing intensify this feeling. (p. 170)

In other words, in a situation of social unrest, interactions reinforce and heighten the unrest. If one group, for example, shouts "Let's get him," others model this behavior and usually adopt the same feelings and ways of expressing them. The reactions of these others increase the fervor of the original group, which in turn excites the rest of the crowd even further. In the absence of widespread unrest, such a reaction would never begin. Three types of circular reactions are milling, collective excitement, and social contagion.

In a *milling* crowd, people move about aimlessly. Milling tends to make people preoccupied with one another and less responsive to the usual sources of stimulation. Like hypnotic subjects who become increasingly preoccupied with the hypnotist, milling individuals grow more preoc-

cupied with others in the crowd and become increasingly inclined to respond quickly, directly, and without thinking.

Collective excitement takes place when milling reaches a high level of agitation. People in the grip of collective excitement are emotionally aroused. They respond on the basis of their impulses, they are likely to feel little personal responsibility for their actions, and under the influence of collective excitement they may behave in an uncharacteristic manner (Blumer, 1939).

Social contagion comes about wherever milling and collective excitement are intense and widespread. What is fascinating about social contagion is that it can attract people who were initially just indifferent spectators. They get caught up in the excitement and become more inclined to become involved. Unlike Le Bon's theory, this theory does not suggest the existence of a group mind. Rather, people's interactions tend to heighten in intensity until the group is capable of spontaneous behavior.

The Emergent Norm Perspective

The *emergent norm perspective*, first proposed by Turner and Killian (1957), emphasizes how norms influence crowd behavior and how new norms emerge and are maintained. Whereas Le Bon and Blumer stress similarities in the behavior of crowd members, the emergent norm perspective focuses on differences in crowd member behavior. As Turner and Killian (1972) state,

> An emergent norm approach reflects the empirical observation that the crowd is characterized not by unanimity but by differential expression, with different individuals in the crowd feeling differently, participating because of diverse motives, and even acting differently. (p. 22)

According to this view, crowds do not behave as a homogeneous unit. Observers may think they act as a unit, but divergent views and

Collective behavior is the spontaneous and unstructured response of a group of people to a specific event. At a rock concert in Cincinnati, hundreds of fans rushed forward when the doors were opened. Eleven people were trampled to death and countless others were knocked down and crushed. Shown here are the covered body of one known dead and a group of firefighters working to revive other young people who were victims of the collective response.

behaviors may go unrecognized or be dismissed as unimportant. When attention is focused on the acting crowd, people frequently overlook those who remain silently on the sidelines, those who passively lend their support, and those who express little excitement. People behave differently because they act in accordance with different norms. Norms influence all social conduct, and new norms arise during novel situations such as mob actions or riots. Some may accept norms that make violence and looting acceptable. Others may define the situation differently and choose to leave or remain uninvolved.

The process by which norms emerge occurs daily in any context of human social interaction and communication. All of us are dependent on those around us to define and determine what a given event means. When others in the group shout, run, or express fear, we are likely to feel tremendous pressure to conform to their behavior. An untrained observer may note the one dominant behavior and describe the group members as unanimous in their definition, mood, and behavior. More careful observation, as emergent norm theory suggests, would reveal that unanimity is an illusion and that differential expression does take place. The problem of accounting for differential expression is illuminated by Turner (1980), who cites the following example, a first-hand account of an adult male with his young son and daughter in a toy department of a store:

Suddenly there was a loud and continuous hissing noise from the center of the room, a few cries of fear, and in an instant the entire basement room was cleared of shoppers and clerks alike. I was astonished and even amused at the panicky flight of women shoppers and clerks. I felt no fear — it sounded to me as if one of the automatic sprinkler heads had been broken, which was nothing to be afraid of. I looked down at my daughter, who was holding my hand and looking rather wide-eyed, but giving no sign of fear. I looked across the room for my son, but could see no one in the room. I felt quite concerned lest he be hurt or frightened, being alone in the crowd. I looked for the broken sprinkler so that I could cross the room to find him without getting drenched. There was no sign of water, so I walked with my daughter toward the center of the room where the hissing was still coming from. Then I saw the gas escaping from the hydrogen container used to inflate toy balloons.

As I started to walk out across the room, I felt a sudden strangeness — was there something wrong with me? Why did I feel no fear when a hundred or so people had run in panic from the room? Still I felt no fear, but I began to reexamine the situation. No, the amount of gas in the one container could not possibly be dangerous in a room so large, with a high ceiling. Furthermore, both doors leading upstairs were wide open, and they were wide doors. There would be plenty of natural air circulation. And yet, there I was with my daughter who simply mirrored my confidence, the only ones left in the basement. Could my reasoning really be right — could everyone else's fear be unjustified? I could find no flaw in my reasoning — but I began to wish that I did feel some fear. Then I felt the responsibility for my daughter. There was no danger — but if anything *did* happen to hurt my daughter, all these other people would be around to say that I brazenly carried her into danger.

I turned back, walked quickly to the nearest exit, told my daughter to walk to the first landing (half a flight up), and wait right there while I went and found her brother. Then I hurried across the room toward the other exit, feeling immensely relieved. When I was halfway across the room the hissing stopped; and then I saw Santa Claus, who had also not left the room. Suddenly I felt normal again — someone else had seen the situation the same way I had. . . . The violence of my sense of relief at this moment has been paralleled by few other experiences in my lifetime. As people began filing back in, I met my son at the door, listened to him assure me spontaneously that he just ran because everyone else did, as we walked back to the other exit, where my daughter waited obediently. (pp. 31–44)

The Game Perspective

The *game perspective* on crowd behavior suggests that crowd members think about their actions and consciously try to act in ways that will produce rewards (Berk, 1974). Unlike other theories, which assume that crowds behave irrationally, game theory stresses the importance of rational decisions. People weigh the rewards and costs of various actions and choose the course that is most likely to lead to a desired end. Looting, for example, may yield a reward such as a television set. If few people are looting, the chances of arrest may be fairly great, and a potential looter may choose not to take the risk. If, on the other hand, there are thousands of people looting stores, the chances of arrest are quite low and the person may decide to join in. Milling about before engaging in violent action may be used as a time for assessing various courses of action and evaluating the strength of support. According to this perspective, violence is not necessarily irrational. It may be the result of a conscious decision that it will be useful in acquiring a desired end: civil rights, jobs, housing, new leaders, or something else. When many people desire the same goal, collective action can increase their chances of achieving it.

Spatially Diffuse Collective Behaviors

Spatially diffuse collectives are collectives that form among people spread over a wide geographical area. The most common types are known as masses and publics.

Masses and Mass Behavior

A *mass* is a collective of geographically dispersed individuals who react to or focus on some common event. We often hear the term "mass" in speech: mass media, mass communication, mass hysteria. The millions of people who watch the Super Bowl or World Series on television or listen on radio constitute a mass. The thousands of people who rush to the store to buy an item rumored to be in short supply constitute a mass. Although dispersed over a large geographical area, they are reacting to a common event.

Members of a mass come from all educational and socioeconomic levels. They are anonymous, and they interact little or not at all. A mass has no established rules or rituals, no shared or common ideology, no hierarchy of statuses or roles, and no established leadership (Blumer, 1939).

Fads and fashions are specific types of diffuse collective mass behaviors. Generally, they arrive suddenly and disappear quickly, but they may attract great interest from large numbers of people during their tenure. A *fad* is a superficial or trivial behavior that is very popular for a short time. Some examples of fads are flagpole sitting, crowding into telephone booths, using hula hoops, dancing the jitterbug, twist, or frug, swallowing goldfish, streaking, and more recently buying cabbage patch dolls. Most of these fads were harmless and had no long-range social consequences.

A *fashion* is a temporary trend in some aspect of appearance or behavior. Fashions resemble fads but they tend to be more cyclical. They are generally thought of as influencing styles of dress, but there are also fashions in music, art, literature, and even sociological theories. To be "in fashion" is to wear the style of hair and the types of clothes that advertisers are pushing and that are currently in vogue. At any given time, hemlines may be long or short, neckties may be wide or narrow, and hair styles may be straight or curly.

Fads and fashions provide many people with a sense of excitement, feelings of belonging, or a source of identification and self-esteem. Fads and fashions, however, are also big business. Packaging pet rocks, opening a disco club, and selling the latest clothes are ways of making money. Although fads and fashions may seem trivial to the average consumer, they can bring large profits to those who take advantage of them.

Mass hysteria and panic are two other types of diffuse collective mass behaviors. *Mass hysteria* is a widespread, highly emotional fear of a potentially threatening situation. A *panic* occurs when people try to escape from a perceived danger. A recent example of mass hysteria and panic took place at Three Mile Island beginning on Wednesday, March 28, 1979, and continued for several weeks. The incident involved a series of events at the nuclear power plant at Middletown, Pennsylvania. The fear was that a total meltdown of a power unit would cause serious radiation contamination of all people in the area and the destruction of all plant life over a vast land area. When news of the event first broke, commercial telephone lines were jammed with calls to and from people living near the Three Mile Island area. Newspapers around the country carried maps of the area that showed 5-, 10-, and 20-mile concentric circles of danger and reported that evacuation would be the only hope of avoiding contamination. By noon Friday, just two days after the event, the governor of Pennsylvania recommended the immediate evacuation of all pregnant women and preschool children living within 5 miles of the area. By evening that plan was expanded to include everyone within a 20-mile radius. By this time, vast numbers (actual percents and numbers unknown) had already departed, many going to stay with relatives and friends in neighboring states or other areas. To lessen the extent of mass hysteria and panic and convey an impression that all was "safe and under control," President Carter visited the reactor site on Saturday, March 31.

How serious was this event to the residents of the area? *Science News* reported in November

Fads and fashions are two forms of mass behavior that people enthusiastically pursue. Fads are usually short-lived variations in behavior whereas fashions, although similar to fads, change less rapidly, are less trivial, and tend to be more cyclical. Fashion may involve the arts and literature, but it most often affects clothing and adornment. Some fads and fashions enjoyed by Americans over the past three decades include: 3-D eyeglasses worn by movie-goers in the fifties — and making a comeback in the eighties; tailored suits, briefcases, and running shoes for young women professionals on the go; and home-exercise or physical-fitness equipment and a variety of other health products and activities for improving both the mind and body.

of 1979 that according to the President's commission on the accident at Three Mile Island, there was immediate short-lived mental distress produced among certain groups of the general population living within 20 miles. The results of a representative sample of interviewees showed that a substantial minority, perhaps 10 percent, experienced "severe demoralization" at the time of the accident and in the weeks that followed.

Publics and Public Opinion

A public is another type of spatially diffuse collective. Blumer (1939) defines a *public* as a group of people who are confronted with an issue, who do not agree on how to address the issue, and who discuss the issue. Publics have no culture and no consciousness of themselves as a group. Voters, consumers, magazine subscribers, and stockholders are separate publics. Although these people are geographically dispersed, they share a concern about an issue. As they discuss the issue in order to resolve their differences about it, a certain public opinion begins to prevail.

Public opinion is defined variously as any opinion held by a substantial number of people or as the dominant opinion in a given population. Public opinion is especially complex in mass cultures where many publics have differing viewpoints. Some publics want their tax money to go to defense, others would prefer to see it spent on social programs. Some publics favor abortion, others oppose it. These conflicts of interest multiply as cultures become more complex. In simpler cultures most decisions about new issues can be made on the basis of traditional folkways and mores.

The formation of public opinion is influenced by a wide range of factors. Organizations such as the political parties, the National Organization of Women, and the National Rifle Association have a profound effect on public opinion. The mass media are also influential. They do not merely report the news, they can also create it. By choosing to discuss a certain issue, the media focus people's attention on it. If their reporting tends to favor one side of the issue, they may succeed in shifting public opinion in that direction. Opinion is further influenced by a population's cultural values and ethnic and social makeup. Leaders from business, government, or religion also shape public opinion, and it is interesting that elected leaders, who were put in office by the public, often try to use their office to influence those who elected them. Because public opinion is so important in contemporary social life, there is considerable interest in how it is measured.

Knowledge of public opinion is generally obtained through the use of polls, which are a form of survey research (see Chapter 2). A public opinion poll is a sampling of a population representative of a geographical area, of a group of interest to the pollster, or of a society as a whole. The pollster asks the sample population a series of questions about the issue of concern. In most polls, the responses are provided in advance, and the respondents simply state whether they agree or disagree with a statement or answer a yes-no question. These responses are then tabulated and reported to the sponsoring agency.

In recent elections, pollsters have been criticized for announcing results before the voting is completed, but in most cases increasingly refined polling techniques enable pollsters to make very accurate predictions. There are a number of potential problems in taking accurate polls, however. The sample to be polled and the questions to be asked must be carefully selected because answers to ambiguous or loaded questions may not reflect true opinions. Even those who support a woman's right to abortion might find it difficult to answer yes to a question such as "Do you favor the murder of helpless unborn children?" A question phrased in this way will not

"FRANKLY, I DON'T CARE ONE WAY OR THE OTHER ABOUT VOTER APATHY"

yield representative responses. Polls may also force people to express opinions on subjects they know nothing about. Another problem is that they do not attempt to assess a person's reasons for giving a yes or no response.

Those who sponsor polls often use the results to influence public opinion, which may be done through the use of *propaganda,* attempts to manipulate ideas or opinions by presenting limited, selective, or false information. The purpose is to induce the public to accept a particular view. Propagandists rarely present opposing or alternative views, and when they are presented, they are usually distorted. Propaganda tries to influence people by playing on their emotions rather than by discussing the merits of the various positions, but if it diverges too far from known facts or personal beliefs, the public may simply dismiss it as nonsense.

The use of propaganda in the early 1980s was evident in the controversy over requiring that biblical as well as evolutionary versions of creation be taught in the public schools. Each side issued statements that played on emotions, that diverged from known facts, and that contained limited and selected information. Each side had the goal of inducing people to accept its own point of view. Those who believe in the literal biblical interpretation that God created all matter and energy in six days are not swayed by those who present fossil evidence of evolution covering a time period of millions of years. And those who believe in the separation of church and state are not swayed by the argument that evolution is as much a religious belief as the creation theory. If propaganda is to be successful, it must not conflict too strongly with a person's existing values and beliefs.

Another way to manipulate public opinion is through *censorship*, prohibiting the dissemination of some type of information. A community may try to prohibit sex education, X-rated movies, or the sale of pornographic magazines. A car manufacturer may refuse to release information on a potential danger in a car's construction. Government officials may withhold controversial information, as the United States government did when it kept secret the bombing of Cambodia during the Vietnam war. Censorship manipulates public opinion not by presenting distorted or incomplete information, as in propaganda, but by withholding information that might influence public opinion.

Social Movements

A *social movement* is a collective effort to bring about social change and establish a new order of social thought and action. Movements involve more than a single event or community, they begin during periods of unrest and dissatisfaction with some aspect of society, and they are motivated by the hope that the society can be changed. Initially, social movements are poorly organized. They have no identity, and their actions are often spontaneous. As they develop, however, they acquire an established leadership, a body of customs and traditions, divisions of labor, social rules and values, and new ways of thinking. This process of institutionalization leads to the development of formal organizations and, ultimately, new social systems.

Types of Social Movements

In the United States, a number of new movements have developed in the last few decades, including the civil rights movement, the women's liberation movement, the ecology movement, the peace movement, the gay liberation movement, and the nuclear freeze movement. Each one involves a collective effort to

bring about social change and establish a new social order. Various authorities have used different schemes to classify such movements. Turner and Killian (1972) organize them in terms of their orientation. Value-oriented movements advocate social changes concerning various groups that result in broader adherence to the central values of the larger society. The civil rights, gay liberation, and women's movements, for example, are efforts to fulfill the American values of equality, freedom, and justice. Power-oriented movements aim to achieve power, recognition, or status. The Nazi movement in Germany and the Bolshevik revolution in Russia are extreme examples of this type of movement. Participant-oriented movements focus on personal rewards and fulfillment for their participants. Back-to-nature and evangelical movements are of this type.

Actually, there are as many different kinds of movements as there are goals. Reactionary movements advocate the restoration of the values and behaviors of previous times. Conservative movements attempt to protect the status quo and resist change. Resistance movements are aimed at preventing or reversing changes that have already occurred. Reformist movements try to modify some aspect of society without destroying or changing the entire system. Revolutionary movements believe in the overthrow of the existing social order as a means of creating a new one. Nationalistic movements hope to instill national pride and a sense of identity with one's country. The goal of utopian movements is to create the perfect community. Religious movements want to convert or modify the existing belief system in accordance with a religious principle. Expressive movements would like to change people's emotional reactions to help them cope with prevailing social conditions. Some movements have several purposes or combine the features of several types of movements. Regardless of the way they are categorized, they all involve collective efforts to initiate (or sometimes resist) a new order of social thought and action.

The Development and Life Cycle of Social Movements

Social movements develop most frequently in complex, nontotalitarian societies. They evolve through a series of stages that closely parallel those suggested by Smelser as preconditions of the development of any type of collective behavior. Blumer (1939) divided the development of movements into four steps: social unrest, popular excitement, formalization, and institutionalization. These stages are idealized types, of course, because development varies considerably from one movement to another.

The stage of *social unrest* parallels Smelser's stages of conduciveness and structural strain. This stage is characterized by unfocused restlessness and increasing disorder (Turner and Killian, 1972). Often, we are unaware that others share the same feelings and concerns. Rumors abound, and we become increasingly susceptible to the appeals of agitators. These agitators do not advocate any particular ideology or course of action; rather, they make people more aware of their discontentment and raise issues and questions to get them thinking.

Social unrest is followed by the stage of *popular excitement*. During this period, unrest is brought into the open. People with similar concerns begin to establish a rapport with one another and openly express their anger and restlessness. Then the group begins to acquire a collective identity, and more definite ideas emerge about the causes of the group's condition and how the situation can be changed. Leaders help define and justify feelings, identify the opposition, and point out obstacles that must be overcome. They also offer a vision of what things could be like after the movement succeeds. In the past, movements like these have

Social movements are one form of collective effort for bringing about social change. During the 1980s, an immense military build-up among the world's super powers led to demonstrations and collective expressions of opposition.

SOCIOLOGISTS AT WORK
Public Opinion Research

A. Emerson Smith is the founder, director of research, and one of the major stockholders of Metromark Market Research Inc. in Columbia, South Carolina. This firm gathers information on public opinions and preferences for companies with products to sell to the public. Smith is also a sociologist.

How did Emerson Smith become a marketing researcher? "I did not make a real decision to go into this area," he says. "It just happened that way." In 1974 Smith was an assistant professor at the University of South Carolina, in Columbia. He and another sociology professor, Frank K. Brown, began talking about possible applications for their extensive background in sociology. They wanted something new. So they started a nonprofit research organization called Sociology Research Associates. "Our goal was to do contract work for local and state government agencies. We rented an office, got a phone, had some letterhead printed up, and made arrangements to share a secretary with an architect we knew. We chose nonprofit status because of our training in sociology. We didn't know of one sociologist who worked *as a sociologist* for a profit-making organization.

"Nearly all the work we did in those days was survey research for state agencies and city governments. In 1977 we did some research for a department store chain as part of a survey for the state of South Carolina. This department store asked us to do some surveys in other cities in the southeast, and suddenly we found ourselves doing marketing research. This prompted us to list ourselves in the Yellow Pages as marketing researchers.

"Before 1978 we were listed under the heading *Public Opinion Analysts*. This was the only heading we could find where sociologists would fit, and we were the first ones to use this heading in South Carolina. But we found that we were not getting any calls based on this listing. When we decided to list ourselves under the heading *Marketing Research and Analysis*, we felt that we were not really trained for marketing research, so we went to the university library and looked at all the marketing research periodicals. We discovered that marketing researchers were using many of the methods of sociology and social psychology. In fact, we saw areas where the methods of sociology could be used but weren't. We found that many people in marketing research had business and marketing backgrounds but little training in research methods or statistics."

In 1979, Smith and his colleagues incorporated their business as Metromark Market Re-

fallen to social reformers such as Martin Luther King, charismatic leaders such as Gandhi, and prophets such as Christ. In other instances, it is a group of individuals that clarifies the issues, provides direction, and stirs up excitement. In these cases, the movement becomes increasingly better organized.

During the third stage, *formalization*, a formal structure is developed and rules, policies, and tactics are laid out. The movement becomes a disciplined organization capable of securing member commitment to stable goals and strategies. At this stage, movements make concerted efforts to influence centers of power (Turner and

search Inc. and dissolved Sociology Research Associates.

Smith's job is to plan, conduct, and analyze surveys for companies that have a problem marketing a product or service or are thinking of marketing a new product. "The bulk of my time," he says, "is spent reviewing data and writing summary reports for clients.

"All of our work involves applications of our training in sociology. The marketing director of a department store chain came to us with this problem: Several other downtown stores in a city in Tennessee had decided to close their doors and move to a proposed mall in a fast-growing residential suburb. What proportion of the department store's customers would transfer their business to the new mall? How many new customers could the store expect to attract if it moved to the mall? Many of the downtown store's customers were elderly and poor, and many of the mall's customers would be younger and more affluent. How should the store's current merchandise selection change if it moved to the mall? What changes in advertising and marketing would the store have to make? How far would customers travel to come to the mall store? How much of the family clothing business could a store in the mall have after the first year there?

"First we looked at Census data to see the population changes in this city from 1970 to 1980. This involved application of our training in demography. Then we sent interviewers into the downtown store to ask customers about their shopping habits, and we did telephone interviews of adults within a ten-mile radius of the mall. Here we used our training in survey research. We asked about shopping habits, driving habits, preferences in clothing, and what forms of advertising they paid most attention to in making shopping decisions. We needed to know who made the decision to go to a specific store to shop, so advertising could be directed at these decision-makers. Our background in sociology helped us understand family decision-making."

They also needed to advise their client on possible problems in closing the downtown store. Energy issues and possible downtown revitalization would affect this decision, and their training in urban development and social change found an application here. But perhaps the most important application Smith found for his training as a sociologist, in this and in all his projects, was in the area of statistical techniques. "While I was sitting through six undergraduate and graduate courses in social statistics, I wondered how in the world this was going to be useful to me. Now those statistics courses and textbooks (which I kept) are invaluable."

"We don't try to sell ourselves as sociologists," Smith sums up. "We try to sell the skills we have acquired in our sociological training. Our clients don't care that we have Ph.D. degrees or that we have published in academic journals. Our clients just want to know if we can apply our skills to help them create and sell a product that will make them money."

Killian, 1972). The stable organization of the movement and the establishment of various programs and committees serve to keep members involved after the initial urgency has died down. The leadership shifts from agitators, reformers, or prophets to statesmen or intellectual leaders and administrators. The statesmen develop the ideology, symbols, and slogans that keep the movement alive. The administrators work on procedures, tactics, and organization. It is at this stage that movements often split into factions or break down completely due to differences of opinion over such questions as how the movement should proceed, how radical its tactics should be, and what type of concessions can be granted.

In the formalization stage, it becomes clear that the success of social movements requires more than just successful leadership. A group of committed followers is also needed. It has traditionally been assumed that followers are drawn from the ranks of the discontented, the deprived, the frustrated, and the angry. A more recent perspective, *resource mobilization theory*, suggests that the success of a social movement depends not only on those who benefit from it directly but also on their ability to mobilize other individuals and groups to contribute time, money, and influence to the cause even though they may not directly benefit.

Oberschall (1973) argues that mobilization results, not from the recruitment of large numbers of isolated individuals, but from the recruitment of blocs that are already highly organized and politically active. Gamson (1975) agrees, arguing that collective resources are more important than personal goals in shaping a movement and that one of the most important resources is groups that are already organized. The success of the civil rights movement, for example, depended on the effective mobilization of churches, state and federal agencies, and government leaders, as well as white sympathizers. Martin Luther King and his followers could not have been so successful alone. Likewise, the women's movement, to be effective, needed the support of legislation, the mass media, political leaders, men, and existing groups that supported feminist goals.

If adequate resource mobilization takes place, social movements reach the final stage in the life cycle of social movements, *institutionalization*. During this stage, the movement becomes integrated into society. It may have a permanent office and personnel hired to continue its efforts. At this point, it may have accomplished its primary purpose and disappear into the network of

institutions that already exists. In other instances, the success of a movement leads to the development of new social movements. Some movements never reach this stage — they are suppressed by formal or informal powers and disappear or go underground. At the institutional stage, unrest, discontent, and popular excitement have largely ceased and are replaced by formal offices, organized groups, and structured activities.

The Life Cycle of the Women's Movement

Articles on the origins of the women's liberation movement indicate that this group passed through the four stages typical of movement development. According to Jo Freeman (1973), four factors were essential to the emergence of this movement in the mid-1960s. (1) There was an established network for communication about women's issues. (2) This network could be used to convey the ideas of the new movement. (3) A series of crises galvanized people using this network into action. (4) Subsequent organizing efforts formed the groups into a movement. These four elements reflect the stages of development discussed in the previous section.

Social unrest, stage one, began during the nineteenth century, when organizations such as the Women's Trade Union League, the Federation of Women's Clubs, and the Women's Suffrage Association worked to obtain equal rights. By the 1960s, most of these organizations were relatively small, but the National Women's Party, started in 1916, and other groups remained dedicated to feminist concerns. These organizations served as a lobbying group for the Equal Rights Amendment and helped bring the unrest into the open (the popular excitement stage). During the 1960s, existing and newly formed groups, composed of women who shared similar perceptions and concerns and faced similar crisis situations, began to organize nationally (the formalization stage). Leadership came, not from an individual, as in some social movements, but from a number of sources, and the National Organization for Women (NOW) and its sister organizations were formed. These national organizations began to make use of the media and legal and political means to express their views (resource mobilization) and developed formal rules, policies, tactics, and discipline. Like many social movements, NOW split into several factions in the late 1960s. Today, there is evidence of institutionalization, and in many ways the movement has become an integral part of society. There is widespread sensitivity toward sexist language in textbooks and the media. Affirmative action programs encourage the employment of women, and they are moving into roles formerly considered the province of men. This is not to say that the movement has met all its goals. Many would argue that institutionalization will not be achieved until an equal rights amendment is added to the Constitution.

Summary

Collective behavior is spontaneous, loosely structured, and transitory. Institutionalized behavior, by contrast, is more orderly and has stable goals, expectations, and values. There are two types of collective behavior: spatially proximate, in which people are in face-to-face contact or geographical proximity, and spatially diffuse, in which people are dispersed over a wide geographical area.

Certain conditions increase the likelihood of collective behavior. Smelser described six of them: (1) structural conduciveness, the existence of conditions or situations in which collective behavior is possible; (2) structural strain, some type of frustration, stress, conflict, or dissatisfaction in society; (3) generalized belief, a shared understanding of the reasons for the strain and stress; (4) precipitating factors, events that trigger a

collective response; (5) mobilization for action, in which individuals or groups encourage participation in collective behavior; and (6) the initiation of social controls to counter the conditions just listed.

The most common type of spatially proximate collective behavior is the crowd. The characteristics of crowds are anonymity, suggestibility, contagion, and emotional arousability. There are four types of crowds. A casual crowd such as a street gathering has a momentary existence and little unity. The participants are simply drawn to an event by a common interest. A conventional crowd, such as spectators at a baseball game, follows established social norms and rules. An expressive crowd, like a religious revival or festival dance, is distinguished by physical movement as a form of release. Finally, acting crowds, such as mobs or rioters, are often aggressive and hostile. In acting crowds, the four characteristics of crowd behavior occur in an extreme form.

There are four major theories of acting crowd behavior. The classical theory of Le Bon posited the existence of a collective or group mind that has a regressive influence on behavior, which tends to be irrational, irritable, and impulsive. Blumer's interactionist theory focused on social interactions and a circular reaction process that generates milling, collective excitement, and social contagion. The emergent norm theory of Turner and Killian emphasized how norms influence crowd behavior and how the emergence of new norms causes a divergence of crowd views and behaviors. Berk's game theory stressed the rational decision-making process involved in crowd behavior and suggested that people consciously weigh the rewards and costs associated with various kinds of collective activity.

In spatially diffuse collectives, people who are widely dispersed focus on a common event. The groups who watch a certain television show or buy a given item are considered masses — although they are geographically separate, they participate in a common behavior. Fads and fashions are mass behaviors that large numbers of people participate in for a brief period. Mass hysteria takes place when a potentially destructive or threatening event causes a widespread, highly emotional fear. Sometimes these fears are accompanied by panic, mass flight, or attempts to escape.

A public is a spatially dispersed group confronted with a common issue but divided about how to address it. As the issue is debated or discussed, a variety of public opinions develop, which vary from one public to another. Opinions are influenced by such factors as dominant cultural values, the mass media, group affiliations, and social backgrounds. They can be measured by a type of survey research known as polling. Propaganda and censorship are two ways of manipulating public opinion.

Social movements are organized collective efforts to bring about social change and establish a new order of social thought and action. Turner and Killian classify movements in terms of their orientation, while other authorities use different classification schemes. As social movements develop, they generally go through four distinct stages: social unrest, popular excitement, formalization, and institutionalization. Although all social movements grow through roughly the same process, the goals of different movements can vary considerably. Their success is heavily dependent on their ability to effectively mobilize resources. The life cycle of the women's movement illustrates this process.

Key Terms

acting crowd
casual crowd
censorship
classical perspective
collective behavior

collective excitement
conventional crowd
crowd
emergent norm perspective
expressive crowd
fads
fashions
formalization
game perspective
generalized belief
institutionalization
institutionalized behavior
interactionist perspective
mass
mass hysteria
milling
mobilization for action
mobs
operation of social control
panic
popular excitement
precipitating factors
propaganda
public
public opinion
resource mobilization theory
riots
social contagion
social movements
social unrest
spatially diffuse collectives
spatially proximate collective
structural conduciveness
structural strain

Suggested Readings

Deckard, Barbara Sinclair. **The Women's Movement: Political, Socioeconomic and Psychological Issues, 2d ed.** *New York: Harper & Row, 1979.* A book about changes in the social, economic, and political status of women during the past and present in their struggle for liberation.

Le Bon, Gustave. **The Crowd: A Study of the Popular Mind.** *London: Ernest Benn, 1895; Dunwoody, Georgia: Norma S. Berg, 1968.* An early classic on collective behavior.

Perry, Joseph B., Jr. and M. D. Pugh. **Collective Behavior: Response to Social Stress.** *New York: West Publishing, 1978.* An introduction to the field of collective behavior covering theoretical developments and research results.

Piven, Frances Fox and Richard A. Cloward. **Poor People's Movements: Why They Succeed and How They Fail.** *New York: Pantheon Books, 1977.* A book about protest movements among the poor in the United States, including the civil rights and welfare rights movements, industrial workers, and the unemployed.

Pugh, Meredith D. **Collective Behavior: A Sourcebook.** *New York: West Publishing, 1980.* A collection of twenty-four articles on collective behavior covering theory, disaster research, collective violence, and social movements.

Smelser, Neil J. **Theory of Collective Behavior.** *New York: The Free Press, 1962.* An important, systematic theoretical work on collective behavior that attempts to explain the conditions under which it occurs and the forms it takes.

Turner, Ralph and Lewis M. Killian. **Collective Behavior, 2d ed.** *Englewood Cliffs, N.J.: Prentice-Hall, 1972.* A textbook that covers the nature and emergence of collective behavior and the organization and functioning of crowds, the public, and social movements. It also contains a section of selected readings.

Wright, Sam. **Crowds and Riots: A Study in Social Organization.** *Beverly Hills, Calif.: Sage, 1978.* The results of a three-year study of crowds and riots.

Zald, Mayer M. and John D. McCarthy. **The Dynamics of Social Movements.** *Cambridge, Mass.: Winthrop, 1979.* Papers delivered at a 1977 symposium at Vanderbilt University on tactics, resource mobilization, and the social control of movements.

CHAPTER 19

Population and Ecology

We have come to a turning point in the human habitation of the earth.

— Barry Commoner

If you are like most people, you worry about the population a great deal, even though you may not realize it. By "population" we mean the number of people in a society. The population affects your chances of finding a job and a spouse. If you do marry, it is likely to influence the age of your spouse, whether you have children, and how many you will have. It may also affect your chances of being promoted, your taxes, the age at which you will retire, and your income after retirement. Sometimes we also worry about population problems in the larger world. Poverty, disease, accident and death rates, world hunger, the problems of crowded cities, vanishing farmlands — all are population problems. Lest this all sound too gloomy, we should point out that some of the most practical things we can do to resolve problems involve studying the population in hopes of influencing it. By understanding the size, age, sex ratios, and movements of the population, we may be able to better understand our own lives and plan sensible social policies to shape the world's future.

Figure 19-1 is a population pyramid, a graph that shows how many males and females from each age category there are in the United States today. Find in the left-hand column the category containing the year you were born, noting that the bars extending to the left and right represent the males and females born in those years. By looking at the bottom of the graph, you can determine the percentage of people of your age and sex in the population. If you were born between 1965 and 1969, the bottom line tells you that about 8 percent of the population consists of people your age — 4 percent male and 4 percent female. Notice also how the pyramid bulges out for the years between 1955 and 1964 and how it

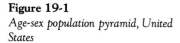

Figure 19-1

Age-sex population pyramid, United States

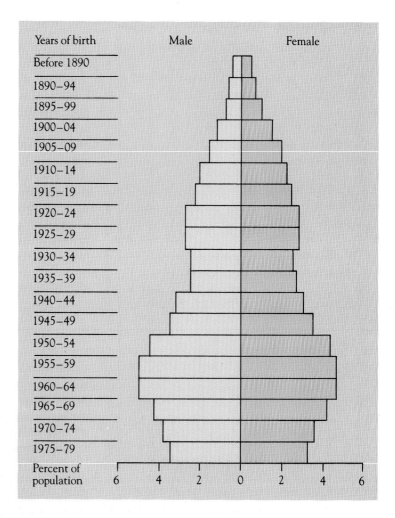

becomes smaller again in later years. The bulge represents the people born during the baby boom.

Why were so many people born in the middle of this century? During the depression of the 1930s and World War II in the 1940s, many people postponed having children. After the war, the country was both peaceful and affluent. Those who had postponed having children began families, and those who were just entering

their twenties began having children too. Because the times were so affluent, some people decided to have three or four children instead of just two.

How has the baby boom affected your life? If you had been born when it began, you might not have gone to nursery school because they were full. Schools were crowded, and you might have gone to elementary school in a temporary classroom building. If you had gone to school at the end of the baby boom, your school might have closed shortly after you left it. Some students, especially those in suburban areas, watched their elementary schools close, went to a junior high school that was closed while they were there, moved to a second junior high, and saw that one close before they had finished senior high school.

Baby boom children had to compete for space in college. When they completed their education, unemployment rates were high because so many people were competing for jobs and because only a small part of the work force was retiring to create more job openings. The drop in the unemployment rate in 1984 was largely a result of a drop in the number of young people entering the job market. The unemployment rate may continue to drop as more older people — those born after 1920 — begin to retire in the mid-1980s. The vacancies they leave may be filled by those born during the baby boom, but they are more likely to be filled by people born later because industry prefers to hire younger workers at lower wages.

The baby boom generation caused great changes in fashion. Miniskirts became the vogue because manufacturers began to design clothes for this age group when they were very young, and only the very young look good in miniskirts. Youngsters born during this time represented a big market, and manufacturers catered to them. It became stylish to be thin because adolescents tend to be thin during their period of rapid growth, and a whole nation dieted to look like adolescents. Previously the mark of beauty was to have a more well-developed figure like Marilyn Monroe or Betty Grable. Now that the baby boom generation has grown older, clothing manufacturers are changing styles to meet the market for clothes for more mature figures, and the miniskirt has been replaced by stretch blue jeans with a fuller-cut thigh and an elastic waist. Also, the health club business is growing rapidly because this age group wants to stay thin and look

Health clubs and physical fitness centers have become popular over the past few years — with the baby boom generation especially. Members enjoy a wide variety of activities and regularly scheduled events such as swimming, aerobics, and nautilus exercises as shown here.

young. Today, there is more emphasis on makeup and hair color, and the fuller, more mature figure is coming back into style.

Women born during the baby boom are more likely to marry at an older age or to stay single than was true in earlier generations. Why? Because women traditionally marry older men, and a look at the population pyramid shows that there is a shortage of older men for these women. Women born late in the baby boom or after it have many older men to marry, so they may marry at a younger age.

Men born late in the baby boom who want to follow the normative practice of marrying younger women face a shortage. They may set a new trend by marrying slightly older women.

Imagine that bulge in the population pyramid when the baby boom reaches age sixty-five or seventy. Think of how many people will be on Social Security! By the time they reach that age, they will have held and may still hold powerful positions in business and government. Moreover, because they will be a large voting bloc, they may be able to control decisions about continuing the support of Social Security benefits. Since the smaller population just younger than the baby boom may have a large tax burden to help support all the people in retirement, it is to be hoped that the younger population will be fully employed. By studying population and predicting how it will affect our lives, we are able to tailor public policy planning to accommodate these shifts in population trends.

Demography and the Study of Population

Demography is the study of the size and makeup of the human population and how it changes. Demographers want to know how many babies are being born, what diseases there are in the population, how long people live, whether they stay in the same place or move about, and whether they live in remote regions or crowded urban areas. This information makes it possible to recognize changing trends in the population and help plan social policies. Where will new houses and jobs be needed? What diseases should be investigated most thoroughly? How many elderly will require care in 1995? It is questions such as these that are addressed by demographers.

Collecting the Data

Demographers use many statistics in their work. After all, their main concern is counting people. In fact, the word "demography" is often used to refer to the study of population statistics. The statistics demographers use are fortunately rather straightforward and easy to understand, and they are also readily available.

Societies have always realized how important it is to know about their members and since early times have kept some form of *census*, a count of the population with a record of the age and sex of its members. From such records estimates of early populations can be made and studied. For hundreds and sometimes thousands of years, family lineages have been recorded and passed on orally to keep track of who was born to whom. Records of deaths can be found in early Greek and Egyptian accounts. The Bible says that Mary and Joseph were on their way to be counted in a Roman census when Jesus was born.

Modern nations keep much more reliable records of their populations. The first census in the United States was carried out in 1790, and censuses are still carried out once every ten years with questionnaires mailed to all known households. In addition, interviewers search door to door for those who are not contacted or do not respond by mail. A smaller census is made every year, which may be more accurate than the ten-year census because it is based on a carefully chosen random sample of the population and it is done by expert interviewers who use every available method to ensure its accuracy.

In addition to population counts, *vital statis-*

Francis W. Edmunds' painting The Census Taker *(1854) depicts such a person as he visits a home to record the names and ages of everyone in the family. Often family members could not read, write, or accurately spell their names; sometimes they were not sure how old they were. Even though these older records are not entirely accurate, they have been used by many American families to trace their family history.*

tics — records of all births, deaths and their causes, marriages, divorces, certain diseases, and similar data — are recorded in each state and reported to the National Center for Health Statistics. Most modern nations keep records as accurate as those of the United States. Underdeveloped nations also attempt to record their populations, and although data from these countries may be relatively inaccurate, they provide enough information to study world population trends.

Three variables can cause the size of the population in a given region to change: (1) births, (2) deaths, and (3) migrations. Demographers measure these factors in terms of their rates. *Fertility* is a measure of the rate at which people are born. *Mortality* is a measure of the rate at which people die. *Migration* is the movement of people into or out of a geographical area. To understand how populations change, it is necessary to understand how demographers measure these factors.

Fertility

Fertility data indicate the rate at which babies are born. The crude birth rate is simply the number of births per 1,000 population, but if we want to predict how many babies will actually be born, more information is needed. We must know the *age-sex composition* of the society, the number of men and women in the population, along with their ages. A population with few women will have few children. The ages of the women are especially important because young girls and older women do not have babies.

In most societies, the number of men and women is about equal. About 105 males are born for each 100 women, but women live longer than men. Thus there may be more men at younger ages, but there are more women in older groups. During the childbearing years, the number of men and women is usually about equal except in societies suffering from wars in which large numbers of men are killed or in societies experiencing a great deal of migration. Areas that men move out of have a surplus of women, whereas the areas they move into have a surplus of men, and a society with unequal numbers of men and women will have a low birth rate. There was an imbalance of this sort in the Soviet Union because so many men were killed during World War I, the Civil War of 1917–1921, World War II, and the repressive era following World War II. As a result, many women were left without husbands and did not have children, and the birth rate dropped dramatically. For years the Soviets kept secret their great loss of manpower and low birth rates, but the latest available information indicates that they are now comparable to the United States in birth rates and population size.

Demographers generally assume that women are fertile from age fifteen to age forty-nine. They also know that more children are born to women in the middle of their childbearing years, but some women in their childbearing years choose not to have children, and few have as many as they potentially could. A woman's potential for bearing children is called her *fecundity*. Although women can potentially have twenty to twenty-five children, very few have this many.

Fertility varies greatly among societies and among subcultures within societies. The Hutterites, a religious group in the northwestern United States, apparently have the most children of any American subculture. The mean number of children reported by women between forty-five and fifty-four years old was 10.6 (Eaton and Mayer, 1953). Swedish women have the fewest children, fewer even than women in the United States, who have one of the lowest birth rates in the world (Heer, 1975).

The number of children born in a society is affected by three major factors: wealth, environment, and societal norms about marriage and children. Generally, richer nations have lower birth rates and poorer nations have higher birth rates. The same relationship between wealth and birth rates holds within nations: the upper classes usually have lower birth rates than the poor classes.

Fertility rates are also different in rural and urban areas. Women in rural areas usually have more children than those in cities. In rural areas, children are needed to help with farm labor, but in modern urban areas, children are not productive. Rather, they are an expense to house, feed, clothe, and educate. They may also decrease a family's income because a parent may have to stay home to care for them. Many demographers believe that the birth rate of the world will decline and perhaps drop sharply as underdeveloped nations become more industrialized and urban.

A society's norms regarding the value of children and the age at which marriage is considered acceptable have a strong effect on fertility rates. In countries where women marry young the birth rates are higher than those where they marry later because of differences in the number of childbearing years. Norms about the number of children a family should have and about the acceptability of birth control and abortion also affect the birth rate. Separation by war, working away from home, and conflicts between spouses reduce the birth rate, whereas abstaining from intercourse during the menstrual cycle may make intercourse more likely during fertile periods and result in an increased birth rate.

A low or high fertility rate will of course affect the number of people born into the population, but this is only one of several factors that influence population size. Mortality and migration rates are also influential.

Mortality

Mortality, the rate of death in a population, can be measured very simply. The crude death rate is the number of deaths in a given year per 1,000 population. Like the crude birth rate, however, the crude death rate does not provide enough information to predict how many people will die or to compare death rates among populations. For a more accurate estimate of the death rate, demographers consider age and sex. A population with many old people will have a higher death rate than a comparatively young population, and because women live longer than men, a population with many women will have a lower death rate. Demographers often use an *age-adjusted death rate*, a measure of the number of deaths at each age for each sex, usually per hundred thousand living at that age. Demographers can also compute life expectancy by predicting how many of each *cohort*, or age group, will die at each age.

Mortality, like fertility, varies with wealth. When people, especially infants, have adequate food, housing, and medical care, they are less likely to die of disease. The rate of infant mortality, death in the first year of life, was very high in the Middle Ages, but now it is lower and the average life expectancy has been greatly increased. Infant mortality is low and life expectancy high in more developed nations like the

The birth rate is higher in rural areas and in poorer classes. This large North Carolina family is both rural and poor. A large number of children is often considered an asset, as they can help a great deal with family chores and, as they grow older, provide security to their parents.

United States, Canada, and European countries. People in Norway, Sweden, and the Netherlands have the longest life expectancy. An infant boy in these countries can expect to live seventy-two years, an infant girl seventy-eight years. The death rate is higher and the life expectancy shorter in India, Africa, South America, and Southeast Asia, where poverty is widespread. Death rates also vary by class within nations. In the United States, poor people have a higher rate of infant mortality and a shorter life expectancy than the rich, and blacks, a larger proportion of whom are poor, have more infant mortality and a shorter life expectancy than whites, as discussed in Chapter 11.

Migration

Migration includes both *immigration*, movement into an area, and *emigration*, movement out of an area. Migration is harder to define and measure than birth or death rates. How far must one move and how long should one remain in a place to be considered a migrant? In the United States, moving within a county is not considered migration, but moving from one county to another is. Migrant workers who travel about the country doing farm labor are not technically considered migrants because rather than remaining in a new location after the work season is over, they return to their original starting point and take up jobs in that area.

Why do people move? Demographers speak in terms of push factors and pull factors. *Push factors* are those that push people away from their homes: famines, wars, political oppression, loss of jobs, or bad climate. Austria, for example, reported that the number of emigrants from Poland increased dramatically during the recent labor and economic troubles. *Pull factors* are those that make a new place seem more inviting: the chance to acquire land or jobs, the discovery of riches such as gold or oil, or the chance to live in a more desirable climate. Discoveries of gold in California, for example, drew fortune seekers from all over the world.

There have been migrations since early in history when waves of migrants moved out of Asia into the Middle East and eastern Europe. Later, tribes moved further into Europe, spreading their culture as they moved. It is assumed that these waves of migration were caused by push factors such as changes in climate, changes in food supply, or pressure from increasing pop-

ulations in Asia, and pull factors such as Europe's warmer climate.

The population of Europe increased slowly throughout the Middle Ages. When Columbus discovered America, a new wave of migration began. It started slowly, but it is estimated that over 60 million Europeans eventually left Europe. Many later returned, so the net migration, the actual population change, was much lower (Heer, 1975).

Between 1820 and 1970, 46 million migrants entered the United States (Thomlinson, 1976). In a single peak year, 1854, a total of 428,000 immigrants came to this country. This group consisted mainly of Irish leaving their country because of the potato famine and Germans leaving as political refugees. A second peak was reached around the turn of the century, when immigrants averaged a million a year. Most of the Europeans who entered the United States at that time were from Italy or other southern and eastern European countries.

Another great migration was of a different sort. Between 1619 and 1808 400,000 Africans were forced to migrate to the United States as slaves. Between 10 and 20 million Africans were brought to the entire Western Hemisphere (Thomlinson, 1976).

Immigration restrictions were first imposed in the United States in 1921 and again in 1924 to slow the rate of immigration. During this period, most immigrants were from Canada, Mexico, Germany, the United Kingdom, or Italy. After 1965, immigration quotas were relaxed and a new wave of immigrants, many from Southeast Asia, entered the country.

Migration within the United States has also been extensive. Throughout this country's history, people have moved from the East to the West and from rural to urban areas. After World War I, for example, when immigration was restricted and the supply of laborers entering the country was limited, northern cities recruited southern blacks to fill labor jobs, but many more blacks moved to northern cities than there were jobs for. Most recently, people have been migrating from northern to southern (or Sunbelt) cities such as Houston, Phoenix, and Charlotte, North Carolina.

Rate of Population Change

The rate of population change is determined by all the factors discussed above. If the birth rate is high and the mortality rate is low, the population increases. If the mortality rate is high compared with the birth rate, the population will decline. As shown in Figure 19-2, countries in which the population is very young, such as Mexico, can be expected to grow rapidly as children mature and have children of their own. In Sweden, where there are more older people, the population will grow slowly, but the large

Figure 19-2
Population pyramids of a young population (Mexico) and an older population (Sweden)

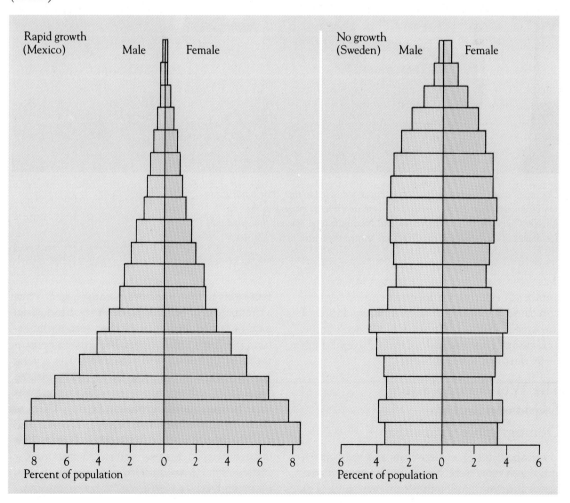

The recent wave of immigrants to the United States led to this mass naturalization ceremony, when 9,700 immigrants were sworn in as citizens at the Los Angeles Coliseum. U.S. Immigration and Naturalization officials processed the documents of each new citizen as they all waited their turn in the hot sun.

number of elderly who need to be cared for may be a cause for concern. The overall population of the world more nearly resembles Mexico's and is expected to grow rapidly because of overall high birth rates and low death rates.

The World Population Explosion and the Demographic Transition

Until about two hundred years ago, both birth and death rates were very high. As a result, the size of the world population remained stable. For every person who was born, someone died. Then a dramatic change took place. First, in industrial nations in the early part of the nineteenth century, the death rate dropped because of improvements in nutrition and sanitation. For several generations, however, the birth rate remained high. (This is the period when what we now refer to as the population explosion began.) Then, in about 1850, the birth rate began to decrease also and the rate of population increase slowed. This change from high birth and death rates to low birth and death rates with a period of rapid population growth in between is known as the *demo-*

Figure 19-3

World birth and death rates (estimated)

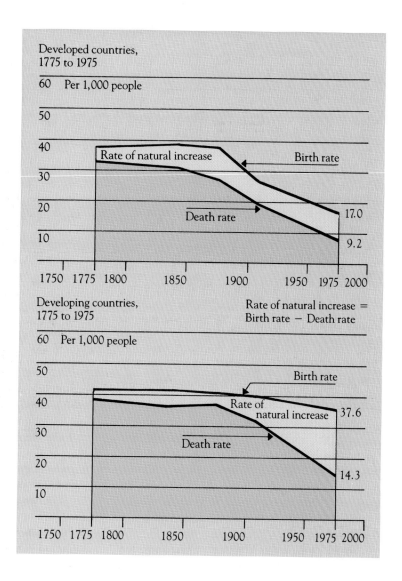

Developed countries, 1775 to 1975

60 Per 1,000 people

50

40

Rate of natural increase   Birth rate

30

20   Death rate   17.0

10   9.2

1750 1775 1800   1850   1900   1950 1975 2000

Developing countries, 1775 to 1975

Rate of natural increase = Birth rate − Death rate

60 Per 1,000 people

50   Birth rate

40   Rate of natural increase   37.6

30   Death rate

20   14.3

10

1750 1775 1800   1850   1900   1950 1975 2000

graphic transition. It occurs as a society evolves from a traditional premodern stage to a modern industrial stage; most European nations and other industrial countries have already passed through it. Other countries, particularly those in the Third World, still have very high birth rates. It is in these countries that population growth continues at very high rates (see Figure 19-3). While it had taken the human race from the beginning of history to 1850 to reach a population of one billion people, it took only an additional one hundred years to reach 2 billion, and now, only thirty years later, the population stands at about 4.5 billion (see Figure 19-4).

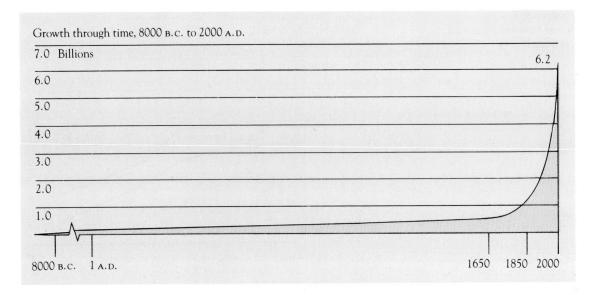

Growth through time, 8000 B.C. to 2000 A.D.

Figure 19-4
World population growth

Population Density

The population explosion has dramatically increased the number of people in the world, but migrations have not distributed people evenly over the face of the earth. While the population is sparse in many areas of the world, in some regions it is extremely dense. Such areas cannot provide the natural resources needed to maintain their population.

The United States, although it has absorbed millions of immigrants, has a relatively low population density. In some remote areas, the density is only five people per square mile. In major cities during the business day, on the other hand, the population density is as high as 100,000 people per square mile. For the whole country, the density is sixty people per square mile.

The other highly industrialized nations of the world have a higher population density than the United States. In Europe, it is very high.

France has an average of 252 people per square mile; West Germany, 642 people per square mile; and Belgium, 842 people per square mile — higher even than Japan's very dense average of 811 people per square mile. The Netherlands is the most densely populated country in Europe, with 1,000 people per square mile.

The developing nations are less densely populated than European countries, and are not highly industrialized, and therefore have less wealth to support themselves. China, the largest nation in the world, now has a population of over one billion people, but its area is so great that its population density is only 278 people per square mile. There are places in the Third World where the population density is so very high that the land cannot begin to support the human life in the area, and the poverty is devastating. Bangladesh, the most densely populated country in the world with 1,530 people per square mile, is also one of the poorest countries.

Population and Ecology

How large a population can survive on the earth's resources? The study of the interrelationships between living organisms and the environment is called *ecology*. In the case of human beings, the concern is that the environment will not be able to support human life with the necessary food, water, and other basic necessities if the population should get too large.

Interestingly, theories about the relationship between population and the environment were initially developed during a period when it was feared that there were too few people to produce what society needed. Between 1450 and 1750, European traders were exporting Europe's products in exchange for gold and silver. In some areas, however, one-third to one-half of the population had been killed by the plague. Many writers argued that if the population were larger, there would be a better ecological balance. More products could be produced and exported, which would bring more gold and silver to the merchants. If the population were large enough, labor would be cheap, wages could be kept low, the people would have little to spend, and increases in imports would not be needed. Thus all increased production could be traded for gold, silver, or merchandise valuable to the traders.

The political activity of this period was designed to encourage a high birth rate. The birth rate did increase, and by 1750, writers had begun to worry about overpopulation. The most famous of these writers was Thomas Malthus.

Malthus's Theory of Population

Thomas Robert Malthus (1766–1834) argued in his *Essay on the Principle of Population* that because of the strong attraction between the two sexes, the population could increase by multiples, doubling every twenty-five years. According to *Malthusian theory*, the population would increase much more rapidly than the food supply. Two people might have four children, these four children might have sixteen children, and so on. Furthermore, Malthus believed that the

The world population explosion has led to a dramatic increase in the population density of many countries. Unfortunately, the supply and distribution of food is inadequate to provide the minimal nutritional requirements for many of the people. One example, that of Bangladesh, is shown here.

more intensively land was farmed, the less the land would produce and that even by expanding farmlands, food production would not keep up with population growth. Malthus contended that the population would eventually grow so large that food production would be insufficient, and famine and crowding would cause widespread suffering and increase the death rate, which is nature's check on overpopulation. Malthus suggested as an alternative that the birth rate be decreased, especially through postponing marriage until a later age.

The debate about Malthusian theory has continued down to the present. Writers such as John Stuart Mill and the economist John Maynard Keynes supported his theory. Others have argued against it. Karl Marx, for example, contended that starvation was caused by the unequal distribution of the wealth and its accumulation by capitalists.

Malthus's contention that food production could not increase rapidly was much debated when new technology began to give farmers much greater yields. In fact, the French sociologist Dupreel (1977) argued that an increasing population would spur rapid innovation and development to solve problems, whereas a stable population would be complacent and less likely to progress.

During the depression of the 1930s, the debate changed somewhat because the birth rate fell sharply in industrial nations. Some predicted that the human species would die out, first the Caucasians, then other races. Schemes were proposed to encourage families to have more children by giving them allowances for each child born. Many economists, however, believed that even in societies with smaller populations, people could prosper and industry could grow if the wealth were redistributed to increase consumption by poor families. Government spending on programs for the poor and unemployed could be increased, and low interest rates could be used to encourage spending on houses, cars, and other consumer goods. These demand-side economic programs were widely adopted during the Great Depression.

The birth rate rose sharply after World War II, especially in the underdeveloped nations; people starved in Bangladesh, Africa, and India. Birth control programs were instituted, and it was argued that the only way to eliminate starvation was to reduce the birth rate.

World Food Distribution Today

Before World War II, Africa, India, and Asia exported grain to other nations, primarily to the industrial nations of Europe (George, 1977). Why, then, are people in these underdeveloped nations starving today?

Some analysts argue that the land in overpopulated areas has been farmed too intensively to provide food for large populations and thus has been ruined. Even the United States with its comparatively low population density has lost 10 to 15 percent of its farmland through soil erosion since the time of the European immigration (Humphrey and Buttel, 1982). In parts of Asia, Latin America, and Africa, the problem is much worse because overuse of the land is causing it to deteriorate very rapidly. In Africa, the size of the Sahara Desert is increasing by 30 miles a year because the land cannot sustain the population using it.

Other observers of the world food situation have criticized American corporations for creating the world food shortage. They contend that because we had a surplus of grain, we encouraged underdeveloped nations to grow nonfood cash crops such as cotton and rubber or nonnutritious foods such as coffee, tea, and sugar. The United States would lend money and supply fertilizer and farm equipment only to nations who agreed to grow products it needed. In Brazil, for example, the United States encouraged soybean production, but American corporations own all the soybean processing plants and receive most of the profit from soybean production.

In the last few decades, many underdeveloped nations have become increasingly dependent on American grain imports because they use their land for nonfood products. In the 1970s, the price of grains rose dramatically, and critics argue that the United States, having acquired a monopoly of the food supply, increased prices to make enormous profits. Today, the cash crops grown by other nations cannot be sold at prices high enough to buy all the grain needed from the United States. Thus poor people everywhere starve because they do not have land on which to grow food or money to buy food, even when enough food is produced in the world to feed all its people.

Population and Other Natural Resources

Food production and distribution is only one of the problems that occurs as the world population increases. Humans need water just as they need food, and the earth's large human population is rapidly polluting the available water. Waste from modern life, including the many chemicals that are now produced each year, find their way into small streams and large seas, making the water unfit for human consumption. It also makes water unfit for fish, thereby eliminating any hope of turning to the sea for a source of additional food. Because of the pollution of waters and overfishing, the supply of fish has been decreasing since 1970 (Brown et al., 1976).

The increased population also affects the air we breathe. As the population increases, more and more rural areas become densely settled and atmospheric pollution is exacerbated by the toxic elements emanating from cars, planes, industrial smoke, and other sources. Almost every human activity generates dust, and these particles become airborne, seed clouds, and increase rainfall. In New England in recent years, pollution from midwestern industries has caused acid rain to fall, killing fish and changing the composition of the land on which it falls. Another pollution-related problem is that as the cloud cover increases with airborne pollutants it has a "greenhouse effect," holding warmth from the sun close to the earth rather than letting it escape into the upper atmosphere. As a result, the cli-

An ecological concern of many citizens focuses on the quality of the air they breathe. Sometimes, particularly in and around major urban industrial areas, the air becomes so concentrated with automobile exhaust, smoke, and other pollutants that heavy haze and smog result.

An Unwanted Baby Boom

Liu Chunshan, an illiterate peasant from Shandong Province, had a problem: a four-year-old daughter and a wife who was pregnant in violation of the state's one-child-per-family policy. After a soothsayer told him the new baby would be a son, Liu threw his daughter down a well. He watched while she drowned, ignoring her tearful pleas of "Papa, Papa." "Without a son, the generations cannot be passed on and we remain childless," he said later. Caught and convicted, he was sentenced to 15 years in prison. And his wife gave birth to a second daughter.

One after another such horror stories make the papers in China. Despite efforts to stop female infanticide, the practice has become an ugly side effect of the country's efforts to control a runaway population. Family-planning officials are up against relentless demographic pressure: more than half of China's 1 billion people were born since 1949, and a vast "baby boom" generation is now reaching childbearing age. The state toughened its family-planning policy in 1979 to cope with an impending "echo boom." Even that may not be enough to meet China's goal of limiting the population to 1.2 billion by the year 2000. Now Chinese officials are taking harsher measures to enforce the one-child-per-family rule. The 1982 constitution makes practicing birth control a civic duty, and the state has launched vigorous abortion and sterilization campaigns.

Fines

The strategy is based on a system of incentives. Couples who pledge to have one child are granted monthly bonuses, priority in school enrollments, jobs and housing; those who have more than one are subject to stiff fines, have their paychecks docked and lose benefits and raises. The plan has worked fairly well in urban areas. The irony is that China's economic reforms are undermining the incentives in the countryside. New agricultural policies allowing peasants to keep much of what they produce have made large families profitable — and many peasants wealthy enough to pay the fines. As one farmer told

mate of the earth will become warmer and icebergs may begin to melt, which could raise the sea level and flood coastal areas.

Our forests are also being rapidly depleted. Trees are cut down to make room for people, to provide fuel, and to provide wood for houses, furniture, and other products. The loss of forests not only means the loss of these wood products but also affects the ecological balance between the earth and the atmosphere.

As these natural resources are lost — and the loss will be rapid if we do not use resources wisely — conflict will occur. People who lack the necessary resources to survive will fight those who do have resources. Although conflict in the world is expressed in political terms and we hear about the United States fighting "communist expansion" in the Middle East or in Latin America, these conflicts are not based on political ideology. They are conflicts over scarce resources. The United States' involvement in the Middle East is motivated largely by our desire to safeguard our supplies of oil. The war between India and Pakistan arose because they did not have the resources to supply the needs of their peoples. Latin-American countries such as El Salvador and Nicaragua cannot provide for the peasants who have been driven off their land by the larger agriculturalists — a dilemma that induces revolution. If conflict is to be ended, increasing population must be accompanied by an end to the unregulated freedom to pursue wealth and a more equitable rationing of the world's scarce resources.

People's Daily, "If we produce more children, that's our business and nobody can interfere."

The most sensitive issue is where birth control leaves off and human-rights violations begin. There have been reports of pregnant women forced to undergo abortions as late as the eighth month of pregnancy. Last year even women expecting their first child without permission were presssured to take "remedial measures." Sterilization is increasingly common as well; 10 million such operations were performed between January and August last year. Officials in Peking deny the practice is obligatory, which would violate United Nations guidelines and jeopardize China's request for additional U. N. family-planning aid. But officials in some provinces have proclaimed that compulsory sterilization for at least one parent of two-child families is indeed part of China's official family-planning policy.

Prime Minister Zhao Ziyang publicly condemned female infanticide in 1982. No one knows how widespread the practice has become since then; but Chinese newspapers report that in some rural areas the ratio of male to female children is as high as 5 to 1. The problem is rooted in economic reality: lacking a nationwide retirement system, Chinese peasants rely on their children to support them in later years. Sons represent old-age insurance, while daughters traditionally support their husbands' families.

"Social Cost"

The practice is likely to persist until China establishes a pension system — or relaxes its one-child-per-family rule, something authorities say will not be possible until the baby-boom generation passes out of childbearing years. In the meantime, some women are illegally removing birth-control devices; some families are sending children to live with grandparents in distant provinces. Others have reportedly even murdered meddling family-planning cadres. China "could achieve the numerical population goal by the year 2000 — but it would be at tremendous social cost," says University of Chicago sociologist William Parish. The alternative is also bleak. As Chinese couples are constantly reminded, unchecked population growth will mean shortages of jobs, food, clothing, housing and services for them and, for China, a future no brighter than the present.

Political Policies on Population

Although a more even distribution of resources would solve some of the world's hunger problems, and careful planning would help us preserve what resources we still have, ultimately our population must be controlled. Current government policies are aimed at reducing the birth rate to improve the standard of living. After World War II, Japan initiated a program legalizing abortion and encouraging contraception. Soon afterward, India and most other Asian nations began such programs. In the 1960s, the United States began to offer millions of dollars' worth of contraceptive aids, especially intrauterine devices and birth control pills, to underdeveloped countries requesting help in controlling their populations. The federal government also provided funds to states to open family planning clinics and disseminate information about contraceptives in this country. These programs have succeeded in reducing birth rates in many nations, but they have also been severely criticized, for several reasons.

First, some of the contraceptive methods used in underdeveloped nations are those considered unsafe and banned in the United States. Users in other countries, not warned of the dangers, unknowingly risk infection, heart attacks, strokes, and death when they use these contraceptives. Second, lowering the birth rate in underdeveloped nations deprives parents of children, who are an asset in rural areas. They can help carry water and grow food on family

Monitoring Population Trends

Mathew Greenwald is director of the social research services department of the American Council of Life Insurance (ACLI). He and the ten-person staff he supervises have an unusual responsibility. Their job is to monitor how our society is changing today and to predict how it will change in the future. Their conclusions are used in constructing insurance policies and preparing for the future of the insurance business.

"Whole life policies can run for fifty or sixty years," Greenwald explains, "so we have an interest in the long view. People will be collecting on some of the policies we're selling now in the year 2045. Of course, some aspects of the social world are so volatile that it's difficult to say what will be happening fifteen years from now. But we can make some forecasts. For example, we know that Social Security will be in trouble in 2011. That's when the first year of the baby-boom generation, those born in 1946, will be retiring. We also expect important medical breakthroughs in such areas as cancer research. Certain trends in computerization and global economics will probably also continue. Thus, while there's a lot we can't know, some trends can be accurately predicted, and the more we know the easier it is to make decisions."

"The primary purpose of life insurance is to replace income if a family breadwinner dies or is disabled, so the insurance business is bound up with many basic social institutions," Greenwald says. "We use survey research to keep track of a number of trends on an ongoing basis, including attitudes toward death, retirement, and family responsibility. We also use demographic data about factors such as health, birth rates, death rates, divorce rates, and the number of women working." As you might expect, major social developments influence the sales of life insurance policies. "Now that families are more dependent on wives' income, women are buying much more insurance than they did previously. We're also finding that sales among blacks and Hispanics are increasing as these groups become more affluent."

The group Greenwald supervises also contributes to the public debate on bioengineering

plots and care for their parents in illness and old age. Thus we see that policies used to reduce poverty in Japan could well increase poverty in underdeveloped countries. When planning policy, it is crucial to consider all the factors at work in the countries that will be affected.

Zero Population Growth

The goal of current world population policy is *zero population growth*, which is achieved when parents have only two children, just enough to replace themselves. If this practice were followed, the population would remain the same generation after generation. In reality, of course, some people do not have children and some children die before reaching adulthood, so zero population growth could be attained if couples averaged slightly more than two children each. Given current rates of infant mortality and the number of women who actually have children,

and medical ethics. "Researchers are now working on replacements for something like twenty-seven parts of the human body," he says. "As some of these do develop we'll have to deal with a number of controversial ethical issues. Will these replacement parts be available only to the affluent? Should they be available to everyone? How should "test-tube" babies be covered in the mother's health insurance? On a more fundamental level, now that we've developed the ability to prolong life in some cases, when can we say that a life has ended? Under what circumstances should it be prolonged? There are lives at stake in some of these matters. We as a society have to make decisions on these issues or the insurance business will be affected by what is decided."

In addressing complex questions such as these, Greenwald draws heavily on his training in sociology. He has a Ph.D. from Rutgers University. "The sociological perspective is of crucial importance," he says. "It's really a certain type of logic, a guide for analysis. It gives me a structure for assessing situations. I might approach a family-related problem by looking at it in terms of statuses and roles, for example. More concretely, my training is useful in developing questionnaires and doing survey research. It's helped me with my interviewing skills, understanding what questions needed to be asked. In my coursework, I've found my classes in methods and statistics useful.

My work in theory, health, population, and the family has also been very valuable."

In addition to following demographic trends, Greenwald and his department often undertake special projects. One recent study concerned the public's sense of control over key aspects of their lives. Their findings? "Sadly, we found that people feel they have less control than they did ten and fifteen years ago, especially over the long term. This is probably a result of a number of factors — inflation, a volatile economic system, Watergate, Vietnam. It's unfortunate. People who don't feel that they have much control are less likely to take a stand and try to change the situation — they don't take advantage of the control they do have. As concerns the insurance business, there's evidence that feelings of lack of control are associated with ill health."

When it comes to sociologists, Greenwald predicts that in the future more will be working in business, for two reasons. "First," he says, "is that academic work is in short supply — the field is simply overcrowded. Sociologists are going to have to move into new areas to find work. Second, business is becoming more sophisticated and can make better use of sociological analysis. An advanced degree won't be necessary. An M.A. is useful, but a Ph.D. is not essential. A B.A. would be good for entry-level jobs."

the population would remain stable if couples averaged 2.1 children.

The 2.1 zero growth rate is maintained in Japan and many European countries. In the United States the rate has been dropping; in 1980, it was 2.2, just a bit above the zero growth rate. Many underdeveloped nations have much higher birth rates, however, so the world population explosion is continuing.

Increasing population and associated ecolog-

ical problems will continue to be crucial issues in the future. A more equal and careful distribution of resources is essential to prevent starvation and pollution. If hunger is caused by the practices of capitalists, reducing the population will not prevent the world's poor from starving. This relationship between population and ecology illustrates the need for a sociological understanding of the interrelationships between population size and social institutions.

The concern over the rapid growth of world population has led to concentrated efforts by most countries of the world to establish family planning centers and birth control clinics. Many developing nations have established national policies and programs aimed at limiting population growth. Here a trained health worker meets with a group of women in India to educate and discuss ways to control fertility.

Summary

The size of the population affects each of us quite personally. Whether we are born into a growing or a shrinking population has a bearing on our education, the age at which we marry, our ability to get a job, the taxes we pay, and many other aspects of our lives.

Demography is the study of population statistics. Demographers study census data on the number of people in the population and records of births and deaths to compute the birth and death rates. Their goal is to understand how the population is changing.

The crude birth and death rates are computed by determining the number of births and deaths per 1,000 people. Neither of these measures takes age or sex into account, but these factors also influence the number of births and deaths.

Populations remain stable when people are born at the same rate that they die. They increase when the birth rate exceeds the death rate and decrease when the death rate exceeds the birth rate. They may also change through migration. Push factors are conditions that encourage people to move out of an area, while pull factors encourage people to move into an area.

The population explosion of the last two hundred years occurred because of improvements in nutrition, medicine, and sanitation, which lowered the death rate. In industrial nations, the birth rate has also dropped, but rapid population growth continues in many Third World countries. Population densities vary greatly in different parts of the world.

Ecology is the study of the interrelationship

between organisms and the environment. Malthus argued that because the population grows faster than the food supply, starvation is inevitable if population growth is not controlled. Although his arguments have received much support through the years, critics contend that the world produces enough food to feed everyone but that food is distributed unequally.

Some underdeveloped nations raise cash crops that neither feed the people nor bring in enough money to buy food. Some observers believe that the United States, which is the world's largest food exporter, encouraged other countries to grow nonfood cash crops and then, having cornered the grain market, raised prices to increase profits.

Other problems affecting food production vis-à-vis population stem from pollution of the air and water and the destruction of forests. Most nations are now attempting to reduce their birth rates, and contraceptives have been distributed throughout the world for this purpose. It is expected that the size of the population will decrease as the world becomes urbanized, and it is hoped that eventually the world will reach zero population growth, calculated to be an average of 2.1 children per family. Until this goal is reached, the size of the population and the distribution of food will continue to be major problems.

Key Terms

age-adjusted death rate
age-sex composition
census
cohort
demographic transition
demography
ecology
emigration
fecundity
fertility
immigration
Malthusian theory
migration
mortality '
pull factors
push factors
vital statistics
zero population growth

Suggested Readings

Heer, David M. **Society and Population.** *Englewood Cliffs, N.J.: Prentice-Hall, 1975.* A concise overview of the study of population and demography.

Humphrey, Craig R. and Frederick R. Buttel. **Environment, Energy, and Society.** *Belmont, Calif.: Wadsworth Publishing Co., 1982.* Although the title of the book implies that energy is the first concern of the authors, their discussions of population and food supplies are excellent.

Jones, Landon. **Great Expectations. America and the Baby Boom Generation.** *New York: Ballantine Books, 1981.* A detailed description of the impact of the baby boom on American society.

Overbeek, Johannes (ed.). **The Evolution of Population Theory.** *Westport, Conn.: Greenwood Press, 1977.* A collection of articles on population, beginning with Malthus's theory and including a sampling of later writers who agreed or disagreed with him. It is interesting to note how long the population debate has continued with few new twists in the arguments.

Simon, Julian L. **The Ultimate Resource.** *Princeton: Princeton University Press, 1981.* Simon argues the less popular view that an increasing population can be valuable and that the human mind can create ideas to develop and supply the ever-increasing amounts of resources needed for a growing population.

Thomlinson, Ralph. **Population Dynamics. Causes and Consequences of World Demographic Change.** *New York: Random House, 1976.* A comprehensive text on population.

Valentey, D. I. (ed.). **The Theory of Population. Essays in Marxist Research.** *Moscow: Progress Publishers, 1978.* The Soviets are serious students of population. This collection of essays translated into English will help you understand their point of view.

CHAPTER 20

The Changing Community

To live is good. To live vividly is better. To live vividly together is best.
— Max Eastman

The towns and cities of the United States and the rest of the world have been changing rapidly for many years. The communities in which many of you were brought up have probably undergone dramatic changes during your lifetime, or even since you entered college. Some of these changes are readily apparent: one of your favorite old buildings may have been razed to make way for a new office complex, or perhaps a new park has been created near your home. Other changes, although less tangible, are equally important. The streets you played on as a child may now be considered unsafe after dark. You may have trouble finding a summer job because several large businesses have left your city.

The reasons for changes such as these are many. We touched on a number of them in earlier chapters. Form of government, the family, changing gender roles, bureaucracies, ethnicity — the list of factors that influence the communities we live in is endless. Past and present trends in community living, their causes, and the problems they have brought are the subject of this chapter.

The Origin and Development of Communities

A *community* is a collection of people within a geographic area among whom there is some degree of mutual identification, interdependence, or organized activity. This term is applied by sociologists to a variety of social groups, including small North American Indian tribes, towns, communes, and large urban centers. As we will show, urban communities have become larger and more diverse throughout the course of human history.

Early Community Development

The first communities, which originated over 35,000 years ago, were small bands that hunted and foraged for food. Their means of subsistence dictated the size and activity of the group: they were nomadic, moving frequently to new areas as food ran out. There were few status distinctions among members of these communities, although males and older persons had somewhat higher status and more power than others. Apparently there was little conflict between hunting and gathering bands. We find little evidence of war-making tools or group attacks (Lenski, 1966). This rather idyllic form of community predominated for about 25,000 years.

Roughly ten thousand years ago, humans learned to produce and to store their food. This "Neolithic revolution," as it was called, ushered in the era of horticultural communities. *Horticulture* was essentially small-scale farming that relied on tools such as the hoe to till the soil. Though horticulture was tedious, back-breaking work, it doubled the number of people the land could support — from one to nearly two persons per square mile (Davis, 1973). Stable communities developed around fertile agricultural regions, and in the more fertile areas a surplus of food was produced, which freed some members of the community from agricultural activities. As agricultural techniques improved, horticultural communities became larger and more diverse. Craftsmen who produced the tools and implements necessary for survival were the first specialists in history (Childe, 1951). It was during this era, which lasted about seven thousand years, that the first urban communities emerged.

An urban community is one in which a number of people are not engaged in the collection or production of food (Ucko et al., 1972). The earliest cities, which developed along the fertile banks of the Tigris and Euphrates rivers, were small by modern standards. Cities could grow only as large as the food surplus allowed; that is, the release of a number of people from agriculture required that the remaining members produce more than before. Ancient Babylon, for example, had a population of 25,000 and covered roughly three square miles; Ur, one of the oldest known cities, had about 5,000 people and covered less than a square mile (Cook, 1969; Davis, 1970). Urban communities grew slowly for the next several thousand years because of the inefficiency of horticultural techniques — it took about fifty horticulturalists to produce enough surplus to support one urban resident — and also because of the primitive political and social organization (Davis, 1973).

Preindustrial Urban Communities

The introduction of metals, the invention of the plow, the use of animals for transportation and farming, and the refinement of irrigation techniques helped usher in a new era in human history around 3000 B.C. — the Agrarian Age (Lenski, 1966). The development of writing and counting and the evolution of political and social organizations were also essential to the spread of agrarian society. These technological advances increased surpluses, so more people were freed from agriculture. Cities grew larger and their activities became more diverse. Around 1600 B.C., Thebes, the capital of Egypt, had a population of over 200,000. Athens had a population of 150,000 or so during the same period (Childe, 1951). By the first century A.D., Rome had an estimated population of over half a million.

This trend of urban growth was not to continue, however. Rome fell in the fifth century, and subsequent wars and plagues reduced the size of cities. The rate of agricultural innovation was slow because human energies were directed toward the technology of war. The social system became more rigid: status and occupations were determined on the basis of heredity rather than achievement or ability.

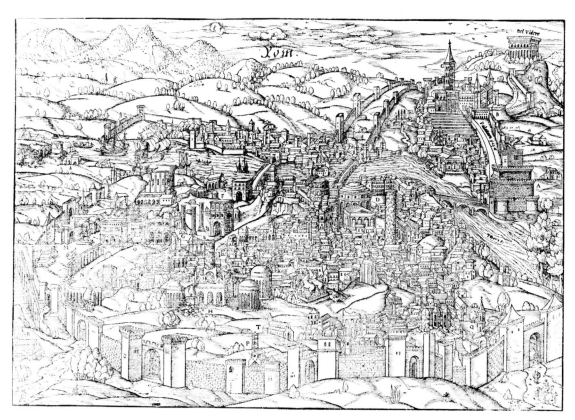

Preindustrial Rome differs radically from Rome today or other cities in industrialized societies. Rome became the largest of all the preindustrial cities, yet its population never numbered more than a few hundred thousand people. Beyond size, these cities served as crossroads for trade and as centers of learning and innovation. They encouraged a non-agricultural occupational specialization and a more rigid division of labor by sex in the creation of goods. Class systems were basically closed with little social mobility.

In the eleventh century, cities, especially those along natural routes and junctures, began to flourish after feudal wars subsided. As the food surplus increased, the population in the cities became more specialized. In fourteenth-century Paris, for example, tax rolls listed 157 different trades (Russell, 1972). In addition to craftsmen, cities also had specialists in other areas such as government, military service, education, and religion. Each major urban activity led to the development of an institution devoted to its performance, and churches, shops, marketplaces, city halls, and palaces became the prominent features of medieval cities.

Community Development in the Industrial Era

It was not until the end of the eighteenth century that cities began to grow rapidly, due largely to the effects of the industrial revolution. The social and economic forces that converged at this time eventually changed Western Europe and later the United States from rural to urban societies. The growth of the number of people who live in urban rather than rural areas and the subsequent development of different values and lifestyles are referred to as *urbanization*. Agricultural innovations — crop rotation, soil fertilization, and the selective breeding of animals — brought larger and larger surpluses. At the same time, the development of manufacturing in the cities attracted many people. As the nineteenth century progressed, cities became much larger and grew into centers of commerce and production, but they were at the same time the locus of poverty and disease. Also, as migration from rural areas increased, the city population became more heterogeneous. The variety of occupations, ethnic backgrounds, dialects, and lifestyles in these urban areas stood in sharp contrast to the relatively homogeneous populations of small towns and rural communities. Population diversity, poverty, cramped living quarters, inadequate garbage disposal and sewage facilities, and other social and economic problems placed a tremendous strain on the urban political order. Cities became centers of unrest. Riots and revolutions, strikes by workers, and numerous clashes among members of different social groups were a significant part of nineteenth-century urban history. Many of the problems that arose in European cities during this era persist to some degree in Western nations and in a differing way in Third World nations.

Third World Urbanization

Prior to 1900, urbanization outside of Western Europe and North America was limited in both scale and extent to colonial expansion. Throughout this century, however, the situation has been changing dramatically. During the last fifty years, the urban population of the developed regions increased by a factor of 2.75 while in the Third World countries it increased by a factor of 6.75 (Berry, 1973). Urbanization was fastest in the least developed countries. In Latin America and Africa, the urban population increased eightfold.

By the end of World War II, the colonial powers had relinquished control to the governments they had created. In each developing nation, one city became the focus of change and progress. Because these cities had improved health conditions and facilities, more jobs, and better education, they drew masses of people. The newly created governments, usually controlled by military juntas or totalitarian regimes, were unable to keep pace with this rapid growth, however, and those who had moved from the country found that they had exchanged lives of rural poverty for lives of urban poverty.

Much of this Third World urban growth became concentrated in "squatter" settlements. People would settle temporarily — squat — along railways, highways, the banks of streams, or on vacant government land. Most major cities in developing countries have squatter areas: Manila in the Philippines; Calcutta, India; Lima, Peru; Saigon, Viet Nam. Although these areas lacked all the basic amenities, were physically decrepit and highly disorganized, and became centers of squalor, illiteracy, sickness, and human depravity, they played an important role in solving the housing shortage and the other complex problems associated with migration from rural to urban centers. On closer examination, they were found to provide access to the jobs and services of the central city. Many squatter areas developed highly organized self-help efforts over a period of a few years. The residents gave shelter, security, and assistance to one another, and many of these settlements provided opportunities to continue rural values and ways of living, thereby easing the transition to the density and fast pace of the city.

To Western observers the solution to these "problem" areas was to relocate them and provide housing, usually outside the central city limits. These solutions rarely solved the problems of most squatters, however, for they involved heavy interest, maintenance, and transportation costs and did not originate in the self-help efforts of the squatters themselves. Often funded by developed nations, these efforts tended to follow patterns established in the Western world, ignoring the values and priorities of the Third World residents themselves. They also tended to overlook the importance of urban community services and failed to follow through on a long-term basis with a commitment to the residents themselves. In most Third World countries, one of the residents' high priorities is to own or have a secure right to the land they occupy. These problems, which have existed in most Third World countries throughout this century, are more severe today than ever before because of rapid population growth.

Urbanization in the United States

The industrial revolution began approximately half a century later in the United States than it did in Western Europe. The major population shift from rural to urban areas did not begin here until the Civil War. An urban area, according to the United States Census, is a city or town that has at least 2,500 inhabitants. In 1800, 6 percent of the population of the United States lived in urban areas (see Table 20-1). This figure rose to 20 percent by 1860. The period of greatest urban development took place during the sixty-year period between 1860 and 1920; by the latter date, slightly more than half the population lived in urban areas. This figure has continued to in-

Squatter areas are common in most major cities of developing countries. Many families with no money or resources migrate to urban centers in search of jobs and food. Having no place to live, they construct a shelter from discarded wood or tin. Poor sanitation and health conditions prevail which leads to high rates of disease, sickness, and death.

Table 20-1

Urban population: 1800–present

YEAR	URBAN POPULATION[a]	PERCENT URBAN
1800	322,000	6
1820	693,000	7
1840	1,845,000	11
1860	6,217,000	20
1880	14,130,000	28
1900	30,160,000	40
1910	41,999,000	46
1920	54,158,000	51
1930	68,955,000	56
1940	74,424,000	57
1950	96,468,000	64
1960	124,899,000	70
1970	149,325,000	74
1980	167,051,000	74

[a] All numbers and percentages are rounded.

SOURCE: U.S. Bureau of the Census, *Statistical Abstract of the United States: 1984*, 104th ed., U.S. Government Printing Office, Washington, D.C., 1983, no. 32, p. 32.

crease until today about three of every four Americans live in an urban area.

Why do people live in cities? The answer is that an increasing number of jobs in our society are nonagricultural. Thus the shift of the population from rural to urban areas has paralleled the growth of jobs and opportunities in the industrial and service sectors. Because of their early industrial and commercial development, northeastern states such as New York and Pennsylvania were among the first to urbanize. A few years later, midwestern cities such as Chicago and Detroit became large urban centers. The western states experienced strong urban growth only after World War II as a result of the growth of the defense industries. Today the South and Southwest are our fastest growing regions. As can be seen in Figure 20-1, in the last decade the population of the West increased by 24 percent

and that of the South by 20 percent. Population projections by Census demographers (*Statistical Abstract: 1984*, no. 14) for the decade between 1980 and 1990 show an additional 22 percent growth in the West (from 43 to 53 million) and a 16 percent growth in the South (from 75 to 88 million). This growth in the Sunbelt states contrasts with a projected 2.1 percent growth in the North Central region and a 1.7 percent decline in the Northeast region. A number of businesses have relocated in the Sunbelt because of the economic advantages this area offers: primarily low wage scales, few problems with unions, cheap land and energy, and low taxes. As history demonstrates, people want to move to areas that provide, or at least are perceived as providing, good employment opportunities. A number of Sunbelt businesses have been advertising their job openings in city newspapers in the "Snowbelt" states, and they have attracted many skilled specialists to Sunbelt areas. This loss of industry and commerce in Snowbelt cities has magnified their social and economic problems.

The Metropolitan Community

The large, densely populated cities of the early 1900s have given way to the growth of metropolitan areas. The U.S. Bureau of the Census describes a *Metropolitan Statistical Area* (MSA) as a large population nucleus together with adjacent communities that have a high degree of social and economic integration with that nucleus. The metropolitan community is the organization of people and institutions that performs the routine functions necessary to sustain the existence of both the city and the area around it.

The growth of metropolitan areas has been rapid and dramatic (see Table 20-2). Numerous areas in Florida, Texas, Arizona, and California, for example, have had a 40 to 65 percent increase in the past decade. Because of new developments in technology, in transportation, and in social structures, the concentration of large numbers of people has become possible. These same developments have also enabled a population dispersed over a wide area to become part of a larger, integrated community.

Metropolitan growth was caused initially by a shortage of space for industrial development, new housing, and new highways. Businesses were forced to design their facilities to fit the space that was available. Because streets were narrow and heavily congested, the transportation of goods was tedious and costly. Room for storage and loading was scarce. The land adjacent to the cities was ideal: it was inexpensive, taxes were low, and businesses could design their facilities to suit their needs. The development of the steam engine and, later, the electric trolley facilitated the transportation of goods and employees over a wider area (Hawley, 1971). After the

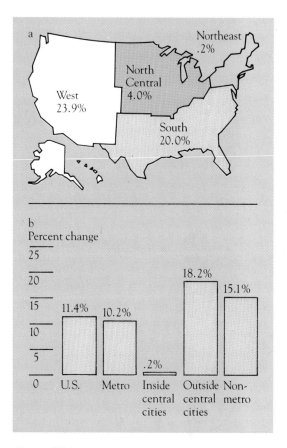

Figure 20-1
(a) Resident population — percent change: 1970 to 1980. (b) Metropolitan/Nonmetropolitan population: 1970 to 1980.

1920s, the increase in motor vehicles and the accompanying growth of highway systems stimulated unprecedented metropolitan development. Trucking became an important method of moving goods and supplies (Dobriner, 1970). As manufacturing and industry moved to the suburbs, so did the people and a variety of small businesses and stores. After World War II, hundreds of suburbs developed, each of which

Table 20-2

Population growth in metropolitan areas and the selected Sunbelt states, in millions

	1970	1980	GROWTH, %
High growth Metropolitan Statistical Areas			
West Palm Beach–Boca Raton	349	577	65.3
Phoenix	971	1,509	55.4
Orlando	453	700	54.4
Tucson	352	531	51.1
Austin	360	537	48.9
Tampa–St. Petersburg–Clearwater	1,106	1,614	46.0
Houston	1,891	2,736	44.7
Miami–Fort Lauderdale	1,888	2,644	40.0
San Diego	1,358	1,862	37.1
Riverside–San Bernardino	1,139	1,558	36.8
Anaheim–Santa Ana	1,421	1,933	36.0
Salt Lake City	684	910	33.1
Denver–Boulder	1,238	1,618	30.7
Atlanta	1,684	2,138	27.0
Dallas–Fort Worth	2,352	2,931	24.6
State populations			
Nevada	489	800	63.8
Arizona	1,775	2,718	53.1
Florida	6,791	9,746	43.5
New Mexico	1,017	1,303	28.1
Texas	11,199	14,229	27.1
California	19,971	23,668	18.5
Oklahoma	2,559	3,025	18.2

SOURCE: U.S. Bureau of the Census, *Statistical Abstract of the United States: 1984*, 104th ed., U.S. Government Printing Office, Washington, D.C., 1983, no. 23, pp. 20–22.

had its own government, school system, and public services. The suburban growth paralleled a slower growth and recently a decline in the population of central cities.

Table 20-3 shows the size of the twenty largest cities in the United States in 1970 and 1980 and the percentage of population change in the past decades. Several changes are noteworthy. More than half of these cities declined in population. The greatest declines were in Cleveland

and Detroit, major industrial and blue-collar cities in the northern Midwest of the United States. The greatest gains were all Sunbelt or "new technology" cities: San Jose, Phoenix, Houston, San Diego, and San Antonio. Concern over flight from the cities to the suburbs and the death of the large city is not universal, however. Northern industrial cities such as New York, Boston, Detroit, and Cleveland declined in population over the past decade, but southern cities

Significant characteristics of cities and metropolitan communities include density of population and the congestion of people. Jobs, shopping, and theatres in selected areas cause masses of people to leave their residential communities and descend upon the central city. Visibly absent from the hustle and bustle of these congested areas are large numbers of children and elderly persons.

such as Los Angeles, San Diego, Houston and others grew.

A metropolitan area that extends beyond the city and the Metropolitan Statistical Area is the *megalopolis,* which is a continuous strip of urban and suburban development that may stretch for hundreds of miles. One example exists between Boston and Washington, D.C. on the East Coast. This megalopolis covers ten states, includes hundreds of local governments, and has a population of nearly 50 million. Other megalopolis areas are forming between San Francisco and San Diego on the West Coast and between Chicago and Pittsburgh in the Midwest. Sometime in the next fifty years, half the United States population may live in one of these three enormous population conglomerations.

Nonmetropolitan Growth

During the first seventy years of this century, metropolitan populations grew far more rapidly than nonmetropolitan ones. Between 1970 and 1980, however, while the population increased by 23.2 million, 7.5 million of that growth (a 15.1 percent change) was in nonmetropolitan areas (*Statistical Abstract: 1984,* p. xvii). As can be seen in Figure 20-1B, the greatest percentage change occurred outside central cities (18.2 percent) while the growth inside central cities was a mere .2 percent. Virtually all metropolitan areas grew significantly less and nonmetropolitan areas grew significantly more during the 1970s than they had previously. Why are these changes taking place?

In some ways, the same factors that stimulated the development of the suburbs (cheap land, low taxes, ease in commuting) are responsible for the growth of rural areas. Manufacturing development is one factor, but more important is the growth of specialized areas of recreation and retirement. Scenic areas and those with hospitable climates have grown considerably in recent years, and a number of "retirement communities" have sprung up in Florida, Arizona, and

Table 20-3

Size and population change of twenty largest U.S. cities: 1970–1980

	1970 POPULATION	1980 POPULATION	POPULATION CHANGE: 1970–1980, %
1. New York, N.Y.	7,896,000	7,072,000	− 10.4
2. Chicago, Ill.	3,369,000	3,005,000	− 10.8
3. Los Angeles, Calif.	2,812,000	2,967,000	5.5
4. Philadelphia, Pa.	1,949,000	1,688,000	− 13.4
5. Houston, Tex.	1,234,000	1,595,000	29.3
6. Detroit, Mich.	1,514,000	1,203,000	− 20.5
7. Dallas, Tex.	844,000	904,000	7.1
8. San Diego, Calif.	697,000	876,000	25.5
9. Phoenix, Ariz.	584,000	790,000	35.2
10. Baltimore, Md.	905,000	787,000	− 13.1
11. San Antonio, Tex.	654,000	786,000	20.1
12. Indianapolis, Ind.	737,000	701,000	− 4.9
13. San Francisco, Calif.	716,000	679,000	− 5.1
14. Memphis, Tenn.	624,000	646,000	3.6
15. Washington, D.C.	757,000	638,000	− 15.6
16. Milwaukee, Wis.	717,000	636,000	− 11.3
17. San Jose, Calif.	460,000	629,000	36.9
18. Cleveland, Ohio	751,000	574,000	− 23.6
19. Columbus, Ohio	540,000	565,000	4.6
20. Boston, Mass.	641,000	563,000	− 12.2

SOURCE: U.S. Bureau of the Census, *Statistical Abstract of the United States: 1984*, 104th ed., U.S. Government Printing Office, Washington, D.C., 1983, no. 29, pp. 28–30.

other states. Finally, the growth of rural areas is the outcome of a traditional "antiurban" mentality. The move to the suburbs resulted in part from negative attitudes toward city living because of crime, decay, pollution, and other problems. At the same time, people have a positive attitude toward suburban living because of the clean air, low crime rate, and open space. As suburbs become more congested and experience some of the same problems as large cities, however, the entire metropolitan area comes to be regarded as an area to escape from. Also, nonmetropolitan growth is limited by job and time constraints. Many people cannot leave the metropolitan area because they are tied to their jobs

and many cannot move farther from the city because commuting would become too costly and time-consuming. The nonmetropolitan population of the 1980s will probably consist mainly of the affluent who can afford to move, those who have flexible work schedules that permit long travel times, and those who are not tied to jobs, such as the elderly.

Urban Ecology

In recent years, "ecology" has come to be associated with the biological and "natural" world of plants and animals and how they are affected by pollution and other environmental influences, but it is also concerned with populations and communities. In this context, it is the study of the interrelationships of people and the environment they live in. *Urban ecology* is concerned not only with urban spatial arrangements but also with the processes that create and reinforce these arrangements.

Urban Processes

Urban areas are not static; they change continually. The urban environment is formed and transformed by three processes: (1) concentration and deconcentration, (2) ecological specialization, and (3) invasion and succession.

The term *concentration* refers to increasing density of population, services, and institutions in a region. As people migrate to the city to find jobs, living quarters become scarce and the institutions that serve the people become strained. This starts an outward trend, called *deconcentration* as land values and taxes increase and services and public facilities decline. As a result, the core of the city — the central business district — eventually comes to consist of businesses that use space intensively and can afford to pay the economic costs, usually prestigious department and retail stores, financial institutions, high-rise luxury apartments, and other profitable ventures.

People, institutions, and services are not randomly distributed in the city. Different groups and activities tend to be concentrated in different areas. This phenomenon is called *ecological specialization*. Commercial and retail trade concerns are generally found in a different part of the city than manufacturing and production. Similarly, public housing and low-rent tenements are not located near suburban residences. The basic principle at work is that people and institutions usually sort themselves into spatially homogeneous groups. As we have indicated, this homogeneity may result from economic factors: people gravitate toward places they can afford. Personal preference is also influential, as is evi-

dent from the existence of ethnic communities and areas that attract people with a particular lifestyle such as Greenwich Village and Chicago's Gold Coast.

Changes in community membership or land use result from *invasion* by other social groups or land users, which leads to *succession* as the old occupants and institutions are replaced by the new. We can give a number of examples of this process. As cities increased in size, areas that consisted originally of single-family dwellings were converted to commercial or industrial use. A recent example is the displacement of residents in an ethnic community called "Poletown" in metropolitan Detroit by a huge automobile assembly complex. Perhaps the most notable case of invasion and succession is that which is reflected in the changing racial composition of central cities. The "white flight" of the 1960s and 1970s changed the racial composition of large cities such as Detroit, Atlanta, and Washington, D.C. from predominantly white to predominantly black. A related development is the "ghettoization" of inner cities, which occurs as minorities become trapped in central cities that have diminishing tax bases, deteriorating housing, and inefficient public services.

Urban Structure

The three ecological processes just discussed are the basis for different models of urban structure. One of the most influential models during the early development of ecological theory was the *concentric zone model*, developed by Ernest W. Burgess (Burgess, 1925) in the 1920s (see Figure 20-2). According to this theory, a city spreads out equally in all directions from its original center to produce uniform circles of growth. Each zone has its own characteristic land use, population, activities, and institutions. At the center of the city is the business district, which consists of retail stores, civil activity centers, banks, hotels, and institutional administrative

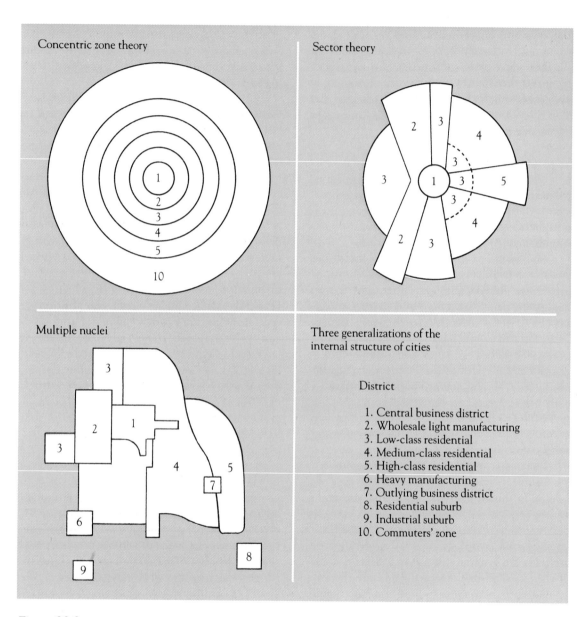

Concentric zone theory

Sector theory

Multiple nuclei

Three generalizations of the internal structure of cities

District

1. Central business district
2. Wholesale light manufacturing
3. Low-class residential
4. Medium-class residential
5. High-class residential
6. Heavy manufacturing
7. Outlying business district
8. Residential suburb
9. Industrial suburb
10. Commuters' zone

Figure 20-2
Ecological models of urban structure

offices. Zone 2, the transitional zone, contains older factories, wholesale and light manufacturing businesses, and low-rent tenements. It is in this zone that immigrants or migrants are likely to live when they first arrive in the city. At the turn of the century, first-generation European immigrants made their home in this zone, but today it is populated by minorities: blacks, Hispanics, and other ethnic groups. Zone 3 marks the edge of the residential areas and consists of progressively more expensive houses and apartments, ending finally with the commuter zone.

Since its formulation, Burgess's zone theory has come under considerable attack. Many cities do not fit the concentric zone pattern, which is more characteristic of commercial-industrial cities than of administrative cities. Commercial-industrial cities are those built around industry, for example, Detroit, Cleveland, Pittsburgh, and so forth. These cities have a high proportion of blue-collar workers. Administrative cities such as Washington, D.C. or New York City rely heavily on government, education, and nonindustrial businesses. Also, it seems to more accurately describe cities like Chicago that developed at the turn of the century than cities like Houston that are developing today (Schnore, 1965).

There are two major alternatives to Burgess's theory. One is the *sector model* formulated by Hoyt (1939). According to Hoyt, the city is organized into pie-shaped wedges radiating from the central business district. Patterns of land use — industrial, high-income residential, and low-income tenement — tend to extend outward from the city core in internally consistent sectors or wedges. An industrial zone might radiate from the core in one wedge and spread into the suburbs, whereas high-income housing might push from the core in another wedge. Hoyt noticed this pattern in several large cities, notably Minneapolis and San Francisco.

The third theory of spatial growth rejects the idea of a single urban core or center, main-

taining instead that areas of different land use have different centers. This is the *multiple nuclei model* formulated by Harris and Ullman (1945). In their view, each area expands from its center, and the form of expansion may fit either the concentric or sector zone models. In many ways, the multiple nuclei model describes the growth of metropolitan areas better than the growth of central cities.

These three models do not reflect every possible variety or pattern of growth. Urban expansion is influenced by a variety of factors, including rate of migration into the city, cultural and historical precedents for urban development, and the physical characteristics of the land. As a result of these and other factors, Latin American cities, for example, do not fit American growth patterns, and cities built near major waterways grow differently from other cities (Thomlinson, 1969). Sociologists today are developing more complex models of urban development that take into account a wide variety of factors, including social, economic, and cultural variables.

Life in Cities and Suburbs

Metropolitan areas, urban areas, cities, and towns are generally defined and described in terms of population. But the term "community" suggests some degree of interdependence, mutual identification, or organization of activities. The emergence of urban communities has altered human lifestyles and values. The size, complexity, and density of urban communities have given rise to new forms of social organization, new behaviors, and new attitudes. One of the major questions sociologists have grappled with is why urban communities are different from rural areas in so many ways, rather than just the fact that they are larger and more densely populated. Sociologists have long recognized that there are qualitative differences between urban and rural life, and Ferdinand Tönnies (1887), a German sociologist, made a distinction in this regard nearly a century ago. He called small, rural villages of his boyhood gemeinschaft (communities); the centers of activity he called gesellschaft (associations).

A *gemeinschaft* community is characterized by a sense of solidarity and a common identity. It is a primary community rooted in tradition. Relationships between neighbors are intimate and personal, and there is a strong emphasis on shared values and sentiments, a "we" feeling. People frequently interact with one another and tend to establish deep, long-term relationships. Small towns and communes generally have many of these characteristics.

A *gesellschaft* community, in contrast, is based on diverse economic, political, and social interrelationships. It is characterized by individualism, mobility, impersonality, the pursuit of self-interest, and an emphasis on progress rather than tradition. Shared values and total personal involvement become secondary. People live and work together because it is necessary or convenient, and people are viewed more in terms of their roles than as unique individuals. In a large city, for example, one is likely to interact with a policeman as a public servant or authority figure who has certain stereotyped characteristics and obligations. In a small town, on the other hand, one would be likely to know a policeman personally. Rather than viewing him as a manifestation of a certain form of authority, one would know him as an individual with certain unique character traits. Historically, there has been a shift from gemeinschaft to gesellschaft relationships as a result of role specialization and, more generally, of bureaucratization. In the nineteenth century, Weber labeled this as a change from a traditional to a rational society. In the twentieth century, American sociologists have used these ideas as a springboard for their own theories. In the next two sections, we will examine some of

these theories about the quality of life in cities and suburbs.

City Life

One American sociologist, Robert Redfield (1941), developed a typology similar to those formulated by ninetenth-century scholars. He distinguished a *folk society*, which is small, isolated, homogeneous, and kin-oriented, from an urban society, which is large, impersonal, heterogeneous, and fast-paced. Around the same time, Louis Wirth, a colleague of Redfield's at the University of Chicago, described the effects of large numbers, density, and heterogeneity on urban life. In "Urbanism as a Way of Life" (1938), Wirth argued that as the population in an area becomes denser, lifestyles diversify, new opportunities arise, and institutions develop. At the same time, density increases the number of short-term, impersonal, and utilitarian social relationships a person is likely to have.

According to Wirth, these three factors — large numbers, density, and heterogeneity — create a distinct way of life called "urbanism." The distinctive characteristics of urbanism are an extensive and complex division of labor; an emphasis on success, achievement, and social mobility, along with a behavioral orientation that includes rationality and utilitarianism; a decline of the family and kinship bonds and a concurrent rise of specialized agencies that assume roles previously taken by kin; a breakdown of primary relationships and the substitution of secondary group control mechanisms; a replacement of deep, long-term relationships with superficial, short-term relationships; a decline of shared values and homogeneity and an increase in diversity; and finally, segregation on the basis of achieved and ascribed status characteristics.

Milgram (1970) has focused on the effects of urbanism. In midtown Manhattan, for example, someone can meet 220,000 people within a ten-minute walking radius of his or her office and

Tönnies described two contrasting orientations to social and community life. One orientation, termed gesellschaft, he saw as relationships that occur contractually and are based on formal, impersonal, and legal terms. The other, gemeinschaft, referred to relationships that occur "naturally" and are based on informal, personal, and nonlegal terms. Gesellschaft is more typical of large cities, whereas gemeinschaft is more typical of small villages.

not recognize a single person! Such an experience, says Milgram, may cause "pyschic overload" and result in the detached, "don't get involved" attitude that is frequently cited as a part of big city life. There have been a number of recorded incidents, for instance, in which people have been mugged, raped, or beaten in plain view of pedestrians who refused to help the victim.

These views of urban life give the impression that it is cold, violent, and alienating. City living conditions have been viewed by scholars as the cause of crime, mental illness, aggression, and other serious problems, but recent studies by sociologists have questioned the validity of this assessment. Certainly these negative aspects of city life do exist; the real question is how typical or widespread they are. Several studies have found that there is considerable cohesion and solidarity in the city, particularly in neighborhoods where the residents are relatively homogeneous in terms of social or demographic characteristics. The findings of early sociologists may have accurately described the central core of American cities such as Chicago during periods of rapid growth. Contemporary research illustrates that a variety of lifestyles and adaptations can be found in cities.

A fine example of research on the diversity of urban lifestyles has been presented by Herbert Gans (1962). He argues that there are at least five types of residents in the city: cosmopolites, singles, ethnic villagers, the deprived, and the trapped.

Cosmopolites usually choose to remain in the city because of its convenience and cultural benefits. This group includes artists, intellectuals, and professionals who are drawn by the opportunities and activities generally found only in large urban centers. They are typically young, married, and involved in upper-middle-class occupations.

Singles like to live in the city because it is close to their jobs and permits a suitable lifestyle. The central city, with its nightclubs and "singles only" apartments, offers a basis for social interaction. It gives singles opportunities to make friends, develop a social identity, and eventually find a mate (Starr and Carns, 1973). Many of these people are not permanent urban residents; they live in the city only until they marry, at which time they move to the suburbs.

The third group identified by Gans, ethnic villagers, generally consists of working-class people who have chosen to reside in specific areas of the city. Their neighborhoods often develop a distinctive ethnic color as shops, restaurants, and organizations spring up. The Chinatowns in New York and San Francisco and the Polish communities of Chicago and Detroit are neighborhoods of this type. Because of their strong ethnic ties, they usually do not identify strongly with the city, nor do they engage in many of the cultural, social, or political activities. Their identity and allegiance are tied to the ethnic group and local community to a far greater extent than to the city. A strong emphasis is placed on kinship and primary group relationships, and members of other groups are often perceived as intruders or outsiders.

The fourth group, the deprived, is composed of the poor, the handicapped, and racial minorities who have fallen victim to class inequality, prejudice, or personal misfortune. They live in the city because it offers inexpensive housing and holds the promise of future job opportunities that will enable them to move to a better environment.

Finally, the trapped are those who cannot afford to move to a newer community and must remain in their deteriorating neighborhoods. The elderly who live on pensions make up most of this group, and since many have lived in the city all their lives, they tend to identify strongly with their neighborhoods. The deprived and the trapped are the most frequent victims of the problems of the city. They are more likely to be the targets of assault, mugging, extortion, and other crimes than other city residents. In high crime areas, many of these people live isolated lives and are terrified by the ongoing violence in their neighborHoods.

Suburban Life

The dominance of *suburbs*, communities surrounding and dependent upon urban areas, is a recent phenomenon, although the population movement to the suburbs began at the end of the last century. Suburbs grew as a result of both push and pull factors. The problems of the city

Urban lifestyles are very diverse. Many singles, young couples, and young professionals choose to live in the city not only because it may be close to where they work but because it permits them to live a more independent lifestyle.

drove residents to the suburbs, while the positive aspects of suburban life — clean air, low taxes, large lots, and a chance to own a home — attracted people. Since the move involved a substantial capital investment, this transition was made primarily by the affluent.

The growth of the suburbs was also influenced by technological developments, especially those in transportation. Before the 1920s, trains and electric trolleys were the major means of mass transportation to and from the central city. Accordingly, the first pattern of suburban growth was star-shaped as communities sprung up along the railway and trolley corridors radiating from the center of the city. The automobile gave the suburban movement a significant boost by permitting the development of land not located near a railway or a trolley corridor.

After World War II, the suburbs took on a different appearance. The increased affluence of American workers and the mass production of relatively inexpensive housing enabled many lower-middle-class and blue-collar families to become suburbanites. The type of housing that emerged in the post–World War II suburbs, called "tract housing," was based on mass production techniques. Neighborhoods and sometimes whole communities of similar houses were constructed. As the population began to shift to the suburbs, so did the retail trade and small businesses. The result was an unprecedented growth of suburban shopping centers.

The rapid growth of suburbs in the 1950s and early 1960s caused a great deal of concern among many social commentators. Suburban life was characterized as a "rat race" dominated by a preoccupation with "keeping up with the Jones's." Suburbanites were seen as anxious,

Suburbs have been said to offer the best of both urban and rural life: the varied activities and events of the city and the quiet, open spaces of the country. To lower costs and thus make suburban home ownership available to an increasing number of moderate-income persons, housing developers often used mass production technology. Today a large number of housing tracts bear witness to this residential cloning.

child-oriented, status-seeking people who lead empty, frustrating lives (Bell, 1958; Gordon et al., 1961; Mills, 1951). The typical suburbanites were viewed as more concerned with household gadgets, status symbols, and getting into the "right" organizations than with understanding the world around them or achieving individuality. These views generated what sociologists call the "myth of suburbia." Recent research has given us reason to doubt that the patterns of behavior found in the suburbs are due to suburban residence and even that there is a distinctly suburban way of life.

The suburbs and the people who live there (sometimes called "suburbanites") are actually quite diverse. Harris (1971) captured some of this diversity in his categorization of suburbs on the basis of income levels and growth rates. He found four types: the affluent bedroom, the affluent settled, the low-income growing, and the low-income stagnant. The first two types are populated by upper-middle-class residents who are typically white, Protestant, and Republican. They tend to find suburban living quite satisfactory, although boring in some respects. The latter two categories are dominated by blue-collar workers. One finds a larger proportion of nonwhites, Democrats, and Catholics in these communities. People in all categories gave as their primary reason for moving to the suburbs the desire to own a home. The second most important reason was to find a suitable environment in which to raise children. Other factors common to all suburbanites were a desire for open spaces and for a less hectic pace.

Do people change when they move from the city to the suburbs? Is there evidence of a *conversion effect*, a radical shift of interest and lifestyle? Berger (1960) and Cohen and Hodges (1963) found that blue-collar families had similar values, behavior patterns, and psychological orientations whether they lived in the city or in the suburbs. Similarly, Gans (1967) found that middle-class suburbanites in Levittown were not

plagued by the stereotypical problems of boredom, unhappiness, and frustrated status seeking. He found instead that they were generally happy, well adjusted, and involved in family and social activities. In short, there is little evidence of a conversion effect.

The differences in the lifestyles of the city and the suburbs should be thought of as differences of degree, not of kind. Suburban residents tend to be more family-oriented and more concerned about the quality of education their children receive than city dwellers (Bell, 1958). On the other hand, because the suburbs consist largely of single-family homes, most young and single people prefer city life. Suburbanites are usually more affluent than city residents and more apt to have stable career or occupational patterns. As a result, they seem to be more hardworking and achievement-oriented than city residents. They may also seem to be unduly concerned with consumption, since they often buy goods and services that offer visible evidence of their financial success. The career involvement and the consumption patterns, however, are related more to social class position than to a mythical "suburban mentality" (Seeley et al., 1972). Suburbanites are also more involved than city residents in local social activities (Marshall, 1973; Tallman and Morgner, 1970), which is probably due partly to the demographic homogeneity of suburbs and partly to suburbanites' concern for their neighborhoods and schools.

In recent years, the number of blacks who live in the suburbs has increased sharply. In the last decade, the rate of black suburbanization increased by over 33 percent compared with a 10 percent increase for whites (U.S. Bureau of the Census, 1978, Table F). There is little evidence, however, that the suburbs are becoming racially integrated. Since the median income of blacks is still considerably lower than that of whites, most blacks cannot afford to move into the suburbs where most whites reside. Instead they are mov-

ing into the older suburbs with lower property values that whites are leaving behind in their search for better suburban communities. Though whites often react strongly to blacks who move into their suburban communities because they are perceived as being different, there is reseach evidence that blacks who move to the suburbs have values and lifestyles similar to those of their white neighbors (Austin, 1976).

Urban Problems

The most severe problems in urban areas are found in the central cities: poverty, unemployment, crime, noise and air pollution, waste disposal, water purity, transportation, housing, population congestion, and so on. Although the suburbs are by no means immune to these problems, they generally do not experience them to the same degree as central cities. The central cities are beset by a number of crises, some of which are becoming worse. In this section, we will discuss three problems: poverty and unemployment, crime, and schooling.

Among the most serious issues facing cities today are the related problems of poverty and unemployment. The economic vitality of central cities has diminished over the years as industry, affluent taxpayers, and jobs have moved out. The result has been a steady deterioration of housing and public services and the loss of high-paying jobs. The least fortunate of city residents are forced to live in slums. *Slums* are overcrowded streets or sections of a city marked by poverty and poor living conditions, which result from the dirt, disease, rodents, and other health hazards that accompany concentrations of housing with poor plumbing, garbage disposal, and sanitation facilities (National Commission on Urban Problems, 1972). Slum residents are often victims of social injustice and personal misfortune: racial minorities, the elderly, women who head large families, and addicts. Slum living has a number of detrimental effects on health: residents of slums are more likely than other city

dwellers to contract diseases and to become seriously ill; they have poorer overall health and shorter life spans as well (Schorr, 1970; Ways, 1971); and they are also more apt to have poor self-images and experience psychological problems such as depression and alienation (Polk, 1967; Lander, 1971).

The term ghetto is relevant to an understanding of urban poverty and unemployment. A *ghetto* is an area, usually a deteriorating one, in which members of a racial or ethnic minority are forcibly segregated. Urban areas that are no longer of interest to the more affluent majority tend to become ghettos. A ghetto is a social and economic trap that keeps members of the minority group within a controllable geographic area. In a sense, an urban ghetto is the counterpart of an Indian reservation, and there is evidence that black ghettoization is increasing today. During the last decade, the number of whites in central cities declined by 7 percent while the number of blacks increased by 15 percent (*Statistical Abstract: 1984*, no. 27). As a result of this change, blacks, many of whom are poor, constitute a numerical majority in several large cities, including Washington, D.C. (70.3 percent), Atlanta (66.6 percent), Detroit (63.1 percent), Newark (58.2 percent), and New Orleans (55.3 percent) (*Statistical Abstract: 1984*, no. 29).

The jobs that the less affluent central city residents are qualified for are usually low-paying and scarce, and the unemployment rate is twice as high as the rate in the suburbs. The departure of industry and manufacturing jobs has left inner-city residents with jobs characterized by high turnover, low wages, and few opportunities for advancement. It is not unusual to find a person who heads a family and works fulltime but barely earns enough to stay above the poverty line. With recent cuts in federal aid to job-training programs, it is unlikely that the situation of these city residents will improve in the near future.

Crime is another serious urban problem. In the 1970s, crime was ranked as the nation's number one social problem, especially by residents of cities of more than a million and there is evidence that it is increasing. A comparison of burglary rates in the mid-1960s and mid-1970s, for example, found an increase of nearly 200 percent (Wilson and Boland, 1976). Crime has often been viewed as essentially an urban problem, one that is especially common in large cities. There are several justifications for this view. Illegal vice activities like prostitution, gambling, and the use and sale of narcotics are found more generally in large cities where there is greater anonymity (Wolfgang, 1970). In addition, the methods of control are different in large cities and small towns. While towns rely on internalized values and primary group pressure for enforcement, cities depend on abstract laws and impersonal, bureaucratic agencies such as the police (Dinitz, 1973). When high density, heterogeneity, and anonymity are combined with poverty, a physically decayed environment, and other characteristics of inner-city living, there is great potential for deviance and violence.

Not all areas of a city experience the same crime rate or the same types of crimes. The highest crime rates are found in the inner-city sectors, while the rate decreases as one moves toward the fringes of the urban area. Zonal differences in crime tend to persist, however, even when the physical characteristics and the occupants of a zone change.

Using sociological research as a guide, one might argue that there are several ways of reducing urban crime. Increased police surveillance is often an important political issue in cities, but there is some evidence that it has little if any effect on the crime rate. Since high crime areas are located in similar areas in different cities — generally the most poverty-stricken areas — one might argue that providing the people in these areas decent living conditions and meaningful jobs would have a greater impact on crime than increasing the size of the police force. One could

also argue that voluntary neighborhood organizations in high crime areas might not only provide role models of lawful behavior but also create a sense of community that is frequently lacking in these areas (Wilson, 1968).

A third urban problem area is schooling. City schools are faced with two major problems today: inadequate financing and disorder and violence. The cost of a public school education rose by over 150 percent in the last decade (Coleman and Kelly, 1976), and many cities have had a very difficult time keeping pace with the accelerating costs. This difficulty is accentuated by inequalities in school funding: urban schools have a much lower per student expenditure allowance than schools in the suburbs (Berlowitz, 1974). City schools have reacted to this funding problem in several ways. In some areas, school bond increases have been used to retain financial solvency. In recent years, however, an increasing percentage of school bond proposals are being rejected by irate taxpayers (Coleman and Kelly, 1976). As a result of the fiscal crisis, many schools are forced to use outdated or damaged curricular material. It was recently discovered that one Detroit school was using history books that made reference to Lyndon Johnson as president! Reductions in staff and salary are another means of dealing with the financial woes. This "solution" has been a factor in recent teacher strikes and walkouts, which are becoming more frequent (Browne, 1976). Staff and salary cutbacks also seem to be related to the morale problems found in many inner-city schools.

School disorder, especially violence, is increasing. Incidents that rarely occurred a generation ago happen today on a fairly routine basis in many city schools: theft, extortion, physical attacks on fellow students and teachers, and vandalism (U.S. Department of Health, Education and Welfare, 1978). In some schools, the halls are routinely patrolled by police officers; in others, the doors of classrooms are locked during class hours to prevent intruders from entering; still

other schools have unannounced locker checks to confiscate drugs and weapons. One explanation for the increase in school crime is that schools are no longer immune to the day-to-day problems of the city. Solving some of the problems that cause crime on the streets would therefore probably reduce crime in the schools. Another explanation is that the schools themselves are responsible for disorder. Deteriorating buildings, prejudiced teachers, curricular tracking, and pessimism about the future may all produce an atmosphere of despair and anger (Rist, 1970). Without adequate funds to buy better equipment and hire more qualified teachers, this problem is likely to persist.

Urban Rejuvenation: Problems and Prospects

What can be done to help our cities survive? Has the central city outlived its use? These are a couple of the serious questions addressed by scholars concerned about the future of our cities. Some feel that the future is dim. Hauser (1977) thinks that the present crises many cities are experiencing will worsen as the tax base continues to erode, buildings and homes continue to deteriorate, and "tax rebellions" become more frequent. Sternlieb (1977) has compared the function of the central city of the future to that of a sandbox: as the city loses its economic functions, it becomes a place to keep the American poor in check by periodically giving them new "toys" — welfare and relief programs. Other scholars are less pessimistic. Banfield (1974) argues that the urban crisis is not becoming more severe but that cities are simply not recovering at the rate we expected them to. He suggests that the financial drain in large cities could be alleviated by redrawing city boundary lines to include all metropolitan residents for tax purposes or by charging nonresidents for their use of city services. He admits that although these ideas are economically feasible, they are politically explosive.

Downtown Revitalization

One's view of the problems and prospects of the city depends greatly on whether the central business district or residential areas are being considered. Many business districts are being revitalized. Most cities, even those in the Northeast and Midwest, are experiencing significant new business construction. In Chicago, over a billion dollars of construction is planned before 1985. Detroit recently built a new sports arena as well as a "Renaissance Center," a huge complex including a hotel, offices, and a variety of retail shops. Since the downtown areas of our cities are a major center of white-collar employment, financial firms, insurance companies, and private and government services, the future of these areas is relatively secure.

Downtown revitalization programs tend to have a greater impact on white-collar jobs than blue-collar ones, however. The number of white-collar jobs in cities is increasing, but the number of blue-collar jobs continues to decline (Kasarda, 1976). Since the revitalization of the central business district creates a need for well-educated, highly skilled employees, many inner-city residents who have weaker credentials do not directly benefit from these types of economic programs. This has made many city residents angry because they feel that their problems and concerns are secondary to the plans of affluent city and suburban residents. Citizen groups such as ACORN (The Association of Community Organizations for Reform Now) have voiced the concerns of many people, stressing that urban rejuvenation must include residential neighborhoods as well as the business district and must create jobs for all city residents regardless of their levels of skill or education.

Urban Renewal

Urban renewal is, at least in theory, the residential counterpart of downtown revitalization. According to the Urban Renewal Act of 1954, the major goal is to rebuild and renovate the ghettos and slums of American cities, but urban renewal projects have had several shortcomings. First, local urban renewal agencies were given the power by the federal government to define which areas were "blighted" and therefore qualified for renewal. Generally, the better areas of the slums were developed while the worst were allowed to remain. Sometimes the reason for this selection was the perception that one area was more likely to produce income than the other. Shopping centers and high-rise apartments for the middle class, for example, often replaced low-income housing. Ironically, many of the residents whose homes were razed did not benefit at all from the structures that were erected (Greer, 1965). Second, the act specified that the people displaced by urban renewal should be relocated in "decent, safe, and sanitary" housing in other areas of the city. In a number of instances, the new neighborhoods were just as bad as the old ones, and the relocation often destroyed an existing sense of community with friends and neighbors (Ryan, 1973).

The case of the Pruitt-Igoe Housing Project in St. Louis exemplifies some of the problems associated with urban renewal projects (Newman, 1972). The project, which had cleared some of the city's slum dwellings by 1955, consisted of thirty-three buildings, each eleven stories high. It was lauded as a model for all future public housing projects because of its design and use of innovative structures. By 1970, however, the project had become a symbol of all the negative aspects of public housing. The physical deterioration and destruction of elevators, laundry rooms, and stairways was considerable. Residents were afraid to leave their apartments because of the frequency of robbery and rape. The absence of public bathrooms on the ground floors resulted in foul-smelling hallways. Gradually, most of the occupants fled the project, and even the most desperate welfare recipients were unwilling

During the past decade many American cities have undergone downtown revitalization. Detroit, for example, has demolished many of its old downtown structures. In their place the city has built apartment complexes and malls, planted trees and shrubs, and along the Detroit River erected a "Renaissance Center." The Center, which appears in the background of this photo, consists of a major hotel surrounded by six office towers, a plaza often used for ethnic festivals, an auditorium for concerts, a hall for major auto/home/industrial shows, and a sports complex for professional hockey.

to tolerate the living conditions. The government finally closed down the entire project and later razed it. The basic problem was that human values and lifestyles were not fully considered in the project's design. The high-rise construction isolated residents from one another; the architectural design left too much open space (halls, elevators, laundry rooms) that no one felt responsible for and that made surveillance of children and adolescents very difficult.

Other means of housing the poor were legislated after the problems with urban renewal projects were publicized in the 1960s. Most of them received mixed reviews. Title 235 and Title 236 of the Housing and Urban Redevelopment Act provided direct subsidies to low-income families so that they could either buy their own homes or else rent apartments of their choice. Section 8 and the Experimental Housing Allowance Program were implemented in the early 1970s to help low-income tenants pay their rent. In both cases part of the rent was paid by the

The Edible City

City farming and the design of new self-reliant neighborhoods to supplant the current urban sprawl could be the solution to increasing demands on the land, says Richard Britz, a landscape architect and author of *The Edible City Resource Manual.*

Urban development causes a 10–15 percent annual decrease in the productivity of American soil (34 percent of the prime U. S. farmland was converted to urban or water use between 1967 and 1975), a trend that is likely to continue as the population increases. But with creative design of "edible" garden cities rather than the typical urban tracts, the land will not lose its productivity. Meanwhile, existing urban areas

that are unproductive and dependent on outside sources for all food and energy can be transformed into self-sufficient block farms, as is being done now in Eugene, Oregon.

In these pilot projects in several of Eugene's low-income neighborhoods, Britz and others demonstrate how cooperative urban farming can improve the quality of life. The edible city means more than a collection of backyard gardens, but a union of neighboring families working for better food, better health, reduced crime, improved education, energy conservation, reduced pollution, and more efficient housing design.

"We can learn to increase our humanity rather than decrease it

by increasing intensity of land use," Britz writes in the *Resource Manual,* based on the Eugene projects. "As we bind ourselves to economic realities generated by increased density, our street trees can produce food through careful management, and even the streets can be reclaimed as we garden the north-south passageways most exposed to the sunlight."

The Whiteaker neighborhood project in Eugene was funded in 1979 by a $146,000 grant from the National Center for Appropriate Technology. The project was designed to put people to work producing essentials in their own communities, and the strategy in each neighborhood was based on the geographical and climatic conditions of the area (for example, nearness to a water source).

In one neighborhood, trees were planted along a corridor of heavy automobile traffic to help decrease airborne pollutants and

government, either to the tenant or directly to the landlord.

A recent federal plan that is becoming increasingly popular is *urban homesteading.* Homesteading programs sell abandoned and foreclosed homes to private families for between one and 100 dollars if they agree to live in the house for at least three years and to bring the house up to code standards within eighteen months. Though the program is less than a decade old and has limited funds, it has had a significant effect on a number of cities, but there have been pitfalls. Individuals and lending institutions are reluctant to invest in houses surrounded by vandalized,

rundown buildings, and despite the low purchase price, repairs may be quite expensive. Recently, the Department of Housing and Urban Development has acted to alleviate these problems by buying up and making modest repairs on entire neighborhoods. If the federal government were to continue its commitment to urban homesteading in the 1980s, some of our deteriorating neighborhoods could probably be transformed. At the time of this writing, however, this type of commitment by the federal government appears highly unlikely.

A growing number of urban neighborhoods are being rejuvenated by *gentrification.* Since the

noise levels. Eventually, this urban "forest" could be suitable for a small-scale logging industry.

In another neighborhood, residents asked the city to divert traffic around the area, reducing noise and pollution, and began a neighborhood farm in addition to their private gardens.

The projects in Eugene are still in their early stages and could take more than a decade — if all goes right — to reach the level of self-sufficiency that Britz and his colleagues envision. Among the actions Britz urges are: In Phase One, the first five years, residents jointly buy the center lot of their neighborhood block and build farmhouses and greenhouses; renovate homes to accommodate solar panels and wood stoves; buy food collectively; plant food trees; develop their gardens; build shelters for rabbits and chickens; recycle and compost household wastes; and build windmills.

In the second phase, years five through nine of the project, neighbors convert streets and driveways for more food-growing and recreation; increase the capacity of housing by renting out garages, basements, and lofts or converting some of this space to offices, thus allowing businesses to move closer to the residents; build beehives to ensure pollination of the gardens and the food-producing trees; sell private cars and buy community vans or trucks; and dig a pond to begin aquaculture farming.

In the third phase, the tenth year and beyond, nearly all residents would be employed within the neighborhood. Residents would have developed complete on-site waste recycling systems and would be nearly sulf-sufficient in energy and food production.

The development of edible cities would shorten "energy loops" by encouraging people to produce goods locally, harness local low-grade energy (such as the sun, wind, and wood), recycle wastes and handle disposal locally, and rely less on motorized vehicles and more on human-powered transportation — walking or bike riding.

More than energy or land conservation is at stake, Britz says. The true benefit of edible cities will be the changes in the human condition: people will have a sense of belonging to and being responsible for the area in which they live. They will become healthier by living in less-polluted environments, by eating more nutritious food, and by enjoying more exercise as they abandon their cars. And their children will learn the values of cooperation and neighborliness, sharing energy, materials, and ideas.

mid-1970s, middle-class people have been moving into and repairing old rundown homes at their own expense. Notable examples of this are found in Chicago's Newtown, the Mission District of San Francisco, and Atlanta's Ansley Park. These people are generally young, white, childless couples who work in the city. They tend to have different values than their suburban counterparts. Many do not want to have families and most are turned off by the sameness and the lack of charm of suburban housing (Bradley, 1977). This trend may continue in the future with the increasing costs of transportation and suburban housing.

Urban Planning

Most of our urban development has occurred without a long-term commitment to community living or a strong theoretical understanding of it. Urban planning is a field of study concerned with urban physical structures and spatial configurations and their effects on human attitudes and behavior. Two traditional goals of this field are the reduction of population density and the creation of appealing community structures.

Urban planning became a concern in the nineteenth century when many large cities in Europe and the United States were experiencing severe problems because of rapid industrial and population growth. One early influential figure was Ebenezer Howard. Howard, in *Garden Cities of Tomorrow* (1902), argued that the ideal was to develop cities that combined the benefits of both rural and urban living. All new towns, or "garden cities" as he called them, would be built on undeveloped land in accordance with scientific principles. Population density, a factor he felt was responsible for urban blight, would be carefully controlled. Cities were also to be surrounded by a greenbelt, an area preserved for farming and recreation, thus limiting the outward growth of the city. Howard's ideas have had a significant impact on the theoretical orientations of several generations of urban planners whose major focus has been the construction of "new towns" that have a careful mixture of houses, entertainment areas, businesses, and industries.

One of the most popular critics of this view is Jane Jacobs (1961). She feels that urban planners who are trying to create "garden cities" are actually eliminating some of the characteristics that make urban life unique. Cities are naturally diverse and innovative, and attempts to zone various activities into distinct areas and to establish routine patterns of behavior will only create a dull, stagnant, social and economic environment. She suggests four ways to create a healthy, diverse urban environment:

1. Urban districts should serve several functions, and different parts of a district should be active at different times. This diversity and activity will attract people and make the streets safe at all hours of the day.

2. Most blocks should be short; there should be frequent opportunities to turn corners. This will prevent residents from walking the same, long monotonous streets. This would also encourage shops and small businesses to open up on previously untraveled streets, adding to the diversity of the area.

3. Old and new buildings should be mingled in the district. This intermingling is necessary so that high and low yield economic enterprises can coexist in the same area. Low-profit businesses, such as art shops and foreign restaurants, can rarely afford the costs of large, modern buildings whereas high-profit enterprises such as banks or chain supermarkets can.

4. The district must have a sufficiently dense concentration of residences and people. In constructing residences, extremes should be avoided. Too much density creates turmoil and reduces the ability of residents to enjoy the diversity; too much open space, on the other hand, makes surveillance difficult. This may lead to inappropriate or deviant behavior (pp. 143–151).

A number of modern new towns have been carefully designed and monitored. Columbia, Maryland, located between Washington, D.C., and Baltimore, is an example of a city developed with human needs and lifestyles in mind. When it is fully developed it will house 110,000 people in ten "villages," each containing four neighborhoods. Each neighborhood has its own elementary school and recreational facilities, and the villages form a circle around a plaza with a shopping center, office buildings, and medical facilities. The community has also made a conscious attempt to achieve racial balance; a little less than a quarter of the residents are black (Rouse, 1971).

Other, more recent new towns have not been as successful as Columbia, and federal cutbacks in funding for development have led to the demise of more than half a dozen new towns. Soul City, North Carolina, is one of the latest to be foreclosed by HUD. The lesson to be learned from these recent experiences is that the successful development of planned communities requires a long-term investment of money, perhaps as long as fifteen or twenty years, by the federal government. With its present economic woes, our government is unlikely to make such a commitment in the near future.

Picture the city of the future. Will it resemble this city of the future, as depicted in the movie Metropolis? Will our living environment be totally controlled by artificial lighting, cooling, and heating? Will millions of people live on confined geographical areas? Will personal relationships in urban areas be increasingly impersonal and contractual? Urban planners, including sociologists, will need to design the types of communities that combine the available resources with societal values and group preferences.

Diversity of Values

Although urban planners should be sensitive to the diverse values and lifestyles of the people who live in urban communities if they are to achieve their goals, they have not been completely successful in this area, and they have been criticized as having a distinct middle-class bias (Gans, 1968). This point can be illustrated with findings about the design and use of space.

Most planners assume that people like a considerable amount of open public space and clearly demarcated areas of private space. Among many blue-collar and minority groups, however, the distinction between public and private space is blurred, and social interactions tend to flow more freely across private and public regions than they do in middle-class environments (Freid and Gleicher, 1961). The effects of spatial arrangements on behavior are also class-related, as was illustrated in a study by Newman (1972). He found that two adjacent housing projects in New York with similar population densities and residents had significantly different rates of

SOCIOLOGISTS AT WORK
Banking and Community Relations

Daniel S. Voydanoff is director of the Urban Affairs Department of the National Bank of Detroit. His position is a new one — it didn't exist until he was promoted to it. His job reflects the growing recognition in the business community that corporations must devote more attention to the public's changing needs and how they influence business policies and practices. Businesses must also explain their needs and concerns to the public. He is well served in these roles by his education: he has a masters degree in sociology from Detroit's Wayne State University.

How does Voydanoff's background in sociology help him in his work? He applies his methodological and analytical skills and his ability to work with demographic information — skills he learned through his MA program — in a broad spectrum of tasks. "Most business MBA programs don't provide sufficient background in

survey methodology, statistics, social and organizational theory, and applying demographic information to business," he says. "Sociology is particularly important in providing a broad basis of understanding and sensitivity to social issues and problems."

A recent focus has been his bank's policy concerning neighborhood and housing needs in Detroit. "Our policy recognizes that neighborhood and merchant associations have a strong role to play in the conservation of neighborhoods, housing stock, and the merchant base in the city. Without their existence, individual residents and merchants have little voice when dealing with large institutions, public and private, that are adversely affecting their interests. Much of our community relations programming is directed to strengthening such organizations. The bank has also assumed a strong role in

crime and maintenance problems. The only difference was that the one with few crime and maintenance problems was smaller than the other; it had six-story rather than mostly thirteen-story buildings. The reader might generalize these findings to our earlier discussion of the Pruitt-Igoe Project.

That urban planners and the less affluent have different spatial preferences has also been noted with regard to the structure of individual apartments. An experiment in which Hispanic

residents of a New York tenement conferred with an architect about the redesign of their apartments revealed that the residents did not like the large areas of open space in an apartment that middle-class couples prefer; that they wanted an apartment entrance that did not open directly into the living room; and that they liked an apartment in which the kitchen was isolated from the rest of the house by a wall or door (Zeisel, 1973).

Sensitive design of new urban places can

special economic development projects."

The department Voydanoff directs has a number of general responsibilities. These include, among others, "monitoring public and community issues affecting the bank and its customers; appraising bank policies, operations, marketing programs, and products as they affect customers, consumers, and the community; assuring appropriate corporate participation in economic development and community betterment efforts; and conducting community programs designed to help fulfill community needs."

His department also advises the bank's executive management on matters related to public issues and stays in "ongoing contact with outside organizations and interest groups to maintain sensitivity to issues and concerns affecting the corporation and the community."

Voydanoff was promoted to his current position from the directorship of his bank's Marketing Planning and Research Department, and before that he spent seven years doing research for a credit union trade association. He found his background in sociology useful in this work, too. His department's responsibilities included designing surveys and analyzing their results as well as

initiating, directing, and analyzing research to produce reliable information for executive decisions. His department undertook such tasks as investigating the characteristics, attitudes, and behavior of the retail and corporate banking markets; evaluating the effectiveness of advertising, public relations, and civic and urban affairs programs; assessing customer satisfaction with products and hours; and evaluating proposed new products, services, and marketing programs.

There is little traditional connection between sociology and business, but Voydanoff believes that "university sociology departments and their students should be encouraged to develop career paths into business. It is important to recognize the necessity of 'job evolution' when career paths are absent," he says. "The urban affairs job evolved out of the marketing job because of my interest in social and urban issues affecting the bank and the application of bank resources in their solution. Corporations have a stake in the favorable resolution of public issues affecting them, and in the economic and social well-being of their local communities. Sociology provides an excellent academic background for these functions."

greatly enhance the satisfaction city residents derive from their surroundings. Newman (1972) offers five guidelines for achieving this end:

1. Design buildings of no more than six stories in which not more than a dozen families share the same stairwell.
2. Acknowledge definitions of space that reflect the values of the inhabitants and the community to which they belong.
3. Position apartment windows so that residents

can easily survey the interior and exterior public areas of their environment.
4. Construct buildings in a manner that does not stigmatize the inhabitants and allow others to perceive their vulnerability and isolation.
5. Increase the safety of residents by locating residential developments in functionally sympathetic areas away from areas that would provide a continual threat. (p. 9)

The development of attractive, functional physical surroundings cannot be accomplished without a long-term commitment by the government to aid our ailing cities. The rejuvenation of the city also requires the creation of jobs and opportunities for inner-city residents. In the last two decades major steps have been taken toward the realization of these goals.

Summary

Urban communities can exist only when there is a group of people to grow and process food for the urbanites. A degree of social organization is also necessary to transform overcrowded people into a social group that behaves in an orderly and predictable manner. The first urban communities developed approximately ten thousand years ago during the horticultural era. This development was possible because of increased food production and the creation of regular surpluses. Several thousand years later, technological advances — the plow, the use of animals, counting, and writing — and the increasing complexity of social and political organization enabled cities to grow to unprecedented sizes. The fall of Rome in the fifth century A.D. marked the beginning of a precipitous decline in city size and complexity that lasted for nearly six hundred years. Urban communities did not begin to grow substantially again until the late eighteenth century with the dawn of the industrial age. Urban populations increased dramatically, and within a few decades more people lived in cities than in rural areas. In the United States, this population shift took place between 1860 and 1920.

Today, three-fourths of our population live in urban areas, which have increased in size as well as in number. The rapid industrial and population growth in large cities during the early part of this century caused people and industry to move from central cities to the sparsely populated areas outside of them. This process resulted in the modern metropolis. A Metropolitan Statistical Area (MSA) is a large population nucleus together with adjacent communities that have a high degree of social and economic integration with that nucleus. A megalopolis results from the overlap of two or more metropolitan areas. Since the mid-1970s, nonmetropolitan areas have been growing at a faster rate than metropolitan areas.

Urban ecology is the study of the spatial configurations of communities and their effects on social life. Three models of spatial growth — the concentric zone, the sector zone, and the multiple nuclei zone models — have been used to describe structural changes in the urban environment.

Cities and suburbs, in contrast to popular stereotypes, have quite diverse populations. Early sociologists believed that city living was unhealthy and encouraged family breakdown, violence, and depersonalization. Recent research, however, shows that a variety of people and lifestyles are found in the city. A number of people prefer the city because of its social and economic advantages. Suburban life is also quite diverse and suburbanites do not differ in lifestyle or values from city residents with similar demographic and social characteristics.

Our cities face a number of problems today, notably poverty and unemployment, crime, and inadequate schools. Attempts to remedy these problems are not likely to succeed without a considerable influx of money and the creation of social and economic opportunities. The downtown areas of many cities are being revitalized, and a number of residential neighborhoods are being given a new appearance as a result of urban renewal, urban recovery, and urban homesteading projects. The field of urban planning may play an important role in the future of our cities and can have a significant impact on the quality of urban social and cultural life if it is sensitive to the needs and values of different groups of city residents.

Key Terms

community
concentration
concentric zone model
conversion effect
deconcentration
ecological specialization
folk society
gemeinschaft
gentrification
gesellschaft
ghetto
greenbelt
horticulture
invasion
megalopolis
Metropolitan Statistical Area
multiple nuclei model
sector model
slums
suburbs
succession
urban ecology
urban homesteading
urbanization

Suggested Readings

Abrahamson, Mark. **Urban Sociology, 2d ed.** *Englewood Cliffs, N.J.: Prentice-Hall, 1980.* An introduction to urban sociology.

Banfield, Edward. **The Unheavenly City Revisited.** *Boston: Little, Brown, 1974.* This controversial book examines the problems of American cities. The author contends that the sort of programs undertaken in the last decade will not solve these problems.

Blackwell, James E. and Philip S. Hart. **Cities, Suburbs and Blacks: A Study of Concerns, Distrust and Alienation.** *Bayside, N.Y.: General Hall, 1982.* An empirical investigation of urgent concerns, priorities, health needs, alienation, and distrust of the power structure as identified by nearly one thousand suburban and urban black Americans.

Clark, Kenneth. **Dark Ghetto.** *New York: Harper & Row, 1965.* An analysis of the problems of the ghetto in relation to the educational, political, religious, and economic institutions of our society.

Hawley, Amos. **Urban Society.** *New York: Ronald Press, 1971.* An analysis of the structural and demographic forces that influence the city. The author takes an urban ecological approach.

Karp, David A., Gregory P. Stone, and William C. Yoels. **Being Urban: A Social Psychological View of City Life.** *Lexington, Mass.: D. C. Heath, 1977.* A look at some neglected aspects of the urban scene from a symbolic interaction perspective.

Liebow, Elliot. **Tally's Corner.** *Boston: Little, Brown, 1967.* A descriptive study of black men in the inner city of Washington, D.C. and how they adjust to urban life.

Lottman, Herbert. **How Cities Are Saved.** *New York: Universe Books, 1976.* An analysis of the sources of the present urban crises and the author's prescription for solving them.

Mumford, Lewis. **The City in History.** *New York: Harcourt Brace Jovanovich, 1961.* An analysis of the conditions that led to the development of Western cities. The author traces the history of a number of urban problems.

Palen, J. John. **City Scenes: Problems and Prospects, 2d ed.** *Boston: Little, Brown, 1981.* An integrated collection of provocative essays on urban problems and issues.

Wirth, Louis. **"Urbanism as a Way of Life,"** **American Journal of Sociology.** *44 July 1938:1–24.* This article outlines the major ideas of one of the early American theorists about urban life.

CHAPTER 21

The Nature of Social Change

The art of progress is to preserve order amid change and to preserve change amid order.

— Alfred North Whitehead

In our rapidly changing society, sociology is largely the study of *social change*, changes in the structure of society and in its institutions. This chapter is devoted to a discussion of the approaches that are used to understand social change, with an emphasis on changes in social structures and social institutions.

Sociologists have tried to answer three basic questions about social change. The earlier sociologists wanted to know whether social change was good or bad. As societies change, do they get better or do they deteriorate? Writing at the beginning of the industrial revolution, they saw their traditional family-oriented society vanish and watched it being replaced by urbanization and factory work.

Today, we are more likely to accept social change, but we are still interested in the reasons for it. Thus the second basic question is, What causes the change? And, like the early sociologists, we are still concerned with the third question: What happens to the people in a society when their society changes?

Theories of Social Change

The Evolutionary Theory of Change

During more optimistic periods of our history, social change was regarded as progress. When society changed, it was assumed to be getting better. As discussed in Chapter 2, evolutionary theory suggests that societies evolved from the simple and primitive to the more complex and advanced, just as animal life progressed from the simplest one-celled organisms to the most complex animal, the human being. Herbert

Spencer, a classic evolutionary theorist, lived in England at a time when Great Britain was a powerful, progressive nation. Spencer believed that Great Britain was the most advanced of societies and that eventually all nations on earth would evolve to the level of his society. He believed that as a society grows, the functions of its members become more specialized and better coordinated into the larger system, just as when animals increase in size, they develop millions of body cells to serve specific complex functions, all of which are interrelated.

Spencer was very influential for many years, especially in the United States where growth was equated with progress. It was assumed that growth would unquestionably lead to a better society and that a lack of growth would lead to deterioration.

Evolutionary theory is less popular today. Growth may create social problems rather than social progress, and Spencer's optimistic theory is regarded with some skepticism. Conflict theorists are among those who do not believe in the continuous evolution of progress.

Conflict Theory of Social Change

Conflict theorists are in many ways as optimistic as evolutionary theorists, but they do not assume that societies smoothly evolve to higher levels. Conflict theory suggests that societies progress to a higher order as oppressed groups improve their lot. In this view, conflict is necessary and conflicting groups must struggle to improve their lot (Coser, 1956).

Karl Marx was a conflict theorist who predicted the revolt of the masses under capitalist economic systems, but Marx was by no means a pessimist. He saw the upcoming conflict as a stage of development that would lead to a higher order. Although social change was not synonymous with social progress, progress could eventu-

ally be hoped for. Marx was very optimistic compared with some cyclical theorists of his own day and of ours.

Cyclical Theories of Change

The most pessimistic cyclical theorists think that decay is inevitable. One such theorist was the historian Oswald Spengler (1918), whose *cyclical change theory* suggests that every society is born, matures, decays, and eventually dies. The Roman Empire rose to power and then gradually collapsed, just as the British Empire grew strong and then deteriorated. Spengler contended that social change may take the form of progress or of decay but that no society lives forever.

Most sociologists believe this view is too rigid and that although societies may have cycles of change, the cycles are not preordained. Pitirim Sorokin (1889-1968), a Russian social theorist who lived through the Russian Revolution of 1917, did not equate change with progress, but neither did he believe that all societies are inevitably destined to decay. He noted, rather, that societies go through various stages. At different stages, he suggested, they emphasize religious beliefs, scientific beliefs, or the pleasures of art, music, and the beauty of nature. They shift from one cycle to another, moving first in one direction, then in another as the needs of the society demand. The fact that a society is changing does not necessarily mean that it is progressing or decaying; change does not necessarily tend in a certain direction. Sorokin is still respected for these ideas and has greatly influenced the attempts of structural-functionalists to explain social change.

Structural Functionalism and Social Change

As you know, structural-functionalists believe that society is a balanced system of institutions, each of which serves a function in maintaining society. Structural-functional theory

The Roman Empire was once powerful and wealthy. Many people believe that wealthy nations inevitably decline because they spend their wealth and energy in frivolous ways, on extravagant parties, meals, and entertainments. Such an explanation, however, is too simple a theory to explain social change.

suggests that when events outside or inside the society disrupt the equilibrium, social institutions make adjustments to restore stability. An influx of immigrants, a natural disaster, a famine, or a war may disrupt the social order and force the social institutions to make adjustments. Like Sorokin, the structural functionalists do not necessarily consider social change per se to be good or bad — rather, it is the process through which societies lose and regain their equilibrium.

The term "cultural lag" is often used to describe the state of disequilibrium. When an event such as an increase in population or a depletion of natural resources causes a strain in a society, it takes some time for the society to understand the strain and alter its values and institutions to adapt to the change. Just as the human body must adjust its functioning to adapt to changes, societies adjust to maintain and restore themselves.

Social Change Theory: A Synthesis

Few theorists today are so optimistic that they believe societies inevitably improve, and few are so pessimistic that they believe societies inevitably decay. Most integrate the ideas of Sorokin, the structural functionalists, and the conflict theorists. Societies do change, but the

changes are not necessarily good or bad. Societies attempt to remain stable, and although a stable one is usually better than a chaotic one, stability sometimes causes harsh conditions, injustice, and oppression. When this happens, conflicts arise and society is forced to change, perhaps for the better.

Change and stability, then, are processes that can take place simultaneously in any society. At any given time, one or the other will dominate, depending on the society's needs. Change is inevitable, and it is often beneficial.

What Causes Social Change?

Sociologists believe that social systems change when powerful internal or external forces influence them such that the previous social order can no longer be maintained. But societies are complex, interdependent systems of values, norms, and institutions; they are often amazingly resistant to change and rarely transformed by the ideas or behavior of a single person. When a major change does occur, however, it influences the entire society and each social institution must adapt to the new order.

Sociologists have determined that *ecological changes* — variations in the relationship between population and geography — are the most powerful sources of social change, although social innovations and conflicts may also cause major changes in societies.

Population, Geography, and Ecology

A population change can bring dramatic social changes. The decreasing death rate over the past two hundred years, for example, has caused an enormous increase in the size of the population. The average age of the population has also increased. While the size of the population has grown, the birth rate has been decreasing, which means that there are relatively few children in

many societies and that social programs will be oriented more toward the older population than toward children.

Societies that were once sparsely populated are now crowded, so people have been migrating to new areas with more space. When they migrate, they bring with them the ideas and customs of their old culture, which are often new to the society they enter. The migrants not only increase the size of the population but also influence it culturally. The spread of one culture to another as populations migrate is termed *cultural diffusion.*

A geographic change may also cause migrations. In Chapter 19, we noted that great waves of Asians migrated to the Middle East and Europe long before written history began. It is assumed that this migration was largely the result of changes in the Asian climate, perhaps increasing cold weather or severe droughts. Geographic changes have been a major source of social change: volcanic eruptions ended the society at Pompeii, an earthquake and fire destroyed San Francisco in 1906, and the drought in the southern United States during the 1930s caused migrations to Southern California. These migrations were movingly portrayed by John Steinbeck in *The Grapes of Wrath.*

Natural disasters can cause both environmental and social changes. Although small fires and floods may not affect the larger society, they have a great impact on the local community. People caught in a natural disaster may be left without friends, relatives, or resources. They may have to abandon their community or completely rebuild it.

Today, many geographic changes and natural disasters are induced by the inhabitants of a region — for example, the size of a population using a geographic area may deplete its natural resources. Ecological changes of this sort are now a far greater source of social change than migrations or natural disasters.

Destruction of buildings can change the lives of people, whether that destruction is caused by war or a natural disaster. These photographs show the destruction of war in Beirut and a flood in Malibu. The difference is that in Beirut there is little hope of restoring the building that has been lost — or peace and order. In Malibu the building can be replaced and life can go on as before.

The growing population of the United States has dramatically changed this country's geography. Consider, for example, the history of the small town of Williamsport, Pennsylvania (Humphrey and Buttel, 1982). In the mid-nineteenth century, the increasing population of the East Coast needed lumber for houses, and the Susquehanna Boom Company began to harvest timber in Williamsport, which was located in a wilderness region of the Appalachian mountains on the west branch of the Susquehanna River. The company built a boom one-quarter mile wide and seven miles long in the middle of the river to hold lumber for transport to eastern cities. Thirty-five mills were started, and thousands of immigrants came to the area to find work. The mill owners got wealthy, but the workers, who labored fourteen hours a day for very poor pay, were discontented. Union leaders entered the area, strikes broke out, and the state militia was called in to subdue the strikers. Williamsport became a violent town.

The timber was soon cleared from the mountains, and the branches left behind made excellent tinder. When lightning struck the mountains, they burned. When it rained on the bare mountains, the soil washed away and ruined the area for agriculture. The region could no longer support a large population, and people began to move out at the end of the century.

The resources of Williamsport attracted its population, but the ecological relationships between the population and the environment led to dramatic social changes. The population grew stratified and violent as resources were used up, and the society changed again when the resources were depleted. The area has continued ever since to decline in population.

A more recent ecological disaster, described by Kai Erikson (1976), took place at Buffalo Creek in West Virginia. Waste material from mining operations had been piled on a mountainside, and behind it the mining company had created a vast pond of waste water accumulated from mining operations. The heap of slag collapsed, and the slag and water, churned together, crashed down the side of the mountain in a twenty-foot wave. As Erikson describes it,

> It did not crush the village into mounds of rubble, but carried everything away with it — houses, cars, trailers, a church whose white spire had pointed to the slag pile for years — and scraped the ground as cleanly as if a thousand bulldozers had been at work. (p. 29)

Those who survived were left without family, friends, or community; they were dazed, angered, isolated, and apathetic. Those who could, created new lives; their old lives had been destroyed forever.

Discoveries and Inventions

Discoveries and inventions have caused far-reaching changes in modern societies, which are becoming increasingly technological. Discoveries and inventions are called *innovations*, changes that offer something new to society and that alter its norms or institutions. A *discovery* is the act of finding something that has always existed but that no one previously knew about. The discovery of America led to the great migrations from Europe and the creation of a new country. The discovery of gold and other scarce resources in the West led Americans to continue their migration. Infection is no longer a leading cause of death since the discovery of penicillin. The discovery of oil today leads to great social changes in the areas where it is found.

An *invention* is a device constructed by putting two or more things together in a new way. Henry Ford invented the automobile assembly line by putting together knowledge and materials already known. This advance permitted him to mass-produce cars and bring about widespread social change.

The Automobile, the Assembly Line, and Social Change

The automobile has altered individual lifestyles and precipitated a number of social changes. Because the automobile was developed hand-in-hand with the assembly line, it changed the nature of work. Since assembly lines were more economical when large quantities were produced, companies had to create public demand — that is, socialize people into buying their automobiles.

The automobile has also affected international relationships because it requires oil, and our demand for oil has far outstripped the supply available within the United States. As our discussion will show, each change creates other changes, and today our society is very different from what it was at the turn of the century.

The Automobile and Social Control

When cars became common in the 1920s, the nature of the American family began to change rapidly. Cars provided people with a measure of privacy and anonymity never before possible and removed them from the social control of the community. Young people could escape the watchful eyes of family and community by leaving town and pursuing recreation in other towns. Dating became commonplace and moved beyond the control of the family. There was less emphasis on proper introductions to suitable people and evenings spent chaperoned by family members. As a result, there was a dramatic increase in premarital sex, and the twenties marked the first major sexual revolution in this country.

Adults also began to travel more and change their lifestyles. While previously the church had been the center of both religious and social life for many people, adults with automobiles began to take Sunday drives instead of going to church, and they were able to travel to more distant places for recreation. They were also free to live a distance from work if they had a car for transportation. Where once it had been considered suspect for a family to live outside of town — people would question what suspicious kind of activity a family might pursue in a remote area — the automobile made it possible for families to work in town while living in the country. The move to the country grew rapidly and removed people further from the watchful eyes of neighbors and the social control small towns provided.

Creating Demand

Mass production becomes more economical as larger quantities of goods are produced. Cars are made more cheaply when constructed in

(Above) courtesy, Museum of Fine Arts, Boston

Scenes of Tremont Street in Boston show changes since 1843, when families with children and dogs lived in the city and could enjoy a leisurely stroll along the street. Now families live in the suburbs and bring their cars to the city where office buildings have replaced homes. The streets and sidewalks now are busy and noisy.

The George Washington Bridge pictured here is but one example of the vast numbers of costly road and bridge systems designed to facilitate our lives. Yet traffic is snarled everywhere, and little relief will be possible without more efficient transportation systems.

large numbers, which increases the industry's profit margin. Once produced, of course, the cars must be sold — a market must be found for them.

General Motors has long been in the business of creating a market for its automobile prod-

ucts. By the 1920s, most people who wanted and could afford a car had bought one, and General Motors needed new markets (Snell, 1976), so they began to produce buses. They bought interurban electric railways and urban trolley systems, dismantled them, and replaced them with buses. By 1949, General Motors, working with companies such as Greyhound, Standard Oil of California, and Firestone Tire, had replaced more than one hundred electric transit systems with buses.

Buses were slow, inefficient, dirty, and expensive to operate. People did not enjoy riding in them. Furthermore, when they were bombarded with advertisements encouraging them to buy cars not just as a means of transportation but as status symbols, they turned from using public transportation and bought automobiles. In the meantime, the automotive industry lobbied to have the federal interstate highway system constructed. Between 1945 and 1970, state and local governments spent $156 billion to build hundreds of thousands of miles of roads. Only 16 miles of subway were built during the same period. Thus the automobile became a necessity as a means of transportation, and Americans bought them in ever-increasing numbers. As a result, the auto business became the major U.S. industry.

With the rise of the auto industry, alternative modes of travel became less popular. Public transportation systems began to deteriorate. Bunke (1983) estimated that New York City alone needs $100 billion to repair its transportation system. Intercity transportation systems have also declined. Most railroad systems that were not destroyed and replaced by bus lines have gone bankrupt or fallen into such disrepair that they may have to be abandoned.

Ironically, the road system that was built to accommodate the widespread use of the automobile and contributed to the neglect and destruction of railroads is itself on the verge of disintegration from neglect. The bridges alone in our road system require an estimated $41 billion to repair, and while the present road system verges on collapse, few new roads are being built. As the population continues to increase, the use of the automobiles grows, and all these cars must compete for space on the deteriorating road system. Major traffic jams are more and more common as roadways approach their capacity for handling traffic. Also, a condition known as "gridlock" is increasingly common. A gridlock occurs when traffic chokes major arteries and roads leading to them to the point where nothing is able to move in any direction.

The Assembly Line and the Nature of Work

The revolution in traditional modes of travel was only one of the areas dramatically altered by the automobile industry. The assembly line changed the nature of the workplace forever. To produce cars efficiently, manufacturers have tried to make assembly lines as fast and as automatic as possible. The more efficiently and predictably space, time, and workers are used, the more economically automobiles can be produced.

One assembly plant, built at Lordstown by General Motors in 1970, was designed to provide three remarkable improvements in efficiency (Rothschild, 1973). First, the assembly line made use of the most modern automated equipment to perform some routine tasks. Robots were used to weld steel parts together and worked far more rapidly than humans. Second, the assembly-line process was made more efficient with computers, which carefully analyzed every stage in the assembly-line process. Each step was measured to the second, every second of time was planned, and every movement of the workers was timed. The assembly line itself moved up and down so that workers did not have to reach up or bend down, which increased the workers' speed

because they did not need time to move. The third innovation was computer control of the work process. Computers controlled the assembly line, scanned the work area, detected problems instantly, and otherwise supervised the work.

This great efficiency in assembly-line production made the job intolerable for workers. They no longer worked in teams for the satisfaction of producing a product. Instead, they worked for computers, which controlled their every move and reported every move not prescribed. If workers saw a problem on the assembly line such as a tool not functioning properly or a machine spraying paint in the wrong direction, they reported it to the computer, not to a human boss. Many employees felt that they too were expected to perform like robots.

The assembly line has recently taken a new turn. Increasingly, workers are being replaced by computers, not just being controlled by them. There are now only about 5,000 industrial robots in the United States, but conservative estimates suggest that 70,000 more will be in place by the end of this decade (Coates, 1983). Robots work a twenty-four hour shift, so each one is capable of replacing a minimum of three people required to cover three shifts in a twenty-four hour day. Robots can also work straight through the weekend, thus eliminating forty-eight more human hours of labor, and they can work faster than humans without lunch and coffee breaks, so in reality they can replace even more people. The 70,000 new robots, then, could replace a minimum of 210,000 people in jobs. If other, more rewarding jobs were available, the arrival of the robots would be welcome, but it is very possible that such jobs will not be available.

Automation may also replace many white-collar workers. Already computers can make phone calls, read mail, write letters, keep the books, and do much of the office work required by business. It may be that one day soon only management level workers will have jobs, and

Many office workers are shown here using computers, but as computers become more sophisticated, they will be able to do the work of most of the people in this office. Perhaps someday only one worker will remain to receive the printout from the computer; others will be displaced from their jobs.

everyone else will be unemployed or self-employed in whatever work is to be found.

The Automobile and the Environment

Another area of social change brought about by automobiles concerns environment. The heavy use of automobiles and diesel buses causes pollution, and smog from automobile emissions has become a serious problem in American cities. The bad urban air burns the eyes, damages lung tissues, and increases the levels of lead and other poisons in the human body and in food products. It has been estimated that five hundred Los Angeles residents die every year of diseases caused by auto-produced smog (Snell, 1976). It is not known how many deaths occur nationally because of pollution.

The automobile has also vastly increased our need for oil. The United States, even though it has huge supplies of oil, uses so much that it must import more.

Oil is the major pollutant of the ocean (Mostert, 1976), and huge tankers routinely dump oil into the sea. It is not known how much oil tankers dump, but the most conservative estimate is that the total is well over a million tons a year. When oil leaks, spills, or is purposely dumped from tankers, it poisons, smothers, burns, or coats sea plants and animals and kills them. The oceans of the world from the Arctic to the Antarctic are slowly being covered with oil slicks, and to date there is no effective way to clean them up.

In addition to the oil dumped during routine operations, hundreds of accidents involving tankers take place at sea each year, and they cause far more serious problems than dumping. In one accident, in May of 1970, a Norwegian tanker carrying a full cargo of oil ran aground and burst into flames off the Spanish coast. The oil burned with such intensity that the flames

started a fire storm. Winds created by the heat reached hurricane force, lifted the oil into the air, and carried it to high altitudes. A few days later the oil rained down on coastal farmlands as a fine mist, damaging homes, gardens, crops, and pastures. Grazing cattle died from eating the oil-covered grasses. Fortunately, much of the oil fell in uninhabited areas, and the ship involved was only a small tanker. An accident of this type would be much worse if it involved a larger ship near a populated area.

Our need for oil as a fuel is so great that the United States is willing to go to war to protect its supply from foreign oil fields. Since World War II, this country has built up a vast military force, and the government has vowed to use it to protect oil-producing nations that sell to the United States. It has also sold billions of dollars' worth of arms to these nations, including Iran under the Shah and Saudi Arabia.

Thus we see that the United States has become so economically dependent on the automobile and on oil that it is willing to pollute land and sea, further the arms race, and threaten to go to war to prevent economic disaster. It is obvious that these factors have serious sociological consequences.

Other Energy Sources

Because the automobile uses such great quantities of oil, it is not available for other uses, and new sources of fuel must be found to heat our homes and run our industries. Some people believe that nuclear power should be used to solve our energy problems. Others do not, and its advantages and disadvantages have been hotly debated. The debate centers around two basic problems.

The first problem is the current safety of nuclear energy plants. Those who believe they are safe argue that although a nuclear reactor accident could be dangerous, the probability of an accident is very small. A person is more likely to die from an earthquake, hurricane, tornado, or from being hit by a meteorite than as a result of a nuclear accident, proponents contend. Even if an accident did happen, it would be contained within the power plant. In the very unlikely case that the accident was not contained and radioactive steam did escape, there would be enough warning to evacuate the population and minimize deaths and illnesses.

Those who believe that nuclear reactors are unsafe argue that the chance of an accident is very great and cite the many accidents that have already taken place in power plants. They also argue that an accident could have catastrophic consequences. A reactor not operating normally could become so hot that it would explode, filling the air with enormous quantities of radioactive dust that would rain down on large areas as it was carried by the wind. Critics believe that both the number of immediate deaths and the illnesses leading to cancer and premature death would be enormous.

The second problem is the disposal of nuclear waste. Reactors create waste that remains dangerous to human life for hundreds of years, and everyone agrees that there is no good way to dispose of it. Proponents argue that a way will be found to dispose of the wastes; opponents say that we may not find a way. If we don't, we may kill or injure the next generation of the earth's population.

The Uses of Sociology

Although we do not usually think of the disposal of nuclear waste as related to the invention of the automobile, the mass production of cars created the need to sell them, which in turn gave rise to fuel and pollution problems that technology has not been able to solve. Sociologists who study society from a historical perspective, observing the relationship between increasing automobile use and today's energy problems, are likely to be frustrated by our practice of solving

Dodging Celestial Garbage

The North American Aerospace Defense Command (NORAD), which is responsible for providing early warning against aerial attacks, estimates that some 3,800 pieces of junk are currently circling the earth.* Total weight of this space-age garbage: six tons. Two-thirds of the nuts, bolts, oxygen cylinders, broken solar panels, dead satellites, spent rocket boosters and other litter is in geosynchronous orbit 22,300 miles from the earth's surface, where it will remain indefinitely. One-third of the circling scrap is in low earth orbit, only 120 to 300 miles overhead.

Most of the space garbage consists of nonfunctioning satellites and space probes launched from earth. There is also fragmentary junk, resulting from midspace collisions between spacecraft and meteorites. Astronauts have dumped sewage, food containers and spent oxygen cylinders overboard. On rare occasions, space walkers have accidentally dropped objects in space. Astronaut Ed White lost a shiny white glove during the Gemini 4 flight in 1965. George ("Pinky") Nelson fumbled away two tiny screws while repairing the Solar Maximum Mission satellite during the shuttle flight.

Objects in low earth orbit circle freely until the slow wear of molecular friction and the force of gravity cause them to reenter the earth's atmosphere at a blazing 18,000 m.p.h. and subsequently burn up. That was the fate of the first man-made satellite, the 184-lb. Soviet Sputnik 1, which incin-erated in the heat of re-entry three months after its historic launching on Oct. 4, 1957.

Since then 9,695 man-made objects have fallen from orbit, but the number that survived the atmospheric plunge to hit the earth is unknown. Shards have landed on more than a dozen nations, including Zambia, Finland and Nepal. As early as 1961, Premier Fidel Castro indignantly charged that a re-entering chunk of a U.S. spacecraft had struck and killed a Cuban cow. A year later, a 21-lb. metal cylinder landed at the intersection of North 8th and Park streets in Manitowoc, Wis. The debris was later identified by the U.S. Air Force as a fragment of Soviet Sputnik 4, launched two years earlier. It was the first certified piece of space litter to hit the U.S. In 1963 a charred metal sphere with a 15-in. diameter turned up on a sheep ranch in New South Wales. It was part of a Soviet

problems as they arise rather than trying to find long-range solutions. These solutions might require better technology — to control auto emissions, clean up oil spills, or dispose of nuclear wastes — but more effective solutions can be developed if we understand the social basis of the problems and change our system of transportation.

Our transportation problems are caused in part by a cultural lag in our awareness of the need for safe public transportation. Social planning could help us change our social systems and improve the situation. Those who have a vested interest in our current system might resist change, which would create a certain amount of conflict, but such conflict might be beneficial to society. Sociologists, by helping us understand social change, can help us direct it.

Modernization in Underdeveloped Nations

Evolutionary theorists tend to assume that today's underdeveloped nations in Africa, South America, and other areas that do not have mod-

space vehicle, but the U.S.S.R. never claimed it.

The probability of space rubble hitting a person is so small that Lloyds of London considers the odds impossible to calculate. Nevertheless, in 1969 a Japanese freighter in the Sea of Japan was struck by wreckage from a Soviet spacecraft. There were reports from Tokyo that five crewmen were seriously injured. They remain the first and only victims of debris from space.

More serious than the danger to earth is the threat that space debris poses for satellites and other extraterrestrial conveyances. Shuttle 10 returned to earth last February with a pea-size pit in its windshield. NASA has reserved judgment on the cause, but the dent is probably the result of a micrometeorite strike or a fragment of titanium, beryllium or other space-age material striking the craft.

Orbital space has become so crowded in recent years that launched objects frequently pass within 30 miles of one another. NASA intentionally sent off the most recent shuttle at the earliest possible opportunity in April to make sure that the orbiter would fly no closer than 130 miles to Soviet space station Salyut 7. Said a Kennedy Space Center launch technician: "We have had a kind of unwritten agreement with the Soviets to keep our launch vehicles at least 200 kilometers away from their birds."

Despite measures taken to prevent accidents, two U.S. satellites collided in 1965, scattering a cloud of debris in their wake. Evidence suggests that in 1981 Cosmos 1275, a Soviet navigation satellite, was blown into 135 fragments by an errant piece of space debris. In 1975 a metallic U.S. communications balloon deflated after colliding with a junk fragment.

The success of the Solar Max satellite repair mission provided a potential solution to some of the orbital traffic headaches. NASA has suggested that on future missions space-walking astronauts may be able to collect some of the space junk with grapples, rope it in line like freight cars, attach the tethers to rockets and propel the material either into the earth's oceans or to special garbage dumps in space. One possible site: the moon. "Who knows?" says one NASA official. "A junkyard out there could be a good place for us to find spare parts one day."

*Even that count is incomplete, since NORAD did not include objects that have escaped the earth's gravitational clutches, such as the abandoned Viking lander on Mars or Pioneer 10, which last June flew beyond the outermost planet of the solar system.
SOURCE: *Time*, 21 May 1984.

---

ern industry, such as is found in Europe and North America, will pass through the same stages that industrialized nations passed through in their quest for *modernization,* the process whereby preindustrial countries emerge as urban societies with lower birth rates, more goods and services, better nutrition and health care, improved housing, and a share of some luxuries.

A closer comparison, however, suggests that contemporary nations may not be able to take the same course as those that are already industrialized. Since the United States developed into an industrial society, it has had a vast supply of natural resources, including excellent land for agriculture and minerals such as iron and coal. The United States can also bring in the labor it requires through immigration and stop immigration when no more workers are needed.

Third World nations that have not modernized are developing in a very different environment. Death rates in these nations have been decreasing sharply while birth rates have generally remained high. Even where the birth rate has dropped, rates of infant mortality are low and the population is growing rapidly. As the population increases, so does the demand for food and

shelter, but the supply of these necessities has not increased, and dysentery and pneumonia are common, especially among children. The need for more medical care thus puts further strain on the resources of the population.

Many underdeveloped nations simply lack natural resources. Tropical forests and arid deserts cannot easily be developed to produce grain. Oil, coal, iron, and lumber are unavailable in many countries. Many of these items must be purchased from other countries to meet the needs of the ever-growing native population. To purchase these necessities, Third World countries have borrowed enormous sums and now have huge debts to Western banks, especially to the large banks in the United States.

To pay these debts, Third World countries have tried to develop cash crops that can be exported to pay for the goods the country must buy. These agricultural products are usually not foods, but such products as coffee, cotton, and flowers; and since the land has been taken over for cash crops, the native population no longer has land to grow food for themselves. They do not have jobs in agriculture either, because most of the work is done with farm machinery. Part of the rural population has moved into the already crowded cities hoping to find work, but often they live in the streets or in makeshift homes that provide little shelter.

Work in the city is scarce, since manufacturing requires natural resources. Even when a newly developing nation can produce goods that are competitive on the market, they may find markets closed to them. Textiles and clothing, for example, can be produced very inexpensively in many underdeveloped nations because they have many workers who will work for extremely low wages. As a result, their clothing is cheaper than any produced in the United States. To counteract this differential and to protect its own industry, the United States limits the amount of foreign clothing that can be imported.

Inasmuch as underdeveloped nations cannot compete with the large multinational industries, they sometimes invite those industries to come into their countries to do business, hoping to provide employment for the natives and income for the country. But this is rarely successful. Employment opportunities are usually too few and limited to the lowest-paying jobs. When the goods are exported, the profits go to the multinational corporation and not to the host country.

Thus, while the United States developed its industry with control over its population, abundant natural resources, and no competition from other world industries, developing nations have tried to modernize with too large a population, a shortage of natural resources, and highly developed competition from worldwide industries. Not surprisingly, they have been unable to support their people. In trying, they have gone into debt to such an extent that the world banking system is threatened by bankruptcy from the unpaid debts of these nations.

The assumption that underdeveloped nations will develop into industrial nations is overly optimistic. The very different circumstances existing between the underdeveloped and the developed world have rendered old patterns of modernization unworkable. Third World nations will need to find a new pattern of development and will undoubtedly need the aid of developed nations if they are to succeed in their efforts to support their populations.

Social Change and the Individual

How does social change affect the individual? In developing nations, increasing population and the removal of people from their land have had a devastating effect on the individual. Whenever social change is so disruptive to the social order that individuals cannot obtain the basic necessi-

Clothing is manufactured much more cheaply in Asian countries, because labor is inexpensive. Here a woman works in a massive factory cutting out dozens of garments at a time. These garments will be sold at low prices, and the profits will go to the owners of the factory. If the factory is American owned, rather than locally owned, the underdeveloped nation will benefit little from the industry.

ties of life, change can be terrifying. But what are the effects of social change when it is generally perceived as progress? This question has always been of interest to sociologists.

Most early sociologists believed that industrialization alienates people from their work and from one another. Durkheim was one of the few who believed that complex industrial societies would have a positive effect on human relationships. Noting that peasants were moving to European cities in large numbers, he recognized that this changed the nature of their labor. Peasants had been self-sufficient and performed all of the work necessary to meet their personal needs, while in the city, work was specialized and workers were not self-sufficient. Each person specialized in a particular product and then traded that product for money to meet personal needs. Thus the cobbler sold shoes and bought food and clothing. In *The Division of Labor* (1893),

Durkheim endorsed the move toward specialization, arguing that this interdependence would create a more integrated society.

Marx, on the other hand, was concerned that the move from agrarian to industrial societies would alienate people from their work. The goods produced would be owned by the factory owner, not the worker. Marx believed this arrangement was so unfair that it would not survive. Workers would rebel and a more equitable system of work would be developed.

Tönnies (1887), whose theories we discussed in Chapter 20, was also concerned that interpersonal relationships would suffer in industrial society. Peasant society, he contended, was characterized by gemeinschaft relationships in which people knew one another totally, while in urban society they would be strangers. Those who worked together would know nothing about their coworkers' families or religious or political

views, for example. Tönnies referred to these impersonal relationships as gesellschaft.

Weber was concerned about the increasing rationalization of society. The traditional beliefs of the family were rapidly disappearing, and in Weber's day society was becoming more bureaucratic. Decisions were no longer being based on traditional family concerns. The system in which people performed tasks according to their capabilities and were taken care of when they were unable to be productive gave way to one in which decisions about employment were made on the basis of the employer's needs. Employees were hired or fired regardless of their own needs for work, income, or self-respect.

Sociologists realize that modern socialization encourages individuals to behave in a fashion compatible with industrial society. In the nineteenth century, when frontiers were being conquered and industries were being built, people were encouraged to be highly innovative, and even those who were the most ruthless were needed to tame the frontier and build the new industries. Also, people on the frontier far from neighbors did not have to worry about being popular, getting along with others, cooperating, or making a good impression. They did, however, need the skill and wit to stay alive.

The same skills were needed in the business world. Businesses were small, and whether one owned a store or began a small factory, survival depended on one's own skill and hard work. The most successful industrial leaders of the nineteenth century, the so-called robber barons, were noted for their extreme ruthlessness.

Today, the nature of work has changed dramatically. Most people work in corporations with many other individuals. In a large corporation, a competitive person who lives by skill and wit and is concerned exclusively with his or her own survival makes many enemies and can create chaos rather than cooperation.

The type of manager corporations seek today, according to Maccoby (1977), is the *gamesman*, the person who is highly competitive and innovative but who prefers to function as the leader of a team. The gamesman thus occupies a position similar to that of a quarterback on a football team. Interestingly, football surpassed baseball as the most popular American sport in the mid 1960s. The more individualistic sport of baseball has given way to a type of sport requiring a team effort and cooperation. It seems that changes in the way we spend our leisure correspond to changes in the types of managers sought in the job market.

Television and the other mass media have also affected individual lifestyles. The media encourage us to buy cosmetics and designer clothes, and we watch programs depicting middle-class lifestyles. We listen to news broadcasts that tell us what is important in the world. As a result of the mass media, there are probably fewer eccentric individualists in society — most of us have learned the ideal of the middle-class lifestyle.

The Future

Futurists, people who attempt to describe what the future will be like, range from the most pessimistic doomsayers to the greatest optimists. The doomsayers predict an economic depression far worse than the depression of the 1930s. The wisest investment, they say, is to buy a piece of land in a very remote part of the country, build a substantial shelter that will be well hidden from the hordes of the poor and starving who will be roaming the countryside when the economy collapses, and bury near the shelter a supply of dehydrated food, guns, and other basic equipment needed to survive alone in the wilderness.

The optimists predict an end to poverty and drudgery and believe that human innovation will solve our problems. Alvin Toffler (1981), in his book *The Third Wave*, suggests that computers may make a more individualistic society

Writers and filmmakers have often fantasized about the future. Woody Allen's movie Sleeper *offered a satirical view of the future, in which elements of present-day society exist side by side with futuristic elements. No one really can predict the future, but most likely it will fall somewhere between the visions of the pessimists and those of the optimists.*

possible. People will be able to remain at home and earn their livings by telecommunications, creating for themselves and their children a more unique and creative individual lifestyle.

Sociologists are more hesitant to make predictions. One realistic method of determining what the future will be like is to analyze the possibilities and problems that it might hold and use social planning to strive for future goals and avoid future disasters.

Etzioni (1980) followed this course in making his predictions. He argues that society should make choices and plan for a future that will provide a satisfactory lifestyle to its members. Our economy is currently based on the consumption of vast amounts of goods, and we are using up our natural and economic resources. Meanwhile, our factories, transportation systems, roads, railroads, and bridges are deteriorating rapidly. We must choose either to continue to spend

money on goods or to spend hundreds of billions of dollars to modernize our factories and build an efficient transportation system. This rebuilding would reduce the hazards of pollution and improve the quality of life for all, but it might mean we would have to cut back on our consumption of goods.

Etzioni used the typical approach of sociologists in his study of social change, which is to try to understand the social system. Our social system is based on a profit-oriented economy, and we manufacture products that can be sold for a profit. Our system functions to support a cycle of production and consumption, but it does not support modernization of factories or an efficient use of resources unless such actions provide a profit. By understanding that our system now functions only when profits are made, it is possible to predict what will happen if we continue to function as we have in the past. We will use up

SOCIOLOGISTS AT WORK
Consulting on Energy Conservation

E. Denise Stokes is an associate with Planergy, Inc., a group of energy management and conservation consultants in Austin, Texas. She has a doctorate in sociology and demography from the University of Texas. Since 1982, she has been using her expertise to help utilities and consumers use energy more efficiently.

"We do most of our work for electric and gas utilities," she says. "The utilities are regulated by state governments, which are trying to encourage conservation and control costs. Certain states are beginning to take a utility's record on conservation into account when they consider requests for rate increases and during other phases of regulation. Some of our recent work has been to evaluate utility conservation programs. On this type of project, one of our roles is to ensure that the evaluation fulfills both the state's and utility's planning needs and requirements. We try to get as much of the information we need from the data available at the utility itself, and then we devise a plan to collect any additional information."

How is a background in sociology useful to an energy consultant? "A knowledge of survey methods, questionnaire development, and sampling design is critical in developing accurate surveys on energy conservation and load manage-

ment," Stokes explains. "I find informal interview techniques and general research skills valuable in collecting information from sources in government and business. And I need statistical expertise for countless projects, including writing the proposals used to get work, analyzing the data we collect in surveys, evaluating the research done by others, and making forecasts of potential savings for various conservation programs."

Stokes says that her studies of the structure and functioning of formal organizations have proven fruitful as well. "Knowing how bureaucracies work helps me get information from state government. I know that the best person to ask for a certain piece of information is not necessarily the person you know has it. Often it's easier to get if from secretaries or staff members, who are not as busy and who may actually be the ones putting the information together anyway. One branch of a bureaucracy often doesn't know what the others are doing. A department that is supposed to have information may not have it, but you may be able to get it from some other department.

"My demographic training also ranks high in value," she says. "As part of our evaluation, we

all our resources. Yet innovations can be made, institutions can be changed, and values and goals can be altered: a society can change its course and move in a new direction. We cannot today optimistically assume that progress will inevitably be made and that we do not have to plan to reach our goals. Neither is there reason to be so pessimistic that we resign ourselves to becoming

victims of a social system in decline. Furthermore, we cannot blithely assume that society will run its course from good times to bad and then bounce back to good times again; we could in the meantime destroy all life on earth. By understanding how societies function, we can make choices, alter our social institutions, and develop lifestyles that will reduce conflict, avoid ecologi-

assess whether a given conservation program has reached all types of energy consumers with our surveys — homeowners as well as apartment dwellers, members of different racial and ethnic groups, and people at all income levels. And because consumer conservation is influenced by socioeconomic factors, we can then make recommendations on how to improve program effectiveness."

One of Stokes's recent projects was to evaluate an earlier conservation survey conducted by Planergy. In the earlier project, questionnaires were mailed to all of a utility's customers to obtain a profile of their energy use and offer them conservation recommendations. Questions covered a variety of topics — the temperature the house was kept at, the number of people in the house, the number of windows and the direction they faced, and so on. When the questionnaires were returned to Planergy, the results were analyzed by computer and the respondents were mailed information on how they could improve their energy efficiency. Stokes's task was to evaluate the effectiveness of this program. In her follow-up survey, she asked questions designed to find out whether consumers were satisfied with the earlier project and whether those surveyed made or planned to make any changes as a result of the evaluation. When they did not make changes, her job was to evaluate why not.

Once a project has been completed, Stokes writes up a report that goes to the utility. In some cases, she suggests that a conservation program be modified to improve cost effectiveness; in others, she suggests ways of improving a program's promotion to make sure it's reaching those it is intended for. Sometimes an evaluation turns up problems of a distinctly sociological bent. One Texas utility, for example, offered to repair broken air conditioners belonging to elderly people for free, but they found that they had trouble getting their customers to take advantage of their service. Several organizations that worked with the elderly had said they would help, but they had backed out at the last minute, and it appeared that they distrusted the utility's intentions. Stokes had to determine how the problems had arisen and help get the service to the people who would benefit from it.

Has her work given Stokes insight into energy use in the United States in the years ahead? "The trend is definitely toward conservation," she says. "I may be biased because I deal mostly with people interested in conservation, but it seems to me that individual households are more conservation-minded. Whenever somebody is renovating a home today, saving energy is always a consideration because they get their money back so quickly. This is also reflected in government programs. Now that the federal government is less active in this area, the states are really getting serious about it. By providing services to people who work directly to solve our energy problems, I have the opportunity to learn firsthand what factors spur our formal organizations to act and react."

cal devastation, and support human life in the ever-increasing numbers that seem inevitable. We can plan to use our resources wisely. The authors hope that this introduction to the study of sociology has sparked your own sociological imagination so that you can think about "the good life" in terms of social as well as individual accomplishments.

Summary

Society is changing so rapidly that sociology has become in many respects the study of social change. Evolutionary theory proposes the optimistic view that change is progress, that growth is always good, and that stagnation leads to decay.

Conflict theorists are also optimistic about social change, but they believe that conflict will occasionally arise to correct adverse social developments. The outcome of such conflict, they say, will be better social systems.

Cyclical theories can be very pessimistic. They assume that societies grow, reach a peak, and then inevitably decay. Some cyclical theories, however, do not assume that change is always for the better or the worse. Societies move back and forth, they contend, emphasizing first one value, then another as the needs of the society change.

Structural functionalists have been concerned primarily with stability, but they recognize that society changes occasionally. Often, a change that affects one social institution will be followed by cultural lag, a disruption in the functioning of society until other institutions adjust to the change.

Most sociologists agree that society is orderly and that social institutions function to maintain order. They also agree that conflicts may arise when the existing social order causes hardship for the members of a society but that such conflicts can be beneficial.

Some major causes of social change and conflict are population changes, geographic changes, changes in the ecology, discoveries, and inventions. Population changes that have altered modern society include a decrease in the death rate, which has caused a population explosion and increased the number of older people; a decrease in the birth rate, which has decreased the number of young people; and migration, which has brought different cultures into contact with one another, spreading the ideas of one culture to another. We call this overlapping cultural diffusion.

Geographic changes such as droughts or increasing cold weather may cause people to migrate. Natural disasters such as floods, tornados, hurricanes, or fires can also precipitate sudden changes in societies. Today, many geographic changes are caused by the human population and its activities. Ecology is the study of the relationship between the population and the environment. Populations that strip an area of natural resources often undergo dramatic social changes.

Discoveries and inventions, which are human innovations, also change society. The discovery of resources not previously known and inventions that used resources in new ways brought about the industrial revolution. The invention of the automobile changed American lifestyles, relationships to family and community, the nature of work, the size of corporations, the use of fuels, ecology, and our willingness to go to war. Even with the diffusion of modern technology, it is unlikely that today's Third World nations will develop as industrial nations did because they lack important natural resources and must compete with the well-established industries of the industrial nations.

Changes in modern industry have changed the nature of human relationships. From the peasant's concern for family and community we moved to a period of competitive individualism, and we are now moving into an era of competitive team play. In the future, it is hoped that we will be able to plan innovations that will improve our ecology and our ways of relating to one another.

Key Terms

cultural diffusion
cyclical change theory
discovery
ecological changes
gamesman
innovations
invention
modernization
social change

Suggested Readings

Critchfield, Richard. **Villages.** *New York: Doubleday, 1981.* Advances in agriculture and contraceptive techniques have brought progress to some underdeveloped villages, but this book suggests further reforms to improve life in underdeveloped countries.

DiRenzo, Gordon J. **We, The People: American Character and Social Change.** *Westport, Conn.: Greenwood Press, 1977.* This collection of essays discusses how social changes affect the changing American character.

Erikson, Kai T. **Everything in Its Path: Destruction of Community in the Buffalo Creek Flood.** *New York: Simon & Schuster, 1976.* A moving story of what happened to the people in one community after a disaster.

Humphrey, Craig R. and Frederick R. Buttel. **Environment, Energy and Society.** *Belmont, Calif.: Wadsworth, 1982.* Two sociologists review the problems of environment and energy and discuss social changes needed to overcome them.

Miles, Ian and John Irvine (eds.). **The Poverty of Progress: Changing Ways of Life in Industrialized Societies.** *Elmsford, N.Y.: Pergamon Press, 1982.* Chronic diseases, suicide, homicide, stress, tooth decay, environmental devastation, and nuclear annihilation are all discussed as risks that have developed along with modern economic systems.

Ward, Barbara. **Progress for a Small Planet.** *New York: Norton, 1979.* This book optimistically argues that the world can progress and solve its present problems of pollution, malnutrition, and economic inequality.

Wright, James D. and Peter Rossi. **Social Science and Natural Hazards.** *Cambridge, Mass.: Abt Books, 1981.* These authors, who studied natural disasters over a period of a decade, concluded that disasters do not cause social change.

The Information Society: The Path to Post-Industrial Growth

by Graham T. T. Molitor

Social change affects every institution in a society. The most dramatic social change today involves communications and information — television, computers and data processing, for example. The changes in technology have had an impact on the family, the economy, political regulation, international trade, and religion. People who like to predict the future must consider the impact of technology on all areas of social life, as is done in the following article.

Runaway inflation, slowed economic growth, lagging productivity, and the depression of traditionally strong industries are now focusing much-needed attention on America's economic plight. But such immediate concerns distract people from the underlying transformation of the American economy that has given rise to these dislocating effects.

Simply stated, agriculture and manufacturing no longer constitute the foundation of the economy. A new economic order has emerged — one based not on material goods but on information.

The much-heralded post-industrial society has been with us since the mid-1950s. As modern technologies and innovations restructure the economy, they bring with them a host of new issues that demand response.

A new universe of policy questions now confronts society. Choices must be made about how best to invest scarce time and resources to encourage economic progress, and about the pervasive influence of computers and electronic data processing on such issues as individual privacy. These choices will help determine America's future economic and social health.

Many people still believe that America remains in the group of the Industrial Revolution. Such a notion is far out of date. The high point of American work force employment in manufacturing, commerce, and industry came not during World War II, as most people might guess, but in 1920, when 53% of the work force was so employed. In that year, 28% of the workers were engaged in agriculture and extractive industries, and 19% were employed in information, knowledge, education, and other service enterprises.

The distribution of the work force in contemporary America is far different. By 1976, only 4% were engaged in agriculture, 29% were in manufacturing, 50% — fully one-half — were in information, and 17% were in other service occupations.

Economically, politically, and socially, the importance of manufacturing is fading fast. By the year 2000, a mere 2% of the American work force will work in agriculture, 22% will be in manufacturing, and 66% — two-thirds — will be allied with information. An additional 10% will provide other services.

This is a basic profile of post-industrial society. As it takes shape, America will continue to suffer from the structural dislocations of an economy adjusting to new economic underpinnings.

Pre-industrial society — America before World War I — depended on labor in drawing resources from nature's bounty.

In industrial society — America in the middle of the century — man-machine combinations used energy from the natural environment to transform nature into a technical environment. This form of economic activity depended heavily on energy.

The Knowledge Revolution

But now, in post-industrial society, the major resource is knowledge. Intangibles have replaced tangible material goods as the dominant factor in commercial enterprise, the central assets, and the primary source of wealth and power. A new set of "knowledge industries" are on the rise. They include a vast range of endeavors:

☐ All aspects of the printing and publishing trades.

☐ The communications and telecommunications industries — broadcasting, periodicals, journals, libraries, accounting, teleprocessing, word processing, and so forth.

☐ Communications and knowledge professionals, including journalists, research scientists, engineers, social scientists, and educators on all levels from pre-school to postgraduate and from trade school to on-the-job training. Also included are policy researchers, think-tank workers, and swelling numbers of professionals whose primary contributions are their brains, not their brawn.

☐ Last, and crucially important, are the companies engaged in the research, manufacture, and distribution of communications equipment — such firms as AT&T, Xerox, IBM, Control Data, RCA, Texas Instruments, and even Exxon (fast becoming a major factor in communications high technology).

Information processing equipment, supplies, and services expenditures alone are likely to reach $62 billion during 1981. The annual growth rate of 12–15% makes it a standout amidst other faltering sectors.

The companies involved are blue chips in more than one sense of the term. They are destined to be the business giants of the future, eventually eclipsing the older industrial giants, such as General Motors, that dominated a bygone age.

The production, understanding, and control of knowledge have become essential, especially in the advanced nations. Knowledge and information industries are fast becoming the decisive factors in the growth of the productive forces of nations.

The knowledge revolution already has invaded other areas of the economy. Livestock are fed by computer from computer-controlled diets. The most productive automobile factories in existence, in Japan, are also the most highly automated. Robotics is taking over.

Drastic Changes for Society

A wide range of new and emerging information technologies will reshape many facets of society. Some of these innovations will mean drastic changes for the transportation industry. Americans are not far away from the time when people will conduct many of their transactions — banking, shopping, and even jobs — electronically. People will no longer have to commute to work, but will communicate instead. High energy costs will encourage the rapid introduction of elaborate electronic home entertainment systems.

The desperate need for more efficient use of resources will also accelerate such trends. In no small part, these developments will eventually reduce energy requirements.

In the past, technology has always solved problems of limited resources. For example, futurist Buckminster Fuller reminded us in his 1969 book *Utopia or Oblivion* that a one-quarter-ton communications satellite outperformed 150,000 tons of transoceanic cable. Since then, the cost and efficiency of commercial communications satellites has improved drastically and further advances already on the horizon assure continued remarkable improvement. The Federal Communications Commission's approval last December of launching 20 to 26 domestic communications satellites will add substantially to the eight satellites presently in orbit.

The information revolution promises a vast new range of potential home information services — electronic fund transfer systems, electronic shopping, electronic mail terminals, interactive TV, pay cable TV, teleconferencing, video recorders, and home computers.

Bringing electronic data processing within the reach of mass marketing grows ever closer as costs decline. During 1980, microprocessor costs declined at an annual rate of 22%, information storage costs fell by a 40% rate, and communications equipment dropped at an 11% clip. As costs dropped, sales grew. The work horse, personal home computers, grew at an astounding rate of 60% in 1980.

These telecommunications services are destined to become the dominant source of information received by U.S. citizens, eventually displacing the current dominance of the ubiquitous TV set, telephone, radio, phonograph, and tape recorder.

New Technologies Evolve

Historically, newer, more efficient and convenient communications media have supplanted established ones. At first, the more advanced medium supplements the earlier one; then the earlier mode wanes as the new technology becomes the dominant source or conduit of information.

This pattern has held true from the time language replaced guttural communication and gesticulation as the primary means of communication to the present day, the most recent dramatic example being when television replaced radio and the printed word as the primary source of information.

Television is without a doubt the dominant communications medium today. The average person spends more time watching TV than following any other single leisure-time pursuit. The number of daily household viewing hours increased from 4.6 hours in 1950 to 6.2 hours in 1977.

Most households have more than one TV set (an average of 1.67 per household in 1979), and nearly every household has at least one — an estimated 98% of American households did in 1978.

The tremendous decline in the cost of TV sets has made them increasingly available to the masses. Initially, sets cost $500; current prices run under $100.

Within any communications medium, improved versions regularly supplant the old. Years ago, large-screen black-and-white televisions succeeded smaller-screen models. In turn, color TV replaced black-and-white TV.

Innovations in the works promise an exciting future for television. The number of TV channels available will greatly expand with the growth of cable TV, satellite broadcast TV signals, and microwave and other exotic transmission modes.

Video recordings and two-way (interactive) cable TV will provide still another means for expanding the versatility and richness of the information and entertainment available from TV. Flat-screen, full-wall projection television and even holographic (3-D) projection systems show technological promise.

While current activity focuses on television, the stage already is set for the emerging communications modes to dominate and supersede it.

Telecommunications — and particularly the advent of computers as a main element in information handling — is already creating waves.

Electronic data processing (EDP) will become the next step in a long line of innovations in communications.

EDP is probably not the last step in this process. The coming years may see some startling developments in areas exploiting potential powers of extrasensory perception (ESP) and parapsychological phenomena. One can only imagine the effects of technologies that provide information in advance of the actual occurrence of events.

But for the foreseeable future, computers will provide the largest changes. The information revolution is upon us. What steel, petroleum, and the induction motor were to the industrial revolution, computers and semiconductors will be to the post-industrial society.

The Information Business

At this point, America is by far the world leader in information industries. Information equipment sales for 1980 are estimated at $30.5 billion in the U.S., contrasted with $8.6 billion in the second-ranked nation, Japan.

America leads all other countries by large margins in the production of computers. Value of production in U.S.: $13.3 billion; in second-ranked Japan: $2.9 billion (1979 figures).

As market dominance in the new information growth sector steadily grows in importance, new rivalries loom on the horizon, particularly for the United States, Japan, and West Germany. World economic and political leadership will increasingly depend on competitive advantage in the new growth sectors.

Although the U.S. now leads, some indicators suggest that the country's competitors are rapidly catching up. In a knowledge-based economy, research and development are especially important and can be indicators of coming innovations and future economic progress. In the U.S., the funds spent on research and development have declined in the last few years. West Germany increased R&D expenditure as a percentage of gross national product by approximately 50% from 1964 to 1978. During the same period, Japan's increased by 30%. The U.S. underwent a 23% *decline*.

The U.S. has been making relatively lesser commitments in other areas of investment with long lead times, such as the numbers of graduates in science and high-technology disciplines and investments in new plants and equipment.

Patents, whether applied for or granted, indicate advances in applied science and engineering and are another crude indicator of technological progress. They provide tangible evidence of successful research and development and represent an important step toward commercial application.

While simple quantitative counts of patents do not reflect the potential of the inventions, they do give a rough guide to the number of innovations one can expect in the next few years. In this era of the information-based economy, such innovations are important to economic progress.

More patents are granted annually in the United States than in any other country in the world. In recent years, the gap has been closing. In 1965, the U.S. granted more patents than Japan and West Germany combined. But by 1977, the number of patents granted in Japan alone was fast approaching the number of U.S. patents granted.

Patent applications tell another story of recent Japanese growth. In 1965, Japan and West Germany together accounted for about 50% more patent applications than the United States. By 1970, Japan and West Germany accounted for almost twice the number of patents applied for in the U.S. Japan alone had 50% more patent applications than the U.S. in 1977.

These factors imply that America's leadership position could decline over the next few years. While U.S. industries lead in many categories, their lead could be lost. Japan is playing "catch-up ball." Japan's long-term game plan, with active government support and active encouragement of huge Japanese vertical and horizontal combines (with antitrust immunity), accounts for the fact that an increasing number of Japanese firms are to be counted among the world's largest electronics manufacturers. "Japan, Inc." is a formidable competitor.

Japan openly avows the goal of seeking world domination of global telecommunications. America needs a similar government resolve to spearhead global market penetration, superiority, and dominance in critical information industries. Japan and its far-flung affiliates already control production in many telecommunications categories, both electronic and optical.

The World Marketplace

America might do well to reassess its antitrust policy. World economics has radically altered in the post-World War II period.

The Communist countries centralize all trade with non-Communist countries in just a few state trading companies. No more than 10 or 15 companies in Russia or China trade with the rest of the world.

Open cartel registries in Western European countries encourage industrial combinations to attain a parity of scale for effective competition in world markets.

Government-assisted multiple-industry collaborators in Japan strive to penetrate world markets. Centrally planned economies other than Communist nations (e.g., France) also focus economic strength in world markets.

Perhaps the most significant factor of all is the growing importance of regional trading blocs. The most important of these is the Euro-pean Economic Community. Member country integration of internal and external trade relations makes their impact in certain sectors, such as agriculture, extremely effective.

Not to be overlooked is the growing significance of commodity-oriented trading authorities. The most notable is the Organization of Petroleum Exporting Countries (OPEC), but it is not the only one.

These realities of competition in a changed world market call for economic power on a scale larger than ever. New legal guidelines that encourage rather than hobble and hamper large-scale economic units are indicated if the U.S. is to remain a meaningful and major economic world power. Parity of scale among economic competitors is crucially important.

The success of current antitrust suits aimed at breaking up America's biggest communication companies — notably AT&T and IBM — would surely adversely affect U.S. economic competitiveness and advance the global position of giant combines in Japan, Germany, and elsewhere.

Governmental regulatory tethers of other sorts also may hamstring the ability of U.S. firms to compete against other huge organizations that presently dominate world markets.

At the same time, the government should continue efforts to encourage competition *within* the communications industry. Emergent communications technologies, such as cable TV and satellite transmission, although still in infancy, are certain to grow by leaps and bounds. Federal policies should encourage competition between these new media as well as with the old. Fostering inter-industry competition should promote better service, a variety of choices, and lower prices.

Regulating Communications Media

Without a doubt, the government will be involved with the communications industry in many ways. In the past, as new communications technologies and products reached the market, abuses by promoters eventually led to government regulation.

This century has experienced three major cycles in which new communications technologies came to the fore:

- Low-cost, mass-circulation "penny press" at the turn of the century.
- Radio during the early 1900s.
- Television in the mid-1900s.

In each case, over-zealous promotion and advertising led to excesses and abuses. Self-regulatory efforts eventually gave way to government-mandated standards.

TV content and advertising, for instance, have been under siege in recent years by consumer critics. During the 1970s, American advertisers responded by undertaking self-regulation. The National Advertising Review Board, an industry supreme court of advertising review, was created. Better Business Bureau budgets and responsibilities increased. The National Association of Broadcasters TV code was updated. Numerous business association and private company codes of broadcasting ethics were revamped. Federal regulatory and legislative solutions are moving toward mandating action should serious shortcomings in these efforts become evident.

Regulating Electronic Data Processing

This same pattern will undoubtedly hold for this century's fourth emerging communications technology, as electronic data processing (EDP) becomes more widespread. Information technologies, like most innovations, entail both positive and negative effects.

Society will have to sort through many of these developments to decide how to deal with them. The far-reaching consequences of EDP will result in an overwhelming number of public policy issues. In fact, Public Policy Forecasting, Inc., has identified an astounding number of these issues — nearly 2,000 — and studied the directions many are likely to take.

For example, the integration of information systems steadily centralizes data, as well as the power implicit in the control of knowledge. At the same time, other developments, such as interactive, two-way telecommunications, push society toward decentralization. A free democracy depends in no small measure on maintaining an appropriate balance between the centralization and decentralization of information and knowledge. This is one area of upcoming public debate.

The amassing of large and detailed personnel dossiers of various kinds that EDP allows will draw increasing concern. The consolidation of this information through central computer banks will draw particular criticism. Citizens increasingly will need to be protected from unreasonable invasions of privacy.

The growing bodies of financial and economic data about bank customers and credit card users will prompt legislation to protect them from unwarranted invasions of privacy. More safeguards, particularly those restricting unauthorized use and third-party access, will be established. Tighter rules governing unauthorized access to or burgeoning dissemination of personal medical records will be imposed.

Employee privileges to inspect personnel records will be vastly expanded, including rights to: examine, hold, and copy their files; be consulted concerning the release of records or use of them for purposes other than those originally intended; correct, update, or submit their point of view on controversial matters; and restrict the scope and kinds of information allowed to be filed. Stiffer penalties for violations, simpler and more convenient civil processes, and judicial safeguards will be provided to assure fulfillment of these provisions.

Stricter Safeguards

Stricter safeguards governing the release of criminal records will be imposed. More laws expunging "blots" in criminal records for one-time follies will be enacted.

A continuing lightning rod for public policy concern involves America's headlong plunge toward the checkless-cashless society. The arbitrary power of "gatekeepers" controlling access to credit approval and ratings will be constrained so as not to unreasonably deny citizens access to financial exchange systems.

The more widespread the use of computers becomes, the greater will be the opportunity for fraud, embezzlement, trespass, and other criminal abuse. New computer crime control laws are coming.

Private sector eavesdropping and covert surveillance in all its myriad forms will be restricted. Concurrently, the use of these measures by law enforcement officials will be facilitated, especially in cases involving organized crime, narcotics offenses, and national security.

Polygraph and personality testing — either as a precondition of hiring or of continuous employment — will be discouraged. However, laws allowing their use at the subject's option (and free of coercion) will grow in number.

Computer-dialed telephone solicitations, so-called "junk calls," already have been prohibited in certain jurisdictions — Great Britain, for example. The further diffusion of reasonable controls is likely.

Freedom of information laws, sunshine legislation, and the like, still riding high, may fade with adverse experiences of openness and as memories of Watergate wane. The pendulum will swing back toward government secrecy. Too much openness will be seen as frustrating forthright action; the need to safeguard personal information will be given keener attention; and Cold War dictates will impose national security restrictions. Arrogant and wanton secrecy in government, however, will not be tolerated.

Royal commissions, White House task forces, and investigatory committees of all kinds already have begun to address these and other issues. Further government interest and action are coming.

The information revolution is causing fundamental economic, political, and social changes, both domestically and around the world. The changes raise new issues society has never before had to consider. As computers come to pervade all areas of life, the next 20 years should see some lively debate over these public policy issues, as people must decide how much the privacy of the individual must be protected, how much openness in government and business is necessary, whether or not large communications companies should be broken up or allowed to grow to a scale competitive with those of other countries, what portion of its resources the U.S. needs to devote to research and development, and how to support information technologies to advance economic growth.

With the number, magnitude, and complexity of the issues to be resolved, one thing is certain: despite the current anti-regulatory mood, further government involvement in the information sector is inevitable.

SOURCE: From *The Futurist*, April 1981, published by the World Future Society, 4916 St. Elmo Avenue, Washington, D.C. 20014.

Exploring a Career in Sociology

In a competitive job market, the more you know about what options are available to you, the better your chances of finding a job. We hope that the twenty-one profiles of "Sociologists at Work" in the preceding chapters have not only stimulated your interest in sociology, but also provided a sense of the range of career options open to you. Although they are but a small sampling, these sociologists clearly represent some of the many areas in which their knowledge, perspective, and methodologies can be applied. Traditionally, the vast majority of sociologists have chosen to teach and conduct their research in an academic setting. Although most sociologists continue to do so, an increasing number are electing to apply their skills to the government, business and industry, health services, and welfare and other nonprofit agencies. According to the American Sociological Association's 1977 publication *Careers in Sociology,* "sociology's career potential is just beginning to be tapped," and "many sociologists predict that the next quarter century will be the most exciting and most critical period in the field's 150-year history."

What career opportunities are available to graduates with various levels of training as we head toward the 1990s? What options might you consider if you choose to pursue your studies? This appendix provides a brief overview, followed by a list of sources — both organizations and publications — from which you can learn more about what sociologists are doing today, how you might make the best use of your training, plus a few tips on job hunting.

Degrees in Sociology: How Far Will You Go?

Once you decide to major in sociology, how far will you go? A B.A.? An M.A.? A Ph.D.? We hope the following information, drawn from conversations with other sociologists and from publications of professional sociological associations, will help you make this decision.

If you are thinking about beginning your career after four years of college, you might consider the following positions for which you would be qualified with a bachelor's degree. They are drawn from a list in the American Sociological Association brochure *Majoring in Sociology.*

- interviewer
- research assistant
- recreation worker
- group worker
- teacher (if certified)
- probation and parole worker
- career counselor
- community planner
- statistical assistant
- social worker (not certified)

Several of these positions and others like them begin as entry-level jobs but may lead to positions of increasing responsibility through on-the-job training and advancement. These types of jobs are available in a wide variety of settings — public and private welfare agencies, hospitals, research institutes, consulting firms, retail stores, corporations, schools, residential treatment centers, and federal, state, and local government departments. You would do well to investigate these different settings to determine which environment you would prefer to work in. Taking full advantage of school internships, volunteer work, and summer and part-time jobs can help you make this choice while allowing you to gain valuable practical experience and establish contacts during your undergraduate years. Once you have chosen to major in sociology, visits to your school career placement office, state and local employment agencies, federal job information centers, and the personnel departments of businesses and corporations can provide you with specific job descriptions as well as general information in areas that interest you. As you plan your course work, discuss your interests and goals with your professors. They can help you select the courses that will best prepare you for your chosen career. Whether you begin work after four years of college, seek advanced training, or pursue professional training in some other field, your undergraduate studies in sociology can be a valuable asset: they can provide you with a greater understanding of people and organizations — both of which you will deal with in almost every aspect of your life.

If you decide to go on to graduate studies, you have a broad spectrum of subjects from which to choose a particular area of expertise. Your special interest may lie, for example, in the sociology of the family, urban or rural life, education, health, gerontology, occupations, environmental issues, racial issues, stratification, religion, sports, government, the military, or law enforcement. Your approach to your specialty may involve concentrating on social organization, human ecology, demography, or methodology.

The 220 graduate programs in the United States offering master's degrees in sociology vary considerably in strengths and weaknesses, requirements for a degree, settings, and orientations. Review school catalogs carefully, talk with your instructors, visit as many schools as you can, and talk to alumni, if possible. You should find the graduate program that is strongest in your area of special interest and the one best suited to your career objectives.

Would you like to research population trends for the Census Bureau in Washington? Would you like to evaluate the effects of treatment programs in a rehabilitation center? Would you like to teach? Some graduate programs emphasize preparation for an academic career, and others are designed specifically to prepare students for careers in applied sociology in government or business.

According to Dr. Alexander Boros of Kent State University, the first program offering a master's degree in applied sociology was developed at Kent State in 1969. Similar programs are now offered in over a third of the nation's graduate schools. They place major emphasis on the application of sociological skills in a variety of settings. Many universities provide, in addition to core courses in theory, research, and statistics, training in (1) research for the practitioner, including evaluation research, (2) program designing/planning, (3) grant writing, (4) in-service training, and (5) clinical roles (counseling). At Kent State, students apply their training by doing an internship in an agency, where they work on a specific project and complete it within a forty-day time limit. Instead of a thesis, students write an "applied monograph," which consists of a log of their daily activities, a report on their project to the agency, and a report on the project from a sociological perspective. In addition to this close involvement with one agency, students spend one day a week visiting the sites of other internships, where they observe and evaluate activities and programs. Seventy-six students graduated from the Kent State program between 1970 and 1981. Just a few examples of their current jobs from a list by Dr. Boros will give you an idea of some of the career options open to you with a master's degree in sociology.

□ vocational rehabilitation specialist with the Veterans Administration

□ coordinator, deaf-blind services, with a city society for the blind
□ educational consultant for a regional council on alcoholism
□ Affirmative Action officer at a state university
□ administrator at a state home for the deaf
□ urban planning consultant, self-employed
□ researcher with the state Department of Health
□ research assistant at a private interviewing service
□ teaching associate at a state university
□ marketing administration coordinator at a banking equipment company

Our "Sociologists at Work" hold degrees at all levels, from B.A. through Ph.D. As you can see from their career paths, they play rich and varied roles in today's society. As consultants, researchers, policy planners, administrators, clinical counselors, teachers, social critics, and program evaluators, they work in areas as broad and diverse as the discipline they have chosen.

Finding out about Jobs

How do people find out about their jobs? Talk with a few successful job hunters and the answer will be "in every way imaginable. . . ." Consider some of our "Sociologists at Work," for example. Henry Lewis found out about his job as a group leader and counselor at New Horizons Ranch and Center from a friend in the criminal justice system who knew Henry had a B.A. in sociology and wanted to work with people. Carroll De Weese learned about his position with General Motors from a posting on a sociology department bulletin board. Joanne Willette got her job with a management and government consulting firm by finding a company she was interested in working for and writing to the president of the company.

Plan your job hunting strategies around your three main resources: people, job listings, and referral agencies.

One of the most successful strategies is developing a network of contacts whom you can call to ask about openings and who may call you when they hear about a job which might interest you. Building up such a network may involve several kinds of activity. Many leads arise out of social contacts — conversations with friends, friends of friends, and even strangers. You may want to establish a file of the names and phone numbers of whoever does the hiring at companies and agencies where you'd like to work (and use the file *often*). It is almost always worthwhile to attend meetings of professional organizations where you can meet people already working in the field.

Let your professors know you are looking for a job — a referral and recommendation from a professor helped secure the jobs of several of our "Sociologists at Work." Get in touch with anyone you've previously worked for during summer internships, on summer and part-time jobs, or while doing volunteer work. Never underestimate the power of word-of-mouth in your job search.

The alumni of your school are often a good source of information about careers. The career placement office probably keeps a file of alumni organized by type of career (e.g., government, publishing, public relations, etc.). The alumni included in these files are usually willing to talk to students about what they do and how they got started. Write to people who have careers in fields that you find interesting. Follow up your letter with a phone call. Don't be discouraged if the person you call is too busy to talk with you at that time — many jobs have peak periods of activity. Ask if you could call again in a couple of weeks. It is best to approach these interviews as opportunities for gathering information rather

than for lobbying for a job. You are more likely to receive a positive response to your request for an interview if you express an interest in learning more about the company or job. If after the information interview, however, you think that you would like to work at that company, say so in your thank you note. You never know when a job opening might come up and the person you talked with may very well remember your note and your interest.

While you're keeping your ears open and staying in touch with your contacts, watch for job listings and postings. Most sociology departments have bulletin boards set aside for job postings. Check these as well as postings in departments of education, theology, and social work, which often list social service jobs for which a degree in sociology can be an advantage. Visit your school's career placement office where you'll find counseling as well as lists of available positions. Don't ignore the most obvious and current list available — the newspaper want ads. If you don't see the particular job you're looking for, you can use the ads to build up your contact network by obtaining the names and addresses of agencies, businesses, and organizations where you might want to look in the future. Check the phone book and the local Chamber of Commerce for additional possibilities. Since many companies issue weekly listings of job openings, find out how to get hold of them. Professional organizations (see some below) often list jobs in newsletters or distribute employment bulletins.

Make the best use you can of public and private employment agencies. Register with the best agency in town — preferably one to whom the employer, and not you, pays the fee — and contact it on a regular basis. Register with state and local employment agencies and hound them for results. Don't forget the federal job information center in your area, where you can find out about federal jobs for which your degree qualifies you. Job hunting requires energy, imagination, endurance, and the most complete and current information you can obtain.

Applying for Jobs: Résumés and Cover Letters

You've gathered information about companies and careers you are interested in and have a list of places to contact. You've seen a job posting that interests you. What is the next step?

Put together a résumé of your skills and experience. Since people have written entire books on writing résumés, we will list only a few pointers here. (Check with your placement office or school library for more detailed information sources.) Depending on how many different career areas you are considering, you will probably want to have several versions of your résumé. If you are considering a job in public relations, for example, you should emphasize your experience dealing with people; if you are considering a job with a computer company, you should point up your experience with computers. In any case, start by listing jobs you've held (including part-time and summer jobs); honors or awards you've won; offices you've been elected to; extracurricular activities you feel are relevant; and any courses that may be appropriate. Once you've compiled your list condense and organize it so that it will provide the potential employer with an easy-to-read summary of your skills and experience.

Most résumés also include information about the schools you've attended and sometimes your career objectives. Go through several books on résumé writing for guidelines on format and style, as well as the pros and cons of including career objectives and personal information. Ideally, the résumé should be only one page and neatly typed. At the interview you can elaborate on your experience and any other pertinent information.

If you think of job hunting in terms of exchange theory, you will get a sense of what is involved in the process. Basically, you must convince the potential employer that you have skills that could be of value to his or her company. You want to exchange those skills for the opportunity to hold a job (with its attendant benefits). The employer wants to exchange the job for the use of your skills, which will benefit the company. Therefore, the more homework you do to determine what skills a company is looking for, the better your chances of getting a job. Most companies consider computer skills, word processing, and typing as pluses. Other skills are not so clear cut. Your knowledge of French, for example, might be of value if the company you are looking at has dealings with French-speaking clients, but for many companies your knowledge of French won't make a difference one way or the other. In such cases, there is no need to point out in your cover letter that you are fluent in French and have traveled extensively in France.

A degree in sociology can be of great benefit to companies, but you must think of concrete benefits in order to present it in your cover letter. Think of some of the things you have studied as a sociology major such as your awareness of the impact of social change on society that could be applied to government, environmental, or public service jobs. You have learned about the importance of roles and statuses that give you insights into areas involving advertising campaigns or public relations strategies. Your knowledge of research methods and statistics can be applied to any type of job requiring the analysis of data. These are just a few examples. If you have very little work experience, pointing out how you feel your degree prepares you for a particular job will be extremely important.

The cover letter that accompanies your résumé can be as important as the résumé itself in getting an interview. The type of cover letter you write will depend on the person you are writing to and your purpose for writing. You may be writing to respond to a specific job opening you read about in the newspaper. You may be writing to a specific person whose name was given to you by a contact about possible job openings. Or you could be writing to a personnel office to request an interview. In each of these cases the letter should be slightly different. The cover letter serves to catch the attention of the reader so that he or she will look at your résumé and respond to it.

Be sure to state why you are writing in the first paragraph of your letter. If you are writing in response to a specific job opening, you should state what the position is and where you saw it advertised. If you are writing to someone whose name was given to you by a contact, be sure to give the name of that contact. If you are writing to a personnel office, however, your task is a little tougher. Try to find out something about the company and include it in your letter. You might, for example, mention how successful a new product of their's appears to be based on an article you read in *The Wall Street Journal*. A special touch like this will separate your letter from the run-of-the-mill inquiry letters, and it will show that you have done some homework on the company.

Organizations

Among the best sources of information about any field and its career potential are its professional organizations. In the United States, sociologists are organized on the national, regional, and state level, as well as by special interests. These groups provide a variety of services and activities directed toward the furthering of sociology. Career prospects and opportunities are a frequent topic of discussions and reports at an-

nual meetings and workshops and in newsletters and journals. Most of these organizations welcome student members.

Below are some of the groups you can contact for additional information.

The American Sociological Association (ASA)
1722 N Street NW
Washington, D.C. 20036

The American Sociologial Association represents sociologists on the national level and comprises the largest sociological organization in the United States, with a total membership of almost 14,000 in 1982. Founded in 1905, it is "an organization of persons interested in the research, teaching, and application of sociology; the Association seeks to stimulate and improve research, instruction, and discussion, and to encourage cooperative relations among persons engaged in the scientific study of society" (ASA brochure). Within ASA are several "sections" organized by special interest, such as the Practice Section, the Medical Section, and the Social Psychology Section. ASA also provides a Teaching Resources Center and conducts an annual meeting, attended by thousands of people. Hundreds of research papers and reports are read at the meetings, and sociologists have the opportunity to share new ideas, make important contacts, and discuss new developments in the field. In addition, the association provides an employment service at the annual meetings. At other times during the year, members of ASA organize workshops devoted to specific concerns, such as one held in December 1981 on "Directions in Applied Sociology." The ASA newsletter, *ASA Footnotes*, is distributed to members nine times a year and contains career information, reports on the activities of ASA, departmental news, and organizational reports and proceedings. The association also publishes a monthly employment bulletin, several professional journals, a teaching newsletter, and a series of studies on areas of sociological concern. As the largest network of sociologists in the United States, ASA provides the most comprehensive clearinghouse for information about the field.

The Society for Applied Sociology (SAS)
c/o Dr. Alexander Boros
Department of Sociology
Kent State University
Kent, Ohio 44242

Founded in 1979, the Society for Applied Sociology was formed primarily to give an organizational role to sociologists employed outside academia and to promote interest in applied sociology. According to one of its founders, Dr. Alexander Boros, members "seek to promote social and cultural change with the sociological perspective. " SAS publishes the quarterly *Applied Sociology Bulletin*, which provides conference updates, reports on activities in the field, presents position papers, and lists job openings in applied settings. A journal and annual conferences are being planned for the future.

The Clinical Sociology Association (CSA)
c/o Dr. Jonathan Freedman
Hutchings Psychiatric Center
P.O. Box 27
Syracuse, N.Y. 13210

The Clinical Sociology Association was founded in 1978 to promote the establishment of a profession of clinical sociology. According to CSA's Fall 1979 newsletter, *Clinical Sociology*, the group's goals are "(1) to promote the application of sociological knowledge to intervention for individual and social change; (2) to develop opportunities for the employment and utilization of clinical sociologists; (3) to provide a meeting ground for sociological practitioners, allied professionals, scholars, and students; (4) to develop training, internship, certification, and other activities to further clinical sociological practice; and (5) to advance theory, research, and

methods for sociological interventions in the widest range of professional settings." In addition to many other features, each issue of the quarterly *Clinical Sociology Newsletter* highlights the career path and work of a practicing clinical sociologist.

Other Special Interest Organizations

There are several other sociological organizations with activities and services similar to those mentioned above and directed to areas of special interest and concern. Among these are the Rural Sociological Association, the Association of the Study of Religion, the Society for the Study of Social Problems, the Gerontological Society of America, the National Council on Family Relations, and the American Criminological Association. Current addresses for these groups may be obtained through the ASA.

Regional and State Organizations

There are several regional organizations (for example, the North Central Sociological Association, the Eastern Sociological Association, the Midwestern Sociological Association, the Pacific Sociological Association, and the Southern Sociological Association) as well as approximately twenty-five state associations, such as the D.C. Sociological Association. These groups generally hold annual meetings, conduct workshops in areas of special concern, and publish journals or newsletters. Some provide employment services and career information. For the past several years the D.C. Sociological Association, for example, has conducted an annual workshop devoted to employment opportunities for undergraduate sociology majors. Potential employers talk to students about where and how they would employ a person with a bachelor's degree in sociology. Current addresses for these groups may be obtained from ASA or your sociology professors.

Publications

The following publications may be ordered through ASA at the address listed above.

□ *Majoring in Sociology: A Guide for Students.* Contains information on how to apply to a college and secure a degree in sociology, what programs are offered in sociology departments, how and where to seek employment information, and what areas a sociology student might choose to specialize in. (Single copies are free.)

□ *Careers in Sociology.* Provides a description of the various careers in sociology and an understanding of the scope of the field. (Single copies are free.)

□ *Embarking on a Career: The Role of the Undergraduate Sociology Major.* Provides job-hunting strategies for the undergraduate sociology major. (Single copies are free.)

□ Reprints from *ASA Footnotes.* The following articles provide career information and are available for a nominal fee.

□ Hollin, Albert E. "ASA Committee Makes Recommendations for Expanding Employment Opportunities," *ASA Footnotes* 5(7) (October 1977):1, 8.

□ Jacobs, Ruth. "Job Hunting Hints Given to Undergraduate Majors," *ASA Footnotes* 3(1) (January 1975):1, 12.

□ Manderscheid, Ronald W. "Training for Federal Careers," *ASA Footnotes*, January 1978.

□ Orzack, Louis H. "Rutgers Searches for Non-Academic Jobs for Sociologists," *ASA Footnotes* 2(9) (December 1974):4.

□ Wilkinson, Doris. "Employment Projections, Job Seeking Tips for Undergraduate, Graduate Sociology Trainees," *ASA Footnotes* 6 (August 1978):6-7.

□ Wilkinson, Doris. "A Synopsis: Projections for the profession in the 1980's," *ASA Footnotes*, April 1980.

□ *Directory of Departments of Sociology.* A reference book listing departments of sociology in 1,936 institutions in the United States and Canada. Information includes name and address of departments, chairperson, telephone number, number of members of sociology faculty, number of undergraduate majors, and number of graduate students. Try the Department of Sociology for this. ($10)

□ *Guide to Graduate Departments of Sociology* (published yearly). Listing of departments of sociology offering master's and/or doctoral degrees. Includes information on faculty as well as special programs, tuition costs, and student enrollment statistics, along with a listing of recent Ph.D. dissertations and current positions. ($4 for students)

□ *Federal Funding Programs for Social Scientists.* A guide to federal funding opportunities; contains a description of more than fifty programs that support social science research.

□ *ASA Employment Bulletin.* Monthly listing of positions available in academic and applied settings; sent free of charge to all sociology departments. While positions listed generally call for graduate training, reading several issues can give you a sense of specific job descriptions of openings available to sociologists.

The following articles have appeared in professional sociological journals as noted and should be available in your school library:

Teaching Sociology

□ Lutz, Gene M. "Employment and a Liberal Arts Undergraduate Degree in Sociology," *Teaching Sociology* 6(4) (July 1979):373-390.

□ Schultz, C. C. "The Occupation of the Undergraduate Sociology Major," *Teaching Sociology* 2 (October 1974):91-100.

□ Vaughan, Charlotte A. "Career Information for Sociology Undergraduates," *Teaching Sociology* 7 (October 1979):55-64.

□ Watson, J. Mark. "Would You Employ Sociology Majors: A Survey of Employers," *Teaching Sociology* 9(2) (January 1982): 127–135.

The American Sociologist

□ Foote, N. N. "Putting Sociologists to Work," *American Sociologist* 9 (1974):125–134.

□ Gelfund, D. E. "The Challenge of Applied Sociology," *American Sociologist* 10 (February 1975):13–18.

□ Street, D. P. and E. A. Weinstein. "Problems and Prospects of Applied Sociology," *American Sociologist* 10 (May 1975):65–72.

The following publications of the Federal Bureau of Labor Statistics are available at your regional office of the Bureau of Labor Statistics by writing to Superintendant of Documents, Dept. 34, U.S. Government Printing Office, Washington, D.C. 20402.

□ *Federal Career Directory: A Guide for College Students.* Lists federal careers by type and agency and includes qualifications, descriptions, and projected openings for federal jobs.

□ *Occupational Outlook Handbook.* Provides information under the following categories for several hundred professions: nature of work, working conditions, places of employment, training, other qualifications, advancement, employment outlook, earnings, related occupations, sources of additional information.

Additional Sources of Information

□ "Working with People: Careers in Sociology." Contact the Department of Sociology and Philosophy, Tennessee Technical University, Cookville, Tenn. 38501.

□ *NELS Bulletin.* Monthly listing of positions available in the criminal justice system and social services. Write to the National Employment Listing Service, Criminal Justice Center, Sam Houston State University, Huntsville, Tex. 77341. Lists job descriptions, qualifications, salaries, and persons to contact.

□ "Clinical Sociology," a special issue of *The American Behavioral Scientist* (March–April 1979). Several articles describing aims and practice of clinical sociology. May be ordered through Sage Publications, P.O. Box 5024, Beverly Hills, Calif. 90210.

Glossary

absolutist view The view that there is wide agreement about social norms and that certain behaviors are deviant regardless of the social context in which they occur.

achieved status A social position obtained through one's own efforts, such as teacher, graduate, or wife.

acting crowd A crowd that acts on the basis of aroused impulse and thus one that may be volatile, aggressive, and dangerous.

activity theory The theory of aging that suggests that elderly persons who remain active will be the best adjusted.

age-adjusted death rate The number of deaths occurring at each age for each sex, per 100,000 people of that age who are living.

ageism Prejudice and discrimination based on age.

age norms Expectations about the behavior considered appropriate for people of a given age.

age-sex composition The number of men and women in the population, along with their ages.

aggregate group Any collection of people together in one place; participants interact briefly and sporadically.

Anglo-conformity A form of assimilation in which the minority loses its identity completely and adopts the norms and practices of the dominant WASP culture.

animism The religious belief that spirits inhabit virtually everything in nature and control all aspects of life and destiny.

anomie theory The view that deviance arises from the incongruence between a society's emphasis on attaining certain goals and the availability of legitimate, institutionalized means of reaching these goals.

anthropology The study of the physical, biological, social, and cultural development of humans, often on a comparative basis.

applied science Areas of science in which the knowledge gained from the "pure" sciences is put into practice.

artifacts Physical products or objects created through human actions.

ascribed status A social position assigned to a person on the basis of a characteristic over which he or she has no control, such as age, sex, or race.

assimilation The process through which individuals and groups forsake their own cultural tradition to become part of a different group and tradition.

associational group A group of people who join together to pursue a common interest in an organized, formally structured way.

authoritarian personality theory The view that people with an authoritarian type of personality are more likely to be prejudiced than those who have other personality types.

authority Power accepted as legitimate by those it affects.

barefoot doctors People chosen by the peasants in the communes in Communist China to provide medicine and treat simple illnesses and emergencies. They receive three to eighteen months of training.

beguines Communes of peasant women who did not choose to marry and who took vows of celibacy; these communes existed during the Middle Ages.

behaviorism The study of observable behavior in humans and animals; behaviorism is distinguished from theories that draw inferences about nonobservable motivations.

behavior modification The process of changing behavior by altering the response to the behavior; for example, a behavior that has been rewarded in the past will cease if the rewards are stopped.

bilateral A descent system in which influence, wealth, and power are assigned to both sides of the family.

bourgeoisie The class of people who control the means of production and use capital, natural resources, and labor for their own profit.

Buddhism One of the world's principal religions; adherents follow the teachings of Buddha, the enlightened one who preached a doctrine of "Four Noble Truths."

bureaucracy A hierarchical, formally organized structural arrangement of an organization based on the division of labor and authority.

capitalism An economic system in which all of the means of production are privately owned.

caste system A system of stratification in which

one's social position is ascribed at birth, one's value is assessed in terms of religious or traditional beliefs, and in which upward social mobility is impossible.

casual crowd A crowd that is high in anonymity but low in suggestibility, contagion, emotional arousal, and unity.

categorical group A group of people who share a common characteristic but do not interact or have any social organization.

censorship Prohibiting the availability of some type of information.

census An official count of the number of people in a given area.

charismatic authority Authority granted to someone on the basis of his or her personality characteristics.

Chicago school An approach developed by Cooley, Mead, Thomas, and others in the 1920s that emphasized the importance of social interactions in the development of human thought and action.

Christianity One of the principal religions of the world, followers of which profess faith in the teachings of Jesus Christ.

church An institutionalized organization of people who share common religious beliefs.

citizen One who is considered a member of a state and who is entitled to the privileges and freedoms granted to members of the state.

city-state A city and the surrounding area ruled independently of other areas.

class consciousness Awareness among members of a society that the society is stratified.

classical conditioning A form of training that involves pairing one stimulus with another to elicit a certain response; for example, a dog will learn to salivate at the sound of a bell if the bell is consistently rung when the dog is presented with food.

classical perspective A view of acting crowd behavior that suggests that people in a crowd lose their conscious personalities and act impulsively on the basis of their instincts rather than reason.

class system A system of stratification found in industrial societies in which one's class is determined by one's wealth and in which vertical social mobility is possible.

closed system A system of stratification in which there is no movement from one rank to another.

cohort A particular age group in the population.

collective behavior The spontaneous, unstructured, and transitory behavior of a group of people in reaction to a specific event.

collective excitement In the interactionist perspective on crowd behavior, the stage when milling reaches a high level of agitation.

community A collection of people within a geographic area among whom there is some degree of mutual identification, interdependence, or organization of activities.

compulsory public education Publicly funded education that is mandatory until a certain age.

Comte's law of human progress Comte's notion that all knowledge passes through three successive theoretical conditions: the theological, the metaphysical, and the scientific.

concentration An urban ecological process in which population, services, and institutions come to be gathered most densely in the areas where conditions are advantageous.

concentric zone model A model of urban structure showing that cities grow out equally in all directions from their original centers, producing uniform circles of growth that have their own distinctive land use, population, activities, and institutions.

concept An abstract system of meaning that enables us to perceive a phenomenon in a certain way.

conceptual framework A cluster of interrelated concepts for viewing a phenomenon and describing and classifying its parts.

conflict theory A social theory that views conflict as inevitable and natural and as a significant cause of social change.

Confucianism One of the world's principal religions, found mainly in China, adherents of which follow the teachings of Confucius.

conjugal families Families consisting of a husband and wife, with or without children.

contest mobility A competitive system of education in which those who do best at each level are able to move on to the next level.

control group In an experiment, the group not exposed to the independent variable that is introduced to the experimental group.

conventional crowd A crowd such as the spectators at a baseball game, the members of which are anonymous but share a common focus and follow established social norms and rules.

conversion effect A radical shift of interests and lifestyle that occurs when people move from one type of area to another, as from an urban area to a suburb.

counterculture A subculture that adheres to a set of norms and values that sharply contradict the dominant norms and values of the society of which that group is a part.

credentialism   The practice of requiring degrees for most high-paying jobs, whether or not the degrees actually signify skills necessary to accomplish the jobs.

crime   A violation of a criminal statutory law accompanied by a specific punishment applied by some governmental authority.

crowd   A temporary group of people in face-to-face contact who share a common interest or focus of attention.

cults   Extreme forms of sects that call for a totally new and unique lifestyle, often under the direction of a charismatic leader.

cultural complex   A combination of related cultural traits; for example, kissing, holding hands, and sharing verbal intimacies are parts of a love complex.

cultural diffusion   The spread of one culture's ideas and customs to another culture as populations migrate.

cultural lag   The tendency for changes in nonmaterial culture to occur more slowly than changes in technology and material culture.

cultural pluralism   The situation in which the various ethnic groups in a society maintain their distinctive cultural patterns, subsystems, and institutions.

cultural relativism   The belief that cultures must be judged on their own terms rather than by the standards of another culture.

cultural traits   The smallest meaningful units of culture.

cultural transmission theory   The theory that a community's deviance may be transmitted to newcomers through learning and socialization.

cultural universals   Aspects of culture that are shared by all people, such as symbols, shelter, food, and a belief system.

culture   The system of ideas, values, beliefs, knowledge, norms, customs, and technology shared by almost everyone in a particular society.

cyclical change theory   The view that societies go through a cycle of birth, maturation, decline, and death.

deconcentration   Movement outward from the city because of increases in land values and taxes and declines in services and public facilities.

demand-side economy   A political and economic policy designed to put more money into the hands of consumers so that they can spur the economy by buying more goods and services.

democracy   A power structure in which people govern themselves, either directly or through elected representatives.

democratic socialism   An economic system in which the means of production are owned primarily by individuals or groups of individuals; goods and services vital to the society, such as transportation systems and medical care, are owned and run by the state.

demographic transition   The change from high birth and death rates to low birth and death rates with a period of rapid population growth in between; this transition occurs as a society evolves from a traditional premodern stage to a modern industrial stage.

demography   The statistical study of population, especially data on birth rates, death rates, marriage rates, health, and migration.

denominations   Well-established and highly institutionalized churches.

dependency ratio   The ratio between the number of persons in the dependent population and the number of people in the supportive or working population.

dependent variable   A variable that is changed or influenced by another variable.

development theory   A perspective that emphasizes the life cycle and various stages of transition with specific tasks to be accomplished at each stage.

deviance   Variation from a set of norms or shared social expectations.

differential association theory   The theory that deviance results when individuals have more contact with groups that define deviance favorably than with groups that define it unfavorably.

differential reinforcement   The view that the acquisition and persistence of either deviant or conforming behavior is a function of what behaviors have been rewarded or punished.

direct relationship   A relationship between two variables in which an increase in one variable is accompanied by an increase in the other; compare with *inverse relationship*.

disclaimers   An aspect of our maintaining our presentation of self in which we deny behavior that contradicts how we wish to be viewed.

discovery   The act of finding something that has always existed but that no one previously knew about.

discrimination   Overt unequal and unfair treatment of people on the basis of their membership in a particular group.

disengagement theory The theory of aging that suggests that as people get older, they and the younger people around them go through a period of mutual withdrawal.

displacement A process occurring in split labor markets in which higher-paid workers are replaced with cheaper labor.

diversification The corporate practice of entering business in a variety of areas of manufacturing in order to protect profits; a decrease in profits in one type of business might be made up by an increase in profits in another type, for example.

downward mobility A move to a position of lower rank in the stratification system.

dramaturgical approach An approach to the study of interaction in which interaction is compared to a drama on stage; the importance of setting and presentation of self are emphasized.

dysfunctions In structural-functional theory, factors that lead to the disruption or breakdown of the social system.

ecclesia An official state religion that includes all or most members of society.

ecological change Change brought about by the way a population uses the natural resources available to it.

ecological specialization The concentration of homogeneous groups and activities into different sections of urban areas.

ecology The study of the interrelationships between living organisms and the environment.

economic determinism The idea that economic factors are responsible for most social change and for the nature of social conditions, activities, and institutions.

economics The study of how goods, services, and wealth are produced, consumed, and distributed.

ecumenism The trend for different denominations to join together in pursuit of common interests in a spirit of worldwide Christian unity.

egalitarian The norm of authority in the family in which decisions are equally divided between husband and wife.

ego In Freudian theory, the part of the personality that reconciles the desires of the individual with the demands of society.

emergent norm perspective A view of collective behavior that emphasizes how new norms emerge and influence the behavior of crowds.

emigration Movement of people out of an area.

endogamy A marriage norm requiring people to marry someone from their own group.

Equal Rights Amendment (ERA) A proposed amendment to the Constitution of the United States giving equal rights to women; it was not ratified.

estate system A system of stratification based on a family's relation to the land; practiced in Europe during the Middle Ages. People were born to a certain rank — noble, serf, or slave — but there was some opportunity for rank to change.

ethnic antagonism Mutual opposition, conflict, or hostility among different ethnic groups.

ethnic groups Groups set apart from others because of their national origin or distinctive cultural patterns such as religion, language, or region of the country.

ethnocentrism The view that one's own culture is superior to others and should be used as the standard against which other cultures are judged.

euthanasia Sometimes called mercy killing; deliberately ending a person's life to spare him or her suffering from an incurable and agonizing disease.

evolutionary theory A theory of social development that suggests that societies, like biological organisms, progress through stages of increasing complexity.

exchange theory A theory of interaction that attempts to explain social behavior in terms of reciprocity of costs and rewards.

exclusion Attempts to keep cheaper labor from taking jobs from groups that receive higher pay.

exogamy A marriage norm requiring people to marry someone from outside their own group.

experimental design A scientific procedure in which at least two matched groups, differing only in the variable being studied, are used to collect and compare data.

experimental group In an experiment, the group to which an independent variable is introduced; this variable is not introduced in the control group.

expressive crowd A crowd characterized by the physical movement of its members, as with a dancing crowd at a party.

expressive role A role that emphasizes warmth and understanding rather than action or leadership; traditionally associated more with women than with men.

extended family A family that goes beyond the nuclear family to include other nuclear families and relatives such as grandparents, aunts, uncles, and cousins.

external controls   Pressures or sanctions applied to members of society by others.

fads   Superficial or trivial behaviors that are very popular for a short time.

false consciousness   Lack of awareness of class differences and acceptance of upper-class rule.

family   A group of kin united by blood, marriage, or adoption who share a common residence for some part of their lives and assume reciprocal rights and obligations with regard to one another.

family life cycle   A series of stages families pass through, each of which involves different responsibilities and tasks.

family of orientation   The nuclear family into which one was born and in which one was reared.

family of procreation   The nuclear family formed by marriage.

fashions   Temporary trends in some aspect of appearance or behavior. Fashions resemble fads but tend to be more cyclical.

fecundity   A woman's potential for bearing children.

fee-for-service   A medical payment system in which the physician is paid for each visit and each service rendered.

fertility   A measure of the rate at which people are being born.

fetal monitoring   Measuring the vital signs of the infant as it is being born.

folk society   A community described by Redfield as small, isolated, homogeneous, and kin-oriented.

folkways   Norms of conduct of everyday life that bring only mild censure or punishment if they are violated.

formal external controls   Formal systems of social control applied to the individual by others; examples include courts, police, and prisons.

formalization   The stage in the development of social movements in which a formal structure is developed and rules, policies, and tactics are laid out.

formal organization   A large social group deliberately organized to achieve certain specific, clearly stated goals.

Freudian theory   A theory developed by Sigmund Freud that explains human behavior in terms of unconscious biological drives.

frustration-aggression theory   The theory that prejudice results when personal frustrations are displaced to a socially approved racial or ethnic target.

game perspective   A view of crowd behavior that suggests that members think about their actions and consciously try to act in ways that will produce rewards.

gamesman   The type of manager sought by corporations today: a person who is highly competitive and innovative but who prefers to function as the leader of a team.

gemeinschaft   A traditional community characterized by a sense of solidarity and common identity and emphasizing intimate and personal relationships.

gender roles   The cultural concepts of masculinity and femininity that society creates around gender.

generalized belief   A stage in the development of collective behavior in which people share a common identification and interpretation of a problem.

generalized other   The assumption that other people have similar attitudes, values, beliefs, and expectations. It is therefore not necessary to know a specific individual in order to know how to behave toward that individual.

genocide   The deliberate destruction of an entire racial or ethnic group.

gentrification   The rejuvenation of urban neighborhoods by middle-class people who move into and repair run-down houses.

geographic mobility   Movement from one geographic area to another.

geography   The study of the physical environment and the distribution of plants and animals, including humans.

geriatrics   The subfield of gerontological practice that deals with the medical care of the aging.

gerontology   The systematic study of the aging process.

gessellschaft   A modern community characterized by individualism, mobility, and impersonality, with an emphasis on progress rather than tradition.

ghetto   An area in a city in which members of a racial or ethnic minority are forcibly segregated.

greenbelt   An area surrounding cities that is preserved for farming and recreation and that limits the growth of cities.

Gross National Product (GNP)   The total value of the goods and services a nation produces in a year.

group marriage   A form of marriage in which several or many men are married to several or many women.

Health Maintenance Organization (HMO)   A prepaid health care plan in which a fee is paid in advance for all necessary health care.

heroic medicine   Dramatic medical treatments such as bleeding, blistering, or administering poisonous laxatives.

Hinduism   One of the world's principal polytheistic religions, with no religious hierarchy but a close involvement with society and the cosmic order; it is practiced mainly in India and Pakistan.

history   The study of the past; social history is concerned with past human social events.

horizontal mobility   A move from one job to another that does not raise or lower one's position in the stratification system.

hospice   A home for terminally ill patients in which the emphasis is on providing a comfortable, supportive environment for the patient and the patient's family.

horticulture   Small-scale farming that relies on tools such as the hoe to till the soil.

human relations school   A form of industrial management in which the workers' psychology, peer pressures, and attitudes toward management are taken into account.

hypochondriac   A healthy person who believes he or she is ill.

hypothesis   A statement about the relationship between variables that can be put to an empirical test.

id   In Freudian theory, the collection of biological drives that motivate behavior.

ideal culture   The norms and values that people profess to follow.

ideal type   A model of a hypothetical pure form of an existing entity.

idioculture   The system of knowledge, beliefs, behaviors, and customs that is unique to a given group.

immigration   Movement of people into an area.

incest   Socially forbidden sexual relationships or marriage with certain close relatives.

independent variable   A variable that causes a change or variation in a dependent variable.

inequality   Differences between groups in wealth, status, or power.

informal external controls   Pressures applied by peers, friends, parents, and other people with whom one associates regularly that are intended to encourage one to obey rules and conform to social expectations.

in-group   A social group to which people feel they belong and with which they share a consciousness of kind.

innovation   Changes that offer something new to a society and alter its norms or institutions.

institution   A stable cluster of values, norms, statuses, and roles that develops around a basic social goal.

institutional discrimination   The continuing exclusion or oppression of a group as a result of criteria established by an institution.

institutionalized behavior   Recurrent behavior that follows an orderly pattern with a relatively stable set of goals, expectations, and values.

institutional racism   Racism that is embodied in the folkways, mores, or legal structures of a social institution.

instrumental role   A role that emphasizes accomplishment of tasks such as earning a living to provide food and shelter; traditionally associated more with men than with women.

integration   The situation that exists when ethnicity becomes insignificant and everyone can freely and fully participate in the social, economic, and political mainstream.

interactionist perspective   A view of crowd behavior that emphasizes how people in crowds reinforce and heighten one another's reactions.

internal controls   Learned patterns of control that exist in the minds of individuals and make them want to conform to social norms.

invention   A device constructed by putting two or more things together in a new way.

inverse relationship   A relationship between two variables such that an increase in one variable is accompanied by a decrease in the other; compare with *direct relationship*.

Islam   One of the world's principal religions, followers of which adhere to the teachings of the Koran and of Muhammad, a prophet.

Judaism   The oldest religion in the Western world and the first to teach monotheism; today, the Jews are both an ethnic community and a religious group.

kinship   The web of relationships among people linked by common ancestry, adoption, or marriage.

labeling theory   A theory that emphasizes how certain behaviors are labeled "deviant" and how being given such a label influences a person's behavior.

laissez faire   An economy in which there is no government planning or intervention.

language The systematized use of speech and hearing to communicate feelings and ideas.

latent functions The unintended consequences of a social system.

laws Formal, standardized expressions of norms enacted by legislative bodies to regulate certain types of behaviors.

left wing A group in American politics that is motivated by political or religious moral issues and that seeks to radically alter the distribution of power and wealth in order to provide equality for the disadvantaged.

legal authority Authority based on a system of rules and regulations that determine how a society will be governed.

life chances The opportunities a person has to improve his or her income and lifestyle.

life expectancy The average years of life remaining for persons who attain a given age.

life span The biological age limit beyond which no one can expect to live.

lifetime jobs An employment practice in which workers are guaranteed a job for a lengthy period of time.

lobby An organization of people who want to influence the political process on a specific issue.

looking-glass self A process occurring in social interaction. It has three components: (1) how we think our behavior appears to others, (2) how we think others judge our behavior, and (3) how we feel about their judgments.

macrosociology A level of sociological analysis concerned with large-scale units such as institutions, social categories, and social systems.

Malthusian theory The theory proposed by Thomas Malthus that population expands much faster than the food supply, resulting in starvation for much of the population when it grows too large.

manifest functions The intended consequences of a social system.

market economy An economy in which the price and production of goods are determined by what people are willing to pay in the marketplace.

Marx and social conflict Karl Marx believed that social conflict — class struggle due to economic inequality — was a fundamental social process and an important source of social change.

mass A spatially diffuse collective in which geographically dispersed persons react to or focus upon some common event.

mass expulsion Expelling racial or ethnic groups from their homeland.

mass hysteria A form of diffuse collective behavior involving a widespread, highly emotional fear of a potentially threatening situation.

mass media Forms of communication intended for a large audience such as television, popular magazines, and radio.

matriarchal A family structure in which the wife dominates the husband.

matrilineal A family structure in which descent and inheritance are traced through the mother's line.

matrilocal A family norm that newly married couples should live with the wife's family.

mean A measure of central tendency computed by adding the figures and dividing by the number of figures; also known as the average.

median A measure of central tendency that half the figures fall above and half the figures fall below; also known as the midpoint.

medical center A major hospital that trains new physicians, conducts research, and provides tertiary medical care.

medical model of illness A model of illness in which sickness is viewed as an individual problem requiring individual treatment.

medical view The view that deviance is essentially pathological evidence that a society is unhealthy.

megalopolis A continuous strip of urban and suburban development that may stretch for hundreds of miles.

melting pot A form of assimilation in which each group contributes aspects of its own culture and absorbs aspects of other cultures such that the whole is a combination of all the groups.

Metropolitan Statistical Area A county or group of counties with a central city with a population of at least 50,000, a density of at least 1,000 persons per square mile, and outlying areas that are socially and economically integrated with the central city.

microsociology The level of sociological analysis concerned with small-scale units such as individuals in small group interactions.

middle range theory A set of propositions designed to link abstract propositions with empirical testing.

migration Movement of people into or out of an area.

millennialism The belief prevalent among certain sects that there will be a dramatic transformation of life on earth and that Christ will rule the world for a thousand years of prosperity and happiness.

milling The stage in the development of crowd behavior during which people move about aimlessly, grow increasingly preoccupied with others, and become increasingly inclined to respond without thinking.

minority group A group subordinate to the dominant group in terms of the distribution of social power; such groups are defined by some physical or cultural characteristic and are usually but not always smaller than the dominant group.

mobilization for action A stage in the development of collective behavior during which people are persuaded to join the movement.

mobs Emotionally aroused groups ready to engage in violent behavior.

mode The most frequent response in a body of data.

modernization theory The view that the status of older people declines with modernization.

modified-extended family structure The family structure in which individual nuclear families retain considerable autonomy yet maintain connections with other nuclear families in the extended family structure.

monogamy The marriage of one man to one woman.

monotheism The belief in one god.

moral view The view that deviance is immoral and antisocial.

mores Norms of conduct associated with strong feelings of right or wrong, violations of which bring intense reaction and some type of punishment.

mortality A measure of the rate at which people die.

mortification of self Stripping the self of all the characteristics of a past identity, including clothing, personal possessions, friends, roles and routines, and so on.

multinational corporations Corporations that do business in a number of nations.

multiple nuclei model The model of urban development showing that cities have areas of different types of land use, each of which has its own center or nucleus.

municipal hospital A hospital built and operated by a city or county.

mysticism The belief that spiritual or divine truths come to us through intuition and meditation, not through the use of reason or via the ordinary range of human experience and senses.

nation-states Large territories ruled by a single political institution.

nature-nurture debate A longstanding debate over whether behavior results from predetermined biological characteristics or from socialization.

neolocal A family norm that newly married couples should establish residences separate from those of both sets of parents.

noblesse oblige The obligation of the rich to give to the poor and suffering.

norms Formal and informal rules of conduct and social expectations for behavior.

nuclear families Families in which two or more persons are related by blood, marriage, or adoption and who share a common residence.

observational research Research in which the researcher watches what is happening and makes no attempt to control or modify the activity being observed.

oligarchy Government by a small elite group.

open system A system of stratification in which it is possible to move to a higher or lower position.

operant conditioning Conditioning in which a behavior is repeated because it has been reinforced in the past.

operational definition A definition of a concept or variable such that it can be measured.

operation of social controls A stage in the development of collective behavior in which the mass media, government, and other groups try to suppress or influence collective behavior.

organic solidarity Durkheim's term for the integration of society that results from the division of labor.

organizational group See *associational group.*

organized crime Groups expressly organized to carry out illegal activities.

out-group A group to which people feel they do not belong; they do not share consciousness of kind, and they feel little identity to the group.

panic An attempt to rapidly escape from a perceived danger.

parties Organizations in which decisions are made to reach certain goals, the achievement of which affects society.

pathological illness An illness in which the body is clearly diseased or malfunctioning in some way.

patriarchal A family structure in which the husband dominates the wife.

patrilineal A family system in which descent and inheritance are traced through the father's line.

patrilocal A family norm that newly married couples should live with the husband's family.

peer group An informal primary group of people who share a similar or equal status and who are usually of roughly the same age.

Peter Principle The notion that in a hierarchy, employees tend to rise to their level of incompetence.

Piagetian theory The theory that children pass through a series of qualitatively different stages in the development of their ability to think; these stages are associated with biological development.

placebo effect A benefit arising from a patient's belief that a medicine will have a beneficial effect.

planned economy An economy in which the production and prices of goods are planned by the government.

play According to Mead, a way of practicing role taking.

Political Action Committees Organizations formed to raise money for a political campaign.

political parties Groups of citizens formed with the express intent of gaining control of the political body of the state.

political pluralism A political system in which many diverse groups have a share of the power.

political science The study of power, government, and the political process.

politics The use of power to determine who gets what in society.

polyandry The marriage of one woman to more than one husband at the same time.

polygamy The marriage of one man or woman to more than one person of the opposite sex at the same time.

polygyny The marriage of one man to more than one wife at the same time.

polytheism The belief in and worship of more than one god.

popular excitement The stage in the development of a social movement when social unrest is brought into the open and people with similar concerns begin to organize.

power The ability to control or influence the behavior of others, even without their consent.

power elite A small group of people who hold all of the powerful positions and cooperate to maintain their social positions.

precipitating factors A stage in the development of collective behavior during which an event triggers a collective response.

prejudice A preconceived attitude or judgment, either good or bad, about another group; prejudices usually involve negative stereotypes.

presentation of self The way we present ourselves to others and how our presentation influences others.

priests Religious leaders who owe their authority to the power of their office.

primary care givers The health professionals who provide the first general, overall care the patient needs.

primary group A small, informal group of people who interact in a personal, direct, and intimate way.

primary labor market The labor market reserved for people who will advance to high-level positions.

primary medical care The first general, overall care the patient needs.

primary workers Workers who produce raw materials such as food or minerals.

principle of legitimacy Malinowski's idea that every society has a rule that every child should have a legitimate father to act as the child's protector, guardian, and representative in society.

profane That which belongs to the realm of the everyday world; anything considered mundane and unspiritual.

projection A psychological explanation of prejudice that suggests that people transfer responsibility for their own failures to a vulnerable group, usually a racial or ethnic group.

proletariat The laborers who serve as the instrument of production for the bourgeoisie.

propaganda An attempt to manipulate the ideas or opinions of the public by presenting limited, selective, or false information.

prophets Religious leaders who have authority on the basis of their charismatic qualities.

proposition A statement of the relationship between two or more concepts or variables.

proprietary hospital A hospital that is privately owned, usually by physicians or hospital corporations.

Protestant ethic The view associated with the Puritans that hard work is valuable for its own sake; according to Weber, the Protestant ethic is responsible for the high value placed on capitalism in the United States.

psychology The study of human mental processes and individual human behavior.

public A group of people who are confronted with an issue, who do not agree on how to address the issue, and who discuss the issue.

public opinion Any opinion held by a substantial number of people or the dominant opinion in a given population.

pull factors Natural or social factors that cause people to move into an area.

pure science The area of science in which knowledge is sought for its own sake with little emphasis on how the knowledge might be applied.

push factors Natural or social factors that cause people to move out of an area.

quality control circles Meetings at which workers discuss ways of improving production and set policy to reach their goals.

racial group A socially defined group distinguished by selected inherited physical characteristics.

racism Discrimination based on racial characteristics.

radicalism Labor groups joining together in a coalition against the capitalist class.

random sample A sample selected in such a way that every member of a population has an equal chance of being chosen.

range The span between the largest and smallest amount of a variable.

real culture The norms and values that people actually follow and practice. The real culture may or may not be the same as the ideal culture, which represents the norms and values people profess to follow.

reference group A group with which people identify psychologically and to which they refer in evaluating themselves and their behavior.

relativistic view The view that deviance can be interpreted only in the sociocultural context in which it occurs.

reliability The extent to which repeated observations of the same phenomena yield similar results.

religion An organized community of believers who hold certain things sacred and follow a set of beliefs, ceremonies, or special behaviors.

religiosity Intensity of religious feeling.

resocialization Socialization to a new role or position in life that requires a dramatic shift in the attitudes, values, behaviors, and expectations learned in the past.

resource mobilization theory The theory that the success of a social movement depends not only on those who benefit from it directly but also on their ability to mobilize other individuals and groups to contribute time, money, and influence.

right wing A group in American politics that consists of conservative people who want to preserve the traditional ways of life.

riots A form of collective behavior involving mass violence and mob action.

"roleless" role A position in society that is not associated with any expectations about performance; used to describe the position of the elderly in modern industrial society.

roles The social expectations or behaviors associated with a particular status.

role taking Assuming the roles of others and seeing the world from their perspective.

sacred Involving objects and ideas that are treated with reverence and awe.

sample A number of individuals or cases drawn from a larger population.

Sapir-Whorf Hypothesis The hypothesis that societies with different languages perceive the world differently because their members interpret the world through the grammatical forms, labels, and categories their language provides.

scapegoating A psychological explanation of prejudice that involves blaming another person or group for one's own problems.

scientific management A method of managing assembly-line workers such that their every movement is efficient.

scientific method A procedure that involves systematically formulating problems, collecting data through observation and experiment, and devising and testing hypotheses.

secondary care givers Those who provide more specialized care than that provided by a general practitioner.

secondary group A group in which the members interact impersonally, have few emotional ties, and come together for a specific practical purpose.

secondary labor market The labor market in which jobs pay poorly, there is little job security, and there are few promotions or salary increases.

secondary medical care Care that is more specialized than that the general practitioner provides.

secondary workers Workers who produce manufactured goods from raw materials.

sector model An explanation of the ecology of cities as a series of pie-shaped wedges radiating from the central business district, each with its own characteristics and uses.

sects Religious groups that have broken away from a parent church, follow rigid doctrines and fundamentalist teachings, and emphasize "otherworldly" rewards, rejecting or deemphasizing contemporary society.

secularization The process through which beliefs concerning the supernatural and religious institutions lose social influence.

segregation The separation of a group from the main body; it usually involves separating a minority group from the dominant group.

self-fulfilling prophecy The process described by Robert Merton in which predictions about behavior influence behavior so that those predictions come true, thus confirming the original prophecy.

senility A mental infirmity associated with the aging process.

serial monogamy Marriage to a number of different spouses in succession, but only one at any given time; also called sequential monogamy.

sexual harassment Sexual advances made by co-workers or superiors at work.

shamanism The religious belief that certain persons (shamans) have special charm, skill, or knowledge in influencing spirits.

sick role A set of expectations, privileges, and obligations related to illness.

significant others Persons that one identifies with psychologically and whose opinions are considered important.

slums Sections of a city marked by poverty, over-crowding, substandard housing, and poor living conditions.

social change Changes in the structure of a society or in its social institutions.

social class A category of people who have approximately the same amount of power and wealth and the same life chances to acquire wealth.

social contagion A stage in the development of crowd behavior during which the crowd's response to a common event increases in intensity and the crowd's behavior moves others to behave in the same way.

social dynamics Comte's term for social processes and forms of change.

social facts Reliable and valid items of information about society.

social gerontology A branch of gerontology that focuses on the social and cultural factors related to age and the aging process.

social group A group in which people physically or socially interact.

socialism An economic system in which the means of production are owned by all the people through the state.

socialization The process of learning how to interact in society by learning the rules and expectations of society.

social learning theory The view that deviant and conforming behavior are strongly influenced by the consequences that follow them.

social model of illness The view that much disease is caused by social conditions and that it can be cured by changing social conditions.

social movements Collective noninstitutionalized efforts to bring about social change and establish a new order of social thought and action.

social psychology The study of how individuals interact with other individuals or groups and how groups influence the individual.

social science A science that has as its subject matter human behavior, social organization, or society.

Social Security The federal program that provides financial support for the elderly.

social statics Comte's term for the stable structure of a society.

social status The amount of honor and prestige a person receives from others in the community; also, the position one occupies in the stratification system.

social stratification The ranking of people according to their wealth, prestige, or party position.

social system A set of interrelated social statuses and the expectations that accompany them.

social unrest The stage in the development of social unrest that is characterized by unfocused restlessness and increasing disorder.

social work The field in which the principles of the social sciences are applied to actual social problems.

societal unit See *categorical group.*

society A group of interacting people who live in a specific geographical area, who are organized in a cooperative manner, and who share a common culture.

sociobiology The study of the biological and genetic determinants of social behavior.

sociocultural learning theories Theories that deal with the processes through which deviant acts are learned and the conditions under which learning takes place.

socioeconomic status (SES) An assessment of status that takes into account a person's income, education, and occupation.

sociological perspective A way of looking at society and social behavior that involves questioning the obvious, seeking patterns, and looking beyond the individual in an attempt to discern social processes.

sociology The study of human society and social life and the social causes and consequences of human behavior.

spatially diffuse collectives Collectives that form among people spread over a wide geographical area.

spatially proximate collectives Collectives in which people are geographically close and physically visible to one another.

Spencer's evolutionary scheme Herbert Spencer's belief that human societies evolve according to the principles of natural selection from relative homogeneity and simplicity to heterogeneity and complexity.

split labor market A labor market in which some jobs afford upward mobility and others do not.

sponsored mobility A system of education in which certain students are selected at an early age to receive advanced education and training.

statistical group A group formed by sociologists or statisticians; members are unaware of belonging and there is no social interaction or social organization.

statistical illness An illness in which one's health varies from the norm.

statistical view A perspective on deviance that defines deviant as any variation from a statistical norm.

stereotypes Widely held and over-simplified beliefs about the character and behavior of all members of a group that seldom correspond to the facts.

stratified sampling Sampling in which a population is divided into groups and then subjects are chosen at random from within those groups.

structural assimilation One aspect of assimilation where patterns of intimate contact between the guest and host groups are developed in the clubs, organizations, and institutions of the host society.

structural conduciveness The extent to which a society's organization has the conditions that make a particular form of collective behavior possible.

structural functionalism The theory that societies contain certain interdependent structures, each of which performs certain functions for the maintenance of society.

structural strain Any conflict or ambiguity in a society's organization that causes frustration and stress; often seen as a precondition for collective behavior.

subcultures Groups of persons who share in the main culture of a society but also have their own distinctive values, norms, and lifestyles.

suburbs The communities that surround a central city and are dependent on it.

succession An urban process of replacing old occupants and institutions with new ones.

superego In Freudian theory, the part of the mind that incorporates social rules.

supply-side economy A political and economic policy designed to put more money in the hands of the rich so they will spur the economy by investing in more competitive manufacturing systems.

survey research A quantitative research technique that involves asking people questions about the subject being surveyed.

symbol Something that is used to represent something else, such as a word, gesture, or object used to represent some aspect of the world.

symbolic interaction theory The social theory stressing interactions between people and the social processes that occur within the individual that are made possible by language and internalized meanings.

systematic sampling Obtaining a sample from a population by following a specific pattern of selection, such as choosing every tenth person.

taboos Mores that prohibit something.

technology The application of nonmaterial and material knowledge by a society to maintain its standard of living and lifestyle.

temporocentrism The belief that one's own time is more important than the past or future.

tertiary medical care Long-term care requiring complex technology.

tertiary workers Workers who provide a service, such as doctors, lawyers, politicians, police officers, and secretaries.

theodicy The debate over why an omnipotent and good God allows evil to exist in the world.

theory A set of logically and systematically interrelated propositions that explain a particular process or phenomenon.

totalitarianism A power structure in which the government has total power to dictate the values, rules, ideology, and economic development of a society.

totemism The worship of plants, animals, and other natural objects as gods and ancestors.

traditional authority The right to rule granted to someone on the basis of tradition, as with a patriarch or king.

trained incapacity The situation that exists when the demands of discipline, conformity, and adherence to rules render people unable to perceive the end for which the rules were developed.

unionization The process of organizing workers to improve their wages and working conditions.

upward mobility Movement in the stratification system to a position of greater wealth, status, and power.

urban ecology   The study of the interrelationships between people in urban settings and the social and physical environment in which they live.

urban homesteading   A federal plan in which abandoned and foreclosed homes are sold to private families at extremely low prices if they agree to live in the house and bring it up to code standards.

urbanization   The growth of the number of people who live in urban rather than rural areas and the process of taking on organizational patterns and lifestyles characteristic of urban areas.

validity   The extent to which observations actually measure what they are supposed to measure.

values   Ideas and beliefs shared by the people in a society about what is important and worthwhile.

variable   A characteristic such as age, class, or income that can vary from one person to another; a concept that can have two or more values.

variance   A descriptive statistic that tells how the data are spread over the range.

verstehen   Understanding human action by examining the subjective meanings that people attach to their own behavior and the behavior of others.

vertical mobility   Movement to a position of greater or less wealth, status, or power in a stratification system.

vital statistics   Records of all births, deaths and their causes, marriages, divorces, and certain diseases in a society.

voluntary association   An organization people join because they share the organization's goals and values and voluntarily choose to support them.

voluntary hospital   A nonprofit hospital that treats patients who need short-term care.

welfare capitalism   A mixed economy in which private and public ownership are both practiced extensively.

women's movements   The social movements led by women to gain political and economic equality.

xenocentrism   The belief that what is foreign is best and that one's own lifestyle, products, or ideas are inferior to those of others.

zero population growth   A population policy that encourages parents to have no more than two children to limit the growth of the population.

References

Adams, Gordon. "The Iron Triangle," *The Nation*, Oct. 31, 1981.

Adorno, T. W., Else Frenkel-Brunswik, Daniel J. Levinson, and R. Nevitt Sanford. *The Authoritarian Personality*. New York: Wiley, 1950.

Agran, Larry. "Getting Cancer on the Job," *The Nation*, Apr. 12, 1975.

Akers, Ronald L. *Deviant Behavior: A Social Learning Approach*, 2d ed. Belmont, Calif.: Wadsworth, 1977.

Akers, R. L., M. D. Krohn, L. Lonza-Kaduce, and M. Radosevich. "Social Learning and Deviant Behavior: A Specific Test of a General Theory," *American Sociological Review* 44 (August 1979):636–655.

Albrecht, Stanley L., Darwin L. Thomas, and Bruce A. Chadwick. *Social Psychology*. Englewood Cliffs: N.J.: Prentice-Hall, 1980.

Allport, Gordon. *The Nature of Prejudice*. Boston: Beacon Press, 1954.

Atchley, Robert C. "The Process of Retirement: Comparing Men and Women," in Maximiliane Szinovacz, ed., *Women's Retirement: Policy Implications of Recent Research*. Beverly Hills: Sage Publications, 1982, pp. 153–168.

Atchley, Robert. *The Social Forces in Later Life: An Introduction to Social Gerontology*, 3rd ed. Belmont, Calif.: Wadsworth, 1980.

Austin, Sarah. "Crisis in New York City," *The New York Times*, Jan. 4, 1976, p. 40.

Ayensu, Edward S. "A Worldwide Role for the Healing Powers of Plants," *Smithsonian* 12 (November 1981):86–97.

Bales, Robert F. "The Equilibrium Problem in Small Groups," in Talcott Parsons, et al., eds., *Working Papers in the Theory of Action*. Glencoe, Ill.: The Free Press, 1953.

Bandura, A. "Vicarious Processes: A Case of No-Trial Learning," in L. Berkowitz, ed., *Advances in Society Psychology*, vol. 2. New York: Academic Press, 1965, pp. 1–55.

Banfield, Edward. *The Unheavenly City Revisited*. Boston: Little, Brown, 1974.

Barry, Brian and John D. Kasarda. *Contemporary Urban Ecology*. New York: Macmillan, 1977.

Bart, Pauline B. "Rape as a Paradigm of Sexism in Society — Victimization and Its Discontents," *Women's Studies International Quarterly* 2 (1979):347–357.

Bean, Frank D. "The Baby Boom and Its Explanations," *The Sociological Quarterly* 24 (Summer 1983):353–365.

Becker, Howard S. *Outsiders: Studies in the Sociology of Deviance*. New York: The Free Press, 1963.

Becker, Howard S. "The Labeling Theory Reconsidered," in Paul Rock and Mary McIntosh, eds., *Deviance and Social Control*. London: Tavistock, 1974.

Bell, Wendell. "Social Choice, Life Styles, and Suburban Residences," in W. Dobriner, ed., *The Suburban Community*. New York: Putnam, 1958.

Bem, S. and D. Bem. "Training the Woman to Know Her Place: The Power of a Nonconscious Ideology." In S. Cox, ed., *Female Psychology: The Emerging Self*. Chicago: SRA, 1976, pp. 180–191.

Berg, Ivar. *Education and Jobs: The Great Training Robbery*. New York: Praeger, 1970.

Berger, Bennett. *Working Class Suburbs*. Berkeley, Calif.: University of California Press, 1960.

Berk, Richard A. *Collective Behavior*. Dubuque, Iowa: Brown, 1974.

Berlowitz, Marvin S. "Institutional Racism and School Staffing in an Urban Area," *Journal of Negro Education* 43 (Winter 1974):25–29.

Bernard, Jesse. *The Female World*. New York: The Free Press, 1981.

Berry, Brewton and Henry L. Tischler. *Race and Ethnic Relations*. Boston: Houghton Mifflin, 1978.

Berry, Brian, J. L. *The Human Consequences of Urbanization*, New York: St. Martin's Press, 1973.

Bierstedt, Robert. *The Social Order*, 3rd ed. New York: McGraw-Hill, 1970.

Biggar, Jeanne. "The Sunning of America: Migration to the Sunbelt," *Population Bulletin* 34 (March 1979):128–144.

Bilge, Barbara and Gladis Kaufman. "Children of Divorce and One-Parent Families: Cross-Cultural Perspectives," *Family Relations* 32 (January 1983):59–71.

Billingsley, Andrew. *Black Families in White America*. Englewood Cliffs, N.J.: Prentice-Hall, 1968.

Blake, Judith. "Family Size and the Quality of Children," *Demography* 18 (1981a):421–442.

Blake, Judith. "The Only Child in America: Prejudice Versus Performance," *Population and Development Review* 7 (March 1981b):43–54.

Blau, Peter. *Exchange and Power in Social Life*. New York: Wiley, 1964.

Blau, Peter M. and Otis Dudley Duncan. *The American Occupational Structure*. New York: Wiley, 1967.

Blau, Peter M. and Richard C. Scott. *Formal Organizations*. San Francisco: Chandler, 1963.

Blau, Zena Smith. *Aging in a Changing Society*, 2d ed. New York: Franklin Watts, 1981.

Blumer, Herbert. "Collective Behavior," in Alfred McClung Lee, ed., *Principles of Sociology*. New York: Barnes & Noble, 1939.

Bonacich, Edna. "Abolition, the Extension of Slavery, and the Position of Free Blacks: A Study of Split Labor Markets in the United States, 1830-1863," *American Journal of Sociology* 81 (November 1975):601-628.

Bonacich, Edna. "Advanced Capitalism and Black/White Race Relations in the United States: A Split Labor Market Interpretation," *American Sociological Review* 41 (February 1976):34-51.

Bonacich, Edna. "A Theory of Ethnic Antagonism: The Split Labor Market," *American Sociological Review* 37 (October 1972):547-559.

Bose, Christine E. and Peter H. Rossi. "Prestige Standings of Occupations as Affected by Gender," *American Sociological Review* 48 (June 1983):316-330.

Bowles, Samuel and Herbert Gintis. *Schooling in Capitalist America.* New York: Basic Books, 1976.

Bradley, Donald. "Neighborhood Transition: Middle Class Home Buying in an Inner-City, Deteriorating Neighborhood." Paper presented at the annual meeting of the American Sociological Association, Chicago, Sept. 1977.

Brown, Lester R., Patricia L. McGrath, and Bruce Stokes. "The Population Problem in 22 Dimensions," *The Futurist,* October 1976.

Browne, James. "Power Politics for Teachers, Modern Style," *Phi Delta Kappan* 58 (1976):158-164.

Bunke, Harvey C. "An America in Need of Repair," *Business Horizons,* November-December 1983.

Burgess, Ernest W. "The Growth of the City," in Robert E. Park and Ernest W. Burgess, eds., *The City.* Chicago: University of Chicago Press, 1925, pp. 47-62.

Burke, Ronald J. and Tamara Weir. "Relationship of Wives' Employment Status to Husband, Wife and Pair Satisfaction and Performance," *Journal of Marriage and the Family* 38 (May 1976):279-287.

Burris, Val. "The Social and Political Consequences of Overeducation," *American Sociological Review* 48 (August 1983):454-467.

Burstein, Paul. "Equal Employment Opportunity Legislation and the Income of Women and Non-Whites," *American Sociological Review* 44 (June 1979):367-391.

Caplovitz, David. *The Poor Pay More.* New York: The Free Press, 1963.

Careers in Sociology. Washington, D.C. American Sociological Association, 1977.

Cashion, Barbara G. "Female-Headed Families: Effects on Children and Clinical Implications," *Journal of Marital and Family Therapy* (April 1982):77-85.

Centers, Richard. *The Psychology of Social Classes.* Princeton, N.J.: Princeton University Press, 1949.

Chambliss, William J. *Crime and the Legal Process.* New York: McGraw-Hill, 1969.

Chambliss, William J. and Robert Seidman. *Law, Order and Power.* Reading Mass.: Addison-Wesley, 1971.

Charon, Joel M. *The Meaning of Sociology.* Sherman Oaks, Calif.: Alfred Publishing, 1980.

Cheal, David J. "Intergenerational Family Transfers," *Journal of Marriage and the Family* 45 (November 1983):805-813.

Chesler, Mark A. and William M. Cave. *A Sociology of Education: Access to Power and Privilege.* New York: Macmillan, 1981.

Childe, V. Gordon. "The Urban Revolution," *Town Planning Review* 21 (April 1951):3-17.

Cicourel, Aaron. *Social Organization of Juvenile Justice.* New York: Wiley, 1968.

Coates, Vary T. "The Potential Impacts of Robotics," *The Futurist,* February 1983.

Cohen, Albert K. and Harold M. Hodges, Jr. "Characteristics of Lower Blue-Collar Class," *Social Problems* 10 (Winter 1963):307-321.

Coleman, James and S. D. Kelly. "Education," in W. Gorham and N. Glazer, eds., *The Urban Situation.* Washington, D.C.: The Urban Institute, 1976.

Coleman, James S. et al. *Equality of Ed-ucational Opportunity.* Washington, D.C.: U.S. Government Printing Office, 1966.

Coleman, James S. et al. *Youth: Transition to Adulthood.* Report of the Panel on Youth of the President's Science Advisory Committee. Chicago: The University of Chicago Press, 1974.

Collins, Randall. "A Conflict Theory of Sexual Satisfaction," *Social Problems* 19 (Summer 1971):3-21.

Collins, Randall. *The Credential Society: An Historical Sociology of Education and Stratification.* New York: Academic Press, 1979.

Cook, Robert. "The World's Great Cities: Evolution or Devolution?" in P. Meadows and E. Mizruchi, eds., *Urbanism, Urbanization and Change.* Reading, Mass.: Addison-Wesley, 1969.

Cooley, Charles H. *Human Nature and the Social Order.* New York: Schocken, 1964 (Scribner's, 1902).

Cooley, Charles H. *Social Organization.* New York: Scribner's, 1909.

Coser, Lewis. *The Functions of Social Conflict.* New York: The Free Press, 1956.

Cowgill, Donald. "Aging and Modernization: A Revision of the Theory," in J. Gubrium, ed., *Late Life: Communities and Environmental Policy.* Springfield, Ill.: Charles C Thomas, 1974.

Cowgill, Donald and Lowell Holmes. *Aging and Modernization.* New York: Appleton-Century-Crofts, 1972.

Cumming, E. and W. Henry. *Growing Old: The Process of Disengagement.* New York: Basic Books, 1961.

Dahrendorf, Ralph. *Class and Class Conflict in Industrial Society.* Stanford, Calif.: Stanford University Press, 1951.

Davis, Karen. "Equal Treatment and Unequal Benefits: The Medicare Program," *Milbank Memorial Fund Quarterly* 53(4)(1975):449-458.

Davis, Kingsley. "Extreme Social Isolation of a Child," *American Journal of Sociology* 45 (1940):554-565.

Davis, Kingsley. "Final Note on a Case

of Extreme Isolation," *American Journal of Sociology* 50 (1947):432–437.

Davis, Kingsley. "The First Cities: How and Why Did They Arise?" in K. Davis, ed., *Cities: Their Origin, Growth, and Human Impact.* San Francisco: W. H. Freeman, 1973.

Davis, Kingsley and Wilbert E. Moore. "Some Principles of Stratification," *American Sociological Review* 10 April (1945):242–249.

Davis, Wayne H. "Overpopulated America," *The New Republic,* Jan. 10, 1970, pp. 13–15.

Denton, John A. *Medical Sociology.* Boston: Houghton Mifflin, 1978.

Dinitz, Simon. "Progress, Crime, and the Folk Ethic," *Criminology* 11 (May 1973):3–21.

Dinnerstein, Leonard and David M. Reimers. *Ethnic Americans: A History of Immigration and Assimilation.* New York: Harper & Row, 1975.

Dobriner, William. "The Growth and Structure of Metropolitan Areas," in Robert Gutman and David Poponoe, eds., *Neighborhood, City and Metropolis.* New York: Random House, 1970, pp. 190–205.

Dohrenwend, Bruce P. and Barbara Snell Dohrenwend. "Sex Differences and Psychiatric Disorders," *The American Journal of Sociology* 81 (May 1976):1447–1454.

Dollard, John, et al. *Frustration and Aggression.* New Haven: Yale University Press, 1939.

Domhoff, G. William. *The Higher Circles: The Governing Class in America.* New York: Random House/Vintage, 1971.

Domhoff, G. William. *The Powers That Be: Process of Ruling Class Domination in America.* New York: Random House/Vintage, 1979.

Douglass, Richard L. "Domestic Neglect and Abuse of the Elderly: Implications for Research and Service," *Family Relations* 32 (July 1983):395–402.

Dowd, James. "Aging as Exchange: A Preface to Theory," *Journal of Gerontology* 30 (September 1975):584–594.

Dowd, James. *Stratification Among the Aged.* Monterey, Calif.: Brooks/Cole, 1980.

Dowie, Mark. "Pinto Madness," *Mother Jones,* vol. II, no. VIII, September–October 1977.

Dowse, Robert E. and John A. Hughes. *Political Sociology.* New York: Wiley, 1972.

Duberman, Lucile. *Social Inequality: Class and Caste in America.* Philadelphia: Lippincott, 1976.

Dubos, Rene. *Man Adapting.* New Haven, Conn.: Yale University Press, 1965.

Dupreel, Eugene G. "Demographic Change and Progress," in Johannes Overbeek, ed., *The Evolution of Population Theory.* Westport, Conn: Greenwood Press, 1977, pp. 80–85. Originally published in 1922.

Durkheim, Emile. *The Division of Labor in Society.* New York: The Free Press, 1947. Originally published in 1893.

Durkheim, Emile. *The Elementary Forms of the Religious Life.* New York: The Free Press, 1926. Originally published in 1915.

Eaton, Joseph and Albert J. Mayer. "The Social Biology of Very High Fertility Among the Hutterites: The Demography of a Unique Population," *Human Biology* 25(3) (September 1953):206–264.

Ehrenreich, B. and D. English. *For Her Own Good: 150 Years of the Experts' Advice to Women.* Garden City, N.Y.: Anchor Books, 1979.

Elkin, Frederick and Gerald Handel. *The Child and Society: The Process of Socialization,* 3rd ed., New York: Random House, 1978.

Encyclopedia of Associations, vol. 1, 16th ed. "National Organizations of the U.S." Detroit: Gale Research Co., 1981.

Encyclopedia of Associations, vol. 1, 18th ed., "National Organizations of the U.S." Detroit: Gale Research Co., 1983.

Engels, Frederich. *The Origin of the Family, Private Property and the State.* Chicago: Charles H. Kerr, 1902.

Erikson, E. H. *Childhood and Society.* New York: Norton, 1963.

Erikson, Kai J. *Everything in Its Path. Destruction of Community in the Buffalo Creek Flood.* New York: Simon & Schuster, 1976.

Eshleman, J. Ross. *The Family: An Introduction,* 3rd ed. Boston: Allyn & Bacon, 1981.

Eshleman, J. Ross. *The Family: An Introduction,* 4th ed. Boston: Allyn & Bacon, 1985.

Etzioni, Amitai. *A Sociological Reader on Complex Organizations,* 3rd ed. New York: Holt, Rinehart & Winston, 1980.

Farley, Lin. *Sexual Shakedown.* New York: Warner Books, 1978.

Feagin, Joe. *Racial and Ethnic Relations.* Englewood Cliffs, N.J.: Prentice-Hall, 1978.

Feagin, Joe R. *Racial and Ethnic Relations,* 2d ed. Englewood Cliffs, N.J.: Prentice-Hall, 1984.

Featherman, David L. and Robert M. Hauser. "Changes in the Socioeconomic Stratification of the Races, 1962–1973," *American Journal of Sociology* 82 (November 1976):621–651.

Feldman-Summers, Shirley and Gayle C. Palmer. "Rape as Viewed by Judges, Prosecutors and Police Officers," *Criminal Justice and Behavior* 7 (March 1980):19–40.

Fine, Gary Alan. "Small Groups and Culture Creation: The Ideoculture of Little League Baseball Teams," *American Sociological Review* 44 (October 1979):733–745.

Fischoff, Ephraim. *The Sociology of Religion.* Boston: Beacon Press, 1963.

Flacks, Richard. *Youth and Social Change.* Chicago: Markham, 1971.

Form, William H. and Joan Rytina Huber. "Ideological Beliefs on the Distribution of Power in the United States," *American Sociological Review* 34 (February 1969):19–36.

Fox, Karen D. and Sharon Y. Nickols. "The Time Crunch: Wife's Employment and Family Work," *Journal of Family Issues* 4 (March 1983):61–82.

Freeman, Harold. *Toward Socialism in America.* Cambridge, Mass.: Schenkman, 1979.

Freeman, Jo. "The Origins of the Women's Liberation Movement," *American Journal of Sociology* 78 (January 1973):792–811.

Fried, Marc and Peggy Gleicher. "Some Sources of Residential Satisfaction in an Urban Slum," *Journal of the American Institute of Planners* 27 (November 1961):305–315.

Fromm, Erich. *The Sane Society.* New York: Holt, Rinehart & Winston, 1965.

Galbraith, John Kenneth. "Why Arms Makers Must Be Checked," *Scholastic Update,* Apr. 29, 1983:19–20.

Gamson, William A. *The Strategy of Social Protest.* Homewood, Ill.: Dorsey Press, 1975.

Gans, Herbert J. *More Equality.* New York: Pantheon Books, 1972.

Gans, Herbert J. *The Urban Villagers.* New York: The Free Press, 1962.

Gardner, R. A., and B. T. Gardner. "Teaching Sign Language to a Chimpanzee," *Science* 165 (1969): 644–672.

Gelfand, Donald E. *Aging: The Ethnic Factor.* Boston: Little, Brown, 1982.

Gelles, R. J. "The Myth of Battered Husbands and New Facts About Family Violence," *MS.,* October 1979:65–73.

George, Susan. *How the Other Half Dies. The Real Reasons for World Hunger.* Montclair, N.J.: Allanheld, Osmun, 1977.

Glassner, Barry and Bruce Berg. "How Jews Avoid Alcohol Problems," *American Sociological Review* 45 (August 1980):647–664.

Glazer, Nathan and Daniel P. Moynihan. *Beyond the Melting Pot,* 2d ed. Cambridge, Mass.: Mass. Institute of Technology Press, 1970.

Goering, John M. "The Emergence of Ethnic Interests: A Case of Serendipity," *Social Forces* 48 (March 1971):379–384.

Goffman, Erving. *Asylums: Essays on the Situation of Mental Patients and Other Inmates.* Garden City, N.Y.: Anchor/Doubleday, 1961.

Goffman, Erving. *Encounters.* Indianapolis, Ind.: Bobbs-Merrill, 1961.

Goffman, Erving. *Interaction Ritual, Essays on Face-to-Face Behavior.* Garden City, N.Y.: Doubleday/Anchor, 1967.

Goffman, Erving. *The Presentation of Self in Everyday Life.* Garden City, N.Y.: Doubleday/Anchor, 1959.

Goldberg, S. and M. Lewis. "Play Behavior in the Year-Old Infant: Early Sex Differences," *Child Development* 40 (1969):21–30.

Goode, William J. *World Revolution and Family Patterns.* New York: The Free Press, 1970.

Goodin, Robert E. *Manipulatory Politics,* New Haven: Yale University Press, 1980.

Gordon, Milton. *Assimilation in American Life.* New York: Oxford University Press, 1964.

Gordon, Milton M. *Human Nature, Class and Ethnicity.* New York: Oxford University Press, 1978.

Gordon, Richard, Katherine Gordon, and Max Gunther. *The Split Level Trap.* New York: Bernard Geis Associates, 1961.

Goring, Charles. *The English Convict.* London: His Majesty's Stationery Office, 1913.

Gouldner, Alvin W. *Patterns of Industrial Bureaucracy.* New York: The Free Press, 1954.

Gove, Walter R. and Michael R. Geerken. "The Effect of Children and Employment on the Mental Health of Married Men and Women," *Social Forces* 56 (February 1977):66–76.

Gove, Walter R. and J. F. Tudor. "Adult Sex Roles and Mental Illness," *American Journal of Sociology* 78 (January 1973):812–835.

Greeley, Andrew M. and Paul B. Sheatsley. "Attitudes Toward Racial Integration," *Scientific American* 225 (December 1971):13–19.

Greer, Scott. *Urban Renewal and American Cities.* Indianapolis, Ind.: Bobbs-Merrill, 1965.

Griandjean, Berke D. "History and Career in a Bureaucratic Labor Market," *American Journal of Sociology* 86 (5) (March 1981):1057–1092.

Guterman, Stanley S., ed. *Black Psyche: Modal Personality Patterns of Black Americans.* Berkeley, Calif.: Glendessary Press, 1972, p. 87.

Hare, A. Paul. *Handbook of Small Group Research.* New York: The Free Press, 1976.

Harris, Chauncey. "Suburbs and Suburban Life-Styles," *Time,* June 13, 1971, p. 78.

Harris, Chauncy and Edward L. Ullman. "The Nature of Cities," *Annals of the American Academy of Political and Social Science* 242 (November 1945):7–17.

Harris, Diana K. and William E. Cole. *Sociology of Aging.* Boston: Houghton Mifflin, 1980.

Hartmann, Heidi. "Capitalism, Patriarchy, and Job Segregation by Sex," in Nona Glazer and Helen Youngelson Waehaer, eds., *Woman in a Man-Made World,* 2d ed. Chicago: Rand McNally, 1977, pp. 71–84.

Hauser, Phillip. "Chicago — Urban Crisis Exemplar," in J. John Palen, ed., *City Scenes.* Boston: Little, Brown, 1977, pp. 15–25.

Hawke, Sharryl and David Knox. *One Child by Choice.* Englewood Cliffs, N.J.: Prentice-Hall, 1977.

Hawley, Amos. *Urban Society: An Ecological Approach.* New York: Ronald Press, 1971.

Hayes, C. *The Ape in Our House.* New York: Harper & Row, 1951.

Hazard, John N. *The Soviet System of Government,* 5th ed. Chicago: The University of Chicago Press, 1980.

Heer, David M. *Society and Population.* Englewood Cliffs, N.J.: Prentice-Hall, 1975.

Heilbroner, Robert L. *The Making of Economic Society.* Englewood Cliffs, N.J.: Prentice-Hall, 1980.

Hine, Virginia H. "Dying at Home: Can Families Cope?" *Omega* 10 (1979–1980).

Hobbs, Daniel F., Jr. "Parenthood as Crisis: A Third Study," *Journal of Marriage and the Family* 27 (August 1965):367–372.

Hochschild, Arlie Russell. "The Sociology of Feeling and Emotion: Selected Possibilities," in Marcia Millmav and Rosabeth Moss Kantor, eds., *Another Voice*. Garden City, N.Y.: Doubleday/Anchor, 1975, pp. 280–307.

Hogan, Dennis P. and David L. Featherman. "Racial Stratification and Socioeconomic Change in the American North and South," *American Journal of Sociology* 83 (July 1977):100–126.

Hodge, R. W., P. M. Siegel, and P. H. Rossi. "Occupational Prestige in the United States, 1925–1963," *American Journal of Sociology* 70 (November 1964).

Hoffman, L. W. and I. F. Nye. *Working Mothers*. San Francisco: Jossey Bass, 1974.

Homans, George. *Social Behavior: Its Elementary Forms*. New York: Harcourt, Brace and World, 1961.

Howard, Ebenezer. *Garden Cities of Tomorrow*. London: Faber & Faber, 1902.

Hoyt, Homer. *The Structure of Residential Neighborhoods in American Cities*. Washington, D.C. Federal Housing Administration, 1939.

Humphrey, Craig, R. and Frederick R. Buttel. *Environment, Energy and Society*. Belmont, Calif.: Wadsworth, 1982.

Hunt, J. G. and L. L. Hunt. "Race, Daughters and Father-loss: Does Absence Make the Girl Grow Stronger?" *Social Problems* 25 (February 1977):90–102.

Hunt, Janet G. and Larry C. Hunt. "Racial Inequality and Self-Image: Identity Maintenance as Identity Confusion," *Sociology and Social Research* 61 (July 1977):539–559.

Jacobs, Jane. *The Death and Life of Great American Cities*. New York: Random House, 1961.

Jacquet, Constant H., Jr., ed. *Yearbook of American and Canadian Churches*. Nashville: Abingdon, 1979.

Jencks, Christopher. *Who Gets Ahead? The Determinant of Economic Success in America*. New York: Basic Books, 1979.

Jones, James M. *Prejudice and Racism*. Reading, Mass.: Addison-Wesley, 1972.

Kantor, Rosabeth M. *Men and Women of the Corporation*. New York: Basic Books, 1979.

Karier, Clarence J. "Testing for Order and Control in the Corporate Liberal State," in N. J. Block and Gerald Dworkin, eds., *The I.Q. Controversy, Critical Readings*. New York: Pantheon Books, 1976, pp. 339–373.

Kart, Cary S. *The Realities of Aging: An Introduction to Gerontology*. Boston: Allyn & Bacon, 1981.

Kasarda, John. "The Changing Occupational Structure of the American Metropolis," in Barry Schwartz, ed., *The Changing Face of the Suburbs*. Chicago: University of Chicago Press, 1976, pp. 113–136.

Keith, Jennie. *Old Age as People*. Boston: Little, Brown, 1982.

Keller, Suzanne. *Beyond the Ruling Class. Strategic Elites in Modern Society*. New York: Random House, 1968.

Kellogg, W. N. and L. A. Kellogg, *The Ape and the Child*. New York: McGraw-Hill, 1933.

Kelly, Delos H. *Deviant Behavior: Readings in the Sociology of Deviance*. New York: St. Martin's Press, 1979.

Kerner Report. *National Advisory Commission on Civil Disorders*. New York: Bantam Books, 1968.

Kessler, Ronald C. and James A. McRae, Jr. "Trends in Sex and Psychological Distress," *American Sociological Review* 46 (August 1983):443–452.

Kinloch, Graham C. *The Dynamics of Race Relations: A Sociological Analysis*. New York: McGraw-Hill, 1974.

Kitano, Harry H. L. *Race Relations*, 2d ed. Englewood Cliffs, N.J.: Prentice-Hall, 1980.

Kitsuse, John I. "Societal Reaction to Deviant Behavior: Problems of Theory and Method," *Social Problems* 9 (Winter 1962):247–256.

Knapp, M. "The Activity Theory of Aging: An Examination in the English Context," *Gerontologist* 17 (1977):553–559.

Koff, Theodore H. *Hospice: A Caring Community*. Cambridge, Mass.: Winthrop Publishers, 1980.

Kohn, Melvin L. "Bureaucratic Man:

A Portrait and an Interpretation," *American Sociological Review* 36 (June 1971):461–474.

Kraut, Robert E. "Deterrent and Definitional Influences on Shoplifting," *Social Problems* 23 (February 1976):358–368.

Labovitz, Sanford and Robert Hagedorn. *Introduction to Social Research*, 3rd ed. New York: McGraw-Hill, 1981.

Lander, Bernard. "Towards an Understanding of Juvenile Delinquency," in H. Voss and D. Petersen, eds., *Ecology, Crime, and Delinquency*. New York: Appleton-Century-Crofts, 1971.

Leach, Jim. "PAC's Americana: The Threat of Political Action Committees," *USA Today*, May 1983:10–12.

Leavitt, Ruby R. "Women of Other Cultures," in Vivian Gornick and Barbara K. Moran, eds., *Women in Sexist Society Studies in Power and Powerlessness*. New York: New American Library, 1971.

Le Bon, Gustave. *The Crowd: A Study of the Popular Mind*. London: Ernest Benn, 1895, 2d ed., Dunwoody, Ga.: Norman S. Berg, 1968.

Lederer, Laura, ed. *Take Back the Night: Women on Pornography*. New York: Morrow, 1980.

Lee, Gary R. "Age of Marriage and Marital Satisfaction: A Multivariate Analysis with Implications for Marital Stability," *Journal of Marriage and the Family* 39 (August 1977):493–503.

Lee, Gary R. "Marriage and Morale in Later Life," *Journal of Marriage and the Family* 40 (February 1978):131–139.

LeMasters, E. E. "Parenthood as Crisis," *Marriage and Family Living* 19 (November 1957):352–355.

Lemert, Edwin. *Social Pathology*. New York: McGraw-Hill, 1951.

Lemon, B. L., V. L. Bengtson, and J. A. Peterson. "An Exploration of Activity Theory of Aging: Activity Types and Life Satisfaction Among In-Movers to a Retirement Community," *Journal of Gerontology* 27 (1977):511–523.

Lengermann, Patricia M. "The Founding of the American Sociological Review: The Anatomy of a Rebellion," *American Sociological Review* 44 (April 1979):185–198.

Lenski, Gerhard. *Power and Privilege.* New York: McGraw-Hill, 1966.

Lenski, Gerhard. *The Religious Factor.* New York: Doubleday, 1961.

Levison, Andrew. *The Working-Class Majority.* New York: Coward, McCann and Geohegan, 1974.

Lewis, Jerry M. "A Study of the Kent State Incident Using Smelser's Theory of Collective Behavior," *Sociological Inquiry* 42 (1972):87–96.

Lieberson, Stanley and Arnold R. Silverman. "The Precipitants and Underlying Conditions of Race Riots," *American Sociological Review* 30 (December 1965):887–898.

Lipset, S. M. and Reinhard Bendix. *Social Mobility in Industrial Society.* Berkeley: University of California Press, 1967.

Litt, Edgar. "Civic Education, Community Norms, and Political Indoctrination," *American Sociological Review* 28 (February 1963):69–75.

Lopata, Helena Z. *Polish Americans: Status Competition in an Ethnic Community.* Englewood Cliffs, N.J.: Prentice-Hall, 1976.

Lueptow, Lloyd B. "Social Structure, Social Change and Parental Influence in Adolescent Sex-Role Socialization: 1964–1975," *Journal of Marriage and Family* 42 (June 1980):93–104.

Lynd, Robert S. and Helen Merrell Lynd. *Middletown.* New York: Harcourt, Brace and World, 1929.

Lynd, Robert S. and Helen Merrell Lynd. *Middletown in Transition.* New York: Harcourt, Brace and World, 1937.

Maccoby, Michael. "The Changing Corporate Character," in Gordon J. DiRenzo, ed., *We, The People: American Character and Social Change.* Westport, Conn.: Greenwood Press, 1977.

Macklin, Eleanor D. "Nonmarital Heterosexual Cohabitation: An Overview," in Eleanor D. Macklin and Roger H. Rubin, eds., *Contemporary Families and Alternative Lifestyles.* Beverly Hills: Sage Publications, 1983, pp. 49–74.

Madsen, William. *The Mexican-Americans of South Texas.* New York: Holt, Rinehart & Winston, 1964.

Malinowski, Bronislaw. "Parenthood: The Basis of Social Structure," in V. F. Calverton and Samuel D. Schmalhausen, eds., *The New Generation.* New York: Macaulay, 1930.

Manion, O. V. *Aging: Old Myths Versus New Facts.* Eugene, Ore.: Retirement Services, Inc., 1972.

Manis, Jerome G. *Serious Social Problems.* Boston: Allyn & Bacon, 1984.

Margolis, Diane Rothbard. *The Managers: Corporate Life in America.* New York: Morrow, 1979.

Markle, Gerald E. and Ronald J. Troyer. "Smoke Gets in Your Eyes: Cigarette Smoking as Deviant Behavior," *Social Problems* 26 (June 1979):611–625.

Marshall, Harvey. "Suburban Life Styles: A Contribution to the Debate," in L. Masotti and J. Hadden, eds., *The Urbanization of the Suburbs.* Beverly Hills, Calif.: Sage Publications, 1973.

Martin, Wilfred B. W. and Allan J. Macdonell. *Canadian Education: A Sociological Analysis.* Scarborough, Ont.: Prentice-Hall of Canada, 1978.

Marx, Karl and Friedrich Engels. *Communist Manifesto.* Baltimore: Penguin Books, 1969. Originally published 1848.

Masters, William H. and Virginia E. Johnson. *Human Sexual Inadequacy.* Boston: Little, Brown, 1970.

Masters, William H. and Virginia E. Johnson. *Human Sexual Response.* Boston: Little, Brown, 1966.

Maykovich, Minako K. *Medical Sociology.* Palo Alto, Calif.: Mayfield Publishing, 1980.

McKinlay, John B. and Sonja M. McKinlay. "Medical Measures and the Decline of Mortality, in Peter Conrad and Rochelle Kern, eds., *The Sociology of Health and Illness: Critical Perspectives.* New York: St. Martin's Press, 1981, pp. 12–30.

McNeely, D. L. and John L. Calen, eds. *Aging in Minority Groups.* Beverly Hills: Sage Publications, 1983.

Mead, George Herbert. *Mind, Self and Society from the Standpoint of a Social Behaviorist,* Charles Morris, ed. Chicago: University of Chicago Press, 1934.

Mead, Margaret. *Sex and Temperament in Three Primitive Societies.* New York: Morrow, 1935.

Mechanic, David. *Medical Sociology,* 2d ed. New York: The Free Press, 1978.

Medvedev, Z. A. "Aging and Longevity: New Approaches and New Perspectives," *Gerontologist* 15 (1975):196–201.

Medvedev, Z. A. "Caucasus and Altay Longevity: A Biological or Social Problem," *Gerontologist* 14 (1974): 381–387.

Merton, Robert K. *Social Theory and Social Structure.* New York: The Free Press, 1949, rev. eds., 1957 and 1968.

Merton, Robert K. *Sociological Ambivalence and Other Essays.* New York: The Free Press, 1976.

Milgram, Stanley. "The Experience of Living in Cities," *Science* 167 (Mar. 13, 1970):1461–1468.

Miller, Herman P. *Rich Man, Poor Man.* New York: Thomas Y. Crowell, 1971.

Mills, C. Wright. *The Power Elite.* New York: Oxford University Press, 1958.

Mills, Charles W. *White Collar: American Middle Classes.* New York: Oxford University Press, 1951.

Mol, Hans. *Identity and the Sacred.* New York: The Free Press, 1976.

Money, John. *Love and Love Sickness: The Science of Sex, Gender Difference, and Pair-Bonding.* Baltimore: The Johns Hopkins University Press, 1980.

Money, J. and Anke A. Ehrhardt. *Man and Woman, Boy and Girl: The Differentiation and Dimorphism of Gender Identity from Conception to Maturity.* Baltimore: Johns Hopkins University Press, 1972.

Moss, H. "Sex, Age and State as Determinants of Mother-Infant Interaction," *Merrill-Palmer Quarterly* 13 (1967):19–36.

Mostert, Noel. "Supership," in Jerome H. Skolnick and Elliott Currie, eds., *Crisis in American Institutions,* 3rd ed. Boston: Little, Brown, 1976, pp. 286–304.

Mumford, Lewis. *The Transformation of Man.* New York: Collier, 1962.

Murdock, George P. *Social Structure.* New York: Macmillan, 1949.

Murdock, George P. "World Ethnographic Sample," *American Anthropologist* 59 (August 1957):664–687.

National Commission on Urban Problems. *Building the American City.* Washington, D.C.: U.S. Government Printing Office, 1972.

National HMO Census, June 30, 1983. Excelsior, Minn.: Interstudy, 1984.

National Opinion Research Center, *General Social Surveys, 1972–1982: Cumulative Codebook.* Chicago: National Opinion Research Center, 1982.

Nelson, Mary. "Why Witches Were Women," in Jo Freeman, ed., *Women. A Feminist Perspective.* Palo Alto, Calif.: Mayfield Publishers, 1975, pp. 335–350.

Newman, Oscar. *Defensible Space.* New York: Macmillan, 1972.

Newman, William M. *American Pluralism: A Study of Social Groups and Social Theory.* New York: Harper & Row, 1973.

Noel, Donald L. "A Theory of the Origin of Ethnic Stratification," in Norman R. Yetman and C. Hoy Steele, eds., *Majority and Minority: The Dynamics of Racial and Ethnic Relations.* Boston: Allyn & Bacon, 1975, chap. 2.

Novak, M. *The Rise of the Unmeltable Ethnics.* New York: Macmillan, 1972.

Novak, Michael. "White Ethnic," in Norman R. Yetman and C. Hoy Steele, eds., *Majority and Minority: The Dynamics of Racial and Ethnic Relations.* Boston: Allyn & Bacon, 1975.

Nuehring, Elane and Gerald E. Markle. "Nicotine and Norms: The Reemergence of a Deviant Behavior," *Social Problems* 21 (April 1974): 513–526.

Oakes, Jeannie. "Classroom Social Relationships: Exploring the Bowles and Gintis Hypothesis," *Sociology of Education* 55 (October 1982):197–212.

Oberschall, Anthony. *Social Conflict and Social Movements.* Englewood Cliffs, N.J.: Prentice-Hall, 1973.

Ogburn, William F. *Social Change.* New York: Viking, 1950.

Olson, David H., Hamilton I. McCubbin, and Associates. *Families: What Makes Them Work.* Beverly Hills: Sage Publications, 1983.

Orcutt, James D. "Deviance as a Situated Phenomenon: Variations in the Social Interpretation of Marijuana and Alcohol Use," *Social Problems* 22 (February 1975):346–356.

Ortiz, Flora Ida. *Career Patterns in Education: Women, Men and Minorities in Public School Administration.* New York: Praeger, 1982.

Orum, Anthony M. *Introduction to Political Sociology: The Social Anatomy of the Body Politic.* Englewood Cliffs, N.J.: Prentice-Hall, 1978.

Ouchi, William G. *Theory Z: How American Business Can Meet the Japanese Challenge.* Reading, Mass.: Addison-Wesley, 1981.

Park, Robert E. and Ernest W. Burgess. *Introduction to the Science of Sociology.* Chicago: University of Chicago Press, 1921.

Parsons, Talcott. "Definitions of Health and Illness in the Light of American Values and Social Structure," in E. Gartly Jaco, ed., *Patients, Physicians and Illness,* 3rd ed. Glencoe, Ill.: The Free Press, 1979.

Parsons, Talcott. "The School Class as Social System: Some of Its Functions in American Society," *Harvard Educational Review* 29(4) (1959):297–318.

Parsons, Talcott and Robert F. Bales. *Family, Socialization and Interaction Process.* New York: The Free Press, 1955.

Parsons, Talcott and Edward A. Shils, eds. *Toward a General Theory of Action.* New York: Harper & Row, 1951.

Patterson, Orlando. "Context and Choice in Ethnic Allegiance," in Nathan Glazer and Daniel Moynihan, eds., *Ethnicity.* Cambridge: Harvard University Press, 1975, pp. 305–345.

Pearce, Diana M. "The Feminization of Ghetto Poverty," *Society* 21 (November–December 1983):70–74.

Peter, Lawrence J. and Raymond Hull. *The Peter Principle.* New York: Morrow, 1969.

Pirenne, Henri. "Stages in the Social History of Capitalism," *American Historical Review,* vol. XIX (July 1914):494–515.

Piven, Frances Fox and Richard A. Cloward. *Regulating the Poor: The Functions of Public Welfare.* New York: Vintage Books, 1971.

Polk, Kenneth. "Urban Social Areas and Delinquency," *Social Problems* 14 (Winter 1967):320–325.

Quarantelli, E. L. and Russell R. Dynes, "When Disaster Strikes: It Isn't Much Like What You've Heard and Read About," *Psychology Today* (February 1972):67–70.

Queen, Stuart A. and Robert W. Habenstein. *The Family in Various Cultures,* 4th ed. Philadelphia: Lippincott, 1974.

Quinney, Richard. *Criminology.* Boston: Little, Brown, 1979.

Radke, Marian J. and Helen G. Trager. "Children's Perceptions of the Social Roles of Negroes and Whites," *The Journal of Psychology* 29 (1950):3–33.

Reasons, Charles E. and William D. Perdue. *The Ideology of Social Problems.* Sherman Oaks, Calif.: Alfred Publishing, 1981.

Redfield, Robert. *The Folk Culture of Yucatan.* Chicago: University of Chicago Press, 1941.

Reiss, Ira L. "The Universality of the Family: A Conceptual Analysis," *Journal of Marriage and the Family* 27 (November 1965):443–453.

Riccio, James. "Religious Affiliation and Socioeconomic Achievement," in Robert Wuthnow, ed., *The Religious Dimension: New Directions in Quantitative Research*. New York: Academic Press, 1979, pp. 199–231.

Ridley, F. F., ed. *Government and Administration in Western Europe*. New York: St. Martin's Press, 1979.

Riley, Matilda White, Anne Foner, Beth Hess, and Marcia L. Toby. "Socialization for the Middle and Later Years," in David A. Goslin, ed., *Handbook of Socialization Theory and Research*. Chicago: Rand McNally, 1969, pp. 951–982.

Rist, Ray. "Student Social Class and Teacher Expectations: The Self-Fulfilling Prophecy in Ghetto Education," *Harvard Educational Review* 40 (August 1970):411–451.

Roethlisberger, Fritz J. and William J. Dickson. *Management and the Worker*. Cambridge, Mass.: Harvard University Press, 1939.

Rokeach, Milton, Patricia W. Smith, and Richard I. Evans. "Two Kinds of Prejudice or One?" in Milton Rokeach, ed., *The Open and Closed Mind*. New York: Basic Books, 1960, pp. 132–168.

Roos, Patricia A. "Marriage and Women's Occupational Attainment," *American Sociological Review* 48 (December 1983):852–863.

Root, Waverley and Richard de Rochemont. *Eating in America: A History*. New York: The Ecco Press, 1976.

Rose, Vicki McNickle and Susan Carol Randall. "The Impact of Investigator Perceptions of Victim Legitimacy on the Processing of Rape/ Sexual Assault Cases," *Symbolic Interaction* 5 (Spring 1982):23–36.

Rosenthal, R. and L. Jacobson. *Pygmalion in the Classroom: Teacher Expectation and Pupil's Intellectual Development*. New York: Holt, Rinehart & Winston, 1968.

Ross, Catherine E., John Mirowsky, and Joan Huber. "Dividing Work, Sharing Work, and In-Between: Marriage Patterns and Depression," *American Sociological Review* 48 (December 1983a):809–823.

Ross, Catherine E., John Mirowsky, and Patricia Ulbrich. "Comparison of Mexicans and Anglos," *American Journal of Sociology* 89 (November 1983b):670–682.

Rossides, Daniel W. *The American Class System: An Introduction to Social Stratification*. Boston: Houghton Mifflin, 1976.

Rothman, Robert A. *Inequality and Stratification in the United States*. Englewood Cliffs, N.J.: Prentice-Hall, 1978.

Rothschild, Emma. *Paradise Lost — The Decline of the Auto-Industrial Age*. New York: Random House, 1973.

Rothstein, William G. *American Physicians in the Nineteenth Century: From Sects to Science*. Baltimore: Johns Hopkins Press, 1970.

Rouse, James. "The City of Columbia," in Victor Fisher and Herbert Graves, eds., *Social Science and Urban Crises*. New York: Macmillan, 1971.

Rubin, J., F. Provenzano, and Z. Luria. "The Eye of the Beholder: Parents' Views on Sex of Newborns," *American Journal of Orthopsychiatry* 44 (1974):512–519.

Russell, John. *British Medieval Population*. Albuquerque: University of New Mexico Press, 1972.

Ryan, Edward. Cited in Marc Fried and Peggy Gleicher, "Some Sources of Residential Satisfaction in an Urban Slum," in Sandor Halebsky, ed., *The Sociology of the City*. New York: Scribner's, 1973.

Schaefer, Richard T. *Racial and Ethnic Groups*. Boston: Little, Brown, 1979.

Schiller, Bradley R. "Stratified Opportunities: The Essence of the 'Vicious Circle'," *American Journal of Sociology* 76 (November 1970):426–442.

Schnore, Leo. "The Socioeconomic Status of Cities and Suburbs," in L. Schnore, ed., *The Urban Scene*. New York: The Free Press, 1965.

Schorr, Alvin. "Housing and Its Effects," in D. Gutman and R. Popenoe, eds., *Neighborhood, City and Metropolis*. New York: Random House, 1970.

Schur, Edwin M. *Interpreting Deviance: A Sociological Introduction*. New York: Harper & Row, 1979.

Scott, Marvin and Stanford Lyman. "Accounts," *The American Sociological Review* 33 (December 1968):46–62.

Secord, P. F. and C. W. Backman. *Social Psychology*. New York: McGraw-Hill, 1964.

Seely, Gordon M. *Education and Opportunity: For What and For Whom?* Englewood Cliffs, N.J.: Prentice-Hall, 1970.

Seeley, John, R. Sim, and E. Loosley. "The Home in Crestwood Heights," in J. Kramer, ed., *North American Suburbs: Politics, Diversity, and Change*. Berkeley, Calif.: Glendessary, 1972.

Serbin, L. and K. O'Leary. "How Nursery Schools Teach Girls to Shut Up," *Psychology Today* 9 (December 1975):56–58.

Sewell, William H. "Inequality of Opportunity for Higher Education," *American Sociological Review* 36 (October, 1971):793–809.

Sewell, William H., Robert M. Hauser et al. *Education, Occupation, Earnings*. New York: Academic Press, 1975.

Shackley, Pamela and Constance Staley. "Women in Management Training Programs: What They Think About Key Issues," *Public Personnel Management Journal*, 9(3), 1980.

Shanas, Ethel. "The Family as a Social Support System in Old Age," *The Gerontologist* 19 (April 1979):169–174.

Shattuck, Roger. *The Forbidden Experiment: The Story of the Wild Boy of Aveyron*. New York: Farrar, Straus & Giroux, 1980.

Shaw, Clifford R. and Henry D. McKay. *Delinquency Areas*. Chicago: University of Chicago Press, 1929.

Sheldon, William H. *The Varieties of Human Physique*. New York: Harper, 1940.

Sheldon, William H., Emil M. Hartl, and Eugene McDermott. *Varieties of Delinquent Youth*. New York: Harper & Row, 1949.

Shortridge, Kathleen. "Working Poor Women," in Jo Freeman, ed.,

Women. A Feminist Perspective. Palo Alto, Calif.: Mayfield Publishers, 1975, pp. 242–253.

Simmons, Roberta G., Leslie Brown, Diane M. Bush, and Dale A. Blyth. "Self-Esteem and Achievement of Black and White Adolescents," Social Problems 26 (October 1978):86–96.

Simpson, George Eaton and J. Milton Yinger. Racial and Cultural Minorities: An Analysis of Prejudice and Discrimination. New York: Harper & Row, 1972.

Smelser, Neil J. "Theoretical Issues of Scope and Problems," in Robert R. Evans, ed., Readings in Collective Behavior. Chicago: Rand McNally, 1969, pp. 89–94.

Smelser, Neil J. Theory of Collective Behavior. New York: The Free Press, 1962.

Smirlock, Michael L. "Working Women in America: Factors Which Influence Their Participation and Attachment to the Labor Force," American Economist, 24 (Fall 1980)(2):47–52.

Smith, Adam. The Wealth of Nations. New York: The Modern Library.

Smith, Douglas A. and Christy A. Visher. "Sex and Involvement in Deviance/Crime: A Quantitative Review of the Empirical Literature," American Sociological Review 45 (August 1980):691–701.

Snell, Bradford. "American Ground Transport," in Jerome H. Skolnick and Elliott Currie, eds., Boston: Little, Brown, 1976, pp. 304–326.

Sorokin, Pitirim A. Social and Cultural Dynamics. Englewood Cliffs, N.J.: Bedminster Press, 1962.

Spates, James L. "Counterculture and Dominant Culture Values: A Cross-National Analysis of the Underground Press and Dominant Culture Magazines," American Sociological Review 41 (October 1976):868–883.

Spengler, Oswald. The Decline of the West. New York: Knopf, 1962. Originally published in 1918.

Spitz, Rene A. "Hospitalism," The Psychoanalytic Study of the Child 1 (1945):53–72; and "Hospitalism:

A Follow-Up Report," ibid. 2 (1946):113–117.

Spitzer, Steven. "Toward a Marxist Theory of Deviance," Social Problems 22 (June 1975):638–651.

Spradley, James P. and Brenda J. Mann. The Cocktail Waitress. Woman's Work in a Man's World. New York: Wiley, 1975.

Srole, Leo. "Measurement and Classification in Socio-Psychiatric Epidemiology: Midtown Manhattan Study (1954) and Midtown Manhattan Restudy (1974)," Journal of Health and Social Behavior 16 (December 1975):347–364.

Stadtman, Verne A. Academic Adaptations: Higher Education Prepares for the 1980s and 1990s. San Francisco: Jossey-Bass, 1980.

Stark, Rodney and William Sims Bainbridge. "Secularization and Cult Formation in the Jazz Age," Journal for the Scientific Study of Religion 20 (December 1981):360–373.

Starr, Paul. The Social Transformation of American Medicine. New York: Basic Books, 1982.

Starr, Joyce and Donald Carns. "Singles and the City: Notes on Urban Adaptation," in J. Walton and D. Carns, eds., Cities in Change. Boston: Allyn & Bacon, 1973.

Sternglanz, S. and L. Serbin. "Sex-Role Stereotyping in Children's Television Programs," Developmental Psychology 10 (1974):710–715.

Sternlieb, George. "The City as Sandbox," in J. John Palen, ed., City Scenes. Boston: Little, Brown, 1977, pp. 73–91.

Suchar, Charles S. Social Deviance: Perspectives and Prospects. New York: Holt, Rinehart & Winston, 1978.

Sumner, William G. Folkways. New York: New American Library, reprint ed., 1980. Originally published in 1906.

Sung, Betty Lee. Mountain of Gold. New York: Macmillan, 1967.

Sutherland, Edwin H. Principles of Criminology. Philadelphia: Lippincott, 1939.

Sutherland, Edwin H. "White-Collar Criminality," American Sociological Review 5 (February 1940):1–11.

Sutherland, Edwin H. and Donald R. Cressey. Criminology. Philadelphia: Lippincott, 1970.

Szymanski, Albert. The Capitalist State and the Politics of Class. Cambridge, Mass.: Winthrop Publishers, 1978.

Tallman, Irvin and Ramona Morgner. "Life-Style Differences Among Urban and Suburban Blue-Collar Families," Social Forces 48 (March 1970):334–348.

Taylor, Frederick Winslow. Scientific Management. New York: Harper & Row, 1911.

Teachman, Jay D. "Early Marriage, Premarital Fertility, and Marital Dissolution," Journal of Family Issues 4 (March 1983):105–126.

Terkel, Studs. Working People Talk About What They Do All Day and How They Feel About What They Do. New York: Pantheon Books, 1974.

Thio, Alex. Deviant Behavior. Boston: Houghton Mifflin, 1978.

Thomlinson, Ralph. Population Dynamics. Causes and Consequences of World Demographic Change. New York: Random House, 1976.

Thomlinson, Ralph. Urban Structure. New York: Random House, 1969.

Thornton, Billy, Michael A. Robbins, and Joel A. Johnson. "Social Perception of a Rape Victim's Culpability: The Influence of Respondents' Personal-Environmental Causal Attribution Tendencies," Human Relations 34 (March 1981):225–237.

Tobias, S. "Math Anxiety: Why Is a Smart Girl Like You Counting on Her Fingers?" Ms. 5, September 1976:56–59.

Toffler, Alvin. The Third Wave. New York: Bantam Books, 1981.

Tönnies, Ferdinand. Community and Society, trans. C. P. Loomis. New York: Harper & Row, 1963. Originally published in 1887.

Troeltsch, Ernst. The Social Teachings of the Christian Churches. New York: Macmillan, 1931.

Tumin, Melvin. "On Social Inequality," American Sociological Review 28 (February 1963):19–26.

Turk, Herman. "Interorganizational Networks in Urban Society: Initial Perspectives and Comparative Research," *American Sociological Review* 35 (February 1970):1–19.

Turner, Castellano B. and Barbara F. Turner. "Gender, Race, Social Class, and Self-Evaluations Among College Students," *The Sociological Quarterly* 23 (Autumn 1982):491–507.

Turner, Jonathan A. *Sociology: Studying the Human System.* Santa Monica, Calif.: Goodyear, 1978.

Turner, Jonathan H. *The Structure of Sociological Theory.* Homewood, Ill.: The Dorsey Press, rev. ed., 1978.

Turner, Ralph H. "New Theoretical Frameworks," in Meredith D. Pugh, ed., *Collective Behavior: A Source Book.* New York: West Publishing, 1980, pp. 31–41.

Turner, R. H. "Sponsored and Contest Mobility and the School System," *American Sociological Review* 25 (December 1960):855–867.

Turner, Ralph H. and Lewis M. Killian, eds. *Collective Behavior.* Englewood Cliffs, N.J.: Prentice-Hall, 1957; 2d ed., 1972.

Ucko, Peter, Ruth Tringham, and G. W. Dimbleby, eds. *Man, Settlement, and Urbanism.* London: Duckworth, 1972.

U.S. Bureau of the Census. *Current Population Reports,* Series P-20, No. 288, "Fertility History and Prospects of American Women: June 1975." Washington, D.C.: U.S. Government Printing Office, 1976.

U.S. Bureau of the Census. *Current Population Reports,* Series P-20, No. 341, "Fertility of American Women: June 1978." Washington, D.C.: U.S. Government Printing Office, 1979.

U.S. Bureau of the Census. *Current Population Reports,* Series P-20, No. 378, "Fertility of American Women: June 1981." Washington, D.C.: U.S. Government Printing Office, 1983a.

U.S. Bureau of the Census. *Current Population Reports,* Series P-20, No.

380, "Marital Status and Living Arrangements: March 1982." Washington, D.C.: U.S. Government Printing Office, 1983b.

U.S. Bureau of the Census. *Current Population Reports,* Series P-20, No. 381, "Household and Family Characteristics: March 1982." Washington, D.C.: U.S. Government Printing Office, 1983c.

U.S. Bureau of the Census. *Current Population Reports,* Series P-23, No. 128, "America in Transition: An Aging Society." Washington, D.C.: U.S. Government Printing Office, 1983d.

U.S. Bureau of the Census. *Current Population Reports,* Series P-60, No. 140, "Money Income and Poverty Status of Families and Persons in the United States: 1982." Washington, D.C.: U.S. Government Printing Office, 1983e.

U.S. Bureau of the Census. *Current Population Reports,* Special Studies P-23, No. 75, "Social and Economic Characteristics of the Metropolitan and Nonmetropolitan Population: 1977 and 1970." Washington, D.C.: U.S. Government Printing Office, November 1978.

U.S. Bureau of the Census. *Statistical Abstract of the United States: 1982–83,* 103d ed. Washington, D.C.: U.S. Government Printing Office, 1982.

U.S. Bureau of the Census. *Statistical Abstract of the United States: 1984,* 104th ed. Washington, D.C.: U.S. Government Printing Office, 1983.

U.S. Department of Commerce, Bureau of the Census. *Current Population Reports,* Series P-60, 197. "Money Income and Poverty Status of Families and Persons in the United States, 1980." Washington, D.C.: U.S. Government Printing Office, 1981.

U.S. Dept. of Health and Human Services. *Health United States: 1980.* Washington, D.C.: U.S. Government Printing Office, 1981.

U.S. Department of Health, Education and Welfare, *Violent Schools — Safe Schools.* Washington, D.C.: U.S. Government Printing Office, 1978.

Van den Berghe, Pierre L. *Human Family Systems. An Evolutionary View.* New York: Elsevier, 1979.

Van Den Berghe, Pierre L. *Man in Society: A Biosocial View,* 2d ed. New York: Elsevier, 1978.

Vanfossen, Beth E. *The Structure of Social Inequality.* Boston: Little, Brown, 1979.

Veevers, J. E. "The Moral Careers of Voluntary Childless Wives: Notes on the Defense of a Variant World View," *The Family Coordinator* 24 (October 1975):473–487.

Vitarello, James. "The Red Lining Route to Urban Decay," *Focus* 3(10), (1975):4–5.

Vold, George B. *Theoretical Criminology.* New York: Oxford University Press, 1958.

Wade, Richard C. "How the Media Seduced and Captured American Politics," *American Heritage,* February–March 1983:47–53.

Waller, Willard. *The Family: A Dynamic Interpretation.* New York: Cordon, 1938.

Waller, Willard and Reuben Hill. *The Family.* New York: The Dryden Press, 1951.

Ware, Helen. "Polygyny: Women's Views in a Traditional Society, Nigeria, 1975," *Journal of Marriage and the Family* 41 (February 1979):185–195.

Warner, W. Lloyd and Paul S. Lunt. *The Status System of a Modern Community.* New Haven: Yale University Press, 1942.

Ways, Max. "How to Think About the Environment," in J. Hadden et al., eds., *Metropolis in Crisis.* Itasca, Ill.: F. E. Peacock, 1971.

Weber, Max. *The City.* New York: The Free Press, 1958.

Weber, Max. *From Max Weber: Essays in Sociology,* trans. and eds., H. Gerth and C. Wright Mills. New York: Oxford University Press, 1946.

Weber, Max. *The Protestant Ethic and the Spirit of Capitalism,* trans., Talcott Parsons. New York: Scribner's, 1930. Originally published in 1905.

Weber, Max. *The Protestant Ethic and the Spirit of Capitalism,* trans., Talcott Parsons. New York: Scribner's, 1958.

Weiler, Stephen J. "Aging and Sexuality and the Myth of Decline," in Robert W. Fogel et al., eds., *Aging: Stability and Change in the Family.* New York: Academic Press, 1981, pp. 317–327.

Weinberg, M. *Minority Students: A Research Appraisal.* Washington, D.C.: U.S. Government Printing Office, 1977.

Weitz, Rose. "Feminist Consciousness-Raising, Self-Concept and Depression," *Sex Roles* 8 (February 1982):231–241.

Weitzman, L. J., D. Eifler, E. Hokada, and C. Ross. "Sex Role Socialization in Picture Books for Preschool Children," *American Journal of Sociology* 77 (1972):1125–1130.

Westhues, Kenneth. *Society's Shadow: Studies in the Sociology of Countercultures.* Toronto: McGraw-Hill Ryerson, 1972.

Westoff, Charles F. and Elsie F. Jones. "The Secularization of U.S. Catholic Birth Control Practices," *Family Planning Perspectives* 9 (September–October, 1977):203–206.

Whorf, Benjamin L. "The Relation of Habitual Thought and Behavior to Language," in *Language, Culture and Personality.* Menasha, Wisc.: Sapir Memorial Publication, 1941.

Williams, Peter. *Popular Religion in America; Symbolic Change and the Modernization Process in Historical Perspective.* Englewood Cliffs, N.J.: Prentice-Hall, 1980.

Williams, Robin M., Jr. *American Society: A Sociological Interpretation,* 3rd ed. New York: Alfred Knopf, 1970.

Williamson, John B., David A. Karp, and John R. Dalphin. *The Research Craft: An Introduction to Social Science Methods.* Boston: Little, Brown, 1977.

Wilson, E. O. *Sociobiology.* Cambridge, Mass.: Harvard University Press, 1975.

Wilson, James Q. "The Urban Unease: Community vs. City," *The Public Interest* 12 (Summer 1968):25–39.

Wilson, James W. and Barbara Boland. "Crime," in W. Gorham and N. Glazer, eds., *The Urban Situation.* Washington, D.C.: The Urban Institute, 1976.

Winch, Robert F. *Mate Selection.* New York: Harper, 1958.

Winch, Robert F., Thomas Ktsanes, and Virginia Ktsanes. "The Theory of Complementary Needs in Mate Selection: An Analytic and Descriptive Study," *American Sociological Review* 19 (June 1954):241–249.

Wirth, Louis. "Urbanism as a Way of Life," *American Journal of Sociology* 44 (July 1938):3–24.

Wolfgang, Marvin. "Urban Crime," in J. Wilson, ed., *The Metropolitan Enigma.* Garden City, N.Y.: Doubleday, 1970.

World Almanac and Book of Facts, 1982. New York: Newspaper Enterprise Association, 1981:251.

World Almanac and Book of Facts, 1984. New York: Newspaper Enterprise Association.

Wray, Joe D. "Population Pressure on Families: Family Size and Child Spacing," *Reports on Population Family Planning* 9 (August 1971):403–461. Published by The Population Council, New York.

Yinger, J. Milton. "Countercultures and Social Change," *American Sociological Review* 42 (December 1977):833–853.

Zeisel, John. *Sociology and Architectural Design.* New York: Russell Sage Foundation, 1973.

Zelditch, M. Jr. "Role Differentiation in the Nuclear Family," in Parsons, Bales et al., eds., *Family, Socialization and Interaction Process.* New York: The Free Press of Glencoe, 1955.

Zirkel, P. A. "Self-Concept and the Disadvantage of Ethnic Group Membership and Mixture," *Review of Educational Research* 41 (1971): 211–225.

Zwerdling, Daniel. "The Food Monopolies," in Jerome H. Skolnick and Elliott Curie, eds., *Crisis in American Institutions,* 3rd ed. Boston: Little, Brown, 1976, pp. 43–51.

Figure Credits

(Continued from page iv)

Chapter 4, Figure 4.1, p. 89: From *New Rules: Searching for Self-Fulfillment in a World Turned Upside Down*, by Daniel Yankelovich. Copyright © 1981 by Daniel Yankelovich. Reprinted by permission of Random House, Inc.

Chapter 7, Figure 7.1, p. 186: Federal Bureau of Investigation, *Uniform Crime Reports*, 1982, U.S. Government Printing Office, Washington, D.C., p. 5.

Chapter 10, Figure 10.1, p. 273: U.S. Department of Commerce, Bureau of the Census, *Current Population Reports*. Series P-60, No. 127, "Money Income and Poverty Status of Families and Persons in the United States: 1980," Washington, D.C.: U.S. Government Printing Office, 1981.

Chapter 11, Figure 11.1, p. 292: Adapted from U.S. Bureau of the Census, *Current Population Reports*, Series P-23, No. 128, "America in Transition: An Aging Society," U.S. Government Printing Office, Washington, D.C.: 1983, p. 3. *Figure 11.2, p. 294:* U.S. Bureau of the Census, *Current Population Reports*, Series P-23, No. 128, "America in Transition: An Aging Society," U.S. Government Printing Office, Washington, D.C.: 1983, Figure 5, p. 5. *Figure 11.3, p. 305:* Diana K. Harris and William E. Cole, *Sociology of Aging*. Copyright © 1980 Houghton Mifflin Company. Used with permission. *Figure 11.4, p. 306:* U.S. Bureau of the Census, *Current Population Reports*, Series P-23, No. 128, "America in Transition: An Aging Society," U.S. Government Printing Office, Washington, D.C.: 1983, Figure 14, p. 11.

Chapter 12, Figure 12.2, p. 347: U.S. Bureau of the Census, *Statistical Abstract of the United States: 1984*, 104th ed. U.S. Government Printing Office, Washington, D.C., 1983, p. 63. *Figure 12.3, p. 351:* U.S. Bureau of the Census, *Statistical Abstract of the United States: 1984*, 104th ed. U.S. Government Printing Office, Washington, D.C., 1983, p. 63.

Chapter 13, Figure 13.1, p. 385: "The Gallup Opinion Index," *Religion in America: 1981*. Princeton, N.J. The Gallup Organization, Inc. and the Princeton Religion Research Center, Inc., Report No. 184, January 1981, p. 36. Reprinted by permission.

Chapter 14, Figure 14.1, p. 410: U.S. Bureau of the Census, *Statistical Abstract of the United States: 1984*, 104th ed., U.S. Government Printing Office, Washington, D.C., 1983, No. 209, p. 137.

Chapter 15, Figure 15.1, p. 438: U.S. Bureau of the Census, *Statistical Abstract of the United States: 1984*, 104th ed., U.S. Government Printing Office, Washington, D.C., 1983, No. 204, p. 262.

Chapter 19, Figure 19.1, p. 544: Population Reference Bureau, no date. *Statistical Abstract of the United States: 1980*, Washington, D.C.: U.S. Government Printing Office, 1980, p. 29. *Figure 19.2, p. 551:* Reprinted from "The Nature of Cities" by Chauncy D. Harris and Edward L. Ullman in vol. 242 of *The Annals* of the American Academy of Political and Social Science, November 1945. By permission. *Figure 19.3, p. 553:* Population Reference Bureau, Washington, D.C. *Figure 19.4, p. 554:* Population Reference Bureau, Washington, D.C.

Chapter 20, Figure 20.1, p. 571: U.S. Bureau of the Census, *Statistical Abstract of the United States: 1984*, 104th ed. U.S. Government Printing Office, Washington, D.C., 1983, p. xvii. *Figure 20.2, p. 576:* Reprinted from "The Nature of Cities" by Chauncy D. Harris and Edward L. Ullman in vol. 242 of *The Annals* of the American Academy of Political and Social Science, November 1945.

Photo Credits

Chapter 1. p. 4: © G. Rancinan/Sygma; *p. 7 (left):* © Horst Shafer/Peter Arnold, Inc.; *p. 7 (right):* Kent Reno/Jeroboam, Inc.; *p. 9 (top):* Owen Franken/Stock, Boston; *p. 9 (bottom):* © John Lei/Stock, Boston, Inc.; *p. 17:* © George W. Gardner, 1984. All rights reserved; *p. 20:* © Donald Dietz, 1984; *p. 21:* Detroit Police Department, Crime Prevention Section.

Chapter 2. p. 26: Library of Congress; *p. 29:* The Granger Collection; *p. 31:* The Bettmann Archive; *p. 32:* Culver Pictures; *p. 34:* United Press International/The Bettmann Archive; *p. 35:* © Robert Merton; *p. 39:* © Billy Barnes/Jeroboam, Inc.; *p. 41:* Rhoda Sydney/Monkmeyer Press Photo Service; *p. 43:* The White House.

Chapter 3. p. 50: © Brent Jones 1984; *p. 53:* Jean-Claude Lejeune/Stock, Boston, Inc.; *p. 55:* Roland Neveu/Gamma-Liason; *p. 58:* © Jane Scherr/Jeroboam, Inc.; *p. 59:* Traver/Gamma-Liason; *p. 61:* © Marion Bernstein 1984; *p. 65:* Courtesy of AT&T Technologies; *p. 66:* Philip Jon Bailey/Taurus Photos.

Chapter 4. p. 80: The Granger Collection; *p. 83 (top):* Hugh Rogers/Monkmeyer Press Photo Service; *p. 83 (bottom):* © Alan Carey/The Image Works; *p. 84:* © Vic Cox/Peter Arnold, Inc.; *p. 87:* Universal Pictures/Museum of Modern Art, Film Stills Archive; *p. 91:* © Erika Stone/Peter Arnold Agency; *p. 93:* W. Campbell/Sygma; *p. 94:* Kent Reno/Jeroboam, Inc.; *p. 95:* David A. Burnett/Stock, Boston, Inc.; *p. 99:* Harvey Barad/Monkmeyer Press Photo Service; *p. 101:* Drawing by Mankoff; © 1982 The New Yorker Magazine, Inc..

Chapter 5. p. 106: Micheal Rizza/The Picture Cube; *p. 113 (top):* © Jeffrey Blankfort/Jeroboam, Inc.; *p. 113 (bottom):* Raoul Hackel/Stock, Boston, Inc.; *p. 115:* Copyright © 1984 by Longshadow Books; reprinted by permission of Longshadow Books, a division of Simon & Schuster, Inc.; *p. 116 (top):* © Abigail Heyman/Archive Pictures, Inc.; *p. 116 (bottom):* David L. Miller/Monkmeyer Press Photo Service; *p. 119:* © Elizabeth Hamlin, 1984; *p. 122:* photo by Steve Lipofsky/courtesy of the Boston Celtics; *p. 125:* Reprinted by permission: Tribune Media Services.

Chapter 6. p. 132: Gabor Demjen/Stock, Boston, Inc.; *p. 135:* United Artists/Museum of Modern Art, Film Stills Archive; *p. 138:* Peter Vandermark/Stock, Boston, Inc.; *p. 140:* Jamie Cope; *p. 144:* David S. Strickler/Monkmeyer Press Photo Service; *p. 148:* Document/Gamma-Liason; *p. 149:* Photo courtesy of the National Broadcasting Company, Inc.; *p. 151:* © Rebecca Colette/Archive; *p. 153:* Bernard Charlon/Gamma-Liason; *p. 155:* Kent Reno/Jeroboam, Inc.

Chapter 7. p. 160: Robert V. Eckert/EKM-Nepenthe; *p. 162:* Elliott Erwitt/Magnum; *p. 165:* Bob Bouchal/Little, Brown & Co.; *p. 168:* Peter Simon/Stock, Boston, Inc.; *p. 171:* Larry Lambert/Picture Group photo; *p. 174:* Jill Freedman/Archive Pictures, Inc.; *p. 176:* Photo courtesy of the National Broadcasting Company, Inc.; *p. 178:* © Richard Younker 1981/Click-Chicago; *p. 180:* Ethan Hoffman/Archive Pictures, Inc.; *p. 187:* Gamma-Liason.

Chapter 8. p. 204: Eddie Adams/Liason Photo Agency: *p. 206 (top):* Jeffrey Blankfort/Jeroboam, Inc.; *p. 206 (bottom):* Hugh Rogers/Monkmeyer Press Photo Service; *p. 209:* Sylvia Plachy/Archive Pictures, Inc.; *p. 211:* Doonesbury, Copyright, 1984, G. B. Trudeau, Reprinted with permission of Universal Press Syndicate. All rights reserved.; *p. 213:* United Press International; *p. 214:* Mary Ellen Mark/Archive Pictures, Inc.; *p. 217:* © Alan Carey/The Image Works; *p. 219:* © Marion Bernstein 1984; *p. 224:* © Diane Graham-Henry 1981/Click-Chicago.

Chapter 9. p. 230: Ethan Hoffman/Archive Pictures, Inc.; *p. 233:* photo by Edwin Levick/Library of Congress; *p. 235:* © Brent Jones 1984; *p. 237:* Abigail Heyman/Archive Pictures, Inc.; *p. 240:* The National Archives; *p. 241:* John Running/Stock, Boston, Inc.; *p. 243:* Charles Harbutt/Archive Pictures, Inc.; *p. 245:* © Universal Pictures/Museum of Modern Art, Film Stills Archive; *p. 251:* Peter Jordan/Liason Photo Agency; *p. 252: Trail of Tears* by Robert Lindneux, courtesy of Woolaroc Museum, Bartlesville, Oklahoma; *p. 257:* © Charles Harbutt/Archive Pictures, Inc.

Chapter 10. p. 264: Gamma-Liason; *p. 267:* © Deborah Gewertz, Dept. of Anthropology-Sociology, Amherst College; *p. 268:* From the Twentieth Century Fox Release, "Mr. Mom," © 1983 Sherwood Productions, Inc. All rights reserved.; *p. 271:* International Museum of Photography at George Eastman House; *p. 274 (top):* Mimi Forsyth/Monkmeyer Press Photo Service;

p. 274 (bottom): Rhoda Sydney/Monkmeyer Press Photo Service; *p. 276:* Peeter Vilms/Jeroboam, Inc.; *p. 279:* Frank Siteman/EKM-Nepenthe; *p. 280:* © Mark Antman/The Image Works.

Chapter 11. p. 286: Sovfoto/Eastfoto; *p. 289:* Frank Siteman/Stock, Boston, Inc.; *p. 291:* Sovfoto/Eastfoto; *p. 293:* L. Druskis/Taurus Photos, Inc.; *p. 296 (left):* Patrick Ward/Stock, Boston, Inc.; *p. 296 (right):* David S. Strickler/Monkmeyer Press Photo Service; *p. 299:* Pam Hasegawa/Taurus Photos, Inc.; *p. 300:* Clara Peller in her "Where's the Beef?"™ role/Wendy's International, Inc. 1984.; *p. 301:* Diane Walker/Gamma-Liason; *p. 309:* Courtesy of Hospice of Cambridge, Mass.

Chapter 12. p. 328: Alain Keler/Sygma; *p. 332:* © Anthony Howarth/Daily Telegraph Magazine/Woodfin Camp & Associates; *p. 334:* Malcolm S. Kirk/ © Peter Arnold, Inc.; *p. 337:* Ginger Chih/Peter Arnold, Inc.; *p. 339:* © Charles Harbutt/Archive Pictures, Inc.; *p. 340:* Alen MacWeeney/Archive Pictures, Inc.; *p. 343:* Jane Kramer/EKM-Nepenthe; *p. 349:* B. Prepper/Peter Arnold, Inc.; *p. 357:* © Martha Stewart/The Picture Cube.

Chapter 13. p. 362: Owen Franken/Stock, Boston, Inc.; *p. 365:* © Kal Muller 1982/Woodfin Camp & Associates; *p. 367:* © Jacques Jangoux/Peter Arnold, Inc.; *p. 368 (left):* Unitarian Universalist Association; *p. 368 (right):* Diego Goldberg/Sygma; *p. 373:* United Press International/The Bettmann Archive; *p. 377:* Philippe LeDru/Sygma; *p. 379:* © R. Darolle/Sygma; *p. 382:* Peter Arnold/Peter Arnold, Inc.; *p. 384:* Keya/Gamma-Liason.

Chapter 14. p. 390: © Bill Stanton 1984/International Stock Photography, Ltd.; *p. 393:* Peter Arnold/Peter Arnold, Inc.; *p. 395:* David S. Strickler/Monkmeyer Press Photo Service; *p. 397:* University of Virginia Information Service/Photo by Ed Roseberry; *p. 398:* Culver Pictures; *p. 403:* Bryce Flynn/Picture Group photo; *p. 406:* © Brian Seed 1982/Click-Chicago; *p. 407:* © Marion Bernstein 1984; *p. 409:* United Press International.

Chapter 15. p. 416: Daniel Simon/Gamma-Liason; *p. 419:* United Press In-

ternational; *p. 421:* Culver Pictures; *p. 424:* Don Wright/The Miami News/Tribune Company Syndicate; *p. 426:* Alain Nogues/Sygma; *p. 433:* Elaine Isaacson/Picture Group photo; *p. 435:* Wide World Photos; *p. 437 (top):* United Press International; *p. 437 (bottom):* Jerry Berndt/Picture Group photo; *p. 439:* Daniel Brody/Stock, Boston, Inc.

Chapter 16: p. 444: © 1982 Andrew Popper/Picture Group photo; *p. 447:* Courtesy of BritRail Travel International, Inc.; *p. 451: Pat Lyon at the Forge* by John Neagle/Courtesy, Museum of Fine Arts, Boston, Herman and Zoe Oliver Sherman Fund; *p. 453;* Mark Godfrey/Archive Pictures, Inc.; *p. 457:* Jean-Pierre Laffont/Sygma; *p. 461 (top):* United Press International/Bettmann Archive; *p. 461 (bottom):* Wide World Photos; *p. 466:* © Gail Harvey/Picture Group photo.

Chapter 17. p. 470: !DEAWORKS PRESENTATIONS/Boston; *p. 473:* The Granger Collection; *p. 475:* Wide World Photos; *p. 476:* Illustration © 1982 Henry R. Martin, reprinted from *First Aid for Hypochondriacs* © 1982 by James M. Gorman, Workman Publishing, N.Y. Reprinted with permission of the publisher.; *p. 480:* Alan Price/Taurus Photos, Inc.; *p. 483:* © Mark Tuschman 1984; *p. 485:* © 1984 William Thompson/Limited Horizons; *p. 488:* Ray Solomon/Monkmeyer Press Photo Service; *p. 489:* © Joan Lifton/Archive Pictures, Inc.; *p. 491 (top):* Central Office of Information, London; *p. 491 (bottom):* Alice Grossman/The Picture Cube; *p. 493:* © Jorge Garcia Crasto 1984.

Chapter 18. p. 516: Mattison/Gamma-Liason; *p. 519:* Bill Tiernan/Sygma; *p. 521:* Wide World Photos; *p. 523:* Sydney Byrd/© Peter Arnold, Inc.; *p. 525:* Library of Congress; *p. 528:* United Press International; *p. 531 (left):* J. B. Eyerman © 1973 Time, Inc.; *p. 531 (right, top):* Chris Pullo/Monkmeyer Press Photo Service; *p. 531 (right, bottom):* Curtis/Peter Arnold, Inc.; *p. 533:* By John Fischetti © 1972 Chicago Daily News. Courtesy of News America Syndicate; *p. 535:* © Charles Gatewood/The Image Works.

Chapter 19. p. 542: © Sharon Fox/

Name Index

Subject Index